ROLLS-ROYCE

ROLLS-ROYCE

Compiled by Peter Garnier and Warren Allport from the archives of AUTOCAR

Hamlyn
London · New York · Sydney · Toronto

This edition published in 1978 by
The Hamlyn Publishing Group Limited
London · New York · Sydney · Toronto
Astronaut House, Feltham, Middlesex, England

Copyright © I.P.C. Business Press Limited 1977, 1978.
ISBN 0 600 37612 5
Printed in Great Britain

Contents

Introduction	6
1904	Paris Salon	8
1905	Current models described	10
1905	Rolls-Royce 10 h.p.	14
1905	Tourist Trophy Race	20
1905	Tourist Trophy car	23
1905	8-cylinder Landaulet	27
1906	Tourist Trophy Race	30
1906	New 40/50 engine	32
1906	The Silver Ghost	34
1909	Next Year's refinements	38
1913	London–Edinburgh car	39
1914	Alpine Trial	40
1915	Alpine car described	42
Pictorial–India	44
Pictorial–at War	45
1919	Post-War 40/50	46
1920	40/50 on the road	47
1921	Luxurious 2-seater 40/50	50
1921	40/50 on the road	52
1922	Lightweight 40/50	55
Pictorial–colour	57
1922	20 h.p. 6-cylinder	61
1924	Servo brakes described	65
1925	New Phantom	69
1925	New Phantom road impressions	72
1926	20 h.p. 6-cylinder Road Test	75
1925	A Fascinating Phantom	81
1928	40/50 for H.R.H. The Prince of Wales	82
1929	20 h.p. 6-cylinder Road Test	85
1929	Advance of the Sportsman's Coupé	87
1929	Phantom II described	88
1931	New cars for 1932	94
1931	20/25 h.p. Road Test	97
1932	20/25 h.p. modifications	99
1933	Phantom II Continental Road Test	101
1935	20/25 Touring Saloon Road Test	103
1935	12-cylinder Phantom III described	106
1936	Phantom III Road Test	109
1938	Driving the Phantom III	112
1938	25/30 h.p. Wraith described	116
1939	Detail in a Wraith	119
1939	Wraith on the Road	122
1946	Silver Wraith described	125
1947	Hooper all-enveloping coachwork	135
1948	Research and development	136
1949	Silver Dawn for Export	144
1949	Silver Wraith Sedanca Road Test	145
1950	Phantom IV for H.R.H. Princess Elizabeth	148
1953	Silver Dawn Road Test	152
1955	Silver Cloud described	156
1956	Craftsmanship–Freestone & Webb	162
1956	Silver Cloud refinements	166
1957	Silver Wraith Park Ward Limousine	169
1958	Silver Cloud Road Test	171
1959	6¼-litre Vee-8 engine	175
1959	Phantom V Limousine	179
1960	Phantom V for H.M. The Queen	182
1960	Silver Cloud II Road Test	183
1962	Silver Cloud III described	189
1963	Methods at Crewe	192
1973	Phantom VI Black Cherry	198
1963	Silver Cloud III Road Test	203
1965	Silver Shadow described	208
1967	Silver Shadow Road Test	217
1971	Corniche described	222
1972	Ultimate in luxury–Phantom VI	224
1974	Corniche Road Test	228
1975	Camargue described	234
1976	Silver Shadow Road Test	242
1977	Silver Shadow II described	248
1978	Royal Phantom VI	252
Index	255

'There's no such thing as good enough...'

(Henry Royce)

The Hon. C. S. Rolls

Sir Henry Royce

THE ROLLS-ROYCE STORY really begins before there were cars bearing that name when, in 1884, F. H. Royce, a former railway apprentice and electrical engineer, set up at the age of 21 an electrical firm in Cooke Street, Manchester, with A. E. Claremont. They started making lampholders, then electric bell sets and progressed to dynamos and cranes. By March 1899 the firm, started with £70 capital, had orders worth £20,000 on their books and had become Royce Ltd. The reason for this rapid rise in the fortunes of the company can be attributed to their products which already possessed the Rolls-Royce qualities of complete reliability and apparently never wearing out.

By 1903 the infant motor industry had progressed a long way from the early cars of the 1890s but cars were still noisy, unreliable and lacking smoothness. The secondhand 10 h.p. Decauville which Royce purchased in that year, although one of the better small cars, was no exception. He lost no time in introducing improvements, even though the car suffered in reliability by being used as a mobile test bed. The first Royce car had many features in common with the Decauville, for Royce was far more of an improver than an innovator. It had a 10 h.p. two cylinder engine with a bore and stroke of 95 × 127 mm. This car was largely built by Royce and his two apprentices Platford and Haldenby, for there were few component suppliers in those days. On 1 April 1904 the 10 h.p. took to the road and made an uneventful trip of 15 miles.

Two more experimental Royce cars soon followed, the second going to A. E. Claremont and the third to Henry Edmunds, a director of Royce Ltd. Edmunds was an experienced motorist who at once recognized the merits of the little Royce car, and it was he who persuaded his friend the Hon. C. S. Rolls to go to Manchester to meet Royce and try the car. Rolls was very impressed and arrangements were made for his partner Claude Johnson, the first secretary of the Automobile Club of Great Britain and Ireland (now the RAC), to have a trial run. Rolls and Johnson were eminently suitable to launch a new make of car as they had an established business selling Panhard et Levassor and Minerva cars and were well known in motoring circles, having taken part in the 1900 1,000 Miles Trial. An agreement, dated 23 December 1904, was drawn up between C. S. Rolls and Co. and Royce Ltd. whereby Rolls and Co. took all the cars produced by Royce and these cars were called Rolls-Royce. The agreement also stated that Royce would supply four different chassis: a 10 h.p. two-cylinder at £395, a 15 h.p. three-cylinder at £500, a 20 h.p. four-cylinder at £650 and a 30 h.p. six-cylinder at £890.

On 16 March 1906 C. S. Rolls and Co. ceased to exist and a new company called Rolls-Royce Ltd. was formed with a capital of £60,000. A. E. Claremont was chairman and F. H. Royce, C. S. Rolls, C. G. Johnson and A. H. Briggs directors. This move meant that Rolls and Johnson could now devote all their time to promoting and selling Rolls-Royce cars. Royce Ltd., however, continued to manufacture electrical equipment until about 1933.

In May 1906 C. S. Rolls, driving a 20 h.p. with Massac Buist (an early Editor of *The Autocar*) as navigator, beat Charles Jarrott's record of 37 hours 30 minutes between London and Monte Carlo by one and a half minutes—despite a wait of 3hr 11min for a boat. Rolls averaged 27.3 m.p.h. for the 771 miles from Monte Carlo to Boulogne. In June Claude Johnson's 30 h.p. Rolls-Royce was the only six-cylinder car to lose no marks in the 1,187-mile Scottish Reliability Trial, and in September 1906 Rolls won the Isle of Man TT at an average speed of 39.3 m.p.h. December 1906 saw the introduction of the 20 h.p. Rolls-Royce to the USA with Rolls winning the Five Miles Silver Trophy for cars of 25 h.p. at the Empire City Track, New York.

By that time it had become obvious that the company must expand as the Manchester works were unable to keep pace with orders. To finance this the nominal capital was increased to £200,000 and Rolls-Royce became a public company. In addition to his other work, Royce became involved in designing the new Derby factory which was opened in July 1908. Royce still found time to complete another new model, the six-cylinder 40/50 h.p., which was announced at the 1906 Olympia Motor Show and was available with a long or short chassis. This model, commonly called the Silver Ghost, was so superior to any previous Rolls-Royce that in 1907 the company decided to to cease production of all the other models and concentrate their efforts on making the 40/50 h.p. the best car on the market.

In May 1907 The Silver Ghost averaged 20.86 m.p.g. from London to Glasgow on the Scottish Reliability Trial, while in June it completed a 15,000-mile RAC-observed run, 14,371 miles being completed without an involuntary stop. The story of this famous car is told on pages 26-29.

By that time C. S. Rolls had begun to lose interest in the cars and had turned his attention to ballooning and flying. It was while taking part in a flying meeting at Bournemouth on 12 July 1910 that he was killed. Soon after this Royce was taken ill; years of work with irregular meals and sleep were beginning to take their toll. Claude Johnson came to the rescue, taking Royce abroad to convalesce, and reorganizing the factory so that Royce could continue his vital design work without ever being near Derby. That this continued to work so well, with Royce living at West Wittering in the summer and at Le Canadel in France in the winter—right up to his death in 1933—was in no small measure due to Claude Johnson's organizing genius.

In 1911 a modified Silver Ghost with cantilever rear springs, tapered bonnet, enlarged carburettor and a higher compression ratio was driven from London to Edinburgh on top gear (it had a three-speed gearbox) achieving a fuel consumption of 24.32 m.p.g. At Brooklands the same car reached 78.26 m.p.h. However, the three-speed gearbox caused

consternation in 1912 when James Radley's Silver Ghost failed to climb a 1-in-4 section of the Katschberg during the Austrian Alpine Trial and two passengers had to alight. This was a blow to Rolls-Royce prestige, so three works cars in addition to Radley's were entered for the 1913 event which they completely dominated. In June 1913 Carlos de Salamanca won the Spanish Grand Prix in a Silver Ghost and E. Platford of Rolls-Royce came third, the cars winning a number of awards between them.

During the 1914-18 war Rolls-Royces did valuable work as staff and armoured cars but with the end of hostilities it was evident that the Silver Ghost era was coming to an end. In 1922 a supplementary small 20 h.p. model was introduced, beginning the two-model policy that was to be followed for many years. By 1925 time had caught up with the Silver Ghost, and it was succeeded by the New Phantom, the first of a long line of Phantoms which continue to the present day. The death of Sir Henry Royce on 22 April 1933 just after his 70th birthday was not the disaster for the works which it would have been in 1910, though of course a sad loss for the company and his colleagues. By then the Phantom II and smaller 20/25 h.p. models were well established and the Rolls-Royce design team were able to carry on with Royce's policies of continual testing and improvement.

There is a widely held belief that the initials R-R on the radiator were changed from red to black as a sign of mourning for Royce. However, Rolls-Royce say that actually the change was planned well before his death in deference to the wishes of customers who considered that red clashed badly with the colour of the paintwork of many cars.

Almost 12 months before Royce's death, work had started on a completely new Rolls-Royce model with a V12 engine using much of the knowledge derived from the company's aero engine work. Though Royce was never to see the finished product—the first experimental car was not on the road until June 1934—the project had his approval. Certainly Hives in the experimental department, and chief engineer A. G. Elliott, put into the hands of Rolls-Royce customers one of the finest Rolls-Royce models of all in the new Phantom III, even though there are those who say that had Royce been alive the servicing arrangements might have been more practical. The model broke new ground for Rolls-Royce being their first to use independent front suspension—something that posed problems for some coachbuilders. However, Park Ward had already patented a steel body framework to counteract the flexing of the chassis.

The Phantom III era did not last long and upon the outbreak of war in 1939 Rolls-Royce under the leadership of Ernest Hives turned all their attention to making Merlin aero engines and the tank derivative called the Meteor. Wartime work gave Rolls-Royce a chance to cover many miles in a range of prototype cars.

Claude Johnson

Lord Hives

David Plastow

At the end of hostilities Rolls-Royce's car manufacturing plant was relocated in the war-time Crewe aero-engine factory whence all post-war Rolls-Royce and Bentleys (the marque was acquired in 1931) have emerged.

In 1949 a Rolls-Royce version of the Bentley Mk VI was announced and became the first Rolls-Royce to be built entirely in the works—the body coming from Pressed Steel. Chassis were, of course, available and continued to be so right up until the end of the Silver Cloud series in 1965. That year marked another major milestone in the development of the modern Rolls-Royce with the introduction of the current Silver Shadow series embodying much advanced technology. This model in its latest form is the mainstay of the current Rolls-Royce range and was supplemented in 1971 by the 2-door and convertible coachbuilt Corniche models.

Just as the Rolls-Royce company had nearly been undersubscribed in 1906, so the world held its breath when Rolls-Royce Ltd. were forced to call in a receiver in 1971. The story might have ended there, but with the aero engine interests taken over by the Government, the re-formed Rolls-Royce Motors Ltd. went public in 1973. Since then the car division—the new company also make Continental light aero engines and diesel engines among other products—have gone from strength to strength. Newest model is the prestige Camargue launched in April 1975 and now being built at the rate of about two a week. In 1975 Rolls-Royce car production topped the 3,000 mark for the first time and produced a pre-tax profit of £3.4 million. World demand for the company's cars comfortably exceeds supply and under the leadership of group managing director David Plastow Rolls-Royce Motors have succeeded in the difficult task of making perfection pay.

Model	Years in Production	Engine Size (c.c.)	No. of Cyls.	Bore × Stroke (mm)	Gears	Wheelbase ft in.	Length ft in.	Chassis Weight (lb)	Where Built	No. Made	Notes
Royce 10 h.p.	1904	1,800	2	95 × 127	3	8 1	10 0	1,344	M	3	Experimental models based on Decauville.
10 h.p.	1904	1,800	2	95 × 127	3	8 1	10 0	1,204	M	16 }	Production Rolls-Royce model with classic
	1905-1906	2,000	2	100 × 127	3	8 1	10 0	1,204	M		radiator shape. Three survive.
15 h.p.	1905	3,000	3	102 × 127	3	8 7	–	1,456	M	6	Three cylinder blocks. One car survives.
20 h.p. (Light)	1905-1906	4,000	4	102 × 127	4	8 10	11 9	1,512	M	40 }	Paired cylinder blocks. Light model used by
(Heavy)	1905-1906	4,000	4	102 × 127	3	9 6	12 11	1,680	M		Rolls in 1905-6 TT races. One survives.
30 h.p. (Short)	1905-1906	6,000	6	102 × 127	4	9 8½	13 1	1,904	M	37 }	Three blocks of two cylinders. Biggest of
(Long)	1905-1906	6,000	6	102 × 127	4	9 10	13 2¾	1,960	M		unit-construction models. One survives.
Legalimit	1905-1906	3,500	V8	83 × 83	3	8 10	–	2,240	M	3½ }	First V8-engined Rolls-Royce. Little sales
Invisible engine	1905-1906	3,500	V8	83 × 83	3	7 6	–	–	M		success so model dropped. None survives.
40/50 h.p. (Short)	1906-1908	7,036	6	114 × 114	4	11 3½	15 0	2,464	M		Start of Rolls-Royce "one model" policy.
(Long)	1906-1908	7,036	6	114 × 114	4	11 11½	15 7¼	2,540	M		Two blocks of three cylinders. Pressure feed
	1908-1909	7,036	6	114 × 114	4	11 11½	15 7¼	2,540	D		bearing lubrication. London-Edinburgh type
	1909-1913	7,428	6	114 × 121	3	11 11½	15 7¼	2,540	D	6,173 }	(cantilever rear springs, higher compression,
	1913-1915	7,428	6	114 × 121	4	11 11½	15 10¼	2,856	D		larger carburettor, tapered bonnet) available
(Short)	1918-1925	7,428	6	114 × 121	4	12 0	15 10¼	3,800	D		from 1911. Electric starting from 1918 and
(Long)	1918-1925	7,428	6	114 × 121	4	12 6½	16 4¾	3,800	D		four-wheel brakes from 1924.
40/50 h.p. USA (Short)	1921-1925	7,428	6	114 × 121	4	12 0	15 10¼	3,800	S		Manufactured completely at R-R factory in
(Long)	1921-1925	7,428	6	114 × 121	4	12 6½	16 4¾	3,800	S	1,703 }	USA. Production continued after introduction
(Short)	1925-1926	7,428	6	114 × 121	3	12 0	15 10¼	3,800	S		of New Phantom in England. Coachbuilders
(Long)	1925-1926	7,428	6	114 × 121	3	12 6½	16 4¾	3,800	S		like Brewster fitted stylish bodies.
20 h.p.	1922-1925	3,127	6	76 × 114	3	10 9	14 10	2,542	D	2,940 }	First overhead valve R-R. Starts "two model"
	1925-1929	3,127	6	76 × 114	4	10 9	14 10	2,635	D		policy. Horizontal radiator shutters.
New Phantom (Short)	1925-1929	7,668	6	108 × 140	4	12 0	15 10¼	4,000	D	2,212 }	Ohv six-cylinder with detachable head. Gear-
(Long)	1925-1929	7,668	6	108 × 140	4	12 6½	16 4¾	4,000	D		box as separate unit. Four-wheel brakes.
New Phantom USA (Short)	1926-1931	7,668	6	108 × 140	4	11 11½	15 10¼	4,000	S	1,241 }	Built entirely in USA with left-hand drive
(Long)	1926-1931	7,668	6	108 × 140	4	12 2½	16 4¾	4,000	S		until closure of American factory in 1931.
20/25 h.p.	1929-1932	3,669	6	83 × 114	4	10 9	15 1	2,653	D	3,827 }	Six cylinders in single block. Vertical
	1932-1936	3,669	6	83 × 114	4	11 0	15 0	2,915	D		radiator shutters.
Phantom II (Short)	1929-1935	7,668	6	108 × 140	4	12 0	16 8	3,810	D	1,767 }	Continental model on short chassis with
(Long)	1929-1935	7,668	6	108 × 140	4	12 6	17 4	3,810	D		stiffer suspension from 1931.
25/30 h.p.	1936-1938	4,257	6	89 × 114	4	11 0	15 9	2,930	D	1,201	More powerful version of 20/25 h.p.
Phantom III	1936-1939	7,340	V12	83 × 114	4	11 10	17 7	4,050	D	717	Independent front suspension, alloy engine.
Wraith	1938-1939	4.257	6	89 × 114	4	11 4	16 11	3,038	D	491	Small R-R with independent front suspension.
Silver Wraith	1947-1951	4,257	6	89 × 114	4	10 7	16 8	4,732*	C	1,144 }	Hydraulic front brakes, pressed steel wheels.
(Short)	1951-1952	4,566	6	92 × 114	4	10 7	16 8	4,732*	C		Optional automatic gearbox from 1952
(Long)	1951-1955	4,566	6	92 × 114	4	11 1	17 2	5,124*	C	639 }	and optional power-assisted steering from
	1955-1959	4,887	6	95 × 114	4	11 1	17 2	5,404*	C		1956. All had coachbuilt bodies.
Silver Dawn	1949-1951	4,257	6	89 × 114	4	10 0	16 0	2,740	C	760 }	First R-R sold with factory finished Pressed
	1951-1955	4,566	6	92 × 114	4	10 0	16 7½	4,100*	C		Steel body. Auto gearbox standard from 1953.
Phantom IV	1950-1956	5,675	8	89 × 114	4	12 1	19 1½	3,300	C	16	Supplied to Royalty and Heads of State only.
Silver Cloud I	1955-1957	4,887	6	95 × 114	4	10 3	17 7¾	4,368*	C	2,238 }	Final development of 114 mm stroke six-
(Short)	1957-1959	4,887	6	94 × 114	4	10 3	17 7¾	4,368*	C		cylinder. Pressed Steel body and automatic
(Long)	1957-1959	4,887	6	95 × 114	4	10 7	17 10¾	–	C	121	transmission.
Silver Cloud II (Short)	1959-1962	6,230	V8	104 × 91	4	10 3	17 8	4,558*	C	2,417 }	Power-assisted steering standard. V8 engine
(Long)	1959-1962	6,230	V8	104 × 91	4	10 7	18 0	–	C	299	with self-adjusting hydraulic tappets.
Phantom V	1959-1968	6,230	V8	104 × 91	4	12 0	19 10	5,600	C	832	All had coachbuilt limousine bodies.
Silver Cloud III (Short)	1962-1966	6,230	V8	104 × 91	4	10 3	17 7	4,558*	C	2,044 }	More powerful V8 engine and Pressed Steel
(Long)	1962-1965	6,230	V8	104 × 91	4	10 7	18 0	–	C	253	body. Coachbuilt cars continued to Mar. 1966.
Silver Shadow	1965-1968	6,230	V8	104 × 91	4†	10 0	16 11½	4,636*	C	1,483 }	All-independent suspension, disc brakes, mono-
	1968-1970	6,230	V8	104 × 91	3	10 0	16 11½	4,636*	C	2,472	coque construction. Coachbuilt cars from 1967.
(Long)	1967-1970	6,230	V8	104 × 91	3	10 4	17 3½	4,731*	C	77	Federal Safety interior from 1969, and
	1970-1977	6,750	V8	104 × 99	3	10 0	16 11½	4,850*	C	15,380	bigger engine with more power.
(Long)	1970-	6,750	V8	104 × 99	3	10 4	17 3½	4,945*	C	–	
Silver Shadow II	1977-	6,750	V8	104 × 99	3	10 0	17 0½	4,930*	C	–	Revised version with rack and pinion steering.
Corniche	1971-	6,750	V8	104 × 99	3	10 0	16 11½	5,018*	C	–	Coachbuilt version of Silver Shadow.
Phantom VI	1968-	6,230	V8	104 × 91	4	12 1	19 10	6,010*	C	–	Available only with coachbuilt body.
Camargue	1975-	6,750	V8	104 × 99	3	10 0	16 11½	5,175*	C	–	Coachbuilt prestige model.

All engines are water cooled in-line units except where stated to have vee configuration. Figures for lengths and weights are approximate only and varied from car to car according to the type of coachwork fitted. * Indicates weight for complete car with standard body. Cars were built as follows: M Manchester, D Derby, S Springfield USA, C Crewe. † Lhd export cars had 3-speed gearboxes.

BRITISH EXHIBITS AT THE PARIS SALON.

Another All-British Car.

Messrs. Rolls and Co., Ltd., are also to be congratulated upon exhibiting their new machines for the first time by showing "all-British" cars in the midst of France's best. On the stand of this company are found a 10 h.p. Rolls-Royce chassis, a 10 h.p. car, a 15 h.p. chassis at present without motor, a 20 h.p. car, and a 30 h.p. motor. The 10 h.p. two-cylinder car has a cylinder bore of 95 mm. and stroke of 127 mm., the three cylinder 15 h.p. 100 mm. by 127 mm., the 20 h.p. four cylinder 95 mm. by 127 mm., and the 30 h.p. six-cylinder 95 mm. by 127 mm. The engine of the three-cylinder car has separate cylinders, but the other motors have their cylinders cast in pairs. A special feature in the construction of the engines is that the exhaust ports are placed at the lowest points of the valve chambers, the object being to get the burnt products away in as direct a manner as possible. All the parts of all the above types of motors are interchangeable. The simplicity of the detachment of the exhausts and inlet pipes is also a notable feature. The induction valves are actuated by tappets *à la* 1903 Mercedes, the lay shaft for this duty being on the left of the engine, that for the exhausts on the right. The crankshafts of all the engines have bearings between each crank. Ring and pressure lubrication are fitted to crankshaft bearings. The engine and gear box are carried on a channel steel underframe, and a sheet metal apron serves to preserve the engine from mud and dust. The clutch is of the internal coned type with no end thrust, and a universal joint is placed between the clutch and the primary gear shafts. The change-speed gear is of the sliding sleeve type with direct drive on top speed, and with the secondary gearshaft idle when the top speed is in. The propeller shaft has well designed universal and telescopic joints at both ends. A good feature in the design of the car is the production of the driving bevel wheel pinion within the differential gear case rearward, where it is supported by a bearing of ample length. The live axle follows somewhat on the design of the Decauville or New Orleans, in which the road wheels rotate on extensions of the live axle sleeve, the live axle itself passing right through to the outside of the hub, and rotating the wheel by means of a lock-nutted cross head. High-tension ignition is used with one coil only, a high-tension distributer being fitted. The whole of the ignition apparatus is contained in a box on the dashboard, the contact cams being rotated from a worm by worm wheel and spindle off one of the lay shafts. The advance and retard of the ignition is obtained by an ingenious but simple method of rotating the primary contact cam, thus obviating any movement of the wire leads, which are immovably fixed. The lubricator, which serves crankshaft, gearshaft, and driving bevel pinion bearings, is carried on the dashboard, and is fitted with a belt-driven positive pump. The design and workmanship of these cars are excellent throughout, and the exhibit reflects great credit on those responsible for its being beneath the roof of the Grand Palais.

The chassis of the 10 h.p. Rolls-Royce car. This will be seen in the Salon and for the first time at any exhibition.

A Rolls-Royce car which will be exhibited in the Salon. The car body is by Cann, Ltd., a London firm, who make a special feature of motor car body building, and is designed to afford a side entrance to the rear seats on a comparatively short wheelbased chassis. As will be seen, this is accomplished by swinging the left front seat outwards.

"My Touring Reminiscences," by Hon. Chas. S. Rolls, forms very pleasant reading in the November issue of *C. B. Fry's Magazine*. The recital commences with his never-to-be-forgotten run from London to Monmouth at Christmas, 1896, in which the car knocked him down and ran over him in the yard of the New Inn at Gloucester, after making a blood-curdling descent of the awesome Birdlip. The run of 140 miles occupied Rolls and his friend no less than three days on the 3¾ h.p. Peugeot, though they landed in time for the Christmas festivities. The sketch also details the weird experiences of running one of the first, if not *the* first, Bollée three-wheeled cars from Victoria Station to Cambridge, which will astonish and amuse all those who have not heard them before. The same issue of this magazine presents an article on the cost of the upkeep of an 18ft. motor boat, 5ft. beam, driven by a 2 h.p. two-cycle petrol engine, and after detailing all the expenses incurred, the writer considers that the annual cost would be somewhere about £7 to £12.

9

ROLLS-ROYCE AUTOMOBILES.

WE HAVE IN A PREVIOUS ISSUE OF *THE AUTOCAR* BRIEFLY REFERRED TO THESE CARS, WHICH ARE OF THE FOLLOWING POWERS: TWO-CYLINDER, 10 H.P.; THREE-CYLINDER, 15 H.P.; FOUR-CYLINDER, 20 H.P.; AND SIX-CYLINDER, 30 H.P. WE HAVE BEEN AFFORDED SUCH OPPORTUNITIES AS NOW ENABLE US TO GIVE A DESCRIPTION OF THE MORE IMPORTANT PARTS OF THE MECHANISM OF THESE CARS.

THE SIX-CYLINDER ENGINE.

Fig. 1 is a longitudinal and transverse sectional elevation, the two forward cylinders being shown wholly in section, and exhibiting the detail which characterises the remaining four. The bore of these cylinders is 100 mm. and the stroke 127 mm., equal to 4in. by 5in., and the six-cylinder engine develops 30 b.h.p. at about 1,000 revolutions per minute. The induction and exhaust valves are all mechanically operated from the right-hand side of the engine by one camshaft H H, the induction valves being set in the crown of the combustion chamber, and operated by the induction valve tappets I and tappet levers T. This is done to give the minimum amount of internal surface, and so avoid cooling the gases, and also to provide ample inspection openings for examining the interior of the cylinders. It will be seen that the fulcrums of the tappet levers T are carried in extensions of the valve domes L, and these domes are held in position by the dogs L¹, which are themselves secured by the single nuts shown, and are, therefore, easily detached and replaced. The cylinders are cast complete with their water-jackets in pairs, and are amply water-jacketed round the combustion chambers, cylinder walls, and valve chambers. The cooling water is fed by the pump to the cylinder jackets through the apertures N N, and the heated water flows away to the radiator through the delivery pipe N¹.

Special attention has been paid to the efficient lubrication of the bearings of both crankshaft and valve camshaft. The oil splashed upwards from the bottom of the crank chamber by the revolving crank case is caught in the oil cups O, and passes by the leads therefrom to the bearings.

The crankshaft, which is formed of a solid forging of nickel steel and machined on all surfaces, is carried in seven bearings—one long bearing at each end, and shorter ones between each crank. The valve camshaft, in addition to a bearing at each end, has a long bearing between each pair of cylinders.

The crank chamber is divided transversely into six compartments by diaphragms running across the case and carrying the central crank bearings. By this arrangement each crank revolves in its own crank chamber, and the necessary oil for its lubrication is retained at a sufficient depth for the purpose when the car is being driven uphill.

The lower half of the crank chamber carries the complete bearings for the crankshaft, and suitable positioned inspection doors (not shown) are provided to permit the examination of the connecting rods, bearings, etc.

The radiator fan R, the spindle of which runs in bearings carried by a bracket attached to the forward cylinder, is belt-driven through the pulleys R¹ R² off the crankshaft G.

The gear actuating the half-time shaft is enclosed in a separate gear case at the forward end of the crank chamber.

The various parts will be readily understood by reference to the index under fig. 1.

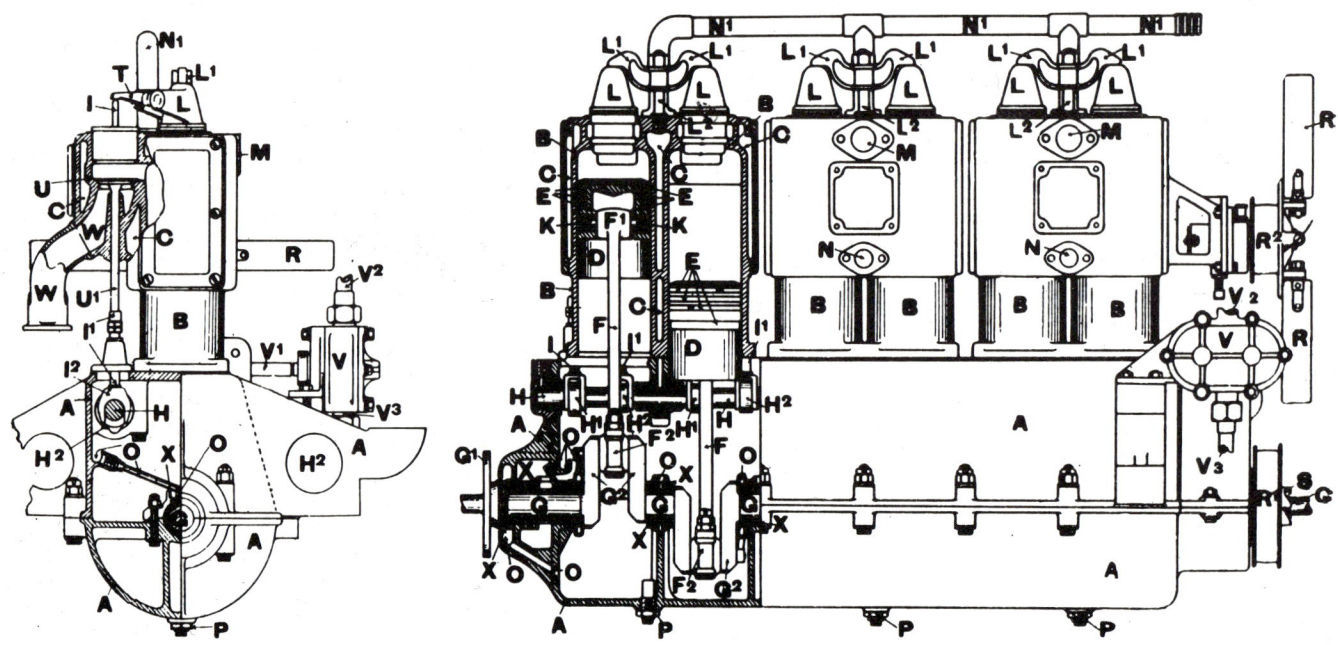

Fig. 1.—Part sectional end view and side elevation of the Rolls-Royce 30 h.p. six-cylinder engine.

A, crank chamber	G2 G2, crank cheeks	L2 L2, induction valve dome dog studs	R2, driven pulley on radiator fan spindle
B, cylinders	H H, camshaft	M M, induction ports	S, starting clutch
C, water jacket spacings	H1, induction cam	N N, entrance to water jackets	T, induction valve tappet lever
D, pistons	H2, exhaust cam	N1 N1, water delivery to radiator tank	U, exhaust valve head
E, piston rings	I, induction valve tappet	O, oil cups and leads	U1, exhaust valve stem
F, connecting rods	I1, exhaust valve tappet	P P, oil drain plugs to crank chamber	V, water circulating pump
F1, little end bearing	I2, guide fork of exhaust valve tappet	R R, vanes of radiator fan	V1, pump spindle
F2, big end bearing	K, gudgeon pin	R1, driving belt pulley for fan	V2, delivery pipe
G, crankshaft	L L, induction valve domes		V3, suction pipe
G1, flange for attachment of flywheel	L1 L1, induction valve dome dogs		W, exhaust pipe
			X, crankshaft bearings

THE 15 H.P. THREE-CYLINDER ENGINE.

The 15 h.p. Rolls-Royce engine is of a type somewhat distinct from the three other motors built by this firm. The bore of the cylinders of the 15 h.p. engine is 4in. and the stroke 5in., the designated horse-power being developed at about 1,000 r.p.m.

The cranks are set at 120 degrees, and from the fact of the engine getting an impulse to every two-thirds of a revolution, the running is so smooth and fine that it is difficult to detect the difference between this and the four-cylinder motor. The cylinders are cast separately with their own water-jackets, and the inlet and exhaust valves are placed similarly to those of the engine already referred to. Dash lubrication is depended upon to supply the lubricant to the oil cavities and leads, and ring lubrication is fitted to the end bearings.

Fig. 2.—The lower half of the 10 h.p. crank chamber, with the crankshaft in position. This shows the balancing of the cranks.

The Clutch.

The construction of the clutch used in connection with the four types of Rolls-Royce cars is clearly shown by the vertical section (fig. 3). The outer ring C of the flywheel is cast with a dished web, for the purpose of bringing the attachment of the latter to the flange B B in the centre of the flywheel when the same is made up by the addition of its rear half, which forms the female portion of the clutch. The male portion of the clutch F F, which is of aluminium, is attached to the flange on the clutch sleeve H H by means of the screws shown in the section. It is also provided with a clutch brake ring J J, which, when the clutch is moved inwards for the purpose of declutching, comes into

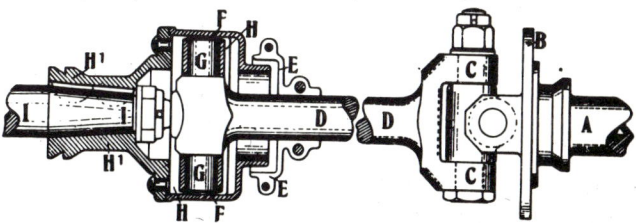

Fig. 4.—Transmission-shaft of the 10 h.p. Rolls-Royce car.

A. primary gearshaft
B, flange upon which the brake drum is mounted
C C, universal joint
D D, transmission-shaft
E E, aluminium dustcap
F, aluminium cap over universal joint
G G, universal joint trunnions
H H, hardened square blocks
H1 H1, jaw piece of cardan joint
I I, driving bevel pinion shaft

contact with a brake, which reduces the speed of its rotation, and accordingly facilitates the changing of the gear. The ball thrust bearing K K is set in the rear of the flange B B to take the thrust of the clutch spring, which, for the sake of clearness, is not shown on the accompanying section. The pressure from the clutch fork ring L L operates upon the clutch through the ball thrust bearing M M. The clutch itself is very easily dismounted for the purpose of cleaning or re-leathering, by withdrawing the set screws E E which hold the two sections of the flywheel rim together.

The Transmission.

We may dismiss the change-speed gear by merely remarking that it is of the usual sliding type, and affords a direct drive on the top gear.

Fig. 3.—Sectional elevation of the Rolls-Royce clutch.

A, engineshaft
B B, flange to which one half of the flywheel is bolted
C C, forward half of the flywheel
D D, rear half of flywheel forming the female portion of the clutch
E E, studs securing C to D
F F, aluminium male portion of the clutch
G G, clutch leather
H H, clutch sleeve and flange
I I, bronze bearing bush
J J, clutch brake ring
K K, clutch thrust bearing
L L, clutch fork withdrawing ring
M M, clutch fork ring ball thrust bearing
N N, universal joint block
O O, universal joint pin
O1 O1, universal joint blocks

ROLLS-ROYCE AUTOMOBILES.

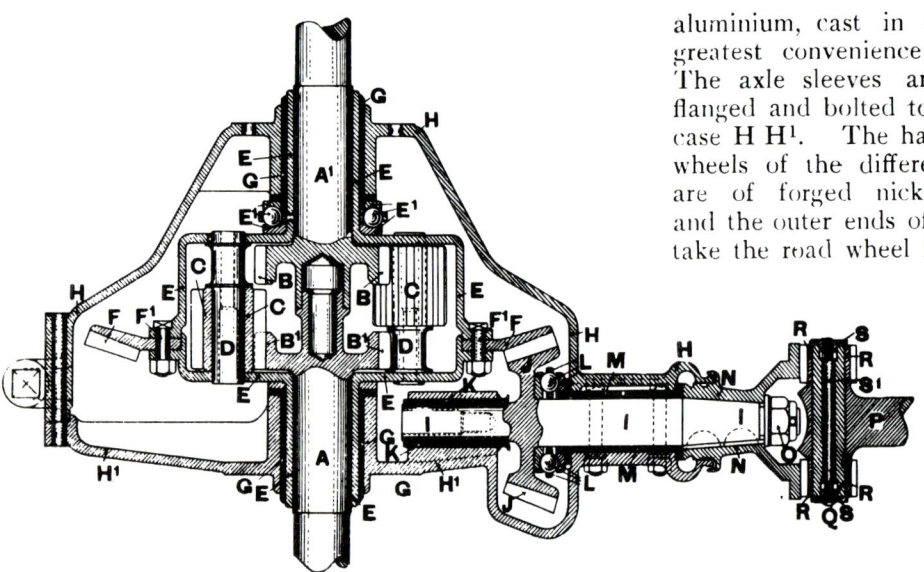

Fig. 5.—Bevel gear drive and differential in section .

A A1, two-piece live axle
B B1, differential centre pinions on the inner ends of live axle
C C, differential pinions or satellite wheels
D D, pins to carry C C
E E, differential gear box
E1 E1, differential ball thrust bearing
F F, bevel toothed ring
F1 F1, securing bolts for F
G G, bearing bushes
H H1, left and right-hand halves of the differential gear case
I I, driving bevel wheel shaft

J, driving bevel wheel
K K, plain bearing for tail of driving bevel wheel shaft
L, driving bevel wheel ball thrust ring
M M, driving bevel wheel shaft plain bearing
N N, universal joint jaw on I I
O, nut locking N to I
P, propeller-shaft end
Q, universal joint pin
R, universal joint block
S S, retaining piece for universal joint block
S1, retaining bolt for S

The Propeller-shaft.

The next part which calls for attention is the propeller-shaft, and fig. 4 is a side elevation and partial section of the shaft employed in the 10 h.p. car. The various parts and their proportions are clearly indicated by the reference table below the drawing. The flange B on the end of the primary gearshaft A is intended for the attachment of a brake drum which is not shown. The attachments between the jaw piece of the cardan joint H1 and the driving bevel pinion shaft I I is of a particularly secure character, for not only is it tapered and held up by means of the keyed nut shown, but is also secured thereto by the two semi-circular keys shown by the full and dotted lines in the section.

The Back Axle and Differential Gear.

The construction of the back axles on these cars will appeal to all who have given this important part of the gear transmission close attention. The left and right-hand halves of the differential gear case H and H1 are in

aluminium, cast in such a form as to afford the greatest convenience and strength for the purpose. The axle sleeves are of solid drawn steel tubes flanged and bolted to the ends of the aluminium gear case H H1. The halves of the live axle with the sun wheels of the differential gear cut solid upon them are of forged nickel steel of the highest grade, and the outer ends of these half axles are arranged to take the road wheel hubs as shown. Four keys are left solid on the end of the shaft to transfer the drive to the wheel hub. The bevel ring F is formed from a solid steel forging, and the driving bevel pinion J which meshes with it is turned solid with its shaft I. It will be noticed that in addition to carrying the bevel wheel shaft I in the long ring lubricated bearing M, the end of the shaft subtending the bevel wheel is carried in another bearing K—a most important and valuable feature in propeller-shaft transmission. A ball thrust bearing E1 is provided behind the case carrying the bevel wheel F and at the back of the driving bevel pinion, as is shown by L.

The inner ends of the half axles run in the long plain bearings G G, and at the outer ends in the long plain bearings in some types, whilst in the higher power cars roller bearings are employed.

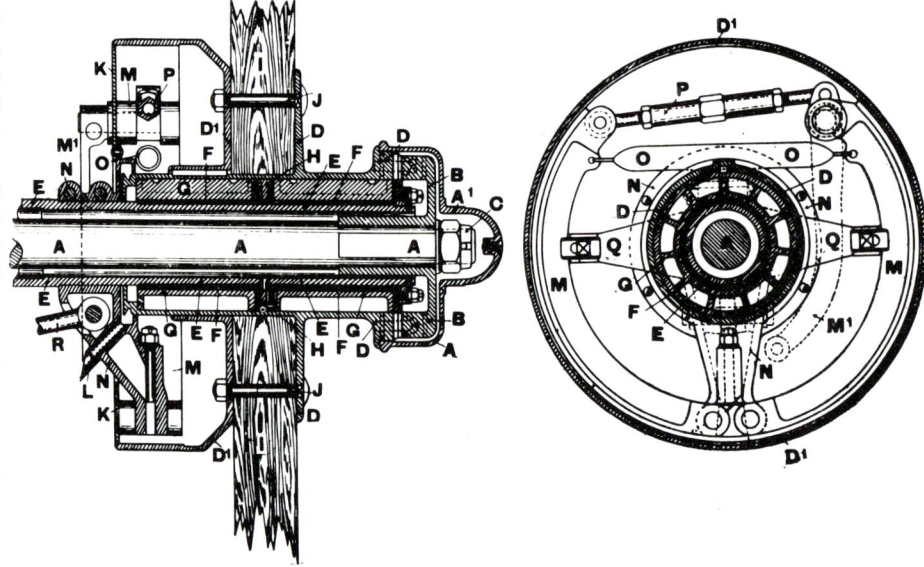

Fig. 6.—Rear axle end bearing and brake.

A A, right-hand half of live axle with squared end
A1, axle cap
B B, driver on end of A
C, nut securing driver on to A
D D, hub flange driven by B
D1 D1, brake drums
E E, axle sleeve
F F, hardened sleeve on which bronze bush revolves
G G, bronze bushes
H H, thrust ring to take side thrust
I I, spokes

J J, hub flange and spoke bolts
K K, brake drum cover plate
L, tube for draining away surplus oil
M M, expanding brake segments
M1, brake lever
N N, bracket carrying brake segments
O, brake spring
P, coupling nut for adjusting brake segments
Q, adjustable brake stops to prevent rattle
R, tension rod

The spring flap bosses are free to oscillate on the axle, thus avoiding any stress or thrust being thrown on the bevel gearing.

The differential gear, it will be seen, is of the planetary type, and is of ample dimensions.

The Rear Wheel Bearings and Brakes.

Fig. 6 shows in transverse and longitudinal section the construction of the rear wheel bearings and brakes. What is now well known as the Decauville practice has been generally followed by the designer of the cars. It will be seen that the live axle A passes free through the axle sleeve E E, and has no bearing upon it. The outer end of the live axle is arranged to take the driver B B, which is connected to the flange of the hub D D by four claws locking into slots on the face of the hub flange. The driver B B is a tight fit on the squared end of the shaft A A, and is secured in position by the pinned nut C. F F are the hardened steel sleeves on which the phosphor-bronze bushes G G revolve. In the centre of these bushes, which are formed with the flanges shown, is placed a thrust ring H H, this thrust ring being inserted to relieve the differential and driving gear of the pressure resulting from turning corners. By reference to the cross section, it will be seen that the phosphor-bronze bushes G G are formed with their radial arms, having certain oil cavities between them. The radial arms have each two semicircular passages cut in them to permit of the oil flowing from one to the other. The phosphor-bronze bushes G G are a tight fit in the hub shell D D, and are further secured to the same by a claw plate bolted to the face of the hub by the lock-nutted set screws shown in dotted lines. The brake drum D is bolted by the bolts J to the outer flange of the hub through the spoke centres, and forms the inner hub flange, although it is not part of the hub itself. The design of the internal expanding brakes is shown in elevation on the transverse section. The segments M M are expanded by a right-

hand movement of the brake lever M¹ shown in dotted lines, the left-hand segments being thrust against the inside surface of the drum through the rod and coupling nut P by means of the short reverse arm of the lever M¹. O O is a strong spiral spring which withdraws the segments from contact with the drum upon the release of the lever M¹. Q Q are adjustable brake stops for the

Fig. 7.—The steering wheel control on the Rolls-Royce cars.

purpose of steadying the brake segments and preventing them from rattling. The segments and stops are carried on the bracket N, which is bolted fast to the axle sleeve E E. The spaces occupied by the radial arms of the bushes G G and their intervening oil cavities can be occupied by ball or roller bearings if desired.

THE AUTOCAR. SEPTEMBER 9TH, 1905.

One day last week Mr. Hodson, of Liverpool, called upon us with the first of the three-cylinder 15 h.p. Rolls-Royce cars which has been turned out. This particular car was fitted with a heavy landaulette body and canopy. Mr. Hodson took us for a short drive so that we could see how the three-cylinder engine ran. It will be remembered that the Rolls-Royce three-cylinder engine is exactly the same as the four, so far as the bore and stroke are concerned, these being 100 × 127 mm. respectively. We were particularly interested in trying this engine, because we have already driven in the two, four, and six-cylinder Rolls-Royce cars. So far as the three is concerned, it is really a satisfactory compromise between the two and the four. The two is one of the smoothest two-cylinder engines we have tried, and we can certainly make the same remark respecting the three-cylinder engine. Of course, it is not so good as the four, though, as far as the smoothness of running is concerned, there is very little in it indeed, but there is not the same range of power that a four-cylinder engine gives. On the other hand, it runs at any speed without vibration, and picks up quickly, besides pulling exceedingly well when working hard at a slow speed. We are told that a great deal of trouble has been taken to get this three-cylinder

pattern right, and from its running we have no doubt whatever that this is so. The single trembler coil and synchronised ignition have not a little to do with the excellent results attained.

Dr. Warre, the late headmaster of Eton, has been presented by old Etonians with the comfortable looking Rolls-Royce phaeton de luxe illustrated above. The brougham top is removable, so that it may be used as an open carriage.

13

1905 Rolls-Royce 10hp

"The most silent two-cylinder car in the world" (1905 CATALOGUE)

By Warren Allport

Photographs: Peter Cramer

Rolls-Royce Motors' two-cylinder under way with Dennis Miller-Williams at the wheel and the author beside him. Note how high the driver sits, with a good view of the road ahead. Both the brake and gear levers are low down and forward necessitating considerable movement to use them.

TODAY, the name Rolls-Royce is synonymous with large, luxury cars offering the ultimate in refinement. The first Rolls-Royce cars were far from this, though the finished products already exhibited the meticulous attention to detail, engineering finesse, and superb finish which have characterized Rolls-Royce cars ever since.

The story of the little, two-cylinder, 10 hp car really begins back in 1903, though then there were no cars bearing the Rolls-Royce name — indeed, the Hon Charles Rolls and Henry Royce had not met. While it is likely that the exploits of pioneer automobilist Rolls were known to Royce, it is certain that Rolls had never heard of the electrical engineering company of Royce Ltd, or its principal.

Royce, with his partner, A. E. Claremont, had been established in Manchester since 1884, in which year Royce had celebrated his twenty-first birthday. They progressed from making lamp holders and electric bell sets to dynamos and electric cranes, the business becoming a limited liability company trading as Royce Ltd from 1894. Five years later the capital of the company had been increased to £30,000 but, with the turn of the century, business was not as good as it should have been for Royce Ltd, mainly due to competitors who were prepared to lower the quality, and price, of their products to obtain orders.

It seems that Royce Ltd's venture into motor car manufacture happened more by chance than anything, following Royce's purchase of a secondhand, two-cylinder, 10 hp Decauville early in 1903. It has been said that Henry Royce was so disgusted by the poor performance of his Decauville, particularly the reliability, that it made him determined to build something better.

In fact the little Decauville was one of the better cars of its day and not nearly so unrefined or unreliable as has been made out, though in common with its contemporaries it did suffer to some extent from mechanical noise

and vibration. Most cars of that time did not tick over at all smoothly due to the difficulties of adjusting ignition and carburation and the inherent poor fuel mixture distribution to the cylinders. Even though 1,500 rpm was likely to be the maximum engine speed, exposed valve gear, frequent and noisy gearchanging, and not inconsiderable gear noise added to the feeling in 1903 that the new-fangled cars were noisy.

Royce was a compulsive tinkerer with all things mechanical, so it was hardly surprising that he should have tried various improvements to the Decauville and build his own machine is not known, but the resultant Royce car, which took shape in the late 1903 and early 1904, borrowed a number of features from the Decauville. Royce's decision to build a batch of three experimental cars was met with some incredulity by his partner, A. E. Claremont, who was struggling to keep the company viable. Suffice it to say that the move was not popular, particularly as it meant "borrowing" mechanics from the electrical side of the business to work on the cars.

September, 1903, saw the first engines being bench tested with entries such as: "exhaust cams taken out and altered to give less lift . . . short connecting rods fitted. Run for about three hours . . . Consumption test with special short connecting rods. Started continuous load of 30 amps, 120 volts, 720 revs." The log book goes on to record that the two gallons of petrol put into the tank were finished after 2¾ hours and continues: " Run with too rich a mixture. Took all top covers off for examination. Found trailing cylinder to be taking more oil than the leading cylinder. Trailing covers, exhaust and inlet, badly caked up with oil. Leading cylinder only thin soot. Mr Royce thinks oiling device might have caused this." So it can be seen that the building of the first three Royce cars — Rolls had not yet come on the scene remember — was not without its problems.

One of the three experimental Royce cars parked outside the Cooke Street, Manchester, works of Royce Ltd., who then proclaimed themselves as electrical and mechanical engineers. Note that apart from the obvious difference in radiator shape between Royce and Rolls-Royce, the two models were otherwise almost identical in appearance and design.

The Royce car

Royce persisted with his experiments and finally, on Friday, 1 April, 1904, the very first Royce car was "hammered" out of the Cooke Street workshop by the employees in the time-honoured way, and made an uneventful 15-mile trip to Royce's home in Knutsford. The second Royce car was used by A. E. Claremont and was subjected to a continuous programme of further Royce "improvements" which marred its reliability somewhat. The third 10 hp model went to Henry Edmunds, who had joined Royce Ltd as a director in 1903 and was a committee member of the Automobile Club (now the RAC) and well known in motoring circles.

To say that Edmunds was impressed by the company's new product is an understatement — in the new car he saw the possibility of a profitable new line if proper marketing arrangements could be fixed up. Two names immediately came to his mind as being ideal for this, if they could be persuaded to take on the new Royce as well as their existing franchises. The names of the two men were, of course, the Hon Charles Rolls and Claude Johnson, secretary of the Automobile Club at the time of the 1,000 Mile Trial of 1900, who were in business as C. S. Rolls and Co, selling Panhard et Levassor and Minerva cars.

Rolls had for some time been wanting to sell a quality, British-made car but had found nothing suitable. He was sceptical, to say the least, when Henry Edmunds told him that he had found such a car in the little two-cylinder Royce and suggested that Rolls should journey to Manchester to try it. This Rolls was most unwilling to do as he thought the journey would be a complete waste of time. Royce was equally adamant that he was too busy at Cooke Street to travel to London to demonstrate the car. Eventually, after some negotiation, Edmunds persuaded Rolls to travel to Manchester with him to meet Royce and try the car. The two Rs met at the Midland Hotel for lunch, followed by Rolls taking the wheel of the 10 hp.

At once he realized that this was no ordinary, rough, two-cylinder car, it had the smoothness and pull of a good four-cylinder. Here was the car he had been looking for. Back in London Johnson was hauled out of bed to have the car demonstrated, and was equally impressed. Rolls made immediate arrangements with Royce Ltd to take their entire output of cars, and an example was shown at the Paris Salon early in December, 1904, as a Rolls-Royce.

A formal agreement, dated 23 December, 1904, between C. S. Rolls and Co and Royce Ltd, stated that Rolls and Co would be supplied with four types of chassis: a 10 hp two-cylinder selling for £395, a 15 hp three-cylinder at £500, a 20 hp four-cylinder at £650, and a 30 hp six-cylinder at £890. The agreement further stipulated that these cars should be marketed under the name Rolls-Royce. The Rolls-Royce car was born.

Engine design

Though the external difference in the radiator shape between the three Royce cars — none of which survive — and the first Rolls-Royce is immediately obvious, there were other differences.

For example, the Royce cars had only two crankshaft bearings while the production Rolls-Royce version had three, and the general finish on the production cars was much better. The Rolls-Royce two-cylinder engine was an in-line unit with a single cast-iron cylinder block, cylinder dimensions of 95x127 mm giving a capacity of 1,800 c.c. The pair of cylinders were water-cooled, the car being equipped with a gear-driven pump and belt-driven fan. Royce had a dislike for belt or chain drives and much preferred a proper gearwheel arrangement, so it was hardly surprising to find the two camshafts operating the valves gear driven from the front of the crankshaft. Overhead inlet and side exhaust valves were used — a system Rolls-Royce kept to well into the 1950s — with the camshaft on the right (driver's side) of the engine operating the two inlet valves via exposed pushrods and rockers and supplying the drive for the ignition distributor, while the camshaft on the left operated the two side

exhaust valves, supplied the drive to the water pump via gears at the front, and drove the oil pump for lubrication via a belt and pulley at the rear.

As can be seen in the cutaway drawing prepared specially for this article by *Autocar* senior artist Vic Berris, the fact that there were only two cylinders meant that a massive flywheel and hefty counter-balance weights were essential in the design. These weights were bolted to the crankshaft web — which ensured that the balance was very accurate. Seeking smoothness, Royce was bound not to design with crank throws in line, though this would have given even power impulses instead of the bang-bang-silence-silence produced by his choice of 180 deg crank throws.

One of the common problems then associated with this firing sequence was that of uneven mixture distribution, the first cylinder to fire tending to receive a richer mixture due to carburettor flooding in the interim between the power strokes. Royce dealt with this by some clever induction manifold plumbing and by fitting his own float-feed type of automatic carburettor. Exhaust gas flow was also aided by placing the exhaust ports as low as possible in the valve chambers, giving a clear exhaust run.

Note the classic proportions of the original Rolls-Royce radiator which did not extend below the chassis frame. Visible on top of the induction pipe (between the plugs) is the tap allowing hand priming. The carburettor itself is low down on the left at chassis height.

Above: Accumulators for the 6 volt electrics are housed in this wooden box on the running board. There is no charging system built into the car. Above right: The twin tremblers for the coil ignition are housed in a box on the dashboard. Right: The front passenger seat swings outwards, and must be held in position, to afford access to the rear seat from beside the driving seat. The actual aperture is masked by the leather flap on the base of the passenger seat in this picture.

1905 Rolls-Royce 10hp

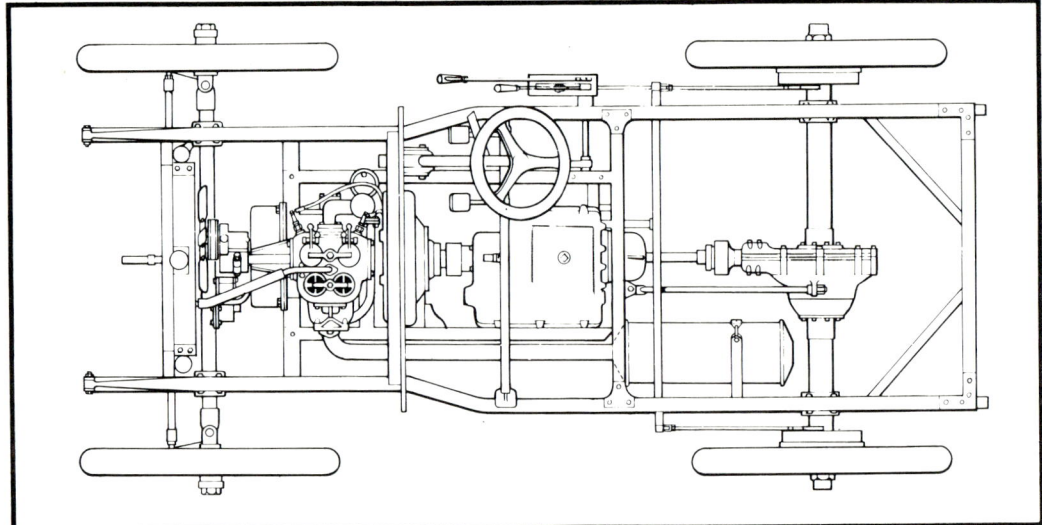

The chassis design itself is quite simple and conventional. Note large gearbox with transmission brake immediately behind it, flexible joint just ahead of live rear axle, tie rod between axle and gearbox, and large silencer.

Lubrication of the nickel-steel forged crankshaft, running in three phosphor-bronze bearings, was by splash and also from the usual battery of drip feeds housed on the dashboard. Whereas the Royce experimental cars had used exhaust gas to pressurize the oil to the drip feeds, the production models had the drip feeds supplied at 4 psi from a spring-belt-driven pump within the dashboard oil tank. There were no less than four drip feeds working off this tank. The two lubricators nearest the driver fed to the engine at eight drips per minute (each), that furthest from the driver looked after the gearbox at four drips a minute, while the remaining feed sent one drip per minute to the clutch.

One of the poorer features of the engine design was the detachable, cast aluminium, lower half of the crankcase which carried the complete crankshaft bearings, not using the block to locate the bearings as is current practice. Even before Royce's first car had been designed, this system of bearing location was thought to give poor rigidity, depending as it did merely on the strength of the lower half of the crank chamber. Claimed advantages, which may have attracted Royce, were good lubrication and ease of repair.

As one would expect, the electrics of the car were particularly good and overcame many of the ignition problems then prevalent. Two separate six-volt accumulators were housed in a wooden box attached to the running board of the car on the driver's side, and these fed the twin-trembler ignition coil — one trembler for each cylinder. A switch on the dashboard selected either of the accumulators — remember there was no dynamo to top up the accumulators, which had to be charged from an external source when the car was at rest — and would be the equivalent of the modern ignition key.

The rotating distributor wipe contact, driven from the inlet camshaft, merely closed the low-tension primary circuit, the interruption of current flow to give the necessary high tension current was effected by the electromagnetic trembler on the coil. This trembler provided a stream of sparks to the plugs as long as the primary circuit was closed. Ignition advance and retard was controlled from a lever on the steering column and was so arranged that a system of levers rotated the primary contact cam at the front of the engine, thus removing any necessity for the ignition wires to move.

Transmission

A leather-lined cone clutch, typical of that fitted to many cars, transmitted the drive to the large gearbox, which gave three forward speeds and reverse. Drive from clutch to gearbox went through a universal joint, no doubt to absorb any movement between engine and gearbox due to the flexing of the lightweight steel chassis frame.

The gearchange was operated by a massive external lever alongside the handbrake. It was of the then common sliding type with a neutral position between each gear, rather than the preferred gate-change to be found on Mercedes of the time, and, of course, on later Rolls-Royces. Various gear ratios were offered depending on the use for which the car was intended, but in each case direct drive was provided in third (top) gear. Just aft of the gearbox was the transmission brake drum operated by the foot brake.

The propeller shaft had a universal joint at the front end and a flexible coupling at the rear. It was, perhaps, in the choice of final drive arrangement that Royce's Decauville influence was most in evidence. The propeller shaft rear flexible coupling passed the drive to a substantial aluminium case containing the bevel gears and differential. The live axle was fully floating, with all the weight of the chassis taken on the drawn steel tubes surrounding the drive shafts, and with the wheel hubs rotating on extensions of the drive shaft tubes. The drive shafts passed right through to the outside of the wheel hub where they were lock-nutted to the wheel. As the 1905 Rolls-Royce catalogue proudly proclaimed: "Chains, with all their objectionable features of noise, wear, tear, etc, have been abolished.".

Other features of the simple chassis not already mentioned include the suspension which was by leaf springs, front and rear, both having seven leaves. The distinctive Rolls-Royce radiator was an important part of the cooling system and used drawn brass tubes with horizontal brass plates acting as cooling surfaces. Royce's concern for lightness is to be seen in the use of aluminium for gearbox, crankcase and differential, and in the drilled rear brake drums, which also had tubes to drain away any oil which found its way past the drive shaft seals. Dust and mud were a bugbear at the time, in spite of an overall 20 mph speed limit, so both engine and gearbox were protected by an undertray, the engine section of which could be removed separately.

The wheels were of the then common wooden artillery type, with detachable steel rims carrying the narrow pneumatic tyres, and already boasted the now familiar hexagonal Rolls-Royce hub nut. Changing a wheel in those days was a common occurrence and meant changing the wheel rim and tyre, rather than the whole wheel as is normal now.

Chassis 20165

The production run of the 10 hp lasted for a mere two years, from 1904 to 1906, during which time some 16 examples were built. The first of these was chassis 20154, the original 1904 Paris Show car, and is now owned by Oliver Langton of Leeds, while chassis 20162 is the property of the Science Museum in London. The third surviving car, which has formed the basis for this article, is chassis 20165 now owned by Rolls-Royce Motors Ltd.

Originally 20165, which still bears its original registration number SU 13, was delivered to Sydney J. Gammell of Aberdeen in 1905. He kept the little Rolls-Royce until 1920, by which time it had covered over 100,000 miles in Scotland, before replacing it with a larger car. He then offered the car to Rolls-Royce as a museum piece in token of its many years of faithful service. The presentation was marked by a luncheon and tour of the Derby works, with Rolls-Royce managing director Claude Johnson there to receive the car on behalf of the company. The 10 hp was then in such excellent working order that 21 June, 1920, saw it arriving at Derby for the presentation after being driven all the way from Aberdeenshire.

For many years after that SU 13 stood in the entrance to the Rolls-Royce service station at Derby, latterly sadly neglected. Following repainting in the early 1960s, SU 13 was for a while exhibited in Rolls-Royce's Conduit Street showrooms or used for dealers' showroom displays, and put in appearances at the Rolls-Royce pageants at Goodwood in 1964 and 1967. More recently the car has been on display at the National Motor Museum, Beaulieu, and, following re-upholstery of the leather seats by Hoopers earlier this year, is now to be found alongside her famous daughter, The Silver Ghost, at Rolls-Royce Motors Ltd's London service depot.

SU 13 as originally returned to Rolls-Royce in 1920. Note single headlamp, hood, windscreen and circular sidelamps.

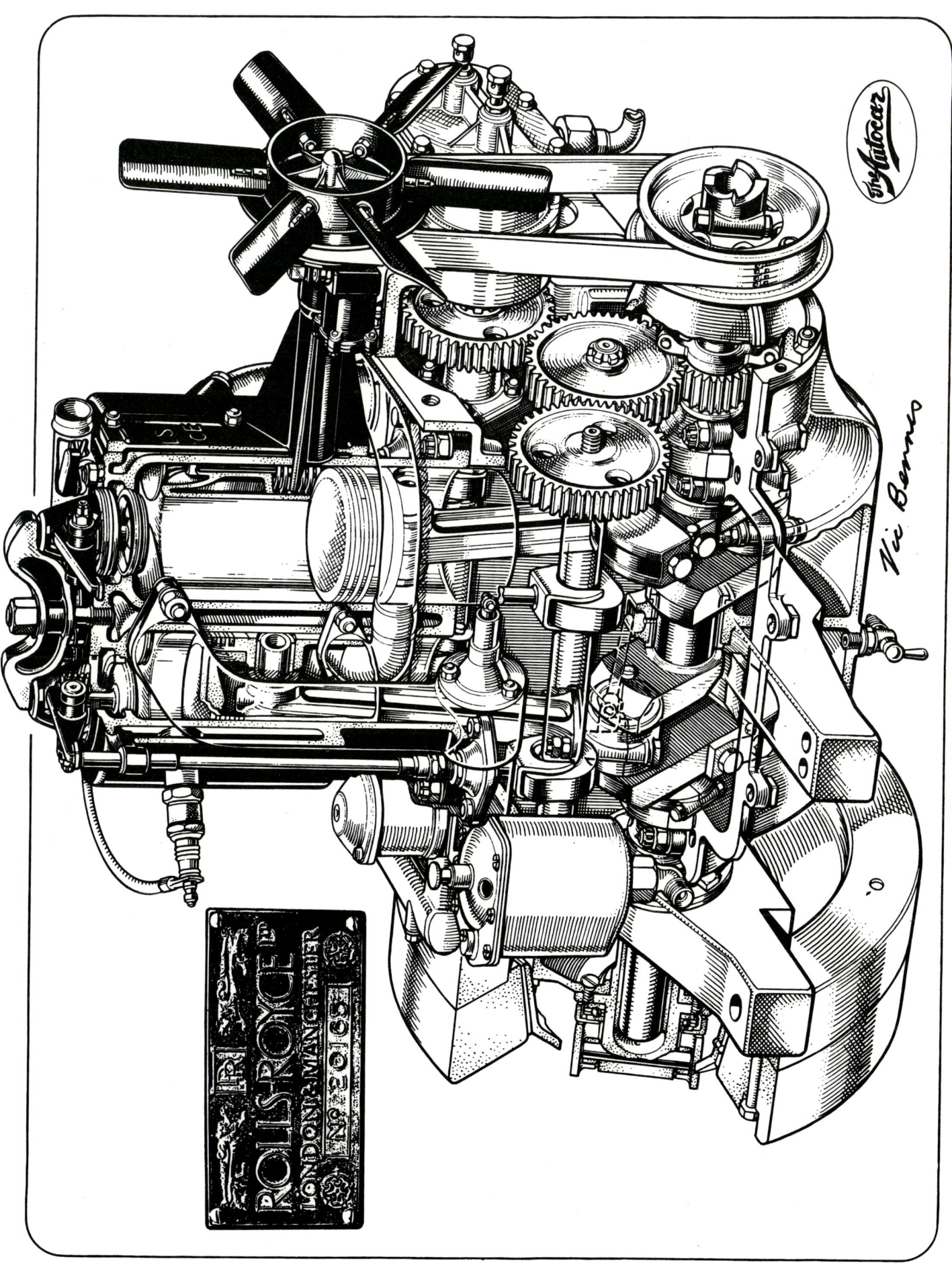

1905 Rolls-Royce 10hp

On the road

It was, therefore, from the Hythe Road service depot that Rolls-Royce Motors group public relations manager Dennis Miller-Williams and myself set out so that I could gain some first hand impressions of SU 13.

The aspect that most interested me was that of silence and lack of vibration — two features of which the reports of the day had made much. Indeed, the 1905 catalogue boasted: "All who have tried one of these cars declare it to be the quietest yet produced. It is certainly unique in this respect. The engine is so accurately balanced, and the carburation so perfect, that when the car is standing still there is an entire absence of noise and vibration, which makes it almost impossible to tell whether the engine is revolving or at rest. The top speed is a 'direct drive', and when running, not a sound can be heard but the rush of air past the car or the 'swish' of the mud on the road."

Starting a 1905 car takes more than the turn of a key in a modern car. First and most important comes the turning of a "key" (tap) under the chassis on the driver's side to allow petrol to pass from the six-gallon tank beneath the driving seat to the carburettor. Since there is no fuel pump, an air pump is provided to pressurize the tank and assist the flow, though Dennis Miller-Williams usually finds the gravity feed adequate. A small button on top of the carburettor is then depressed several times to flood the carburettor before turning the engine over about six times on the starting handle to draw in the mixture. The ignition is now switched on and retarded fully, and the hand throttle set up two or three notches prior to pulling up on the starting handle until the engine fires. Once this happens the ignition is gradually advanced until about three quarters advanced — the normal road running setting. Both the hand throttle (governor) and early/late ignition controls on the steering column have benefited from Royce's attention to detail and are fitted with ratchet mechanisms so they are easy to set up accurately.

Once on the road it was immediately apparent that the 10 hp was not quiet in the now accepted Rolls-Royce manner, nor indeed as silent as the slightly younger Silver Ghost. On the other hand the engine was far smoother than I had imagined, so in that sense at least its claims were not exaggerated. There appeared to be no difference between the two-cylinder and a four-cylinder for smoothness most of the time, though when the engine was pulling the two power strokes could be felt clearly. At other times all that was audible was the quiet "tuf-tuf" of the engine.

Even allowing for the fact that 20165 comes from the final chassis series and is therefore fitted with a slightly larger engine of 2-litres, with a

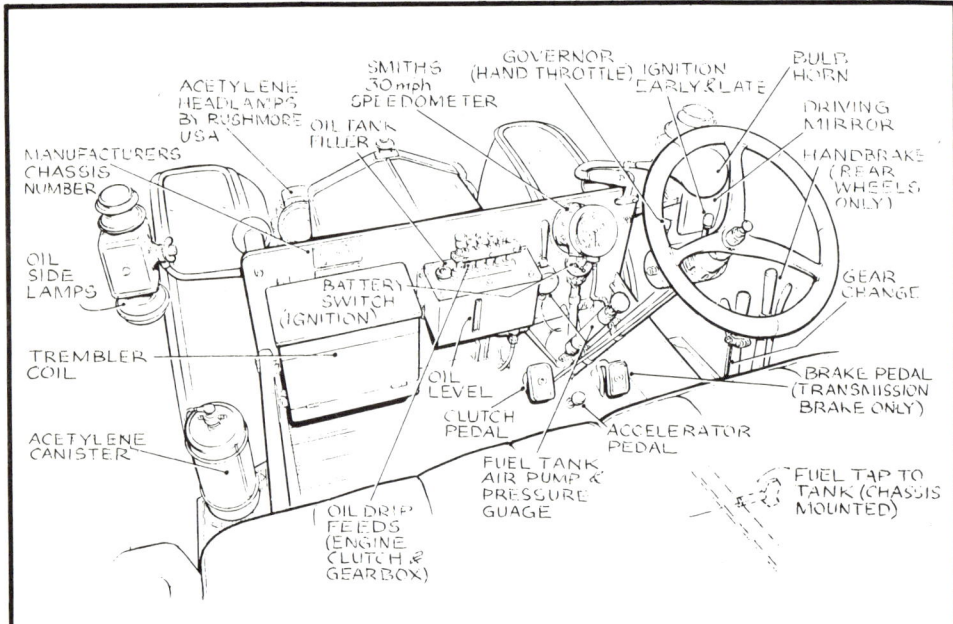

Above: Although the height of the radiator and bonnet are not very great the engine in fact is quite tall and protrudes quite a long way below the chassis frame. Note narrow section pneumatic tyres and the bend in the front axle to bring it below the front of the crankshaft pulley. Left: Controls confronting the driver are not as complicated as they look. Below: The high tail was necessary in 1905 to preserve passengers from the dust cloud that accompanied vehicles on the roads of the time.

100mm instead of 95mm bore, maximum power is still developed at 1,000 rpm which is an incredibly low figure by modern standards. Because the engine is comparatively quiet and works over such a limited rev range, changing gear is none too easy and is not helped by the heavy flywheel maintaining the engine revs when one wishes to change up. Even with two-cylinders there is enough power and flexibility to start in second gear and change up almost immediately to top. Bottom gear is only needed when starting on steep hills or with four people in the car.

Although the footbrake works only on the transmission and is no longer used, the outside handbrake exerts considerable leverage and is more powerful than might be imagined, so stopping presents no problems. The steering is on the heavy side by modern standards and gives the driver far

more feel than motorists nowadays are accustomed to, but otherwise is pleasant enough. The whole aspect of driving is, of course, helped by the high, commanding driving position which gives a view over most modern cars. Originally SU 13 was fitted with acetylene headlamps and oil side and tail lamps for driving at night, but these are no longer used so driving is confined to daylight hours.

As it happened, the day that Dennis Miller-Williams and I selected for our brief run was 1 April, just 73 years to the day after the first Royce car had taken to the road. Our uneventful trip was a tribute to Sir Henry Royce's engineering skill and the longevity of the 10 hp two-cylinder Rolls-Royce, which is today worth well over one hundred times the £395 it cost, with Barker body, in 1905.

So absorbed was Henry Royce in the production of the early Rolls-Royce cars in
the works at Cooke Street, Manchester, that he seldom remembered to eat.
Here amidst 10 h.p. cars being erected "Pa" Royce is being encouraged to
eat a bowl of porridge by one of his devoted employees. Often food consisted
of eggs boiled on the furnace and chunks of bread, and on one occasion
Royce lectured the apprentices on the heat treatment of eggs

FUEL TRIALS IN THE ISLE OF MAN. A fortnight since the Hon. C. S. Rolls took one of his 20 h.p. Rolls-Royce cars to the Isle of Man to conduct some fuel tests over the route on which the Tourist Trophy race is to be decided next September. The purpose of the trial was to ascertain the gear ratios which were most suitable to enable the highest average speed to be maintained, and also the consumption of fuel in relation to the gear used. So far so good, but unfortunately the results are not for publication, so that, beyond saying that the Hon. C. S. Rolls learned a great deal which will undoubtedly be of use to him, not only in the race itself, but in deciding on the design of the car which he will drive in the race, our lips are sealed.

THE AUTOCAR. JUNE 24TH, 1905.

Whilst in Filey for the speed trials, we saw the Hon. C. S. Rolls driving a six-cylinder Rolls-Royce car, similar to that illustrated, and in common with those assembled in front of the Crescent Hotel, remarked upon the beautiful running of the car and its handsome design. The car is a *fac simile* of that exhibited at the show at Olympia, and to our minds it showed to even greater advantage on the road than on a show stand.

RAC Tourist Trophy Isle of Man 1905

THE AUTOCAR. AUGUST 26TH, 1905

SOME TOURIST TROPHY CARS.
THE ROLLS-ROYCE.

The Rolls-Royce Tourist Trophy car. Plan of the chassis.

Our illustrations show the chassis of one of the two Rolls-Royce cars which will take part in the Tourist Trophy competition. So far as dimensions are concerned, the engine is of the firm's standard four-cylinder type, having cylinders of 100 mm. stroke by 127 mm. bore. One or two slight modifications have been introduced, but whether they will be retained or not is at present undecided. We described the Rolls-Royce car in some detail on March 4th and 11th, and it will suffice to say that the main engine accessories, such as carburetter and ignition, are practically unaltered. The real departure from standard practice is in the change speed gear, which embodies two sliding units, giving four speeds forward and a reverse, but the direct drive is not upon the fourth, but upon the third speed. The third speed is therefore the one which absorbs the least power, and is the most efficient, it being intended for use upon moderate inclines, heavy roads, against head winds, and in traffic. That is to say, it is to be used the greater part of the time the car is in motion, the indirect fourth speed only being called into requisition when the conditions are extremely favourable, so that very little power is needed to propel the car. The back axle is of a very strong type, the road wheels running on stationary tubes, the axles having nothing to do but transmit the drive to the wheels. The frame is of pressed nickel steel, and the front axle is a solid nickel steel forging, this metal being very largely used in the R.R. cars. The wheels are provided with 810 mm. by 90 mm. tyres, that is, 32in. by 3½in. The springs are very long, and it will be noted in the plan view that to avoid making the frame unduly long, and to partially obtain the advantage of long springs, the back axle is placed behind the centre of the springs. We hear that the car has been tested for over 500 miles from Manchester northward. It ran without a single compulsory

stop, and although for obvious reasons it is preferred to say nothing about speed, we are assured the petrol consumption was well within the twenty-five

The Rolls-Royce Tourist Trophy car. Side view of the engine.

miles to the gallon limit of the competition, although the car was not driven with any very careful attention to keeping down fuel consumption. It will be seen that the car is not a freak; in fact, it is a very nice-looking machine, and it is to be the model for next year's light 20 h.p. pattern with one or two small modifications.

Photograph by   *Argent Archer, Kensington, W.*

The Rolls-Royce car which has been specially constructed for the Tourist Trophy Race. The Hon. C. S. Rolls was the first entrant for the race with this car, which will be adopted by the firm as a standard type.

TOURIST TROPHY ITEMS.

We hear that a test was made a few days since with one of the Rolls-Royce Tourist Trophy cars upon the London-Oxford Road. After careful fuel measurement, it was found that the car covered exactly fifty-five and a half miles upon two gallons of fuel, representing twenty-seven and threequarter miles to the gallon. As the roads were very heavy and rain was falling for a part of the trial, this is certainly a very satisfactory performance, though Mr. Rolls thinks he can improve upon it by some further adjustments. Despite the low petrol consumption, the car made excellent time, and was found capable of attaining a very high speed upon the flat, so that upon the level parts of the course good time should be made.

The Race SEPT 23RD, 1905.

The first car to be sent off.
The 20 h.p. Rolls-Royce, driven by the Hon. C. S. Rolls.

The second car. No 22, the 20 h.p. Rolls-Royce. In the tonneau the Hon. C. S. Rolls will be recognised, while Mr. Claude Johnson is standing close by. The now famous Arrol-Johnston is in the background.

The 1905 Tourist Trophy

"THERE IS no doubt that the Tourist Trophy Race last week was the most interesting competition which has ever been held in the automobile field. It was an honest attempt to frame regulations which should make the employment of monstrous cars impossible, and also prevent the employment of machines of the exact opposite". In these words, *The Autocar* described the 1905 Tourist Trophy.

The race was run over four laps of the 52¾-mile Isle of Man circuit, the steepest gradient on which was the 2-mile, 1-in-10.8 climb of Snaefell from the "Hair Pin Corner" outside Ramsey. Two 20 h.p., 4-cylinder Rolls-Royce cars were entered, driven by the Hon. C. S. Rolls and Percy Northey. Rolls' engine had a bore and stroke of 100 by 127 mm, developing 20 b.h.p. at 1,000 r.p.m. (compared with Northey's 95 by 127 mm, and 18 b.h.p. at 1,000 r.p.m.). Both had 4-speed gearboxes, giving maxima of 15, 24.5, 37 and 45.5 m.p.h. in the gears. The fastest car in the race, a Napier, was capable of 47 m.p.h. in top, though the fastest practice lap was by a Minerva in 1hr 26min.

During practice, Rolls' car averaged 33 m.p.h. for the 52¾-mile lap, using exactly two gallons of fuel—which was well within the stipulated maximum of 25 m.p.g. With this in view, each car had originally been allowed 8.34 gallons, but this was subsequently increased to 9.25. If the original fuel consumption formula had been adhered to, instead of a combination of speed and consumption, the first and last positions in the final results would have been reversed—the winning Arrol-Johnston coming last and the Dennis, last to finish, would have won.

The two Rolls-Royces started as favourites, though C. S. Rolls' car stripped its gearbox during the opening lap and retired. Percy Northey completed his first lap in 1hr 34min 5sec (32.9 m.p.h.), ". . . able to attone", as *The Autocar* put it, "for the hard luck that Mr. Rolls himself had suffered." His next was in 1hr 32min 32sec (33.8 m.p.h.); and, though his first two laps had been completed in second place to the Arrol-Johnston (the ultimate winner), Northey's third, in 1hr 31min 41sec (34.1 m.p.h.) was faster. His final time was 1hr 32min 8sec, giving him second position overall.

Show Report—Petrol Cars.

C. S. ROLLS AND Co., Conduit Street, W. (97).—We have so recently described the great Rolls-Royce novelty that we need say little more than that an eight-cylinder landaulet is exhibited, and in addition to the landaulet a rather novel form of two-seated car is shown, in which the eight-cylinder engine is placed under a very low wide bonnet. The effect is unusual, and, we must confess, much more pleasant than we should have imagined. This is the Legalimit car, which can be set at will to maintain but not exceed the legal limit of speed. A six-cylinder chassis shows fully all the R.R. points, and also exhibits the Hallé spring wheel, while the four-cylinder car is an example of the famous Tourist Trophy machine which secured second place in the race in September, and which has been bought by our colleague. A particularly interesting feature of the six-cylinder chassis is the change-speed gear, as this has the direct drive on the third speed and the indirect drive on the fourth. As some people have experienced great difficulty in understanding how this—to them—impossible arrangement has been effected, we should

The Rolls-Royce Tourist Trophy car which has been purchased by Mr. Harry J. Swindley.

advise them to examine it, as it will be seen that it is really a very simple matter indeed.

THE 20 H.P. ROLLS-ROYCE TOURIST TROPHY CAR.

AN ALL-BRITISH CAR BOTH IN DESIGN AND CONSTRUCTION, REMARKABLE FOR ITS PERFORMANCE IN THE TOURIST TROPHY RACE, THE NEATNESS, COMPACTNESS, AND FLEXIBILITY OF ITS ENGINE, THE ECONOMY AND EFFICIENCY OF ITS CARBURETTER, ITS SPECIALLY DESIGNED CHANGE-SPEED GEAR, THE LIVE AXLE DRIVE, AND THE CARRIAGE OF ITS ROAD-DRIVING WHEELS ON ITS AXLE SLEEVES.

We are now able to complete the illustrated description of the 20 h.p. Rolls-Royce Tourist Trophy car, the engine of which was described and illustrated in *The Autocar* of March 4th, 1905 (page 324), when we

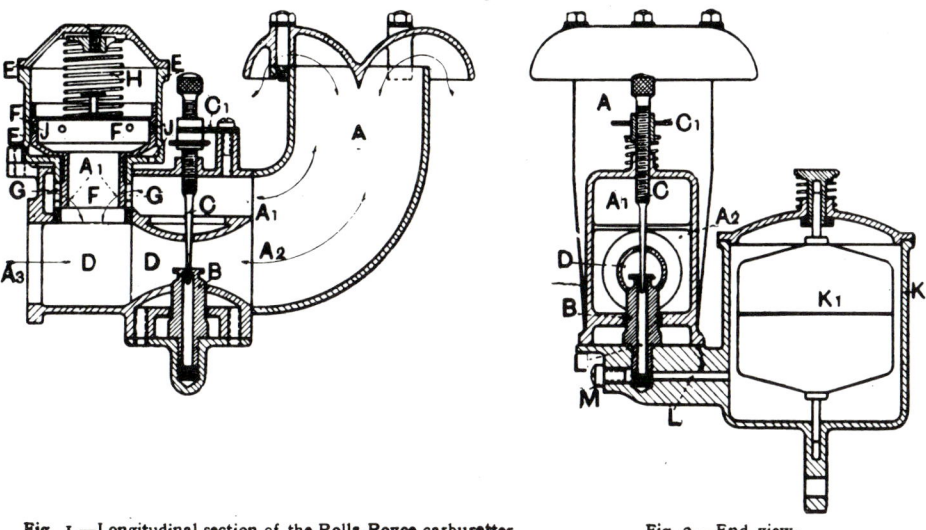

Fig. 1.—Longitudinal section of the Rolls-Royce carburetter.   Fig. 2.—End view.

A, main and auxiliary air inlet
A1, arrow showing course of auxiliary air supply
A2, arrow showing course of main air supply passing over jet
A3, course of carburetted mixture
B, jet
C, taper needle for adjusting petrol supply
C1, locking fork to adjustable needle
D, mixing chamber

E E, automatic air valve box
F F, automatic air valve
G G, air apertures
H H, automatic valve closing spring
J J, vacuum holes
K, float feed chamber
K1, float
L L, petrol passages to jet
M, wash-out to petrol passages

went carefully into the detail of one of the most efficient and quietest internal combustion motors yet fitted to an automobile.

The Carburetter.

The carburetter (see figs. 1 and 2) fitted to the Rolls-Royce cars has, like all other parts of these taking vehicles, been the subject of special design. The apparatus is made in three parts, simply demountable, and placed in a very convenient position. The part marked A is an upturned bend with double-curved top lid to prevent dirt and dust from entering, and at the same time forming easy ingress passages for the induced air supply. It forms a common lead for both the main and auxiliary air feed, the main supply going to the passage over the jet B, as per the arrow marked A_2, and the auxiliary supply by the passage above the jet chamber to the concentric passage surrounding the ports G G, as shown by the arrows marked A_1. A connection not shown, but made within the walls of the apparatus, exists between the interior of the chamber D and that part of the automatic valve box E above the valve F F through the vacuum holes J J. Accordingly the same depression is brought about in the valve box E E as is produced at any time in the mixing or jet chamber D D by the engine suction. Consequently there being a partial vacuum produced in E E, the valve F rises and more or less uncovers the ports G G, so that additional air passes and mingles with the carburetted mixture passing through D D on its way to the cylinders.

Petrol reaches the jet B by the lead L from the float chamber K, the level of petrol therein being governed in the usual way by the float K_1. The delivery of petrol through the jet B is controlled by the adjustment of the needle valve C, which when adjusted can be locked securely in position by the locking fork device C_1. The efficiency and economy of this carburetter have been most completely demonstrated by the performance of the Rolls-Royce car, so skilfully driven by Mr. Percy Northey in the first Tourist Trophy competition.

The Ignition and Distributer.

The engine of this car is fitted with what is generally known, and was described in a recent issue of *The Autocar* (p. 509), as synchronised ignition—that is, a system in which one induction coil only is used, in connection with a distributer, conducting the high-tension current to the cylinders in their proper order. The Rolls-Royce distributer is placed upon the rearward face of the dashboard, in full view of the driver, and in a particularly accessible position, as, indeed, are all the parts of this engine which may at any time require adjustment or attention. Fig. 3 shows the vertical distributer driving spindle rotated off the left-hand half-time shaft by spiral gearing (not shown). This is brought up through a tubular casing K and bearing

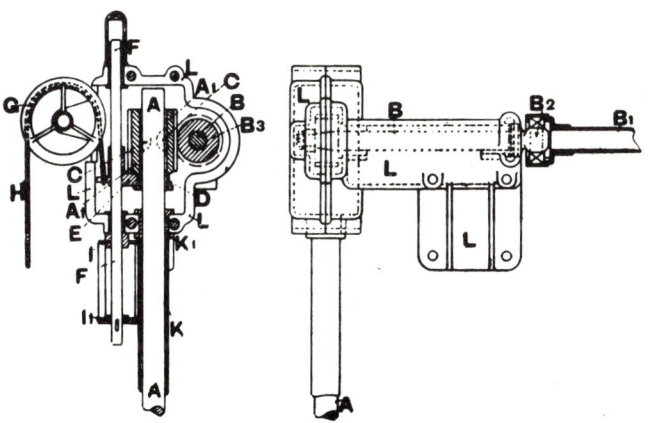

Fig. 3.—Ignition distributer and driving gear.

A A, distributer driving shaft
A1 A1, spirally toothed driving wheel
B, distributer driven shaft
B1, hollow universally jointed shaft connecting B to distributer of dashboard
B2, forward universal joint
C C, keys in special wheel set in slots in distributer shaft
D, collar formed in spirally toothed wheel to take lifting arm E
E, lifting arm
F F, lifting rod carrying lifting arm E
G, pulley carrying tension cord
H, tension cord
I, lifting rod guide and spring carrier
I1, foot of spring carrier
K, distributer shaft casing
K1, guide to distributer shaft
L L, distributer drive case and bracket

guide K_1, to carry at its upper end a spirally-toothed wheel A_1 meshing with a similar wheel B_3 on the forward end of the driven distributer shaft B. This shaft runs in the bearings shown by the dotted lines in the distributer drive case L L.

It will be seen that the driving spiral wheel $A_1 A_1$ is formed as to its lower part with the collar D, into which the lifting arm E attached to the lifting rod F F enters. Around the lower part of the rod F is placed a spiral spring (not shown), which rests upon the cotter carried washer I_1, and abuts against the flange on the lifting rod guide I.

Now to advance the ignition. When the ignition lever is moved forward on the steering wheel, a pull is imparted to the tension cord H, which runs over the pulley G, and is attached to a projecting lug on the lifting arm E. The lifting rod rises in its guides, carrying with it the lifting arm and the spirally-toothed driving wheel A_1. The vertical movement of this wheel, meshed with B_3 as it is, has the effect of rotating the shaft B after the manner of a rack, and so advancing the rotary movement of that shaft, and thus advancing the ignition. The spiral gear is enclosed in the gear case L, and runs in grease.

Change-speed Gear Box.

The special feature of the Rolls-Royce gear box (figs. 4 and 5) is, first, the arrangement ensuring the direct drive on the third and the gear drive on the fourth speed. This arrangement means, therefore, that the direct third is the speed that will be most in use. with this type of car, that with it the vehicle will be fast enough for

the majority of users, and that all reasonable hills encountered in a day's run will be taken without change of gear. The second feature is the employment of ball bearings to both gearshafts, also to the driving sleeve B which carries the driving intermediate wheel S. Both primary and secondary-shafts are hollow, and the

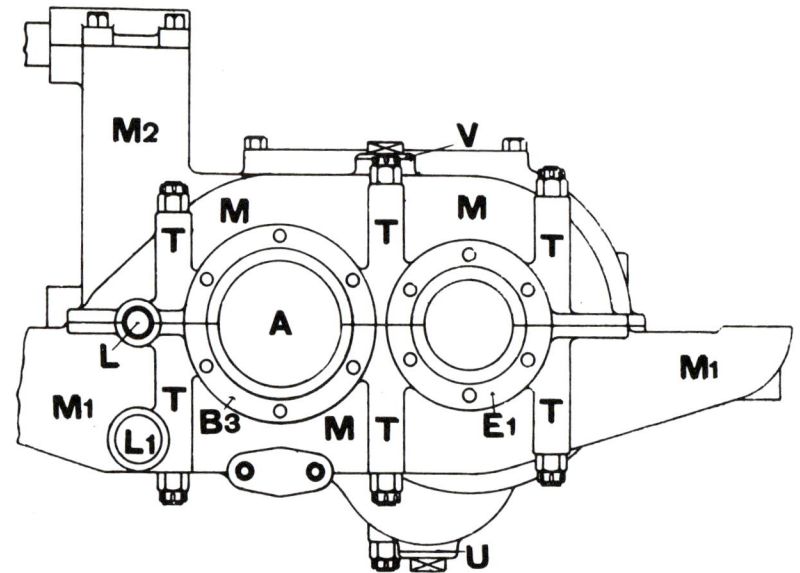

Fig. 4.—End view of gear box.

latter is externally swaged down. At its forward end the primary gearshaft B_1 is carried in a long round-ended bush in the sleeve spindle B, and at its rearward end in a single row ball bearing of large diameter. The secondary-shaft E E is carried in two single row ball bearings, as shown. The driving part of the direct drive third speed clutch 3 is carried on the end of the

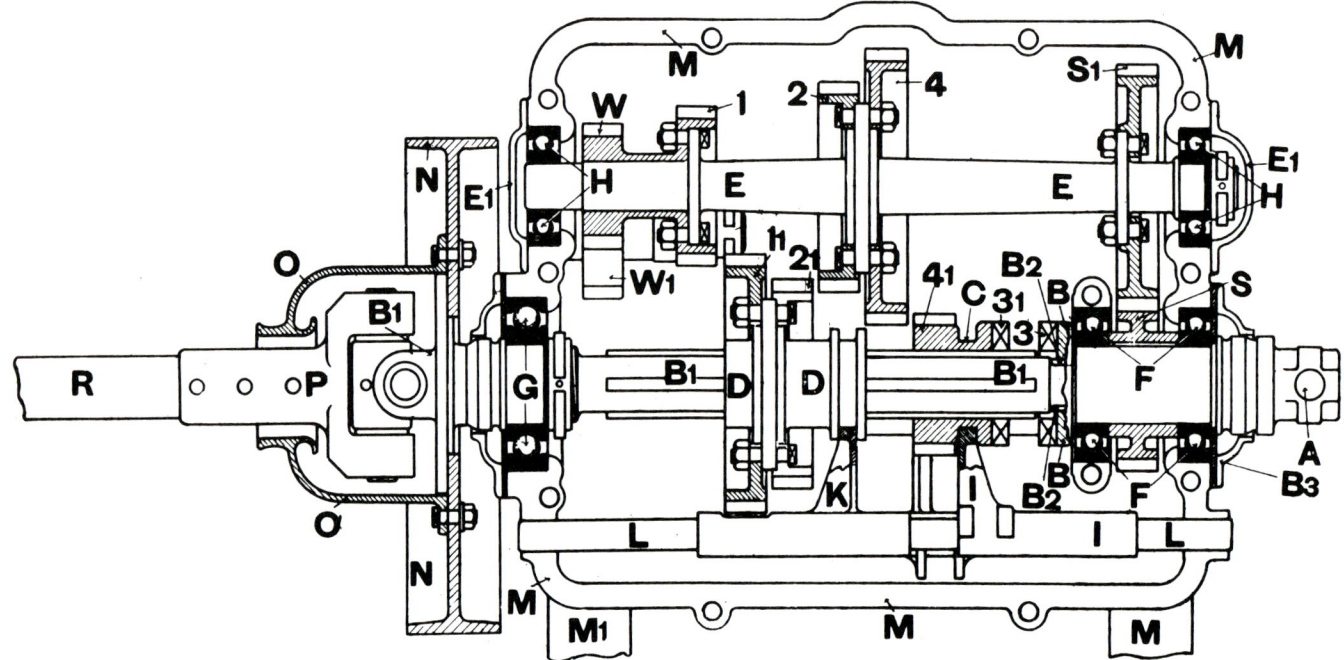

Fig. 5.—Change speed gear-box. Rolls-Royce Tourist Trophy car.

A, clutchshaft joint
B, sleeve spindle part of A carrying half third speed direct drive positive clutch
B1 B1, primary gearshaft with four feathers carrying sliding sleeves C and D, and half universal joint
B2, bushed portion of sleeve spindle B taking turned down end of primary gearshaft B1
B3, dust and oil cap
C C, sliding sleeve carrying half third speed direct drive positive clutch C1, and fourth geared drive driven pinion

C1, dust and oil caps
D D, sliding sleeve carrying first and second speed driven pinions
E E, secondary gearshaft carrying driven intermediate
E1 E1, wheel and first, second, and fourth and reverse driving pinions
F F, ball bearings to sleeve spindle B
G G, ball bearing carrying rear end of primary gearshaft B1 B1
H H, ball bearings to secondary gearshaft E E
I I, striking gear fork to sleeve C
K K, striking gear fork to sleeve D

L L, striking gear fork guide
L1, gear fork striking rod
M M, gear-box
M1, brackets to under frame
M2, tower enclosing change speed rocking levers
N N, pedal applied brake drum
O O, universal joint case
P P, rear half universal joint between primary gearshaft and propeller-shaft
R, propeller-shaft
S, intermediate driving wheel
S1, intermediate driven wheel

T T, gear-box bolt columns
U, gear-box wash-out plug
V, oil filling plug
W W, reverse pinions
1, first speed driving wheel
1¹, first speed driven wheel
2, second speed driving wheel
2¹, second speed driven wheel
3, third speed direct drive positive clutch (driving)
3¹, third speed direct drive positive clutch (driven)
4, geared fourth speed driving wheel
4¹, fourth speed driven wheel

sleeve B, whilst the driving wheels of the three remaining speeds are on the secondary-shaft E E, which is rotating constantly by the meshing of the intermediate toothed wheels S and S_1.

The driven portion of the third speed positive clutch 3_1 and the driven wheel of the fourth geared speed 4_1 are carried on the sliding sleeve C, while the driven wheels of the first and second speed are set upon the sliding sleeve D D.

Now to follow the engagement of the wheels necessary to the production of the four speeds in sequence. It must be taken that the engine is running, that the sleeve B is

Fig. 7.—Details of the bevel and differential gears.

A A, differential gear case	D D, crown or driven bevel wheel	F, ball thrust bearing to E E
$A_1 A_1$, oil retaining cap	$D_1 D_1$, ball thrust bearing to C C	F_1, ball bearing to bevel pinion shaft
B B, bevel gear-case sleeves	E E, driving bevel pinion	G G, rear half of universal joint
C C, differential gear-box	E_1, tail end of shaft of E	H, nut securing G G to E_3
$C_1 C_1$, annular spaces fitted with felt	E_2, plain bearing for E_1	J, oil filling cap
C_2, washers	E_3, tapered end of E taking G	K, wash-out plug
$C_3 C_3$, ball bearings to sleeves on C C		

rotating, and, by the agency of the intermediate wheels S and S_1, E E is also turning. Now, by sliding the sleeve D D rearwards until the wheel 1 is in mesh with 1_1, the drive passes from S to S_1, and from 1 to 1_1, and the first or lowest speed is obtained. If the sleeve D D is slid forward until the wheel 2_1 is in mesh with the wheel 2, then the second speed is obtained, the drive now passing through S S_1 and $2 2_1$. When the sleeve C is moved to the right until half of the positive clutch 3_1 is locked up to the other half of the positive clutch 3, the direct drive third speed is in, and the drive passes straight through the

feathered primary gearshaft B_1 to the propeller-shaft R, the secondary-shaft E running idle. During this neither 4, 2, nor 1 is in mesh with its respective fellows.

To put in the reverse, the sleeve D D is slid rearwards until the wheel 1_1 is in mesh with the wheel W_1, which is carried on a stud immediately below the wheel W on the shaft E, W and W_1 being constantly in mesh. This being done, the drive passes through S and S_1, W and W_1, to 1_1 on the primary gearshaft, with the result that the latter is now rotated in a reverse direction.

The brake band of the pedal-applied brake is applied to the drum N bolted to the rearward outer end of the primary gearshaft B_1. From the web of this drum there extends a dust cover to the universal joint P P. Dust caps to the ends of both gearshafts prevent the exudation of oil and the ingress of dust.

Live Axle Drive.

The vertical section and part sectional elevation of the live axle drive and differential as fitted to the Tourist Trophy Rolls-Royce car (figs. 6 and 7) show clearly the design, and indicate the thought and care devoted to the consideration of this most important part of a live axle car. It will be noticed that with the exception of the tail bearing E_2 of the driving bevel pinion-shaft E_1, the remainder of the bearings, both ordinary and thrust, are ball bearings of a sound and substantial character. The differential gear case itself is, when compared with the generality of such members, found to be much reduced in size. The institution of a plain bearing to the tail of the bevel wheel spindle strikes us as in every way preferable to a single row of balls, as the bearing is placed there pre-eminently as a steady, and it performs its duty there in the best manner. The ball thrust bearings D_1 and F_1 are in each case brought as close as possible to the

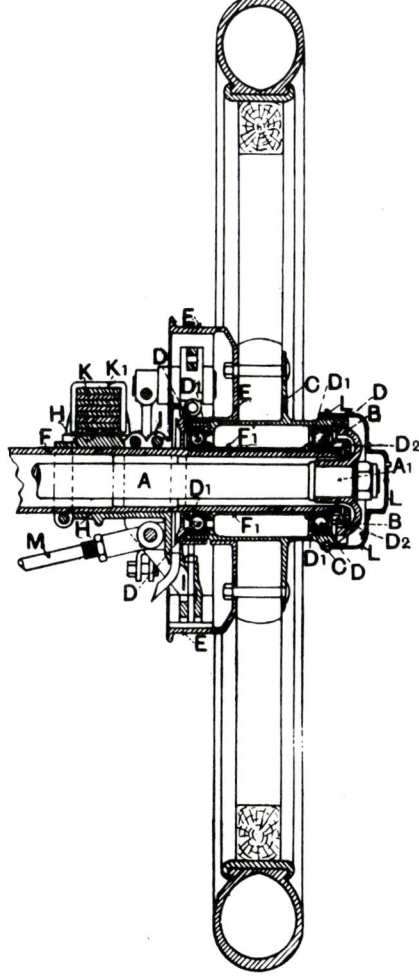

Fig. 6.—Live driving axle.

A, right half live axle
A_1, squared end of live axle carrying road wheel driver
B, road wheel driver
C, flanged portion road wheel hub
D D, ball bearings upon which road wheel hub rotates
$D_1 D_1$, ball races
$D_2 D_2$, ball bearings adjustment
E E, rear wheel brake drum forming part of wheel hub
F F, live axle sleeve carrying spring table, brake bracket, and road wheel bearings
$F_1 F_1$, distance sleeve on live axle sleeve
H H, spring table
I I, road wheel brake bracket
K, car spring
K_1, spring clip
L L, axle cap
M M, rear axle tension rod

member exerting the thrust to be taken. The neat way in which the bevel pinion thrust is packed away within the overhang of the bevel itself is particularly good. Undesirable exudation of oil and grease from the differential gear case is prevented by the filling of the annular spaces $C_1 C_1 C_1$ with soft felt. The bevel-driven ring is most securely bolted to, and forms an actual part of, the differential gear box, as indicated in the figure. Notice should be taken that the differential gear case is fitted with a most conveniently placed grease or oil filler J and a wash-out plug K.

The live axle drive fitted to these cars exhibits several interesting features, not the least being the method in which the road wheel is carried on ball bearings set upon the tubular live axle sleeve F (fig. 6). The ball races are set widely apart, and separated by the distance sleeve F_1, ring and set screw locking adjustment for both bearings $D_2 D_2$ being provided as shown. The live or turning axle A passes right through

the centre of the axle sleeve F to the outside of the road wheel hub, where upon the squared end A_1 is carried the driving dog B. This driver has lugs formed upon its external periphery, which engage with slots cut to take the same in the rim of the road wheel hub flange C, and it is secured upon the squared end A_1 of the driving axle A by the keyed nut shown. Thus the rotary drive is alone performed by the shaft A, no other load or strain being brought upon it.

Within the brake drum E are set the expanding brake segments pivoting on spindles carried by the brake bracket I.

Oil and grease are prevented from escaping from the bearing and brake drum by the axle cap L and the oil catchers and guards fitted to the inner face of road wheel hub. In the matter of thoughtful design and adaptation of means to an end in a light car, we have seen nothing better than this method of drive and this type of road wheel bearing.

In this illustration by the late F. Gordon Crosby, Percy Northey's Rolls-Royce (No. 22), which took second place in the final results of the 1905 T.T., leads the Hon. C. S. Rolls' No. 53. This latter car retired with a stripped gearbox during the opening lap.

THE EIGHT-CYLINDER ROLLS-ROYCE LANDAULET.

Something more than a surprise awaited the guests of Messrs. Rolls-Royce at the dinner to which they were bidden on Friday, the 3rd inst., at the Trocadero. All knew that an announcement of importance was to be made, but the subject was, we are sure, very far removed from all anticipatory opinions. In lieu of detailing the explanatory speeches of Messrs. Royce, Rolls, and Johnson, we place before our readers reproductions of the drawings of the side view, a part vertical section of the new engine, together with reproductions of photographic views of the engine taken diagonally overhead, an upward view of the base chamber, and two views of the high-tension distributer.

A few words as to the incidents which have led to the production of this remarkably designed engine will not be out of place. It will put our readers into possession of the problem laid before that practised engineer Mr. Royce for solution, and our readers can judge for themselves how near in their view of the case he has gone to the proper solution.

In the spring of this year Messrs. C. S. Rolls and Co. resolved to arrange for the construction of a Rolls-Royce petrol-driven landaulet, which should in all desirable particulars come abreast of the electric landaulet for town use, while also being valuable for work in connection with country houses, or for long-distance touring if required. Accordingly the following requirements were tabulated, and put before Mr. Royce, upon which to exert his engineering ingenuity and ability :

In appearance and dimensions the R.-R. landaulet should resemble the best electric carriages in use in London.

Although the landaulet would thus be bonnetless, the engine should be removed as far as possible from the carriage proper.

The engine must be vibrationless.

The motion of the car must be absolutely silent.

The car must be free from the objectionable rattling and buzzing and inconvenience of chains, which also interfere with a really efficient side entrance.

There must be little or no changing of speed.

The engine must be smokeless and odourless.

As we have already suggested, the accompanying diagrams will show how Mr. Royce tackled and solved the problem, particularly as regards the space requirements. The frame of the new Rolls-Royce landaulet is, as usual, of channel cambered steel with suitable cross members, and carrying the engine and change-speed gear box without the intervention of an underframe. In the first instance, as bonnet space forward the dashboard was tabooed, and the length of the vehicle could not be increased, Mr. Royce resolved to place the engine under the footboard instead of under the driver's seat, as has been done in some previous cases. Now, although it is permissible to raise the footboard some few inches from the top of the frame, and this indeed is done in the car under review, it was necessary, in order to place the engine as suggested, to have an engine of but little depth. To achieve this result Mr. Royce determined to adopt an engine of eight cylinders, 83 mm. bore and 83 mm. stroke, and place them four on one side and four on the other side of the crank chamber. These cylinders are inclined at an angle of 45° with the vertical centre line, and at 90° with each other, as shown in fig. 1. Eight small cylinders so disposed were adopted in order that the explosive impulses might be as small, light, and as close together as possible, in order that a practically continuous turning movement (torque)

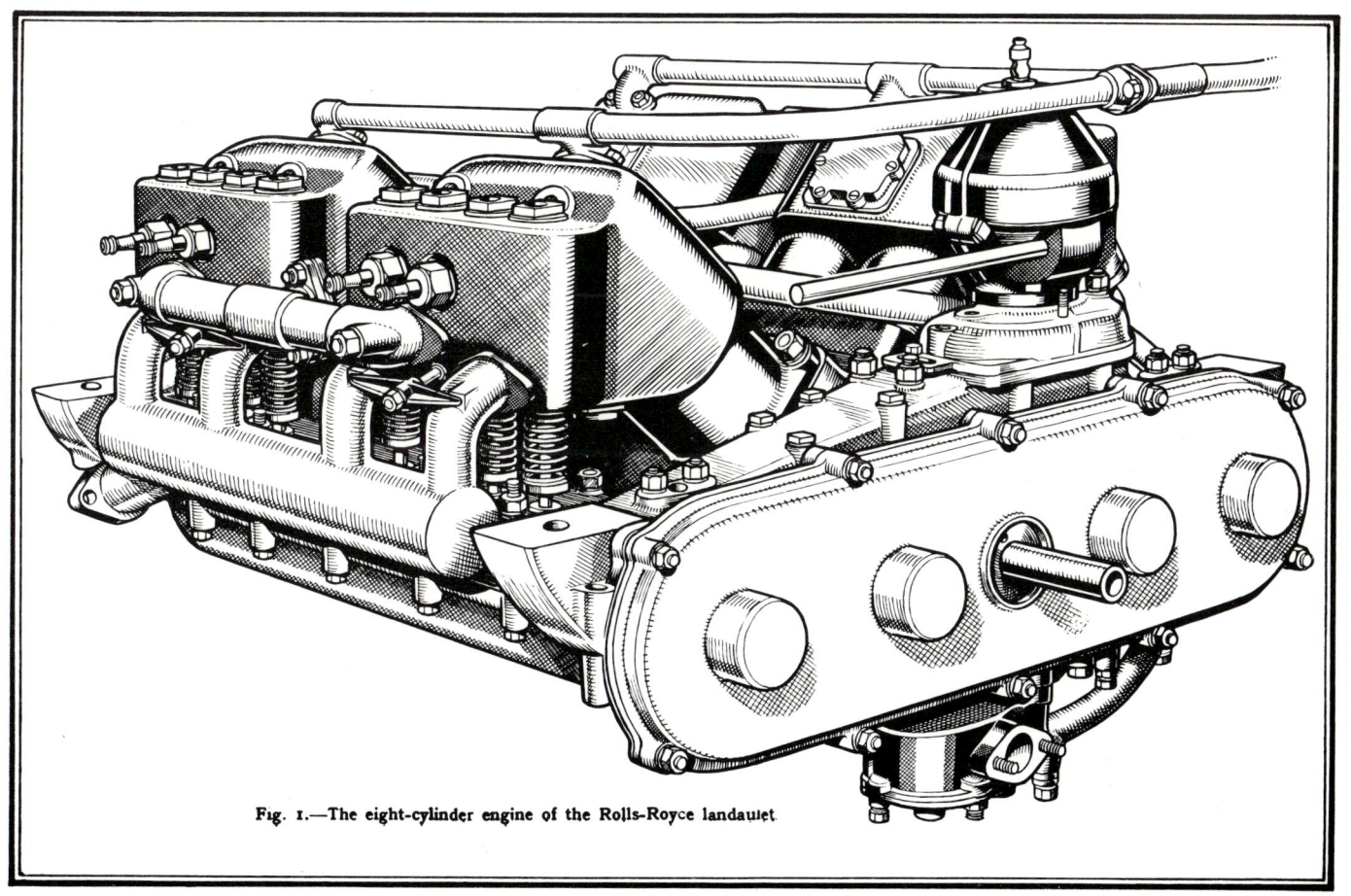

Fig. 1.—The eight-cylinder engine of the Rolls-Royce landaulet.

might be obtained.   By having eight cylinders, and arranging them as above mentioned, it will be realised that the crankshaft receives a rotary impulse every 90° (one quarter of a revolution), and that the impulses and compressions must overlap each other in a much more perfect manner than even in a six-cylinder engine, which hitherto has been accepted as verging upon perfection in this regard.   Further, the eight-cylinder V engine requires but an extremely simple crankshaft, which is comparatively short.   Noiselessness is claimed to be obtained by the fact that with these small cylinders all the moving parts are comparatively light, the exhaust volume per cylinder small and practically continuous, which lends itself to most effectual silencing.

A feature of this engine which will at once strike the mimical critic of inclined engines is the fact that though the cylinders are set in a manner that may not at once appeal to him, yet the valves are vertical in their action.   While the one great objection to inclined cylinders is thereby avoided, it will be noticed, on reference to fig. 4, that the inclined cylinders and vertical valves produce an extremely short port—an object aimed at, it will be remembered, by the inclined valves fitted to the English Daimler engines. It is hardly necessary to draw attention to the fact that

Fig. 2.—Top view of the Rolls-Royce eight-cylinder engine.

each cylinder has its inlet and exhaust valves side by side, and that both are operated by the same camshaft.

The Smoke Nuisance.

It is hoped that by the neat and effectual method of lubrication adopted in connection with the eight-cylinder Rolls-Royce the blue smoke nuisance will never occur.   A small gear pump, worm gear driven off the crankshaft, is placed beneath the forward portion of the crank chamber, and pumps oil from the aluminium oil sump G^1 (holding one gallon) to the main bearings of the engine through holes drilled in the crankshaft and webs, and the oil, still under pressure, arrives at the crank pins, thus ensuring perfect lubrication to all these parts.   At the crank pins the oil is under a pressure of about 15 lbs. per square inch, with the result that sufficient will spurt out around the

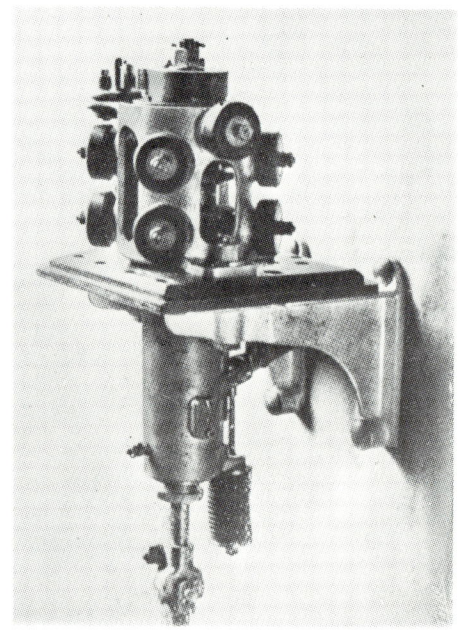

Fig. 3.—The eight-cylinder distributer on the Rolls-Royce engine.

big end brasses, and be thrown by centrifugal force on to the cylinder walls and gudgeon pin bearings. The oil falling into the crank chamber flows at once

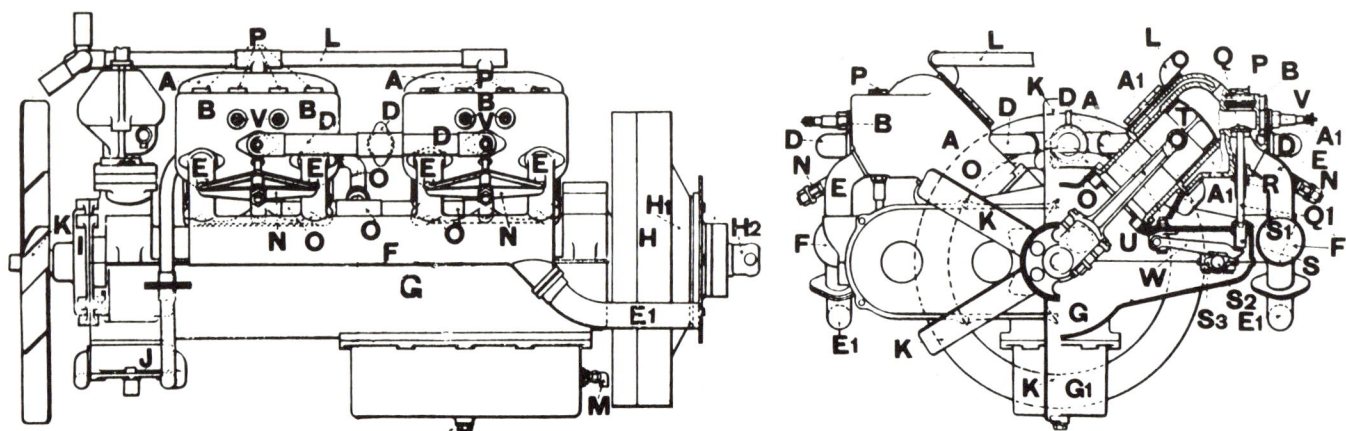

Fig. 4.—Side view and section of the Rolls-Royce eight-cylinder landaulet engine.

A A, cylinders	H, flywheel and clutch	M, oil level cock	S, exhaust valve tappet
A1 A1, water jacket spacing	H1, clutch	N N, exhaust valve and pipe dogs	S1, exhaust valve tappet guide
B B, valve chambers	H2, junction of clutch and gear-shaft	O O, circulating water delivery to cylinders	S2, camshaft
D D, induction pipe	I, half-time gear case	P P, valve caps	S3, exhaust cam
E E, exhaust pipes	J, water circulating pump	Q, exhaust valve head	T, piston
E1, exhaust pipe to silencer	K K, fan to radiator	Q1, exhaust valve stem	U, big end of connecting rod
F, exhaust pot	L L, water delivery from crown of water jackets to radiator	R, exhaust valve stem guide	V, sparking plugs
G G, crank chamber			W, exhaust tappet lifting lever
G1, oil sump			

into the sump G¹, while any surplus oil thrown by the pump escapes back thereto, also by means of a relief valve. As the pump will be made always to throw too much oil, the lead from the relief valve is led up to the dashboard, where it will serve any necessary drip feeds, the oil then passing on through a second relief valve back to the sump.

Synchronised ignition is fitted, but as the firing of eight cylinders in sequence is almost too big a question to demand of one coil and trembler, each set of four cylinders has its own coil and its own distributer, the latter being set one above the other on the distributer spindle, as shown in the illustrations. Otherwise the ignition will be on entirely the same lines as is fitted to the two, four, and six-cylinder Rolls-Royce cars, and which, as the world knows, behaved so well in the Tourist Trophy Race.

The power is transmitted through the ordinary Rolls-Royce clutch and a change-speed gear, giving three speeds forward and reverse, but so flexible will the engine be that its remarkable suppleness, coupled with the utmost elimination of friction, will enable the car to be started and driven always on the top gear, except upon very steep hills. The drive is by propeller shaft to bevel gear on the live axle, the road wheels running on outward extensions of the live axle sleeve, the axle itself having no duty but to rotate the road wheels.

Accessibility has been very carefully studied. It will be remembered that in the early part of this description we referred to a slight upper frame, raised on the upper flange of the main frame to carry the driver's footboards. Removable panels are placed in the sides of this frame, and through these panels uninterrupted access to the exhaust and induction valves and sparking plugs can be obtained. Any necessary attention can be given to the pistons, little ends and big ends of the connecting rods, and crankshaft bearings by dropping off the lower half of the crank chamber, which, though it carries the oil sump, is practically a tray.

It is clear that with the engine under the footboard, and no bonnet, the steering of the eight-cylinder Rolls-Royce landaulet cannot be effected in the ordinary way. The difficulty has been surmounted in a very ingenious and effective manner by running the steering standard proper backwards and downwards from the steering post to a steering box, enclosing the usual worm and nut arrangement. The steering standard is rotated by the steering post by means of special bevel gearing enclosed in a special gear box on about the centre of the steering wheel post.

THE AUTOCAR. DECEMBER 2ND, 1905.

Flashes.

Last week we were very much interested to have the opportunity of trying the first Rolls-Royce eight-cylinder landaulet. It appears to us to be quite an ideal town carriage, as smooth-running as an electric vehicle, and almost as quiet. In fact, it is able to do all that the best electric carriage would do, with the advantage of having a considerably greater speed when necessary, and a very much larger range of action. The points which struck us over and above the smooth running of the engine were the ease of control; the very wide lock, which, combined with a short wheelbase, enabled the car to be turned in an ordinary road without tacking; and last, but not least, the remarkable range of speed which can be obtained by the throttle alone. The car would run in perfect smoothness behind a crawling cab on the top speed, and then, with a touch of the throttle, make for an opening in the traffic, and in less time than it takes to write it would be running at twelve or fourteen miles an hour; in fact, the acceleration and retardation through the throttle alone were all that could possibly be desired. With a new type of engine, it is well known that the extreme refinement of running cannot be obtained unless a very long period is devoted to adjustments and tuning, and we think it remarkable that at the first trial so smooth a running engine should have been evolved. Of course, it should be understood that the eight-cylinder machine is designed for town work mainly. It can be used, and will be used, in the same way that a brougham or landaulet would be used in the country, but for average touring requirements the ordinary four-cylinder and six-cylinder vertical engines are entirely satisfactory to their users.

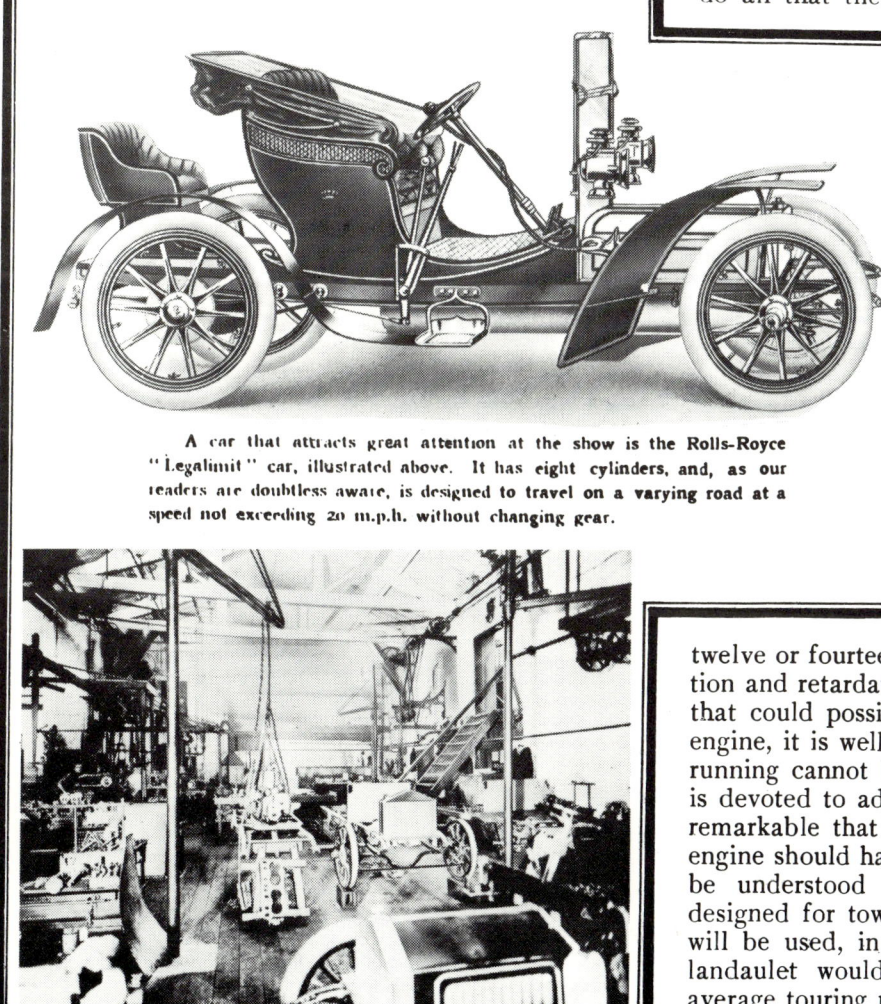

A car that attracts great attention at the show is the Rolls-Royce "Legalimit" car, illustrated above. It has eight cylinders, and, as our readers are doubtless aware, is designed to travel on a varying road at a speed not exceeding 20 m.p.h. without changing gear.

Cook Street, Manchester works in 1904

RAC Tourist Trophy 1906

TOURIST TROPHY CARS. The Rolls-Royce cars for the Tourist Trophy Race have already been over the Isle of Man course under the control of the Hon. C. S. Rolls and Mr. Northey, who are here depicted at the point from which they start off on the race by gravity.

Scene at the starting point of the race, the winner getting ready.

Photograph by   *Argent Archer, Kensington, W.*

A snapshot of the winner of the Tourist Trophy as he negotiated a bend on the mountain ascent at full speed. The effect of the corner and incline is somewhat peculiar, as it seems to cut the road off immediately behind the wheels.

THE RACERS' OWN EXPERIENCES.

The Hon. C. S. Rolls, Rolls-Royce.

My experiences in the race are probably the least interesting of the lot, for I was the happy possessor of a perfect piece of mechanism, which had treated me so well in practice that I never had a moment's anxiety as to getting through all right. I anticipated an interesting struggle with Mr. Napier, and I had a feeling of genuine regret when I saw this good sportsman stranded at the side of the road. I came across one or two other cars in the race going very fast, but I was confident they were over-driving. There is no doubt the Automobile Club has, by the Tourist Trophy Race, produced in this country an ideal type of touring vehicle. With a car like the Rolls-Royce, for instance, the extraordinary ease of control, the speed at which one can run up to a corner, and the rapidity with which one can pull up, make it as much pleasure to drive as a racing monster, while there is no fatigue in driving, very little risk of punctures, no big tyres to manipulate (I had 90 mm. on back and front), and practically no cost of upkeep.

I would like to thank *The Autocar* for its most kind congratulations, but as I had nothing to do but sit there and wait till the car got to the finish, the credit is obviously due to Mr. Royce, the designer and builder, I am happy to think it has again been shown how utterly unnecessary it is for a Britisher desiring to purchase a good motor to spend his money in foreign goods and in the support of foreign workmen, instead of trusting his own country, which is the leading engineering country of the world.

TOTAL TIMES AND AVERAGE SPEEDS.

No.	Name of Car and Driver.	Actual Time. H. M. S.	Average Speed. M.P.H.	Position.
4.	ROLLS-ROYCE (Hon. C. S. Rolls)..	4 6 0¾	39.3	1
23.	BERLIET (— Bablot)	4 32 58½	35.4	2
2.	DARRACQ (A. Lee Guinness)	4 42 48½	34.2	3
15.	CLEMENT (G. Brand)	4 47 20	33.6	4
17.	BEESTON HUMBER (T. C. Pullinger)	4 56 1½	32.7	5
18.	COVENTRY HUMBER (L. Coatalen)	5 0 52½	32.1	6
1.	ARROL-JOHNSTON (John S. Napier)	5 22 1	30.0	7
25.	SIDDELEY (A. E. Crowdy)	5 47 19	27.8	8
32.	SCOUT (J. Percy Dean)	6 57 18¼	23.2	9

AVERAGE SPEEDS ATTAINED ON EACH CIRCUIT.

No.	Name of Car.	First Round. m.p.h.	Second Round. m.p.h.	Third Round. m.p.h.	Fourth Round. m.p.h.
1.	ARROL-JOHNSTON ...	38.4	17.6	39.5	40.2
2.	DARRACQ	28.4	35.1	37.1	36.8
3.	DARRACQ	34.0	34.2	32.5	—
4.	ROLLS-ROYCE	40.2	39.8	39.4	38.1
5.	ROLLS-ROYCE	21.3	—	—	—
6.	MINERVA	25.0	—	—	—
7.	MINERVA	35.6	35.2	—	—
8.	JAMES AND BROWNE	27.0	26.8	—	—
12.	ARGYLL	—	—	—	—
15.	CLEMENT	33.3	34.9	33.5	33.2
17.	BEESTON HUMBER ..	32.7	32.9	32.8	32.4
18.	COVENTRY HUMBER	33.4	31.5	32.1	32.0
23.	BERLIET	34.9	35.2	35.7	35.9
24.	SIDDELEY	31.6	—	—	—
25.	SIDDELEY	32.3	19.4	30.7	35.6
26.	BERLIET	32.4	31.6	27.6	—
27.	THORNYCROFT	29.9	29.9	27.9	—
28.	STAR	27.7	28.6	—	—
29.	DEASY	—	—	—	—
31.	VINOT	29.0	29.9	30.9	—
32.	SCOUT	24.0	17.7	29.1	25.2
33.	STAR	30.2	30.0	—	—
35.	CLIMAX	24.3	—	—	—
36.	SWIFT	34.7	—	—	—
37.	HARDMAN	25.6	28.8	27.1	—
38.	BIANCHI	28.9	37.2	—	—
46.	ACADEMY	27.0	27.0	26.9	—
47.	S.C.A.R.	33.2	34.4	—	—
48.	VICI	—	—	—	—

A TOURIST TROPHY CAR IN THE UNITED STATES. The Hon. C. S. Rolls on Mr. Northey's 20 h.p. Rolls-Royce Tourist Trophy car at the Empire City Track, New York, where he recently won the five miles race for cars of 25 h.p. and under. Rolls's time for the five miles was 5 mins. 51¼ secs., the fastest mile being covered in 1 min. 7 secs.

THE NEW 40-50 H.P. ROLLS-ROYCE ENGINE.

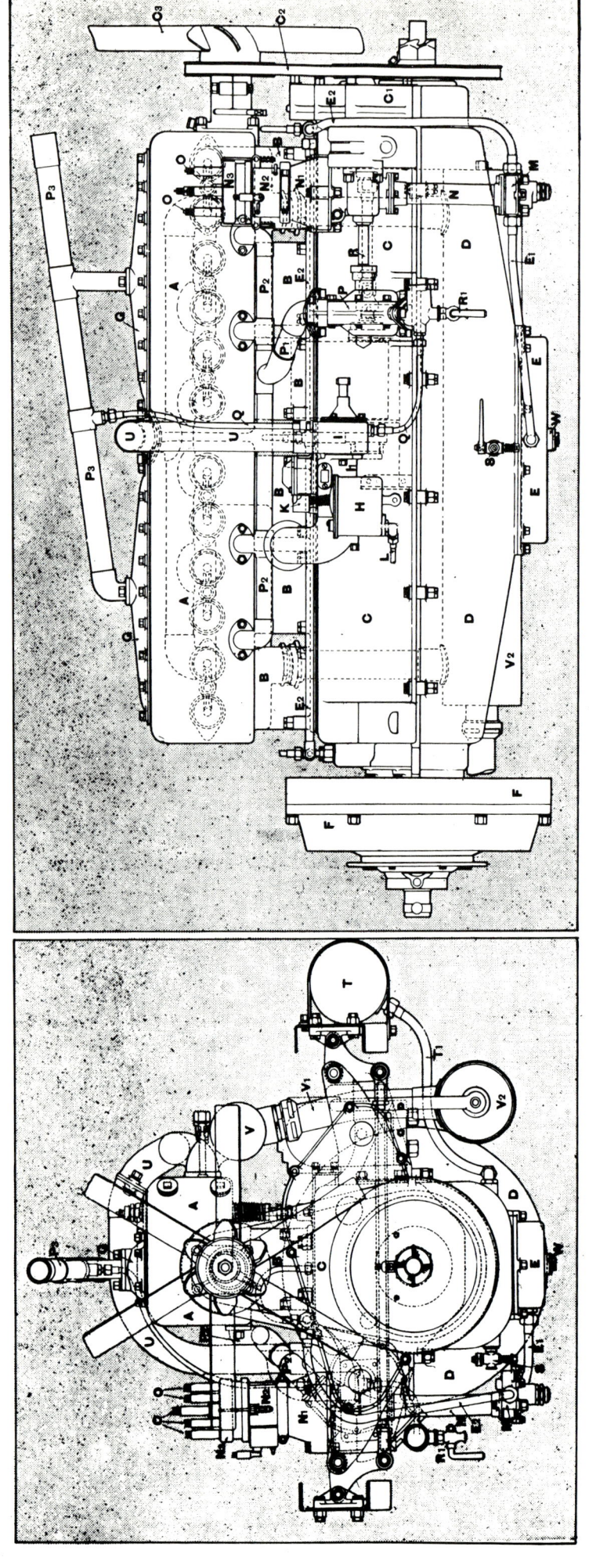

Fig. 1.—Side and end views of engine.

A A, water-jacketed portion cylinder castings, each containing three cylinders
B B, cylinder barrels
C C, upper half of crank chamber
C₁, half-time gear case
C₂, fan belt and driving pulley
C₃, radiator fan
D, lower half of crank chamber

E E, oil sump
E₁, oil suction pipe
E₂, oil delivery pipes
F, flywheel and clutch
G G, water chamber covers
H, float feed chamber of carburetter
I, throttle chamber
I₁, jet and automatic valve chamber

K, petrol feed adjustment screw
L, petrol feed pipe
M, oil force pump
N, column containing oil pump spindle
N₁, governor case
N₂, contact making box
N₃, distributer
O O, high tension current leads

P, water circulating pump
P₁, water delivery pipe
P₂ P₂, water delivery pipes to cylinders
P₃ P₃, water delivery pipe from cylinders to radiator
Q Q, carburetter water jacket pipes
R, water pump spindle
R₁, drain cock to water system

S, crank chamber oil level cock
T, lubricating oil reservoir
T₁, pipe from same to crank chamber
U U U, induction pipe
V, exhaust pot
V₁, exhaust pipe
V₂, silencer
W, wash out plug

Anything appertaining to automobile mechanism which issues from the works at Manchester under the direction of that finished and talented engineer, Mr. Ed. Royce, is certain to attract the immediate attention of the motoring world. Therefore a few points dealing with the new 40-50 h.p. six-cylinder Rolls-Royce engine, which made its first bow to the world at Olympia, are certain to interest our readers. Read in conjunction with the accompanying line diagrams, a very fair idea of its design can be gathered.

The cylinders, which are cast in groups of three, have 4½in. bore by 4½in. stroke, and are claimed to develop 48 h.p. at 1,200 revolutions per minute. With regard to the water-cooling, each cylinder is completely water-jacketed all round, no two adjacent cylinders being without water between them. The group method of casting the cylinders does away with external joints, so that these do not exist to maintain or leak. The valve chambers are placed along the left-hand side of the engine, one camshaft serving to operate all the valves, and

perform sundry other duties hereinafter mentioned. The inlet and exhaust valves are both of nickel steel, and interchangeable.

Mr. Royce has provided bearings of extreme size in the centre and ends of the engine. No bearing at all is found in the centre of the two groups of three cylinders. The crankshaft is turned up out of a solid nickel steel forging, and machined on all surfaces. The bearings, both for crankshaft and crank pins, are provided with an anti-friction lining carried in a phosphor-bronze bush, and are provided with "liners" in the joints, to facilitate the adjustment for wear.

Lubrication System.

The lubrication system followed in connection with the new six-cylinder Rolls-Royce engine is practically the same as that so successfully employed in connection with high speed reciprocating steam engines. The positive feed oil pump, which is skew-driven off the camshaft, delivers oil under pressure to the main bearings, and thence through the hollow crankshaft to the crank pins and gudgeon pins. By means of an easily adjusted valve placed upon the pump cover, a constant pressure of oil is maintained in the oil leads independently of the oil in the reservoir under the crank chamber, to which the oil runs through a filter after dropping from the bearings.

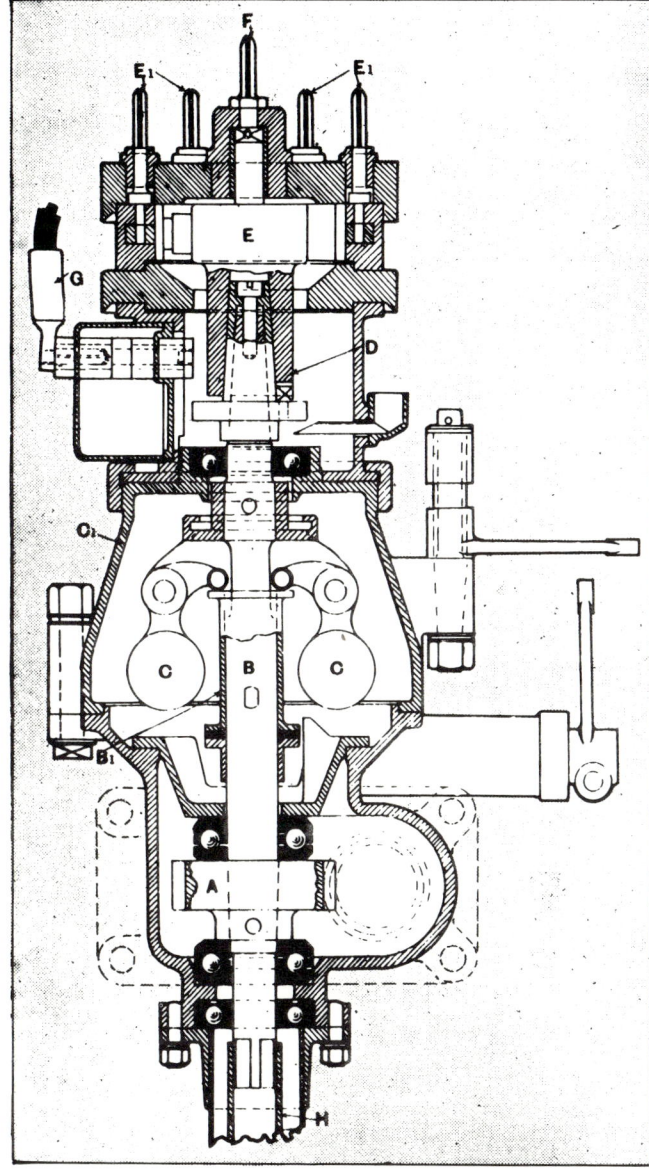

Fig. 2.—Distributer and governor.

A, driven spiral wheel on governor spindle
B, governor spindle
B1, sleeve carrying governor
C C, governor balls
C1, governor case
D, commutator
E, high tension distributer
E1, high tension leads to sparking plugs
F, high tension lead from coil
G, primary lead to contact maker
H, connecting tube to oil pump spindle

In this new engine, the rotating commutator hitherto employed so successfully in the Rolls-Royce engines has been departed from, on the ground that the wipe contact commutator has the defect of making contact at slightly irregular periods. In order to avoid this, the low-tension portion of the Rolls-Royce commutator is now made with platinum points, operated by a cam, which separates them, and, again, allows them to come into contact with each other at exact intervals. Having no desire to tutor Mr. Royce (who is as famous an electrician as he is an engineer), we should like, in passing, to state that the rotary wipe contact commutator fitted to the Rolls-Royce T.T. car (1905) which we have now had in use for nine months, has done so well that, excepting one occasion upon which the coil was in fault, we have—for the odd 3,000 miles we have driven the car—never heard the engine misfire. However, we bow to Mr. Royce's superior discernment, and we have no doubt, good as the rotating commutator was, the new one is better.

The carburetter fitted to this new engine differs but slightly from that described in connection with last year's car, the only difference being that the automatic air valve, in lieu of being of piston form, is now made conical, which eliminates the friction occurring in a piston valve fitting throughout its length. By this alteration, the valve is rendered extremely sensitive, and prevents the dust which might get upon the faces from making the valve stick.

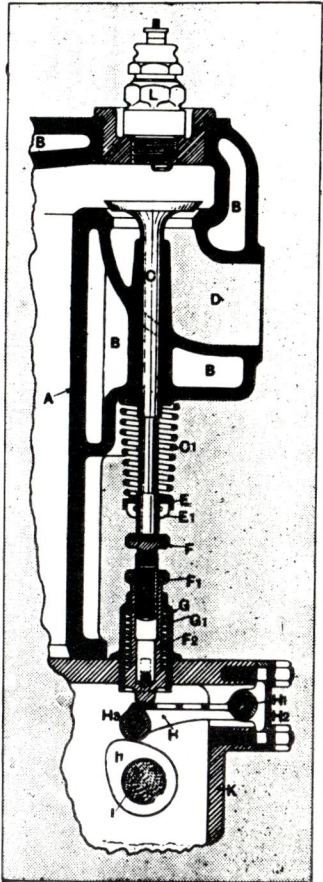

Fig. 3.—Section through inlet valve.

A, cylinder wall
B, water spaces
C, valve
C1, valve spring
D, inlet port
E, spring cup
E1, cotter
F, valve lift adjusting set screw
F1, lock nut
F11, tappet
G, tappet guide
G1, tappet return spring
H, rocking lever carrying friction roller
H1, rocking lever pivot
H11, rocking lever base attached to crank chamber by two set screws
H111, friction roller
I, camshaft
I1, cam
K, crank chamber walls
L, sparking plug

The induction and exhaust valves are operated by means of rocking levers pivoted at one end, and fitted at the other with a friction roller lying between the valve spindle and the cam, as shown in fig. 3. These levers are fitted in pairs, one inlet and one exhaust, mounted on one base, and attached to the crank chamber by studs. The introduction of the friction roller lever is claimed to do away with the side pressure which is exerted on the lifter slides when cam and tappet rod come into actual contact, and is now taken by a pivot, on which the lever hinges.

The engine is suspended from the frame by brackets at the rear end and a special arrangement of levers at the forward end as shown in fig. 1, which allow the members of the frame relative movement to one another for the negotiation of rough roads without involving extra strain on the arms of the crank chamber.

THE SILVER GHOST STORY

By Warren Allport

There is only one Silver Ghost, though later 40–50 h.p. Rolls-Royces have been known as Silver Ghosts. Here we trace the story of this 1907 car, the most famous of all Rolls-Royces

FOR many years now the name Rolls-Royce has been synonymous with all that is best in motoring and so great is the prestige accrued by this make that many manufacturers of articles not in any way connected with motoring have called them the Rolls-Royces of their kind. This enviable reputation – not only for excellence of design and finish but also for reliability in service – was not achieved overnight but was built up over a period of time. When Henry Royce's first experimental 10 h.p. car took to the road on 1 April 1904 the name Rolls-Royce was unknown in the motoring world but at that time Rolls had a partner in the business of C. S. Rolls & Co. by the name of Claude Johnson. The latter was well known to a number of prominent Edwardian motorists having been secretary of the Automobile Club of Great Britain and Ireland (later the RAC) and organizer of the 1900 1,000 Miles Trial. It was natural therefore that Johnson should work with Rolls in publicizing the exploits of the early Rolls-Royce cars.

In an era when the wealthy travelled with maids and valets it was important to have a large car, and for this reason seven-seater bodies were often fitted on chassis. Up to 1906 the largest model produced by Rolls-Royce was the 30 h.p. six-cylinder which was somewhat underpowered when fitted with a heavy body and loaded with passengers and luggage. A longer-chassis version of the 30 h.p. was clearly what was needed but would have had a very poor power to weight ratio, so Royce set about the design of a completely new 40–50 h.p. model which would meet the demands of the carriage trade. It was this model which, expertly publicized by Claude Johnson who had in the meantime become general managing director of the newly-formed Rolls-Royce Ltd., established the Rolls-Royce reputation for engineering excellence on a level that few other car manufacturers have ever reached. One particular car, The Silver Ghost, did much to make that reputation and the story of this one car – probably the best known of any Veteran or Vintage car and the best known Rolls-Royce – is the subject of this article.

Above: The Silver Ghost on a Scottish mountain pass during the 2,000-mile Trial in May 1907. Note the rough surface of the road and the leather aprons which served as weather protection for the passengers. Below: The stripped 40–50 h.p. chassis at Olympia in November 1906

The Silver Ghost

It is thought chassis 60551, the thirteenth six-cylinder 40–50 h.p. Rolls-Royce to be built at the original Cooke Street, Manchester, works, was in fact the polished chassis which appeared on the Rolls-Royce stand at the Olympia Motor Show in November 1906. At the Show, the chassis attracted considerable attention, for not only was it better built and finished than the majority of its competitors but it incorporated a number of important technical innovations. The six-cylinder 7,046 c.c. engine was the normal side-valve of the period with non-detachable cylinder heads; but there the resemblance stopped for the cylinders were cast in two blocks of three (instead of singly or in pairs) and the very stiff crankshaft ran in seven bearings with pressurized oil feed to the crankshaft, big ends and gudgeon pins. An important point with non-detachable cylinder heads was that the tappets, valve guides and springs were not enclosed and were easily accessible for adjustment. The engine itself had special mountings at the front which allowed for flexing of the chassis frame without straining the engine – most engines of the day were bolted straight into the chassis with perhaps half-a-dozen bearer arms – while the efficient two-jet Royce carburettor and separate manifold for each block of three cylinders (in effect a dual exhaust system) helped to provide exceptionally smooth running.

This, then, was the type of car with which Claude Johnson set out to establish the Rolls-Royce name. He had a habit of bestowing pet names on cars and called chassis 60551 The Silver Ghost. While most people today refer to 40-50 h.p. Rolls-Royces built up to 1925 as Silver Ghosts, this is not correct. In their day they were known simply as 40-50s and it was only with the advent of the New Phantom (also a 40-50 h.p.) in 1925 that the earlier cars were called Silver Ghosts to avoid confusion. So, in fact, there is only one Silver Ghost; The Silver Ghost – silver because the metal parts were silver plated and the body finished in silver (aluminium) paint, and ghost by reason of its extraordinary silence.

The first reference to The Silver Ghost in *The Autocar* is dated 20 April 1907 and reads as follows: "The new six-cylinder 40-50 h.p. Rolls-Royce has made its appearance in London. . . . The running of this car at slow speeds on the direct third is the smoothest thing we have ever experienced, while for silence the motor beneath the bonnet might be a silent sewing machine. The cylinders are 4½in. by 4½in., and at 1,000 rpm the speeds are 14, 22, 38 and 47 mph; the highest is a geared fourth. A little trial run up a certain well-known test hill, which has an average gradient of 1 in 11 for 850ft., with 72ft. of 1 in 7·8, showed this superb car to be able to take this rise at a speed of 26·1 mph. The car is delightfully sprung, and the steering is so arranged that upon taking pressure off the steering wheel the car runs in a straight line." The car had left the works on Saturday 13 April and was therefore still very new. Claude Johnson had had it fitted with a special Roi-de-Belges type of touring body executed by Barker & Co. who held the royal warrant.

Further impressions of the car were given in *The Autocar* for 27 April 1907. Again the testers were very impressed with the ride and silence and wrote: "At whatever speed this car is being driven on its direct third there is *no* engine so far as sensation goes, nor are one's auditory nerves troubled, driving or standing, by a fuller sound than emanates from an eight-day clock. There is no realization of driving propulsion; the feeling as the passenger sits either at front or back of the vehicle is one of being wafted through the landscape. . . ."

The 2,000-mile Trial

In May 1907 the Silver Ghost with Claude Johnson at the wheel took part in a public test against a White steam car driven by Frederick Coleman. They then drove from Hatfield to Darlington and then on to Glasgow. Then they covered the routes selected for the first two days of the Scottish Trials, including Rest and Be Thankful hill with acute hairpin bend which Johnson negotiated without difficulty three times forward and twice backward. The Silver Ghost went on to cover the remaining part of the 774 miles of the Scottish Reliability Trial course without incident. Then the return journey to London began from Glasgow by way of Edinburgh and crossing the border at Carter Bar (1,250ft). Arrival in London was followed by a run to Bexhill as at the beginning of the 2,000-mile trial, climbing both Test Hill and Handcross on third gear. On the completion of the 2,000½ miles The Silver Ghost had acquitted herself well, having been driven from the south coast to Scotland in top gear

and having achieved a flying ¼-mile of 52·94 mph on the Bexhill track on which she was also driven at a timed speed of 3·4 mph in top gear. On the trip to Scotland a fuel consumption of 20·86 mpg had been achieved – not bad for a six-cylinder 7-litre car that was no lightweight at 4,382lb (39cwt 14lb) including passengers and all luggage, and comparing favourably with the previous best consumption over a distance of 200 miles by a six-cylinder car of 18·78 mpg. On one of the two-gallon economy tests 23·25 mpg was achieved.

The whole of this performance which lasted for 12 days was under the official supervision of the RAC whose report showed that a total of 1 hour 28 minutes was spent on adjustments in motor houses including attention to the coil, carburettor, brakes and replacement of the accumulators on two occasions.

The 15,000-mile Trial

This performance would to some people have been sufficient proof of the excellence of the Rolls-Royce 40-50 h.p. car, but Claude Johnson was not such a man and so he continued with his plan to put The Silver Ghost over much of the ground already covered as an entrant in the Scottish Reliability Trial and then go on under official observation to set up a new long-distance record, the existing record then standing at 7,089 miles non-stop. The 2,000-mile Trial had ended on 14 May, and Friday 21 June saw The Silver Ghost with Johnson yet again at the wheel leaving London for Glasgow under the official observation of the RAC.

On reaching Glasgow the car then took part in the 747 miles of the Scottish Reliability Trial and won

the gold medal for excellence in hill climbing, reliability and fuel consumption. In this trial the Rolls-Royce beat the six-cylinder Darracq, Hotchkiss and Belsize and the four-cylinder Mercedes, Berliet and Ariel. However, it was during the Scottish Trial that the only involuntary stop occurred when on a very rough section of road the petrol tap shook itself shut causing a delay of 1 minute.

Nothing daunted, Johnson continued to run The Silver Ghost like a train, starting for London after the trial on 1 July. The route was Glasgow, Airdrie, Edinburgh, Dunbar, Berwick, Darlington, Boroughbridge, Leeds, Bradford, Manches-

ter, Newport, Coventry and London. On arrival at London the car turned round and retraced its steps over the 512-mile route. For five weeks the car ran thus covering about 410 miles a day (about 2,460 miles a week) and completing the route 27 times. Running was day and night non-stop except for the early part of the trial when the car ran about 12 hours a day and Sundays when the car was locked up in a garage. On Tuesday night, 9 July, Johnson had completed 4,558 miles at the wheel and handed over to a team of three other drivers: the Hon. C. S. Rolls, Eric Platford (one of Royce's original apprentices) and Reginald Macready.

The record

"All going well, the 'Silver Ghost' will beat the world's reliability record in the early hours of Friday morning next. 17 miles south of Newport in Staffordshire, on its way south from Manchester to London. Will you come? I shall be driving." This was the message from Claude Johnson to *The Autocar* and accordingly Harry J. Swindley followed in a sister Rolls-Royce 40-50 h.p. to witness the breaking of the record in the early hours of the morning of 19 July at the crossing of the Wolverton and Cannock roads to the south of Newport. Finally on the night of Thursday 8 August the 15,000 miles were successfully completed beyond St Albans, making 14,371 miles covered without an involuntary stop except for tyre changes.

No doubt many manufacturers would have been well content with this achievement, but Rolls-Royce publicist Claude Johnson had arranged that at the conclusion of

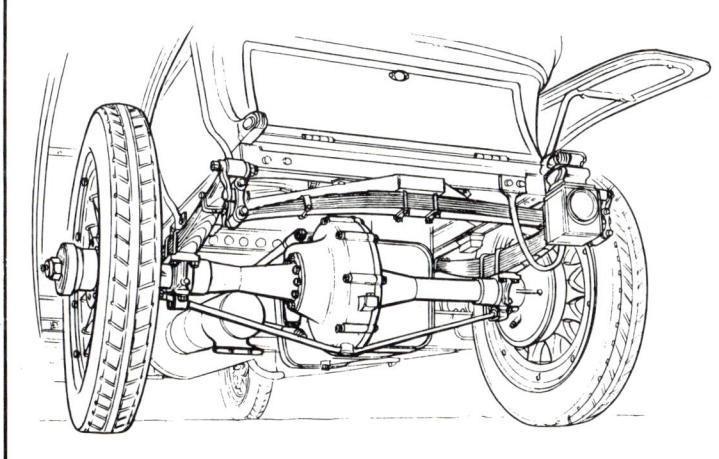

This unusual rear suspension with transverse leaf spring is found only on very early 40-50s built prior to November 1907

the trial the car should be handed over to the RAC's engineers, stripped and the wear measured so that any repairs needed "to render it equal to new" might be carried out – the car being in excellent running order at the conclusion of the trial. The aim of all this was, of course, to establish that the cost of upkeep of a Rolls-Royce was not very great.

The RAC produced a very detailed report of The Silver Ghost's performance on the 15,000-mile trial showing that 40 hours 13 minutes had been spent in work on the car in the motor houses during the five weeks of the run. These may be summarized as follows: Brake adjustment (8 times)

2hr 16min; Ignition system 8hr 9min 30sec; Carburettor 2hr 27min; Petrol tank and pressure system 3hr 28min; Lubrication system 30min; Miscellaneous (including grinding in all 12 valves) 7hr 13min 30sec; Replacements and additions 16hr 9min. The replacements included 6 rubber buffers (four to back springs, two to front), screen stays, nine magneto plugs, fan belt, offside front hub flange and four bolts, magneto and coil. In addition a cap was fitted to the petrol tank and a new petrol tap, with connections to enable pressure in the tank to be maintained automatically or by hand, was added. Running costs worked out at £281 8s 4d for the 15,000 miles, including tyre costs of £187 12s 6d, giving a cost per mile of 4½d (1½d without tyre costs). Petrol consumption was 15·7 mpg and the 995·41 gallons used (at 15·7d per gallon) cost £62 10s, while oil consumption was 956 miles per gallon at a cost of £2 14s 11d. The total bill for all repairs, and replacements during the trial and at the RAC (including labour at 2s 2d per hour) came to just £28 5s 0½d.

The result of the RAC's mechanical examination was a real triumph for Rolls-Royce for The Silver Ghost showed no wear measurable by micrometer in the engine, transmission, brakes or steering gear. The RAC report stated "Had the car been in the hands of a private owner no replacements would have been considered necessary but to bring the car up to a condition indistinguishable from new" certain parts were replaced and the valves were reground. One of the rear spring shackle pins was found to be worn 0·0005in., the pin of the steering cross tube was 0·004 slack and the universal joint of the magneto drive showed slight backlash. Both front steering pivot pins had worn 0·005in. and the propeller shaft rear universal joint had worn 0·0005in. Claude Johnson had put the Rolls-Royce 40-50 h.p. in a position which ensured the success of the model for many years to come.

In September 1907, Johnson took the Silver Ghost on holiday to Cornwall and in 1908 the car was sold to A. M. (Dan) Hanbury, one of Rolls-Royce's travelling inspectors. During his ownership it covered some 500,000 miles but little is known of the car until just after World War II.

A Complete rebuild

Towards the end of 1947 Air Marshall Sir Alex Coryton mentioned to Rolls-Royce managing director Lord Hives that his father-in-law, Mr Hanbury, needed some parts for The Silver Ghost and asked if Rolls-Royce could help. Lord Hives agreed and on 6 November 1947 Rolls-Royce service manager R. F. Messervey wrote to Dan Hanbury who was then living at Castle Malwood, Lyndhurst, Hampshire, asking what parts were needed. Unfortunately Mr Hanbury died before this was ascertained and his heirs part exchanged the car with Rolls-Royce who collected the old lady from Lyndhurst on a transporter on 27 October 1948 with the speedometer reading 19,974 miles.

At that stage the car was in rather a "used" state and Rolls-Royce's first action was to attend to the outward appearance of the polished engine parts. These included 22 copper pipes and taps and sundry other parts which were polished and lacquered after dent removal by H.

P. Jacobs Ltd. of Brighton. That well-known Veteran and Vintage car enthusiast Stanley Sears had been involved in Rolls-Royce's acquisition of the car and he loaned tyres to get the car on the road for display purposes, although five new Dunlop tyres were soon obtained through the VCC at a cost of £36 5s. While this was happening the car had been sent, on Stanley Sears' recommendation, to H. E. Griffin of Haywards Heath for a coachwork rebuild. A letter from them dated 22 February 1950 estimates the cost of body restoration as £829 1s. The body was in a bad state with rotten framing, joints and panels loose and the wings and sheet metal had been badly repaired and the aluminium corroded and perished. The whole car, including the chassis and axle, was stripped of paint and given seven coats of filler, stopped and faced down, before finishing in aluminium paint. All the plated parts were resilvered and fitted, the tool boxes remade, the floorboards repaired and new carpet fitted. The leather was also patched where necessary.

At their London service depot at Hythe Road, Rolls-Royce undertook a fair amount of the mechanical work including welding and refacing the lower half of the crankcase, overhauling the magneto, replacing all the wiring and removing some non-standard electric wiring, rebuilding the rotted wooden wheels, plugging the many holes in the dash (said to resemble a collander), cleaning the petrol tank and system including the exhaust pressure valve for the automatic fuel supply, relining the central foot brake and rear brakes and skimming drums, and attending to the leaking radiator. A crack in the offside frame member of the chassis was found to have been badly plated and this was stiffened internally and welded so that the repair was not visible – even old Rolls-Royces have their pride. Cost of this work was about £380 retail.

In May 1950 both cylinder blocks were bored out and liners fitted to cure galloping oil consumption. At the same time the crankshaft was reground on seven main and six big end journals and these bearings were remetalled and bored in the crankcase to suit the reground crankshaft.

Early in 1951 Hooper and Co. were entrusted with the re-upholstery of the car in Connolly hide and a complete repaint (including the removal of the body from the chassis). Cost of the Hooper work was £235. This was in preparation for a number of publicity appearances which the restored Silver Ghost was to make, and 1952 saw her at the Brussels motor show where unfortunately damage occurred in transit and repairs (Hooper and Hythe Road) cost £336 7s 11d. Publi-

city appearances continued with little except routine maintenance (including regular soaking of the wooden wheels to stop creaks) and running repairs right up until 1957 when the car was used for the Brooklands track 50 years celebrations. Soon afterwards Great Western Radiators of Islington were asked to repair the radiator to overcome persistent overheating.

October 1961 saw The Ghost used for a commemoration run from London–Edinburgh, to celebrate the 50th anniversary of a 1911 40–50 h.p.'s achievement, and five new tyres were fitted for the event. It was at this time that a set of electric tail and side lamps with wiring and concealed two-pin sockets were fitted. They were subsequently removed in July 1962. Early in 1964 the car was taken off the road for a major engine and transmission overhaul. Upon dismantling the engine, one block was found to be

0·015in. oversize and this was sleeved and bored to standard. At the same time the original cast iron pistons were replaced with aluminium pistons with new rings. This involved machining the small end bushes to suit the larger gudgeon pins and fitting compression plates under the cylinder blocks to make up for the difference in crown height of the new pistons. The idler gears were replaced and timing gears and tappets attended to. The gearbox, clutch coupling, propeller shaft and rear axle were all dismantled and overhauled – this including making up two new rear axle thrust bearings. Again all the electrical wiring was replaced. At the same time the car was repainted and the leather given specialist attention. In June 1964 two fitters spent some 17 hours rewelding the rear axle torque rod top ball joint at Booker Aerodrome after the ball

had sheared and later that year Robert Morley used The Silver Ghost in the film *Those Magnificent Men in Their Flying Machines*.

February 1965 saw yet further renewal of silver plating on the body fittings – this time by Jack Barclay (Service) Ltd – and Park Ward retrimmed the car in green hide. By January 1968 the body was again in need of attention and Hoopers removed the plated fittings for re-silvering by Rolls-Royce, welded and restored the fatigued metal, made up a spare wheel steadying bracket and carried out a complete re-paint – all at a cost of £650. The next year the car went on tour in the USA covering many miles under its own power and it was then that overheating of the rear axle became a problem. This thinned the oil and forced it under pressure past the oil seals, resulting in need for the seals to be replaced. The speedometer was then reading 62,182 miles. Later

the same year trouble began to be experienced with a water leak at the rear of the cylinder block. During 1970 the trouble persisted as did the rear oil seal problem which was finally cured by fitting a breather tube to the differential. By this stage the rebuilt wooden wheels had covered a considerable mileage and a new set was specially made by R. M. Ellis and Son of Five Oak Green, Kent for £360. In spite of the engine water leak AX 201 took part in the Manchester–Blackpool run in June 1972, but by then it was clear that the trouble was serious. Resin treatment was used on the block and was successful in sealing a hairline crack at the rear of the engine, so a plan to take a 1909 engine from the Rolls-Royce apprentices' school and convert it back to 1907 specification for fitting into chassis 60551 was not put into effect. The water leak cured, The Silver Ghost took

part in the Rolls-Royce 70th anniversary celebrations in June 1974.

A working car

From the foregoing it might appear that The Silver Ghost has gone from one rebuild to another since 1948, but it must be remembered that all her life she has been – and still is – a working car which has not been pampered by being kept in a museum. The car had already covered over half a million miles by 1948 and the total mileage now must be in the region of 570,000 so one must expect parts to wear out and need replacing. Riding in the car today is most impressive not only for the commanding view over the other traffic but also because of the smoothness, silence and ride comfort which were not at all exaggerated by those who wrote of the car so many years ago.

Travelling behind the Ghost is an experience too, for the suspension can be seen working hard with large movements while the body hardly moves at all. Nowadays, Rolls-Royce publicity manager Dennis Miller-Williams usually runs on the magneto rather than the two coils when driving the car, and the lack of front wheel braking keeps speed down to about 30 mph. The foot-brake which works on the transmission is used purely as a manoeuvring brake, all normal stopping being done by the massive outside hand-brake lever on the driver's side – and very effective it is too. Modern motorists brought up on starting by turning a key might be surprised to learn that for a cold start the induction pipe under the bonnet has first to be primed, the petrol tank air valve opened (normally it is left in this position) and the tank pressure pumped up to 1–1½ psi by hand before flooding the carburettor and turning the engine over. There is no self-starter of course, so the big engine has to be turned over about eight times on the starting handle to draw in the mixture then coil and magneto are switched in with the ignition retarded. Sometimes advancing the ignition is sufficient to start the engine but if not, a further pull of the starting handle is needed, and then the coil is switched out. When the engine is warm it has been known to perform its party trick of starting "on the switch" without being turned over by hand.

That this car should still be performing so well today after many years and miles have passed beneath her wheels is no small tribute to the soundness of Sir Henry Royce's original design and the quality of British workmanship. Without doubt, Claud Johnson's exploits with The Silver Ghost played a large part in establishing the Rolls-Royce reputation for silence, smoothness, comfort and long life as well as quality of construction and soundness of design. Small wonder then that by 1908 the company were proudly proclaiming "British cars are the best; and the Rolls-Royce is the best British car". □

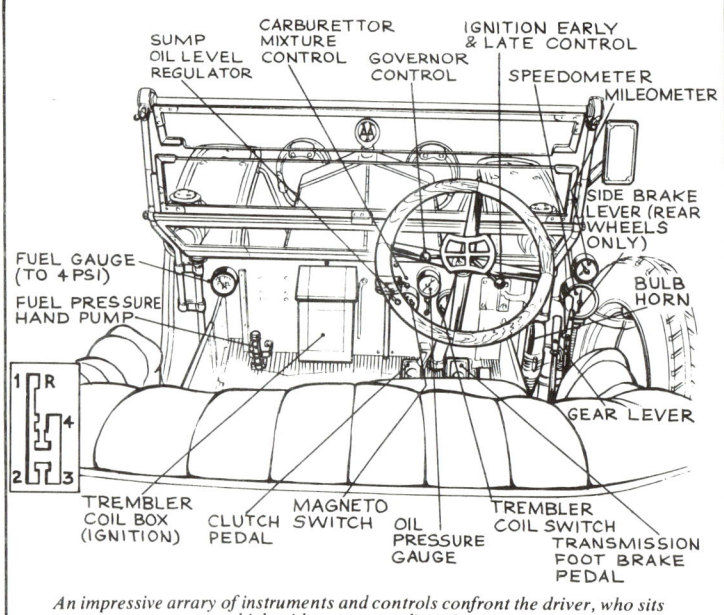

An impressive arrary of instruments and controls confront the driver, who sits high with a commanding view

Specification

Engine: Six cylinders in two blocks of three, 4½ × 4½in. (114 × 114mm) bore and stroke, 7,046 c.c. 48 h.p. developed at 1,200 rpm. Compression 3·2 to 1. Water cooled by pump and fan. Side valves and two sparking plugs per cylinder. Coil and magneto ignition. Nickel steel forged crankshaft running in seven main bearings. Pressure lubrication of bearings, and positive transverse location of bearing caps.
Transmission: Four speeds and reverse with direct drive on 3rd. Overall ratios: 1st 7·67, 2nd 4·51, 3rd 2·708, 4th 2·174, reverse 9·93 to 1. Cone clutch and live rear axle with spiral bevel drive. Wooden wheels running on ball bearing hubs.

Suspension: Front, dead forged axle and 10-leaf springs; rear, fully floating axle and 13-leaf springs. Transverse 11-leaf spring anchored to two diagonal chassis members and ends of leaf springs.
Dimensions: Wheelbase 11ft 3½in., track 4ft 8in., length 15ft 0in., length behind dash 8ft 4in., from dash to centre of rear wheels 7ft 1in. Tyres: 875 × 105mm front, 880 × 120mm rear. Chassis weight approx 22cwt, kerb weight with body 32·9cwt.
Chassis price: £985 in 1907. Value today well over £100,000.

Above: The Rolls-Royce entering Glasgow with Frederick Coleman's White steam car which accompanied it over part of the 2,000-mile route. *Below:* "The Silver Ghost" at the completion of the 2,000 Mile Trial. Claude Johnson is at the wheel and the Hon. Charles Rolls in the rear passenger seat nearest the camera.

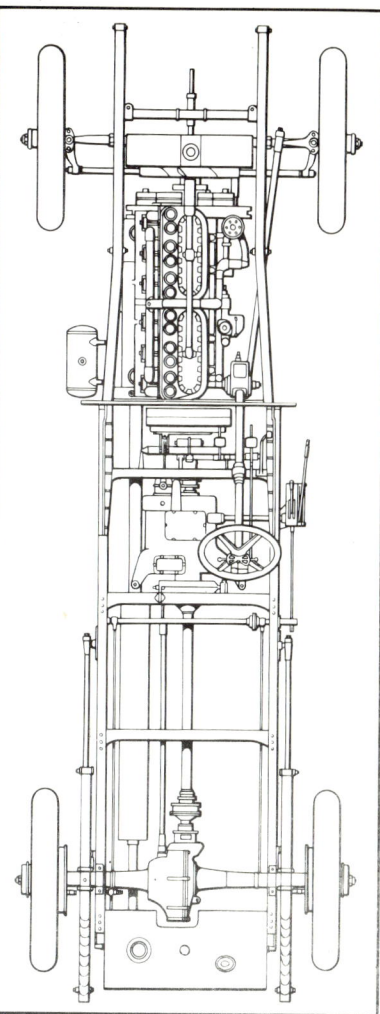

Above: Plan view of the 40/50 h.p. chassis as it was in 1911 with the revised rear suspension which was introduced at the 1908 London Motor Show. *Below:* Max Millar's drawing of "The Silver Ghost" engine with two blocks of three cylinders. Cylinder heads of this square unit were non detachable and the machined nickel-steel crankshaft ran in seven bearings with positive location of the bearing caps. Front, centre and rear crankshaft bearings, camshaft timing wheels and cylinder walls were fed by a pressure lubrication system. Tappets, valve springs and valves stems were not enclosed and the tappet heads had fibre inserts to deaden noise.

Next Year's Rolls-Royce Refinements.

IT is rather early to talk about 1910 cars, but Messrs. Rolls-Royce tell us that all the chassis that can be delivered prior to August 1st are now sold, and from about that date they will begin to deliver the new or 1910 model. In the main the design is unaltered, but among the improvements on the " Silver Ghost " of 15,000 miles fame which will be made are the following:

The height of the frame has now been reduced to 24in. from the ground, measured from the top of the frame. This is undoubtedly an improvement, as it has been effected without reducing the clearance between the ground and the lowest points of the chassis. It

The air pump A and the differential brake compensating gear B.

makes the valves, magneto, carburetter, and pump still more accessible, and reduces the distance between the ground and the floor of the car, thus facilitating the mounting and dismounting of passengers and very considerably improving the appearance.

The front wheel bearings have been increased in size, and the pivot pins which carry the steering wheels have been re-designed and an improved system of lubricating them has been introduced. The Rolls-Royce is one of the few cars which is made without backlash in the steering box, and its beautiful steering is a proof that this backlash, which many makers maintain to be necessary, is not indispensable for good steering, though it is only fair to say that some cars

which have a good deal of backlash steer beautifully also.

The radius rods have been considerably lengthened. The previous shortness was one of the small blemishes in the design, and the improvement will result in a more even braking effort of the rear wheel brakes when the chassis is travelling over rough surfaces.

The petrol tank has been banished from the front seat to the back of the chassis, where it is suspended from projections of the side members of the frame. This will be good news to a number of coachbuilders, as a seat tank always hampers the carriage builder more or less. This tank carries its own filters both inward and outward, and either can be instantly removed for examination or cleansing. The position of the tank necessitates pressure feed. The pressure on the fuel, however, is not maintained by the dirty and somewhat uncertain exhaust system, but by means of a little air pump which is mounted on and driven from the gear box. The pump is of the piston type, and the shaft runs on ball bearings. It has a positive inlet valve, and an automatic delivery valve. It takes its air from a point behind the dashboard where the air is almost entirely free from dust, and a silent acting relief valve is also fitted on the dash, which acts as a safety valve and for releasing pressure when stopping.

The indirect fourth speed has been abandoned, as it was found that so many drivers insisted upon using it at low speeds, thus making the car needlessly noisy. This gear was only intended for use on big open roads, but owing to its abuse it has been decided to abandon it The box has been entirely re-designed, the diameters of all the shafts have been increased, and additional bearings been provided, so that it is extremely quiet.

Shock absorbers are provided. They are of the piston type, and depend for their action upon the flow of liquid through valves. As the shock absorbing cylinder is filled with suitable liquid, such as oil, the piston moves comparatively freely in one direction, because the liquid will flow freely past the valve, but when the motion is reversed the valve automatically closes, and the only means of the liquid escaping is through the space that exists between the piston and the cylinder, the slow action occurring on the recoil.

There are a number of other detail improvements, but we have mentioned the most important.

The testing plant on which Rolls-Royce cars are tested for h.p. at the road wheels.

A Trial of a Rolls-Royce.
With a Short Disquisition on the Number of Speeds.

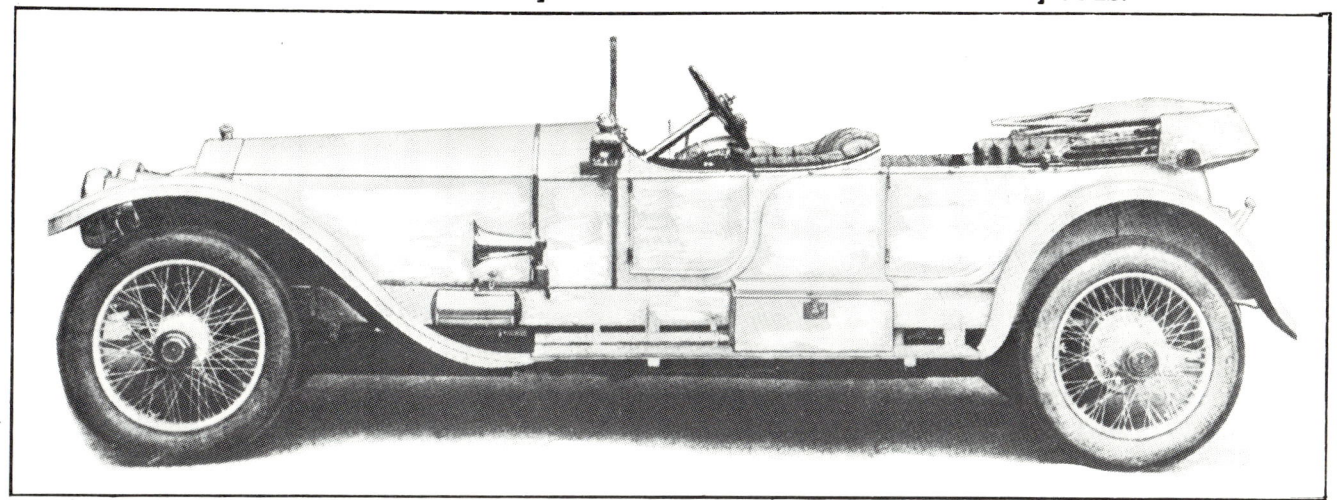

A 40-50 h.p. Rolls-Royce, London-Edinburgh type, a sister car to that referred to in the accompanying article.

THIS trip, most enjoyable and instructive as it proved in every way, arose out of a discussion at the Royal Automobile Club between the writer and Mr. Percy W. Northey, of Messrs. Rolls-Royce, Ltd., on the subject of four-speed gear boxes. Speaking from an experience of a number of good cars fitted with three and four-speed gears, we were somewhat emphatic upon the extreme desirability of a four-speed gear box in any case, premising that, notwithstanding any arrangement of relative ratios between the speeds, the drop from a top speed to a second in the case of a three-speed gear box must of a necessity be too great for the smoothest running.

Now it is, of course, quite well known that the standard 40-50 h.p. Rolls-Royce is fitted with a three-speed gear combination which, with an engine speed of 1,000 revs. per minute, and a bevel gear ratio of 2.9 to 1, gives 11.27 m.p.h. on first, 19.3 m.p.h. on second, and 32.14 m.p.h. on third speed. In respect to our expressed preference for a four-speed gear box even in this case, Mr. Northey proposed that he should, by a selected run on a London to Edinburgh type Rolls-Royce car with six-cylinder engine, 114 × 121 mm. bore and stroke, prove to our satisfaction that, notwithstanding all specious statements to the contrary, the Rolls-Royce combination was perfectly satisfactory. Needless to say, the writer accepted the invitation with pleasure, particularly as his last experience with a Rolls-Royce car was a 100 miles drive at the wheel of the celebrated Silver Ghost of silent memory.

Our recent experience took the form of a circular trip including Titsey and Westerham Hills, and was made with Mr. Northey at the wheel under most enjoyable conditions. The route followed was of our own selection, and was by New and Old Malden, Ewell, Burgh Heath, Reigate, Red Hill, Bletchingley, Titsey, Westerham, Sevenoaks, and back to London *via* Westerham Hill, West Wickham, and Croydon. Hills of dour severity are hard of finding within an easy run of London, but the ascents of the Titsey and Westerham slopes were deemed sufficient for our purposes.

As we have already mentioned, the Silver Ghost of 1907 was the last Rolls-Royce of which we had any personal experience, and good though that good car was, it must be admitted that a gulf of progress separates it from the superlative production of to-day. Naturally, the present car did not suffer under the skilled conning of Mr. Northey, but if one is to experience the best that a car can do, it is obvious that the best possible driver should be at the wheel. From the very moment of starting the silky smoothness yet arithmetically progressive acceleration of the engine was apparent. The car seems to be neither drawn nor thrust, but actually seduced away. It is hard to realise that a power unit in which rapidly reversing reciprocating rectilinear is resolved into rotary motion can so nearly approach in sensation what one imagines a gas turbine ought to be. Nothing but the profoundest study of all the conflicting factors in the problem could achieve such results.

As we have already intimated, stiff hills are hard to find within easy hail of London, but a taste of the sweeping hill-climbing qualities with which the Rolls-Royce is imbued was afforded us in the climb at the end of the stretch of road from Ewell to Burgh Heath by Tumble Beacon. This is a slope which in most medium-powered cars requires a drop from top speed to the next at two points, but for cars that can take it in one mouthful it is a very showy hill. The Rolls-Royce just rolled it out behind it like a machine delivering tape. Indeed, the rapid, sweeping and effortless upward rush was most exhilarating.

Nothing to matter, save good road surfaces and a delightful countryside, then occurs until the summit of Reigate and the crossing of the Pilgrim's Way is reached. The hill being devoid of traffic, the descent was made in a most pleasing manner, the car just melting down the slope, with one or two demonstrations of braking which showed the brakes to be as sweet in application as the running of the car. From Reigate to Westerham the road winds continuously, and though a careful driver reduces speed under such conditions, the taking of the bends served to show how grandly the driving wheels of the Rolls-Royce hold the road, for under such circumstances there was absolutely no sensation of the side dithering of the rear of the car to those occupying the back seats. This is an unusual feature; there are few cars indeed that do not suggest a tendency to outward slip when travelling fast round sharp bends. But the Rolls-Royce seems to be imbued with a wonderful sense of parallelism.

As we have written, Titsey and Westerham hills had been selected, and Titsey was taken before lunch. It is a hill which would have appalled, and did appal, the motorist of seven to ten years ago, and we had

had no personal experience of it since those days. When the Rolls-Royce was really set going at it, we must admit to an amazed disappointment. The hill just faded out before the car and left but the faintest impression of a climb. The second gear was slipped in noiselessly about one-third of the way up, the speed dropped momentarily to twenty-five and then rose to twenty-seven, which was maintained on the steepest part of the hill without a sensation of effort, and immediately the knuckle was passed the top was resumed. This kept the speed constant for a moment, and then it went up rapidly.

After the bewilderment of Titsey, it was not to be hoped that Westerham would do much to maintain its ancient reputation. The approach over the Pilgrim's Way was taken on top easily but intentionally not fast, and top was held until the beginning of the steep bend, and would have been held farther but for the baulking of a cart. Changing down without a sound the speed dropped as on Titsey to twenty-five, and then rose smartly, Hell Corner (1 in 7) being swept round at 27 to 30 m.p.h., with a supreme disregard for its once greatly feared gradient, and this with a full load of four persons of at least average weight.

It is, perhaps, well to add in connection with the Rolls-Royce London-Edinburgh model that when this was first introduced two years ago it was regarded as a high efficiency engine which, compared with the ordinary Rolls-Royce engine, was noisy. We did not try the original London-Edinburgh model, so express no opinion upon this belief, but, so far as the present engine is concerned, while it shows a superabundance of vitality, it is to all intents and purposes a noiseless engine, and it would appear that in the interval Messrs. Rolls-Royce have successfully combined the good qualities of the two engines; that is to say, they have maintained the quietness of what one may call the landaulet engine, and have added to it the vitality of the London-Edinburgh design.

Incidentally, too, it may not be out of place to enlarge somewhat upon the question of gear ratios and the number of speeds, because, while we do not recede in the least from our contention that on the average car four speeds are vastly preferable to three, we as freely admit, as we did when first discussing the question some years ago, that there are a few cars upon which three speeds are all that are necessary; indeed, we should be unfair to the Rolls-Royce if we did not admit that four speeds would have been superfluous upon the distinctly hilly run we undertook, and would have necessitated at least two additional gear changes in covering the stiff route we selected, and that without any corresponding advantage. That being so, it may not be without interest to enquire into the reasons for this apparent contradiction—for it is only apparent and the reasons are quite simple. For three speeds to be quite satisfactory the first essential is that the top direct gear shall not be a high one. It will be seen that the Rolls-Royce meets this requirement. Secondly, as the gear is not high, the engine, although not actually a high-speed engine, is, nevertheless, called upon to revolve at fairly high speeds at times; therefore, to get perfect smoothness of action so that the occupants of the car shall be unconscious of the high speed of the engine, it must be a six-cylinder engine not only with the ability to revolve fast without the smallest commotion or fuss, but, also, with the ability to pull smoothly on the top gear at low road speeds, so that the range on the top speed shall be a very wide one. Thirdly, the engine must be a big and powerful engine, so that when it is dropped on to the second gear it can climb hills which are really steep, steeper than the majority of hills, without a second change. Each one of these basic conditions is met by the Rolls-Royce design, and, in consequence, it is quite satisfactory with three speeds for use in this country.

So far as varied continental work is concerned, which may mean anything from miles of open straight to restarting upon a steep mountain pass with a very heavy load and a treacherous surface, four speeds are necessary, and the new continental model so fitted, which has distinguished itself so strikingly in the recent Austrian Alpine trials, shows that the makers endorse our view.

While speaking of the Rolls-Royce it may be of interest to refer to one refinement in its control which is not generally known, *i.e.*, the governor. The hand throttle on the steering wheel does not exist, but is replaced by a small lever which is marked " Governor." Its functions are in a sense the same as those of a hand throttle, but there is a wide difference, for this reason: the governor lever does not operate directly on the throttle, as in the case of the ordinary hand throttle, but upon the governor. Therefore, if this lever be set to give the engine, say, five hundred revolutions a minute it will make that number of revolutions whether the engine be running light or pulling on any one of the gears, because the governor, being set to a certain speed, will open the throttle and keep it open up to the limit of the power of the engine at any set speed within its range. This means, for one thing, that extraordinarily smooth starting can be obtained by any driver who knows his car. Suppose he is standing on a hill and wishes to restart, all he has to do is to put the governor lever to such a position as to give him the engine speed he wants, and then to release the brake and gently let in the clutch. The engine will take hold and automatically open its throttle to maintain the desired speed; then, of course, once under way the driver can use his foot accelerator as usual.

THE AUTOCAR, July 18th, 1914.

The Alpine Rolls-Royce.
Impressions of a Trial after the Attempt to Destroy its Refinement.

"And she! Oh that I could do her justice."
—*Steam Tactics.*

EVER since the conclusion of the great Austrian Alpine Trial—than which no more strenuous and searching test has ever been imposed on motor cars—the brilliant performance of the Rolls-Royce car, driven with such skill and abandon by Mr. James Radley, has been the subject of general comment. The terrific stress to which cars are subjected in the above trial can only be realised by those who have actually travelled over the route, although the eloquent pen of a Freeston goes a long way towards a mind picture of that *tout ensemble*. The exact state in which a car issues from such a competition must naturally be of great interest, and it is with a view of demonstrating the present condition of the Alpine Rolls-Royce car that Messrs. Rolls-Royce re-purchased it from Mr. Radley and arranged with him to afford us a demonstration of the car's quality. It was therefore with much anticipatory pleasure that we accepted an invitation extended to us by Mr. Claude Johnson to make a trial trip in the now famous Rolls-Royce, conducted by its equally famous driver. The car was to come to us in exactly the same condition as when it finished its great feat. Indeed, when Mr. Radley picked us up he assured us that the bonnet had not been opened since the car left Vienna at the beginning of the Alpine trial. This was indeed evident from the general condition of things, for the unlocking of the bonnet broke a line of dust, and the aspect of the engine within, covered as it was with dust, grit and dead flies, was fearful to behold. Indeed, the engine had been missing somewhat on the drive from the garage, and uniformity was not restored until the dried caked dust had been wiped from the insulation of the sparking plugs.

The demonstrating trip took the form of a run from London to Coventry and back, the Holyhead Road being joined at St. Albans on the outward journey, and the route of Banbury, Oxford, and High Wycombe being taken for the return. Of course there is nothing on either of these routes which could call seriously upon the Rolls-Royce for a single moment. There was nothing to bring it off the sweet top speed, except the desire of Mr. Radley to demonstrate its furious acceleration anywhere on the third. And that acceleration on the steepest bits we encountered was absolutely petrifying. It reminded us of nothing more than the lightning bound of a **suddenly** rowelled steed. Nothing could prevail against its 2,500 (and over) revs. per min.

And then the swift sweep from a crawl on top gear to great speeds on the long straight stretches of the Holyhead Road was not only a sheer delight, but a revelation in progressive speed such as we have never before experienced. And we say it without hesitation, this Rolls-Royce car, with all its strenuous doings in the Austrian Alps thick upon it, without retuning of any sort, without so much as the tightening of a nut, is undoubtedly the most responsive, the most delightful and satisfactory car we have ever handled. There may be better, there is nothing so good in the world that it may not be exceeded, but the better car if it exists has not yet come into our hands. When it does, we will state the fact with equal emphasis. These are the impressions we had while sitting by the side of one of the most skilful drivers by whom it has ever been our lot to be driven; they were more than confirmed, nay, they were intensified, when it became our happy lot to take the wheel on the return journey. How Mr. Radley could bear to put this miracle of mechanical perfection out of his own practised and accustomed hands was more than we could understand, but that he did so gave us the greatest driving delight of our many and varied motoring experiences. On the long straight desolate stretches of road which lie between Banbury and Oxford it flew like a homing pigeon. At topmost speed, it laid pot-holes, ridges, and loose metal "under its most marvellous springs with never a jar." It held the road with the solidity and comfort of a L.N.W. Railway two hours Birmingham express, and it slowed on the application of its sweet brakes as though it had suddenly run into six inches of viscid treacle, while the steering, which was absolutely without back lash, was just as smooth, definite, and easy as steering could be. When we relinquished the wheel to Mr. Radley, he consoled us by an exhibition of fast cornering by taking the bends of Aston Rowant Hill at speed, which is of course made possible by the beautifully light steering with which this car is endowed. Then

its behaviour in the congested Saturday afternoon traffic of the Uxbridge Road was another revelation, for, amongst the trams, motor omnibuses, and cars, it became as tame and smooth on top speed as it had been tremendous and mighty on the long straights of the Banbury-Oxford Road.

It was indeed very hard to realise that this beautifully running car, this combination of smoothness and superabundant life and power, had come through an 1,800-mile Alpine competition in the hands of a Radley, besides having done some 2,400 miles in addition. What we mean is this: that, magnificent driver as he is, Radley does not spare his car in the least: he regards it as having powers to be used, not pampered and nursed. His driving in the Alpine test was an evidence of this, and what we want to bring home is that, after a test of this kind, one would expect the running of a car to be somewhat spoiled till it had been carefully tended and adjusted. Yet the fact remains that this Rolls-Royce without adjustment or cleaning or attention of any kind was running perfectly. There was no sign of "pinking," or insipient knock; one could not hear the valve gear at all; there was not even one noisy tappet out of the twelve; one could accelerate rapidly, almost brutally, without a jar, and one could not detect that anything had been lost in the strenuous competition the car had just passed through. Then, to turn from the engine to the chassis, there were no creaks or groans about the chassis of any kind, while the brakes were as smooth and as powerful as ever. When it is considered what a hard time engines, springs, and brakes get in an Alpine trial, it is possible to realise in some way not merely the remarkable quality of the Rolls-Royce, but the way in which this is proved by the maintenance of this refinement in running after such a persistent attempt to destroy it, for, after all, that is what the Alpine test is.

What particularly interests us is the evolution of what one may call the high-efficiency Rolls-Royce. To go back to about 1911: the car was then, as now, a splendidly smooth running and reliable machine with a reputation which was thoroughly deserved, but it was not what one might call a lively car, and the makers still fostered the impression when they made a lively car that they had produced something which was a little wicked, and a little coarse in its ways, so that it was called "The Scarlet Knave," or "The Sinful Skimmer," or "The Wicked Wraith": it was always given a name to infer that it was very lively and fast, but not quite what a Rolls-Royce should be in refinement and perfection of running in other respects.

Then came the Edinburgh-London-Edinburgh trip under R.A.C. observation, winding up with an eighty mile an hour sprint on Brooklands, and people were astounded that such a fast car under the Rolls-Royce brand had been made; those who were fortunate enough to try it found it ran very smoothly besides being so speedy when it was desired to hurry, and it became an established pattern known as the London-Edinburgh type. Another year elapsed, and it had, as it were, blended with the ordinary engine again; somehow or other the virtues of the two engines had been grafted into one: there was still the silky, noiseless running, plus the abundance of life and power. Surely there was never a more striking example of the benefits of competition between car and car, as the Rolls-Royce has had to meet and beat its Continental rivals and at the same time to maintain its reputation for smooth running, long wear, and ease of control.

An Alpine Rolls-Royce.

Some Particulars of the Chassis and Body.   Special Provision for Tools and Spares.

The " Alpine Eagle" Rolls-Royce car with a sporting type four-seated body, referred to in the accompanying article. The chassis has four speeds, a larger radiator and larger brakes than last year's Rolls-Royce.

A 1915 model Rolls-Royce car with the "Alpine Eagle" four-speed chassis has recently been delivered to Mr. Gerald Herbert, of Coventry. The car is the subject of the accompanying illustrations, from which it will be seen that a sporting type four-seated body has been fitted; this body was built specially to Mr. Herbert's requirements and designs by Messrs. Hamshaw and Co., Leicester, and the workmanship certainly does that firm great credit.

The outline and passenger accommodation of the bodywork were not the only matters by any means to which Mr. Herbert gave special consideration, for quite elaborate, yet extremely practical, arrangements have been made for the accommodation of tools and spares.

The tools have not been placed about the car in a haphazard manner, but those connected with certain operations or adjustments have been grouped together, while those most frequently required have been placed in the more accessible positions. For instance, the tools most likely to be required in connection with

engine adjustments are cleverly arranged on the near side front door, a hinged panel being concealed under normal conditions by a leather flap having its lower end held down by three push buttons. This arrangement is shown in one of the sketches, in which it will be seen that each tool is separately held in position, and free from rattle, by a strap or catch securing it in a bed formed in the panel.

Then in regard to the tools required when changing a wheel, all these are found together in an accessible position under the front seat cushions, or more correctly under the hinged front half of the boards on which the cushions rest. To obtain access to these tools, which include jack, jack handle, wheel spanner, and mallet, the seat cushions are tipped up and the under boards hinged back, as shown in the central sketch.

To refer now to the less frequently required tools, those constituting the next category are to be found in the panel behind the driver's seat. They include tyre levers, sundry special spanners, and a valve spring lifter, but in this compartment there are also spare sparking plugs, spare valves, and other small parts.

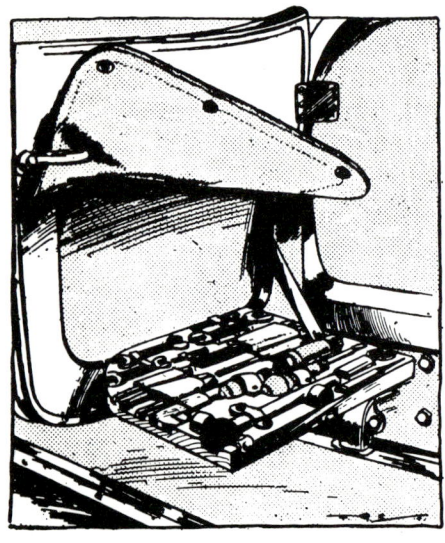  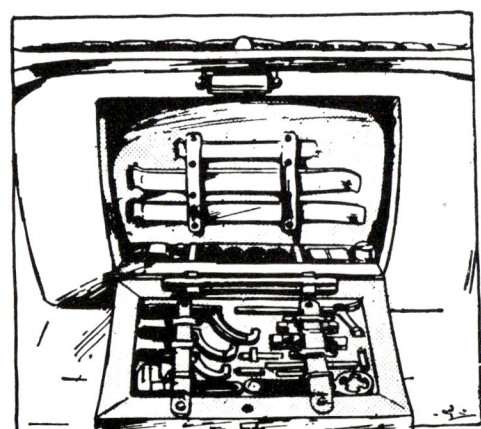

On the left the tool panel secured to the near side front door, the tools being those usually required in making adjustments to the engine. In the centre view is the wheel removing equipment, accommodation for which is provided under the boards below the front seat cushions, the front half of each board being hinged as shown. On the right is seen the provision for tools not often required, a hinged panel being formed behind the driver's seat with an electric light above it.

The off side of the 1915 Rolls-Royce engine as fitted to the "Alpine Eagle" type chassis. On this side, among other details, are the carburetter, water pump, and the contact breaker and high tension distributer of the supplementary ignition. It will be seen that the Klaxon horn is bolted to the dashboard inside the bonnet.

In the side view of the car it will be seen that there are no valances, for Mr. Herbert has had new brackets made to bring the running boards up level with the bottom of the chassis frame. This arrangement allows the underneath parts of the chassis to be more easily inspected without recourse to a pit, causes the car to raise less dust, and, to our mind, improves the appearance of the car as a whole.

The "Alpine Eagle" type Rolls-Royce chassis has certain features differing from the standard four-speed type to render it more suitable for Alpine touring. For instance, the radiator is larger, holding twelve gallons of water, the brakes are larger—the very large diameter of the rear wheel drums can be seen in the side view of the car—and the frame has a tie-rod under each side member to stiffen it to resist the stresses imposed by high speed work on bad roads. On the other hand, all standard models now have four speeds.

To refer to the bodywork, the clean run from the bonnet to the back of the car is apparent in two of the illustrations; a bulbous back has been adopted, but this is not obtrusive; the panelling all round is turned in at the top and meets the upholstery inside and below the extreme edge; the upholstery is in black leather extremely well shaped for comfort, the driver's seat back being more stiffly padded than the other three, so as to afford the driver a firmer "grip" of the car when travelling fast or using the brakes

A practical provision lies in the fact that all the floorboards are detachable, so that any part of the chassis can be inspected and is almost as accessible as though no body were in position.

The body is finished in battleship grey, the bonnet in polished aluminium, and the radiator nickel-plated. No hood has yet been fitted, but provision has been

A threequarter back view of Mr. Gerald Herbert's "Alpine Eagle" Rolls-Royce. This view gives an idea of the shape of the bulbous back. Although a hood is not in position, provision is made for one to be easily fitted if required.

made for it, so that it can easily be fitted if required

Mr. Herbert has covered some 1,500 miles on the car at the time of writing, and expresses great satisfaction with it; the engine is very efficient and lively, and yet "tame"—that is to say, the car can be manoeuvred in a garage or driven through crowded streets as easily as a 10 h.p. light car, or even more easily than many. The steering is perfect and as light as a feather, and the clutch, a fabric-faced cone, as smooth as silk. Altogether the car is one of which its owner may well be proud.

The history of Rolls-Royce cars in India goes back to 1908; but it was the order of the Indian Government for eight cars for the 1911 Delhi Durbar that really put Rolls-Royce on the map there and started the long association of the Indian Rajahs and Maharajahs with the company. Top: This state body was built by Barker and Co. on a London-Edinburgh chassis in 1913 to the order of the Nizam of Hyderabad who subsequently owned a collection of Rolls-Royces. The back part of the body was elevated to provide a raised seat for the Nizam. The seat itself had collapsible armrests and there were four further collapsible seats. The domed roof was finished with silver beading and bordered with a massive silver fleur-de-lys pattern fender. A silver cap of maintenance surmounted the dome. The body was finished in a rich canary yellow with gold mountings and old-gold silk brocade, laces and curtains. Even the lamps, working off a CAV dynamo set, were silver-plated.

Middle: These two 40/50s were bodied by the Regent Carriage Co. Ltd. of Fulham in 1913 to the order of HSH the Maharajah of Alwar. The coupé cabriolet had a roof which folded down making it an open car and was finished in peacock blue with black mouldings and gold lining. Note the rear dickey seat, which could be folded away, for the Maharajah's attendant, the powerful tripod-mounted searchlight on the running board and the serpent horn. The saloon cabriolet, also with folding roof, was vee-fronted and finished in yellow, striped with green edged with gold lining. The upper part of the car and mouldings were also green. Note the unusual circular window of the saloon cabriolet.

Bottom: This Barker cabriolet of 1915 had discs covering the wire wheels and was equipped with dynamo lighting and a special searchlight

Top left: Lady Fitzgerald's gas-driven 40/50 outside St. Margaret's, Westminster for the memorial service to M. Rodin in November 1917.
Top right: A war scarred 40/50 limousine photographed after its return from Russia in 1916 before being converted into an armoured car for further service. This car had been driven over 10,000 miles without mechanical breakdown from Archangel right through northern, central and southern Russia to Erzerum in Turkey and back by the same route on military service.
Above: As an armoured car with the British forces in East Africa in 1916. The car is here loaded as transport to the scene of operations.
Right: In a dug-out close to the firing line in the Dardanelles in 1915, this armoured 40/50 was attached to the British Mediterranean Expeditionary force.

The Post-war 40-50 h.p. Rolls-Royce.

In its Main Points the Chassis Layout is Unchanged. An Electric Engine Starter and Lighting Dynamo are now Fitted.

THE makers of the Rolls-Royce car are not in the habit of permitting detailed descriptions of the famous six-cylinder chassis that bears their name, and for this reason it is not surprising that the first available information concerning the 1919 model should be of a general rather than of a detailed nature.

While, doubtless, in the design of the engine, minor modifications, due to experience gained during the war in aero engine construction, will be found to have been incorporated in its main outlines, established practice has been followed. In the advance specification just published, the bore and stroke of the six cylinders are given as " not less than 4½in. × 4¾in." (approximately 114 mm. × 120 mm., 7,349 c.c.)

The cylinders are cast in two groups of three cylinders each, and side valves are fitted. Lubrication is of the fully forced variety, the carburetter is of the firm's own manufacture, fuel is fed to it by air pressure from a tank at the rear of the chassis, filtered air being forced into the tank by an engine-driven pump, and ignition is by both magneto and an entirely independent accumulator coil and distributer system. The accumulators are charged by a dynamo driven from the front end of the gear box. Water-cooling is by spur gear-driven pump. Although it is by no means unusual to come across Rolls-Royce cars which have been fitted out by their owners with an electric starter, it is a novelty to find that the latter now forms part of the equipment of the standard chassis.

The Chassis and the Price.

Other chassis details include a cone clutch, four-speed gear box, enclosed propeller-shaft, bevel-actuated rear axle, worm and nut steering gear, semi-elliptic front and cantilever rear springs, and detachable wire wheels. Both hand and foot brakes take effect on drums on the driving wheels, the expanding shoes for the hand brake acting in an inner drum concentric with a larger drum for those of the foot brake.

The price of the new Rolls-Royce chassis, with tyres, is to be £1,450. It is hoped that this figure will not have to be advanced, but Messrs. Rolls-Royce, Ltd., reserve to themselves the right to increase it should the cost of tyres, material, or labour make an upward move. In the event of an advance being necessitated, the company will give six months' notice of it, those customers whose chassis are due for delivery within that time being entitled to purchase at the figure originally quoted, while those whose orders cannot be fulfilled until a date more than six months ahead will have the right to cancel them within fourteen days of the receipt of the notice.

Engineering Personnel of a Great Factory.

It must always be of considerable interest to users of a first-class car to know something of the *personnel* responsible for the design and production of such cars. As far as the Rolls-Royce car is concerned, the Engineer-in-Chief is, of course, Mr. F. Henry Royce. Up to March, 1915, Mr. Royce's chief assistant was Mr. T. B. Barrington, who, for six years before the war, was associated with the Rolls-Royce Company. Since March, 1915, he has done war service, and rose to the rank of Lieut.-Colonel, R.A.F., and was awarded the O.B.E. in connection with aero engine design. Lt.-Col. Barrington has now returned to civilian life, and has been appointed chief assistant engineer to Messrs. Rolls-Royce, Ltd.

The other principals associated with Mr. F. H. Royce are Mr. Day and Mr. Elliott, chiefs of the designing staff; Mr. Bailey and Mr. Olley, chief production draughtsmen; Mr. Nadin and Mr. Haldenby, equipment engineers; and Mr. Hall, metallurgical chemist.

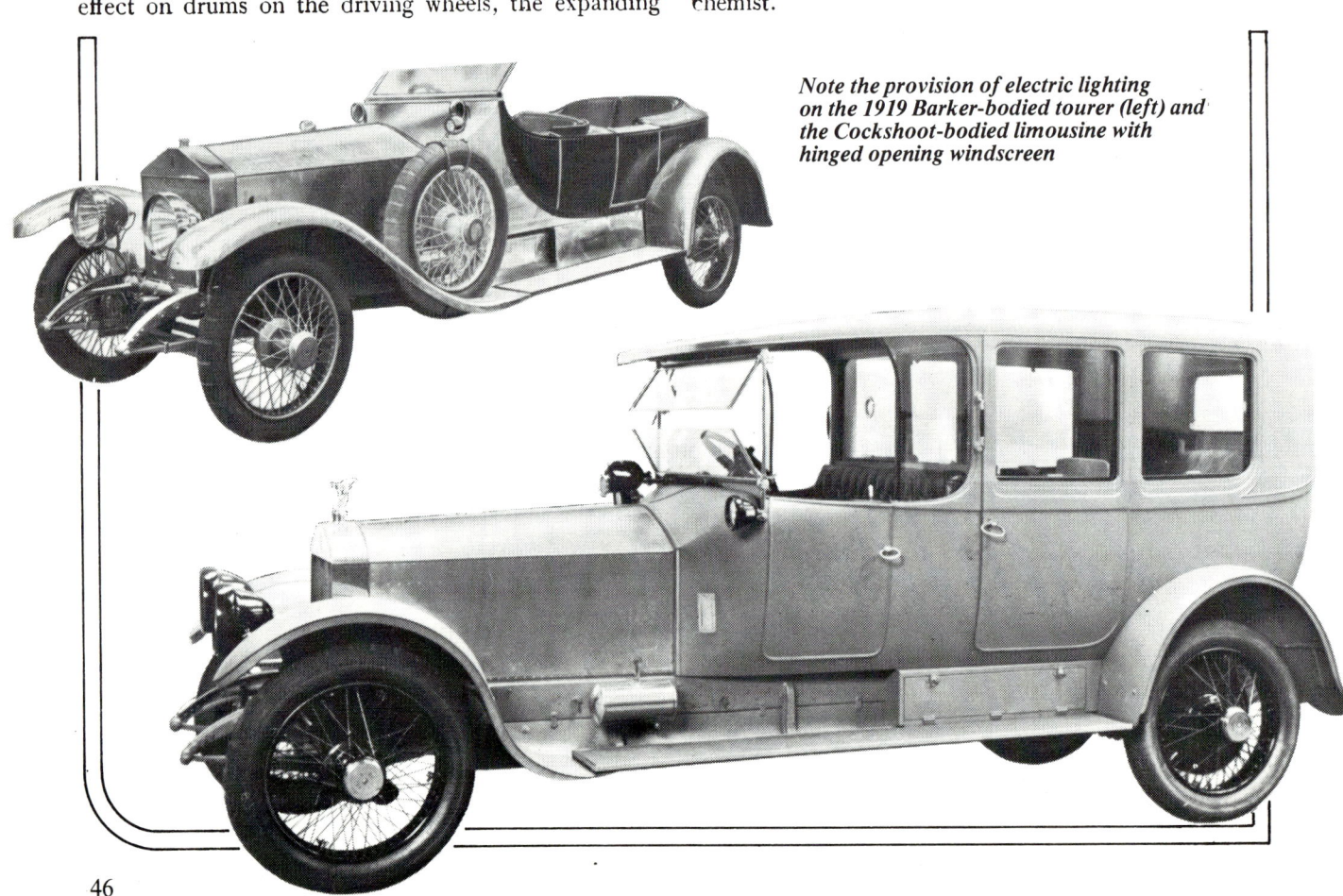

Note the provision of electric lighting on the 1919 Barker-bodied tourer (left) and the Cockshoot-bodied limousine with hinged opening windscreen

A 1920 ROLLS ROYCE on the Road

An Engine which provides Amazing Power for Rapid Acceleration combined with Extreme Smoothness in Propulsion. New Type Cantilever Springs allowing Perfect Comfort, characterise a Remarkable Car.

TWO or three times of late the writer has, in conversation with friends recently returned from India, asked them what was their impression of the Taj Mahal. The reply has invariably been to the same effect: the visitor went to see the Taj assured in his own mind that he would be disappointed in it, merely because its glories had been in advance dinned into his ears *ad nauseam*. In each case, however, the wonderful building more than lived up to its reputation as a compeller of almost reverential admiration.

To some extent, the Taj Mahal and the Rolls-Royce may be regarded as parallel instances of productions as nearly perfect as the wit of man can devise, each suffering from the danger that the ordinary individual will be set against it before he sees it by excessive preliminary laudation.

We had heard many glowing accounts of the capabilities of the 1920 model Rolls-Royce, and when, a few days ago, we set out for a road trial upon the latest type of chassis, equipped with a five-seated open touring body, we were quite prepared to be hyper-critical, and to form the opinion that what had been reported to us represented to some extent the vapouring of the enthusiast partially hypnotised by the name "Rolls - Royce." We will, therefore, at the outset confess that at the end of the day we, who had gone out, if not altogether prepared to scoff at least in somewhat doubting mood, returned unable to do anything but praise.

The latest Rolls-Royce is a distinct advance on anything that has preceded it from the Derby works. One always expects silence, smooth running, and good acceleration, but here are these qualities *in excelsis*.

An induction pipe hand primer, controlled from the dashboard, runs to the central inlet branch. At the rear end of the water pipe outlet is a small pipe leading to the thermometer on the dash.

We were first shaken out of our sceptical mood by our inability when we stepped into the car to determine whether or not the engine was running. That it was we were forced to believe when the car moved away, but it is no exaggeration to say that the engine, when running light, does not cause the slightest perceptible vibration.

Acceleration Extraordinary.

The London traffic was negotiated on top gear throughout, and at one point so slow was our progress that the writer was tempted to step out and walk beside the car. This could be achieved at a leisurely saunter, what time the engine fired steadily and smoothly, while each individual impulse was scarcely appreciable. The acceleration from a slow-walking pace was quite extraordinary, and was achieved without any hesitation even when the throttle was suddenly opened wide.

Outside London one could obtain some idea of the Rolls-Royce's speed. From a pace of 20 m.p.h., we could attain 55 m.p.h. in certainly not more than 200 yards, and it was noteworthy that there was no point in the acceleration where the least hesitation was apparent. The aluminium pistons, doubtless, contribute materially to the liveliness of the engine. Our driver assured us that the car would do 78 m.p.h. on the road, and this we could well believe, though we did not press for the machine to be speeded up to anything like the limit of its gait.

Our run included a few of the Surrey hills, among which we took in the winding road up Box Hill and the steep ascent of Pebble Hill, between Betchworth and Walton Heath. As regards the former, the writer was at the wheel, and it was entirely his fault that third speed was momentarily called for at the hairpin bend. If he had realised that the wonderful lock of the Rolls-Royce had enabled it to negotiate the hairpin, he would not have, as he did, unnecessarily applied the foot brake and brought the vehicle practically to a stop. In this connection, we must make mention of the general excellence of the brakes, both of which, acting on the rear wheel drums, are delightfully smooth yet very powerful.

The Suspension System.

At the foot of Pebble Hill, of which there is a considerable stretch with a gradient of approximately 1 in 6, an early change from top to second speed was made, and the climb was performed over a most indifferent road surface at just over 30 m.p.h. It was a very fine performance, and the absence of vibration with the engine running fast on second was a most agreeable feature.

In addition to the superb pulling power and smoothness of the engine, we would refer particularly to the suspension and the steering. Last year in *The Autocar* we were able to make the first reference to the new type of Rolls-Royce rear cantilever springs. Their design will be appreciated on reference to one of the

(1) Blanking plates are attached to the rear face of the radiator, and a new induction coil is fitted. (2) The large adjustable dashboard ventilator enables the front compartment to be kept at a pleasant temperature. (3) Five leaves only are fitted to the cantilever rear springs. (4) The new instrument board has, in addition to the customary fittings, a hand wheel for opening and closing the scuttle ventilator, and on the right of the switchboard a thermometer is provided for indicating to the driver the temperature of the cooling water of the engine.

accompanying illustrations, but we may mention that the bottom leaf is split longitudinally from the trunnion to the back of the spring, it being claimed that the slot so formed has the effect of holding the car steadily on the road when cornering at high speed. Whatever the cause may be, the result in this respect is all that can be desired. Rolling, so often encountered with flexible cantilever springs, is absent, while the shock-absorbing qualities of the comparatively thick, curiously shaped leaves must be experienced to be believed.

As regards the steering, we can only say that it is quite perfect—as light as a feather, very positive, and so designed that the front wheels automatically resume their straight-forward position if the driver removes his hands from the wheel after a corner has been negotiated.

So far as the chassis details are concerned, we reproduce illustrations showing the engine, the instrument board, and the large adjustable ventilator on the top of the dash in front of the windscreen. This ventilator is operated by turning the large hand wheel shown in the centre of the instrument board above the switchboard.

Immediately on the right of the switchboard is a thermometer gauge, of which the needle's position is controlled by the heat of the water where it rises from the top of the jacket towards the back of the rear cylinder block. The temperature of the water can be controlled by means of the detachable blanking plates shown attached to the rear of the radiator tubes. On the car tested by us, two of these blanking plates were employed, one at the top and the other at the bottom of the radiator, and the water temperature at the top of Box Hill was approximately 95° C.

On the 1920 model Rolls-Royce, the trembler coil as an independent unit has been replaced by a small induction coil on the front of the dashboard, working in conjunction with a make-and-break disposed just below the high-tension distributer for the battery ignition. Incidentally, the retention of this secondary ignition is a commendable feature.

The very large lock of the front wheels is exemplified by this view of the new 40-50 h.p. Rolls-Royce negotiating the hairpin corner on Box Hill, near Dorking.

In the view of the near side of the engine there is shown passing from the dashboard to a point between the cylinder blocks a long tube. Through this tube it is possible, by means of a hand-operated pump, to prime the induction pipe for easy starting. The same pump that effects the priming is used for generating air pressure in the fuel tank.

In conclusion, we would express our firm conviction that the latest Rolls-Royce is bound to enhance the reputation of Messrs. Rolls-Royce, Ltd., and to confound those who are sometimes heard to allege that the Derby works are content to rely for maintaining their reputation for supremacy upon results secured in the old days when really first-class cars were few and far between.

A LUXURIOUS TWO-SEATER.

A Rolls-Royce Car equipped with a Remarkable Two-seater Body provided with Every Convenience for Touring. Some Notes on a Useful Contribution to the Anti-dazzle Problem.

Mr. F. Lionel Rapson's luxurious two-seater Rolls-Royce, fitted with everything that ingenuity can suggest for the convenience and comfort of the passengers.

THERE are two kinds of luxury in car work, the more usual is the luxury of sumptuous fitting, rich upholstery and beautiful bodywork, the second is the luxury of having proper equipment always ready for the convenience of the car user.

It is in the latter class that the two-seater Rolls-Royce here described falls, and its details are characteristic of its owner, Mr. Lionel F. Rapson. The following are some of the specially interesting points of this unusual vehicle. The egg-shaped tail is divided so that the upper portion can be lifted clear. In the flooring towards the point is a trap door, which, when lifted, discloses a funnel permanently in position for filling the petrol tank. The interior of this tail is spacious enough to house a cupboard containing all spares, oils, etc., cooking utensils, a Kodak photographic outfit and suit and dressing cases. Between the forward portion of the tail compartment and the seats, there is in the body space which is utilised to the last degree. In this region on each side of the body are two doors; in the upper compartment this provides room for six full petrol tins, whilst on the near side there is a small washing tray with hot and cold water laid on from tanks situated above this locker. The lower door on the left hand side of the car affords accommodation for tools. Attached to the running board below the wash basin compartment is a container for spare accumulators. Concealed behind the squabs of the front seats is a locker for containing food, this locker being provided with a proper ventilator, whilst below the instrument board is a sliding shelf which can be pulled outwards to form a table.

Dipping Head Lamps.

Not the least interesting feature of the equipment of this car is the dipping head light arrangement. Both head lamps are mounted on trunnions after the fashion of a gun barrel, and the lamps themselves are provided with controls which enable the driver to tilt them angularly downwards, thus retaining illumination in front of the car, but removing the main beam of light from the range

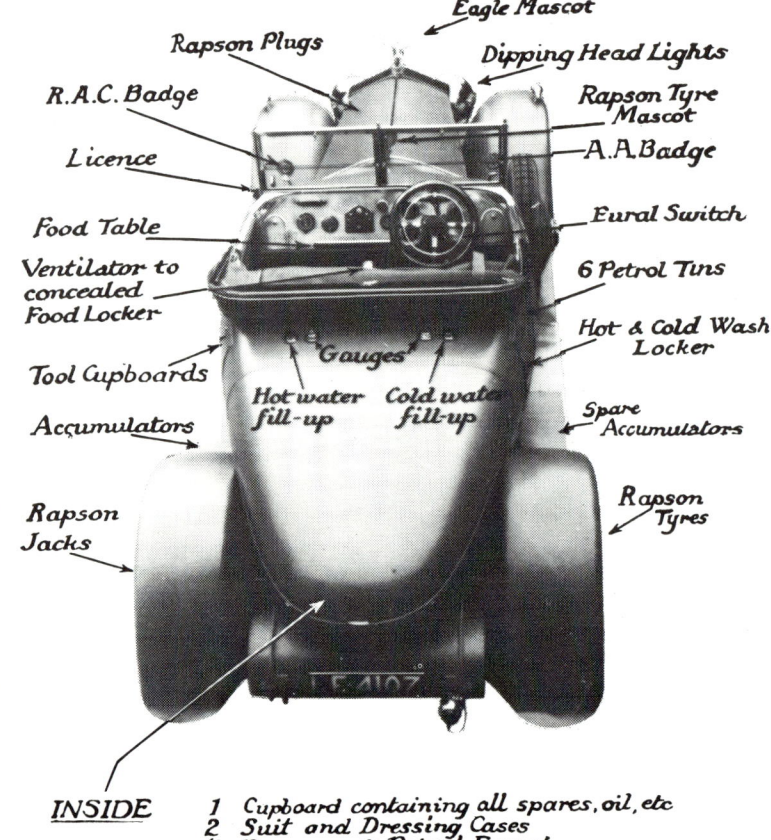

Eagle Mascot
Rapson Plugs
Dipping Head Lights
R.A.C. Badge
Rapson Tyre Mascot
Licence
A.A. Badge
Food Table
Eural Switch
Ventilator to concealed Food Locker
6 Petrol Tins
"Gauges"
Hot & Cold Wash Locker
Tool Cupboards
Hot water fill-up
Cold water fill-up
Accumulators
Spare Accumulators
Rapson Jacks
Rapson Tyres

INSIDE
1 Cupboard containing all spares, oil, etc
2 Suit and Dressing Cases
3 Permanent Petrol Funnel
4 Cooking utensils
5 Kodak Photography Outfit, etc.

Plan view of Mr. Rapson's "Ideal" touring car, indicating the situation of the various points of equipment.

of vision of other road users. This dipping head light was, we understand, used by Mr. Rapson in 1914, when he was head despatch driver on the King's Messenger Service. The car is, of course, fitted with Rapson tyres and Rapson jacks, also Rapson plugs, and it will be seen that a double divided windscreen is used.

In regard to the housing of the spares, by the way, means are provided to carry them all in felt lined lockers and drawers. For sheer comfort and convenience it would be difficult to improve upon the general scheme of this car.

A Test of the Lamps.

With further reference to the Rapson dipping head lights, the principle of which was described in our issue of March 26th, we have now had an opportunity of testing this idea on the road at night, and we frankly admit that we are very favourably impressed with the arrangement.

The great point about the dipping head light is that, while glare from the point of view of approaching traffic is absolutely eliminated, quite a good light remains for the driver of the vehicle to which the lamps are attached. We have both driven behind the dip-

Lockers in the side of the car behind the seats accommodate six spare tins of petrol. On the one side there is a washing basin with hot and cold water, and on the other accommodation for tools. Let into the floor at the point of the tail is a petrol funnel permanently in position above the tank.

ping head lamps and also have stood at various distances on the road ahead of them, and we are confident that, when their possibilities are better appreciated by car manufacturers and by the public, these lamps will be widely adopted as offering a comparatively simple solution of the vexed and very vexing dazzle problem.

We understand that both the Prince of Wales and the Duke of York have intimated to Mr. Rapson their intention to have these dipping head lamps fitted to their new cars, the Prince of Wales deciding to adopt them after a night run on Mr. Rapson's Rolls-Royce on Saturday last.

Note the circular rear window and neat luggage grid over the petrol tank on this 1921 40/50 with Park Ward body. Although a saloon it had a division behind the driving seat and extra folding occasional seats in the rear compartment

ROAD IMPRESSIONS OF THE 1921 ROLLS-ROYCE.

A Test of the Latest Type Chassis, in which are incorporated Various Minor Improvements, including a Modification of the Rear Springs and Thermostatic Control of the Water Temperature.

IN A DEEP CUT SURREY LANE

HAVING recently enjoyed a run of a thousand miles on a 1920 model Rolls-Royce, we availed ourselves with pleasure, a few days ago, of an opportunity to make the acquaintance of the very latest pattern of chassis. Though our trip did not extend to more than some sixty miles, it was carried out over roads widely different in character, and affording a very good general test of the car's ability.

The phenomenal accelerative power of the Rolls-Royce engine, with its comparatively new light pistons, was very thoroughly demonstrated as we threaded our way through London traffic, it being no exaggeration to say that the new car is no whit behind its immediate predecessors in enabling its driver to proceed on top gear at a speed that would not unduly tax the ability of a very slow walker.

To those who have not enjoyed a run through London on a Rolls-Royce it is almost impossible to convey an idea of the quite astonishing manner in which these large cars can thread their way without a change of gear through traffic streams that would on other vehicles call for frequent recourse to the lower ratios. In London the Rolls-Royce on top gear is best comparable with a high-powered steam car, and when the throttle is opened the passenger has the sensation of being pushed by the rear seat squab, gently but forcibly, in the small of the back. Despite the power behind the push, the engine is extraordinarily smooth and absolutely silent.

The Car's Capabilities.

Probably there is no motor car engine made, either at the Rolls-Royce Derby works or at any other factory, that has not a just appreciable periodic vibration at some stage in its range of speed. In this car the only periodicity was experienced between 22 and 25 m.p.h., if the engine was asked to accelerate fast at this point. If the driver was content to allow the speed to increase comparatively slowly, the vibration was not apparent, and, whether accelerating fast or slowly, we were unable to find any other periodicity up to 55 m.p.h., which was the highest speed attained.

DATA FOR THE DRIVER.

40-50 h.p., six cylinders, 114 × 121 mm. (7,410 c.c.). Tax, £49.

Cylinders cast in blocks of three. Magneto and battery and coil ignition, thermostatic water control.

Weight of car less passengers: Front axle, 19 cwt. 2 qr. 20 lb.; back axle, 21 cwt. 24 lb.; total, 40 cwt. 3 qr. 16 lb.

Weight per c.c., .61 lb.

Gear ratios: Top, 3.47; third, 5.4; second 8.05 and first 12.35 to 1.

Spiral bevel final drive.

Springs: Semi-elliptic front. Cantilever rear.

895 × 135 mm. front; 895 × 135 oversize rear tyres. Dunlop detachable wire wheels.

Wheelbase, 12ft. Track, 4ft. 8in.

Fuel consumption, 15 to 18 m.p.g.; tank capacity, 18 galls.

In this connection it should be added that 70 m.p.h. is well within the capability of the latest Rolls-Royce. Doubtless, it is delightful to feel that at 50 m.p.h. one still has 20 m.p.h., as it were, "up one's sleeve," but, save on the Brooklands track, it is seldom possible safely to utilise this reserve in Great Britain. Still, when the car is taken on the Continent, the extra speed is welcome.

In the course of our run, we climbed to Newlands' Corner from the Ripley side, and negotiated the steep portion on top gear, the speedometer needle never falling below 27 m.p.h. This was a remarkably fine performance, for the gradient is very much more severe than it appears at first sight; in fact, we doubt whether any standard touring car could make a better showing on this slope than was put up for our benefit on the Rolls-Royce.

Climbing on Top Gear.

Subsequently, a f t e r passing through Shere, we climbed to Ewhurst Mill, and then made our way into Cranleigh. The most trying gradient encountered was between Cranleigh and Ewhurst on the return journey. We avoided the main road, and came by a lane with a hill of such severity and length—to say nothing of the corners—that we were confident the car would fail to negotiate it on top gear. As a matter of fact, the climb represented the limit possible, but the Rolls-Royce manfully reached the crest, slowly, it is true, but with the engine pulling sweetly and with no sign of distress. All the hills in this neighbourhood are well known to us, and for this reason we were the better able to appreciate this magnificent performance.

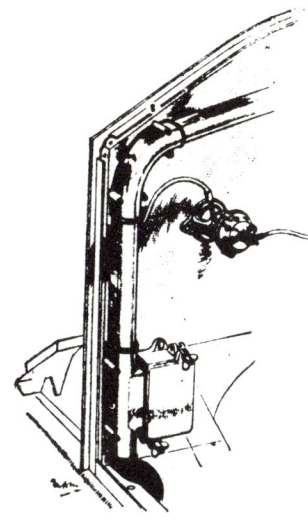

The electric wiring on the front of the dashboard is now neatly enclosed by aluminium channels.

The springing of the latest chassis is beyond reproach, and it is in relation to the springs that one has to record a modification in design. Last year the Rolls-Royce Company fitted to chassis designed for touring bodies five comparatively thick, square-edged leaves for the rear cantilevers. This year, while the number of leaves varies according to the weight to be carried, the number has increased generally to eight, while the tips of the leaves are rounded in the normal manner. Also, the slotted main leaf of the cantilever spring has given place to an unslotted leaf.

Having travelled for several miles as a back-seat passenger over very poor roads, we can say definitely that the comfort behind is practically equal to that in the driver's compartment. Higher praise it would be impossible to give.

Driving Refinements.

We took the wheel for the homeward journey, and found all the Rolls-Royce driving refinements to which we have been accustomed in the past. The steering, in our opinion, is as near perfection as it can be, the controls come easily to hand, and are devoid of lost motion, while the brakes seemed to us to have been improved immensely as compared with those first fitted when the propeller-shaft brake was abandoned some years ago. Very moderate pressure either on the brake pedal or on the hand brake lever was sufficient to check the big car at all speeds, while, should it be necessary to do so, we could lock the wheels with consummate ease.

It is merely repeating an old story to say that the Rolls-Royce is silent in running. In this respect it has always been in the forefront, and in the case of the latest model perhaps the best evidence of silence is that by far the greatest amount of sound is made by the treads of the tyres. One cannot fully realise the quietness of these cars until one has driven them many miles, particularly in populous districts. Then it gradually dawns upon the man at the wheel that he must use the horn far more than is customary, since pedestrians and cyclists otherwise have no warning of his approach, and may at the last moment step or ride in front of the car.

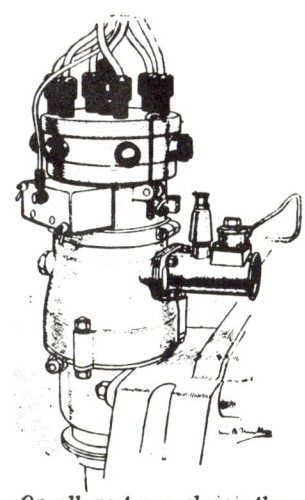

On all post-war chassis the air pressure pump is fitted at the side of the governor gear, below the high-tension distributer.

Thermostatic Temperature Control.

As regards novelties in the latest Rolls-Royce chassis, we have already referred to the alteration in the springs. Apart from this, there is thermostatic control of the water circulation through the radiator. This is purely automatic in action, the thermostat valve opening progressively as the heat of the water in the cylinder jacket rises.

In our opinion, the thermostat is a most admirable addition to the Rolls-Royce, for the temperature of

THE R.-R. POWER UNIT. (Top) The thermostat can be clearly seen in relation to the general run of the water piping. The method of enclosing the wiring on the front of the dashboard is indicated. (Bottom) A detail view of the near side of the engine. Despite the fact that no valve cover plates are provided, this mechanism is absolutely silent.

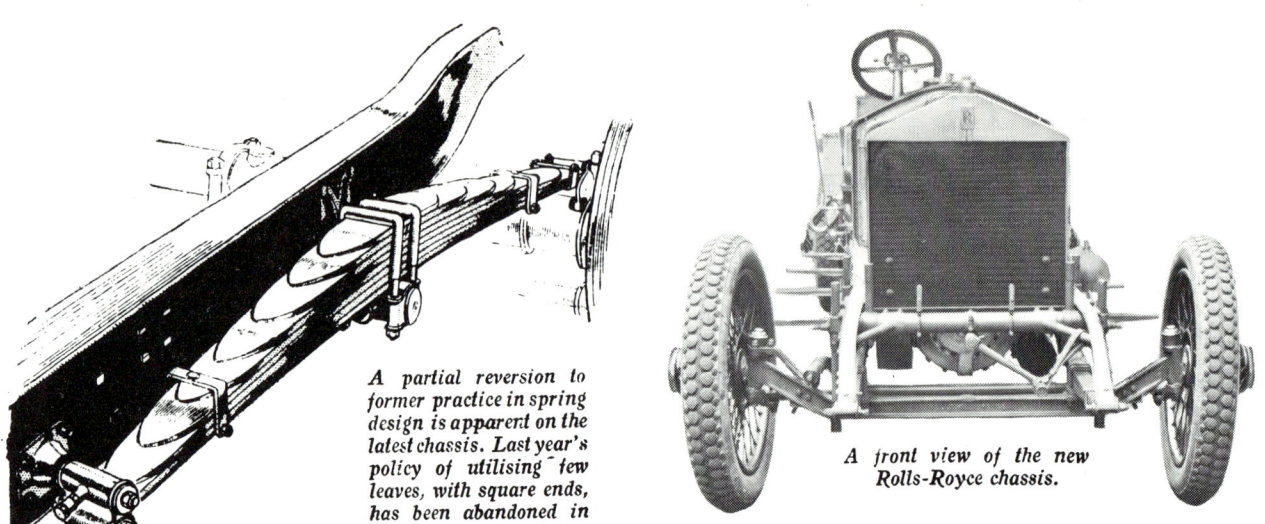

A partial reversion to former practice in spring design is apparent on the latest chassis. Last year's policy of utilising few leaves, with square ends, has been abandoned in favour of the type shown.

A front view of the new Rolls-Royce chassis.

the cylinders when the engine is started from cold very quickly rises to some 80° Centigrade, so enabling the driver to make good use of his engine power practically from the outset. In the past it has been desirable to allow the engine, say, five minutes in which to warm up, and this, though not a very important point, has sometimes been inconvenient.

One particularly pleasing, though not altogether new, feature of the Rolls-Royce is the silence with which the engine starter operates. The starting motor is placed on the near side of the chassis, level with the clutchshaft, to which power is transmitted through a chain. Really, an engine starter on this car seems almost a superfluity, for, at any rate on the vehicle used by us for our trial, we only employed the electric motor once, since, despite about ten stops, we found that on all the other occasions the engine started on the switch.

Our only criticism of the Rolls-Royce has to do with the gear-changing mechanism. It is true that probably not once in the course of a day's run will it be necessary to change from top to third or third to second gear, but, if a change is called for, we think it should be rendered practically foolproof. If we are expecting too much from Mr. Royce in asking him to design a gear box that will enable quiet changes to be made merely by pushing a lever from one slot into another, we think that he himself is to blame, because largely to his genius is attributable the production of a chassis that is so near perfection generally.

This 40/50 cabriolet was built for H.H. The Nawab of Rampur in 1921 by the Cunard Motor and Carriage Co. Ltd.

The Charm of High Power to Weight Ratio.

ON THE HILL IN RICHMOND PARK

A Test of a Rolls-Royce Car with a Powerful Engine and a Specially Arranged Very Light Body.

FOR many years we have insisted that the best results are obtained from a car if the body is made as light as possible, consistent with durability and comfort, and the engine is powerful, for only with a combination of these conditions is it possible to realise the full powers of a car. It does not matter whether it is a large or a small car, and, with certain limits, it does not matter whether the full available power from a given cubic capacity is realised, provided that the ratio of the power to weight is considered.

We were enabled recently to try a machine of which the performance is altogether exceptional. The reason for its success is to be found in the fact that the utmost attention has been paid to the tune of the engine, although it is not in any sense a racing or competition car, and that a very light four-seated body has been installed. The chassis is a 40-50 h.p. 1920 Rolls-Royce, the body resembling in many ways that used during the war in the R.N.A.S., save that it has a large windscreen, a full size hood, a luggage grid, and four comfortable seats. It may be

A precaution for long runs. On Mr. Minchin's Rolls-Royce no fewer than six petrol cans are carried as reserve fuel holders.

mentioned, incidentally, that no fewer than six full petrol cans are carried on a special platform at the rear of the car.

The car in question belongs to Mr. G. R. N. Minchin, of Messrs. Peto and Radford, and the chassis has received particular attention with a view to suiting it to the body. In other words, the springs were not left as they were originally, but were modified to take the lighter load. It would be very difficult to find a finer expression of the modern sporting car than this machine. It can travel up to quite high speeds—its owner claims seventy-five miles an hour if necessary—without the very slightest sign that there is an engine installed and not by so much as the tremor of a footboard can the passengers detect vibration at any time. The response to the throttle, if full advantage be taken of the Rolls-Royce mixture control, is instantaneous, the acceleration being very like that of a fast racing car.

It is noticeable that the seats are placed well within the wheelbase, and, probably as a result of this, the suspension is wonderful, even the

55

most severe shocks being transmitted to the passengers merely as a gradual rise and fall of the body without noticeable jar.

Docile but Powerful.

Although the highest of the Rolls-Royce gear ratios, very nearly 3 to 1, is fitted, the extraordinary thing about the car is that it can crawl on top gear so slowly that there is a distinct pause between the notes of the exhaust, and at a pace which is less than three miles an hour. This must be experienced to be believed, and is quite unique in our experience of cars. From this crawl it is possible by skilful and delicate driving to accelerate gradually for a few yards, and then to pick up speed rapidly and without difficulty.

Both brakes are very good, that operated by the pedal being decidedly better than the hand brake, partly because the lever for the latter is not well placed relative to the driver. This apart, the driving position

How batteries should be treated. Each cell is separate, as the set on Mr. Minchin's Rolls-Royce is experimental, but on the lid, opposite each cell, is the history sheet of that particular cell.

—it may be mentioned that bucket seats are provided — is particularly good, and the machine handles in all its controls as a Rolls-Royce should; one can imagine no higher praise.

Hills are as nothing to the car, for the long gradient of Box Hill was taken comfortably on top gear, corners included, and the climb to Newlands Corner can be tackled on top at a speed never falling below 30 m.p.h. if necessary. Pebblecombe was not climbed so well, partly because the rear wheels slipped a good deal, partly because temporary trouble developed in the fuel feed. At no time whatsoever is there the feeling that the car is cumbersome or hard to handle; instead, it manoeuvres almost exactly like a light car, can be taken in and out of traffic, accelerated, or stopped, with the utmost ease and with absolute certainty.

Taken as a whole, it is the most inspiring form of car to drive, which is a sensation not easily forgotten.

Right: A 40/50 h.p. special vee-fronted cabriolet built in 1922 to the order of His Highness Sawai Kishan Singh Bahadur. Note the wide front door and the much narrower rear door. Below: Sir Charles Higham, MP, stands beside his open-fronted Hooper limousine on a 40/50 h.p. chassis soon after taking delivery of the car in the spring of 1922. His uniformed chauffeur is at the wheel. Note the oil tank on the side of the chassis, the opening windscreen a small oval rear window

1905, 10 h.p. and two cylinders—the first production model

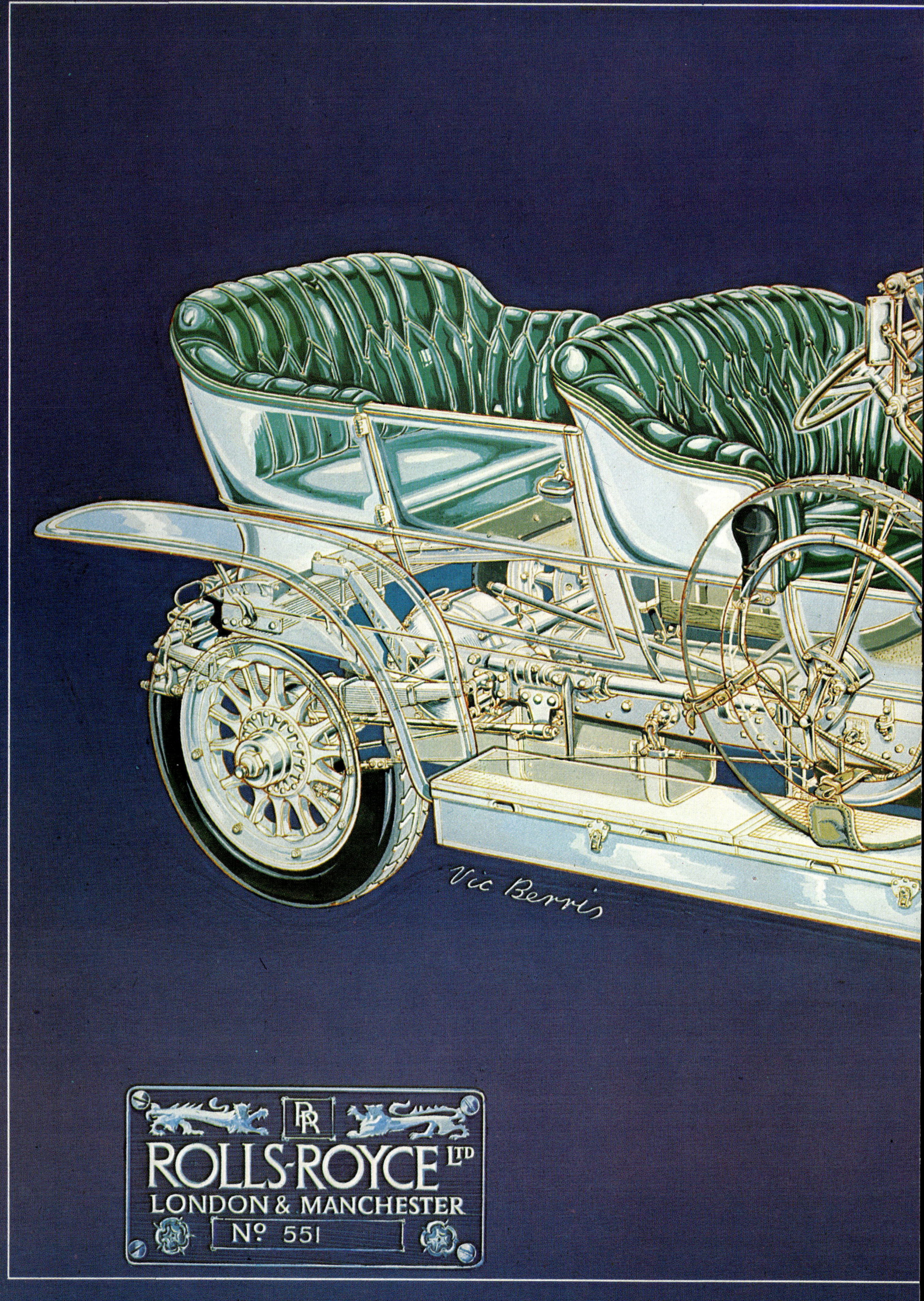

Vic Berris

ROLLS-ROYCE LTD
LONDON & MANCHESTER
Nº 551

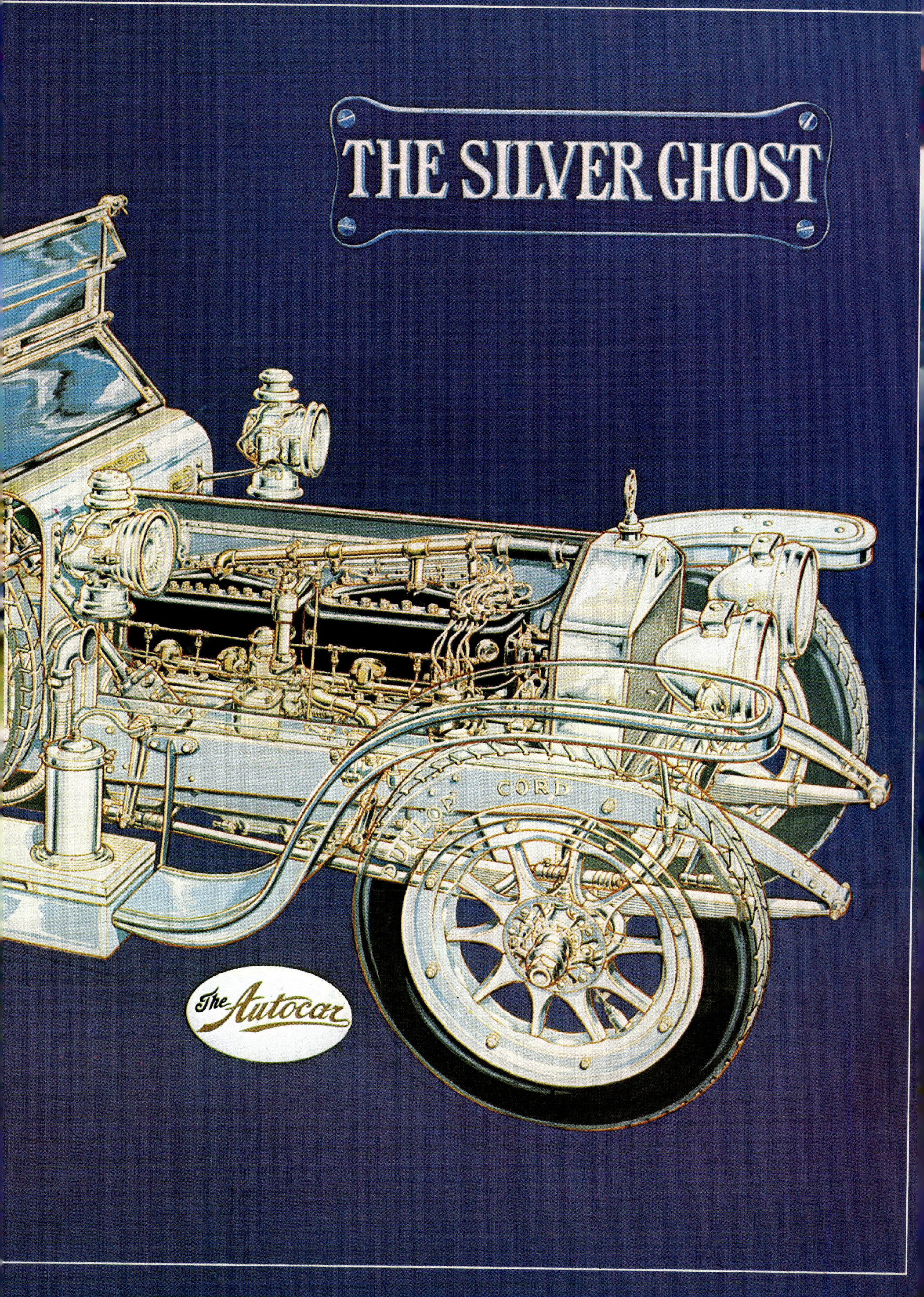
THE SILVER GHOST
DUNLOP CORD
The Autocar

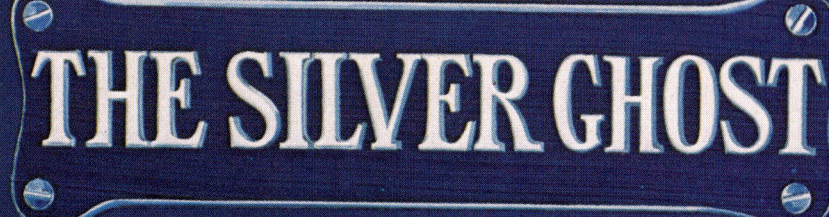

Above: The Silver Ghost at rest in Denham Village. All external fittings are silver plated and the AA badge is original.
Below left: The wood-rimmed steering wheel and instruments are all original.
Below right: Note the height of the Barker body. Tool boxes are built into the running boards and the acetylene cylinder for the headlamps is on the running board ahead of the spare tyre for the detachable rim wooden wheels.

A 20 H.P. SIX-CYLINDER ROLLS-ROYCE.

Technical Details of the Latest Car to Mark the Growing Popularity of the Medium and Small Six-cylinder Engine.   A Light and Lively Chassis designed to Accommodate All Classes of Coachwork.

For years past it has been known that Rolls-Royce, Ltd., have been conducting experiments and research work in connection with chassis of smaller dimensions than those of the world-famous 40-50 h.p. car that bears their name. It has, however, been the policy of the company to test every innovation to the utmost before adopting it, and the work in relation to the new 20 h.p. six-cylinder chassis has afforded further evidence of this method of procedure. The newcomer is, in reality, the result of years of practical experience. It has been tried out not only in this country, but also on the roads of France, and it may be stated definitely that those responsible for its design and construction are entirely satisfied with its capability to uphold the honour of the company and of its 40-50 h.p. "big brother," which, incidentally, it will in no way supersede. It may be remarked that the adoption of battery ignition for the smaller Rolls-Royce is likely to give no small encouragement to those who hold the view that the need for a magneto is becoming less pronounced as the general electrical equipment of motor cars comes nearer to perfection in the way of reliability. In view of the fact that no chassis of the 20 h.p. Rolls-Royce was available for examination in time for an article to be prepared by us for publication this week, the following description of the outstanding features has been compiled by Mr. F. H. Royce, the designer and Chief Engineer to Rolls-Royce, Ltd.

THERE has been no very serious departure in this chassis, but its value is greatly due to the infinite care taken in the design and proportion of the units. Simplicity was one of the aims of the designers, but not at the expense of perfection. Having this in view, no expense has been spared that the parts shall be made as perfect and as lasting as possible within the limit of weight, a leading motto being "spend as much money in the construction as can be done wisely, but not unnecessarily." This chassis is built and tyred to carry open and enclosed bodies up to six seats, and with bodies and wings of moderate dimensions the complete car is capable of high road speed. It is not recommended that this chassis shall carry such heavy bodies as are often fitted to larger chassis. The body space is ample for six seats with moderately raked steering, and the frame length behind the dash is 8ft. 3in.

Special care has been taken to allow of the rear seats being very low considering the diameter of the road wheels, and ample clearance is given for the movement of the back axle, this clearance contributing to the excellence of the car's suspension.

Range of Useful Engine Speed.

The six-cylinder engine has its crankshaft carried in seven bearings, and runs from 150 to 3,000 revolutions per minute without apparent vibration, and, owing to the perfect working of the R.-R. expanding carburetter and carburation system, it pulls with great torque throughout its useful range of speed. The journals and the pins of the crankshaft are bored hollow for lightness and strength, and the crank forgings are machined all over.

The cylinder arrangement, although appearing somewhat usual, is quite unique, as the push rods for the overhead valves are on the opposite side to the ignition plugs, which latter are in an extremely good and accessible position, i.e., they are well in the crown of the combustion chamber, out of the way of oil, and very accessible. The valve gear is particularly silent, and remains so throughout an extended service; this is due

SPECIFICATION.

ENGINE : 20 h.p., six cylinders, 3 × 4½ in. — 76 × 114 mm. — (3,150 c.c.) Overhead valves, push-rod operated. Detachable cylinder head. Battery ignition with automatic advance.
TRANSMISSION : Single dry plate clutch, three-speed gear box, spiral bevel final drive, full floating rear axle.
SUSPENSION : Semi-elliptic front and rear.
STEERING : Worm and nut. Two standard positions for steering column.
WHEELS : Dunlop detachable wire, with 32 × 4½ in. tyres. Wheelbase 10ft. 9 in. Track 4ft. 6in.
WEIGHT : Chassis 18cwt. 4lb.
PRICE : Chassis, £1,100, Open Touring Car, £1,590.

to the great care taken in the design and proportions of the valve operating mechanism.

The cylinders are a *monobloc* casting, as is also the head, which is detachable ; all the valve seats are water-cooled, the joint between the head and the cylinders is most carefully proportioned, and has never given a moment's trouble during prolonged tests. (These have proved considerably more reliable than the usual loose heads on a side-valve engine.) The half-time wheels driving the camshaft and other units are helically cut, and the R.-R. damped spring drive is used, giving a smooth and silent drive through the full range of speed.

The pistons are of aluminium, and, owing to their design, they are light, free from knocks, and not liable to seize. Owing to the careful arrangement of piston rings the wearing surface can be well lubricated without fear of excess of oil entering the combustion chamber. The pressure lubrication is also carried to the little ends of the connecting rods, which are extremely light nickel steel forgings. There are three oil leads to the crankshaft, and the remaining bearings and connecting rod big and little ends are lubricated by the oil passing through the passages in the crankshaft. The valves are made from high-chrome non-corrosive steel. In order to prevent the crank chamber fumes from entering the body, provision is made that these shall be drawn into the induction system.

Carburation and Lubrication.

The carburetter is a modified design of the standard R.-R. expanding carburetter, which has already proved so successful, and has two jets controllable from the instrument board. There is also a third jet for starting purposes, controlled from the instrument board, which gives a mixture of ample strength during starting operations. The induction system is well heated, and the engine has been run successfully on a mixture of petrol and paraffin, although this is not advised in general use. The induction manifold is arranged to give equal distribution at low temperatures, or with poor fuel.

CHASSIS OF THE NEW 20 H.P. SIX-CYLINDER ROLLS ROYCE.

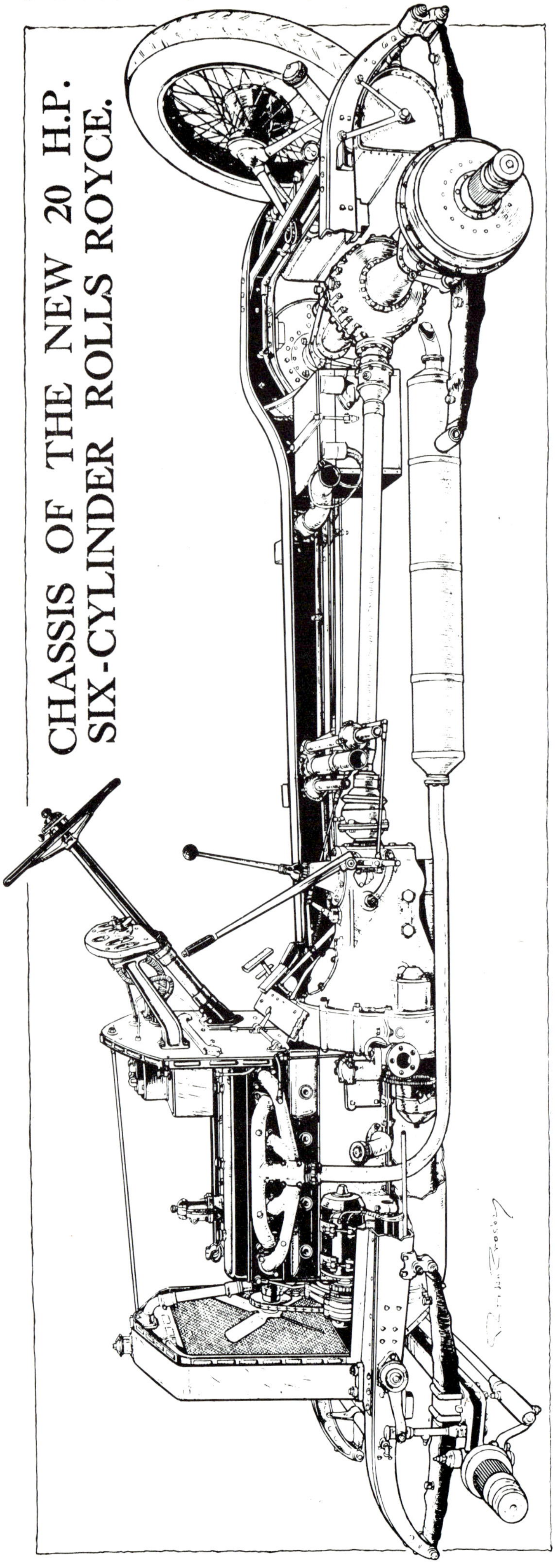

Engine lubrication is by pressure by pump, with float and pointer level indicator, that of the gear box and back axle—which is oil-retaining—by splash. The road wheels and universal joints are oil-retaining, while the details (spring shackles) are lubricated by a *portable* grease injector with rapid connectors.

The oil consumption on this chassis is remarkably low, the car running 1,000 miles to the gallon. This is due to the care given to the oil-retaining in the design of the bearings and oil joints about the whole chassis, and to the design of the pistons, which prevents oil working up into the combustion chambers.

Radiator Shutters Standard.

The radiator, of the honeycomb type, is of ample size, and is fitted with a set of shutters, under the driver's control, so that the water temperature can be maintained in cold weather.

Close behind the radiator an efficient fan is mounted on a spring-controlled support, which maintains a con-

ried on the box, and has its ratchet below the floor-boards, but, unlike the usual arrangement, the teeth are on the lower side of the quadrant, so that no foreign substance can fall and lodge in them and render the ratchet unsafe.

Both brakes are internal expanding, and take effect direct on rear wheel hubs; they are enclosed and protected from road dirt and oil, and compensated by bevel-gear equalisers of R.-R. pattern. The brake shoes are of aluminium, and internal and external adjustment is provided close to the point of wear. The brakes are remarkable for their smooth and effective action; the special R.-R. cams, which have great efficiency and equality, are used to expand the shoes; it is very noticeable how the rear axle steadily keeps on to the road when the brakes are applied, resulting in a straight, powerful, and smooth pull up of the car.

The rear axle is of very light construction, having an aluminium central box, steel tubes with large flanges, and a substantial tie-rod; it is extremely com-

The new 20 h.p. Rolls-Royce. The open touring body is built on smart lines and equipped with a permanently sloping windscreen with adjustable panels. The hood when raised is provided with permanently attached half sides at the rear.

stant tension in the V belt over a large range of movement. The water is circulated by a centrifugal pump fitted with a special form of lubricated double gland, which is remarkable for water retaining and absence of wear. There is a thermometer fitted with a gauge on the instrument board, thus giving complete indication and control of the water temperature, which so largely contributes to efficient running and low petrol consumption.

The clutch is of the single dry-plate type fitted with Ferodo and steel surfaces. It carries four levers revolving with it, so that the thrust is light, and with this and other features its operation is remarkably smooth. Owing to the extreme lightness of the driving member, and its great freedom when declutched, the changing of gears is easy and free from shocks.

Central Control for the Gears.

The gear box, which provides three forward speeds and a reverse, is of the conventional sliding type. The layshaft is driven by helical gears, and has the unusual feature of being supported in three bearings. The driven shaft is also carried in three bearings. The third bearing on the latter shaft almost entirely relieves the spigot bearing, which has in some cases proved unsatisfactory in the more usual form of design. These extra bearings contribute largely to the permanency of the silence of the box, and considerably reduce the tendency to wear. Enclosed in the gear box there is a special worm drive for the speed indicator.

The change-speed lever is controlled by an internal gate, and has a positive interlocking device, as well as the position spring plungers. The interlocking device enables the spring plungers to be very light in action, and the whole change mechanism works with great freedom and delicacy. The hand brake lever is car-

pact for the diameter of the bevel gear. The road wheels are entirely mounted on extensions of the tubes; therefore no part of the rear axle is subject to reverse stresses due to the weight carried, the internal driving shafts being subject to torsional stresses only. The bevel gears are spirally cut, and the pinion is fitted with a third (nose) bearing so that its alignment is maintained.

Front Axle Arrangements.

The front axle is a high tensile alloy steel forging of I section of light and accurate proportions; the stub axles, which are of large diameter, are carefully radiused and bored for strength and lightness. The steering pivots are arranged to give "centre point steering," so as to reduce to a minimum the forces exerted upon the steering gear through rough roads, soft borders to roads, or deflated tyres. The road wheel hubs have special provision to render them oil retaining, and water and mud excluding.

The attachment of the road springs is carried out in a unique manner by the use of a steel sheath which fits keys formed on the axle, transmitting the shocks directly from the axle to the upper plate of the spring to obviate the possibility of shearing the central bolt. The steering arms are attached by the R.-R. system used in the larger chassis.

The steering is by worm and nut, as in the larger R.-R. chassis. The ignition and throttle controls are placed on and above the steering wheel, as in R.-R. practice, but the ignition switch and mixture control are on the instrument board. The longitudinal steering tube is fitted with set-up spring buffers to reduce the force of the shocks reaching the steering box. The well-proportioned steering wheel is notched and covered with black non-conducting covering (including the spokes), so that the steering wheel is pleasant and clean to handle and has a handsome appearance. The thrust bearing is easily adjustable, being on the steering column. The steering joints are of R.-R. design, easily adjustable, and all parts of the bearing are firmly locked after adjustment, so that the blocks do not knock about and become loose in their housing—a unique feature. The steering is fitted in two standard positions—for owner-driving and for chauffeur-driving ; the former is for bodies not exceeding four seats.

The Suspension System.

Both back and front springs are semi-elliptic and very long for the size of chassis. They are extremely carefully fitted, and at the front end of each spring, where the control is taken, they are provided with solid ends having central eyes, to avoid road shocks causing unnecessary and dangerous bending stresses.

The frame is of deep channel section, fitted with a number of tubular cross members to render it more

plicity and weight. For simplicity and robustness the single-wire system is adopted, which permits of the more substantial single-contact lamps and holders being used. For the sake of easily understanding and tracing the various circuits, the installation has been made with coloured wires of the colours shown on the diagram of the wiring in the instruction book. The wiring is carried out in aluminium tubes and channels so as to be well protected. In connection with the head and side lamps special provision is made to support these on the wings by the standard support stays provided with the chassis, and by using these the wiring is enclosed and invisible.

The dynamo has third brush control and cuts in at an extremely slow speed, giving an output which rises rapidly at first (for night running), and afterwards, at high speed, falls to avoid overcharging the battery. It runs with great silence, and even at the highest speed without excessive heat ; it is easily dismounted for cleaning and inspection, and is controlled by an effective

CLOSED COACHWORK.

The standard closed coachwork provided for the new 20 h.p. Rolls-Royce embraces a landaulet (left) and an all-weather body fitted with extremely wide doors.

rigid than usual against twisting, and brackets are provided along the outside for the attachment of the bodywork, so making it unnecessary to use wide and heavy runners in body construction, and permitting the rear seats to be unusually low. Every effort has been made to keep the frame low, and, considering the large road wheels and large road clearance (11in.), this has been extremely successful.

The pedals have long strokes to permit of light operation and avoid frequent adjustments of the operated parts. They are fitted in two positions, corresponding to the two positions of the steering column. So that the pedals can be conveniently placed, the steering column passes through the dash high up, the brake pedal being in the centre.

The instrument board is carried from the dash by brackets in two standard positions, corresponding to the two positions of the steering column. It is fitted with clock, chassis number plate, speed indicator, thermometer gauge, radiator shutter control, mixture control and starting carburetter lever, ammeter, oil pressure gauge, dashboard light, and switchbox. These fittings form part of the standard equipment of the complete car.

The switchbox is fitted with two handles, one controlling the lighting and the other controlling the ignition and dynamo. This switchbox can be locked by the Yale type of key when the ignition is off, and either the lamps are off, or the side and tail lights only burning. It contains a connection socket for the inspection lamp, and also a press-button for the dashboard light.

Except for the accumulator and a few other obvious parts, the whole of the electrical equipment is manufactured by the Rolls-Royce Co., and has been made with the *first object of reliability*, having in view sim-

automatic switch mounted on the distribution board, which is in an accessible position.

The starter motor is of R.-R. manufacture, and is geared to the flywheel with spring drive automatic pinion. There is an extra nose bearing on the motor spindle to prevent excessive deflection and risk of breakage. It is controlled by a pedal-operated switch, which has the unusual feature of being oil-immersed.

The battery, of 12 volts, is carried in the frame, and is accessible and removable through the floor.

On the distribution board the wires, the dynamo, the battery, and the switch box meet together, ample fuses being provided and carefully arranged.

A spare wheel is securely carried at the back of the chassis on a tubular carrier, with aluminium shoes in which the tyre rests. It is important to carry this spare in this position so that its weight can be utilised to make the road wheels more effectively hold the road.

Shock dampers are fitted to both front and rear axles. They are of R.-R. construction, and those at the rear are of the progressive type.

Vacuum Petrol Feed.

The rear tank is suspended in a safe position, being protected by the spare wheel, etc. It is fitted with a side filler and petrol gauge. A very large filter is provided in the petrol tank, which can be removed without emptying the tank. There is also a filter of large area under the carburetter float chamber, also easily detachable.

The vacuum feed tank on the dash is of extra large capacity, which permits the car to run for a long time at slow speed without closing the throttle to obtain the necessary vacuum for refilling. This tank is fitted with a needle valve, so that the petrol can be turned off for safety when necessary.

THE SERVO BRAKES OF THE ROLLS-ROYCE.

A Road Test of their Efficiency. Details of the Actuating Mechanism. Light Operation a Feature

Breasting the summit of Kirkstone Pass (1481 ft.) from Ambleside on the run from London to Glasgow. The road to the left is the easier ascent from Troutbeck.

WHEN the Rolls-Royce Company announced last year its adoption of the principle of brakes on all wheels, considerable interest was evoked. The delay in their final application to cars sold to the public only served to increase curiosity as to the design decided upon, since it was common knowledge that the company, in accord with its usual principles, made a point of testing, over a prolonged period, every known system as well as experimental brakes of its own design. This shows how extremely thoroughly the Rolls-Royce engineers have tackled the job.

It was as long ago as last February that we saw a 40-50 h.p. Rolls-Royce under test on the French Riviera with a six-brake system, the majority of the tests having taken place on the other side of the Channel. First shown to the public at the Paris Salon, the braking system of the Rolls-Royce was a centre of interest at the recent Olympia Show, but hitherto authentic details of the internal design adopted have been withheld. The general arrangement and description of the brakes appeared in *The Autocar* of October 17th, and we are now able to supplement those notes with details of the operation of the servo mechanism employed, together with observations upon their efficacy in practice as a result of an extended run on the latest model car.

Our test was carried out during a two days' run from London, *via* the Lake District, to Glasgow for the Scottish Exhibition, the type of vehicle used being a 40-50 h.p. chassis

Descending Kirkstone Pass toward Patterdale. Brotherswater in the distance.

with a handsome Hooper landaulet body to seat six. On the first day's run a distance of 259 miles was covered without undue effort, Windermere being our halting place ready for an ascent of Kirkstone Pass from Ambleside on the morrow, with further opportunities of testing the brakes on the sharp descent to Patterdale, and again on the narrow and winding roads leading past Brotherswater and Ullswater. It is doubtful if a better all-round testing route could be found in the length, and breadth of the land.

At the outset it can be said that the most striking feature of the new Rolls-Royce braking system is their delicate operation. A mere touch of the pedal is sufficient to arrest the progress of the car, whilst ordinary leg pressure will gently but firmly bring it to a standstill in an incredibly short space, no matter what the speed, and with an absence of wheel skid indicating correct equalisation. Braking power, as such, naturally depends upon the mass of weight, the speed, and the size of brake shoes and drums. The Rolls-Royce system does not necessarily offer quicker stopping powers than the best four wheel brake designs, but, as indicated, it is the silence and sweetness of operation, coupled with the delicate touch necessary to attain that object, that users will most appreciate.

A point is made of the prompt release of the brakes, and there is no doubt about this, for a distinct click is heard as the foot is removed from the pedal, which may be accidental or intentional. In other

a good braking system applied to all wheels has to be experienced to be believed.

A fault of many braking systems is that the power available is considerably reduced when running backwards, but this objection cannot be applied to the Rolls-Royce system, which is equally effective in either direction, as was proved during a test on the single-figure gradient of Kirkstone Pass. Incidentally, this

The 40-50 h.p. Rolls-Royce with six-brake system outside the famous Gretna Green blacksmith's shop, where runaway marriages were celebrated. (Below) The Rolls-Royce at Ullswater.

respects the whole operation of braking is in conformity with the high quality of Rolls-Royce productions.

It may not be generally known that some systems require fairly considerable leg pressure to ensure a quick stop should occasion arise ; it is to minimise this effort that the servo, or mechanical relay, system is occasionally employed. What in effect the engineers of the Rolls-Royce Company have attained is a lightness of operation in keeping with the sensitive steering and general controls of the car, a distinct asset which will be appreciated most by those accustomed to driving far in a day. No sense of fatigue should be felt after long distances at the wheel. So light is the pedal operation that we several times demonstrated that by leaning forward in the driving seat it is possible to pull the car up quickly by merely pressing the brake pedal with the fingers—quite a new experience so far as we are concerned. For a given foot pressure it is claimed that the total braking effect is approximately three times greater than in either two or four wheel brake systems unassisted by servo—and after personal test we can well believe that this is no empty boast.

On many occasions during our first day's run the opportunity was provided, without seeking, for sudden decelerations, once, for instance, when a lorry suddenly reversed out of a blind alley, and at no time were the brakes found wanting, nor was the steering in any way affected. The increased sense of security provided by

long and tiring gradient, used in the M.C.C. London-Edinburgh annual competition, was ascended on second, third, and top gears with four passengers and luggage aboard with the greatest ease, though steam was emitted from the radiator on the crucial stretch near the summit (1,481ft. altitude). Kirkstone Pass in November is usually regarded as a place to avoid, and prominent notices still affirm that it is " unfit for motors." This year, however, the road surface is in excellent order, being firm and smooth for the most part, presumably due to its copious dressing of granite chippings.

To Dim or Dip ?

The car we used was fitted with Barker dipping head lights operated by a long lever conveniently situated in front of the change speed gate. After tea at the Middleton Arms Hotel, Ilkley, lights were needed through Skipton, Settle, and Kendal to Windermere, and it was not difficult to appreciate the contrast with the unsatisfactory practice of blinking the head lights on and off as practised

General arrangement of the Rolls-Royce brakes. Compensating mechanism is provided for the rear, as well as for the front set of shoes.

by the driver of practically every car we encountered. The Barker dipping device not only enabled us readily to avoid inconveniencing oncoming drivers, but actually assisted their progress materially, since the act of reflecting the beam of light almost directly downwards both eliminated dazzle and, at the same time, clearly illuminated the roadsides opposite our car, and thus served to assist the progress of passing vehicles. If more costly than a dimmer, there is no doubt of the efficacy of the Barker dipping device, which possesses benefits for users as well as non-users.

On the run North, on the second day, opportunities were presented to test the speed capabilities of the car, which, though exceeding two tons in weight and in full touring trim, proved itself capable of easily beating a mile a minute gait. Such a speedy closed car needs equally effective braking power, and those who may have been impatient for brakes on all four wheels will now learn that, if outward progress has seemed slow, the Rolls-Royce Company, thanks to prolonged and patient experimental work, have now decidedly attained their object.

Details of the Servo Mechanism.

And now as to the design of the brakes, which, as may be imagined, is distinctly interesting. The servo mechanism, which is the principal feature of the brake system, consists of a disc clutch instead of a set of expanding shoes or a contracting band. The actual movement of the mechanism can best be followed by the diagrammatic sketches, which do not, however, show the exact

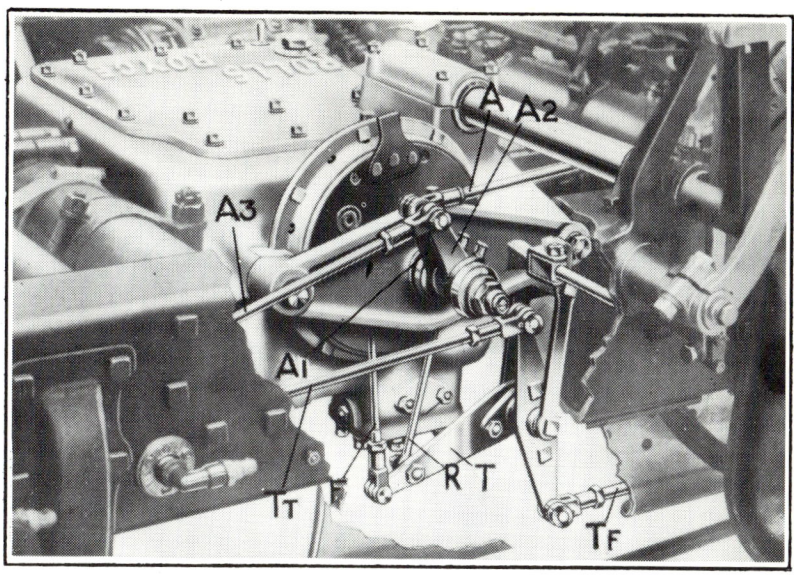

The servo motor and its operating mechanism. A, brake pedal rod; A1, servo-operating lever; A2, rear brake operating lever; A3, rear brake operating rod; F, rod from servo actuating T; R, second rod from servo to T; T, lever operating four wheel brakes; TF, rod to front brakes; TR, rod to rear brakes.

mechanism employed, but indicate the sequence of the successive operations involved.

The driving disc in the servo is rotated through the gear box, via the bevel and the propeller-shaft, when the rear wheels revolve, and in direct proportion to the speed of those wheels. The driven disc has upon it two stops which, if pressed hard against the driving disc, will tend to rotate. If it rotates in one direction one stop pulls rod F, which is attached to a lever in turn secured by rods through pressure equalising devices to the cam operating levers of the four sets of brake shoes in drums on the wheel hubs. In reversing, the driving disc rotates in the opposite direction, and the second stop functions through the medium of the rod R, applying the brakes in an exactly similar manner.

How the Brakes are Applied.

The servo motor is brought into operation in a certain sequence, for the pedal is connected by a rod to a lever—A^1 in the photograph—attached to the shaft of the driven disc, which lever is also coupled to a second lever, A^2, by teeth of ratchet shape. The lever A^2 is connected to the rear brake shoes by a rod. What happens when the pedal is depressed is that the two levers move as one until the rear brakes are applied. Further pressure on the brake pedal then forces the lever A^1 to move still further forward, and the only way in which it can do this is for the ratchet teeth between it and A^2 to move relative to each other. Any movement of the ratchet teeth could only take place if the two levers were to separate. One of them, A^1, is fixed, so it is the other, A^2, which moves to one side, not, of course, sufficiently to disengage the teeth, and in doing so moves the driven disc of the servo motor, to which it is attached, into engagement with the driving disc. Immediately, the servo motor comes into operation as already described, and the brake power is augmented.

It will be noticed at once that there are some interesting features; for example, the rear brake shoes are in contact with the 18in. drums before the servo motor commences to act. When the servo motor does operate, it applies the smaller front wheel brakes and simultaneously

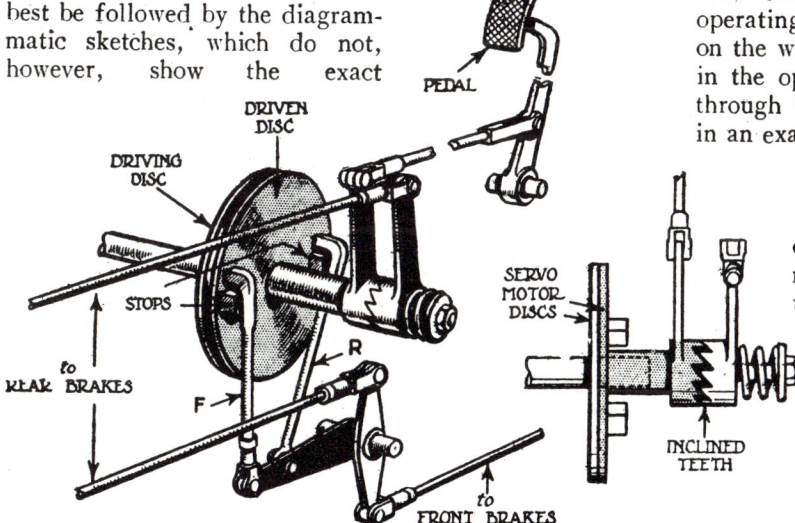

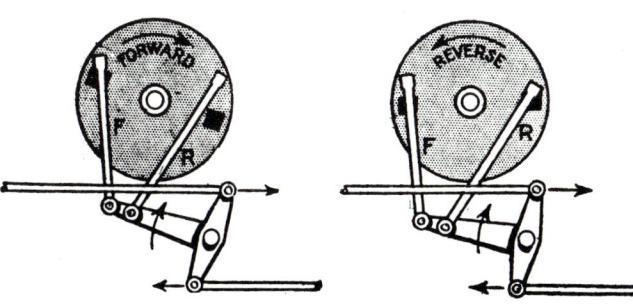

Diagrammatic sketch to explain the operation of the servo motor. The rods F and R are not facsimiles of the actual mechanism, but function in a similar manner, and the spring behind the two levers with ratchet teeth is shown for the sake of clearness.

Details of the front brake operating mechanism, also showing the shock absorber.

increases the pressure on the rear brakes. There is a reason for this sequence of operations and for reduced braking power on the front wheels, since the manufacturers were particularly anxious to avoid locking the front wheels, which might prove dangerous. Therefore, the action of the servo motor, which alone controls the pressure on the front wheel brakes, is dependent on the speed of rotation of the rear wheels. If the latter are locked, the servo motor ceases to operate, and the brake pressure on the front wheels is released so that steering control is possible. The moment the rear wheels revolve again, the servo operates the front brakes.

No Wasted Pressure.

It will be noticed that the force of the braking power is in exact relation to the amount of pressure exerted on the pedal by the driver, and that pressure is not more than would be necessary for rear brakes only, while the pedal travel is quite small. Actually, the braking effect on the car before the servo motor comes into operation is exactly the same as it was when rear brakes only were used; that is, the two rear brakes or all four wheel brakes are alternatively available at the will of the driver.

*Right: In August 1924 a member of **The Autocar** staff accompanied Percy Northey of Rolls-Royce on a Continental trip in a 40/50 which was not equipped with the recently announced front wheel brakes. On many cars these were fitted as a retrospective modification after delivery. The route was from Lyons to Grenoble and took in a number of Alpine passes. Normal cruising speed was 50 mph with a maximum of 72 mph recorded. Here the car, with Northey at the wheel, pauses on the Col du Chat overlooking Aix Les Bains and Lake Bourget.*

Above: A similar tourer with body by Barker pictured in May 1925—still with no front wheel brakes fitted.

Right: An Australian body by Waring Bros. of Melbourne pictured in 1924 on 40/50 h.p. chassis 67 LK which had been erected at Derby in 1923

THE NEW ROLLS-ROYCE.

Overhead-valve Engine, Decreased Bore and Increased Stroke Features of the Latest Chassis, which is Complementary to, and Does Not Supersede, the 40-50 h.p. Side-valve Type.

(Top left) Near side of the engine showing the two exhaust pipes.
(Top right) Hand-controlled shutters are now provided in front of the radiator.
(Bottom) Right side of engine, with the coil ignition, distributor and magneto.

FEW are the firms engaged in the manufacture of motor cars who enjoy quite such a reputation as Rolls-Royce, Ltd. Almost the conjoined names have become the household word for luxury, and every novelist worthy of the name imparts a distinguished air to any character by crediting him or her with the possession of one of this firm's cars.

Consequently any alteration to an existing chassis, or any new component for that chassis, is endowed with an interest extending far beyond that section of the motoring public who are able to buy the car. For more than a year rumour has followed rumour concerning the probable appearance of an overhead-valve-engined 40-50 h.p. chassis until the imminence of such a car became a certainty, and the only doubt was whether it would be announced immediately or next year. Few, however, imagined that the chassis in question would supplement, not supersede, that famous model which we have all known for so long, and which descends in direct line from the famous " Silver Ghost " which did so much to establish the fame of its manufacturers.

The new model, briefly, has a push-rod-operated overhead-valve engine, its cylinders in two blocks of three, with its mechanism neat and most modern. The carburetter is practically the same as on the 40-50 h.p. type, but the ignition is now controlled by mechanism akin to a governor which automatically advances the firing point with the increase in engine speed. As before, there is a vibration damper on the crankshaft forward end. The next change of note is the provision of a disc clutch. Last, but not least, the bore has been reduced from 4½in. to 4¼in., thus making the annual tax £44, and the stroke increased to 5½in. from 4¾in. The price of both old and new types of 40-50 h.p. chassis is £1,850, or £1,900 for the long-wheelbase model.

Fine Details of Design.

It is in the details of the design that the engine is most interesting. The power unit is carried on a special frame slung from the main frame at three points and so constructed that any flexing of the side members will not affect the engine. Infinite pains have been taken to arrange the necessary lever and rod movement for the carburetter and ignition controls, no easy matter with a long engine, and considering the presence of the governor.

In the new car there are two mechanical governors, of which one acts upon the throttle exactly as was the case with the earlier model, but the second controls the ignition advance in relation to the engine speed. There being both magneto and coil ignition provided, great ingenuity has to be used to synchronise the two, especially as the accumulator ignition can be retarded more than the magneto to facilitate slow running.

On the steering wheel is a lever which it is best to imagine first at full advance, in which position the magneto and the coil ignitions are timed at almost full advance; but not quite. On retarding the lever to the halfway position both the distributor for the coil ignition and the contact maker for the magneto ignition are moved a corresponding amount, but at this point the magneto ignition moves no further, additional movement of the ignition lever retarding the coil ignition only, the firing point being then set at well over the dead centre.

Action of the Ignition Governor.

It has been mentioned that the ignition is not at full advance when the control lever is as far forward as it will go. This is because the centrifugal governor driven by

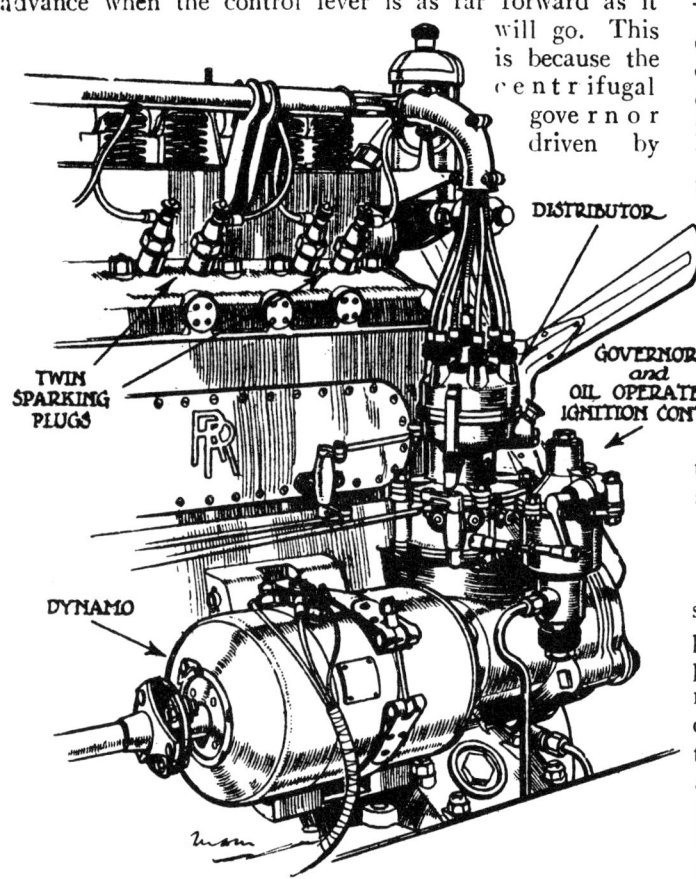

An oil servo motor, operated by the governor, is used to advance the ignition automatically.

the engine is responsible for any further movement. The governor mechanically operates a small piston in a cylinder, sliding it upwards until oil supplied by the engine oil pump can pass through a ring of ports, thus obtaining access to another larger cylinder in which is a piston, and forcing that piston upwards. The upward movement advances both ignitions, and, at the same time, cuts off the supply of oil until a further expansion of the governor once more causes movement. The oil returning from the actuating cylinder—which is in effect a servo motor—serves to lubricate the coil ignition distributor gear.

One cannot but admire the elaborate nature of the little brackets and bearings which support the ignition control, together with the system of a movable fulcrum which

differentiates between the movement of the distributor and that of the magneto.

Another interesting point is the valve gear. The valves are operated by push rods through tappets at one

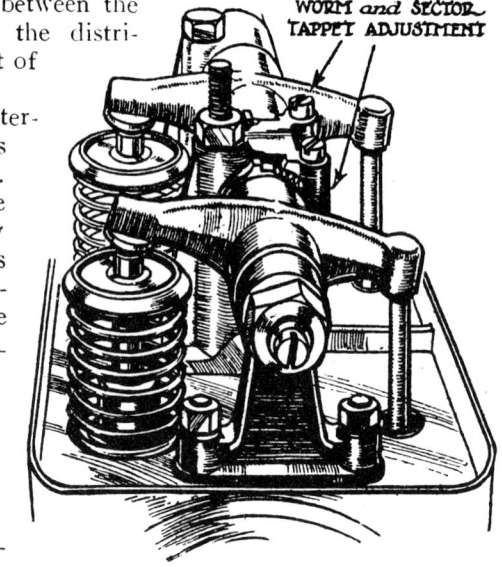

A special eccentric mounting provides micrometer adjustment for the rocking lever clearance.

end, and rocking levers at the other. The tappets have one adjustment, but the chief means of adjustment is an eccentric mounting for the rocking lever axes, and this, incidentally, is provided with a special locking device. The holes in the cylinder head through which the push rods pass have liners which assist to register the head in relation to the cylinders, the head itself being a single piece covering all six cylinders.

Oil is supplied to the engine bearings at 25 lb. pressure through a distributing chamber provided with relief valves so contrived that they divert lubricant at 5 lb. pressure to the hollow axis for the valve rocking levers, and at 1 lb. pressure to the timing gears. Each rocking lever is drilled to lubricate automatically the ball end of the push rod. Even the holding-down nuts of the valve cover can be unscrewed, but not detached from, the cover.

Equal Water Distribution.

Water is circulated by a centrifugal pump with a split gland, and evenly distributed to the cylinders by a pipe inside the jacket. The head is supplied through passages in the gasket, and the water is then taken evenly round the valve ports and out to the radiator. Hand-controlled radiator shutters, operated from the instrument board, have been adopted.

There have been one or two minor alterations to the carburetter. The filter is more accessible and the jet chamber is heated by exhaust gas. The air silencer and automatic extra air valve remain

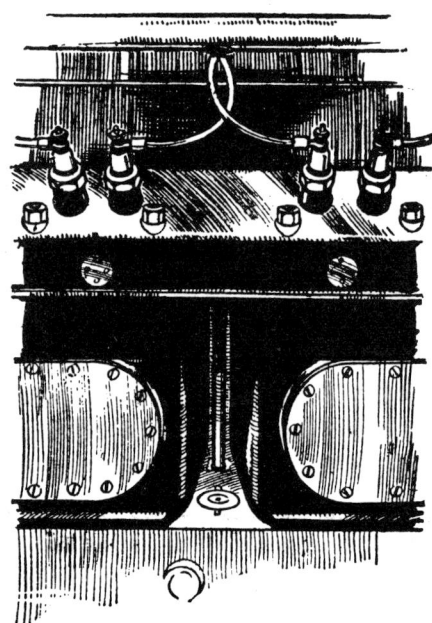

The plugs are carried almost vertically in the head alongside the valve cover.

as before, and small copper pipes drain any fuel which may be deposited in the inlet pipe back to the carburetter. In order that the full effect of the exhaust heating should be available at low speed, a throttle in the exhaust pipe restricts the passage to the silencer when the throttle is closed. As before, a minute separate carburetter, brought into action by a control on the instrument board and bolted to the upper portion of the inlet pipe, is used for starting only.

As regards the disposition of the lighting set, the dynamo is altered in size, single pole wiring is adopted, each wire being a different colour and each circuit supplied with a special marked fuse in a box on the dashboard, which also contains a wiring diagram. The

Hand nut adjustment for the belt drive of the fan.

starting motor, as has hitherto been the case, drives the clutch shaft through a chain.

The remainder of the chassis, including the servo-operated four wheel brakes, is the same as the earlier 40-50 h.p., but the steering wheel is slightly thinner, the gear lever is shorter and the ignition switch is on the instrument board, and is so arranged that the battery or magneto can be used separately.

Finally, the drive is now taken through a single-plate clutch.

It is interesting to record that the new engine has been adopted after Rolls-Royce, Ltd., had carried out extensive and searching tests with a twelve-cylinder V-type engine and a straight-eight.

Windovers Ltd. were responsible for the coachwork on this 40/50 New Phantom built for His Highness the Kumar of Viziangaram in 1925 with many of the fittings in solid gold or silver

IMPRESSIONS OF THE "NEW PHANTOM" ROLLS-ROYCE.

A Road Trial Indicates Further Progress Towards Perfection. Acceleration and Speed Improved Without Sacrifice of Comfort and Refinement.

The "New Phantom" visits Wisley Lake. A fine car in a beautiful setting well known to Metropolitan motorists.

THE Rolls-Royce has a reputation which is a source of legitimate pride to its makers and the cause of no little envy on the part of their rivals. Yet it would be difficult to select any particular point as the origin of the great name justly borne by the car.

The latest model is a very worthy successor to the line of vehicles which have borne the name of Rolls-Royce. Its chief attributes are an extraordinary smoothness, coupled with considerably more power than hitherto, while it is difficult to believe that any other car could be quite so silent. The matter of silence is the more interesting because the new model has push rod operated overhead valves, and it has always seemed as though a certain increase in noise is the natural corollary of any form of overhead valve mechanism. It would be impossible for even the strictest of critics to state definitely that he had heard the valve gear of the new car, and, unless the bonnet had previously been lifted, equally impossible to say, from aural evidence, whether the new engine or the old one was being used.

Exceptionally Quiet Indirect Gears.

It is not, however, only the engine which is silent; the intermediate gears are phenomenally quiet even at speeds as high as 40 or 50 m.p.h. and at full throttle, with the result that it is only just possible to detect from the front seats that an indirect is being used by listening with extreme care, the passengers in the rear having no idea that there has been any change. It is this quality of general silence, coupled to the detail work, which has made the Rolls-Royce unlike any other car when pulling a heavy closed body at a speed of from 20 to 30 m.p.h.; the sensation is near akin to that of coasting down hill with the gear lever in neutral.

Very often the quest of silence has led to a deliberate sacrifice of power, yet there is an undoubted feeling that the new Rolls-Royce engine is more powerful than its predecessor, its acceleration, especially on top gear, having undoubtedly improved. Top gear is the most important of the four, since, without touching the clutch or the ignition lever, the car can be handled the whole time, whether in traffic or not, on this gear alone, and, which is more important, it does not feel as though it wanted any other. On a hill of 1 in 6 the car climbs on second gear at over 20 m.p.h. with five passengers, from a standing start two car lengths from the commencement of the slope. The usual main road hill of 1 in 15 is a really fast top gear climb.

Not "Very Fast," but Quite Fast Enough!

Technically speaking, the Rolls-Royce is not meant to be, and is not, a very fast car considering its engine size, yet it will run quite comfortably at 70 m.p.h. without giving the slightest suggestion that any part of the chassis is working hard, and its maximum is claimed to be in the neighbourhood of 80 m.p.h. At a speed of 40 or 50 m.p.h. the car gives a suggestion that it is not moving by mechanical means at all. As a matter of detail, the carburetter is one of the very few which have no flat spot and respond instantly to the throttle.

The suspension, by grace of the shock absorbers, can be adjusted to suit individual taste, as, indeed, can the whole control of the car to a certain extent. In town, with the shock absorbers loose, the springs are extremely flexible, road shocks practically non-existent; for use in the country, where higher speeds are possible, this would entail a tendency to roll, which can be met and counteracted by a further adjustment of the shock absorbers until the car stiffens for cornering while remaining comfortable.

The new clutch is simpler than the old one, and does not need the famous "stick" at night, yet it is every bit

It would be difficult to conceive of a more attractive ensemble than the latest Rolls-Royce overhead-valve-engined chassis with this graceful five-seated touring body.

as easy to handle. On the car on which we were given a run the clutch stop came into operation too late, but the stop can be set to suit the personal ideas of any individual driver.

The gear change, a point on which there has always been a controversy, is a little easier to handle than hitherto, once one becomes accustomed to the locking mechanism holding the gear lever in its notch, a locking mechanism, by the way, which once and for all prevents any possibility of the gears slipping out of mesh. The same delightful series of tricks can be played by an expert driver with the aid of the speedometer and governor lever, and, incidentally, they are well within the powers of the man whose driving is purely mechanical and not sensitive. Alternatively, the change can be effected with the foot throttle as usual.

this matter, more especially considering the trouble taken to arrange for governors automatically controlling the throttle and ignition, one would like to see a thermostat installed. Cooling, as a matter of fact, is a considerable problem for a car of this type, of which the radiator bears far less proportion to the engine than does the radiator of a smaller car. For nine-tenths of the work done, the radiator is sufficient to keep the engine at its most efficient temperature, naturally a high figure. When

(Above) An example of the detail work. The carrier protects the tank, which has a contents indicator and the filler can be used without difficulty when luggage is in place.

(Above) Shackles on the dumb irons are an unusual feature.

(Left) A very complete tool kit is housed on the running board on the near side.

Few cars have as good a control as the Rolls-Royce, each lever of which can be moved without a sound and with a truly progressive effect on whatever it actuates, but the new automatic advance for the ignition relieves an unintelligent driver of all responsibility without affecting the performance of the car.

That the radiator shutters are hand controlled is admittedly a compromise, and it would inevitably take time before the manual operation would become automatic. In

tackling long, steep hills in very hot weather, however, the shutters have to be used intelligently if boiling is to be avoided, and it is most important to open the four panels, especially provided in the bonnet, for the free

73

escape of hot air. The manufacturers' contention is that, as long as, in exceptional conditions, boiling can take place without the engine being affected and without having to stop for more water, the best compromise has been reached

When one first takes over the wheel, the action of the steering is much more lively than that of most other cars of similar speed and weight, yet the machine can be held comfortably, and the return action given by the inclined pivots is exactly right. A thinner rim to the steering wheel, which even now is scarcely thin to modern eyes, is an improvement.

As to the brakes, the servo motor may at first seem violent to the heavy-footed brigade; but almost at once one learns how little force is necessary, how sensitive are the brakes to the slightest increase in pressure. In a word, the brake power is excellent and the application smooth, backwards or forwards. Owing to the fact that the accumulator ignition can be switched on without the magneto, slow running on top gear is exceptional, and the engine still has that pleasant habit of starting on the switch, albeit the starting motor when used is practically silent, an excellent feature.

As regards detail, it is practically hopeless to go into any one point, for there is not a single minor component of the chassis which has not its interest and is not carried out in a manner suggesting that the designers were able to deal with every problem, great or small, unhampered by the possible cost of solution, intent only on making the best mechanism for the job in hand.

BY A SURREY MILL. The "New Phantom" Rolls-Royce on the banks of the River Mole at Cobham.

AN ULTRA-REFINED "SIX"

Test of the Latest Rolls-Royce " Twenty " Reveals a Car which May be Said to Disarm Criticism. Perfection of Workmanship Apparent throughout the Chassis.

THE latest model of the 20 h.p. Rolls-Royce is a very considerable improvement on its predecessors. A four-speed gear box, right-hand gear lever, servo-operated four wheel brakes, and a number of small details have made the car altogether different from the first model, and it now is much more a smaller edition of the larger car which has made the firm world-famous.

Quite what it is that gives a Rolls-Royce its character would be difficult to define in words, for there is no car in which detail has been more carefully studied or in which it has been proved by experiment carried on over such long periods. Moreover, the very smallest part of the chassis, equally with the largest component, is considered and reconsidered until it is estimated that the best arrangement for the particular duty has been found and adopted. This means, naturally, that those responsible for the work have a relatively free scope ; they are not hindered, as are so many of their rivals, by considerations of what the component in question will cost when it has been evolved. The result, at all events, gives a car which is very near to the ideal of the average motorist—an exceptionally comfortable, silent carriage which is a delight to handle.

Gear Changing a Pleasure.

Delicacy of control is a notable feature. There is no part, big or small, which moves heavily or has not a progressive effect. In fact, to the average driver who is not solely concerned with Rolls-Royce cars, the gear change of the " 20 " is very much lighter and more sensitive to handle than that of many excellent cars. It would, indeed, be difficult to imagine even the possibility of not effecting a quiet change, and a gear change of this nature is a joy. In fact, there is a sense of great satisfaction in handling the car in circumstances where repeated changes of gear improve the performance.

> **DATA FOR THE DRIVER.**
> 20 h.p., six cylinders, 76·2 × 114·3 mm. (3,103 c.c.). Tax, £22.
> **Tested weight of complete car,** less passengers, 28 cwt. 2 qr. 23 lb.
> **Weight per c.c., 1 lb.**
> **Gear ratios :** 16·98, 10·62, 6·89 and 4·55 to 1.
> **Spiral bevel final drive.**
> **Half-elliptic springs.**
> **32 × 4½in. tyres** on detachable wire wheels.
> **Brakes on all four wheels.**
> **Wheelbase, 10ft. 9in. Track,** 4ft. 8in.
> **Fuel consumption, 23 m.p g.**
> **Tank capacity, 14 gallons.**
> **Price chassis, £1,185.**

The gear box has one feature very rarely found, and the more pleasant when it is found. Third and, to an almost equal extent, second gears are almost noiseless ; indeed, the other occupants of the car cannot tell whether the driver is using top or one of the indirects.

High Speed without Fuss.

Very wisely, the car is not designed simply with a view to high speed, but rather to allow the occupants to forget that there is an engine and at the same time to make it possible to maintain that high, steady, smooth speed which results in a surprisingly high average. Until the very end of its range of speed the engine has no period and emits scarcely a sound, and the end of the speed range is well outside the limit of ordinary needs. Take it on any main road in England, and the 20 h.p. Rolls-Royce will run at a steady 40 m.p.h. nearly the whole time, giving never a sign of labouring or stress. At 60 m.p.h. it is still smooth and only very slightly more noisy, though what sound there is will be found to come chiefly from elsewhere than the engine. About 40 m.p.h. is a useful maximum on third, 30 m.p.h. a similar figure for second, and first is the sort of gear that is a real boon in awkward or unfavourable circumstances in very hilly country.

Exactly like the larger Rolls-Royce, the " Twenty " corners smoothly and rides well, the throttle and ignition controls move smoothly and progressively, the mixture control is well worth using, having considerable effect, and, provided the driver does not forget the hand-controlled radiator shutters, the temperature of the cooling water can be maintained at an effective heat the whole time.

A great deal of good design has gone into the servo operation and brake mechanism generally. Servo motors often are apt to be rather violent when first applied, so that at slow speeds in traffic a driver only just accustomed to the car tends to apply the brakes, unwittingly, with too much vigour. This is exactly what the servo on the 20 h.p. Rolls-Royce does not do. As far as the driver can feel, there is no servo, yet, on reflection, it is obvious that the brakes are being applied with much more power than the relatively light pressure on the pedal would generate.

A definite pressure is necessary at low speeds, which is exactly what one wants, for it overcomes the tendency for the servo motor to take control in such circumstances.

Steering connections, front brake and stub-axle design are all characterised by extreme neatness.

The brakes are extremely powerful, and they do not cause the car to slide sideways on a greasy surface as much as some four wheel brakes do, one test on such a surface at 40 m.p.h. resulting in the machine progressing in a definite straight line without a trace of lateral skid. Unquestionably, the brakes do not affect the steering.

From the general point of view, the detail work is beautifully carried out. Every lamp has its own circuit and its own fuse, the fuses being housed in a very neat case. The filler for the rear petrol tank projects well to one side, clearing luggage on the carrier, and, as an instance of the extent to which the detail consideration is carried, the wheels are balanced by counter-weights.

(Top) Instrument board of the 20 h.p. Rolls-Royce. Near the steering column support is the mixture control and the lever operating the radiator shutters. (Bottom) On the dashboard of the car is the fuse box with separate fuses and circuits for each lamp.

Concerning the body, not much can be said, because the purchaser has the choice of any sort of coachwork. The car is a sheer delight with either open or closed coachwork, whether it be used as a town carriage or for country touring.

The 20 h.p. six-cylinder production line at Derby in February 1923 showing chassis being built in fair numbers, even though there was still a considerable amount of hand finishing

1914 40/50 h.p., Alpine Eagle-type tourer

Left: 1905 10 h.p. two-cylinder

Right: 1907 40/50 The Silver Ghost,
Roi des Belges by Barker

Below: 1905 20 h.p. four-cylinder, TT replica

1926: A Phantom I with replica body

1933: A 20/25 h.p. limousine by Hooper

A FASCINATING "PHANTOM."

Sports Weymann Saloon Adds to the Attractions of the Rolls-Royce Chassis.

Sports Weymann four-seater body on a 40-50 h.p. Rolls-Royce " New Phantom " chassis, belonging to Mr. G. R. N. Minchin. H. J. Mulliner and Co. were responsible for the bodywork.

WE recently had an opportunity of trying one of the latest Rolls-Royce " New Phantom " short chassis models belonging to Mr. G. R. N. Minchin and fitted with a special sports-type Weymann four-seater body built by H. J. Mulliner and Co., of Chiswick.

Considering the natural body space limitation on the short chassis, the work has been well done. The seats are extremely comfortable, particularly the two in front, which are separate; the large windows and a skylight combine to make the body very light, the front wind-screen division is below the driver's line of sight, the rear window curtain can be lowered from the driving seat, and Triplex glass is used throughout, while the doors have the new-type Weymann lock, so that three of the four can be secured from inside, and the fourth locked by an ordinary lock and key outside. In case the key is lost, a secret pocket outside the body contains a duplicate.

Guarding Against Heat.

For the occupants of the rear seats, which, by the way, have a centre armrest, two footrests have been provided; these, being lined underneath with patent leather, slide easily on the carpets that cover the Sorbo matting. To keep the car cool while travelling fast in hot weather, a very large scuttle ventilator is provided. In one side of the scuttle is a jack, and in the other side a fire extinguisher, out of the way of the passengers, and underneath the driver's seat cushion is the tool kit, neatly socketed in a wooden box.

The instrument board is fully floating and has a most attractive finish, rather like the machine turning on a

cigarette case. The latest type Lucas screen wiper does not obstruct any portion of the windscreen, while the off-side lamp on the wing has at the back the new Lucas driving mirror. The lines of the body are good, not too square in appearance, and the scuttle blends easily into the bonnet, both radiator and bonnet being higher than usual. The car runs beautifully, and its performance on top gear would be very difficult to equal.

The well-equipped instrument board on Mr. Minchin's Rolls-Royce. In contrast to the black dials of the instruments, the machine-turned metal instrument board is very pleasing.

A 1925 New Phantom four-door saloon by London Improved Coachbuilders Ltd for Mrs Violet Jarrot

THE PRINCE'S NEW CAR
AND TWO OTHER IMPOSING VEHICLES.

Three 40-50 h.p. New Phantom Rolls-Royce Chassis Fitted with Bodywork Typical of Modern Taste in Automobile Design.

BY putting into commission a 40-50 h.p. New Phantom Rolls-Royce with a Weymann saloon body, H.R.H. the Prince of Wales has undoubtedly set the seal of approval on this type of body construction. It is, moreover, a feather in the cap of the bodybuilders, J. Gurney Nutting and Co., Elystan Street, King's Road, Chelsea, S.W.3, of which they are justifiably proud, that this is the third Weymann saloon which they have supplied to the Royal family, for the Duke of York is already the owner of a 21 h.p. Lanchester, while Prince George has a Bentley Six, both of which have been fitted with Gurney Nutting Weymann coachwork.

It is typical of the Prince that he has taken a great personal interest in his new car, and has on occasions visited the works to inspect it in various stages of manufacture. Certainly it is a car of which to be proud, for the massive, dignified lines of the radiator and bonnet blend harmoniously with the artistically simple lines of the four-door, four-light body, giving a well-balanced whole in which no part is brought into prominence.

In fact, the car is one at which every keen motorist would instinctively look twice if he saw it on

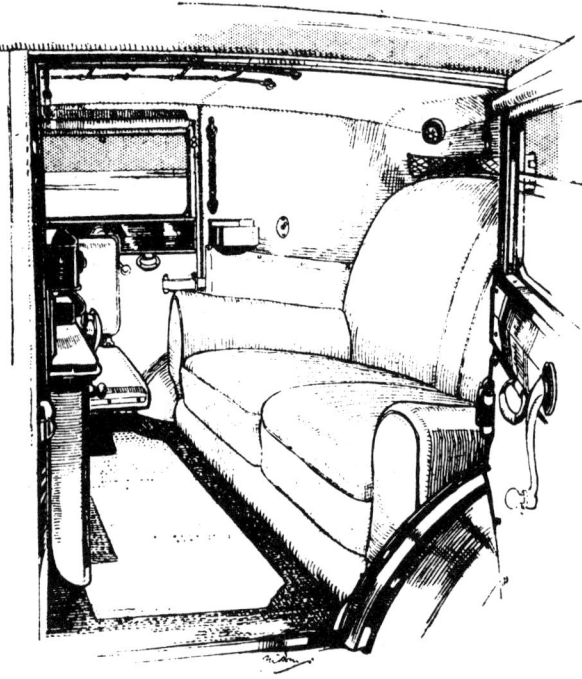

Almost severely simple, although comfortable, is the interior of the Prince's new car.

the road, but it attracts attention by its line alone, for the colour scheme could not be in quieter taste.

From stem to stern the car is black, except for a red line on the wheel discs and the faint blue sheen of the chromium-plated fittings. The domed wings have the side lamps moulded into them, and the two-pane vertical screen has its lower edge curved to conform to the outline of the scuttle, giving the driver a particularly good view of the road, and allowing him to see the front wings. A spotlight is fitted in each of the lower corners of the windscreen, and buffers are fitted at front and rear. A large Brooks trunk has extensible sides so that it can, if need be, contain golf clubs.

In the interior the same quiet taste is displayed, while the seats are designed to afford the maximum degree of comfort, so that even on a long run the occupant should experience no feeling other than of restfulness. The rear compartment is upholstered in biscuit-coloured cloth, and the main seat has permanent arm rests at the sides, with a folding arm rest in the middle, which, when down, transforms the seat into the equivalent of two comfortable armchairs. At the back of the front seat is a rising and falling partition equipped with a winding gear particularly

The Gurney Nutting Weymann saloon which has been built for the Prince of Wales.

The Prince's New Car.

light to operate. In the cabinet work which forms the lower part of this partition there are, in the centre, a locker and tray, and, at the sides, concealed folding occasional seats. Walnut quartered veneer with a wax finish is used for the cabinet work.

Comfort has also been studied as regards the front seats, which are upholstered in soft brown hide. Arm rests are formed on the doors, and there is also a folding arm rest in the centre of the seat. The doors are of good width, particularly those at the front, and, owing to the shallowness of the division in which the occasional seats are housed, the rear doorways are not obstructed in any way. Triplex glass is fitted throughout, and the two rear lights and the division lights are fitted with silk roller blinds.

The interior fittings include roof lights in the

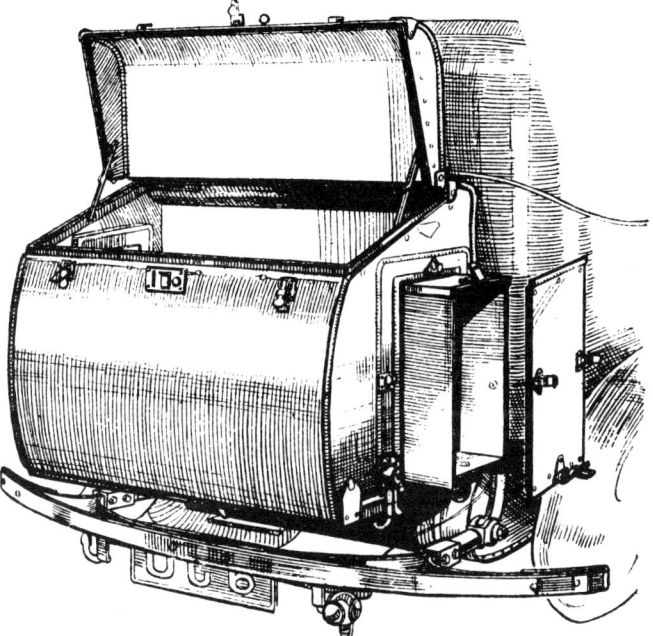

A large rear trunk has extensible sides, so that long articles, such as golf clubs, can be carried by the Prince.

rear corners, a roof net to carry hats, and a small parcel net just above the squab of the rear seat. A direction indicator of the swinging arm type is fitted on each side of the screen, and these are operated by a

Bowden control in the centre of the scuttle, where it over-arches the instrument board. It is thus conveniently placed for the driver, yet does not obstruct his view of the various dials.

One of the features of the Prince's new car is the dummy extension below the radiator.

Coachwork of a distinctly different type is that recently completed by Park, Ward and Co., 27, New Bond Street, W.1, for Mr. Rodney Soher; a coupé-de-ville body, also mounted on a New Phantom chassis, and having a rather Continental appearance. Possibly some critics would ask for a little more headroom, but the angle of the rear seat is so arranged that the occupants have ample headroom when seated, and, after all, the height from floorboards to roof lining is a matter for the choice of the owner.

A Low-built Saloon.

Certainly the low build gives the car a look of compactness which is enhanced by the unobtrusive colour scheme of blue grey, with a dark blue leather top and wings, and black chassis. The extension over the driver is carried by arms which fold inwards over the division in such a way that

Elegance is expressed by every line of this Park, Ward coupé-de-ville. The driver's extension is completely hidden when folded.

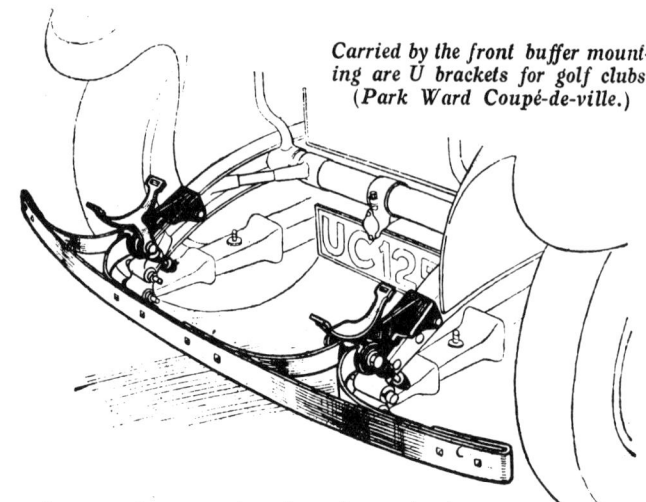

Carried by the front buffer mounting are U brackets for golf clubs. (Park Ward Coupé-de-ville.)

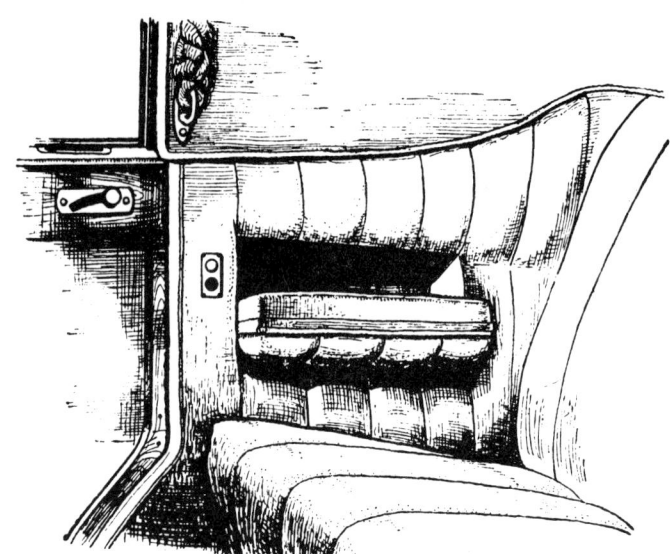

Arm rests which fold up into the upholstery when not required are fitted in the Park, Ward coupé-de-ville.

they do not obstruct the view from the interior. The three-pane front screen is raked slightly, and has side extensions which materially improve the protection afforded. Triplex glass is again used throughout, and all the body fittings are silver-plated.

Blue grey cloth is used for the upholstery and bead lining, and the door panels are of inlaid mahogany, as is the cabinet work covering the two concealed seats behind the front seat. Concealed arm rests are fitted at the sides of the main seat, and roof lights are let flush into the corners. As there is no rear window the occupants sit in a subdued and restful light, but have a good view out through the wide side lights and through the division.

Amongst other fittings are two spotlights, Stephen Grebel side and head lamps, the latter both dimming and dipping, buffers front and rear, lock-up cupboards on each side of the dash, dictaphone, and cigar lighters for the occupants of both front and rear seats. A novelty is the mounting of U-shaped brackets on the front buffer for the reception of a bag of golf clubs.

For the South of France.

Yet a third New Phantom chassis carries open touring coachwork of the type which makes one long for blue skies and all the delights of summer touring. Barker and Co. (Coachbuilders), Ltd., 66-69, South Audley Street, W.1, are responsible for the body, which they have just completed for Rolls-Royce, Ltd., who

are sending the car to the South of France. The colour scheme has been chosen to emphasise the fine lines, and it is cream cellulosed below the waistline, with polished aluminium above, and polished aluminium wings and valances. A note of brightness is introduced by the soft green hide upholstery, and by the neatly fitting hood cover of the same material.

All-weather Equipment.

Both front and rear compartments are comfortable and roomy, and an M.E. screen is provided for the rear passengers, when not required the two portions being housed in a compartment behind the squab of the front seat. Rigid-framed side curtains fit into sockets in the doors and are provided with anti-rattle locking devices. If not required they are stowed behind the squab of the rear seat where they are at any time instantly available.

It should be noticed that the lines of the doors follow the line of the raked two-panel screen, which, incidentally, has an auxiliary centre pillar in view of the roughness of some Continental roads. Flush-fitting ventilators are used in both the top and sides of the scuttle.

These three cars, taken collectively, demonstrate the latest ideas in widely differing British coachwork as designed for mounting on large and high-grade chassis.

This Barker torpedo-bodied 40-50 h.p. Rolls-Royce is finished in polished aluminium above the waistline and has wings and valances to match.

The Autocar

"THE AUTOCAR" ROAD TESTS

20 h.p. ROLLS-ROYCE SALOON

A Car that Combines Performance with Exceptional Refinement.

IN its general characteristics the 20 h.p. Rolls-Royce is very like its larger and possibly more famous relative, the 40-50 h.p. model. That is to say, its qualities are those of a thoroughbred, quietness, smoothness, and ease of control standing out prominently from a background of lesser, but still important, virtues.

Whether the car be stationary with the engine idling, or cruising comfortably at any speed up to 55 m.p.h. or even more, there is practically no engine noise beyond the hiss of the carburetter and a faint murmur from the exhaust. Transmission noise also is non-existent on top gear, and when the indirect gears are brought into play there is only a slight hum as evidence of the fact, the third speed being particularly quiet.

As at all normal speeds the engine is singularly free from vibration, only evincing a slight harshness when forced up to its maximum rate of revolution on the indirect gears, when it naturally becomes audible at the same time, the result is that, as far as the occupants of the rear seat are concerned, the engine might be idle and the car coasting.

It will, perhaps, be imagined that performance has been sacrificed to refinement, but the acceleration figures given in the accompanying table prove

that this is not so. For a car weighing nearly 33 cwt. unladen, and with three up, the figures are distinctly good. As one might imagine from the figures, there is no need to change down from top in traffic, for when an opening presents itself the acceleration on top is rapid enough to allow the opportunity to be seized.

To all intents and purposes, therefore, top gear is sufficient for normal driving when once the car is in motion. Hills of 1 in 10 can be taken in the car's stride by merely depressing the accelerator a little harder, and even on a gradient of 1 in 6½ third gear will suffice to keep up a pace but little below 20 m.p.h. if the change down be made early.

By double declutching a smooth, noiseless change from top to third can be made at 40 m.p.h., so that on a give-and-take road quite a high average speed can be maintained, although the maximum speed is not, for these days, really high. In changing up a perceptible pause in neutral is necessary, but the delicacy of movement of the gear lever is such that the gears can be "felt" and engaged inaudibly with but little skill. It should be remarked that the gear lever is so arranged that in neutral it automatically takes up a position in the centre of the gate.

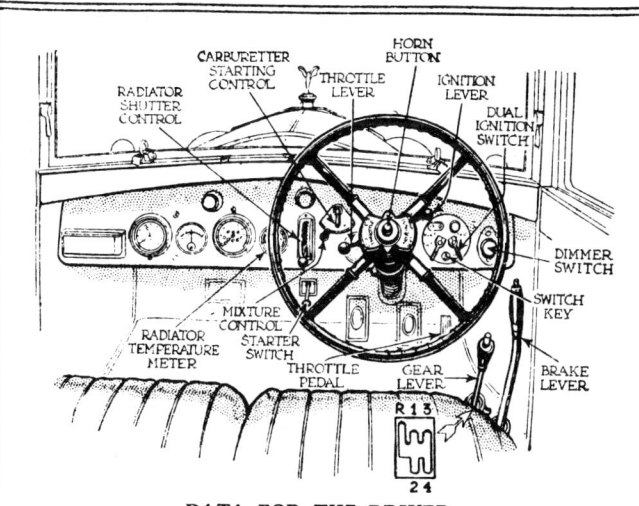

DATA FOR THE DRIVER.

20 h.p., six cylinders, 76.2 × 114.3 mm. (3,127 c.c.).
Tax £22.
Wheelbase 10ft. 9in., track 4ft. 8in.
Overall length 14ft. 10in., width 5ft. 10in., height 6ft. 1in.
Tyres: 32 × 6in. on detachable wire wheels.

Engine—rear axle gear ratios.	Maxima (m.p.h.).	Acceleration (10–30 m.p.h.)
16.98	15	—
10.62	31	7 sec.
6.89	43	8¼ sec.
4.55	65	11¼ sec.

Tank capacity, 14 gallons; fuel consumption, 20–25 m.p.g.
Turning circle, right 45ft. 8in., left 39ft. 2in.
12-volt lighting set cuts in at 12 m.p.h., 10 amps. at 25 m.p.h.
Weight 32 cwt. 3 qrs.
Price, with Weymann saloon body, £1,700.

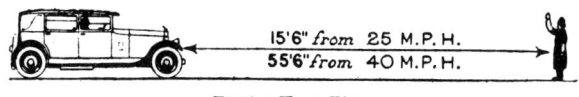

15'6" from 25 M.P.H.
55'6" from 40 M.P.H.

Brake Test Figures.

One of the charms of the Rolls-Royce is the exact and easy manner in which all the controls carry out their work. The clutch is very smooth in action, and calls for only a light pressure on the pedal, the four wheel brakes are operated by a servo mechanism and require the minimum of effort from the driver, while the steering is of the "finger-and-thumb" order and possesses ample self-centring action, straightening up automatically after a corner as the wheel is released. Even the minor controls, such as ignition and throttle levers, mixture control, and the accelerator pedal perform their tasks with meticulous accuracy and no vestige of lost motion, so contributing not a little to the charm of driving the car.

On bad roads the suspension system, which incorporates hydraulic shock absorbers, shows up to advantage, but does not produce a feeling of harshness on better surfaces as is sometimes the case. There is, moreover, no rolling on corners; the car holds the road well and gives the driver the feeling that he can steer to a hair's breadth

As regards the brakes, it should be explained that the servo is as effective on reverse as forwards. From a speed of 25 m.p.h. the car was stopped in a distance of 15½ft. on a tarred macadam road, the surface being dry—a remarkable performance. From 40 m.p.h. also a very good figure was obtained, the distance being 55½ft. Even when stopping so suddenly there was no harshness, nor was there any pull on the steering.

From these acceleration and brake test figures it will be realised that there is no difficulty in keeping up a high average speed, while a long journey can be made without any feeling of fatigue being experienced by the driver, thanks to the lightness of the controls. His mind, too, is always easy as regards the car; for example, should he omit to glance at the thermometer on the instrument board, and forget to open the hand-controlled shutters, he will be reminded of his neglect when the radiator reaches a temperature of about 95 degrees C., as a red warning light then flashes up. Carelessness regarding the fuel supply is also provided for by a tap on the main tank, which gives a reserve supply of two gallons. Again, one has not to be constantly replenishing the oil supply, as a distance of 1,000 miles can be covered without raising the bonnet for this purpose.

As ignition is by coil and battery, a magneto being fitted purely as a stand-by and remaining idle until its quick-acting coupling is engaged, it is worthy of note that the dynamo cuts in at a low speed and charges at 10 amps. at 25 m.p.h. on top gear.

Regarding coachwork little need be said, as it is usual to fit special bodies to the chassis. The car tested had a four-door, four-light Weymann saloon, which proved roomy, comfortable, and quiet, except for a minor rattle apparently from the neighbourhood of the dash, but this would have passed unnoticed on a chassis of less refinement. Allowance should be made also for the mileage covered by the car, which was considerable.

To sum up, it may be said that refinement is the outstanding feature, but that this has not been obtained at the expense of performance. The 20 h.p. Rolls-Royce is, indeed, a very pleasant car to handle, and can suit its paces to the mentality of the driver of the moment.

THE ADVANCE OF THE SPORTSMAN'S COUPE

Details of a Recent Specimen of a Popular Form of Body for an Owner-driver.

THE type of body which has made the quickest rise to popularity in the last two years is the close-coupled saloon—or sportsman's coupé, as it is now more commonly termed. It was during the autumn of 1927 that suggested designs for a wide, two-door sportsman's coupé appeared in these columns, and its special attractions were advanced, coupled with a plea for deep doors, obscuring the then prevalent valances. The effect of those designs and recommendations is now recognisable on every hand.

In the original conception of the design, a separate luggage trunk was arranged at the rear; the tendency is now to have the luggage compartment neatly incorporated in the tail of the body. Such an

Vertical radiator shutters and a wider dash are features of this new 20 h.p. Rolls-Royce. Note the position indicator on the near wing.

Showing the clearance behind the front seats.

example forms the subject of the accompanying illustrations, which depict a new 20 h.p. Rolls-Royce, with a Weymann two-door body, a provisional drawing of which appeared in *The Autocar* of December 21st, 1928. The floor-roof height of this body is 44½in., and in front there are two sliding bucket seats with folding

backs; really luxurious accommodation is provided for two at the rear. Two suit-cases are carried in the streamline tail, space for tools and spares being arranged under the frame on each side and enclosed by the deep doors. In this body there is a Pytchley sliding roof, easily opened or closed on the run; the 41in. doors, in conjunction with the folding back rests to the front seats, provide easy access to the rear compartment.

There is ample leg room, since the floor is "welled."

The colour scheme is black, with green wings and chassis, and green upholstery, lining and carpets inside—a very effective and pleasing combination.

As to the chassis, the dash width is slightly wider than standard, which has resulted in a handsome front appearance, and enabled the bonnet sides to be dropped low and neatly merged with the body sides. All bright parts are chromium-plated as regards both chassis and body fittings, as well as the new Lucas P.100 lamps, incorporated in which is a dimming device actuated by a switch on the dash.

Since the down cushions mounted on air bags provide a lower seating position than usual, a position indicator is mounted on the left wing extremity. This chassis, one of the latest to leave the Derby works, has vertical shutters fitted to the radiator, which is deeper than usual, their operation having a simplified control. The mixture control is mounted on the steering wheel, as in the case of the Phantom, and more rake has been given to the steering column.

Other special points of this very attractive car are leather upholstery, windscreen wipers operating from the bottom of the screen, and divided sliding windows which the owner finds an improvement over the usual winding type.

Coachbuilder's drawing of the 20 h.p. Weymann-bodied Rolls-Royce

T.T. PRACTICE

AT the suggestion of the R.A.C., who are organising the Tourist Trophy Race near Belfast on August 17th, the Northern Ireland Government have agreed that there shall be official practising periods from 10.30 a.m. to 12.30 p.m. on the Wednesday and Thursday preceding the race. Last year, it will be recollected, practice took place in the early hours of the morning.

In connection with this event the R.A.C. has published a leaflet, giving full particulars of train departures and arrivals, all boat sailings, and fares. In addition, the Club has issued a circular concerning particulars of accommodation on the grand stand, together with an application form and a plan of the course. Copies can be obtained free of charge on application to the Secretary, Royal Automobile Club, Pall Mall, S.W.1.

A NEW ROLLS-ROYCE

RUMOURS that a new model Rolls-Royce was on the stocks have been circulating very freely for some time past, and, whether deliberately guided or not, have generally announced the famous Derby firm to be seriously engaged in the production of a new sports model. Since this seemed to indicate a change of policy it was exceptionally interesting, and hotly discussed in all circles where the sports or speed model is of paramount concern—the more so because Rolls-Royce once upon a time did race, and they won immediately upon their entry into the field.

When the new chassis appeared it at once became absolutely certain that it was not a sports model, and that there had been no change of policy whatsoever. But the "Phantom" chassis had been redesigned from beginning to end, with many interesting, and some quite drastic, alterations incorporated to bring the car right in line with modern ideas of chassis detail and arrangement.

The new car is at first sight very little different in appearance from its predecessor, until one notices that the long cantilever rear springs, which have been a feature of the larger model for many years, have given place to big half-elliptics. Probably this is because the difficulty with the cantilever is that of effecting a satisfactory compromise between the free and flexible movement which gives good riding for a town carriage and sufficient firmness and stability for when the car is travelling really fast on the open road.

Exclusive Details of Redesigned Chassis, with Unit Construction of Engine and Gear Box, Open Propeller-Shaft, Half-elliptic Rear Springs and Partial One-shot Lubrication System, to be known as the Phantom II.

Revised arrangement of the carburetter and inlet pipe on the new model.

Closer inspection shows that every component of the car has been treated with that thoroughness for which the firm is famous, and there remains the suggestion that the detail work is carried out regardless of expense. The six-cylinder engine is the same size as that of the "Phantom"—108 × 139.7 mm. bore and stroke, giving a capacity of 7,668 c.c.—a very big engine from the modern point of view, and with all the big engine's capacity for developing a good performance at what are now regarded as low engine speeds. The nominal rated horse-power of the car is 43.3, giving a tax of £44 annually.

The valves are overhead, vertical, and operated by rocking levers, which in turn are actuated by push rods from a camshaft in the side of the crank case. Whereas the earlier car had the ball on the push rod and the socket on the rocking lever, the present machine has the socket on the push rod and the ball, which is adjustable for position to set the rocker clearance, on the rocker, partly because, with the cup so placed, oil is retained therein when the engine stops, while in the older design the joints drained, and there was liable to be some slight noise for a few minutes after the engine had been started.

Internally there has not been much change, and the compression is relatively low considering the size of the

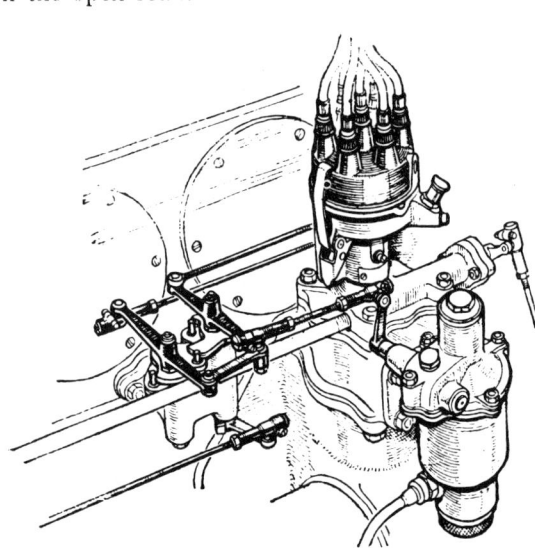

(Left) Compensating control allowing for the variations in range of the battery and magneto advance and the actuation of the governor.

(Right) Connections for the shock absorber arm on the front axle, the arm bearing being lubricated by a one-shot system.

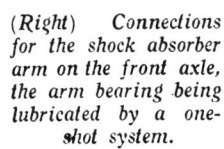

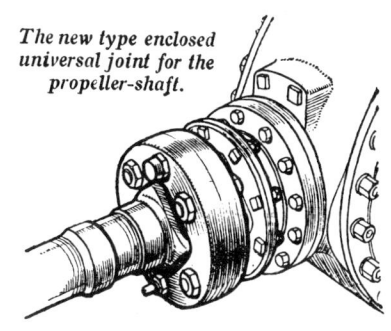

cylinders. The carburetter, which is of Rolls-Royce design, has been placed on the right-hand side of the power unit, and feeds the cylinders through a vertical aluminium pipe attached to a curved fish tail, which is bolted to a long aluminium inlet pipe feeding the ports proper, the mixture thus entering at the top of the pipe and not from below.

Portions of the pipe are warmed by a special water circulation system, and the air-valve chamber of the carburetter also forms the mouth of the crank case breather, being connected by a pipe to the side of the crank case in such fashion that the oil fumes inevitably generated within the crank case pass away through the carburetter. This scheme prevents the fumes reaching the driving compartment through the floorboards, and thus making the interior of a closed body uncomfortable in hot weather.

The main carburetter does not function when the engine is being started, for which purpose there is another miniature carburetter on top of the inlet pipe, with its own jet and its own air intake; being really the equivalent of the slow runner of an ordinary instrument. Fuel is fed to the carburetter by a big vacuum tank supported on the dashboard, which draws its supply from the main fuel tank between the rear dumb irons, using either the main compartment of that tank or a reserve section holding three gallons and brought into operation by a tap on the dashboard. The interesting part of this system is that the vacuum tank depression is maintained not by the depression in

The exhaust pipe is carried down between the dynamo and the magneto, well clear of the floorboards or the radiator.

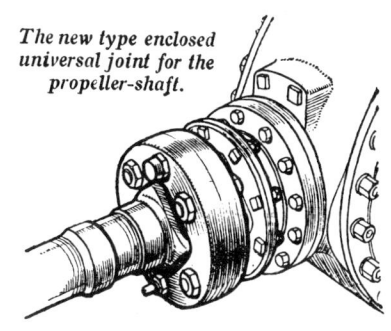

The new type enclosed universal joint for the propeller-shaft.

the inlet pipe, but by an air pump driven from the engine, which maintains the fuel feed whether the throttle is wide open or not.

Between the vacuum tank and the carburetter float chamber is a multi-disc filter, with a metal instead of a glass container. The fuel pipes generally are supported all along the chassis in those beautiful little brackets which remind one inevitably of the traditional bearings laid down in a manual of machine drawings. The tank proper has a big filler on the left-hand side, with a special air vent from the top of the tank to the filler, and the contents of the tank are shown by a gauge on the instrument board.

On the left side of the engine is the distributor for battery ignition, with its automatic advance mechanism controlled by spring-loaded pistons and the pressure of oil. The engine has both battery and magneto ignition, and the ingenious part of the automatic advance is that the range of movement for the two systems is not the same, the battery distributor being retarded considerably more than the magneto, so that with the last-mentioned switched off the slow running can be unusually good.

To advance the two ignitions at different rates there is an ingenious and beautifully laid out series of compensated lever movements which can be operated either by the automatic advance or by a hand control at the centre of the steering wheel. The magneto itself is also on the left of the engine, being at the rear near the dashboard, driven from the dynamo by a long shaft with universal joints. Since a magneto is likely to set up a certain irregular fluctuation in its

Showing the carburetter, pump, battery ignition distributor and governor casing. The circular discs on the cylinder block are inspection covers for the water jackets.

A New Rolls-Royce.

driving shaft, there is a small brake which acts as a constant damper for the drive, the drive itself being taken from one of the big helical-toothed gears of the engine timing. The governor is retained.

The engine lubrication is unusual in that it is so elaborate. What may be termed a distributing chamber is fed by the oil pump, dividing the supply into deliveries at three different pressures, of which the highest naturally goes to the main engine bearings, the second to the overhead rockers, and the third to certain minor engine bearings. Oil flowing from the rocker bearings is prevented by baffle plates from spreading, and drains back to the crank case, through orifices, to the push rods, feeding the tappets on its return journey.

Exhaust Arrangements.

At the middle of the cylinder block, on the left side of the engine, is the exhaust pipe, with three branches to the cylinder ports and an aluminium lagging with a neat metal sheath, so that the heat from the pipe is kept as far away as possible from the driving compartment on one side and from the radiator on the other. The exhaust gases are taken through a pipe to a series of expansion chambers which, combined, are of great size and extend nearly all the way to the rear axle. Thus the tail pipe is very short indeed, and close alongside it is an extra outlet to be brought into operation in countries where to use a free exhaust is not a criminal offence.

Water is circulated throughout the cylinder block and head by a big centrifugal pump passing to a radiator of traditional Rolls-Royce shape, with big metal shutters which can be opened or closed by a control on the instrument board, hand control being deemed more certain where there is a possibility of considerable dust or mud settling on the shutter joints.

The temperature of the cooling water is shown by one of the instruments in front of the driver. One of the great changes in this new car is that the whole power unit is carried by four substantial tubular brackets on the greatly strengthened main frame, the flexible suspension originally adopted having been discarded and, a still more drastic change, the gear box is in one unit with the crank case, the tail end of the gear box having additional support from a frame cross-member.

It is interesting to see a car of this calibre with the now inevitable unit construction, which means that the obvious advantages of rigidity and compactness of the integral system have outweighed the fact that the clutch becomes less accessible and the gear box less easy to handle in the event of its requiring attention. The unit is conventional, with a big bell-housing bolted to the crank case and having inspection covers for access to the clutch operating mechanism and the timing marks.

The gear box itself appears to be considerably smaller than hitherto simply because the shafts lie one above the other instead of side by side, and the disc-type brake servo motor for the brake operation has been

This semi-plan view shows the principal chassis changes: the half-elliptic springs, open propeller-shaft, and unit gear box, and, parallel with the propeller-shaft, the long silencer, which has no baffle plates.

placed on the left-hand side of the gear box and looks tidier than it was, the gear lever being, of course, on the right and not in the centre.

Behind the gear box is a huge tubular propeller-shaft, exposed since the torque is taken through the rear springs, and provided with two universal joints, as well as a big sliding joint at the fore end.

The rear axle itself has been completely redesigned, the centre casing appearing larger, the side sleeves smaller. Here is another interesting point, as the older model had a torque tube enclosing the propeller-shaft, and the tendency to-day seems to be to use the torque tube by preference. The rear brakes now consist of two groups of fabric-lined expanding shoes of the same size and acting on the same drums, a change from previous cars in which the shoes of the hand brake were smaller and had their own drum within the main drum. The difference, of course, is that all shoes now have a common drum, but the brakes are still independent from the commonsense point of view.

As before, the servo controlled by the pedal causes the rear shoes to be applied with greater power than those on the front axle, and the actuation of the front shoes is carried by the front axle, the drums being of big diameter and narrow. It is interesting to see what amounts to a long, thin, coil spring carried round the brake drums to stop any possibility of squeaking.

The front axle has on each side the triangular "torque" member which is coupled to the arm of a big

Rear axle centre casing, in the middle of which, just above the pinion bearing housing, is the single oil nipple for the whole of the rear axle lubrication.

hydraulic shock absorber, the same type of absorber being used for the rear springs.

There have been some alterations to the steering gear, which is lighter to handle than hitherto, while the steering wheel is bigger and has a thin rim. Another most interesting change is that the designers have gone, as it were, three-quarters of the way towards what is called the one-shot system of chassis lubrication. For all the minor bearings coupled to the frame, or in any way connected with

it, are fed by a plunger pump operated by a spring whenever the pump is raised by a pedal on the dashboard. The pump takes its supply of oil from a container on the dashboard and distributes it to the bearings in quantities controlled by special orifices of different sizes.

Further, there is a separate system of lubrication for the front axle components and for the rear axle details, each fed by an oil gun through a single nipple, from which radiate pipes to the various bearings. The universal joints of the propeller-shaft can be filled with lubricant by undoing a plug on one side and forcing oil through a nipple until it overflows at the plug orifice. Not only the spring shackles, but also the spring leaves are fed with lubricant, and each shock absorber spindle has its supply.

The body is mounted considerably lower on the frame than on previous cars, and the ingenious rubber bearings for the body mounting are retained. The instrument board has been tidied considerably, the main instruments being grouped in a sunk panel which is indirectly lighted, the design and shape of the others suiting the general scheme of decoration. The starting motor control is reduced to a very small switch on the instrument board.

The whole chassis is beautifully finished, as might be imagined, the exterior surface of the crank case casting and the general detail work of the brackets and controls being almost of the character one has associated solely with machines designed for exhibition.

The price remains unchanged: £1,850 for the short chassis and £1,900 for the longer wheelbase model.

Brake servo motor and gear box. The apparent reduction in the size of the latter is due to the fact that the shafts are now one above the other, not side by side.

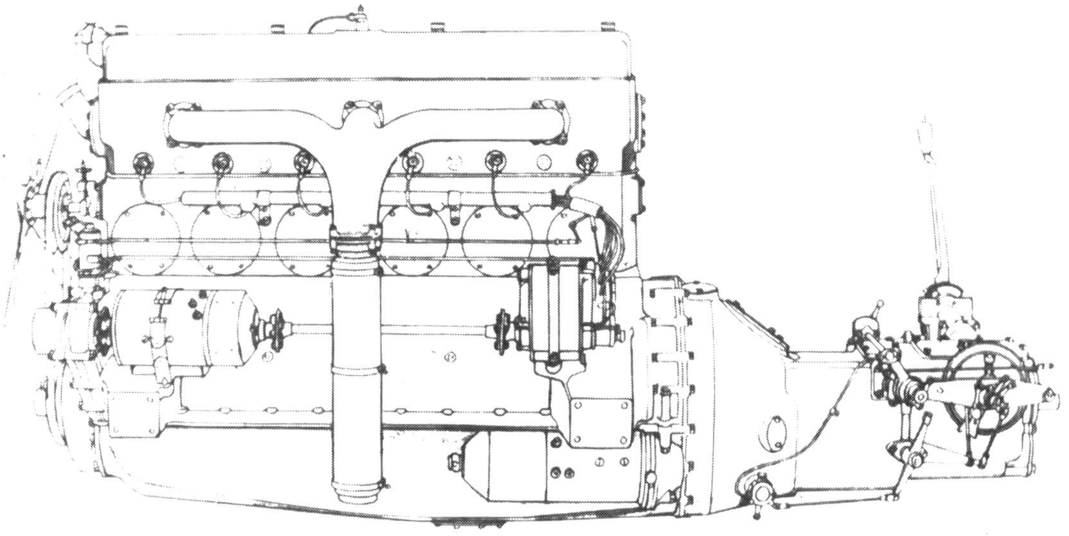

Chassis of the new Rolls-Royce, first described in *The Autocar* of September
20th, one of the most interesting of the new designs which will appear at
the forthcoming Olympia Show.

THE 1930 PHANTOM II.
ROLLS-ROYCE.

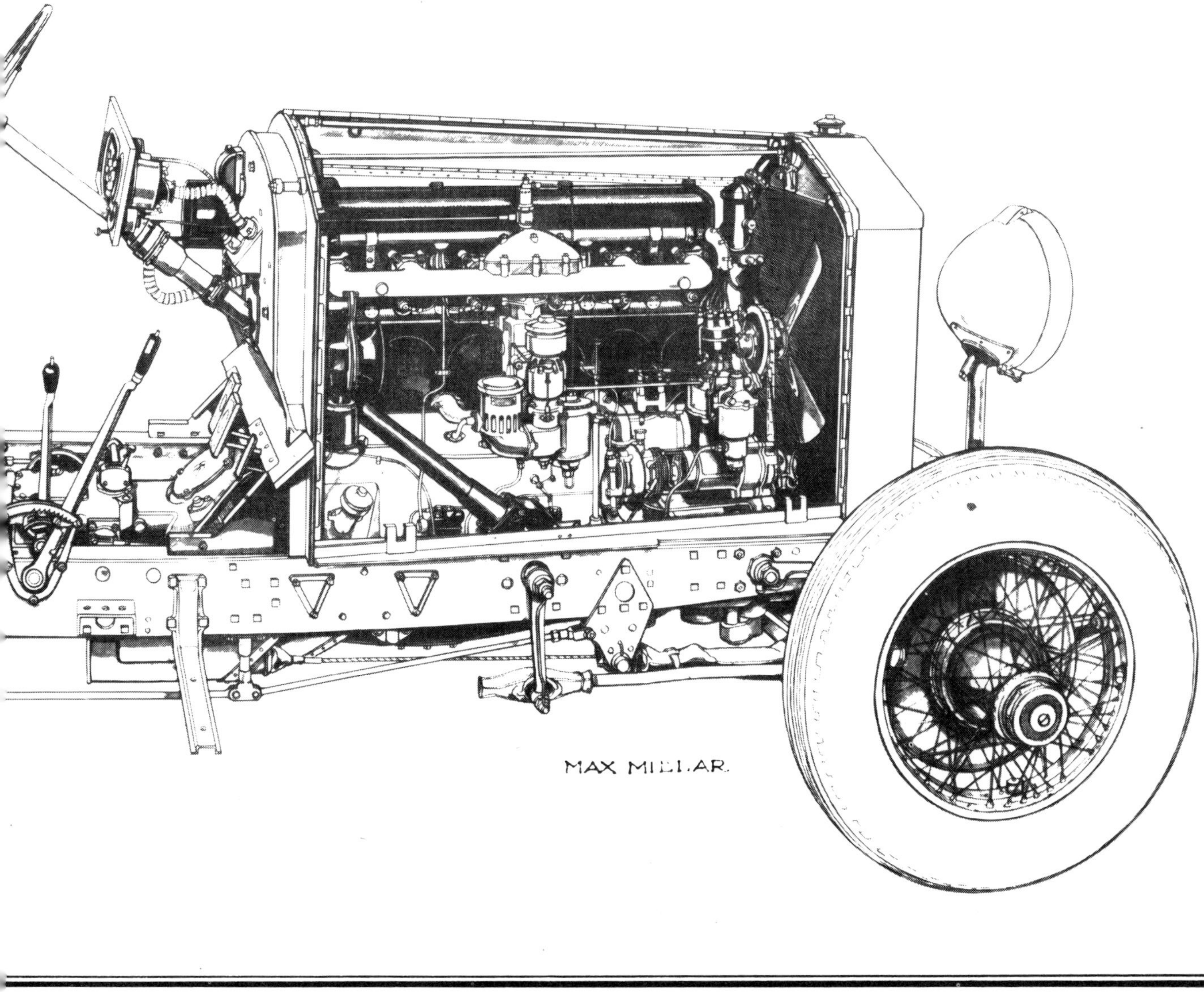

MAX MILLAR.

The salient features are at once apparent. The chassis is lower and the rear springs are half-elliptic. The engine is in one unit with the gear box and the propeller-shaft is open.

ROLLS-ROYCE CA

Improvements to Both Chassis: Increased Performance of 20-25 h.p.: Reduced
Exhibited at Olympia

IN its principal characteristics the design of Rolls-Royce cars remains unchanged, but a number of detail improvements of an important character have been introduced. It is the practice of the company to incorporate any improvements in design as experience dictates, and the examples of the latest chassis which are exhibited at the Paris Salon and will be shown at Olympia embody several modifications which have been introduced since the previous shows.

Dealing with the 40-50 h.p. chassis first, an important change is the adoption of a back axle 1½in. wider than the front axle, which enables a rear seat to be fitted which may be 49in. wide, a dimension sufficient to seat three persons comfortably.

The centralised lubrication system has now been extended to the front and back axles, and the lubrication foot pump has been increased in capacity to cope with this extra demand. The clutch spigot bearing is lubricated automatically from the gear box instead of, as previously, by hand. An Auto Klean filter has been introduced into the engine lubricating system; thermostatic control of the shutters is incorporated in the cooling system. Another detail improvement is a silencer on the carburetter. A new type of dented radiator tube has been devised which, by its delaying

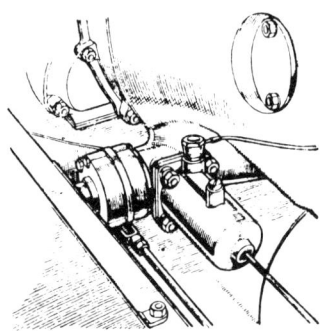

Das'pot in the brake system.

Pipe lines at one side of the front axle, part of the system of one-shot lubrication.

action, gives greatly improved cooling properties.

The electrical system is schemed to provide half-charge for use in the summer months, and full-charge when the demands on the battery are heavy. Wider brake shoes have been adopted for the rear brakes; the positions of the clutch and brake pedals are now adjustable. Extra rake, combined with a large thin-rim steering wheel, are standard, whilst the controls surmounting the wheel are neater and squatter than formerly. The instrument board is neater and more compact in appearance. On the 'dash is a two-way petrol tap controlling the reserve supply, operated from the driver's seat.

Always a handsome car, the Rolls-

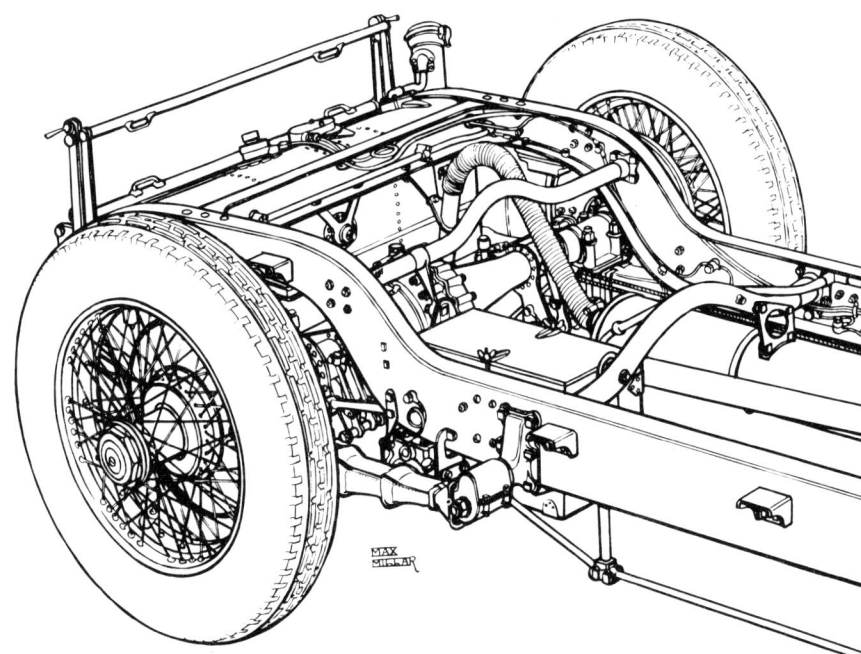

Royce now has the bonnet line slightly raised at the sides, and a lower and wider radiator cap, which still further enhance its good appearance.

Other detail improvements include an apron at the front of the chassis and a

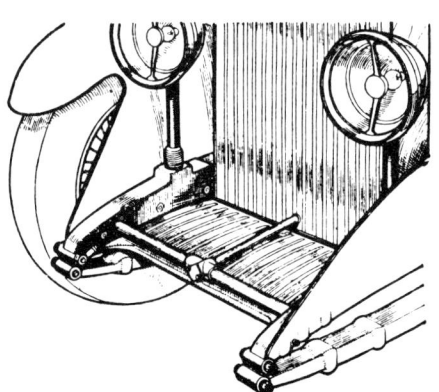

Neat apron joining the dumb irons.

new type of luggage grid which will enable coachbuilders to design an apron to cover the back part of the car, thus giving a clean appearance.

If desired, the larger chassis can be obtained with left-hand steering and central control levers.

This is a matter of very considerable interest, and it should certainly be appreciated by a good many prospective purchasers on the Continent and in America. When a motorist has become accustomed to a left-hand drive car, as in the case of a large number of French and practically all American chassis, he does not willingly change his mount for one with the steering wheel and controls in an unfamiliar position. The Phantom will

now be available for him in a form to which he has been accustomed.

As far as the 20-25 h.p. chassis is concerned, many characteristics of the Phantom are incorporated, including a great rake to the steering column, and large, thin-rim wheel with squat controls, a lower and wider radiator cap, flatter front springs, grouped instruments, and grouped lubrication points. Generally, however, the most important modifications to the 20-25 h.p. chassis do not affect the appearance so much as the performance. With its six-cylinder engine of 82 × 114 mm. (3,669 c.c.) the car has been developed and improved until it is now much faster and has an acceleration far superior to its forerunners. This result has been achieved without impairing the Rolls-Royce qualities of enduring silence, extreme controllability, and docility.

For long past Rolls-Royce owners have desired a car which retained the sweet running qualities of the smaller Rolls-

RS FOR 1932

rices Announced: Complete Standard Cars to be 'or the First Time

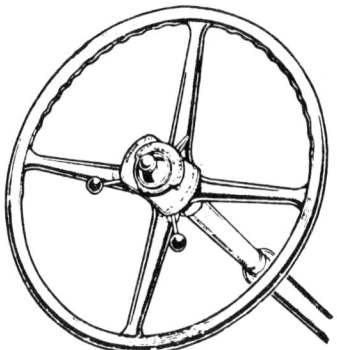

Steering wheel of the Rolls-Royce, showing the jet control.

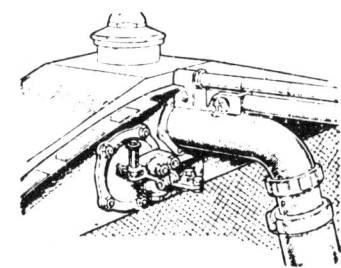

The thermostat which controls the radiator shutters.

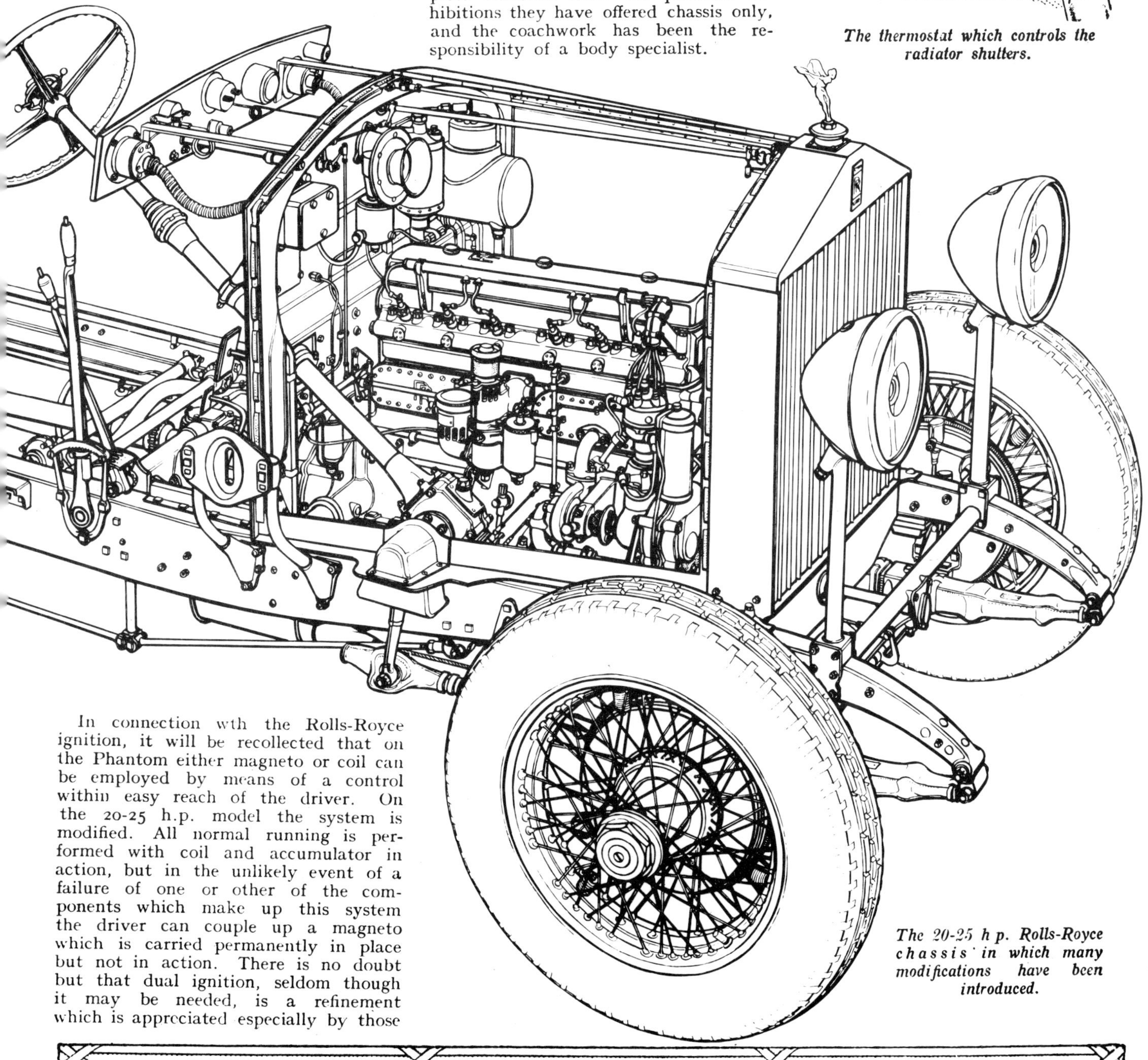

Royce, yet capable of exceeding 70 m.p.h. when occasion demanded. This desire has now been fulfilled, together with a third-gear performance of 50 m.p.h. and much improved acceleration powers. A rise from 10 to 30 m.p.h. on top gear is now possible in slightly less than 10 seconds, depending, of course, upon the type of body fitted.

Throughout the speed range the engine remains cooler than formerly, due to a larger radiator and a modified form of exhaust branch. Other modifications include double-acting hydraulic shock absorbers, front and rear, and alternative ignition systems.

touring abroad far from the nearest service depot for their own vehicles.

The chassis price of the 40-50 h.p. Phantom II has been reduced from £1,850 to £1,750, and that of the long chassis from £1,900 to £1,800, while the 20-25 h.p. model is reduced from £1,185 to £1,050. Two saloon models on the latter chassis now sell at £1,555 and £1,560 for the four- and six-seater respectively. Both of them are standardised models, luxuriously equipped in every way, and fitted with Triplex safety glass.

It is a matter of moment that the Rolls-Royce Company are showing this year at Olympia for the first time complete standard cars. At previous exhibitions they have offered chassis only, and the coachwork has been the responsibility of a body specialist.

In connection with the Rolls-Royce ignition, it will be recollected that on the Phantom either magneto or coil can be employed by means of a control within easy reach of the driver. On the 20-25 h.p. model the system is modified. All normal running is performed with coil and accumulator in action, but in the unlikely event of a failure of one or other of the components which make up this system the driver can couple up a magneto which is carried permanently in place but not in action. There is no doubt but that dual ignition, seldom though it may be needed, is a refinement which is appreciated especially by those

The 20-25 h.p. Rolls-Royce chassis in which many modifications have been introduced.

1931 40/50 h.p. Phantom II with all-weather body by Gill of London. The hood is fully lined and there is a disappearing glass division. When the hood is down the division and side windows may be raised or lowered as needed

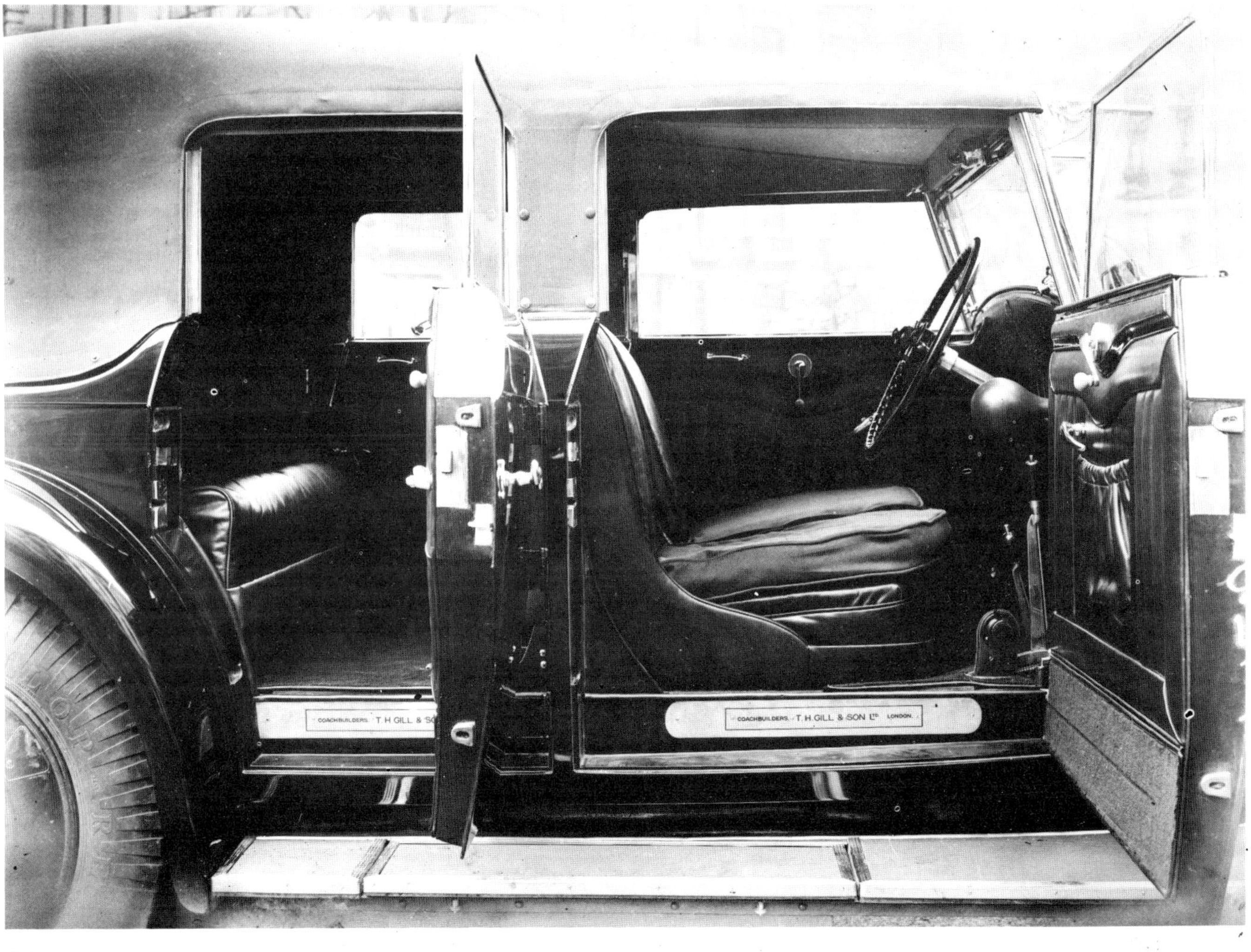

The AUTOCAR ROAD TESTS

The illustration above indicates the size, in feet, of the 25 h.p. Rolls-Royce saloon

No. 644 ($\frac{Post\text{-}War}{Series}$).—25 h.p. ROLLS-ROYCE SALOON

IT is one of the strongest possible tributes to the Rolls-Royce that, much as one expects of it in advance, the fulfilment of those expectations as a result of testing the car is more complete than would be deemed possible.

The driver who has never handled a Rolls-Royce is likely to want to know wherein it differs from the general run of motor cars. That is a point it is impossible to deal with adequately in few words, but the principal impressions concern the extreme delicacy of control, the amazing flexibility on top gear, the silence and quality of the acceleration, and the fact that the engine is as quiet and smooth when the car is travelling at the maximum as it is at lower speeds. In addition, none of the hand controls requires more than the pressure of two fingers and the braking system is probably as near perfection as it is possible to attain.

First, the flexibility of the engine: it is the normal and recommended practice to start the car from rest on third gear, which is effected without opening the throttle at all wide; and starting away on top on the level is possible without any suggestion that the clutch is being abused, so smoothly is the drive taken up. Top gear having been engaged, the car will run on that ratio almost the whole time, with a degree of flexibility that is unbelievable without actually trying the car, for it is possible to throttle down the engine to pull smoothly at so low a speed that the next stage is for the car to stop altogether. It is a feature of the acceleration that it is absolutely clean and free from trace of a flat-spot.

Thus there is ordinarily very little need for a gear box, first speed being re-garded purely as an emergency ratio and second as a gear for restarting on a gradient. But it is typical of the car that the gear change, when used, is delightful to handle, since the lever is exceedingly light to move, there is no suggestion of strong locking springs, yet the teeth can be felt with the utmost sensitiveness. There is an arrangement whereby the gear lever is automatically centred in the gate when in neutral position.

One of the most striking things is that as the throttle is opened and the car accelerated, the driver is unusually conscious of the sound of air rushing against the windscreen as speed is gathered—so unobtrusive is the engine that it cannot be felt during acceleration. Another interesting point is to judge the speed and then refer to the speedometer to check the estimate; in spite of practice with many other machines it is possible to underestimate the figure by as much as 6 to 8 m.p.h.

It is the manner of the car's behaviour which charms and its instant obedience to the driver's every wish as expressed through the controls, but the important point is that there is all the performance most owners can possibly want, for the average at which the Rolls-Royce can be driven comfortably is so much higher in proportion to the maximum than with the majority of ordinary cars, owing to the absence of sense of mechanical effort. Furthermore, as a matter of interest, 50 m.p.h. can be reached on third gear, 35 on second and 21 on first speed, and, although the gear teeth are of straightforward type, nothing above a faint, pleasing hum can be heard on any of the indirect ratios.

The steering is light and the thin-rim wheel cor-

fortable to hold ; there is exactly the right caster action and only occasionally, on poor surfaces, can the slightest movement of the road wheels be felt through the steering wheel itself. The brake operation is assisted by the Rolls-Royce mechanical servo, of course, but apart from the fact that the action is very light the driver is not conscious of the servo, since the shoes can be felt as the pedal is depressed ; the braking instantly affords the greatest confidence.

On this particular car the suspension, with the special double-acting hydraulic shock absorbers, was set to provide an excellent compromise between the needs of what can be termed town carriage work, when softness at low speed is essential, and stability for fairly fast running on the open road. Greater stability is a question of further damping alone, at the sacrifice of a degree of the remarkable comfort at ordinary speeds, which would have the effect of making the car steadier on bends taken at speed, the softer setting allowing some roll.

As to the coachwork, little need be said, since the bodies fitted to Rolls-Royce chassis are invariably a question of individual choice. The body of the 25 h.p. car tested was a metal-panelled Mulliner Weymann four-door, four-light saloon, affording plenty of leg room and having, at the front, two separate and easily adjustable seats of a particularly comfortable type.

The grouped special instruments are indirectly lighted and among them is a fuel tank gauge of the hydrostatic level type. Also there is an engine thermometer. The single-panel screen is made to open on this particular car and has two separate electric wipers.

All through the engine and chassis are exceptionally interesting points of design and, apart altogether from the performance, the detail work shows that wonderful care and forethought, and excellence of material and workmanship, which, in combination, help to explain why no other name

has exactly the same meaning as Rolls-Royce to initiated and uninitiated the world over.

An example of characteristic forethought is the spare magneto, already in position and timed, which can be brought into operation in a matter of seconds in the unlikely event of the coil ignition system failing. All the engine components are remarkably accessible, while everything is beautifully finished, and the wiring and junction and fuse boxes are typical.

Beneath the bonnet also are the vacuum tank for the fuel feed and the reservoir for the centralised system of chassis lubrication. The latter is applied to certain bearings on the chassis, each bearing receiving a supply of lubricant graduated according to its needs, but is not extended to the axles, where relative movement between the axles and the frame might produce a breakage in one of the pipe lines. Instead, on each axle is a single accessible nipple, to which lubricant is supplied in the ordinary way ; thus all the axle units, including brake and steering gear parts, are supplied from two points.

The brake adjustments, both back and front, are remarkably accessible, consisting of individual settings for each drum. The shoes for each wheel are compensated individually.

The radiator shutters are controlled by hand from the instrument board and provide a very sensitive means of regulating the engine temperature. In the instrument panel is a red tell-tale which lights up to give warning when a temperature of 95 deg. C. is reached, should the driver have forgotten to open the shutter control to the normal running position.

The Rolls-Royce has fascination beyond measure ; every single feature spells durability, and the car possesses the modern performance : it is in the manner of delivering this performance that the machine is on a plane altogether superior to the normal style of motor car.

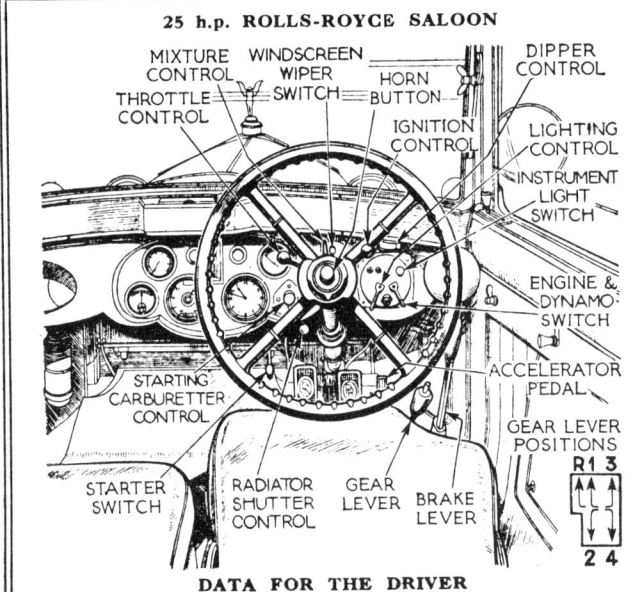

25 h.p. ROLLS-ROYCE SALOON

MIXTURE CONTROL — WINDSCREEN WIPER SWITCH — HORN BUTTON — DIPPER CONTROL — THROTTLE CONTROL — IGNITION CONTROL — LIGHTING CONTROL — INSTRUMENT LIGHT SWITCH — STARTING CARBURETTER CONTROL — ENGINE & DYNAMO SWITCH — ACCELERATOR PEDAL — GEAR LEVER POSITIONS — STARTER SWITCH — RADIATOR SHUTTER CONTROL — GEAR LEVER — BRAKE LEVER

R 1 3 / 2 4

DATA FOR THE DRIVER

25.3 h.p., six cylinders, 82.6 × 114.3 mm. (3,680 c.c.).
Tax £26.
Wheelbase 11ft., track 4ft. 8in.
Overall length 15ft. 1in., width 5ft. 10in., height 6ft.
Tyres : 31 × 6in. on detachable wire wheels.

Engine—rear axle gear ratios.	Acceleration from steady 10 to 30 m.p.h.	Timed speed over ¼ mile.
16.98 to 1		
10.62 to 1	6 sec.	
6.98 to 1	7 sec.	
4.55 to 1	10⅝ sec.	67.66 m.p.h.

Turning circle : 43ft. 1in. (left), 48ft. 6in. (right).
Tank capacity 14 gallons, fuel consumption 18 m.p.g.
12-volt lighting set cuts in at 7 m.p.h., 9 amps. at 30 m.p.h.
Weight : 33 cwt. 2 qr. 21 lb.
Price, with Mulliner Weymann panelled saloon body, £1,815.

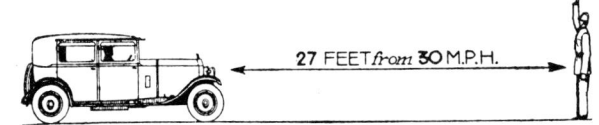

27 FEET from 30 M.P.H.

ROLLS-ROYCE MODIFICATIONS

Synchronised Gear-changing Mechanism Now Fitted on the 20-25 h.p. Model: Increased Power from the Engine, Giving a Higher Maximum Speed

WHEN any question of improvements is mentioned in connection with Rolls-Royce cars it is always known that such alterations as are involved are not just changes for change's sake, or aimed merely to take the passing fancy, but are the result of long experience and intensive testing, and form really worth-while embellishments to the basic chassis. The latest 20-25 h.p. model, which is now available with several detail changes, has the very important addition of a synchronising mechanism for the gear box, whereby the necessity for double-clutching is removed in changing down between top and third, and in changing up between second and third and third and top.

That a device of this nature should have been adopted for a Rolls-Royce means that the makers must be thoroughly satisfied with the results, so the mechanism itself can be taken for granted for the moment, leaving one free to concentrate upon the advantages which it was possible to observe during a short test run.

Starting from rest is normally effected on second gear, if not on third, so smoothly does the drive take up; thus, actually there is no double-clutching called for with the latest car, it being seldom indeed in this country that any ratio lower than third is required. Ease of control is enormously increased, changing down between top and third having been reduced to a process

whereby the clutch is simply taken out and the lever moved to the required position, without sound of any kind and without further acceleration of the engine. It is best, especially when changing down at fairly high speed, to keep the position of the throttle constant, whereby any tendency to jerk as the clutch is let in again, and the drive takes up on the lower ratio, is obviated.

Together with this significant gear box change has come an increase in engine power output, giving better acceleration and, what is quite as important in a way, increased maximum speeds on the indirect gears. It is now possible to run comfortably up to 60 m.p.h. on third and to 35 m.p.h. on second, the full benefit of this increased performance being made available to the owner by the ease of the gear change and by the rapidity with which changes can be made, for no time is lost and the full effect of the acceleration to be gained in dropping down to third is secured.

From the same viewpoint, there is another asset, though this is a side-issue, in that one can change down to third whilst braking, since it is not essential to have the foot on the throttle to secure silent engagement. Even previously, of course, it was possible to brake and change down at the same time, but not with equal facility.

Another advantage is that the gear lever can be slipped into neutral on a long hill, and the car can be allowed to coast; then, when the normal drive is required again, either top or third can be engaged easily and with absolute certainty merely by withdrawing the clutch and pulling the lever into the slot. Silence of Rolls-Royce indirect gears is widely accepted, but the present third speed has been developed to the stage where it is all but inaudible, even on the overrun.

The value of the new mechanism, together with the increased speed on third and the rapidity of the gear change made possible, is scarcely to be over-estimated in considering the maintenance of high average speeds on a long journey, and in this direction those accustomed to the earlier cars have found a very marked advance.

As to the effect of the increased engine power in other ways, it was not possible to test the maximum speed on top gear, though it is hoped that a regular road test of this model can be published later, but on a short open stretch of road the car easily runs up to a reading of 70 m.p.h., and is capable of reaching seventy-five in ordinary conditions, if not a little more.

The renowned silence and smoothness have, of course, been retained, yet it is one of the most difficult things in automobile design to secur greater power and still keep an engine entirely silky and silent. There can be no doubt that the engine still has its charm of effortless running, but with the very great added benefit of increased power.

Another interesting point is that a well-known Surrey hill, which is preceded by a series of bends and has a maximum gradient of 1 in 6½, was climbed comfortably on third gear with two people on board, the run up to the hill being made at about 35 m.p.h., at which speed third was engaged. When, about four years ago, an earlier version, then known as the 20 h.p., was taken up the same hill, with three persons on board, second gear was necessary.

The engine itself remains the same outwardly, as indeed does the chassis as a whole, but the forward mounting of the engine in the frame has been changed, the sub-frame-bearer on which the forward part of the engine rests now being rectangular in shape, whereas previously it was of U construction. The shutters in front of the radiator are opened and closed automatically by a thermostat, there being still the red tell-tale light on the instrument board, which gives warning should the shutters for any reason remain closed and the temperature go up as high as 95 degrees C.

As to the body, that fitted on the car tried was a Park Ward production, representing a scaled-down version of a particularly attractive close-coupled saloon fitted for some time past on the Continental Phantom II chassis.

The chassis price remains at £1,050, and the price of this particular type of complete car is £1,625. Examples of this modified version of the 20-25 h.p. Rolls-Royce chassis are now in regular production.

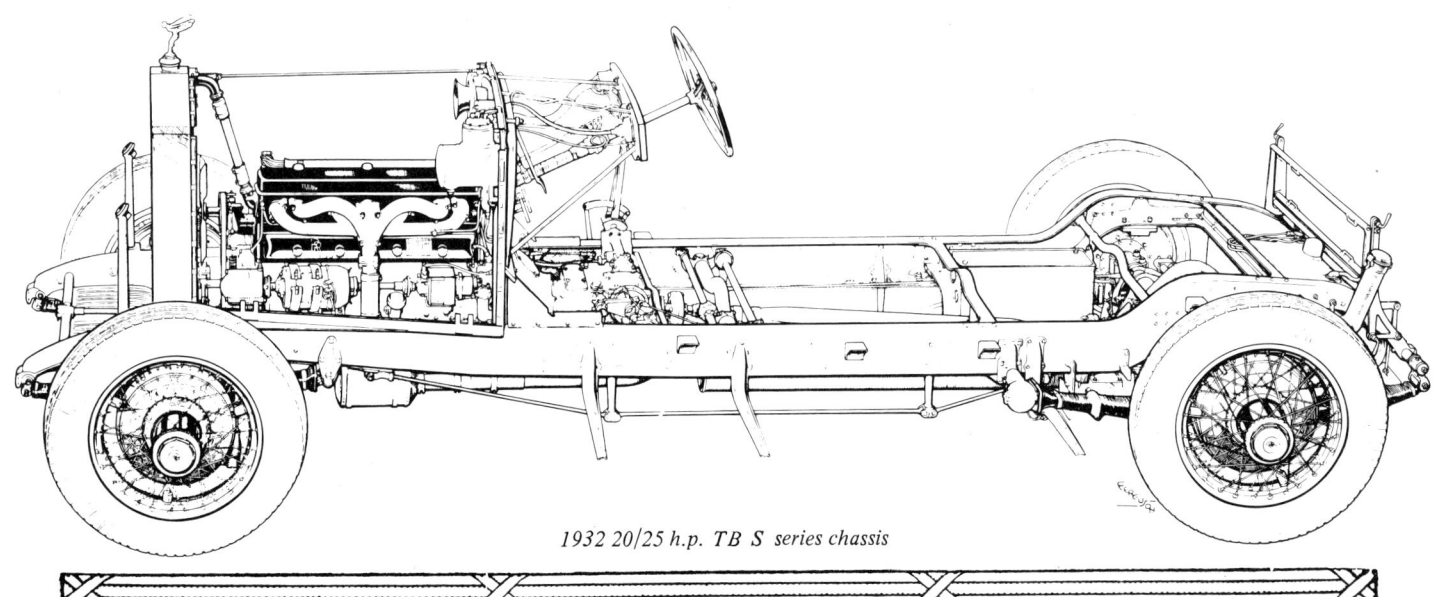

1932 20/25 h.p. TB S series chassis

The Autocar Road Tests

40-50 h.p. PHANTOM II CONTINENTAL ROLLS-ROYCE

Speed, Silence, Tractability, a Wonderful Top Gear Performance, and Unsurpassed Controls

IMAGINATION has to replace reality in the case of the Rolls-Royce where most people are concerned, but quite apart from the twice-fortunate minority that is able to own this renowned car there is undoubtedly very great interest as to what exactly it can do on the road.

The example now dealt with is the Continental Phantom II model, doubly intriguing as being the highest performance Rolls-Royce model at present available, the chassis being shorter, and therefore lighter than that of the normal Phantom II, whilst the body is lower and the wind resistance is thus lessened. Until one has tried and driven the car it is impossible even to begin to appreciate how very good it is. Further, it is not only what the car can do to-day, or to-morrow; day after day the performance can be repeated, whilst the durability is proverbial. That, after all, is no small part of what the buyer of these cars pays for.

First and foremost is the utterly easy way in which the engine does the whole of its work. Admittedly, it is a big engine by present-day standards, but it is a wonderful achievement that on one and the same high top gear ratio a saloon car weighing over 2½ tons laden should be capable of well above a genuine speed of 90 miles an hour and at the same time be so docile as to run without the least trace of snatch at 4 or 5 m.p.h. The engine will tick over so slowly that the individual fan blades can be all but distinguished.

The sheer speed of the car being decidedly interesting, it is worth mentioning that during the timed test the speedometer held a steady reading of 95. The traditional exhaust cut-out is retained, and though not legally to be used on the road in this country, makes an appreciable difference to maximum speed without increasing the noise seriously. For the maximum speed run on Brooklands the cut-out was opened. It seems certain that with the least assist-

JJ 9382

ance from a give and take road the speedometer needle could be got round to the 100 mark.

Over ninety miles an hour in itself is extremely fast for road work, but it is the way in which the car reaches and holds its limit speeds that singles it out from other machines. It is literally true that the engine is not conspicuous at the maximum speed, whilst any speed up to a full 80 m.p.h. simply represents what the car can do in its ordinary running day in day out, as roads permit and the driver's taste and mood dictate. It was found by separate tests that the speedometer was as near to dead accurate as no matter up to 70 m.p.h.

Another thing is the phenomenal top-gear performance, the machine gliding through a town with every suggestion that it is free wheeling, so little can the mechanism be felt. Again, an outstanding impression of the Rolls-Royce is the controls. It is easy to see that the designers realise that equally as important as a very high performance, if not even more so, is the ability of the driver—man or woman—to handle the car the whole time without effort or uncertainty of any kind.

The controls above the steering wheel are a striking instance. The throttle lever and hand control for the ignition operate in quadrants, and each single notch gives definite opening or closing of the throttle or advance and retard of the ignition. There is not a trace of lost movement.

Then, again, the brake operation is a masterpiece of design. There is a mechanical servo alongside the gear box, and the operation is astonishingly light; they are wonderfully powerful brakes when the speed has to be brought down in an emergency, besides being dead smooth in a way that can only be likened, non-mechanically, to silk. It might be said that the Rolls-Royce is as impressive when slowing under the brakes as when accelerating, and equally deceptive.

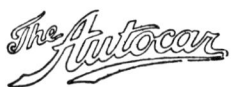

The car is normally started from rest on second or even third gear, the drive taking up as though something far more flexible than uncompromising mechanical connections existed between engine and road wheels, and once moving there are singularly few occasions when it is actually necessary to change down, even when the driver is forced to follow other vehicles slowly up a gradient. Yet the latest cars, and the Continental model in particular, possess a gear box which is thoroughly worth using to increase the performance from an interest point of view, or to make possible a still better average speed. There are few machines indeed in production which can come anywhere near the Rolls-Royce in getting from one place to another really rapidly.

The acceleration on the gears is that of a sports machine; on top gear the pick-up is altogether remarkable. An exceptional car justifies exceptional methods, and additional acceleration figures were taken up to 70 m.p.h. through the gears, these averaging out at 28 sec. Up to 75 m.p.h. is possible on third gear, 70 being easy and comfortable, whilst 45 m.p.h. can be attained on second, first gear being a purely emergency ratio, though high, on which 25 m.p.h. is attainable.

40-50 h.p. PHANTOM II CONTINENTAL ROLLS-ROYCE

DATA FOR THE DRIVER

40-50 h.p., six cylinders, 108 × 140 mm. (7,668 c.c.). Tax £44.
Tyres; 31 × 6.75 on detachable wire wheels.

Engine—rear axle gear ratios.	Acceleration from steady speed. 10 to 30 m.p.h.	20 to 40 m.p.h.	30 to 50 m.p.h.	Timed speed over ½ mile.
11.90 to 1	—	—	—	
6.77 to 1	5⅕ sec.	5⅗ sec.	—	
4.55 to 1	7⅘ sec.	7⅖ sec.	8⅕ sec.	
3.41 to 1	9⅗ sec.	10 sec.	10⅗ sec.	92.31 m.p.h.

Acceleration from rest through the gears to 50 m.p.h., 14⅖ sec.
Acceleration from rest through the gears to 60 m.p.h., 19⅗ sec.
Speed up Brooklands Test Hill from rest (1 in 5 average gradient), 18.19 m.p.h. (on first gear).
15 yards of 1 in 5 gradient from rest, 3⅕ sec.
Turning circle: 48ft. 8in. (left side).
Tank capacity 20 gallons, fuel consumption 10-14 m.p.g.
12-volt lighting set cuts in at 15 m.p.h., 7 amps. at 30 m.p.h.
Weight: 49 cwt.
Price, with Continental touring saloon body, £2,425.

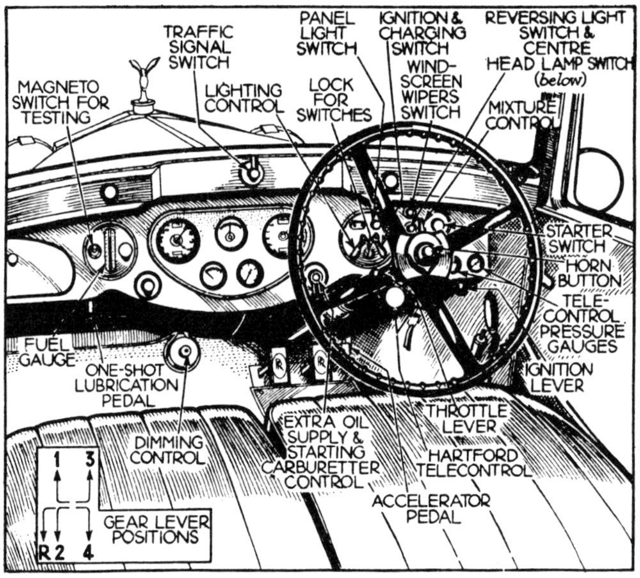
TRAFFIC SIGNAL SWITCH
PANEL LIGHT SWITCH
IGNITION & CHARGING SWITCH
REVERSING LIGHT SWITCH & CENTRE HEAD LAMP SWITCH (below)
MAGNETO SWITCH FOR TESTING
LIGHTING CONTROL
LOCK FOR SWITCHES
WIND-SCREEN WIPERS SWITCH
MIXTURE CONTROL
STARTER SWITCH
HORN BUTTON
TELE-CONTROL PRESSURE GAUGES
IGNITION LEVER
FUEL GAUGE
ONE-SHOT LUBRICATION PEDAL
THROTTLE LEVER
EXTRA OIL SUPPLY & STARTING CARBURETTER CONTROL
HARTFORD TELECONTROL
DIMMING CONTROL
ACCELERATOR PEDAL
1 3
R 2 4
GEAR LEVER POSITIONS

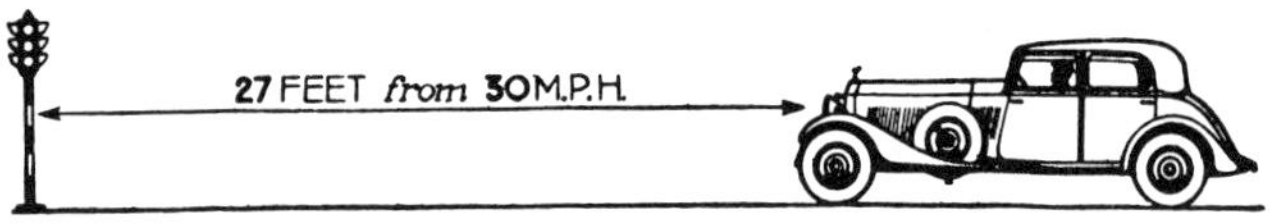
27 FEET from 30 M.P.H.

The gear change has a beautiful synchro-mesh mechanism, so that changing down to third is a matter only of taking out the clutch and moving the lever into third-speed slot, a change which can be effected extremely rapidly at any speed and as quickly back again into top as the lever can be moved. The other gears are normal.

Another point is the lightness and delicacy of the gear change, the pressure of two fingers being sufficient, whilst it is easy to forget up to fairly high speeds that third gear is in engagement, so silent, not just quiet-running, is it.

An important difference of the Continental model is the provision of Hartford shock absorbers for both axles in addition to the hydraulic shock absorbers, and on this particular car the Hartfords are adjustable from the driving compartment by the special Telecontrols, though that is an extra. Thus, there is available a wide range of spring damping between the softness appropriate to running in town and comparatively gently over first-class roads, and the greater hardness of springing required for fast running.

The steering is as light as any on a big car to-day, but absolutely accurate, and reaction from the front wheels is felt only at the highest speeds over a surface such as the worst parts of Brooklands track, and even then there is no discomfort if the wheel is held lightly, as it should be. There is strong but not excessive self-centring action, and to anyone accustomed to driving big cars the Continental Rolls-Royce does not seem unwieldy, or even very big, in fact, in spite of its wheelbase. This, no doubt, is due very largely to the second-to-none controls.

Throughout the car there is, of course, a host of exceptionally interesting features. The engine is wonderful in detail, one of many interesting things being the means adopted, by an oil-operated mechanism, to advance the coil and magneto ignitions—there are two sets of sparking plugs—at different rates up to a certain point. There is now a big air cleaner and silencer for the carburetter, which has made a perceptible difference in the silence of running. The governor is no longer used.

The D.W.S. four-wheel jacking system is fitted.

Coachwork is, of course, a matter of personal choice, but the car in question was fitted with a very pleasing Park Ward four-door saloon of owner-driver type, extremely comfortable in the seats, as would be expected, beautifully finished, and very completely equipped. A sliding roof is provided in this particular body.

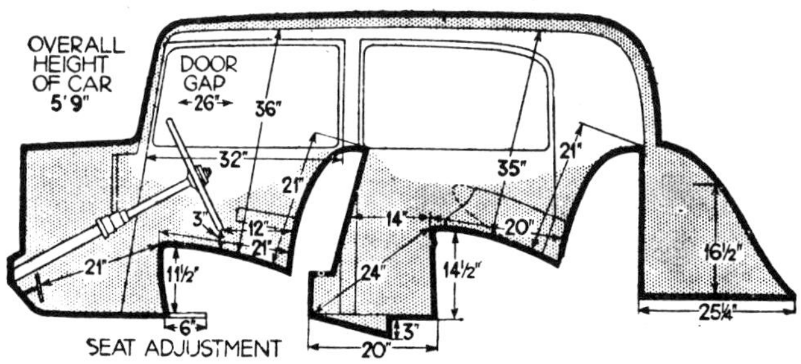
OVERALL HEIGHT OF CAR 5'9"
DOOR GAP 26"
36"
32"
21"
35"
21"
3"
12"
21"
14"
20"
21"
11½"
24"
14½"
16½"
6"
13"
20"
25¼"
SEAT ADJUSTMENT

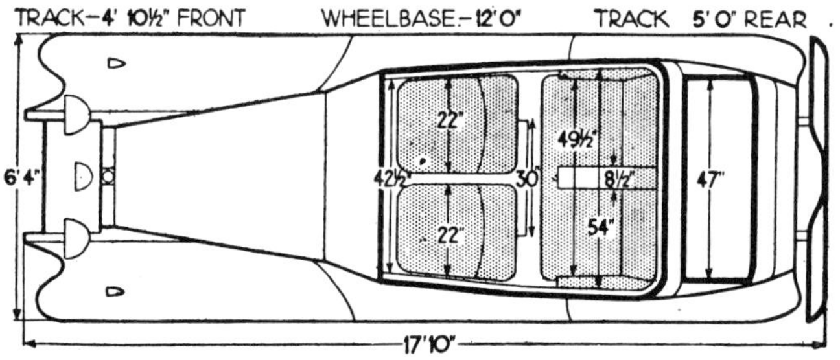
TRACK-4' 10½" FRONT
WHEELBASE-12'0"
TRACK 5'0" REAR
6'4"
22"
42½"
30"
22"
49½"
8½"
54"
47"
17'10"

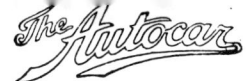

No. 950 (Post-War Series) 20-25 h.p. ROLLS-ROYCE TOURING SALOON

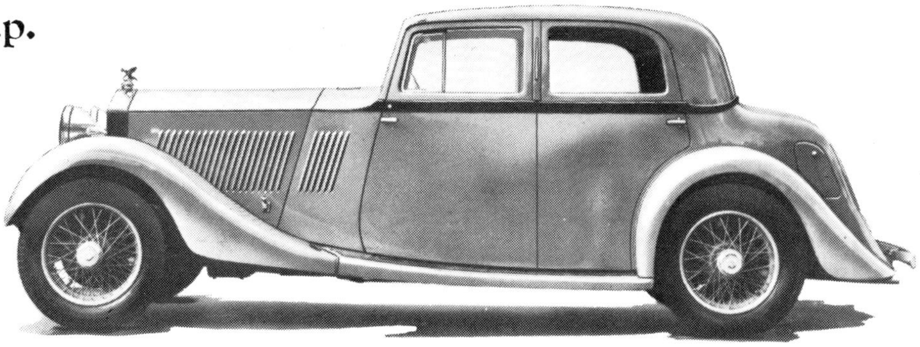

An Experience as Well as a Test : Sensitive Controls, and Top Gear Performance as Outstanding Impressions

TO drive a Rolls-Royce car any appreciable distance is an experience on its own; to drive one several hundred miles, as has been done on this occasion, is to begin properly to appreciate the hidden qualities. Even a short run will, of course, show the silent running that is expected, the ease of handling, and the car's wonderful responsiveness to its controls; but it is necessary to have experience of it in a variety of conditions if the reasons for the existence of what might be called a motoring halo around this name are to be understood.

A tendency whilst driving, and still more in looking back on the car, is to analyse impressions more than usually. It is only reasonable, also, to resist to some extent any inclination to expect too much, for the makers have set themselves so high a standard, which the world has adopted, that the slightest shortcoming, unnoticeable or excused in another car, is liable to be overemphasised.

It has to be borne in mind that the road performance forms but part of the ideals behind the car. It is the lasting powers resulting from the finest workmanship and materials, and the maintained performance built into the car, for which a considerable proportion of the price is paid.

Delicacy of the controls is one of the outstanding impressions retained. They are so far removed on the Rolls-Royce from being necessary evils that the whole handling of the machine is made a pleasure, and a driver strange to the car finds himself instantly at home in it. Second, if it is possible to classify impressions, is the car's top gear performance.

The greater part of the running can be achieved on top gear. This comes from, among other things, a highly developed carburation system in which there is no trace of flat-spot throughout the range; acceleration is regular and evenly responsive to the throttle pedal, and is deceptively good because of the engine's smoothness and quietness. Not infrequently one may glance at the speedometer to discover with surprise that the needle is around 50 m.p.h.—perhaps 5 miles an hour or more than was expected.

In town and up to 40 m.p.h. or so the effect is little short of that of gliding, without evidence of an engine. It seems impossible that as quiet and as easy effect can be maintained at the higher speeds, mechanism being what it is, however exceptionally made. Yet it is only towards 60 m.p.h. that any perceptible increase in the evidence of the engine's existence can be noticed, and even then it is purely a question of comparison with its behaviour at the lower speeds.

The sound of air around the car, especially when running into a head wind, is principally apparent, and it is particularly noted that at 70 m.p.h., or indeed at the maximum of which the car is capable, there is no real further increase in sound from the engine or from any other part of the mechanism.

The top gear abilities at the lowest speeds have been indicated, and even in these days of vast improvement in top-gear flexibility the Rolls-Royce still stands out on its own in that respect, because it shows no vibration, not even a tremor, when given full throttle from a crawling pace on top gear. It has fine power, too, on hills, and in its natural stride at about 50 m.p.h. accelerates extremely well up the main road kind of gradient, again without showing in any way that full throttle is being used.

Continuous improvement is, of course, the keynote of the makers' policy, and it will be seen from the figures given that this present example of the 20-25 h.p. car possesses a decidedly useful maximum speed in addition to its other virtues. To have a maximum of at least 76 m.p.h. in reserve, as was attained with a following wind but on the level on Brooklands track, is ample for the open road. The speedometer was within 1 m.p.h. of accuracy throughout the

DATA FOR THE DRIVER

20-25 H.P. ROLLS-ROYCE TOURING SALOON.

PRICE, with Hooper close-coupled four-five-seater saloon body, £1,658. Tax, £19 10s.

RATING : 25.3 h.p., six cylinders, o.h.v., 82 × 114 mm., 3,669 c.c.

WEIGHT, without passengers, 37 cwt. 3 qr. 20 lb.

TYRE SIZE : 31 × 6.00 in. on knock-off wire wheels.

LIGHTING SET : 12-volt ; automatic voltage control.

TANK CAPACITY : 18 gallons ; fuel consumption, 15-17 m.p.g.

TURNING CIRCLE : (L) 42ft. (R) 47ft. 5in. GROUND CLEARANCE : 8½in.

ACCELERATION.

Overall gear ratios	From steady m.p.h. of 10 to 30	20 to 40	30 to 50
4.55 to 1	10⅗ sec.	11⅗ sec.	12⅘ sec.
6.25 to 1	8 sec.	8⅗ sec.	11⅖ sec.
9.41 to 1	6⅗ sec.	—	—
15.04 to 1	—	—	—

From rest to 50 m.p.h. through gears, 21 sec.

From rest to 60 m.p.h. through gears, 31⅗ sec.

25 yards of 1 in 5 gradient from rest, 6 sec.

SPEED.

	m.p.h.
Mean maximum timed speed over ¼ mile	73.32
Best timed speed over ¼ mile ...	76.27
Speeds attainable on indirect gears—	
1st	18
2nd	25-32
3rd	44-53
Speed from rest up 1 in 5 Test Hill (on 1st and 2nd gears)	14.05

Performance figures of acceleration and maximum speed are the means of several runs in opposite directions.

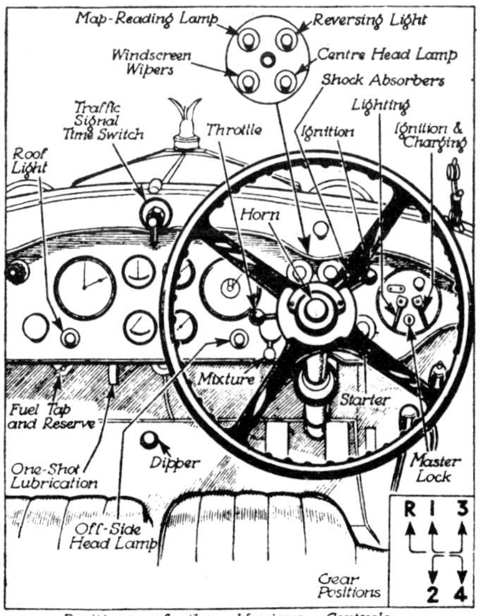

Map-Reading Lamp
Reversing Light
Windscreen Wipers
Centre Head Lamp
Shock Absorbers
Lighting
Traffic Signal Time Switch
Throttle
Ignition
Ignition & Charging
Roof Light
Horn
Mixture
Starter
Fuel Tap and Reserve
Dipper
Master Lock
One-Shot Lubrication
Off-Side Head Lamp
R 1 3
2 4
Gear Positions

Positions of the Various Controls

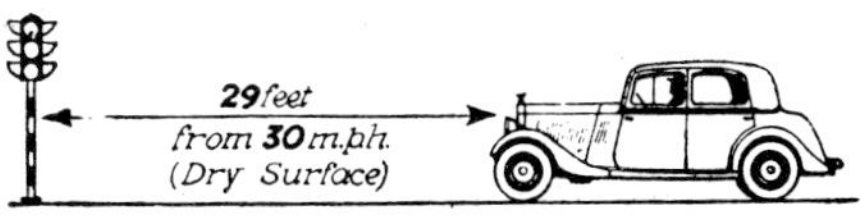

29 feet
from 30 m.p.h.
(Dry Surface)

range, besides which the needle is exceptionally steady at all speeds.

The explanation of the car's undeniable ability to make a very good average speed is the way in which speed is maintained almost irrespective of ordinary gradients and without need for worrying about road surfaces.

Linked up with this matter are the controls, to which impressions keep coming back in considering the car. Steering which has a fairly high ratio is used, and is wonderfully positive and accurate, so that the driver is able to place the car exactly as he wishes. There is no effort necessary to hold it at speed, and this, coupled with steady riding, creates a feeling of complete safety.

The steering has distinct caster action, and besides being finger-light at ordinary and high speeds is not at all heavy when the car has to be manœuvred, or in taking sharp turns. At times, on certain kinds of surfaces, but not at any particular speed, as far as can be discovered, there is a tremor transmitted back to the steering wheel, which however, never becomes pronounced.

Nor can the position of the steering wheel be forgotten. It is not of specially big diameter, nor spring-spoked, but is in just the right position for naturally handling the car and for that feeling of power over the steering which gives instant confidence. It is interesting also to notice that no dictates of fashion have been allowed to interfere with

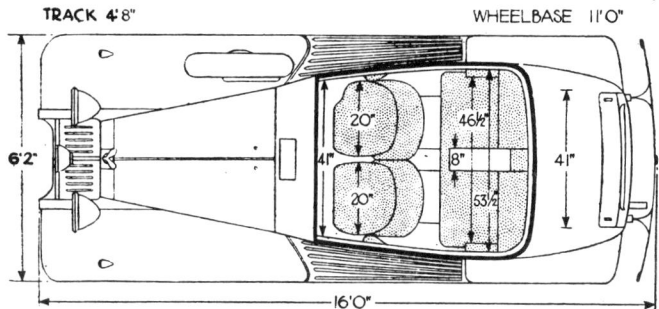

TRACK 4'8"   WHEELBASE 11'0"

driving vision. The edge of the *near-side* wing can be seen, and there is a full view of the right-hand wing. Yet it will not be denied that the body, a Hooper production, has beautiful lines.

Then there are the brakes, again not simply a means of retarding the car, but a sensitive mechanism to which an untold amount of care has been given. The system of operation, as is well known, is by a mechanical disc servo driven from the gear box. Pressure on the pedal, however, first applies the rear wheel shoes, at the same time engaging the servo, which comes in to assist the application principally of the front wheel shoes. It is possible to "feel" the brakes on, and even in making an emergency pull-up, when heavy-footedness is liable to occur, wheels are not locked, and somehow the occupants do not have any real impression of the brakes being applied.

The gear change has synchromesh mechanism for third and top, and the right-hand lever moves with little more than finger pressure, there being spring-loading so that it centres itself in the gate in neutral position. First gear is disregarded unless there should be any question of restarting on a steep gradient or climbing some unusually severe hill approached at low speed with a full load. An entirely smooth getaway is provided by second gear; yet the ratios, including also top gear, are fairly high.

The Rolls-Royce in a part of Surrey sometimes referred to as "Little Switzerland."

The clutch pedal needs very light pressure, and the changes through to third and into top, and down again into third, are as a knife cutting butter, if the analogy may be permitted. Down to second is a normal double-clutching change, and no serious noise results even if the engine speed is misjudged.

It appears to be best from the acceleration point of view if the change up to top is made at not more than about 40 m.p.h.—not because the engine easily becomes harsh on the lower gears, but because the pick-up on top is so ready and it seems to be the proper and intended manner of driving the car. Third cannot be distinguished by ear from top gear.

The system of suspension control from the steering wheel introduced comparatively recently by Rolls-Royce is now fitted to the 20-25 h.p. model, and consists of a finger-tip lever moving over a quadrant which gives eleven different positions, and which has the effect of increasing or reducing pressure in the hydraulic shock absorbers, so stiffening up or softening the springing to meet variations of load and surface conditions. Towards or at the maximum position there is a real firmness about the suspension, as well as added stability for fast cornering.

This particular car is one of the regular models, known as the special touring, or close-coupled, saloon, of which the basic price is £1,625, increased in the present instance by additional equipment. The chassis price is £1,050.

Ventilation and Luggage Accommodation

The seats, both in the support they give and in the softness of the upholstery, are luxuriously comfortable, and the interior equipment is notably complete. To give a detailed list is hardly necessary or feasible. A sliding roof which affords a large opening, and divided forward windows which provide ventilation without draught, may, however, be mentioned. The view in an externally mounted driving mirror was not comprehensive. In the tail there is a large luggage container, designed to take golf clubs also. Permanent four-wheel jacks are standard.

A great deal could be said about the engine, the beautiful finish, the neat arrangement of the auxiliaries, and the

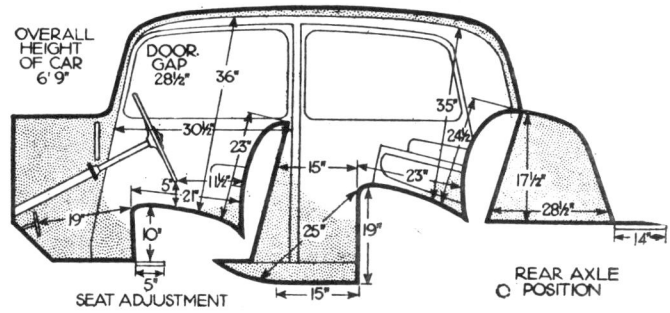

generally practical appearance, also about the electrical gear, much of which is of Rolls-Royce design and manufacture. It must suffice, however, to mention the stand-by magneto, ready timed, so that the car can run on magneto ignition in an emergency; and the fuse or distribution box, which carries a separate fuse for nearly every circuit.

It is easy, having driven the car, and having looked around it—in itself an absorbing occupation—to give full credit to a phrase adopted by the late Sir Henry Royce, "Whatever is rightly done, however humble, is noble."

Famous author
Sax Rohmer and his 1935
Rolls-Royce 20/25 h.p. with
Park Ward sedanca coachwork

The late King George VI,
when Duke of York, inspecting
a 20/25 h.p. chassis during a
visit to the Rolls-Royce works
at Derby in August 1931

Phantom III : New Tw

V Engine of 7.3 litres Capacity :
Suspension : Synchromesh on
Considerably More Room for

Royce, which was once called the "Legalimit."

The purpose of this new design is to make at one and the same time a power unit which is lighter and more compact than any other type of engine possessing the same capacity, the same reasoning which underlies also the adoption of **V** engines for nearly all the racing cars

(Left) Rolls-Royce independent suspension.

(Below) New compensating device at rear end of chassis to check any tendency to roll.

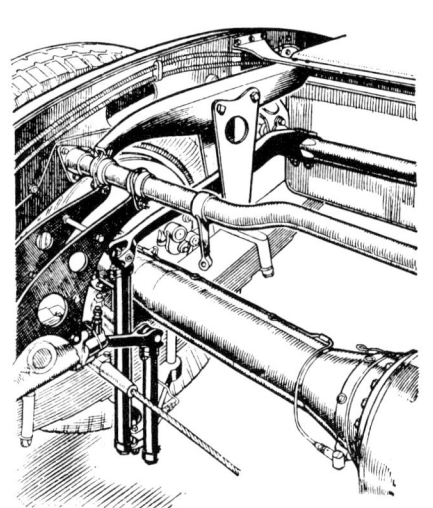

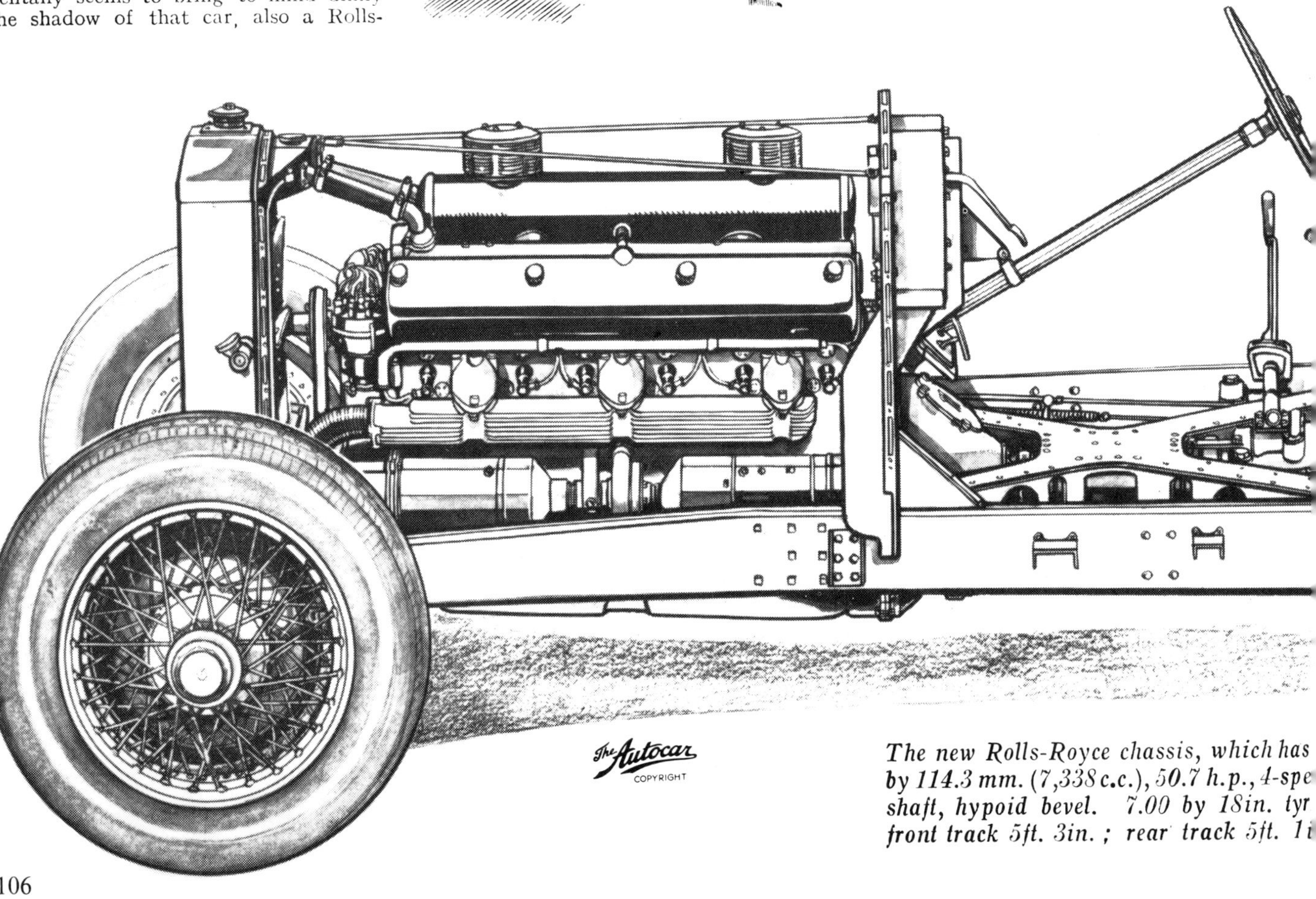

CERTAIN cars have acquired a prestige so great that any radical change in their design is a great moment for the industry as a whole. That is why the decision to give the latest model Rolls-Royce Phantom a twelve-cylinder V engine, and independent suspension for its front wheels, is so very interesting.

To-day, what used to be called complication is of no moment; the multiplication of parts, provided it ensures their better functioning, is definitely of advantage, since we are long past the days when every single component added to a chassis was regarded rather ruefully as an almost certain cause of future trouble. That explains the sudden adoption of the twelve-cylinder engine, a type with which Rolls-Royce, Ltd., is fully familiar owing to its experience with aeroplane engines, and which incidentally seems to bring to mind dimly the shadow of that car, also a Rolls-

being built at the moment. Since the reduction of weight is of the utmost importance, the engine has an aluminium alloy crank case, cylinder blocks, and cylinder heads, the pistons operating in cast-iron liners outwardly in contact with the water of the cooling system. Each cylinder has two valves, and the valves in both blocks are operated by a single camshaft through push-rods and rocking levers, the camshaft being in the centre of the V and gear driven, while aluminium bronze is used both for the valve seats and for the 14 mm. plug holes. All the main and big-end bearings are plain, are, of course, fed with oil under pressure, and are of very great size, and the crankshaft is in static and running balance.

There are four carburetters, with the usual piston controlling the choke size and controlled by the depression in the inlet pipe, the engine being started with the aid of what amounts to a separate carburetter altogether. The exhaust branches, heavily ribbed, pass along to the exhaust pipe at the front end of the cylinder blocks. There are two separate ignition systems, each consisting of a coil and distributor, while 14 mm. plugs have been adopted, and, incidentally, the major electrical components are manufactured by Rolls-Royce themselves.

The entire power unit is mounted on a flexible rubber bed, the disc clutch

The new Rolls-Royce chassis, which has by 114.3 mm. (7,338 c.c.), 50.7 h.p., 4-spe shaft, hypoid bevel. 7.00 by 18in. tyr front track 5ft. 3in. ; rear track 5ft. 1i

elve - Cylinder Rolls - Royce

*Independent Front Wheel
Three of Four Speeds : Price £1,850 :
oachwork on New Chassis*

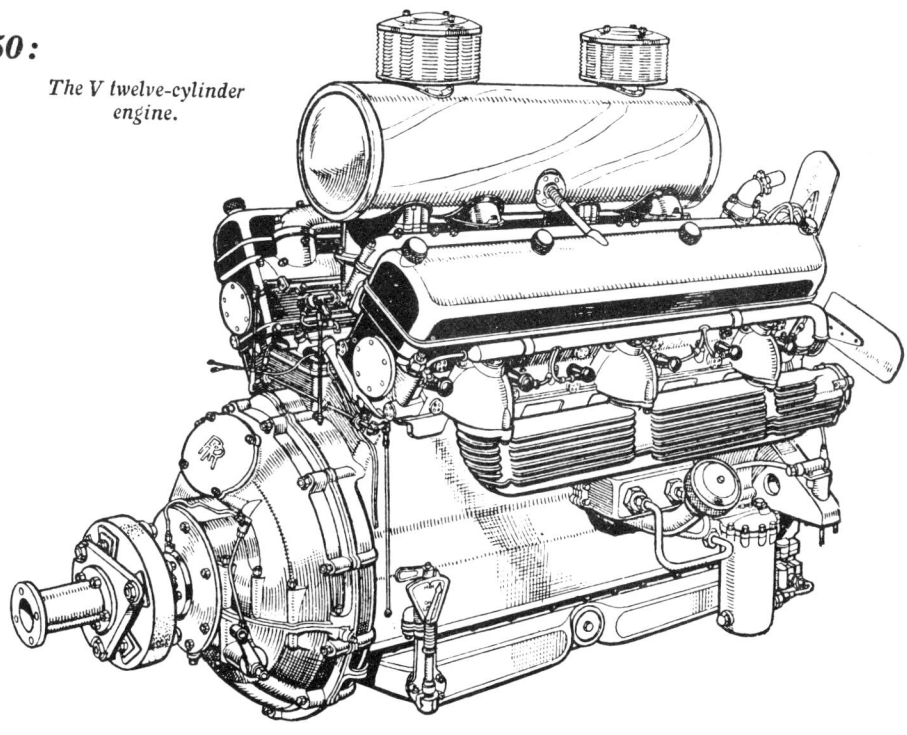

*The V twelve-cylinder
engine.*

housing being attached to the engine,
but the latter being separate from its
gear box. The water temperature control is ensured by a thermostat operating radiator shutters, and the radiator
itself is now slightly farther forward
than hitherto.

Another alteration of considerable
moment is that oil is circulated through
the valve tappets, which are in a sense
telescopic, and so maintain the valve
clearance automatically. The gear box,
which is in light alloy, is also mounted
on rubber, and now has synchromesh
mechanism for second, third and top,
while the reverse train has been made
almost silent in operation. The right-
hand gear lever is, of course, retained,
and at the rear of the gear box is the
housing for the disc-clutch type of servo
motor which, under the control of the
brake pedal, applies the brakes on all
four wheels.

Normal Rear Suspension

From the gear box the drive passes
through a tubular propeller-shaft with
two needle bearing universal joints. The
rear axle, which has a hypoid bevel,
is fully floating, the load from the wheels
being taken direct to the axle casing,
and the torque and drive through half-
elliptic springs of ordinary type backed
by the hydraulic Rolls-Royce shock absorber, which is certainly one of the best
of its kind ever produced, and which can
be regulated at will by the driver from
his seat.

In addition, there is also a device to
check any tendency for the body to roll,
despite the fact that the rear suspension
allows a soft and easy vertical movement in order to absorb any road shocks.
This anti-rolling device consists of a torsion bar set across the frame and coupled
by links and arms to each end of the
rear axle.

Forward, each front wheel is held between a pair of wishbone brackets, and,
therefore, is entirely independent of its
fellow, each being allowed to move without affecting the other, as there is no
tie rod. There are two fore-and-aft rods
from the steering gear running at an
angle, one to each wheel.

Instead of a half-elliptic spring a coil
spring is used to resist the movement of
the wishbone, and is carried horizontally
in a casing full of oil, while the arrangement of the brake actuation is such that
rods in tension running athwart the
frame operate the brake shoes. The
movement of the wishbones is guarded,
of course, by stops, and there is no alteration to the track when the front wheels

move up or down, nor do the wheels
lie over while on a curve. The adoption of independent suspension has
changed the appearance of the front of
the car considerably, and the change is
accentuated, perhaps, because the radiator is slightly farther forward.

Greater stiffness has been added to the
frame by making the side members of
box section, the inner side consisting of
a plate welded in position, and in places
rather deeper than the ordinary frame
web. The steering gear is still worm
and sector, and is now arranged so that
access to the driving seat is considerably
easier.

In this latest chassis there is considerably more room for the coachwork,

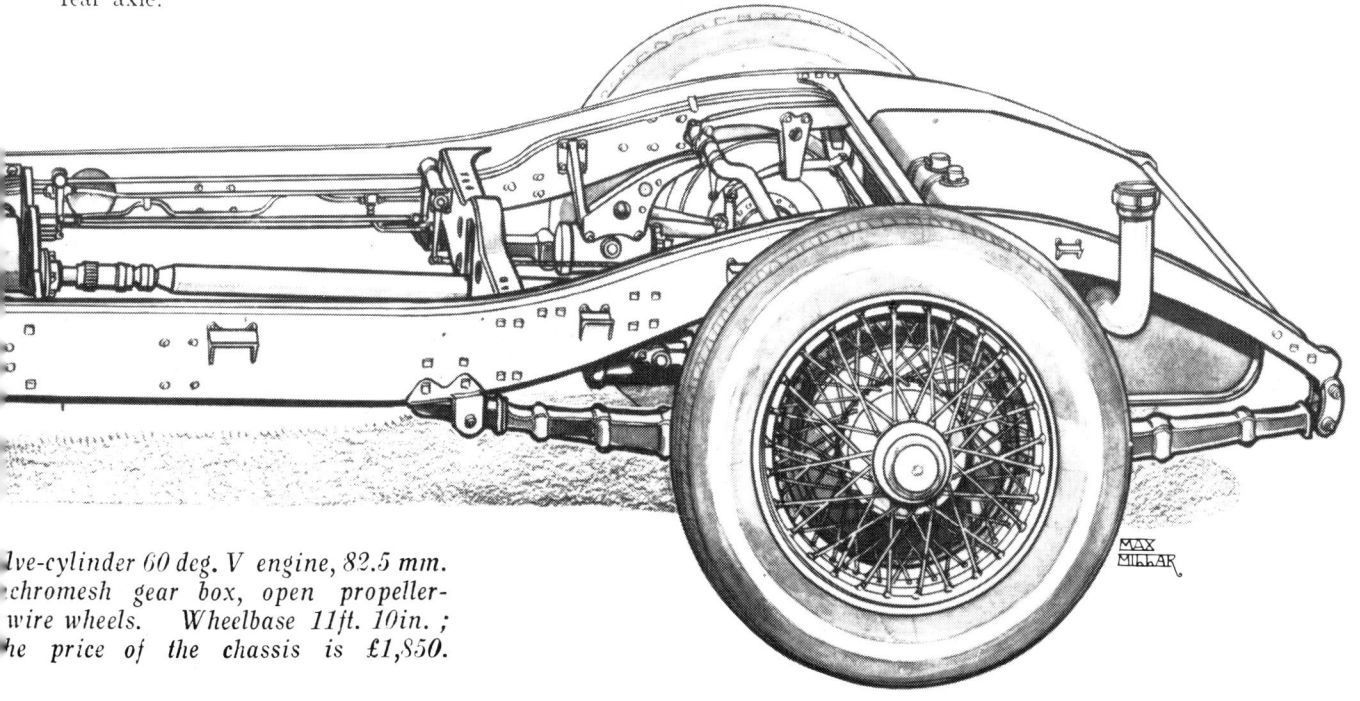

*lve-cylinder 60 deg. V engine, 82.5 mm.
chromesh gear box, open propeller-
wire wheels. Wheelbase 11ft. 10in. ;
he price of the chassis is £1,850.*

partly because of the design of the frame, partly because the power unit is more compact, and the body is better isolated as regards both noise and any possible engine fumes. The track is wider in front than it is at the rear.

As usual, the detail work is extraordinarily thorough, down even to the smallest bracket or lever, and the whole

of the control is beautifully laid out to give a regular effect, and to avoid any lost motion.

Fuel is supplied to the carburetters from the thirty-three-gallon tank at the rear by a splendidly made compound electric pump, the air cleaner and silencer for the carburetters is less unsightly than usual, the fuse boxes, clips

for the pipe lines, and even the smallest detail of the central chassis lubrication system all look as though they have received as much attention as any other component of the engine or transmission, and it certainly appears as though the new machine has gained appreciably in performance, while retaining the smoothness of its predecessors.

Coachwork on Phantom IIIs. Left: 1937 Park Ward sedanca de ville finished in black and ivory and fitted with electrically-operated division. Below: 1937 Barker limousine de ville with their patent sliding de ville extension and metal screen pillars. Below left: 1936 James Young saloon with division built for A. H. Pass of Pass and Joyce Ltd

Below: Rear compartment of the Park Ward sedanca.
Right: Swivelling arm chair occasional seats in a 1937 Rippon limousine

Jack Barclay (left) hands over a H. J. Mulliner sports limousine to dance band leader Roy Fox and Mrs Fox in October 1937

The AUTOCAR ROAD TESTS

No. 1,060
40-50 h.p.
ROLLS-ROYCE
PHANTOM III
LIMOUSINE

The Phantom III seven-seater limousine on the road during the test.

Road Travel In Its Most Advanced and Refined Form Provided by the New Twelve-cylinder Model

SOME cars have to fight their way to fame; others are born to it, because of the reputation of their predecessors and the vast store of knowledge and experience possessed by their builders. Of this noble order is the twelve-cylinder Rolls-Royce Phantom III, which, since it was publicly announced a year ago, has aroused tremendous interest, both academic and practical.

For Rolls-Royce new models are infrequent, and even before the car actually appeared it was known that it must represent years of research and experiment on the part of a firm whose engineers are held in the highest repute the world over.

Phantom II, Phantom I, the old Silver Ghost, have all gone before and were wonderful cars in their time; the V twelve-cylinder Phantom III, Derby's most recent product, puts even these famous prototypes into the background. No Rolls-Royce model has ever failed to charm those trying it, as much for the manner of its performance as for the performance itself. Here, in the Phantom III, true advance has been made, and that is a very striking thing when one remembers the Rolls-Royce models of the past. The V twelve-cylinder is even quieter than its forbears; undoubtedly it is still more flexible on top gear; certainly also it has a wider range of performance of the kind that counts in modern road conditions, its acceleration being, to say the least, thrilling.

Equally, it shows a great gain in riding comfort, allied in an extraordinary degree with stability on the road at all speeds. Never in official state-

ments of the Rolls-Royce Company will any reference be found to the maximum speeds of which their cars are capable; they are built primarily as carriages, with performance by no means a secondary consideration but developed alongside all the features of refinement for which these cars are famous. Thus, in fact, they are as fast as road conditions allow, and the Phantom III in particular has an amazing performance, even from the angle of carefully measured figures. It is most impressive that such a big car as this, with a capacious body that can only be likened to a carriage, should be capable of travelling at over 90 miles an hour if desired, yet retain in the uttermost degree the virtues of flexibility, silence, ease of handling and the maximum of road comfort as at present understood. By no means every user of a Rolls-Royce car wishes ever to travel at speeds of this order, and one would scarcely guess its great possibilities whilst gliding through the streets of a city on top gear.

Perhaps most of all one is impressed by the easy way in which the Phantom III handles. There is no sense of great bulk; the car can be put just where one wishes on the road with an accuracy and delicacy of steering that prove how painstaking has been the design. No conscious effort of hand or foot is needed, and very soon a stranger to it feels at home in the car. This is tantamount to saying that not only do the controls perform their work precisely and lightly, but that they are admirably arranged as to position.

On top gear the twelve-cylinder

DATA FOR THE DRIVER

40-50 H.P. ROLLS-ROYCE PHANTOM III LIMOUSINE.

PRICE, with Pullman limousine body, £2,600 (chassis, £1,850). Tax, £38 5s.
RATING : 50.64 h.p., twelve cylinders, o.h.v., 82.5 × 114 mm., 7,340 c.c.
WEIGHT, without passengers, 51 cwt. 2 qr. 13 lb.
LB. (WEIGHT) PER C.C. : 0.79.
TYRE SIZE : 7.00 × 18in. on centre-lock wire wheels.
LIGHTING SET : 12-volt. Automatic voltage control.
TANK CAPACITY : 33 gallons ; fuel consumption, 10 m.p.g. (approx.).
TURNING CIRCLE : (L. and R.) 48ft. GROUND CLEARANCE : 9in.

ACCELERATION				SPEED	
Overall gear ratios	From steady m.p.h. of				m.p.h.
	10 to 30	20 to 40	30 to 50	Mean maximum timed speed over ¼ mile	86.96
4.25 to 1	7.4 sec.	7.7 sec.	8.2 sec.		
5.59 to 1	5.7 sec.	6.3 sec.	6.6 sec.	Best timed speed over ¼ mile ...	91.84
8.45 to 1	4.2 sec.	5.0 sec.	—		
12.75 to 1	—	—	—	Speeds attainable on indirect gears :—	
From rest to 30 m.p.h. through gears, 5.5 sec.				1st	—
From rest to 50 m.p.h. through gears, 12.6 sec.				2nd	44
From rest to 60 m.p.h. through gears, 16.8 sec.				3rd	73
From rest to 70 m.p.h. through gears, 24.4 sec.				Speed from rest up 1 in 5 Test Hill (on 2nd gear)	20.19
25 yards of 1 in 5 gradient from rest, 4.4 sec.					

Performance figures for acceleration and maximum speed are the means of several runs in opposite directions.

(Left) One of the ignition distributors and one set of six sparking plugs can be seen, also the single carburetter with air cleaner and intake silencer, and, at the rear, the twin electric petrol pumps, fuse box, and wheel spanner (clamped to the steering column). (Right) Part of the instrument board and minor controls.

engine will pull the car at the barest crawl, about 3 m.p.h. Then the throttle pedal can be put straight down, there is a smooth surge of power, and one is aware of no more than that the car is rapidly gaining speed, the speedometer needle moving quickly round its dial. At first it is necessary to refer quite frequently to the instrument to verify the actual speed, for there is no indication of increased effort at 70 as compared with 50 m.p.h., for example. The ease with which this car will run up to high speeds on the open road has to be experienced to be believed, though the test figures give some idea, and it is a remarkable achievement when the whole effortless character of the car's behaviour is taken into consideration.

Too much stress cannot be laid upon the point that this is a vehicle equally capable of satisfying the demands of those who wish to travel comparatively slowly in the greatest possible comfort and of those who choose to drive

The Park Ward seven-seater Pullman limousine.

or be driven at express train speeds where conditions permit. The simile of railway travel seems particularly appropriate, as a matter of fact, for seldom is more motion experienced than might be found in a first-class railway carriage. Also, so entirely unobtrusive is the whole mechanism that passengers not in sight of the speedometer when the car is travelling fast are invariably surprised to learn the figure. Even with the needle on the 80 mark a driver can talk naturally to the passengers and feel no sense of stress. This state of affairs is due not only to the self-effacing running of the car as a whole, but also to the excep-

tional comfort and feeling of safety and stability induced by the suspension, which it will be remembered is independent for the front wheels.

A driver's peace of mind is assured by firm, accurate steering, which is moderately geared, needing three turns from lock to lock, and by the mechanical servo-operated brakes, which achieve prodigies of retardation. In principle these follow the lines of previous Rolls-Royce braking systems, but are, of course, designed to suit the particular needs of the Phantom III. Initial application of the pedal applies the rear wheel shoes and brings the servo motor into engagement, this being driven from the side of the gear box. The servo motor then applies the front brakes and assists the driver's physical application of the rear brakes. It is a system which shows up to extraordinary advantage. A smooth but utterly sure power grips the car, as it were, from high speeds, and pulls the velocity down, yet the driver is scarcely conscious of having applied the brakes. There is no fierceness, no snatch. The actual measured reading obtainable from the customary test speed is no gauge with this car of the phenomenally good braking power that is available higher in the range; although at lower speeds the servo motor has proportionally less effect, it is found in driving at traffic rates that the car can be controlled exactly as one wishes, without disturbing passengers.

Already the comfort and the stability afforded by the suspension have been mentioned. Those to whom a particular method of driving appeals can

A Barker-bodied touring limousine Phantom III which was also driven.

take this big machine round corners in a manner regarded as an attribute of a sports car, for there is hardly a trace of swaying motion. The special Rolls-Royce system of independent front wheel springing—embodying a coil spring at each side, totally enclosed in an oil-filled chamber, and operating against the action of hydraulic dampers which automatically adjust their effect in accordance with road speed—affords a most remarkable combination of comfort and road holding.

At the centre of the steering wheel is a control allowing the driver to regulate the degree of damping applied by the shock absorbers, this working over a range of positions between hard and soft to suit various conditions. The efficacy of this control in giving maximum comfort for low-speed work and the full damping effect for fast running is very definite. Also there are further automatic provisions in the direction of securing stability, consisting broadly of a torsional stabilising bar placed across the rear of the frame and connected to the long rear half-elliptic springs.

Two examples of the Phantom III were tried, one being a touring limousine with Barker coachwork, an owner-driver model, priced at £2,615, the other a chauffeur-driven style of seven-seater Pullman limousine by Park Ward. These cars were found to be capable of an identical top speed. There were differences in weight, the Pullman limousine scaling some 51½ cwt., as against 53 cwt. for the touring limousine, unladen in both cases, but with petrol tanks nearly full. It was the Pullman limousine that was principally driven on the road. Speedometers were checked on both cars, and the instrument on the touring limousine was closer to accuracy than on the other car, showing an error on the high side of 1.5 m.p.h. at 30 and of 2.8 m.p.h. at 60, recording a highest reading of 96 when the maximum speed was being timed by stop-watch.

A point worthy of mention is that on a familiar open road journey, in darkness and on wet surfaces, a greater distance was covered in one hour than has yet been recorded in *The Autocar* Tests over this particular run, and that without employing the maximum speed of the car or causing passengers to become apprehensive.

Interior of the touring limousine, which has a disappearing partition behind the driving seat, folding tables, and special soft floor cushions.

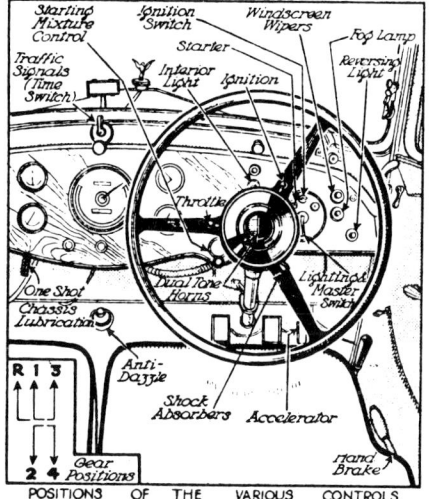

POSITIONS OF THE VARIOUS CONTROLS

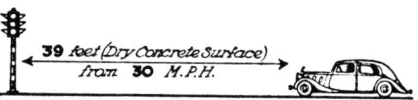

39 feet (Dry Concrete Surface) from 30 M.P.H.

The comfort of riding for the rear passengers is, indeed, quite outstanding.

Excellent driving vision, always a notable Rolls-Royce feature, has been retained, the occupants sitting sensibly high with a good view outwards, and the driver can even see the near-side wing lamp. On this Phantom III there is a change in the placing of the gear and brake levers, which remain, of course, on the right-hand side but are situated further back, in a still more convenient position, where they allow unimpeded entry and exit through the right-hand door, the seat cushion being cut away to accommodate these controls. The hand-brake lever is of cranked shape, and is pulled vertically upwards to the "on" position. Also, there is synchromesh mechanism on second gear as well as on third and top; thus the whole gear change is made easy, for except on a really steep hill the car is started from rest on second, and first gear is disregarded. Thus no data were taken for first gear. Silent running on the gears is another characteristic feature; third, indeed, is indistinguishable from top.

Although there are now standardised body styles on Rolls-Royce chassis, so much variation is possible to meet personal preferences that it is not really useful to describe a particular type in detail. Unusual comfort of upholstery, freedom of movement, and luxury of equipment are expected and unquestionably found. There is one-shot chassis lubrication controlled by a foot-operated lever in the driving compartment.

Naturally there is a wealth of interest in the engine, on which a typically high finish is at once noticeable. The twelve cylinders have dual ignition, with twenty-four sparking plugs, all being used together in the ordinary way. The ignition switch permits either one set of twelve or the other (inlet or exhaust) to be switched in separately for testing purposes. There are two ignition coils and two distributors, each with a twin make and break. Hydraulically operated jacks are fitted, the actuating pump and control valves for the front and rear jacks being found beneath the floor of the front compartment.

Somewhere is an ultimate in the highest expression of road travel comfort and performance, and the Phantom III is beyond question the nearest approach to it as yet.

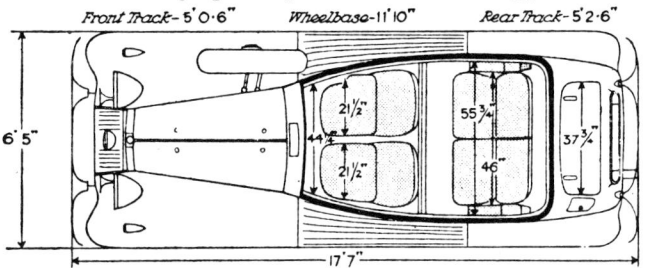

Front Track—5' 0.6"   Wheelbase—11' 10"   Rear Track—5' 2.6"

Seating dimensions are measured with cushions and squabs uncompressed (these apply to the Barker touring limousine).

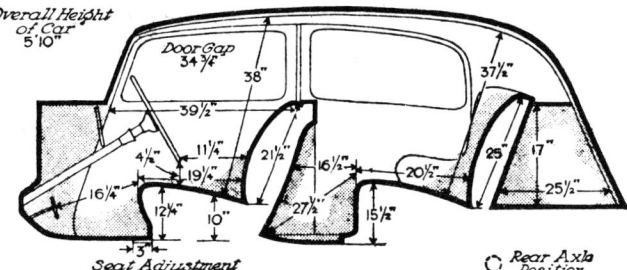

Overall Height of Car 5' 10"

Seat Adjustment   Rear Axle Position

A Phantom

A magnificent Northumberland landscape in the Cheviots country, near Otterburn, seems somehow exactly to set off the majestic light-coloured Rolls-Royce Phantom III.

OF all the points upon which a car is judged, those counting highest are the manner in which the occupants are conveyed upon their journeys and the probability of its continuing to serve an owner satisfactorily. When the car under consideration is priced in the realms of £2,500, and a Rolls-Royce, the best way of forming due opinion on the first of these factors is to take it over a really long journey. As to the second, the reputation of the car is in this instance sufficient evidence.

A twelve-cylinder Phantom III has been put through a searching test from the point of view of displaying ease and comfort of travelling, and consistency of behaviour. In a matter of thirty-seven hours, including a night's rest and sundry stops on the way, it covered more than 700 miles, without in any way providing a test of personal endurance—far from it, indeed, for this machine proves kind to driver and passengers on such a journey. It is a pleasure to have it in one's possession and be faced with a long run over main roads. One feels that there is a certainty of arriving at the destination, and the method of travelling is such as to cause the miles to pass unnoticed.

It is nothing for the Phantom III to average 46 m.p.h. over as much as 475 miles, which was the second day's journey during this test, from Northumberland back to London, by a detour. Yet that run included comparatively slow sections, and crossing London finally. The figure in question is a definite calculation from dividing mileage by running time, and not an approximation. When worked out, it surprised the occupants of the car, including the driver.

The way in which the car sweeps along at high speed with practically nothing to show that mechanism is working, and the absence of any pronounced movement, raise Rolls-Royce motoring far above the ordinary. In spite of the fact that, with three up and the petrol tank full, the weight is not far short of 3 tons (53 cwt. 1 qr. 8 lb. unladen), there is the acceleration of a sports machine for

An idea of the grouping of the instruments and minor controls is given, and also some impression of the beautiful interior finish of the Barker body.

the driver to employ; but he is not conscious by ear of the power that the twelve-cylinder engine is putting forth.

If there is one word which can describe the Rolls-Royce it is "velvet." That is the touch possessed by the engine, the steering, the brakes, and the gear change, in fact by every one of the controls, major or minor. Though the car gathers way really rapidly, and soars easily into the seventies and eighties, it is scarcely believable that the ordinary processes are going on within it.

Then, at the other end of the scale, the car has extraordinary flexibility on top gear. It can keep moving perfectly smoothly on top gear even in slow traffic, and then pull away quickly without a trace of vibration or pinking, as though this were the natural way to handle the car. Yet the ignition advance and retard lever on the steering wheel can be left at the advanced position all the time. The actual minimum on top gear is a 5 m.p.h. quick walking pace.

It is not only a big car with a fine performance. After

in the North

some time has been spent in it, one comes to realise a little of the painstaking work of those responsible in developing every item. Study of the fine instruction manual on the car can tell a great deal about it. From this may be appreciated in some measure the lengths to which the Derby engineers go in making as nearly perfect an example of motor car as long experience, the best materials, and fine workmanship can secure. An example revealed of unseen but important details is the surprising number of oil filters the engine possesses to ensure a clean supply.

As to handling, the Phantom does not feel unwieldy, for there is a balance about it, and the whole control is light. Naturally, it occupies more space on the road than a smaller car, but once acquaintance with it is gained it can be taken accurately through a space only just sufficiently wide, and proves comparatively easy to manoeuvre. The steering lock is good in relation to the wheelbase, and the steering moves easily even with hardly any forward or backward movement of the car itself to assist. A trace of front-wheel

speed of the big car in a fashion that surprises anyone who has not previously experienced this braking system. Yet, as applies to all the other actions, it is a soft effect, free from all trace of fierceness unless the driver "stamps" hurriedly on the pedal, which is needless. If he should, the front brakes—operated by the servo—can be heard to go on, and sometimes, if on a corner at the time, there is a pull on the steering. Braking remains entirely effective even if the engine is not running and the gear lever is in neutral, and the servo operates on reverse, too.

Riding comfort is one of the most important points. The Phantom III has independent front wheel suspension by its own system. For a big and supremely comfortable car this gives a remarkable degree of road-holding. Corners can be rounded without sway or any unpleasant tendency as fast as most drivers ever wish, signs of side roll being evident only if extreme methods are employed.

A passenger who travels in many cars finds that the back seat gives comfort equivalent to that usually associated with a good front seat, both in the freedom from

One of the Latest Examples of the Twelve-cylinder Rolls-Royce Provides De Luxe Motoring on a Northumbrian Test Run of 700 Miles in Two Days

A pleasure to behold and a very wonderful example of advanced automobile engineering, the V twelve-cylinder engine, from the near side.

reaction is felt through the steering at times, but this never amounts to actual kick-back, nor develops at the highest speeds. It is soft but not springy steering, and has exactly the right amount of caster return action, bringing the wheel firmly but gently back through the fingers after a corner. Three turns are needed from lock to lock.

A light application of the brake pedal energises the Rolls-Royce mechanical servo, and brings down the

reaction from the road wheels and as regards minimum disturbance during cornering. There is automatic regulation of the hydraulic shock absorbers, a pump driven from the gear box building up damping pressure as the speed rises. But a hand control on the steering wheel overrides this and allows full damping to be obtained at once if wanted, or the softest effect to be restored for running through a town or over a section of bad surface.

With its flexible, powerful engine, this is a close approach to the single-speed car, and a driver realises that he has covered many, many miles without touching the gear lever. On the other hand, the gear change is a pleasure to handle. The very best kind of synchromesh is provided on second, third and top, and as first gear is never used except for starting on a considerable gradient, it is thus for practical purposes an entirely synchromesh change.

Provided that the movement is not unduly hurried, the upward changes go through beautifully, the lever almost falling into the notches, and similarly downward with suitable adjustment of engine speed. Changes in ratio, especially to third, can be imperceptible to passengers. There is no trace of gear noise from either second or third, and the driver may easily forget that third is engaged. Third gives 65 to 70 m.p.h. comfortably, and second over 40 m.p.h, with more in reserve in both cases.

Both the gear and the hand-brake levers are set in a space cut away, as it were, from the front of the seat cushion. Although in a position where the right hand naturally "finds" them, they do not interfere at all with the driver's use of the off-side door.

Certain information about the measured acceleration of the car is interesting. It shows up strikingly well on top gear, going from 10 to 30 m.p.h. in 7.1 sec., and from 30 to 50 in 7.9 sec., or perhaps still more impressively,

can start from rest on top gear and reach 50 m.p.h. in 19.3 sec. If the gears are used normally in getting away, starting on second in the Rolls-Royce manner, and not forcing the gear change, 50 m.p.h. is attained in 14.1 sec., and 60 m.p.h. in 18.5 sec., as mean figures.

On third 30 m.p.h. can be reached from 10 m.p.h. in 5.5 sec., or the same range of acceleration be achieved on second gear in the very short time of 3.9 sec. From 30 to 50 m.p.h. on third takes 6.3 sec. Such acceleration, rapid though it is, can be used without the engine becoming in the least harsh. Top gear ratio is 4.25 to 1, third 5.59, second 8.44, and first 12.75 to 1.

It is a tribute to the qualities of the Phantom as a whole that in obtaining high average speeds the use of the maximum is not necessary. A highest speedometer reading of 91 was reached on one of the fastest stretches of the Great North Road, above Boroughbridge; the actual maximum was discovered to be above 92 m.p.h. by stop-watch, the speedometer showing 95-96. At 70 the instrument proved to be 3.5 m.p.h. fast, at 50 2.6, and at 30 1.9 m.p.h.

Beautiful Detail Work

In the detail work the Rolls-Royce is a joy to anyone taking even the most superficial interest in the mechanical side of cars. The engine is highly finished, whilst the attention paid to smaller matters is clearly apparent. Attached to the forward face of the bulkhead, under the bonnet, is a very large fuse box which contains a multiplicity of fuses guarding each electrical circuit. Here also is the fluid reservoir for the four-wheel hydraulic jacking system, and the oil container for the centralised chassis lubrication, operated by a lever in the driving compartment.

Engine oil level is shown by a pointer, near which is a spring-loaded lever that enables the sump to be drained without groping beneath the car. The oil filler is large and accessible, and the water system is virtually sealed—that is, the filler cap under the bonnet is tightened home with a spanner—for hardly any water is used, as the addition of less than a pint after 700 miles made evident. Thermostatically operated radiator shutters maintain temperature for a long while when the car is left standing.

Rolls-Royce Electrical Equipment

There are twenty-four sparking plugs in all; to reach those on the inside of the V between the two banks of cylinders a special long spanner is provided in the tool kit. The ignition switch allows either set to be used independently for testing purposes. The electric petrol pumps are also duplicated and a testing switch is again provided. Dynamo, starter, and ignition items—in fact the whole electrical installation except battery, leads, sparking plugs and lamps—are of Rolls-Royce manufacture, as for many years past. The switch-box on the instrument board, embodying the ignition and lighting controls, incorporates a master lock governing all circuits. This renders the entire system "dead" at night, or for parking leaves only the side and tail lamps in circuit.

Another point that endears the car to one is its certainty of starting from cold first thing in the morning, with the mixture lever set to "start" and the hand throttle half

open, and the engine will pull at once. On the long journey mentioned, about 10 m.p.g. was averaged, and a 300-mile range without filling is given, since the tank holds thirty-three gallons of petrol. There is no reserve tap, but when the four-gallon mark is reached a green reminder light on the instrument board is switched on automatically.

This particular car is the touring saloon with division, priced at £2,675, partaking of both an ordinary saloon and a limousine, and thus suitable for either owner or chauffeur driving. The driver's section of the front seat is adjustable fore and aft and in the angle of the back rest, and the partition is almost invisible when lowered. The seat adjustment did not allow an ideal close-up position, as would be possible with entirely separate seats, to be obtained by an average-height driver. Nor was the elbow-rest mounted on the driver's door really convenient.

Ventilation Points

The upholstery is as comfortable as it might be expected to be. The windows of the front compartment in this particular design of body are very deep as well as wide, and there is no special provision for ventilation without draught by means of a partially opened window, a point which one would have imagined would have received attention. Also, the sliding roof is of so large an area that with it fully open considerable wind noise is caused, this being particularly noticeable on a car that is so quiet mechanically.

A practical point is an electrically operated rear window blind, controlled by an instrument-board switch, which moves quickly. This style of body is normally fitted with an electric motor to raise and lower the division also, but this particular car did not have that item of equipment. The beam from the special Lucas head lamps is all that could be wished for, giving both breadth and length of illumination suitable to the car's speed. Twin wind horns produce pleasing soft notes for town use, a stronger note for the open road.

No car attains quite the same quiet impressiveness of appearance. The Rolls-Royce radiator is masterly in its dignity and sets off the whole machine, almost irrespective of the particular style of body it may carry. It is a custom to bestow bouquets upon this car, and sincerity may even be doubted by some; but it does unquestionably deserve them.

H. S. L.

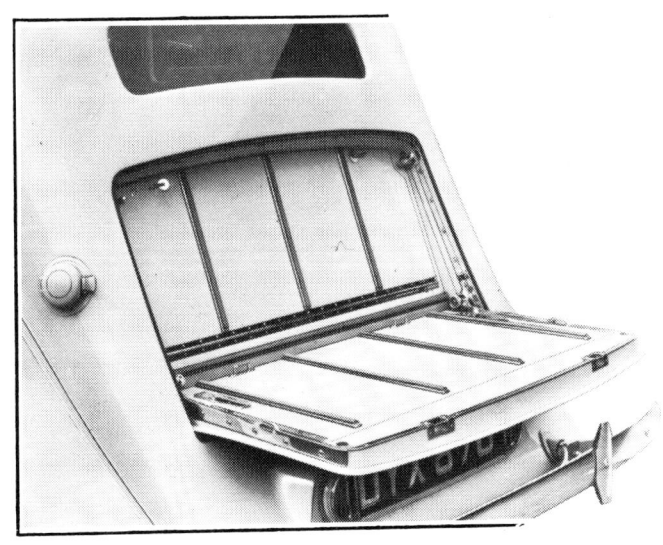

An inner lid to the luggage compartment acts as a seal, and protects baggage carried inside if the main lid is left open as a platform for large trunks.

A 1936 Rolls-Royce Phantom III with Barker body for HRH The Duke of Kent

New Cars Described —

INDEPENDENT FRONT WHEEL SUSPENSION FOR

New Rolls-Royce Wraith

This is the 25-30 h.p. Rolls-Royce Wraith in four-door Special Saloon form, priced at £1,845.

AS is well known, it is not the practice of the Rolls-Royce Company necessarily to introduce improvements in their cars at any set time of year, the process of "refining refinement" going on continuously wherever and whenever possible in the existing remarkably highly developed designs.

There are at the moment, however, decidedly interesting alterations to announce in the smaller of the two cars, the 25-30 h.p. model, which in future is to be known as the Wraith, thus applying to it a designation in keeping with the Phantom name used for the bigger model and the former Silver Ghost.

Most important among these improvements is the adoption on the Wraith of independent front wheel suspension. The system is similar in principle to that used on the 40-50 h.p. Phantom III ever since that model was produced, and consists of horizontal coil springs enclosed in casings which form both a housing for them and the body of the hydraulic shock absorbers. The stub axles, and in turn the wheels, are carried by four radius arms set at a trailing angle. The rear springs are, as before, half-elliptics enclosed in leather gaiters and lubricated from the centralised system. Stability is assisted by the use of a torsion rod coupling between the shock-absorber arms.

Also, there are changes in the steering mechanism, the result of which is to make the car lighter to control. The combination of the independent front wheel springing and the altered steering is to give a much improved "feel" to the machine, making it seem more definitely under control, yet still lighter to handle. The movement which formerly was transmitted to the steering wheel over certain kinds of road surface has been eliminated, and, as a trial of the latest model has indicated, it has become an even more delightful car to drive.

Performance

Although measured figures were not recorded, the impression is received that the performance is almost exactly the same as from the previous 25-30 h.p. model. Handling and riding are the important features that have come in for improvement.

Riding comfort has been increased out of all knowledge by the new suspension, to which have also been added larger-section tyres, now of 6.50in. There is a virtually complete absence of even slight pitching tendency, and the car corners steadily. A passenger in the back seat finds that he can rest his head against the squab while travelling fast without being jarred. Excellent support is afforded by the upholstery.

An increased degree of quietness has been achieved in the gear box, and those who know Rolls-Royce cars will realise that this means a great deal. Also, this smaller model now has synchromesh mechanism on second gear of the four-speed box, as well as on third and top.

Not only is the new gear change thoroughly convenient as regards the placing of the lever, but it is remarkably easy and light to move. Only finger-pressure on the lever is necessary for any change, and the gears slide in without any noticeable resistance being offered. It is impossible to distinguish between second, third or top as regards any gear noise.

Another important point is that the right-hand gear and hand-brake levers have been rearranged so that both are alongside the driving seat cushion and thus out of the way of the door, giving completely free entrance through the driver's door, whilst retaining the now extremely rare feature of right-hand control.

Changes have been made in the system of engine suspension in the frame still further to reduce any transmission of engine vibration or movement of any kind to the occupants of the car. At the front the engine is now supported by a triangular-shaped, arched member, and in rubber mountings at the rear, permitting a controlled degree of flexible movement in the frame.

25-30 h.p. Model Now Receives Characteristic Name : Independent Front Wheel Suspension Adopted : Synchromesh on Second as Well as Third and Top Gears : Rolls-Royce Phantom III Remains Unchanged

Due to the use, as for some time past, of a hypoid form of final drive, in which the pinion is carried below the centre line of the spiral-toothed crown wheel, it is possible to mount the propeller-shaft low and thus provide an entirely flat floor to the rear compartment.

The wheelbase is now 11ft. 4in., against 11ft. previously, and the front track 4ft. 10½in., the rear 4ft. 11½in.; thus increased bodywork dimensions and, in turn, accommodation are allowed. From outside as well as inside the suggestion of a bigger 25-30 h.p. model is given, but the car remains compact, well-balanced, and extremely light to handle in traffic.

Spaciousness

In the case of the saloon that was tried, with a Park Ward body, the rear compartment is so spacious as almost to constitute a small room, there being more than enough leg space and abundant head room and seating width. Particularly noticeable in this body are the slender windscreen pillars, which considerably aid driving vision, in conjunction with a screen which is itself wide and deep. An appreciated provision would be glass louvres over the door windows, allowing a measure of ventilation in wet weather without admitting rain or draught.

Existing features which naturally are retained are a centralised system of chassis lubrication operated from the driving seat, and a hand control at the centre of the steering wheel for regulating the damping provided by the shock absorbers, this having a series of positions between " hard " and " soft " that allows the suspension to be varied according to needs, within certain limits. The lever acts as an overriding control over the automatic regulation of the shock absorbers in accordance with road

speed, by means of a small pump driven from the gear box.

An addition on the latest car is a system of permanently fitted four-wheel hydraulic jacks, which are operated by a lever applied through a trap door in the left-hand section of the front floorboards. There is now no hand-operated ignition control lever, the advance and retard regulation being fully automatic.

The petrol tank is of 18-gallon capacity, and fuel is fed to the carburettor by a duplex electric pump, which is placed in a position inside the frame to insulate it from engine and exhaust heat.

The engine size is 89 by 114 mm., giv-

The enclosed limousine model of the new 25-30 h.p. Rolls-Royce Wraith well maintains the reputation for fine town carriages enjoyed by its makers.

This is the 25-30 h.p. four-door four-light saloon which has decidedly smart lines. Rolls-Royce cars have an excellent turn of speed, quite apart from their world-wide name for silence and refinement.

ing a capacity of 4,257 c.c., the six cylinders having overhead valves operated by push-rods. Both camshaft and crankshaft run in seven bearings. A down-draught carburettor is employed, and a large cylindrical air cleaner-cum-intake silencer is used in the interests of the greatest possible degree of quietness.

An interesting point is that Rolls-Royce themselves make many of the electrical components, including the constant-voltage type of dynamo. The

(**Right**). The control for the hydraulic jacks is in the floor of the front compartment. There is also a foot-operated chassis lubrication control.

(**Left**). The gear and hand-brake levers do not now impede entrance and exit.

The clutch pedal operation also is lighter.

Chassis price remains unaltered at £1,100, and this figure now includes head and side lamps. The head lamps are of the same pattern as fitted to the Phan-

ignition distributor is now on the near side instead of the off side of the engine, where a new external type of oil filter or purifier is mounted.

One of the outstanding features of the design has always been the mechanical servo braking system, this consisting broadly of a plate clutch mounted on the side of the gear box and driven by the transmission. When the brake pedal is depressed the rear shoes are operated normally, and at the same time the servo is brought into operation and the front brakes are applied through it. The servo effect is distributed between front and rear brakes by a balancing lever. On the latest car the brake application is lighter even than before, and the braking effort is remarkably even and effective.

The touring limousine is available with or without a dropping division window and interior heater. In both forms there is a sunshine roof.

The off side of the new Rolls - Royce Wraith engine and gear box, a beautifully finished piece of mechanism.

tom III. Complete car prices of the 25-30 h.p. Wraith are: Enclosed limousine £1,610; saloon with sunshine roof, £1,695, or with division behind the driving seat and interior heater, £1,730; touring limousine £1,625, or with division and heater, £1,660; and what is termed the Special saloon, a four-door four-light style, £1,845, or with division and heater £1,885.

No changes are being made in the twelve-cylinder 40-50 h.p. Phantom III model as compared with those which have been delivered during the past few months. One of the most interesting features is the individual R-R system of independent front wheel suspension, with steering wheel control of the integral shock absorbers.

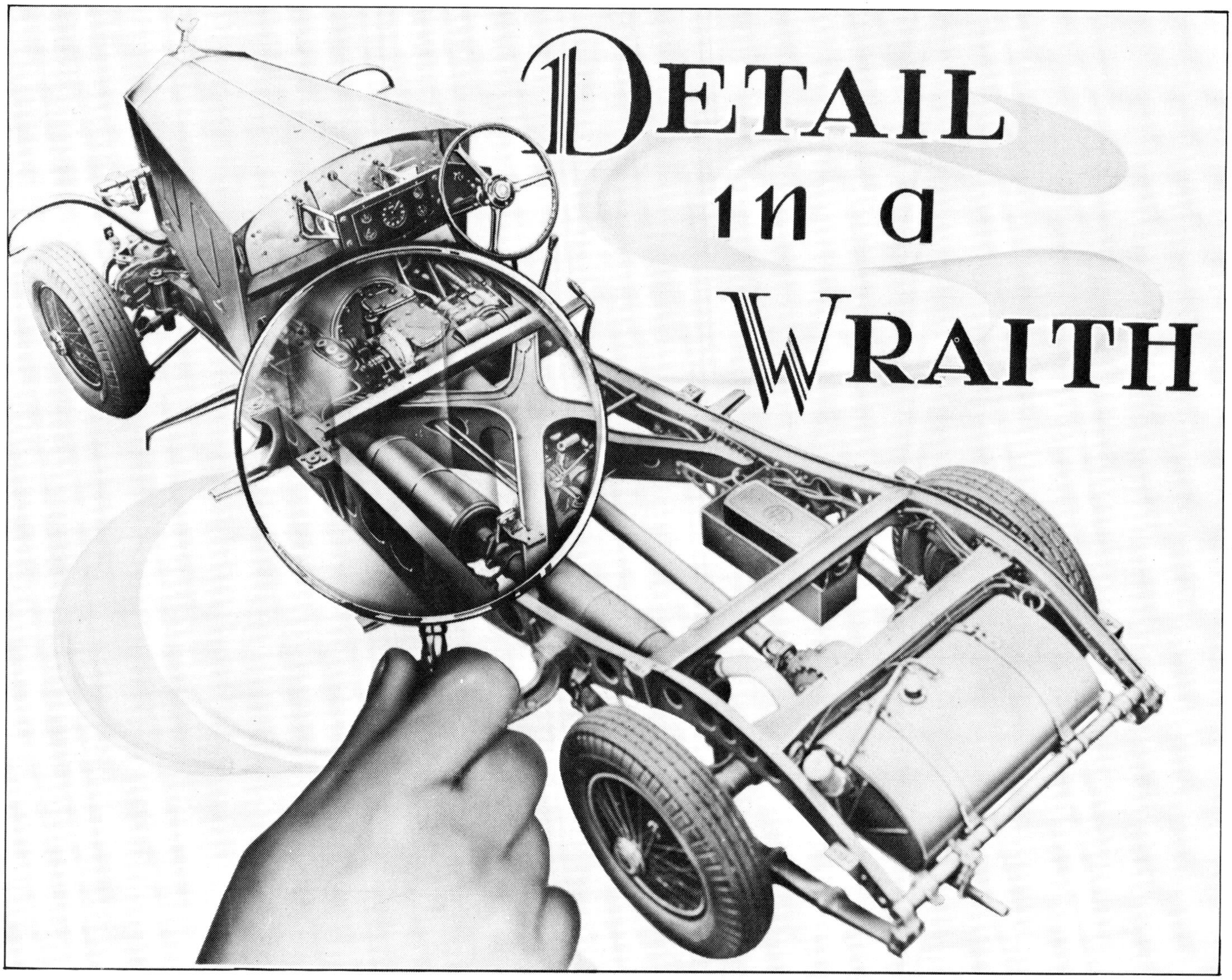

DETAIL in a WRAITH

Extensive Improvements

RECENTLY an imaginative person was heard to describe the running of a Rolls-Royce "Wraith" as being "like floating along on a cloud." The phrase may be a trifle flowery, but there is no doubt that the behaviour of that car does attain a degree of refinement beyond previous experience. This suppression of everything undesirable in the way of sound, noise, vibration and all forms of discomfort in travel is not attained haphazardly. It is the result of most thoroughly conducted research work, some of the main lines of which were recently described in *The Autocar*.

By reason of this unceasing work avenues for improvement are continually being brought to light, and the results are incorporated at the earliest opportunity in the cars made by Rolls-Royce. It happens that extensive improvements in detail have been woven into the 25 h.p. six-cylinder Wraith chassis since it first appeared, but up to the present little or nothing concerning such "inner details" has been published.

The six-cylinder engine has a light alloy cylinder block and detachable head, block and head being beautifully enamel finished, while the crankcase and sump are flawless examples of what a casting can be. Throughout, one notices that surface is held to surface, flange to flange, by many more bolts than are usually employed, to ensure that the contact is complete and that the stresses are evenly distributed. The whole unit is mounted on rubber, the front mounting being high up, while that at the rear is low down, so that the unit moves under torque variation to give the absolute minimum of reaction to the frame, and once more it is appreciated how carefully the design has been studied.

All valves are in the head and operated by push-rods from a camshaft held in substantial bearings at the side of the crankcase, and the barrel-type tappets rotate under the action of the cams partly to ensure a rolling line contact, which is well lubricated, and partly to reduce the high pressure which was found to exist in the earlier type of tappet. The fact that the barrel of the tappet rotates ensures that the lubrication thereof is sufficient. Adjustment for the valve clearance is given at the upper end, because this is most convenient, and the rocker gear ensures the minimum of side stress on the valves.

The latest engine has considerably larger inlet valves than its predecessor, and there is a damped spring drive for the timing gears, partly to reduce noise and consequent wear, partly to enable the engine to run faster without trouble to the valve gear. There are three timing gears only, of which one is of a fabric which is not affected by oil. The crankshaft bearing size has been increased, as also the journal diameter, and the metal used for

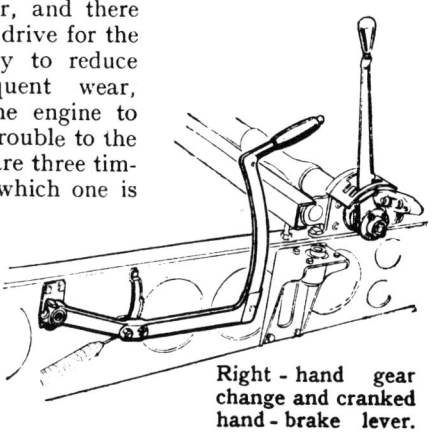

Right - hand gear change and cranked hand - brake lever.

these bearings and for the connecting-rod big-ends is a special alloy of aluminium and tin, provision being made so that in the unlikely event of a rod failing the piston cannot strike the inner part of the head.

Water spaces, both in the head and in the block, have been increased to give a greater water circulation without any chance of steam pockets. There is a steam valve in the radiator, closing the system to atmospheric pressure and causing the water to be subjected to a slight pressure the whole time, and the water pump is driven from the dynamo with a very neat rubber-jointed connection from the delivery pipe to the rear of the engine block. In the block the water is circulated with great care, so that the cooling is even. The radiator filler, by the way, is inside the bonnet, what was the radiator filler being now a mount-

Improvements in the 25-30 h.p. Rolls-Royce Introduced as the Result of Research

ing for the famous Rolls-Royce mascot, and the fan has unequal blade pitch to reduce the noise of operation.

A considerable alteration has been effected by moving the inlet pipe and carburettor to the side of the head opposite to the exhaust ports, which has the additional advantage that the carburettor is well away from the exhaust pipe and the dynamo, so that there is little risk of fire. The carburettor itself has been altered, the choke valve being strengthened and provided with a stop and spring control to relieve the suction when the engine starts, and to prevent the choke valve being bent should there be an explosion in the inlet pipe a spring-loaded relief valve has been incorporated.

Improvements to the governor gear which controls the ignition have resulted in the hand control being eliminated. A spring drive has been placed in the vertical shaft for the ignition distributor to relieve the stress of angular fluctuations, and a spare coil is neatly mounted on a bracket next to the service coil, so as to be handy immediately if required. Rolls-Royce, Ltd., control and manufacture a great deal of the electrical equipment themselves.

Then the capacity of the oil sump has been increased and the oil level indicator made easier to see. The main oil pump has been increased in size and provided with helical gears to reduce noise, there is a by-pass filter on the pressure side of the pump, and the whole system is divided into two circuits, one high, the other low pressure. High pressure is provided for the main bearings and connecting-rods, low pressure for the rockers and the dynamo drive, while the overflow feeds the camshaft gears. Oil from the high-pressure side passes to the by-pass filter, which is controlled by a low-pressure relief valve, and which takes a certain quantity of oil only from the main circulation. No oil connections need be disturbed to remove and replace the filter element.

Changes have also been made to the exhaust system, the pipes and silencers being allowed freedom for the engine movement and room to expand, while the suspension links are of rubber fabric, insulated from the heat. As car heaters are not unusual nowadays, a special water connection is provided on the cylinder head, also on the water pump, for the supply of one of these components.

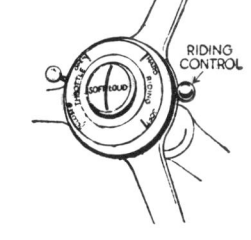

In the bell-housing behind the engine is the clutch, and the linkage between the clutch pedal and withdrawal lever is very carefully laid out to allow for the engine movement on its suspension while the pedal remains unaffected.

As to the gear box, all the gears have helical teeth, which are ground; the synchromesh cones are normally

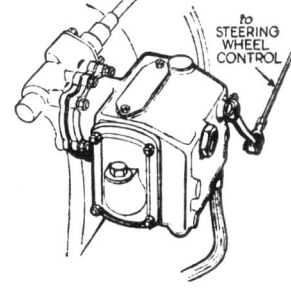

Shock absorbers are controlled from the steering wheel centre.

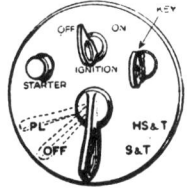

Switchgear panel which incorporates a master switch, shown dotted in "off" position.

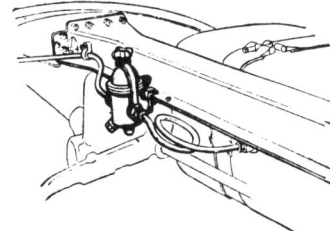

A petrol filter is located near the petrol tank.

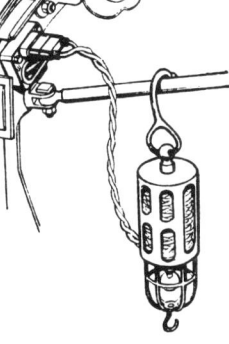

An inspection lamp plug is carried behind the engine bulkhead.

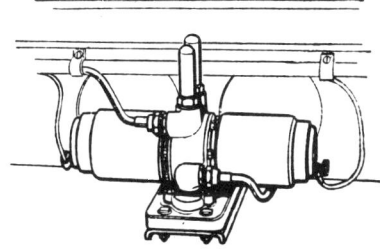

Twin electric fuel pumps are mounted on rubber.

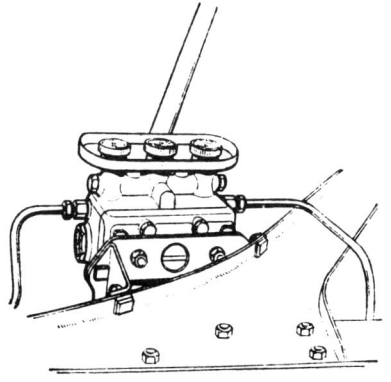

Permanent hydraulic jacking with grouped control valves.

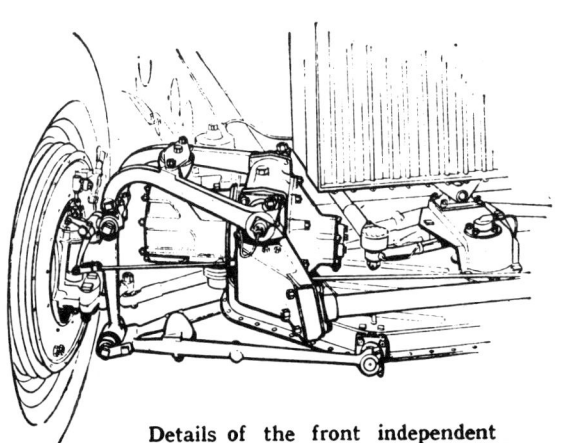

Details of the front independent suspension.

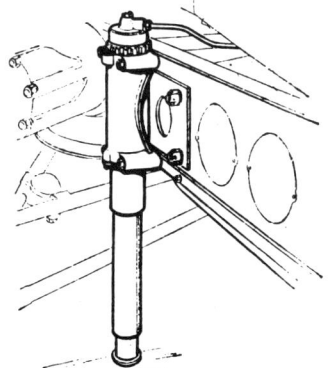

One of the front hydraulic jacks showing the telescopic ram.

From this stripped chassis may be seen the layout of the Wraith independent front-wheel springing.

being enclosed and immersed in oil, and there being in addition shock absorbers operating hydraulically and controlled by a centrifugally operated governor to vary the damping according to circumstances, the action of the damper itself being controlled by the driver. Rolling is minimised by the arrangement of the wishbone brackets and link mechanism, and a very great deal of time and thought have evolved a compromise which is deemed satisfactory, taking into consideration rolling, the lateral movement of the tyre on the road, gyroscopic reaction, and the variation of the caster angle, but which has been none too easy to arrive at since each factor is antagonistic to the other. The whole suspension, by the way, is built up as a unit and then erected in the frame.

At the rear half-elliptic springs are used, the leaves being ground and grooved for oil supplied by the central chassis lubrication system. The springs are insulated by rubber pads between the axle and the leaves, have hydraulic shock absorbers automatically controlled, and there is a rolling bar for lateral stability.

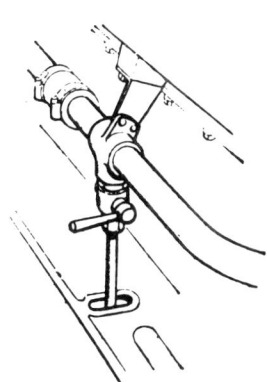

Convenient drain tap for the water system.

held clear of each other to avoid drag, are of exceptionally large diameter, and are operated through a cam mechanism which definitely prevents the dogs being engaged until synchronisation has been effected, so that "scrape" is impossible when changing gear.

Second speed now has synchromesh mechanism, one train of the "constant" mesh gears is not running in neutral, and centre bearings are provided so that light shafts can be used without deflection occurring. A flexible coupling prevents third or top becoming accidentally out of mesh; a universal coupling does the same for second speed, while both during the drive and overrun the reverse gear tends to mesh itself.

Much friction in the gear-operating mechanism has been avoided by the use of needle- and ball-bearings where the load is likely to be heavy, while the right-hand gear lever, being on the frame,

Thumb-screw adjustment for the brakes.

actuates the gears through a universally jointed shaft, so that it is not affected by any movement of the power unit. From earliest dates the Rolls-Royce has had a servo-brake mechanism to provide maximum braking effect for the lightest pedal operation. It is a disc type, having pressure cams with ball-bearing surfaces, and the pressure plates connected together by a spring blade. Direct control to the rear shoes is provided whether the servo is working or not, the servo operation of the front shoes depending on the degree of application of the rear shoes. All the operation is by rod and lever, with the minimum of working joints exposed to mud or flying stones.

Brake drums are stiffened as well as cooled by deep, circumferential ribs, and each brake has an adjustment automatically setting the shoe clearance and easy to get at. Even when the car is washed by a high-pressure hose it should be impossible for water to enter the brake drums.

The front wheels are independently sprung, following the practice adopted for the Phantom III, the coil springs used for the wishbone brackets

The frame of the latest Wraith is of box section with a strong X-shaped centre member, the steel plate used being of thick section but pierced to reduce weight, while welding has replaced rivets throughout. At the rear is the fuel tank, the filler of which can be fitted to any part of the body, while the tank vent carries fumes right away from the body. Fuel is supplied to the carburettor by twin fuel pumps carried low down on the frame on a rubber mounting, and the suction pipes thereto are carried outside the frame, as well as the pipes to the carburettor, to avoid a vapour lock. All parts of the steering gear are lubricated from a central reservoir, the actual gear being a cam and roller.

Considerable care has been taken to arrange that the rear of the body should be brought down. The hypoid gear, for example, makes it unnecessary to have a shaft tunnel, the centre casing projects as little upwards as possible, and the axle itself is of a fully floating type, the dogs being a very close fit to avoid any clicking noises on drive or overrun.

The body itself is mounted on cantilever brackets on rubber, and is really isolated from the chassis frame, for the stiff aluminium dashboard has rubber between it and the body as well. Front wings and radiator form a cantilever construction and are practically one unit, moving with the dashboard. Any engineer who studies the car will be aware that almost every part, however apparently insignificant, has its own special feature and differs considerably in detail from the corresponding component of the average automobile, and the whole serves to show why the name of Rolls-Royce stands so high in the history of motor car engineering.

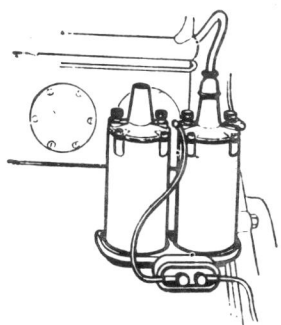

Twin ignition coils make for complete reliability.

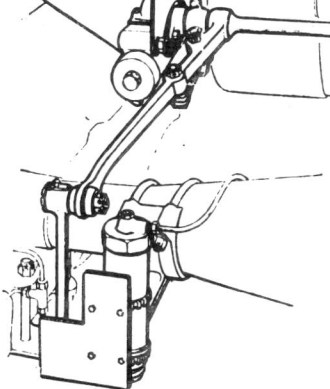

Rear torsion bar stabiliser connected to shock absorber; also jack mounting.

The FORM of a WRAITH

On the Road With the Latest 25-30 h.p. Rolls-Royce, a Car Displaying Many Improvements Over Its Famous Predecessors

IF one quality of the Rolls-Royce is more impressive than another it is consistency. You can drive the car hard all day and by night-time the behaviour will not be in any way different from what it was when you started in the morning—and then you can do the same the next day, and so on, apparently *ad infinitum*.

There will not be any little mechanical noises which suggest that something, however small, has even temporarily lost its adjustment. The oil level scarcely needs to be checked before setting off on another long journey, for the position of the pointer on the side of the crank-case will probably not have altered, and, as to the water level, the infrequent need for inspection is emphasised by the filler now being under the bonnet and having a cap of a type which can be locked up firmly with a spanner.

Minimum Daily Attention

Given fuel and a depression of the one-shot lubrication pedal for the benefit of various bearings all over the chassis, which thus receive oil, it is ready for another long day's motoring.

These points might be regarded as trivial, but whereas it is true that many cars to-day give extremely satisfactory results, the feeling sensed with the Rolls-Royce is of a regularity and true reliability on the mechanical side which is inherent and inevitable.

Experience of the 25-30 h.p. Wraith over more than 700 miles has given rise to these present impressions. This revised version of the smaller Rolls-Royce was introduced last autumn, it will be remembered, and given a type name of the kind the manufacturers choose so effectively. It embodies important improvements introduced as logical steps in the continuous process of development that the Derby firm apply to their cars.

Chief among these new features is the adoption of independent front wheel suspension on the same principle as already employed for some years past on the twelve-cylinder Phantom III. Also, a similar design of gear box to that of the Phantom III is now fitted, this having syn-chromesh on second as well as third and top gears, and the lever set well back against the right-hand side of the driving seat, where it is convenient to reach, yet out of the way of the door.

An Appreciably Bigger Car

Many other improvements are embodied in this latest model of a less obvious nature than the two main points mentioned. They were dealt with in an article that appeared in *The Autocar* of July 7th last. Also, the Wraith is of longer wheelbase and wider track than the 25-30 h.p. model that was current prior to its introduction, the wheelbase being 11ft. 4in., the front track 4ft. 10½in. and the rear track 4ft. 11½in. Thus it comes within inches of the Phantom, of which the wheelbase is 11ft. 10in.

A bigger and far roomier car is certainly noticed by comparison with the previous types. It has gained, too, in impressiveness of appearance, which, said of a Rolls-Royce, means a good deal. The proportioning is admirable, and it is never possible not to rediscover the appeal

of the classically simple but exceptionally effective radiator. None other has quite the same bold but at the same time restrained outline, setting off the whole car and giving a frontal appearance which is known and respected everywhere.

Mechanical work in terms of propelling a motor car is reduced in this machine to a softness and silkiness that approach perfection. One realises that it is not merely a virtually dead-silent engine, in itself an achievement that goes back through years of patient experiment and development, that renders the Rolls-Royce what it is; the other components that sometimes make themselves heard even when an engine is quiet have received the same attention.

Never can anyone sitting in any part of the car detect by ear that there is a back axle transmitting the power and driving the wheels through bevels and pinions. On the pull or on the overrun, whether the throttle is treated lightly or harshly, no trace of a whine or growl or any other sound comes from that axle.

Third Gear Mistaken for Top

Again, third gear is just about as quiet as top, and unless a passenger happens to notice the driver's movement of hand or foot it is easily possible for him to suppose that the car is running on top when in fact it is on third. This is the more readily possible because of the right-hand gear lever, since the actual movement may well be missed. Without taking particular care it is possible to change gear so that not only is there no sound, but also so that the take-up from one gear to another is completely unnoticeable. Second gear, too, attains practically the same degree of quietness, and as first is not used except for starting on a gradient, the whole of the gear changing actually needed is by synchromesh.

Synchromesh is a term which covers a number of forms of assistance to gear changing, broadly of the same principle but decidedly different in the results afforded. The Rolls-Royce system gives a practical certainty of quiet engagement, and, a remarkable point, either as slowly as the driver cares to move the lever or with a rapid action. Though the actual need does not arise frequently in country of average difficulty, there is an inclination to change gear even unnecessarily for the sheer pleasure of handling this delightful gear box, which, considered from all angles, has no present rival.

It is not the object of the Wraith to provide the maximum performance that can be obtained from an engine of the size used. Rather may its purpose be summar-

ised as luxurious comfort of both seating and suspension for all seats, as much performance in terms of acceleration and maximum speed as will ever be wanted by its owners, and the possession of reserve power at all times. These qualities are coupled with a delicacy of control achieved by no other cars than this firm produces.

According to the road and the wishes of those in the car it makes no difference whether the speed be 50, 60, 70 or approaching 80 m.p.h. Whatever be allowed by the road conditions, it is felt that the car is designed to run at that figure. The oil pressure remains at a dead-beat reading, varying only a pound or two according to the speed, and the water temperature hovers over a range of only about 4 deg. with the speed and even the direction of the wind.

Effortless at Over 70 m.p.h.

It seems of little consequence what the precise maximum speed figure is when such astonishingly easy and completely effortless running is available at, say, 75 m.p.h. Speedometer readings between 80 and 84 were reached on two or three occasions, and considerably more was shown once on a definitely favourable stretch of road; but these attainments are far from being the *raison d'être* of the Wraith.

The car feels taut at these higher speeds, the damping provided by the special hydraulic shock absorbers auto-

(Above) By employing a side mounting for the spare wheel, a really large luggage boot is provided. Tools are in a lid tray. (Centre) The beautifully neat engine. Note the large air silencer and cleaner. (Left) Famous all over the world—the square-edge radiator whose basic shape has been constant since Rolls-Royce cars were first manufactured.

EYX 362

matically building up from pressure given by a centrifugally operated pump, this being variable at the will of the driver by means of an overriding finger lever on the steering wheel. So lightly does this control move when depressed clear of the notches in its quadrant that it seems impossible at first to believe that it can be having any effect. That it does make a real and noticeable difference is soon discovered.

This control is typical of Rolls-Royce mechanism. Every lever or pedal moves with a silky lightness of operation, having no lost movement. It is an unforgettable point, though a detail matter, that one notch more or less on the

hand-throttle quadrant alters the tick-over speed of the engine. Ignition control is now fully automatic, there being no advance and retard lever on the Wraith.

As striking as the way in which the car holds high speeds is the manner of its slowing and stopping. There is something very special about the behaviour of the mechanical servo-operated brakes. The pedal needs to be little more than "brushed" with the foot to bring the large and heavy car (weighing 42 cwt. unladen, but with petrol) down from speed under complete control, and, as the foot pressure is increased, the retarding effect obtained is exactly proportional.

Improvements made in the steering have removed the former tendency to road-wheel reaction over certain kinds of surface. It is a fairly low-geared mechanism, but one that affords the utmost confidence, meaning that the driver feels in close touch with the front wheels and able to put the car exactly where he wishes.

Practical and Handsome Body

The body fitted was by Park Ward, a four-light four-door type known as the touring saloon and priced as a complete car at £1,695, the chassis price being £1,100. This is a most practical body in point of seating space and head room, and also of handsome appearance, with a distinctly smart touch added by modern semi-angular treatment of the rear quarters of the roof.

Touring saloon it may well be called in terms of luggage accommodation, for there is a very large boot, the interior of which is virtually unobstructed. The rear seat squab is extended high up so that the passenger may recline, as is permitted by the leg room. The suspension allows him to do so without being jarred; there is no more severe test of back-seat springing. Pull-out footrests are provided, and in the backs of the separate front seats are picnic tables. The driver concerned would have preferred a higher seating position, a matter which could easily be arranged. The steering column is adjustable for rake, it being set at the time in its highest position.

In addition to indirect illumination of the instruments, there is a useful two-way direct lamp which can be shone on to the package locker and near side of the front compartment generally, or to the right, where it illuminates the switch gear, including the master lock for the electrical

The luxurious and spacious Park Ward body includes picnic tables and footrests in the backs of the front seats and companion sets in the quarters.

system. There is a position of this switch where the whole electrical system except this lamp and the electric clock is cut out. Companion sets placed in the rear quarters incorporate mirrors, in conjunction with which there is a small diffused-illumination light. The usual roof lamp switch is fitted, and also, when the side lamps are in use, the roof lights come on if either rear door is opened.

This coachwork style can also be supplied with a drop division between the two compartments, making the car suitable for chauffeur-driving, a sunshine roof being retained, and an interior heater, the price with this additional equipment being £1,730.

Hydraulically operated four-wheel jacks are part of the chassis equipment. Two other points are always impressive—the way in which the car starts from cold in the morning and runs regularly straight away, quickly gaining temperature under the control of thermostatically regulated radiator shutters; and the excellence of the electrical equipment, much of which is made specially for the Rolls-Royce.

It was particularly observed during the run how faithfully the constant-voltage dynamo dealt with the electrical load imposed, a state of balance or slight charge being shown on the sensitive ammeter even when, in difficult conditions at night, all the lamps were in use and the windscreen wipers working, and use was being made of the electrically operated rear window blind.

It is in countless points such as these, quite apart from the excellence of the general road behaviour, that the Rolls-Royce merits the position it holds in general estimation.

H. S. L.

A setting at Tisbury, Wilts, during the test run which shows off the Rolls-Royce profile to advantage.

NEW CARS DESCRIBED

Rolls-Royce
SILVER WRAITH

New Engine with Overhead Inlet and Side Exhaust Valves. Many Outstanding Features in a Superb Chassis

ALL the world knows that Rolls-Royce carry on an unremitting search for engineering perfection in everything they undertake. The qualities which made their aircraft engines famous, and their cars the finest procurable, are the result of hard work scientifically conducted, and of a painstaking attention to details from the large to the most minute. And now a new range of cars is about to appear. In these will be found new ideas as well as further development of carefully established practice which has been proven during the passage of time.

These new cars were designed before the war, and samples then made have been hard at work on various jobs ever since. The engines have been used not only in cars, but in buses and carriers as well. Nearly a million miles have been covered, including 26,000 miles at high speed on European autobahns before the war. Thus, advantage has been taken of a good opportunity to make long-distance and extended time tests before the new designs are offered to the public. It is believed that the new cars are the best that Rolls-Royce have ever built. They have not only an even greater refinement of running than has already been associated with the *marque*, and a remarkable road performance, but also simplicity has been sought. A degree of interchangability of component parts in all models has been introduced, with the object of simplifying and reducing the cost of servicing.

First to be announced is the Silver Wraith, a 4¼-litre six-cylinder chassis which will be fitted with "custom built" coachwork. The main lines of its specification will be found alongside. Before describing it in detail, an impression of the complete car on the road will be of unusual interest. In common with all Rolls-Royce cars, the Silver Wraith has an indefinable something about it, a delicacy of behaviour, which escapes definition in written words. It is a car for the connoisseur in cars. In parallel, can the connoisseur of wines say exactly what it is that causes a particular sample to win his approval?

Perhaps the particular charm of the Silver Wraith lies in the effectiveness with which all the undesirable manifestations incidental to the develop-

ment of power by machinery have been skilfully exorcised. The result is a car which is a sentient being and is like a living thing. An imaginative person might easily believe that the Wraith's feelings could be hurt by a carelessly casual or definitely dangerous driver. Offended dignity might cause it of its own volition to move quietly off to more congenial company! Perhaps such imaginings arise from the extraordinary responsiveness of the car. All the controls work beautifully smoothly and easily; it obeys instantly the slightest wish of the driver, and it obeys exactly. It has perfect manners. And yet underneath that willingness one senses power.

It is when accelerating that this is most evident. There seems to be no limit to its response to the movement of the pedal. Some cars accelerate strongly from low speeds up to a certain point and there they become almost sullen, and unwilling to accelerate further at the same rate. The Silver Wraith appears to be able to maintain its rate of acceleration up to the limit of what the driver wills on the open and suitable stretch of road. And up to the limit imposed by the nature of the road the car maintains its perfect manners. It steers to a hair line, it is exceedingly comfortable and smooth riding, yet it is also entirely stable, and the smooth brakes engender confidence. The innate refinement remains unflurried as the speed rises from the thirties to the eighties. It is a fast car when the driver wishes. Moreover, although it is relatively a large car, the controls are so light and

---

CHASSIS SPECIFICATION

Engine.—Rating 29.4 h.p., 6 cylinders, 89 x 114 mm. (4,257 c.c.). Overhead inlet and side exhaust valves. Detachable aluminium cylinder head with inserted valve seats. Seven-bearing counterbalanced crankshaft with spring-centre flywheel and torsional vibration damper. Steel connecting rods.

Dual downdraught Stromberg carburettor. Pump water cooling with thermostat-controlled radiator shutters. Flexible engine unit mounting.

Transmission.—Dry single-plate centrifugally assisted clutch. Four-speed gear box with synchromesh. Overall ratios: Top, 3.727; third, 5.002; second, 7.514; first, 11.125 to 1. Divided propeller-shaft to hypoid bevel in rear axle with semi-floating shafts.

Steering.—Cam and roller follower.

Suspension.—Independent front suspension with cross-coupled hydraulic dampers. Half-elliptic rear springs, enclosed in gaiters. Rear hydraulic dampers controlled from steering wheel.

Brakes.—Mechanical servo-controlled from gear box. Special form of hydraulic front and mechanical rear operation.

Tyres and Wheels.—7.00 x 16in. Dunlop Fort tyres on detachable disc wheels.

Main Dimensions.—Wheelbase, 10ft 7in. Track, 4ft 10in. Turning circle, 45ft.

This four-light saloon body design for the Silver Wraith chassis emphasises the special appeal of the British luxury car. The absence of running boards will be noted.

Rolls-Royce
SILVER WRAITH
Continued

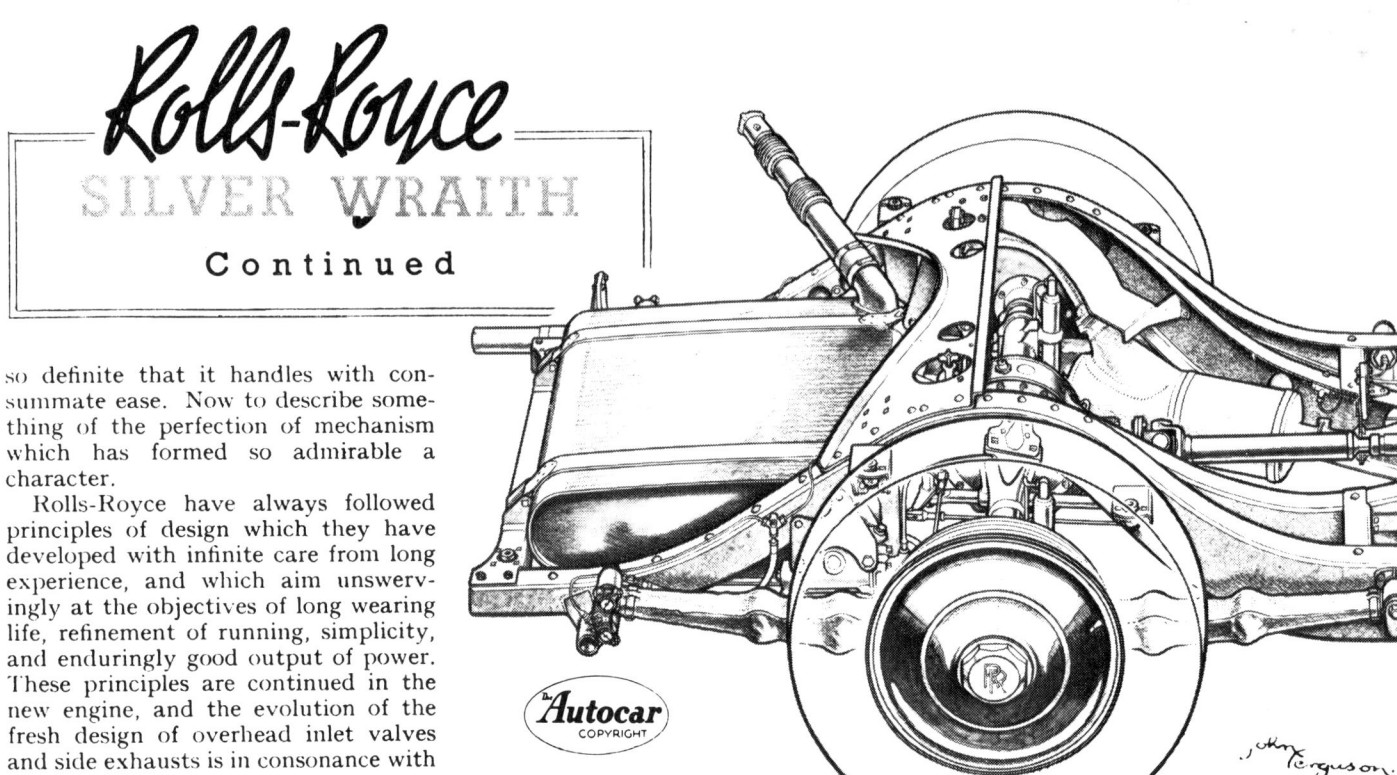

so definite that it handles with consummate ease. Now to describe something of the perfection of mechanism which has formed so admirable a character.

Rolls-Royce have always followed principles of design which they have developed with infinite care from long experience, and which aim unswervingly at the objectives of long wearing life, refinement of running, simplicity, and enduringly good output of power. These principles are continued in the new engine, and the evolution of the fresh design of overhead inlet valves and side exhausts is in consonance with them.

Short Engine Sought

This new valve arrangement is primarily dictated by the desire to obtain a short engine which at the same time affords adequate valve room, good breathing for the inlet valves, even cooling of valve seats, equal thickness of metal walls, good cooling of the sparking plug seats, and less complication of cores in the casting processes.

The arrangement adopted avoids the complications of twin overhead camshafts generally used with hemispherical cylinder heads, and also the restrictions in valve size incidental to overhead valves placed in line and situated in lozenge-shaped combustion chambers. The "under and over" valve arrangement gives adequate

space, and allows large inlet valves to be used. It gives free port space, clear water-ways, and an accessible position for the sparking plug, as well as better accessibility for the valve gear by avoiding congestion.

These are the chief reasons for the adoption of the design. The large inlet valves and clear-run ports enable the cylinders to breathe their full capacity of mixture and hence there is no need to use an extra high compression ratio. That is to say, a full charge of mixture compressed to a reasonable value gives better practical results than a possibly attenuated charge compressed to an assumed high value. The good breathing and full cylinder filling provide a good torque at low speeds as well as

at high, hence the engine attains greater flexibility. The new Silver Wraith six-cylinder engine develops about 137 b.h.p. with open exhaust on the test bed, and about 122 b.h.p. as installed and silenced in the car.

The compression ratio is in the order of 6.4 to 1. The engine has six cylinders of 89 x 114 mm. bore and stroke (4,257 c.c.) and the R.A.C. rating is 29.4 h.p. Although designed to run at a maximum of 4,400 r.p.m., the engine will reach 5,000 r.p.m. without showing signs of valve spring surge and valve bounce, which is a remarkable speed for a car engine of the size concerned. The stroke-bore ratio is 1.25 to 1.

Valve System Details

Details of the new valve arrangement are made clear in the accompanying illustrations, whence it will be seen that the exhausts are at the side of the cylinder block, and are operated by hollow, barrel-shaped tappets of chilled cast iron with relieved faces which bear down upon the specially profiled and "backed-off" cams of a massive solid camshaft. The camshaft is coupled by a two-to-one helical-toothed gear of fabric-reinforced plastic driven from a steel gear on the crankshaft. The object of the tappet face relief and the backing-off of the cams is to ensure a constant rotation of the tappets, which produces a mirror surface on the parts and reduces wear to a minimum, thereby avoiding any need for constant adjustment.

Alternate tappets carry push rods which run up above the cylinder head and engage the ends of tubular rocker arms, the opposite ends of which bear

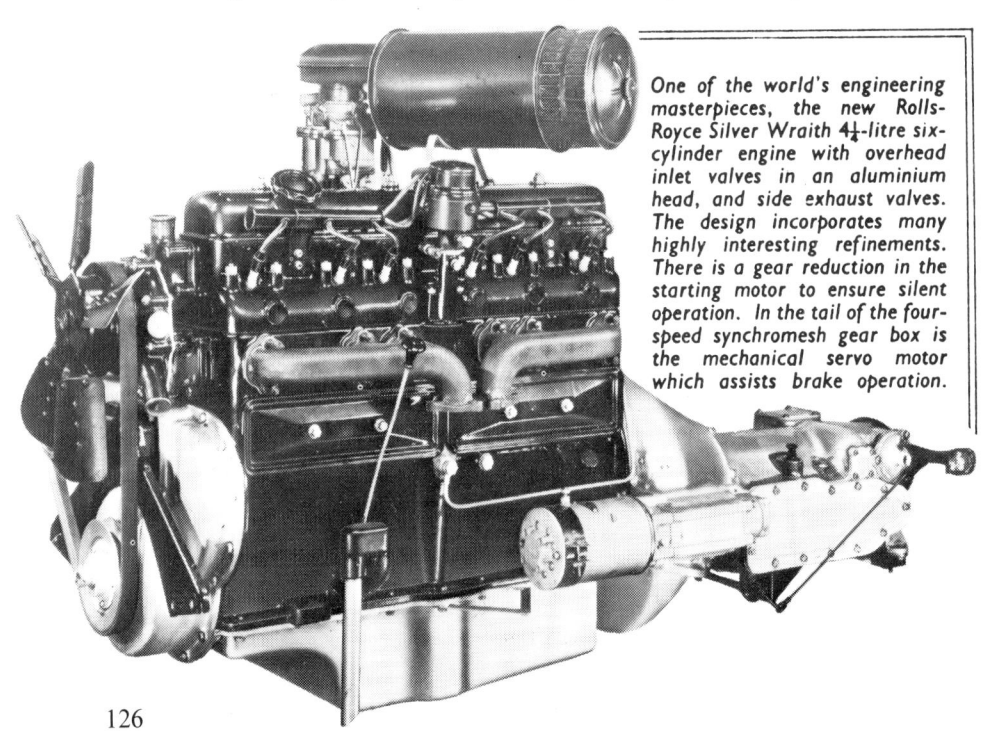

One of the world's engineering masterpieces, the new Rolls-Royce Silver Wraith 4¼-litre six-cylinder engine with overhead inlet valves in an aluminium head, and side exhaust valves. The design incorporates many highly interesting refinements. There is a gear reduction in the starting motor to ensure silent operation. In the tail of the four-speed synchromesh gear box is the mechanical servo motor which assists brake operation.

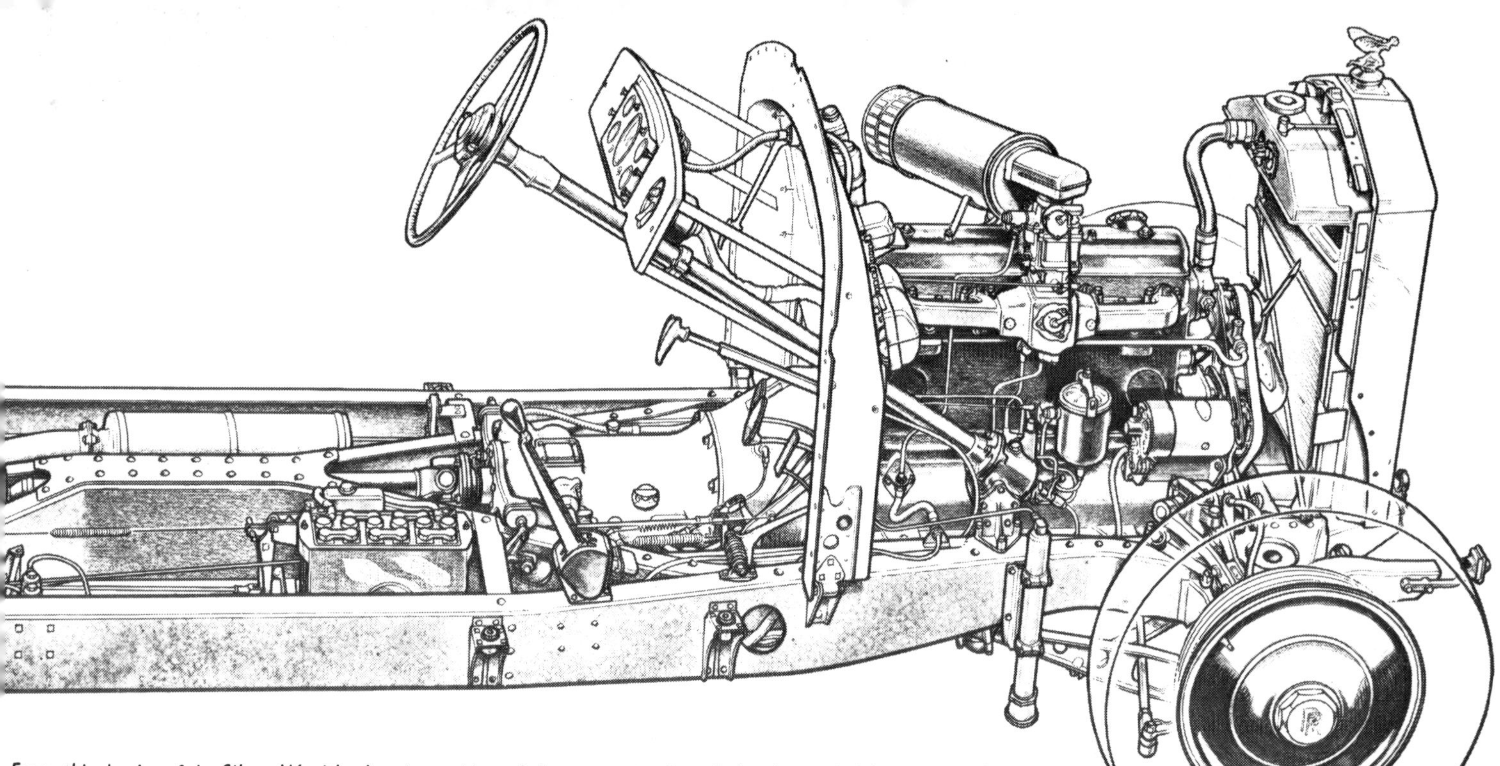

From this drawing of the Silver Wraith chassis an idea of the great rigidity of the deep-sided box-section frame can be obtained. Note also the massive cruciform central bracing, with its unusually stiff centre part. The floating division in the propeller-shaft can be seen just behind this centre.' The two silencers are heavily lagged to prevent noise. In the front is the new 4¼-litre six-cylinder engine with the latest " under and over " valve arrangement. Water temperature in the radiator is governed by thermostatically operated shutters.

upon the inlet valve stems. These rockers are hollow and are pressure fed from the rocker shaft with oil which is conducted to the push rod and valve extremities. The inlet valves are arranged in line along the detachable cylinder head, which is of aluminium alloy. Special inserted valve seats are screwed into position.

As the valve and rocker box contains only six rockers instead of twelve, as would apply with all overhead valves, there is plenty of room and the adjustments are correspondingly accessible. The inlet valves are of considerably larger diameter than the exhausts, and are of a beautifully proportioned tulip shape. They are not heavy. Compound springs are used to return them to their seats, and the outer coil spring is slightly volute; that is to say, the diameter of the top coils is less than that of the bottom ones. This is a special feature which guards against spring surge at high speeds. Provision is made that the inlet valve stems are lubricated in their guides, but that no excess of oil shall percolate through. To this end there is a special form of conical felt washer surrounding the stem at the top of the guide, and this washer is compressed by the abutment disc of the inner spring.

It is noticeable that the valve ports are of large size; the end cylinders have single ports and the inner pairs have siamesed ports, an arrangement which tends to equalise the length of the inlet manifold passages. It is interesting to note that the carburation system treats the engine as two sets of three cylinders, balanced together, and to that end a dual downdraught aero-type Stromberg carburettor is used. The mixture strength is controlled by a bi-metallic strip which ensures flexibility over the entire speed range, with reliable slow running and easy cold starting as well as rapid acceleration. The instantaneous acceleration is very evident on the road.

The central portions of the aluminium inlet manifold are hot water jacketed in connection with the water cooling system of the engine. Before the valves are left a note about the exhaust valves may be added. These are made of a special heat-resisting steel. The swelling from the stem to the tulip head is not a plain geometric curvature, but a carefully calculated grading of diameter which ensures evenness of heat flow and thereby

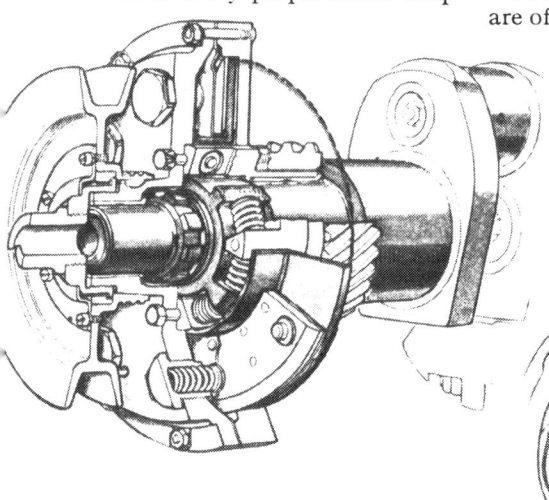

Left: At the front end of the large hollow, counterbalanced crankshaft is this torsional vibration damper, with which is also incorporated a cushioned drive for the timing gear pinion.

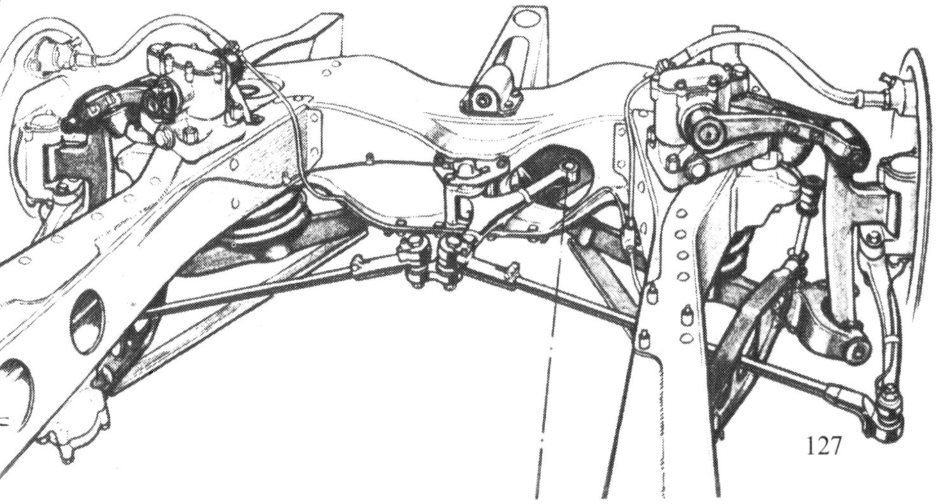

Right: Independent front suspension of the Silver Wraith. The links are made as long as possible so that rubberised bushes can be used without permitting too much flexibility. Note the divided track rod of the steering linkage, which ensures that accuracy of steering is unaffected by the rise and fall of the wheels.

127

Rolls-Royce
SILVER WRAITH
Continued

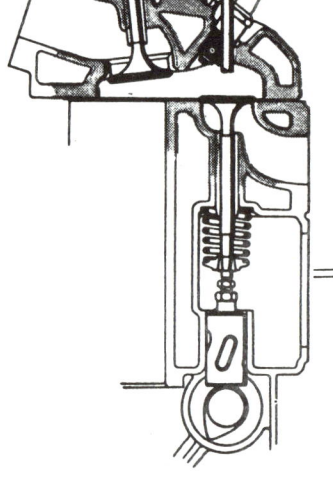

A curved "pan" box-section member of great rigidity forms the front end of the frame. This view shows the partly concealed coil spring of the front suspension and the torsion bar anti-sway coupling between independent suspensions on each side.

avoids overheating at any one point. On both inlet and exhaust valves there is a slight relief at the point where the stem issues from its guide. This ensures that with heavily leaded fuels a fine deposit cannot occur. Heavy deposits break away and disintegrate more easily.

The shape of the combustion chamber is such that the sparking plugs are situated well outside the inlet valve compartment; they enter diagonally and thus are in a very accessible position. It is also noticeable that the distributor head is high up on the engine and is accessibly placed. The use of an aluminium cylinder head naturally saves a good deal of weight, and, indeed, this new engine is remarkably light in relation to its power output, in spite of the rigidity of its design.

A single casting forms the cylinder block, in which there are many points to note. The first, perhaps, is the fact that the upper ends of the cylinder bores are protected against corrosion and wear by a lining of special chromium plating about 0.00075 in. thick. This is a part of the design which aims to produce an engine capable of running 100,000 miles without rebore or major

overhaul. Again, if distortion is to be avoided it is desirable to have the cylinder barrels separated from one another with a free water passage between them. As it is also desirable, and has always been a feature of Rolls-Royce design, to have a substantial bearing between adjacent throws of the crankshaft, the two points work in together. A bearing between adjacent throws gives a rigid support to the crankshaft, and, if the cylinder barrels have water space between them, the engine is not lengthened by the use of inter-throw bearings. Moreover, the transverse walls in the crank chamber which support the bearings also add materially to the general rigidity of the engine.

The crankshaft is a beautiful piece of work, machined all over, counterweighted and balanced. The crank pins are hollow and are closed in by "hour glass" shaped plugs. This arrangement provides chambers into

the recesses of which any sediment or other impurity is flung by centrifugal force, leaving the oil passage clear. Steel is used for the connecting rods, which also are a picture of workmanship; they are machined all over. There is a central web down the rod through which an oil-way is drilled, as the forced feed from the crank journals and the crankpins is carried right up to the floating gudgeon pins. The crankshaft and big-end bearings are of steel-backed Vandervell type, with lead-bronze indium-faced linings. Made of aluminium alloy, the Aerolite-type pistons have fluted skirts. There are two gas rings, and a special slotted scraper ring. Underneath this ring the piston also is slotted.

Spring-Centred Flywheel

Not only is a very special form of torsional vibration damper fitted at the front end of the crankshaft, which additionally safeguards the driving pinion of the camshaft two-to-one gear, but also at the opposite end the flywheel has a spring centre which is specifically designed to damp out oscillation caused by the rocking couples of the throws near that end of the shaft. There is a separate face plate for the 11-in dry single-plate clutch, which is of the Long type with bob weights on the extension of the operating fingers, which give centrifugal assistance to the springs. This arrangement gives a light pedal operating pressure and a smooth take-up, whilst the grip of the clutch increases as the engine speed rises. The clutch pedal is insulated from movements of the engine upon its flexible mounting by neat balance beam linkage.

To return again to the engine, the water cooling system requires some description. Water is circulated by a leak-proof centrifugal pump, which feeds into a flat tube passing from end to end through the cylinder block and directs the cooling medium straight around the exhaust valve seats, after which it passes up to the head and so out to the radiator through the thermostatic valve. The cylinder barrels are cooled by thermo-syphon circulation, and thus the temperature is evenly distributed.

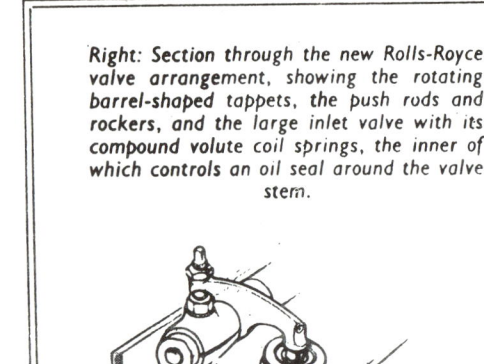

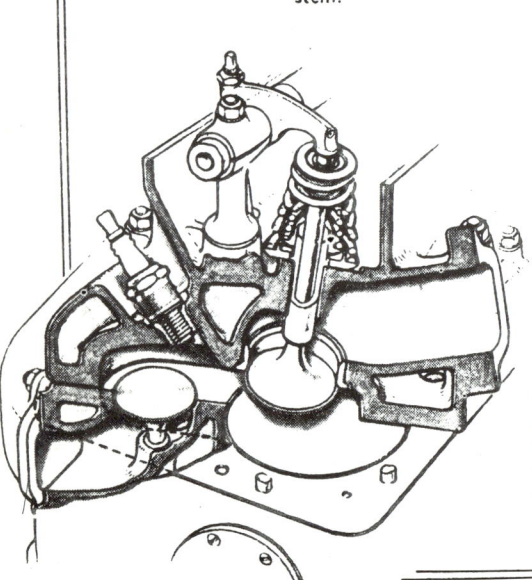

Right: Section through the new Rolls-Royce valve arrangement, showing the rotating barrel-shaped tappets, the push rods and rockers, and the large inlet valve with its compound volute coil springs, the inner of which controls an oil seal around the valve stem.

Left: Layout of the inclined overhead inlet and side exhaust valves. It gives better "breathing" at all speeds, adequate room for large inlets without making a long engine, even cooling of valve seats, good ports, and a well-shaped combustion chamber.

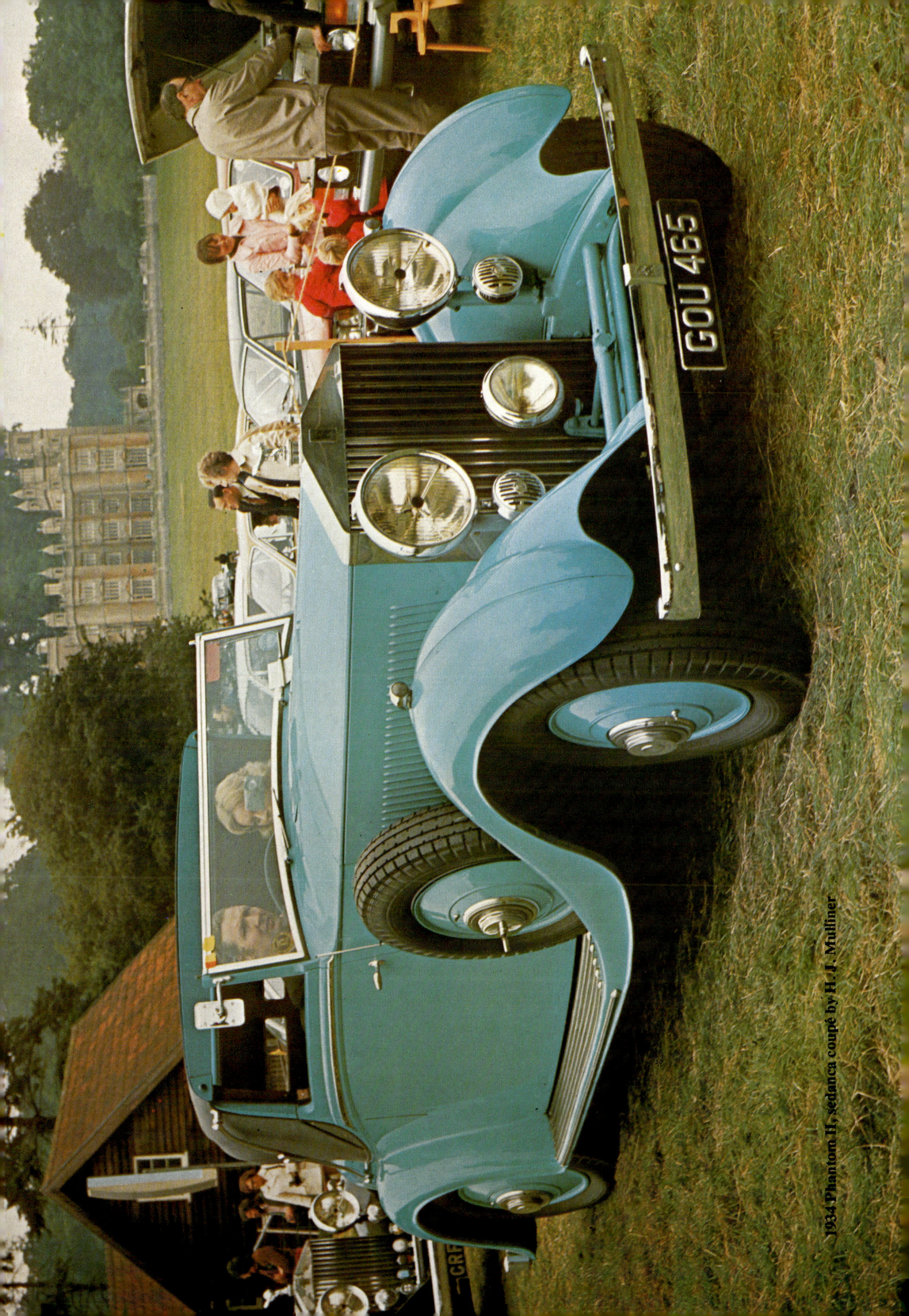

1934 Phantom II, sedanca coupé by H. J. Mulliner

1955 Silver Wraith, limousine
by Freestone and Webb

1932 20/25 h.p., sports saloon by Freestone and Webb

1953 Silver Dawn,
standard steel saloon

One of a pair of Phantom IV straight-eights
in the Royal Mews at Buckingham Palace

The Rolls-Royce is one of the few cars in which water temperature is controlled by a thermostat operating radiator shutters, instead of a thermostat and a radiator by-pass arrangement.

There can be little doubt in the minds of experienced motorists that the radiator shutter system is easily the better, for it precludes the possibility during intense cold of the radiator freezing up while the engine is warm, and it avoids the need for unsightly "blanking off" or covering up part of the radiator. Incidentally the Silver Wraith radiator is still the familiar and classic Rolls-Royce design which has become a hallmark of our national pride.

Lubrication System

Engine lubrication is supplied by a submerged pump, which draws oil from the sump through a filter arranged to float just below the surface; the filter faces downwards, and sludge is not picked up. The oil is forced to a two-stage relief valve, the first stage of which controls the supply under 35 to 40 lb per sq in pressure to the crankshaft and other main bearings. The second stage allows oil at 5 lb pressure to pass to the valve rockers, push rods, and tappets. An external British Filter with a renewable element operates in the by-pass circuit, and ensures that all the oil in the system is kept clean. An electrical tell-tale on the instrument panel records the oil level in the sump, and there is also a dipstick. The oil filter is placed accessibly high on the valve cover.

Giving four speeds, with synchromesh on second, third and top, which is the direct drive, the gear box is of the classic Rolls-Royce type, with helical-toothed ground gears and a one-piece layshaft. In its design the unswerving objective is silence of running, and this is obtained by the rigidity of the box and shafts, the accurately cut gears, and a very close attention to minute details. The box also supplies the drive to the speedometer, the servo motor for the brakes, and the hydraulic over-ride control for the spring dampers. In order to give a free front seat floor the gear change lever is mounted on the right-hand side, beside the driver's seat in a position that is convenient as well as out of the way. It is connected to the gear box by a flexible shaft arrangement to ensure that movement of the power unit is not transmitted.

Engine and gear box form a unit and this is suspended on rubber mountings at two points, the front fairly high, and the rear below the tail of the gear box. The object is to obtain torsional flexibility, and so to prevent engine vibration from reaching the occupants of the car. A tie is fitted to prevent fore-and-aft movement on the mounting. The unit is mounted rather farther forward than in earlier cars, for the dual purpose of increasing available coachwork space and of obtaining a better distribution of weight.

As it is desired to obtain a low floor level, which enables good head room to be given in the body without undue overall height, the open propeller-shaft is divided into two parts. The front portion, below the rear floor, has next to no movement and therefore does not need a tunnel raised from the floor. The rear part is positioned below the rear seat, which is at a higher level than the floor, hence again no space is wasted. As the final drive is by hypoid bevel gear the centre line of the propeller-shaft is low down.

Floating Locating Bearing

One of the most interesting matters from a mechanical point of view is to be found in this propeller-shaft arrangement. At the point where the division is made there is a central locating bearing, but this is not immovably fixed. The bearing is coupled to the frame by two links with rubber-bush bearings. It is thus free to float in a lateral plane. The object is to eliminate vibration. When the joints of a propeller-shaft are running in true axial line, as they do in the zero position of medium car load and flat road surface, there is no angular movement in the joints, and no reactionary vibration. But as soon as the axle rises or falls on a bad surface, or the car is lightly or heavily laden, the joints no longer remain in axial line, and vibration can occur. The flexible mounting allows movement to take place and so absorbs the vibration. This is yet one more reason why the Rolls-Royce obtains that

The inlet side of the 29.4 h.p. Silver Wraith engine, showing the dual downdraught carburettor with its big air cleaner and intake silencer, the inlet manifold, dynamo, and external oil filter. On the side of the gear box housing is the servo, driven from the gear box, which is engaged through a disc clutch when the brake pedal is depressed and multiples the pressure applied by the driver, resulting in light yet positive operation of the brakes.

velvet smoothness which is so entirely characteristic.

There is a change to record in connection with the hypoid bevel rear axle, which has a bevel differential gear. In place of fully floating axle shafts, semi-floating shafts have been adopted. These have "upset" ends, by which is meant that the flanges on the outer ends are forged from the original bar, and are thus integral. These new shafts are solid and large, and are employed with the object of avoiding spring or lost motion in the transmission.

Rigidity is the keynote of the design of the main frame of the car. The side members are of deep section and braced together by a long and stiff cruciform central member, the extremities of which are riveted and welded into the side members to form box sections. Across the extreme front of the frame is a curved cross-member, or "pan," of great strength, and this provides the necessary stiff mounting for the components of the independent front suspension.

Further Suspension Development

This suspension is a further development of the original Wraith design, in which a long link on each side is pivoted close to the centre of the front cross-member, and is inclined rearwardly to a joint at the bottom of the swivel pin yoke piece. A second short link at the head of the yoke has its fulcrum in an hydraulic damper on the top of the frame. Then from the foot of the yoke a long strut runs backwards and inwards to a joint carried below the side member at a point close to the dash. Between the lower link and the pan a stout coil spring is mounted.

The further development of this suspension has been to extend the length of the links and strut so as to enlarge the base of the triangulation. This renders it possible to make a more free use of rubber bushes and so to obtain insulation from road noise and shocks without introducing too much flexibility in the system. The rear springs are long underslung half-elliptics with rolled section leaves which are shot blasted to increase the resistance to fatigue. The leaves are indented and are lubricated from the central chassis lubrication system; they are also enclosed in gaiters.

Mention has been made of the hydraulic dampers used on the Wraith. The front pair are cross-coupled by a torsion bar to prevent roll. The rear ones have an hydraulically operated over-riding control provided from the gear box and set by a small lever at the steering wheel centre. These dampers are of a piston type, but the cylinders are vertical instead of horizontal, the object being to keep the load on the spindle in one direction, and so avoid any tendency to knock.

Rolls-Royce
SILVER WRAITH
Continued

For the steering a cam and roller follower of the Marles type is used in conjunction with Rolls-Royce developments. It is designed to reduce frictional losses to a minimum and to provide light and positive steering at all speeds. The track rods to the swivels are divided and jointed to a central lever which is linked back to the steering gear drop arm. All the joints are spring loaded on half-balls in phosphor bronze bushes.

In the four wheel brake system much interest is to be found. The front brakes are hydraulic, and the rear are mechanical. Both sets are operated through the standard Rolls-Royce servo drive from the gear box, which multiplies the light pressure applied by the driver to the brake pedal. It is perhaps typical of the design of the car that the most suitable parts of specialist brake products should have been adopted to produce the desired combination. For instance, the Girling type transverse expander wedges, adjusters and shoes are used back and front, but the front brakes are operated through Lockheed hydraulic equipment.

To understand the reasons for this arrangement it is necessary to know the Rolls-Royce principle of braking. It is desired to have highly efficient, light-operating brakes which do not "fade" and which remain steadfast and constant. Rolls-Royce prefer to arrange the servo application to take place from an outward source, that is, a mechanical servo motor, which is unaffected by the condition of the brake shoe linings, rather than by a self-servo action of the shoes. Moreover, in order to equalize wear between the two shoes of each brake a mechanical balance linkage is added at a point close to the expanders, so that each shoe is equally applied. The hand brake operates mechanically on the rear wheels only and is applied through a pull-out pistol grip on the right side of the scuttle. *The Autocar* prefers the earlier R.-R. pull-up type of brake lever, though willing to admit that the pistol grip leaves freedom around the seats.

As regards the fuel system, an 18-gallon tank is mounted at the rear of the chassis, and twin electric pumps carry the supply to the dual carburettor.

Power Jacks

Other features of the chassis include permanently fitted hydraulic lifting jacks which are operated by a power-driven pump mounted under the bonnet, and a centralized system of lubrication which attends to all the important parts of the chassis. It is operated by a pedal pump mounted on the dash panel. The electrical equipment is a 12-volt special Lucas system, with automatic regulation of the dynamo output by vibrator control. The starting motor is provided with a geared pinion which gives silent engagement. The battery is of approximately 55 ampere-hour capacity. Twin-tone electric horns are fitted.

In keeping with the policy of insulating the occupants of the car as completely as possible from the transmission of small sounds or minor vibrations from the road wheels and mechanism, a new type of body mounting has been adopted. Attachment is provided at twelve points, where there are rubber bushes mounted on a vertical axis. These are able to afford flexibility of movement up to approximately ⅜in, and they relieve the body accordingly.

Finally, interior heating for the coachwork, including de-frosting and de-misting of the windscreen, and a radio set, are included in the standard equipment of this superb chassis.

ROLLS-ROYCE "SILVER WRAITH" TOURING LIMOUSINE BY HOOPER & CO. LTD.

ROLLS-ROYCE "SILVER WRAITH" DROPHEAD FOURSOME COUPE BY GURNEY NUTTING & CO. LTD.

From the side view the advanced frontal lines are clearly evident, but the design is so well balanced that the car appears much smaller than it really is. The finish is in two tones of bronze; valances are fitted to front as well as rear wheels and the flush-fitting door handles form part of the waist line motif.

R.-R. Transformation

Striking Special Body by Hooper on a Silver Wraith Chassis

HOW many can recognize at a glance the car illustrated on this page? Judging from the very modern lines of the crocodile-type bonnet top, which merges direct into the full-width wings, one might almost suspect an Italian origin. Actually, however, it is a Rolls-Royce Silver Wraith with a unique design of sedanca de ville body by Hooper and Co. (Coachbuilders), Ltd.

Not everyone will care for the very advanced frontal appearance, but there can be no doubt that it is extremely striking. Moreover, the full width at the front results in the actual car looking much smaller than it really is. This effect is probably helped by enclosing by side valances the front as well as the rear wheels. As the front wheels must have clearance at full lock the width over the front wings is 6ft 10in. The overall length is no less than 18ft.

The standard Rolls-Royce radiator and cowl have not been interfered with, and are merely hidden by the curved and swept radiator grille which forms part of the body structure. The head and auxiliary lamps are encased by the front wings but they are not carried by them. The radiator grille, bonnet top and front wings have, of

The extreme front end is supported from the chassis by a tubular framework. The lamps are not, however, carried by the body structure. The bonnet top is of crocodile type and, with the curved radiator grille, it covers in the conventional Rolls-Royce radiator and casing.

course, to be supported at the front and accordingly are carried by a tubular framework which is light but strong.

Another special feature of this car is the mechanism for the sliding de ville extension. This is carried on ball-bearing slides and the portion of the roof panel above the rear door is hinged so that when it is unlatched its front edge moves upwards under a spring loading so that the extension can slide back beneath it. The hinged panel is then, of course, closed down again.

The interior is in typical Hooper style with modern treatment in keeping with the general character of the car. The upholstery is in West of England cloth, in shades of dark and light sand, to blend with the two tones of metalessence bronze of the exterior finish. The front seat is in dark brown leather piped with a lighter shade.

An unusual note is the painting of the interior woodwork to match the exterior finish. The door windows, the partition glass and the rear blind are all electrically operated. There appear to be no external door handles, but in fact the ends of the waist moulding on the doors are flush-fitting handles.

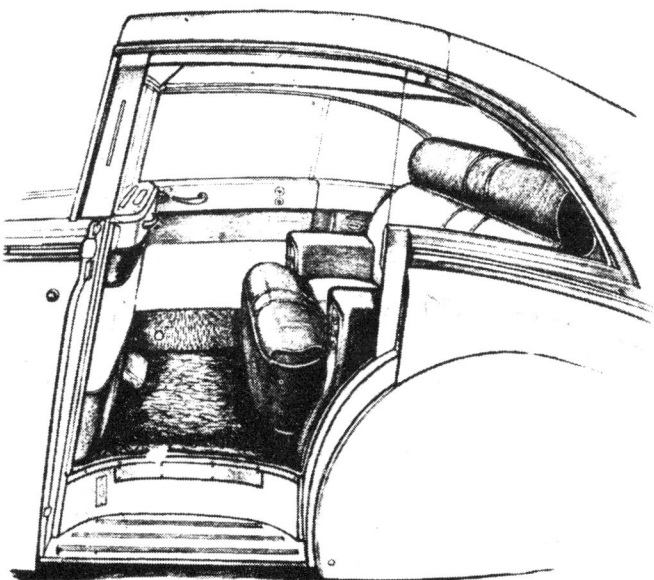

Modern treatment is accorded to the interior, which is upholstered in two shades of cloth of " rolled " type, good use being made of the contrasting colours. Interior woodwork is painted to match the exterior finish.

No Stone Unturned

Unceasing Investigations Carried Out by Rolls-Royce in the Research and Testing Plant of Their Automobile Division

By Montague Tombs
Technical Editor

IN the town of Belper, about ten miles from Derby, and situated in a valley by the side of the River Derwent, there is an unassuming factory premises called Clan Foundry, where the Rolls-Royce and Bentley engineers, designers, testers, and research workers revolve continuously in their special orbits. It is the inner temple of R-R Automobile Division development, and is presided over by "Rm." One regrets at times that the team spirit of R-R is rather against the mentioning of names, which fact hides many a bright intellectual light under a bushel. In the "Clan Belper" they refer to one another by the first and last letters of the surname.

It is a place where there is no room for doubt. Nothing is taken for granted. Should a visitor state what he believes to be a fact, he must be prepared to be able to prove it. If he brought a sample of metal and said that it was so-and-so and had such-and-such physical characteristics, as likely as not that sample would be quietly removed and subjected to immediate tests to prove the truth or otherwise of his assertions. Yet there is nothing of the lion's den about Belper. Rather the reverse. One is made most pleasantly welcome into the bosom of a cheerful and happy family, and it is not for quite some time that an unwary visitor may realise that the conversational ball at the mess room lunch-table is by way of being a punch ball, and might turn into a cannon ball.

Belper is a very human place, although it is steeped in tradition. For instance, you may be sitting with "Rm" in his office. The door opens, a figure in overalls enters. It says, "Eh, have you seen this?" "Well, what about it?" is the reply. "It ain't up to our standards, I don't think." "Right, I'll discuss it at the next technical meeting," is the reply. And the figure goes out satisfied that his comment will be duly investigated.

Behind the Quality Tradition

In short, the same spirit of freedom of speech and search after quality goes right through the organization. Every soul on the ground is intent that nothing should fail on a car once Belper has passed it out as sound. And that tradition, of course, is the reason for Rolls-Royce and Bentley products reaching the highest standards in the world, and maintaining their unique reputation through wars and the broken pieces after the wars.

Although tradition may be an abstract quality, the maintaining of a tradition is very definitely a concrete matter. It has to be carried on every day with wide-awake minds directing skilful hands to operate intricate machinery. No stone must be left unturned. Nothing can be left to chance. In Rolls-Royce engineering, belief has no place; only proof is valid.

Between the tradition behind the products and the products themselves there must be a concrete link. There must be some very definite reason or reasons why these cars not only operate on a higher plane of performance and refinement than any other automobiles in the world, but also maintain their excellence for exceedingly long periods. An owner of an R-R or a modern Bentley is not likely to dispute that his car does actually possess an extraordinary quality which is difficult to define. One has only to drive one of these cars for a few miles to appreciate that the quality is very evidently there. The writer of these notes therefore has been endeavouring to find out what it is that produces this quality. He has found some of the answers, some of the concrete links, in Belper.

Few people outside the organization are permitted to explore all the hidden places in Belper. The writer takes it as a great privilege that he has been allowed to roam with and without a guide in some sections. What a place! It is not, as you might expect, an orderly department full of expensive-looking cream-painted machines with chromium handles and not a speck on the floor. There are things on the floor, but only because someone was working with the apparatus a moment ago. The genius of that place is a masterly gift for improvisation. If a special test rig is wanted, the other Rolls-Royce factories and departments are scoured for convertible components and scraps and pieces, and a rig is made up, exactly as it was wanted, at no very great outlay.

Many New Test Rigs

By this way of working many permanent rigs can be made for the price of one purchased complete from outside, and perhaps not absolutely as required. Hence in the course of time the variety of testing rigs in use has become considerable. It happens that the writer looked over the test rig department just before the war. His recent visit has discovered an entirely new set. It was the habit of Rolls-Royce before the war to purchase, to try, to dissect and to test the best products of other car manufacturers round the world. That practice is continued, and there is not much that R-R do not know about good cars other than their own.

At this point it seems desirable to explain for the benefit of the uninitiated exactly why tests are carried out on these queer machines which are called rigs. Well, most test rigs are contrived as a really quick means of reproducing failures which might be expected to occur, or which have occurred on the road. Normally, R-R expect any component of their vehicles to run 250,000 miles under the most arduous conditions without failing. Obviously, if this mileage had to be covered every time a change was in contemplation, progress would be very slow.

Rigs, in most cases, are brought into operation when a failure has been encountered after, perhaps, 10,000 miles of road work. The distance gives a yardstick for the hours of running on a rig which will cause a similar failure. Hence, by interpolation, the number of hours may be assessed through which a piece must run on its accelerated rig test before breakage. It is the correlation between road work and rig test which is so valuable. Before the war R-R always kept a team of two or three cars running mileage tests on the Continent, where severe conditions

Left: Fig. A. Engine endurance test bed arranged to contribute to the electric mains and to provide shop water heating through an exhaust heat exchanger.

Below: Fig. 2. Apparatus for running a single wheel and tyre on the test drum at various slip angles, cambers, speeds and loads.

with regard to temperature, sustained high speed, and long gradients could be found. Because of difficulties in obtaining fuel these tests are temporarily in abeyance, but in the meantime cars are sent all over the world, including countries such as South America, to check up on their behaviour.

Before describing some of the interesting test rigs which are in use there is one particular instance of adroit improvisation which demands notice. Like everyone else in recent times, the Belper organization had to cope with cuts in fuel and electricity. So Belper secured a suitable large alternating current motor from an aircraft engine test bed, converted it into an alternator with exterior excitation for the field from a railway carriage dynamo, and drove it from a large size experimental car engine. They fitted the engine cooling system with a heat transferring device used in conjunction with the exhaust heat, and so obtained a large hot-water tank to run their shop heating, as well as making their own electricity at mains pressure. This enabled them not only to be independent of the mains, but also to provide a contribution to load shedding. The set-up is shown in Fig. A.

Furthermore, they had obtained a test bed for long-term testing of engines on full throttle. This improvisation was accomplished in little over a week, and one eight-cylinder engine has been running at 1,800 r.p.m., as needed by the generator, developing 120 h.p., for over 1,000 hours—a severe type of test indeed. The heating and electricity supply plant is in a separate building from the main test

Fig. 1. Gear box and transmission test rig, an eight-cylinder engine driving a test gear box which is coupled to an electric dynamometer brake. Rear axles can be tested on this rig.

rig department, and it contains other comprehensive testing plant as well. There is a massive bed upon which gear boxes and rear axles can be tested, either by driving from a powerful electric motor and measuring results on an electric eddy current dynamometer, as shown in Fig. 1, or by driving from a car engine. This engine is also provided with a duplicate set of equipment to provide shop heating. Yet another large electric motor rests on a bed which carries an engine crankcase and cylinder head, but with no pistons and no ordinary crankshaft. This outfit is used for investigating the behaviour of valves and valve gear at high speeds.

Problems of Metal Fatigue

In order to provide the right atmosphere in which to describe the work of Clan Belper, it may be worth while to draw attention to the characteristics of all structural metals and materials. The normal characteristics such as the tensile strength, the elastic limit, the hardness, the rigidity, and the fatigue value are well established, and by the rules the engineer can calculate his designs, and may be sure that his machine will be strong enough in all its parts. But what he cannot be sure of beforehand is the length of time which the machine will last without being halted by some perhaps unexpected minor failure. The killing burden on materials is fatigue. How long can a mechanism survive carrying its load when the load is constantly changing, perhaps reversing? Fatigue is the result of stress reversals. Small stresses under high-speed reversal, such as are caused by fine vibrations, can be most disruptive. Engineers ran afresh into that bother when they first made jet propulsion units.

The primary task of all the test rigs which R-R employ is to reproduce exactly what happens to any part of a machine whilst on duty, to speed up the process, make everything measurable, and produce fatigue, in as short a time as possible, under strict observation.

To progress now to the test rig department proper, the largest apparatus comprises the rolling drums for chassis testing, which are submerged below the level of the floor, and hence do not show up easily in a photograph. A pair of submerged drums can be seen in Fig. 2, but as used for tests on a single wheel. There are two sets, consisting of a pair of wide-faced drums or wheels, set below ground with the upper circumference level with the floor. The drums are a car-track width apart. Each pair can be driven from a variable speed 40 h.p. electric motor, or from the wheels of a car. One set is coupled to a Heenan and Froude water brake.

These drums can be used for many purposes, including the analytical investigation of a complete car or of component parts. Power developed at the road wheels can be measured, or the frictional resistance of the mechanism can be checked in detail. Speeds up to 100 m.p.h. can be used. Cams, or artificial bumps, can be attached to the drums for investigating suspension. There are special provisions for studying tyres, wheels, and brakes. One set of these drums is submerged in an inspection pit and stroboscopic lighting is provided by means of which sight is geared down—so to speak—and fast movement appears to the eye as a slow movement which can easily be followed. This apparatus shows up in a manner sometimes quite alarming how structural parts are bending and weaving under the influence of the cyclic stresses which are being applied to them.

Recently a fresh accessory has been devised for these drums. It was desired to determine whether the movement of a wheel free to rise and fall when rotated by a drum, and kicked upwards by a cam for each revolution of the drum, occurred in a vertical line or not. A single wheel was mounted in bearings at the ends of its spindle attached to the centre of twin half-elliptic springs, one on each side. The springs were carried in long shackles, so that the wheel could choose its own path of rise and fall. Without going into complicated technical details of cause and effect, the net result of this test was to prove that at low speeds the wheel does not rise along a vertical path, but at an angle from the vertical. However, at high speeds the rise is approximatly vertical. If hollows instead of bumps are simulated on the drum, so that the wheel drops from normal instead of rising, similar results, but in the opposite direction, are produced.

Data on Creep Angles

There are a great many uses to which these testing drums can be put, and all sorts of special equipment have been devised to deal with particular problems. An interesting case in point is the rig shown in Fig. 2, already mentioned, which provides a steerable mounting for a single wheel and tyre on one revolving drum. The loading on the wheel can be adjusted to any desired degree, the camber angle of the wheel is variable, and the wheel can be steered to any desired angle, each factor and its reactions being subject to accurate measurement. Tests can be made through a wide range of wheel speeds. This apparatus produces data about slip, or creep, angles of tyres, under a variety of conditions. Recently it has been used for measuring the side load at which alternative types of tyre begin to squeal.

On an automobile the heaviest loads on the steering gear are not, as one might suppose, caused by steering at high speed, but by the effort applied to the steering wheel during parking and manœuvring at low speeds. A special rig shown in Fig. 3 has been devised to test steering gear to destruction under these conditions. With the front wheels resting on the ground, well loaded, and the tyres slightly under-inflated, a rig is attached to the chassis. The rig grips the rim of the steering wheel, and an electric motor is used to drive an hydraulic pump which in turn operates the hydraulic motor gripping the rim. There is a reversing valve in the hydraulic pump. The rig can twist the steering wheel so that the front wheels repeatedly turn from full lock one way to full lock the other. The process goes on until something fails. Usually it is the steering gear that gives way first. Incidentally, the hydraulic mechanism is another spot of improvisation; it used once to rotate the turret in a tank.

138

Fig. 3. Hydraulic pump and reversing motor which twist the steering wheel repeatedly from full lock one side to the other, the tyres being on the ground and the chassis suitably loaded.

Another massive and imposing apparatus is the leaf spring endurance rig shown in Fig. 4. It is used for examining the behaviour of springs as well as for testing their endurance, and is able to cope with two springs at a time. It has equipment to deal with coil and other springs as well as the leaf type. In the head of it is a large cross-shaft driven from an electric motor. At each end of the shaft is a variable-throw crank or swape. A connecting-rod from this runs down to the centre of the spring, if it is half-elliptic, and the spring eyes are shackled at one end and attached to a special shackle at the other. This special shackle is connected to a strong torsion bar spring element, and further connections are made to an indicator which draws a graph upon a chart. Thus the deflection of the

Fig. 4. The leaf spring endurance rig, working on one half-elliptic spring. It can test two springs at a time and can also be used for front suspension coil springs.

Fig. 5. The wheel rim test rig, showing the set-up for measuring stress in rims by strain gauges.

spring is indicated at the same time as the number of oscillations per minute. The investigation can be continued until the spring fails, and its characteristics during the test are recorded.

During the war period R-R had one of their experimental chassis running as a ten-seater bus working all and every day. During the process on two occasions splits in the steel rim of a wheel were encountered. This unusual occurrence was duly noted for investigation when opportunity offered. This was found to be a rather difficult nut to crack. It was not easy to simulate the conditions which caused the failure. Eventually a suitable rig was constructed, and now any tendency to rim weakness can quickly be ferreted out. This wheel rim test rig, as will be seen from Fig. 5, consists of an assembly bed of stout steel girders upon which a pair of rear axles with wheels and tyres can be mounted side by side and parallel to one another. The foremost axle is firmly located, and its spiral bevel pinion is coupled to a powerful electric motor. The second axle is so mounted that it can be slideably adjusted by means of screw jacks to bring the tyres of the one axle into measurable pressure contact with those of the other. Suitable variations in the contact pressure between the tyres, and in the speed of rotation of the wheels, bring about the condition required, and rim flanges which do actually have local weakness are caused to split away.

As very often happens when research is being made, other phenomena are brought to notice. It was so with this rig. The factor of the rapid rise in tractive effect caused by increase in road speed was well known, but the magnitude was not perhaps fully appreciated. The rig showed that the tractive effort required to drive the tyres rises at the rate of the fourth power. Wind resistance of a car rises at the rate of the third power. This in simple language means that the maximum speed of a given car can be more easily raised by changing the tyres to a type offering less tractive resistance than by streamlining the body.

While on the subject of wheels, another interesting rig is shown in Fig. 6. It is concerned with testing the strength and durability of disc wheels. As a matter of fact it does other jobs besides disc testing, but the part with which we are concerned at the moment is the large face plate on the right side. This is mounted on a stout shaft with a large diameter multiple V-belt pulley wheel driven from an electric motor concealed within the guard. It will be seen that the face plate has stout clamps spaced around its circumference. A complete disc wheel is fastened to the face plate by means of the clamps gripping the pneumatic tyre. Then, in place of a hub, a flange is bolted into the centre of the disc. The flange carries a long and massive spindle arm which projects horizontally outwards, and at its far end weights are hung. Then the face plate is rotated.

Importance of Wheel Nut Tightness

The whole disc is thus subjected to constant loads and stress reversals, which can be varied or carried on until somewhere the disc fatigues, and a crack or fracture occurs. This wheel disc testing rig showed up in a marked manner how very important it is that, with a disc wheel bolted to a hub, the securing nuts must be accurately seated and correctly tightened. Lack of uniformity in this can considerably reduce the life of the disc wheel.

We might next take a look at the other side of this particular rig, as shown in Fig. 7. Here is another set-up altogether, which has been called the Iron Lung. It is for testing radiators. A crank on the end of the pulley shaft has a connecting-rod operating a piston in a single cylinder—more ex-aircraft parts—which makes a pump. This pump forces air in cyclic changes of pressure into the radiator to be tested, which is filled with water and otherwise sealed. Weak spots in radiators are very easily discovered with this apparatus. It can determine the amount of linear growth under a pressure of, say, 2 lb per sq in. The cyclic pressure causes the radiator matrix to breathe, and so discovers any spots where fatigue may cause failure. This particular rig is versatile, because other sections of it can be used for endurance tests on various types of ball bearings on brake servo motors.

To be concluded next week

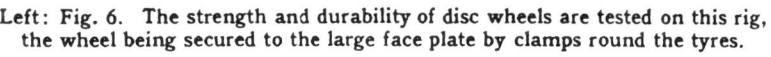

Left: Fig. 6. The strength and durability of disc wheels are tested on this rig, the wheel being secured to the large face plate by clamps round the tyres.

Below: Fig. 7. This is the "Iron Lung," which breathes heavily into a water-filled and sealed radiator, with the object that the cyclic changes of pressure shall find any weak spots in the radiator construction.

IN our continued investigation into the hidden mysteries of the Rolls-Royce automobile research department, its unremitting search for truth, and its genius for improvizing tests and testing machines to get at the truth without needless waste of time or money, it may be noted that amongst all this specially constructed apparatus there is one item which is not an improvization, a large-size Avery spring testing machine, shown in Fig. 8. This is used for general loading and deflection tests. It is true that R-R have made all sorts of special attachments for it, so that they can deal with coil springs, torsion bars, and rubber bushes. Another fitting enables tests to be made of clutch flexible centres in order to determine their correct rating. R-R go to a lot of trouble over springs, and check up carefully on components sent from Crewe as well as on their own experimental work. They want to be certain of the after-effects of processes used in production spring manufacture, such as scragging, shot blasting, and polishing leaves.

One of the factors brought to light by the various rigs for testing road springs was the importance of the correct setting of coil springs for independent front suspension. Where radius arms are employed it is obvious that a coil spring is also bent out of a straight axis when it is compressed. Hence the setting of the angular position of the end coils can materially affect the characteristics of the spring. A rig has been made to determine the correct setting for various types of coil spring.

Hard on the Damper

The complicated-looking piece of machinery shown in Fig. 9 has been specially made for "giving the works" to spring suspension dampers of all types. It can determine their precise characteristics to a fine measurement and check up on their behaviour. The damper is attached to a floating mounting, the movements of which can be measured in detail and recorded, whilst the damper arm is reciprocated by the crank and beam on the left side of the picture. The throw of the arm can be set as required.

Endurance tests on dampers are carried out on a separate rig, which can continue to operate the damper to the limit at which something fails. The damper test rigs have shown themselves to be necessary because damper design, construction and durability have not kept pace with the developments of suspension. Amongst other things the research has shown methods of curing the "squawk" of

No Stone

Fig. 9. This complicated machine can find out all there is to know about the behaviour characteristics of any shock absorber or spring damper.

valves, and has established the imperative need of finding fluids which will maintain their viscosity over the full range of working temperature. A completely satisfactory fluid has not yet appeared.

There is another interesting testing apparatus, Fig. 10, which has been specially made for the purpose of observing the behaviour of grease in front wheel hub bearings. When a car is operating in a mountainous country in a hot climate, and the brakes have to be used hard, front hub bearings can get very hot. So the rig shown in Fig. 10 was devised, with the object of testing greases to discover how effectively they will stay in good condition and remain in place at different temperatures. It operates a loaded hub within a chamber, the temperature of which can be ac-

Fig. 8. The Avery spring testing machine, for which rigs have been made to deal also with coil springs, and even with clutch centres.

Unturned

By Montague Tombs
Technical Editor

Fig. 10. The front hubs grease test rig for running front hubs at high temperatures to determine the behaviour and suitability of various greases.

Fig. 11. Two hydraulic tensometers attached to the gear box for measuring input and output loads of the brake system mechanical servo. The thermo-couple instrument in the background is recording the temperature of the servo rubbing face.

curately controlled. Some rather surprising results were obtained, and in one case the grease being tested changed into a mass of separate brown lumps rather like a breakfast cereal, though probably not so pleasant to eat. And most greases would apparently prefer to exude past the oil seals rather than stay put.

Mention of brakes recalls that when a powerful car is expected to produce fast motoring in such districts as the Alps, the brakes have to go through a gruelling time indeed. Belper conducts detailed research into the efficiency of brake design and the ability of brake linings to resist the nightmare known as "fade," which is the tendency to reduce their co-efficient of friction as they get hot. Additionally there is a rig, shown in Fig. 11, which is used for measuring the load on brake connections, to determine the distribution of load and the frictional losses in the system. It is a portable tensometer employing a low - loss hydraulic cylinder with pressure gauges, which can be hooked up anywhere in the brake set-up. The brake testing apparatus has been valuable in locating the causes of variation in brake performance, particularly after cars have been standing at night out in the open, and the exact nature of the changes in the efficiency of brake linings caused by the formation of moisture in brakes from condensation.

Problems in connection with the water circulation system of the engine are dealt with on a bed carrying the engine and providing a drive for it from a large electric motor, as shown in

Fig. 12. A rig consisting of an electric motor driving the engine whilst everything in connection with water circulation can be measured and tested.

Fig. 12. Above the bed is a water tank, the contents of which can be controlled as regards temperature. The behaviour of water pumps can be exactly checked, and everything relevant to water circulation. This rig resulted in two important discoveries in particular. It drew attention to the fact that if a water pump is to maintain its delivery at high engine speeds, the spring loading on the gland must not be below a certain minimum, otherwise the gland becomes able to lift from its seat and admit air. The second point was the need for close fits between the driving tongue and the driving slots in pump rotors; without close fits freedom from slight chatter cannot be ensured. That may seem a small matter, but on the other hand the almost uncanny quietness of Rolls-Royce engines is secured only by meticulous attention to the elimination of small noises, one by one.

The endurance of water pumps is tested on a branch of the multi-purpose rig which looks after radiators, disc wheels and servo motors, and performs other duties. Fig. 13 shows a water pump mounted to be driven continuously until it fails by a rubber V-belt from a large-diameter flat pulley, whilst taking and returning the water to the tank. Incidentally not everybody knows that a rubber V-belt will convey drive to or take drives from a large diameter flat pulley without flying off.

When a car is intended to be able to give of its best anywhere in the world, a close study of its behaviour in

Fig. 13. A water pump on a rig for endurance test, with sand in the water to determine the effect on the pump.

hot or cold climates and at different altitudes is necessary. One of the major difficulties is to obtain quick and certain starting of the engine under conditions of extreme cold. To deal with this a special trolley, Fig. 14, has been made which will carry a complete engine unit with radiator and fuel tank. This trolley can be run into a cold chamber, and starting tests made at many degrees below freezing point, or even below zero Fahrenheit.

To come to a subject that one does not need to be an engineer in order to understand, there is the smoke tent (Fig. 15). In it the coachwork of the car can be tested for the existence of small chinks, minor orifices and so forth through which it would be possible for draughts, dust or fumes to enter the body. The car is placed in the tent, and then a trolley carrying a large centrifugal fan driven by an electric motor is wheeled in. The fan blows smoke, and its delivery pipe can be directed to any desired point. An observer—an unfortunate man if there are any leaks—gets into the car, shuts all the windows, turns on the lights, and then the flap of the tent is closed, leaving him to his fate. Not that any man of the true faith in Clan Foundry minds putting up with a trifle of asphyxiation in the cause of getting at the truth, the whole truth and nothing but the truth, if by so doing he may advance the cause of R-R.

The world-wide reputation which has been won by

Fig. 14. An engine on the trolley for use in the cold chamber. The rig is used for general experiments on "startability," the torque required to start from cold, and the suitability of the starter engagement mechanism.

Rolls-Royce does not depend only upon the silken silence of the running of the cars or the extraordinarily responsive nature of their performance, or the suaveness of their controls. This reputation is firmly based on the indestructible long life of the cars. They run great distances, 100,000 miles or so, without need of overhaul, and after overhaul will do the same again, *ad infinitum*. This longevity has been won by careful attention to detail—every conceivable detail. Nothing is too large for test, nothing too small. There is a rather quaint test rig, Fig. 16, which discovers the truth about spring clips, such as are used for holding tools in orderly positions in a tool compartment. What is

Fig. 15. The smoke tent, which is used for testing the complete car in order to hunt for leaks into the body through which dust or draught might find entrance.

the difference between a good spring clip and a poor one? How long will a spring clip last? All right. We will take a selection of clips, fasten them down in the usual way, and then engage and disengage suitably sized dummies attached to a reciprocating arm. This process will be continued until the clips have failed, one by one. Of course the same rig can be used for other tests needing a reciprocating load, but there it is in the picture, shaking up the clips.

Losing Power Deliberately

I have kept until the last what is perhaps the most interesting item of all, a specially constructed trailer for absorbing the power developed by a car while travelling along a level road. This power absorbing trailer is shown in Fig. 17. It is a chariot likely to inspire awe amongst bystanders, and inevitably makes one think of Boadicea and the early days of Britain. Once again the trailer is a masterpiece of improvization, built up from the tail end of an old chassis with its rear axle. In the front part are three more axle bevel gear centres; drive from the axle proper is conveyed to the centre of the three, and those on each flank reconvey the drive back to a pair of large improvized dynamos, the output of which can be exactly controlled and measured, so that braking effort of the trailer as a whole can be varied and set at any speed within the available range.

No doubt the best way to describe this machine is to give the gist, without electrical technicalities, of what the R-R Research Department has to say about it.

During the experimental development of i.c. engined road vehicles the need occasionally arises for a means of running the vehicle at full throttle for prolonged periods at a constant and generally low speed. This may be necessary for investigating a vibration or noise which occurs at a particular speed, for checking the work-out mesh of the transmission under maintained driving loads, and in particular for measuring the performance of the cooling system.

In the case of relatively low h.p. vehicles, short-duration tests as above can be done on long hills of sufficient steepness, while cooling tests, which require a total duration of not less than one hour, with a minimum of 10-15 min without interruption at a low speed of 20-30 m.p.h., depending upon the type of vehicle, can be done by towing a second and generally larger vehicle. This, with a low gear engaged and engine overrunning, has enough drag to absorb the surplus power of the vehicle under test.

With larger vehicles with engines of more than three litres capacity it may not be possible to find a second vehicle with sufficient overrun drag to keep the speed down, so that two vehicles have to be towed. This is not a practicable proposition on public roads, although it was possible on Brooklands.

In view of the above difficulties and the urgent necessity for the measurement of cooling performance on post-war cars, it was decided to construct a single axle trailer capable of holding down to 30 m.p.h. the highest-powered vehicle contemplated at that time. The requirements were that the trailer should absorb 100 h.p. at 30 m.p.h., should be remotely controlled from the towing car, and, if possible, have automatic control to keep the speed constant at any desired figure from, say, 20 m.p.h. to 40 m.p.h. irrespective of gradient and power input. As far as possible existing surplus equipment was to be used for the job.

The use of a water brake for absorbing the power offered too many awkward difficulties, whereas the electrical absorption of the power with final dissipation in air-cooled resistances appeared to be much more suitable because (1) The temperature of the resistance elements can be far higher than is convenient with water, making the air-cooled unit small and fans unnecessary; (2) Remote and automatic control are easily arranged, no external source of power is required, and the cables to the car are light. The response of the control should be rapid.

Since suitable surplus electrical equipment was available it was decided to adopt the electrical system. The multiplicity of units in the trailer resulted mainly from the use of existing equipment, but does also give a compact layout. The all-up weight is 27½ cwt.

The main generators are wound rotor three-phase a.c. induction motors normally rated at 45 h.p., 1,500 r.p.m., 200 volts. For use as generators the rotors are fed with d.c. of approximately 40-80 amps at 10-20 volts per machine. The d.c. is supplied by four 7in dynamos, normally of 12-volt, 50-amp capacity.

How Speed is Controlled

For speed regulation a small 12-volt dynamo is belt-driven from one of the main generators and operates a trembling voltage regulator, the contacts of which control the fields of the four 7in exciters and so eventually the output of the main generators. Controllable separate excitation in the field circuit of the small speed-controlling dynamo adjusts the speed at which this dynamo will produce the necessary voltage to operate the regulator. The speed of the trailer is limited to 40 m.p.h., which is 2,110 r.p.m. on the main rotors. In operation the trailer has proved to have more capacity than was expected, and will hold a 4¼-litre Bentley Mk. VI down to 12-15 m.p.h. on top gear and to about 23 m.p.h. on first gear.

Originally the centre of the three axle gear units which transfer the drive from the main propeller-shaft back to the generators had the normal differential. It was found that in this condition one generator would crawl while the other ran at a corresponding overspeed. This differential was therefore locked.

The trailer has now been in use for about three months and has done over 2,000 miles, mainly on cooling tests. It has proved remarkably effective in revealing vibrations, noises and suchlike, at full throttle and low speeds, which are normally not conspicuous because they are passed through so rapidly during acceleration. So far no provision has been made for measuring the power absorbed by the trailer. If this should be required at a later date it would probably be best done by measuring the mechanical load in the attachment between trailer and car.

Fig. 16. Even tool clips have to go through it. This rig repeatedly inserts dummies and retracts them until the clips fail.

Fig. 17. This trailer is a brake on progress, for it is deliberately built to absorb a considerable amount of power by means of electrical resistances — just how much being controllable and measurable.

This new model has a classic economy of line.

EXPORT ROLLS-ROYCE

SILVER DAWN MODEL FOR WESTERN HEMISPHERE

A NEW model by Rolls-Royce is always something of an event, even when it is—like so many things at the present time—for export only. The new Silver Dawn, which was exhibited for the first time at the recent International World's Fair at Toronto, is designed to appeal to those overseas connoisseurs who appreciate the quality of a Rolls-Royce but who do not require a chauffeur-driven car. News of its advert in New York was given in last week's issue.

Basically it comprises the well-tried Silver Wraith engine and chassis, with modifications; for instance, the wheelbase is reduced to 10ft. The suspension remains, as before, independent at the front, embodying wishbones and coil springs, and of conventional half-elliptic pattern at the rear. Hydraulic dampers are employed, those at the rear being adjustable by means of a lever on the steering column. On this chassis is mounted an all-steel body, designed and constructed by Rolls-Royce, Ltd. Another innovation is the installation of the gear lever on the steering column, which is, of course, on the left-hand side; the gear box remains, as before, a four-speed pattern with synchromesh on second, third and the direct-drive top. Right-hand steering with right-hand gear change can be supplied if required.

The braking system also follows Rolls-Royce established practice. There is hydraulic operation at the front, while the rear brakes are mechanically operated. Braking is assisted by a mechanical servo mounted on the side of the gear box and driven by the driven shaft. The result is superlative, for the right foot, instead of doing nearly all the work required to stop the car, does little more than operate the control.

The interior of the body is luxuriously done, the seats being upholstered in leather in "pleating and bolster" style. The front seats are individually adjustable, and in their backs are folding tables for the use of the rear passengers. Complete heating, de-misting and de-frosting equipment is provided, together with a six-valve radio.

The instruments are centrally grouped and include a large-dial speedometer clock, ammeter, fuel gauge and combined oil pressure gauge and water thermometer. There is also a fuel level warning light. The tank capacity is 18 gallons.

It is pleasant to observe that a sliding roof is included in the specification; quarter-light ventilators are also provided in the front windows.

As this is intended to be a model which can, if necessary, be owner-maintained as well as owner-driven, the difficulties of maintenance have been reduced to a minimum. A centrally placed jacking point is to be found on each side, beneath the body sill, while the centralized system of chassis lubrication, including supplies to all necessary points on both the front and rear suspensions, is operated by a pedal mounted on the interior of the bulkhead.

Large bumpers are fitted, together with the over-riders which are such a necessary feature overseas. The head lamps, which have their own fairings merging into the front wing valances, are supplemented by twin driving lamps.

The price of the Silver Dawn will vary slightly according to the duty payable in the particular country to which it is exported; in Toronto, however, it was quoted as $14,000 (£3,500).

Under a neat facia of figured wood is the radio set. The steering column gear change lever is operated by the right hand, and the damper control is in the boss of the wheel. Right: Pleated and bolstered leather is used for the upholstery.

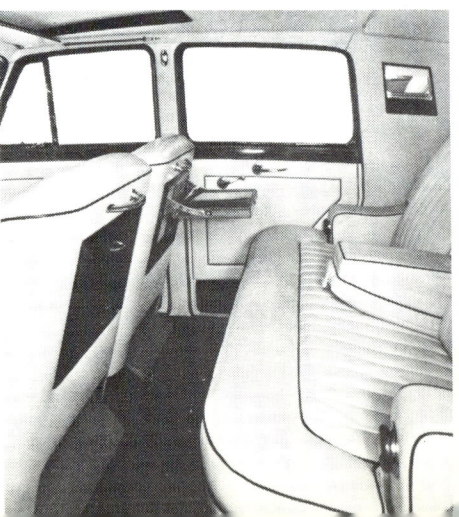

Although the H. J. Mulliner sedanca is a four-light style, with pivoting ventilator panels additional to the drop glasses in each door, it is primarily intended for chauffeur driving. A glass division behind the non-adjustable driving seat is electrically operated.

No. 1393: ROLLS-ROYCE SILVER WRAITH SEDANCA DE VILLE

DATA FOR THE DRIVER

ROLLS-ROYCE SILVER WRAITH

PRICE, with sedanca de ville body, £3,875, plus £2,154 5s 6d British purchase tax. Total (in Great Britain), £6,029 5s 6d.

RATING : 29.4 h.p., 6 cylinders, overhead inlet, side exhaust valves, 89 × 114 mm, 4,256 c.c.

COMPRESSION RATIO : 6.4 to 1. 23 m.p.h. per 1,000 r.p.m. on top gear.

TYRE SIZE : 6.50 × 17in on bolt-on steel wheels with discs. **LIGHTING SET** : 12-volt. **WEIGHT** : 42 cwt 1 qr 0 lb (4,732 lb). **LB. per C.C.** : 1.11.

TANK CAPACITY : 18 Imperial gallons : approximate fuel consumption range, 15-17 m.p.g. (18.8-16.6 litres per 100 km).

TURNING CIRCLE : (L) 44ft 11in ; (R) 46ft 5in. **MINIMUM GROUND CLEAR-ANCE** : 8.125in.

MAIN DIMENSIONS : Wheelbase, 10ft 7in. Track, 4ft 10½in (front) ; 5ft 0in (rear). Overall length, 17ft 2in ; width, 6ft 1in ; height, 5ft 11in.

ACCELERATION

Overall gear ratios	From steady m.p.h. of		
	10 to 30	20 to 40	30 to 50
	sec	sec	sec
3.727 to 1 ..	13.5	12.4	13.0
5.001 to 1 ..	9.5	9.1	10.0
7.520 to 1 ..	6.0	6.6	—
11.113 to 1 ..	—	—	—

From rest through gears to :—

	sec			sec
30 m.p.h.	7.9		60 m.p.h.	24.0
50 m.p.h.	17.2		70 m.p.h.	37.4

Steering wheel movement from lock to lock : 3¼ turns.

WEATHER : Rain, cold ; fresh wind.

Acceleration figures are the means of several runs in opposite directions.

Speedometer correction by Electric Speedometer :—

Car Speedometer	Electric Speedometer m.p.h.	Car Speedometer	Electric Speedometer m.p.h.
10	= 8.5	50	= 48.25
20	= 18	60	= 59
30	= 28.25	70	= 69.5
40	= 38		

Speeds attainable on gears (by Electric Speedometer)

	M.p.h. (normal and max)	K.p.h. (normal and max)
1st ..	14—24	22.5— 38.6
2nd ..	31—44	49.8— 70.8
3rd ..	56—68	90.1—109.4

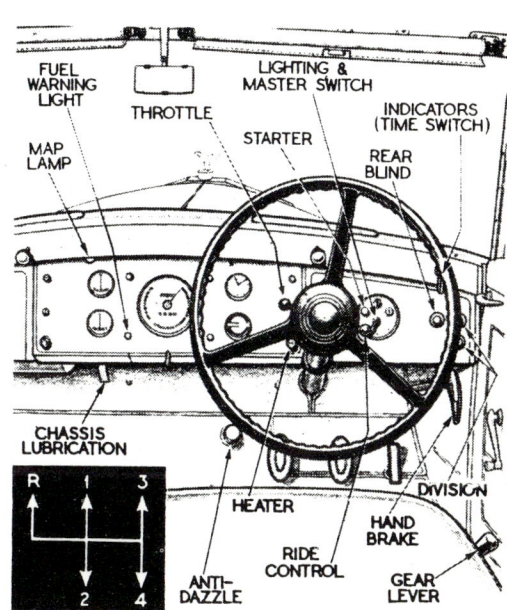

The Autocar ROAD TESTS

FUEL WARNING LIGHT — MAP LAMP — THROTTLE — LIGHTING & MASTER SWITCH — STARTER — INDICATORS (TIME SWITCH) — REAR BLIND — CHASSIS LUBRICATION — R 1 3 2 4 — HEATER — RIDE CONTROL — ANTI-DAZZLE — HAND BRAKE — GEAR LEVER — DIVISION

Described in " The Autocar " of April 5, 1946.

IN a world of shattered monetary values and yet much-improved cars, the Rolls-Royce still stands alone. Perhaps the most striking general thought in considering this supreme machine today is that it has a name more universally known, more universally honoured, as a symbol of quality than that of any other manufactured product, and that is a proud boast, which can be put forward on behalf of a British car. If it can be justified, and there is little doubt that it can, it is because the name stands so extraordinarily high in relation to cars, and without need to call upon the powerful aid of the reputation of the Rolls-Royce aircraft engines.

An opportunity to renew acquaintance with the current Silver Wraith, which with the recently introduced Silver Dawn, of shorter wheelbase and for export only, represents the post-war cars bearing the Rolls-Royce name, has enabled the practical reasons for this tremendous reputation to be re-examined on the road. A natural question asks what it is about a car that should make it cost between £3,500 and £4,000, according to body style, in its country of origin ; and what a reflection it is upon the times that on the actual model that has been tested now, the sedanca

de ville, the home market purchase tax paid to the Government is more than the chassis price.

Detailed answers to that question are of book length rather than within the scope of a Road Test. A great part of the considered reply lies in the past, bearing in mind the research and development and painstaking, restless progress that have gone to develop the Rolls-Royce car seen today. This is not, however, to imply that the design has stood still, for independent suspension was adopted for its predecessor, the Wraith, as long ago as 1938, and even outwardly the present engine and its auxiliaries show a considerable change from that pre-war forerunner, whilst on the export-only car mentioned previously the modern feature of a steering column gear change is available.

The charm, the appeal, the true practical worth of this car among other cars is not that it has the highest performance capable of being derived from 4¼ litres of six-cylinder engine designed and built in the Rolls-Royce manner, a phrase meaning so much, but, as so often has been said, the way in which the car behaves and handles and its day in, day out consistency. The Silver Wraith, with a sedanca body, intended primarily for chauffeur driving, looks a

145

The roof over the front compartment of the body fitted to this particular car can be opened in this smart sedanca de ville style, leaving the side windows for draught prevention.

very big car; yet apart from the matter of manœuvring into a space only just big enough for it when parking at a kerbside, which can never be easy with a large car, the overall dimensions can be practically forgotten.

Rolls-Royce have remembered that a big car, to be serviceable under all conditions and drivable by anyone, must have a superlatively good steering lock, and steering which is never heavy at low speed yet is able to achieve also the difficult opposite task of providing safe control at speeds between 80 and 90 m.p.h. This matter of ease of control has perhaps impressed itself more forcibly on this present occasion even than in past experiences of the R-R.

The driver's position is as it should be. He sits fairly high up, and can see the left wing. The windscreen pillars are thin, and, above all, each control moves lightly yet with precision to the extent that, although it is unnecessary, the driver delights in frequently using the beautifully balanced, clash-proof right-hand gear change with its perfect synchromesh on second, third and top.

To emphasize again the qualities of control, the driver concerned elected, while carrying practically a full load, to take in the dark a narrow winding hill of some length and about 1 in 7 gradient for the sheer delight of controlling the car on the bends, playing between second and third gears for the sake of full performance, and to go out of his way to use an awkward route with a sharp left-hand corner on an appreciable gradient, which he has shirked on occasion in a car of smaller size but clumsier characteristics.

Behind those comments lies an indication of some considerable part of the combination of superlative qualities that Rolls-Royce have put into their car. In some ways, for all its size, it is perhaps the easiest car in the world to drive, out of the small class, because of the lightness and delicacy of the controls.

Part of this aspect, too, is the unique and astonishingly effective braking system. It is unique today for the use of a disc servo, driven from the gear box and engaged by the first depression of the brake pedal, which applies the front hydraulic brakes and then augments the pedal operation of the mechanical rear brakes. The driver is at no time made to realize to his disadvantage that a power application of the brakes is interposed. It is a pleasure in itself to bring the speed down supremely smoothly and

yet rapidly from the eighties with the utmost nicety of pedal pressure, or alternatively to effect in just the same silky manner the ordinary traffic deceleration from 20 m.p.h. at a traffic light. With very little experience of the system this smooth effect can be achieved, but if a driver accustomed to other brakes treads hard he quickly realizes what tremendous braking power is concealed beneath the normally silky effect so readily evoked by the lightest touch on this car's pedal.

The steering ratio is a compromise between low and high gearing in terms of modern practice, and there is strong, but not obtrusive, castor action. Then there is the suspension, as soft as can be wished for a stone sett surface, for instance, never over-soft, however, to permit lateral movement, and always under immediate regulation to suit conditions by finger movement of a lever on the steering wheel, which controls the action of the rear hydraulic dampers. With these set at maximum effect the car feels really taut and can be cornered in a style which would probably surprise anyone with preconceived notions and no knowledge of a current R-R. At this maximum damper setting the steering is seen at its best, too. Sometimes at low speed, on a minimum setting of the dampers, a light steering-wheel shake from road wheel reaction is noticed, though this never amounts to anything that matters.

A remark was made earlier to the effect that the Rolls-Royce does not represent the maximum performance that can be obtained from its engine size. In point of fact, if one considers a journey of either 50 miles or 500, but preferably the latter, it is the fastest and most untiring car in the world with the exception of its close relative the Mark VI Bentley. It gets easily to 80 m.p.h. and can see more, towards the genuine 90 mark, where there is space. It has superb capabilities on top gear up a gradient, an instance being a 1 in 9 hill approached briskly in the forties, and with the same practically full passenger load mentioned earlier, on which it held such a speed that made it unnecessary to think of dropping to third. Second gear will take it up almost any gradient normally encountered and is the regularly used gear for starting purposes. Those who know the R-R already can hardly be surprised by its low-speed flexibility on top gear; in fact this is very striking, in spite of modern improvement in

In these general and close-up views of the rear compartment a good impression is gained of the spaciousness and luxury. Fine quality cloth upholstery, an all but flat floor, very wide door opening, neatly folding occasional seats and tables, a radio built into the division and beautiful walnut veneering are main features of the interior of the H. J. Mulliner body fitted in this instance.

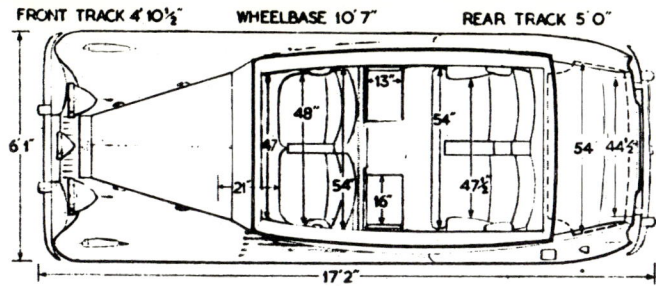
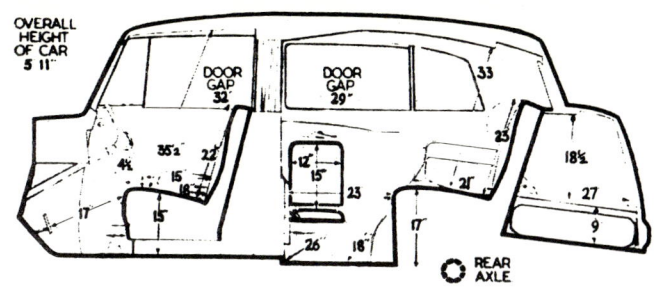

FRONT TRACK 4′10½″   WHEELBASE 10′7″   REAR TRACK 5′0″

OVERALL HEIGHT OF CAR 5′11″   DOOR GAP 32   DOOR GAP 29

REAR AXLE

Measurements in these scale body diagrams are taken with the driving seat in the central position of fore and aft adjustment and with seat cushions uncompressed.

this direction, down to a genuine 5 m.p.h., from which it will accelerate on a snap depression of the throttle pedal. Yet top is a very high gear, in the overdrive category as regards ratio.

When accelerating hard the engine can be felt the merest trifle, but one has to think about the matter to realize that this is so and quote from experience by remarking, "for a Rolls-Royce." Even on the standard British Pool petrol not at any time was there a trace of pinking. Silence of the gears and of the transmission is expected and found.

It might be supposed in some quarters that little information would result from the normal recording of acceleration figures with this car against a stop-watch, but even there something was learned, remarkable consistency in the individual readings being displayed even though the weather conditions were bad for this part of the test. This consistency in detail is repeated on a bigger scale throughout in ownership.

Less than justice can be done to the body, in this instance an H. J. Mulliner sedanca de ville upholstered in leather in the front seats, which in this particular model are non-adjustable, and in the finest cloth in the spacious rear compartment. Lavish use is made of magnificently veneered woodwork, especially in the rear compartment. The division glass and the rear window blind, which is of opaque material, are electrically operated, the division being under the passengers' as well as the driver's control. A heater unit, taking in fresh air from the front, is placed under the left front seat. Three people could travel in the front seat, the gear lever and hand-brake levers presenting no obstruction. The depth of the front windows results in draught being easily caused, but the main windows can be closed and ventilation of the front compartment obtained in cold or wet weather by means of hinged panels.

It would have been preferred for the steering column to have been more sharply raked, as was seen on another current car, a matter of service station adjustment to requirements. The wheel is a large non-spring-spoked pattern with a comfortably notched rim. In the details many lessons are pointed, among them the fact that one Yale

Very considerable as the capacity of the luggage locker is, there is provision for securing the lid firmly open as an additional platform, and a leather-covered roller blind can then be brought down to seal off the interior. Spare wheel and large tools are carried in a separate compartment below.

key serves the electrical master switch lock which can cut off the whole electrical supply, or be used at the side lamp position, the left-side doors of the front and rear compartments separately, the luggage compartment, also the lid of a cubby hole in the facia board. Chassis lubrication can be effected while the car is running by means of a pedal in the left of the driving compartment. Mixture enriching for cold starting is automatic, and after a preliminary depression of the throttle pedal the engine fires at once. With the now unusual hand throttle set partly open the car can be manœuvred from cold out of an awkward garage on the clutch and brake pedals alone. A normal working temperature around 80 deg C is obtained within a few hundred yards, helped by the now unusual feature of thermostatically operated radiator shutters.

The engine exterior displays the neatness and good finish which are inherent in a Rolls-Royce product. The reservoir tank for the chassis lubrication system is seen on the bulkhead. Ignition distributor and oil filler could hardly be more accessible. Above the big air cleaner and intake silencer is a water connection to the interior heater.

There is no concession to current trends in the appearance and confronted once again with the classical simplicity of the famous radiator's impressive proportions, one is inclined to ask why there should be.

ROYAL ROLLS-ROYCE

NEW EIGHT-CYLINDER PHANTOM IV FOR PRINCESS ELIZABETH AND THE DUKE OF EDINBURGH

NEWS of a new Rolls-Royce is always an event, but when the first and, for the present, the only example of the type has been specially produced for the use of members of the Royal Family, it becomes a unique car indeed. Rolls-Royce, Ltd. have been honoured with orders from members of the Royal Family and from many foreign royalties at various times over a long period of years. A Silver Ghost was used by the Duke of Windsor, then the Prince of Wales, after his experience with them during the 1914-18 war, and at the present time the Duchess of Kent uses a Wraith, but this is the first time that a completely new model has been evolved specially for members of the British Royal House. The car has been built by Rolls-Royce in collaboration with H. J. Mulliner to the order of Princess Elizabeth and the Duke of Edinburgh, and will be known as the Phantom IV. It is a limousine of immense size, specially planned to enable the occupants to see and be seen on State occasions, but also equipped with many detail fittings which make for comfortable and convenient use on private journeys.

The line and proportions of the car are so well balanced that its great size is not immediately apparent, but with a wheelbase of 12ft 1in, an overall length of almost 19ft, and a height of over 6ft, it dwarfs most other cars on the road. The rear compartment affords drawing room comfort for two people and has two comfortable occasional seats which fold away into the division when not required. The rear doors are 3ft 2in wide and ease of entry is assisted by the hard-edged body styling which permits a very shallow roof panel. The interior is rendered very light by the generous glass areas, supplemented by a transparent panel in the roof, which can be obscured by a motor-driven blind. At night the interior can be brightly illuminated by a concealed strip light in the roof panel, besides which there are four roof lamps of the normal pattern.

The general style of finish, in keeping with the desires of the owners, is very simple with grey cloth upholstery, a grey curled mohair rug and figured walnut cappings and panel work on the division with banded edges.

In front there are two very large and comfortable arm-

Wide doors allow easy entry to a well-lit interior which enables the occupants to see and be seen. Maximum head room is allowed by the hard-edged body line which permits a very shallow roof structure. The rear seat can be wound forward, and over it is a transparent panel which can be obscured by a motor-driven shutter. Rear blind and division are also motor controlled.

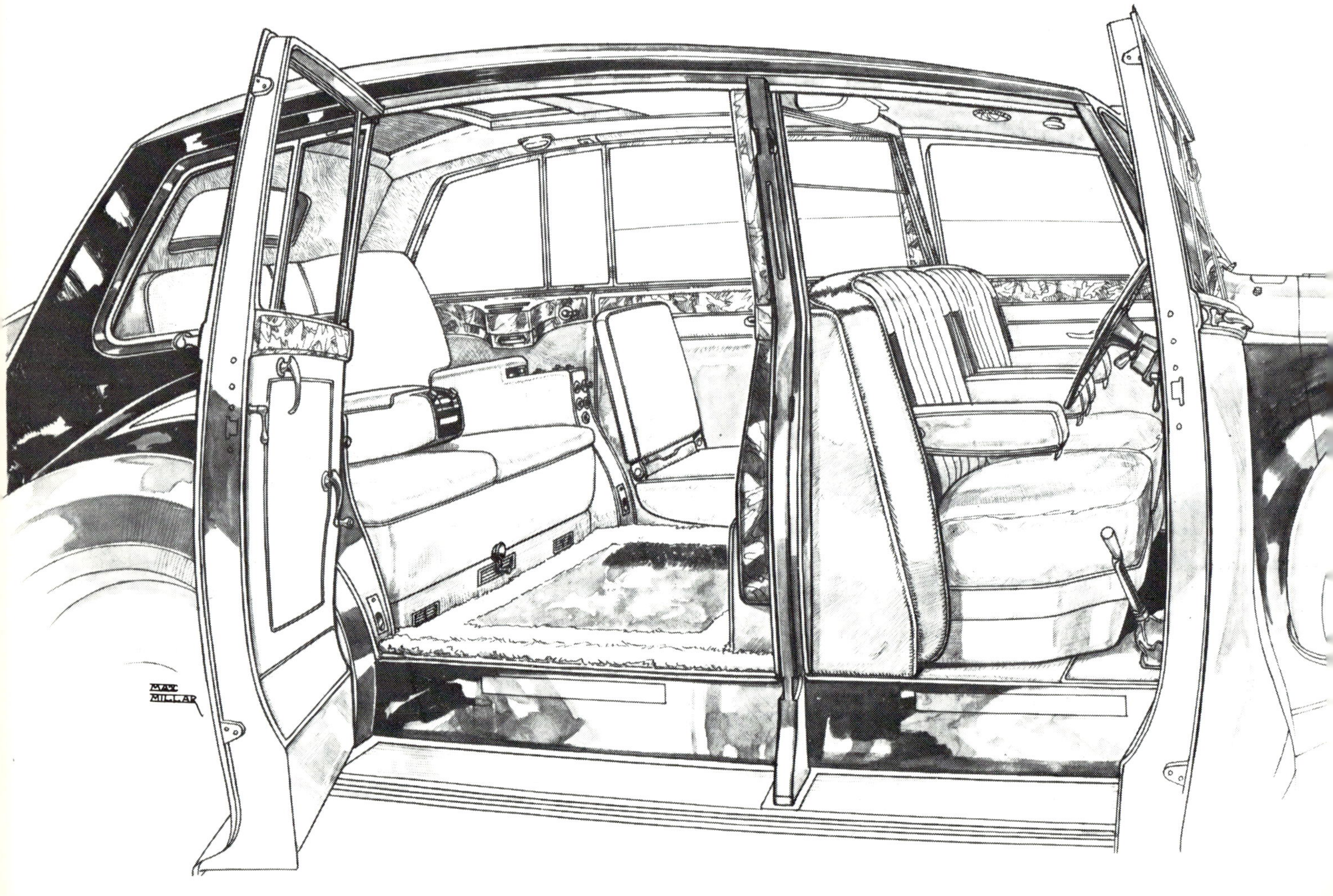

The well-balanced proportions of the limousine coachwork by H. J. Mulliner disguise the great size of the new Phantom IV Rolls-Royce built for Princess Elizabeth and the Duke of Edinburgh. On the roof can be seen the blue police identification light and behind it is a socket in which can be fitted a flag standard or a plaque bearing a coat of arms. On the scuttle can be seen the vacuum-operated radio aerial. The silver statuette of St. George mounted on the radiator is illustrated opposite.

chair seats upholstered in green leather. The driving seat is separately adjustable and a sufficient sliding range has been provided to enable the car to be driven comfortably by a tall driver such as the Duke of Edinburgh himself. Each of the front seats is provided with two arm rests which fold away into the back rest when not required. The provision of such arm rests on the driving seat is, perhaps, surprising, as experience shows that they can restrict the movement of the driver's arms.

Heating and ventilation arrangements are very thorough. Two air intakes, one on each side of the radiator, supply fresh air to ducts which feed front and rear compartments, and there are three heaters, drawing warm water from the engine cylinder head. One heater unit is concealed under the rear seat and feeds warm air through grilles below the

seat, while another, under one of the front seats, also provides a flow of warm air for the rear part of the car through grilles in the division panelling. A third heater under the facia looks after the needs of occupants of the front seats, and there is a separate windscreen demisting system drawing warm air through a duct from an intake behind the radiator matrix. The rear quarter lights incorporate swivelling ventilation panes with a large arc of movement.

Control buttons for the heating system, division, electric window winders and blinds, together with cigarette lighters, hand mirrors and ash trays, are located in the two outer arm rests in the rear compartment. The centre arm rest has built into it the controls for the radio set and also includes a glove box. The radio itself is concealed in the luggage compartment and operates two loudspeakers, one in the cabinet work of the division and another in the driving compartment, which is provided with a separate volume control. A feature of the electrical system is the use of very large separate head lamps which have reflectors set to dip and swivel outwards. A changeover switch on the scuttle makes it possible to switch out one head lamp and dip the other towards the road side according to the rule

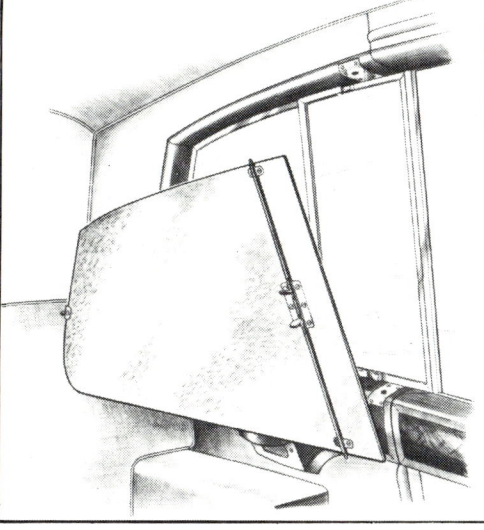

To provide a greater degree of privacy the rear quarter lights and ventilation panels can be obscured by a removable panel. The cabinet work on the division (right) includes two occasional tables and an electric clock which swivels for easy adjustment. In the centre is the radio loudspeaker and below it is a rack for papers which can be locked away when not required.

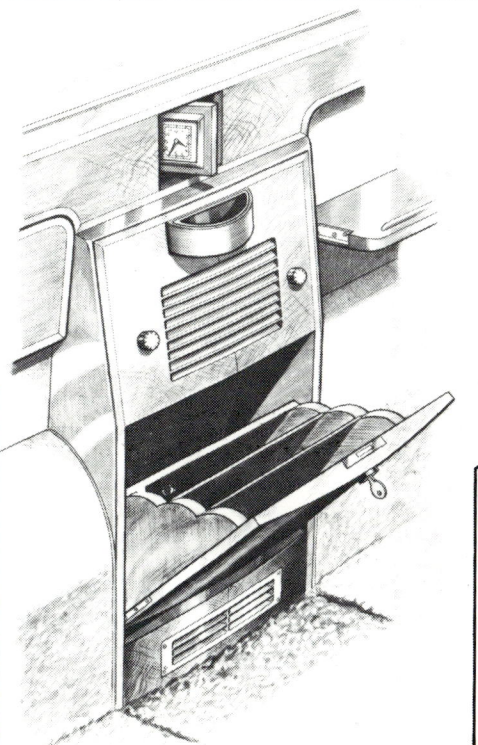

Controls for the many electrical services such as windows, rear blind, drop division and heaters are grouped on the outer arm rests of the rear seat. Cigarette lighters and hand mirrors are also provided.

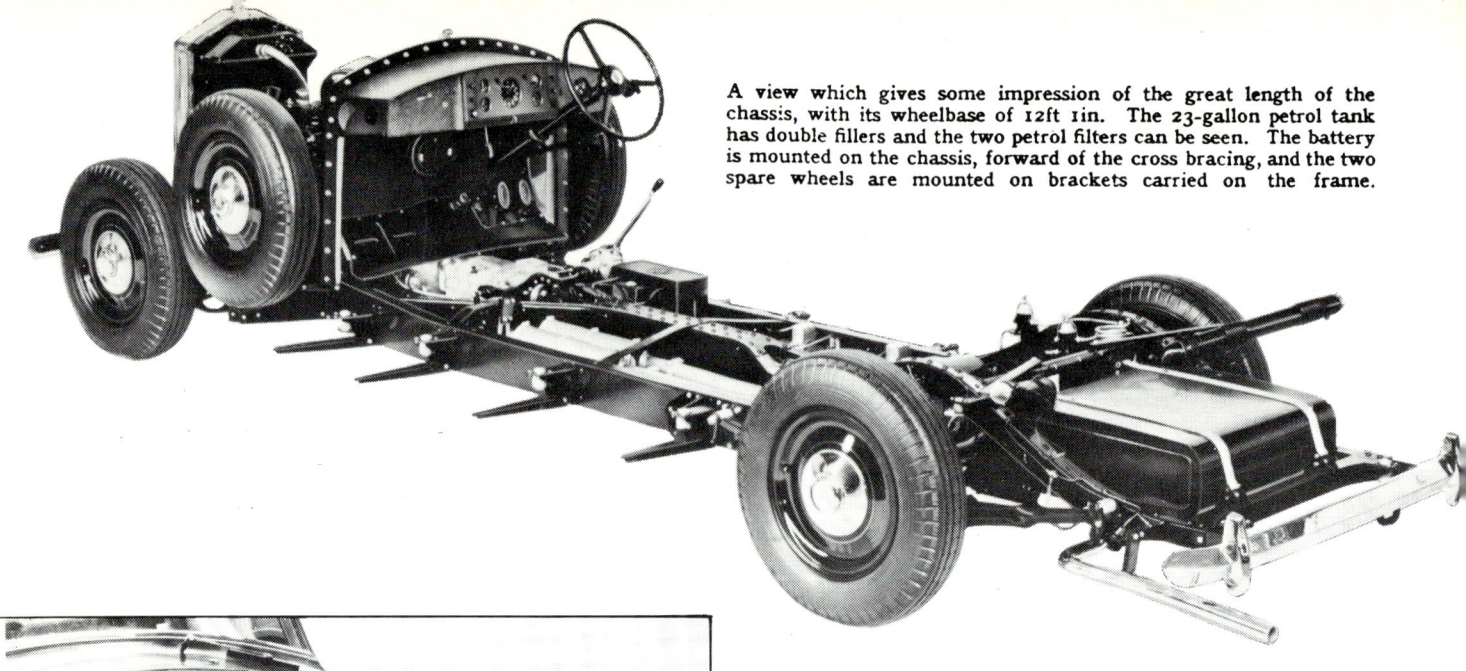

A view which gives some impression of the great length of the chassis, with its wheelbase of 12ft 1in. The 23-gallon petrol tank has double fillers and the two petrol filters can be seen. The battery is mounted on the chassis, forward of the cross bracing, and the two spare wheels are mounted on brackets carried on the frame.

The eight cylinders of the Phantom IV engine are fed by a single downdraught Stromberg carburettor with thermostatically operated mixture control and water heated hot spot. On the scuttle can be seen reservoirs for chassis lubrication and screen cleaning, with one of the air ducts for the ventilation system. Above the engine is the warm air pipe leading from the radiator to the windscreen demister.

The chassis has channel section side members and a large elongated cross bracing, the centre of which is stabilized by massive transverse webs. The front and rear groups of four cylinders feed into separate exhaust manifolds connected to two separate sets of silencers and expansion chambers, which feed finally into a common exhaust pipe. Also visible are the flexible mountings which carry the coachwork, the divided propeller-shaft and the two double fuel pumps.

of the road prevailing in the country where the car is being driven.

The fact that the new chassis is designated the Phantom IV makes it a direct successor to a line of big Rolls-Royce cars stretching back to the immortal Silver Ghost and reaffirms the position of the Rolls-Royce firm as makers of a car which is not only the finest in the world mechanically, but also one which for size, power and performance can justly be regarded as the most magnificent in the world. It is indeed fortunate that the initiative of members of the Royal Family has encouraged production of a worthy successor to the large Rolls-Royces of the past at a time when the taxation policy in this country made it commercially impossible to undertake such a venture.

However, although the chassis is a new model, it was not necessary to start from scratch at the drawing board. It has always been Rolls-Royce policy to anticipate future requirements by building and operating prototypes which provide experience on a wide variety of new developments in engine design, transmission, suspension, braking and other mechanical features. A range of four-, six- and eight cylinder engines with common valve, piston and connecting rod assemblies was designed to the order of the Ministry of Supply some time ago and major components from this range were used in evolving an eight-cylinder car engine which has run for some time in an experimental Bentley chassis. This car has a fantastically high performance which has gained it a legendary reputation in informed motoring circles, and it has been driven for considerable distances by the Duke of Edinburgh himself. Large sums have been offered by foreign customers anxious to possess such a car, but the company decided not to proceed with production in the prevailing conditions. This same engine has, however, provided the basis for the power unit used in the new Rolls-Royce chassis.

The Phantom IV engine, like those of the other Rolls-Royce and Bentley cars now in production, has overhead inlet valves and side exhaust valves and uses a cylinder head of aluminium alloy RR50 with inserted valve seats. The crankshaft is of chrome molybdenum steel and runs in nine main bearings. The crank pins are nitrided and the bearings have thin shells of copper-lead-indium. The crankcase is in cast iron and at the top of each cylinder is a short hard liner of chrome-iron in the area where cylinder wear is normally concentrated. Pistons are in RR53 aluminium alloy and are tin plated, with one compression ring, one L-section scraper and a slotted oil control ring.

There is a helical gear oil pump in the crankcase with feed intake, and a by-pass filter on the outside of the cylinder block. The external pressure relief valve controls the high-pressure feed to main and big-end bearings, camshaft bearings and skew gear drive to oil pump and distributor, with a low-pressure feed to valve gear and timing gears.

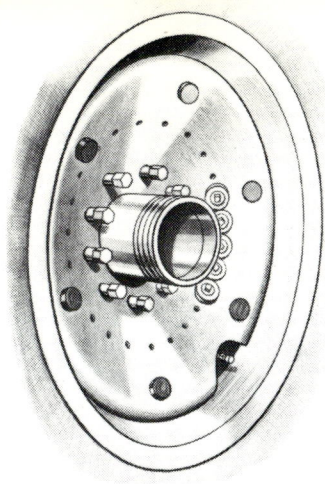

In contrast with the large window and screen areas the rear window on the Royal Phantom IV Rolls-Royce is relatively small and can be obscured by a motor-driven blind. There is a fair-sized luggage locker, the lid of which can be opened flat to carry additional luggage. Wheel changing tools are concealed under the floor of the luggage compartment and small hand tools are carried in a tray lined with moulded rubber under the facia panel.

The steel wheel discs on the Phantom IV are secured by ten mounting studs and are perforated for the addition of balance weights. The five rubber buffers near to the rim are to prevent the nave plate rattling.

SPECIFICATION ROYAL PHANTOM IV ROLLS-ROYCE

Engine.—8 cylinders in line. 88.8 × 114.3 mm, 5,675 c.c. Overhead inlet valves; side exhaust. Compression ratio 6.4 to 1. Single Stromberg downdraught carburettor.

Transmission.—Dry single-plate semi-centrifugal clutch. Four-speed gear box with synchromesh on second, third and top. Right-hand change. Overall ratios: 4.25, 5.71, 8.52, 12.74 to 1.

Suspension.—Independent front by coil springs and wishbones with double-acting hydraulic dampers built into upper wishbones. Anti-roll bar. Rear: rigid axle casing and half-elliptic springs with double-acting hydraulic dampers controlled by a pump driven from the gear box with overriding manual control.

Brakes.—Hydraulic front, mechanical rear with friction servo motor driven from the gear box.

Chassis.—Channel section side members with elongated X bracing in centre.

Fuel System.—23-gallon tank at rear with filler on each side. Two double electrical fuel pumps, one for main system and one for reserve which holds 4 gallons.

Electrical System.—12 volts. R 100 head lamps. Twin fog lamps. Lucas dynamo and starter; Delco distributor.

Wheels and Tyres.—Steel disc wheels; with 7 × 17in Dunlop Fort C tyres.

Dimensions.—Wheelbase: 12ft 1in. Track: (front) 4ft 10½in, (rear) 5ft 3in. Overall length: 18ft 11in. Width: 6ft 5in. Height: (unladen) 6ft 2in. Chassis weight: 3,300 lb.

The cooling system incorporates radiator shutters controlled by a thermostat in the header tank and there is an auxiliary thermostat in the cylinder head which ensures rapid warming up from cold and provides the earliest possible supply of warm water to the interior heating system.

Other features of the chassis design follow the general principles found on the successful Wraith. Front suspension is by coil springs and wishbones with double-acting hydraulic dampers, and the steering is cam and roller with a fore and aft drag link leading from the steering box alongside the engine to a bell crank mounted on the front cross-member, which operates the divided track rod. All bearings in the steering and suspension systems are lubricated from a pedal-operated pump under the facia. The fuel tank at the rear of the chassis holds 23 gallons with four in reserve and the feed is by two double S.U. pumps with a bowl filter element in each fuel line.

Transmission is through a conventional four-speed gear box with right-hand control, and there is the usual Rolls-Royce friction servo motor on the gear box to operate the brakes, those at the front being hydraulically controlled and those at the rear through a mechanical linkage. The rear suspension is by half-elliptic springs with a rigid axle casing and semi-floating shafts.

Every detail on the chassis and coachwork is made and finished in the style which one associates with Rolls-Royce —and the coachbuilders which collaborate with them. No further comment is necessary because it represents the finest work which skill and conscientious craftsmanship can produce. The mascot may be cited as an example of the forethought and thorough care which are brought to bear on the smallest details. It is a specially designed silver statuette of St. George and the Dragon, and is a delightful little work of art, but the first reaction of Rolls-Royce, Ltd. was to propose tests on a bump rig to find out if it would break. As a result, the dragon's head and tongue and the lance have been used to provide firm support for the overhung mass of horse and rider.

Externally the car is finished in dark green with chromium-plated fittings and mouldings. Princess Elizabeth and the Duke of Edinburgh placed the order for the new car through The Car Mart, Ltd., Rolls-Royce retailers, in the normal way, and they do, of course, pay purchase tax, like other British citizens residing in this country. Since the order was placed the purchase tax on cars of this high quality has fortunately been reduced from 66⅔ to 33⅓ per cent, and apart from the very great saving which results in this individual order it is possible to hope that Rolls-Royce may now be encouraged to embark on the production of further examples of this superb chassis. It must be said, however, that at present no other orders are being accepted.

This is the original coloured coachbuilders' drawing by the H. J. Mulliner designer which was submitted by Car Mart when the details of the car were finalized.

No. 1510: ROLLS-ROYCE SILVER DAWN SALOON

The Rolls-Royce Silver Dawn has an elegant body style of traditional British design. In the forward doors are swivelling quarter lights; both doors are hinged from the central pillar. Ventilator panels are placed in the scuttle sides.

The Autocar ROAD TESTS

FOR very many years the name Rolls-Royce has been associated with the best that money can buy. To build up and retain such a reputation is a great feat in the automobile world, where competition is very keen indeed. It must be admitted, however, that if a manufacturer can build cars virtually regardless of cost the problem is somewhat simplified; yet it must be realised that even a very small increase in the standard of finish or performance may increase the cost of production very considerably. The latest representative of this famous name to be put through its paces by *The Autocar* is the Silver Dawn, an owner-driver model with a standard steel production body as distinct from bodies built by coachbuilders to customers' own requirements, as are usually associated with Rolls-Royce cars. Originally available for export only, with left-hand drive, the car can now be supplied in this country.

Now, whereas with some cars the accent is on one particular feature such as performance, fuel economy or luggage space, to name only three items, the Rolls-Royce is designed to provide luxury transport with an all-round excellence. It must achieve and maintain a very high standard in all the desirable features, and not just concentrate on a few, as might be acceptable for a sports car, for example. Such a design must therefore be something of a compromise, yet no one feature must be sacrificed to any marked degree. The most outstanding change between this and previous Rolls-Royce cars that have been tested is that the Silver Dawn can be

supplied with an automatic transmission and two-pedal control. Following in principle the well-known Hydra-Matic transmission, the Rolls-Royce-built automatic transmission has a fluid coupling and a four-speed epicyclic gear box.

There are at present two types of motorist, those who like an automatic transmission and those who do not, but there is little doubt that the majority of purchasers in the large car class appreciate the ease of control that is afforded when it is not necessary to press clutch pedals and operate gear levers. On the other hand, any automatic device must operate on the cause and effect principle, as it cannot think ahead like a well-trained driver. With the Rolls-Royce transmission, however, there is a reasonable amount of driver control.

The 4½-litre six-cylinder engine is particularly smooth. It is also quite lively, bearing in mind the general characteristics of the car, and it can be held comfortably at between 70 and 80 m.p.h. without showing any signs of stress or overwork. It is also extremely docile and the automatic transmission makes the car particularly suited to dense traffic conditions.

For all normal operation the hand selector lever, below the steering wheel, is placed in position 4 and the car is started from rest by releasing the hand brake and opening the throttle. If it is fully depressed, for maximum acceleration, the transmission will automatically change up at speeds of 16, 26 and 52 m.p.h. But if position 3 is selected, although

Left: The deeply and beautifully upholstered seats immediately create an air of luxury. There are adjustable armrests on the doors.

Right: Fine leather and woodwork give an atmosphere. A folding arm-rest is provided in the rear seat and ashtrays are built into the side armrests. Foot-rests are fitted to the backs of the front seats, which also contain folding picnic tables.

The semi-razor edge rear styling matches well with the angular lines of the radiator. Combined stop and tail lights are built into the rear wings, and a flush-fitting door encloses the fuel filler cap in the left wing. Rubber mud flaps are fitted below the rear edges of the front wings.

the change to second and third gears will occur at the same speed, the change up into top gear will not take place until a speed of 59 m.p.h. is reached, even though the throttle pedal may not be held fully open. In position 4 the upward changes can occur at lower speeds, depending on conditions of loading and the throttle position. If position 2 on the hand quadrant is selected the transmission will remain in second gear until a speed of 40 m.p.h. is obtained; it will then change up into top gear. In a similar way, if the position 2 is selected the transmission will not change down unless the speed drops to 40 m.p.h. or below. Position 3 is particularly useful when extra acceleration is required, while position 2— the equivalent to Low Range of the American transmissions—provides a useful measure of engine braking, although the fact that the mechanism changes up at speeds over 40 m.p.h. possibly restricts its utility as a safety measure; on the other hand, it does prevent the engine being over-revved. The change from gear to gear is reasonably smooth, although it can be noticed.

Over all normal types of road surface the suspension provides a very comfortable front and rear seat ride. The Rolls-Royce ride control, comprising a device to vary the settings of the rear spring dampers, enables the damping to be adjusted from a control on the steering wheel (within a limited range) to suit requirements. The roadholding generally is good, and, in spite of a weight distribution bias towards the rear wheels, the car does not tend to oversteer; in

fact, the steering is accurate and enables the driver to control the car within very fine limits. In spite of a fairly large number of turns from lock to lock the mechanism is not particularly light. It does not transmit road shocks, yet there is a useful self-centring action.

The special uniform wear leading and trailing shoe brakes, hydraulically operated at the front, and assisted by means of a mechanical servo, are very effective and require only a moderate pedal pressure. Some slight fade was experienced when the car was driven very hard, but under normal conditions the braking proved to be fully satisfactory.

As one expects with a car of this type, the noise level is particularly low. There is very little engine noise, but some slight transmission noise is noticeable, particularly if the car is driven hard with the gear selector lever in position 2— not a range that would normally be used. The Rolls-Royce is very well insulated in regard to road-excited body noise, and the body does not boom. With all windows closed it is also particularly quiet as regards wind noise, but with the front quarter lights slightly open a certain amount of noise is noticed if the car is driven fast.

Although it is a large car, it is far from being a difficult one to handle, and although ease of control is increased by the use of an automatic transmission, a factor that has an even greater influence is the excellent driving position. Seated fairly high up, the driver has a commanding view and tends to look down at the road and other traffic rather than along the bonnet at the horizon. The end of the bonnet and both front wings can also be seen. The seat itself is particularly well upholstered and gives support just where it is needed. It also has a wide range of adjustment. The relative positions of the steering wheel and pedals are also good and the rubber-covered dip switch provides a rest for the driver's left foot. All-round visibility is very good, and although the driving mirror is small, so that it does not mask a large area of the windscreen, it provides a very satisfactory though much reduced rear view. Two-speed windscreen wipers are fitted; they are effective and cover a useful area of the screen.

Both the oil and radiator filler caps are reached from the left side of the bonnet. A large air cleaner and silencer is mounted diagonally across the engine, and the two-speed windscreen wiper motor is mounted on the left side of the bulkhead.

The interior of the luggage compartment is completely trimmed and finished to Rolls-Royce standards. A separate lower compartment contains the spare wheel and large tools, including an octagonal ring spanner for removal of the wheel nave plates.

The rear compartment is both spacious and well appointed. The rear doors are large enough to permit easy access and they cover the leading edges of the rear wings to prevent passengers' clothes from becoming soiled. There is ample headroom and legroom even when the front seats are well back. The interior of the body is finished in the expected style in leather and polished hardwood; it is automatically illuminated whenever a door is opened. Folding picnic tables are built into the backs of the front seats and a sliding picnic tray is provided in the front compartment.

The many items of equipment that are fitted as standard include a flush-fitting sunshine roof, a rear window blind and a very effective heating and ventilating system designed to benefit all the occupants of the car. There is also an electrical de-froster and de-mister system fitted to the rear window. The main luggage locker is very spacious and it is not necessary to disturb the luggage in order to remove the spare wheel. The eighteen-gallon fuel tank provides a useful range and there is a facia warning light which indicates less than 3 gallons in the tank. The head-lamps give a useful beam, with a satisfactory spread of light. Chassis lubrication is by means of a one-shot pedal in the driving compartment. A single Yale Key serves for all locks, including the admirable lighting and ignition switchbox, doors, luggage compartment, fuel filler, bonnet, and a glove box of moderate dimensions in the facia.

The Rolls-Royce is an expensive car designed for the connoisseur who requires an all-round excellence second to none and is prepared to pay for the best that money can buy in quality of manufacture and finish.

ROLLS-ROYCE SILVER DAWN SALOON

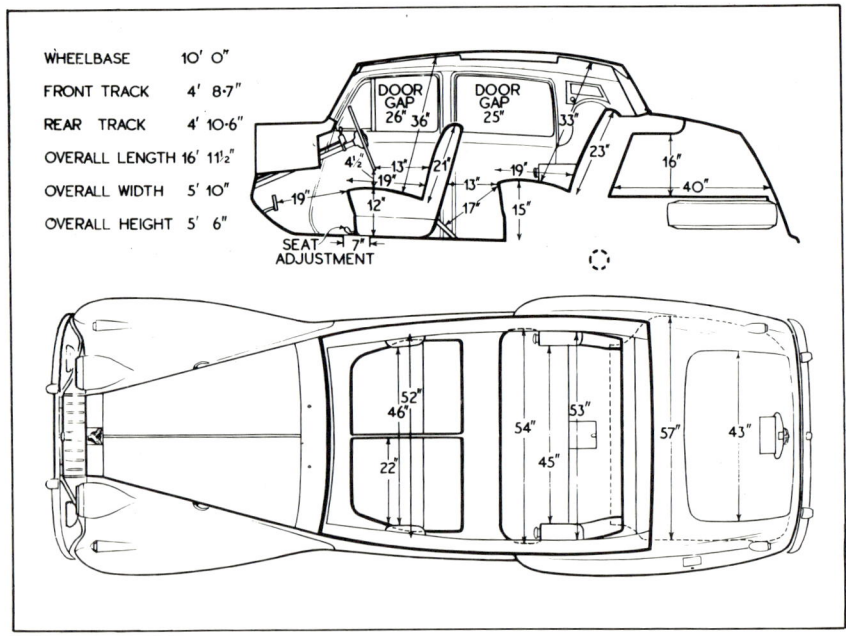

WHEELBASE	10' 0"
FRONT TRACK	4' 8·7"
REAR TRACK	4' 10·6"
OVERALL LENGTH	16' 11½"
OVERALL WIDTH	5' 10"
OVERALL HEIGHT	5' 6"

Measurements in these ⅛in to 1ft scale body diagrams are taken with the driving seat in the central position of fore and aft adjustment and with the seat cushions uncompressed.

PERFORMANCE

ACCELERATION: from constant speeds. Speed, Gear Ratios* and time in sec.

M.P.H.	4 Range	3 Range	2 Range
10—30	4.2	—	5.6
20—40	6.2	—	
30—50	7.0	6.7	—
40—60	9.8	8.7	—
50—70	13.1	12.6	—
60—80	19.4	—	—

*Gear Ratios 3.73; 5.4; 9.82 and 14.23 to 1.

From rest through gears to:

M.P.H.	sec.
30	4.7
50	11.4
60	16.2
70	23.2
80	35.7

Standing quarter mile, 20.4 sec.

SPEED ON GEARS:

Gear		M.P.H. (max.)	K.P.H. (max.)
Top	(mean)	86.5	139.2
	(best)	87.5	140.8
3rd		59	95
2nd		40	64
1st		16	26

(In 4 Range maximum on 2nd and 3rd is 26 and 52 m.p.h.).

TRACTIVE RESISTANCE: 16 lb per ton at 10 M.P.H.

TRACTIVE EFFORT:

	Pull (lb per ton)	Equivalent Gradient
Top	275	1 in 8.1
Third	370	1 in 6
Second	550	1 in 3.9

BRAKES:

Efficiency	Pedal Pressure (lb)
80 per cent	92
70 per cent	70
58 per cent	40

FUEL CONSUMPTION:
14.2 m.p.g. overall for 407 miles (19.9 litres per 100 km).
Approximate normal range 14-16 m.p.g. (20.2-17.7 litres per 100 km).
Fuel, First grade.

WEATHER: Fine; damp surface, wind fresh. Air temperature 60 degrees F.
Acceleration figures are the means of several runs in opposite directions.
Tractive effort and resistance obtained by Tapley meter.
Model described in "The Autocar" of October 16, 1953.

SPEEDOMETER CORRECTION: M.P.H.

Car speedometer	10	20	30	40	50	60	70	80	90	92
True speed	10	20.5	30.5	39.5	49	57	66.5	76	85	87.5

DATA

PRICE (basic), with standard saloon body, £3,250.
British purchase tax, £1,355 5s 10d.
Total (in Great Britain), £4,605 5s 10d.
Extras: Automatic transmission, £70 basic, plus British purchase tax, £29 3s 4d.

ENGINE: Capacity: 4,566 c.c. (278.63 cu in).
Number of cylinders: 6.
Bore and Stroke: 92 × 114.3 mm (3.625 × 4.50in).
Valve gear: Overhead inlet; side exhaust.
Compression ratio: 6.75 to 1.

B.H.P.: — at — r.p.m. (B.H.P. per ton laden —).
Torque: — lb ft at — r.p.m.
M.P.H. per 1,000 r.p.m. on top gear, 22.

WEIGHT: (with 5 gals fuel), 37 cwt (4,132 lb).
Weight distribution (per cent) 48.5 F; 51.5 R.
Laden as tested: 40¼ cwt (4,502 lb).
Lb per c.c. (laden): 0.99.

BRAKES: Type: F, Leading and trailing. R, Leading and trailing.
Method of operation: F, Hydraulic. R, Mechanical (Mechanical servo).
Drum dimensions: F, 12¼in diameter; 2.6in wide. R, 12¼in diameter; 2.6in wide.
Lining area: F, 186 sq in. R, 186 sq in (185 sq in per ton laden).

TYRES: 6.50—16in.
Pressures (lb per sq in): 25 F; 30 R.

TANK CAPACITY: 18 Imperial gallons.
Oil sump, 16 pints.
Cooling system, 32 pints.

TURNING CIRCLE: 41ft 2in (L and R).
Steering wheel turns (lock to lock): 3¼.

DIMENSIONS: Wheelbase 10ft 0in.
Track: 4ft 8.7in (F); 4ft 10.6in (R).
Length (overall): 16ft 11½in.
Height: 5ft 6in.
Width: 5ft 10in.
Ground clearance: —in.
Frontal area: 25.2 sq ft (approximately).

ELECTRICAL SYSTEM: 12-volt; 55 ampère-hour battery.
Head lights: Double dip; 48 watt.

SUSPENSION: Front, Independent, coil springs and wishbones; anti-roll bar. Rear, Half-elliptic.

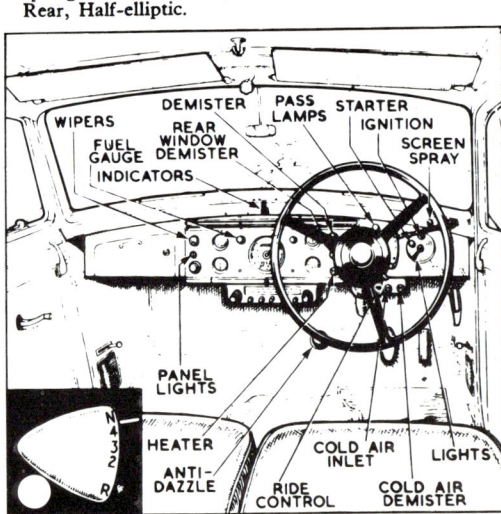

Above **Harold Radford version (foreground) of the Silver Dawn is identifiable externally by the boot treatment. At £5,710 in 1954, it cost £1,105 more than the standard car**

Below left **Complete Countryman picnic equipment in the boot**
Below right **Rear seats fold down to accommodate extra luggage and front seats make into a bed**

NEW CARS DESCRIBED
SILVER

NEW ROLLS-ROYCE AND BENTLEY MODELS

WITH the reputation for making the finest car in the world it is no easy task to introduce a new range of cars that will be better than the models they supersede but cost very little more. Yet with the introduction of the new Rolls-Royce Silver Cloud and the Bentley Series S this is just what has been done. That the nearer one approaches the ultimate the greater will be the standardization is evident by the similarity between the Rolls-Royce and the Bentley.

The automatic transmission, now made standard equipment on all models, remains unchanged. Chassis can be supplied for specialist coachwork. The engine is similar in design to that used on the Bentley Continental.

Cylinder bore diameter has been

of the journal. From there it is conveyed by another drilling to the crankpin, which is cross-drilled to lubricate the big-end bearing. The connecting rod is drilled throughout its length to lubricate the gudgeon pin, and is cross-drilled on the thrust side, below the piston skirt, for cylinder bore lubrication.

At the rear of the back main bearing an oil thrower is now incorporated in addition to the scroll type of oil return. A flange is formed at the rear of the shaft, and to this is attached the flexible disc flywheel which carries the starter ring, and to which is bolted the housing for the fluid coupling used in conjunction with the automatic transmission. At the front of the shaft there is a torsional vibration damper consisting of a metallic mass attached to a thin flange on the shaft by spring-loaded friction linings. In between this and the front main bearing there is the camshaft drive gear; again to reduce the effects of torsional vibration, a spring drive is incorporated in this. Both this

valve seats. To combat the effects of corrosion and reduce pre-ignition the heads of the exhaust valves are given a bright ray treatment. This coats the valve head with 80 per cent nickel and 20 per cent chromium applied with a welding torch.

The most noticeable change to the power unit has been redesigning the cylinder head, the four-port arrangement being replaced by a new six-port head to

increased from 92 to 95.25mm, so that the capacity is now 4,887 c.c. Unified threads are now used for all nuts and bolts. A single casting forms the cylinder block and crankcase, and this is extended well below the crankshaft centre line, the crankchamber being adequately stiffened by the five webs which house the intermediate bearings for the seven-bearing shaft. End thrust is taken by the centre main bearing, and all main bearings have 2.75in journals. The crankpins are 2in in diameter and have an effective width of 1⅛in. Indium-coated lead-bronze steel-backed shells are used for both main and big-end bearings.

The forged crankshaft now has integral balance weights; these are placed on either side of the centre main bearing, on the outsides of numbers 2 and 6 main bearings, and on the insides of numbers 1 and 7 journals. Both main bearing and crankpin journals are hollow, the ends being sealed by bolted-in plugs of stainless steel. On earlier models these plugs were light alloy, but this was changed to prevent adverse effects from leaded fuels. Each main journal has radial drillings which allow lubricant to pass to the hollow centre

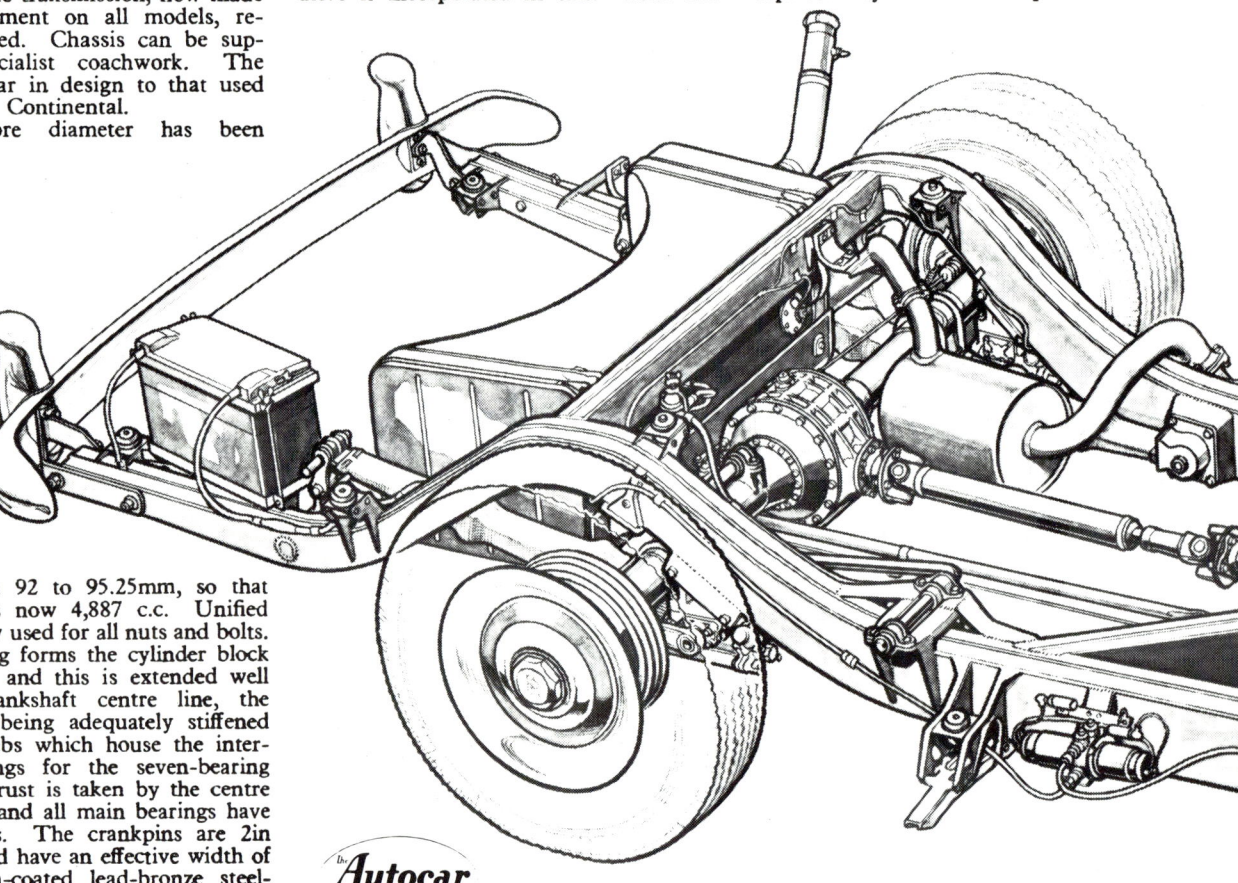

by Autocar COPYRIGHT

gear and the torsional vibration damper are mounted inside the engine front cover.

Full-length cylinder liners, pressed into the bores, provide wear-resisting surfaces for the long split-skirt pistons. These pistons have four rings, the top one being chromium plated.

The well-known Rolls-Royce system of overhead inlet and side exhaust valves is retained, the exhaust valves being produced from KE965 material with Stellite

improve the breathing and permit increased power output. Cast in aluminium, the cylinder head is attached to the block by 37 ⅜in set bolts. By using these in place of the normal arrangement of studs and nuts it has been possible to increase the spanner clearance, particularly on the bolts adjacent to the rocker pedestals. The construction of the cylinder head is interesting: half of the manifold is actually formed in the head itself. The other half,

CLOUD AND SERIES S

containing the flanges for carburettor attachment, is also a light alloy casting, the two parts being held together by 22 studs and nuts. This arrangement results in a fairly simple casting as far as the ports are concerned, and simplifies fettling and inspection.

The inlet valves are 1.85in diameter and have a lift of 0.4in. The corresponding figures for the exhaust are 1.625in and 0.375in. The inlet valves are produced from S65, a nickel chrome alloy steel, and a similar material is used for the inlet valve inserts; these are screwed into place and, once they are in position, the spanner lugs are machined off. Particular attention has been paid to the design of the inlet porting to improve flow, and the internal shape of the inserts is curved, to blend with the line of the inlet porting. This improves gas flow round the back of the valve heads.

Brass inserts are screwed into the head to take the sparking plugs, and these are locked in place by additional screwed rings to prevent the possibility of the insert being removed when the sparking plugs are unscrewed.

Both Bentley and Rolls-Royce models have twin horizontal S.U. carburettors in conjunction with the automatic cold starting device described in the September 19, 1952 issue. Both this unit and the carburettors are different from those previously used on Bentley models. The object of the cold-starting device is to eliminate the manual choke control and the need to raise and lower the carburettor jet block to provide mixture enrichment.

On previous carburettors the jet block was held in place by cork washers which enabled it to be adjusted and also provided a fuel seal. The bottom end of the carburettors has now been completely redesigned, and a new assembly is used with the jet block attached to a rubber diaphragm. This diaphragm permits vertical movement of the jet and provides a better seal. Because of the cold starting device variation of the jet position is required only for initial carburettor tuning.

The carburettors also include a new slow-running adjustment which does not rely on the setting of the main throttle valves in order to produce the correct tickover. Instead, the linkage is adjusted so that when the throttle pedal is released the butterfly valves are closed and the tickover speed is then adjusted by a taper-ended screw which controls the flow through a small port which by-passes the main throttle valve.

The cold starting device has been improved. On the previous model the solenoid which closes the choke valve was in circuit with the starter motor switch;

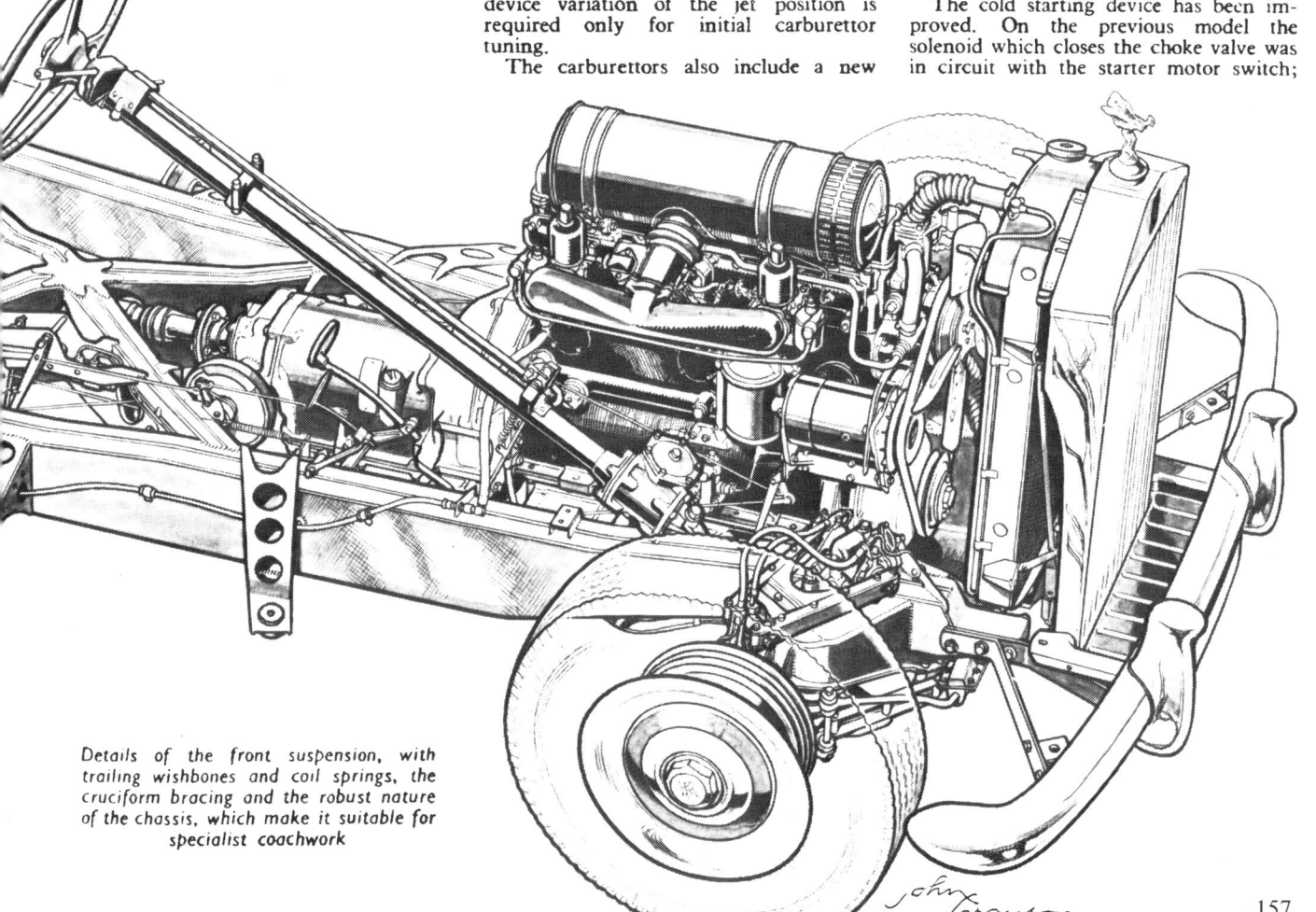

Details of the front suspension, with trailing wishbones and coil springs, the cruciform bracing and the robust nature of the chassis, which make it suitable for specialist coachwork

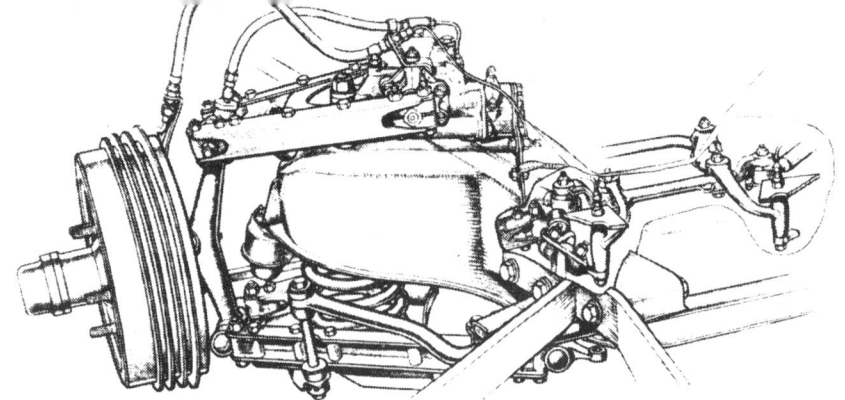

Rolls-Royce layout with single wheel cylinder and compensating link mechanism has been retained. In place of a high-rate spring, special low-rate springs are used on the shake-back stop assembly to enable the friction force to be controlled more accurately, and the friction surfaces for these springs consist of cadmium plating on the web of the brake shoe itself, in conjunction with chromium plated washers. In place of rolled section brake shoes, the linings are riveted to fabricated shoes on the new model.

Previous cars have sometimes been

SILVER CLOUD AND SERIES S
. . . . continued

consequently, as soon as the engine fired and the starter switch was released, the circuit ceased to be energized. The effect could be to stall the engine after a few revs.

To overcome this the solenoid is placed in the ignition circuit; in addition, a pressure-sensitive switch is tapped into the oil gallery which breaks the circuit as soon as the pump produces a given pressure in the oil line. A temperature-sensitive switch is included in the cold-starting circuit to prevent the system from operating at under-bonnet temperatures.

On the new cars automatic transmission, identical with that optionally fitted to the previous model, is a standard feature. The drive from the transmission to the rear axle is by two-piece propeller-shaft with a flexibly mounted centre bearing. The rear section of the shaft consists of conventional Hardy Spicer couplings with a sliding spline just to the rear of the centre bearing. The front section, however, contains a special joint which will slide with the application of only a very light end load, even when it is transmitting full torque. This has been introduced in the quest for complete silence and freedom from vibration.

In designing the braking equipment Rolls-Royce engineers were faced with two problems: first, the performance of

The independent front suspension units consist of half-trailing long and short wishbones, the inner fulcrum bearing for the upper wishbones being formed by the damper unit. The plate welded to the chassis frame and bolted to a plate on the inner end of the damper prevents deflections which could cause a change in castor angle under heavy braking

Although retaining a dignified style, the facia panel has been restyled to give a cleaner appearance

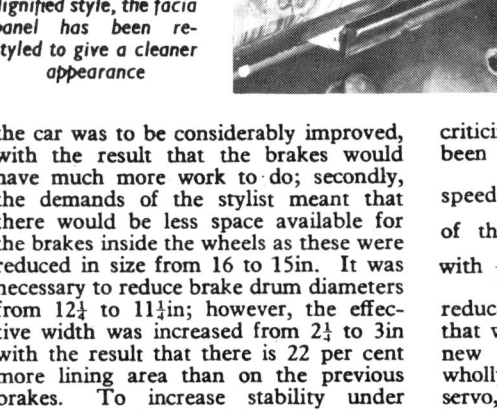
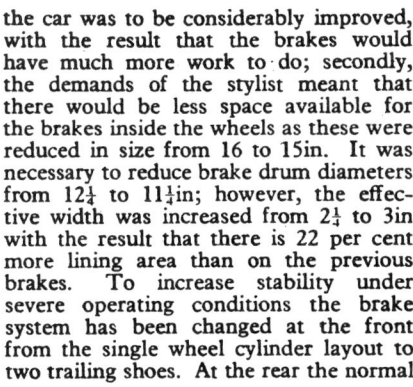

the car was to be considerably improved, with the result that the brakes would have much more work to do; secondly, the demands of the stylist meant that there would be less space available for the brakes inside the wheels as these were reduced in size from 16 to 15in. It was necessary to reduce brake drum diameters from $12\frac{1}{4}$ to $11\frac{1}{4}$in; however, the effective width was increased from $2\frac{1}{4}$ to 3in with the result that there is 22 per cent more lining area than on the previous brakes. To increase stability under severe operating conditions the brake system has been changed at the front from the single wheel cylinder layout to two trailing shoes. At the rear the normal

criticized because of servo lag. This has been rectified by increasing the servo speed so that the motor now runs at $\frac{1}{5.6}$ of the propeller-shaft speed compared with $\frac{1}{10.5}$. This modification has also reduced servo noise and the slight judder that was sometimes experienced. In the new system the front brakes depend wholly upon hydraulic operation by the servo, and 60 per cent of the rear braking is so applied; the remaining 40 per cent at the rear is applied mechanically direct from the brake pedal (the old figure was 50 per cent). The total distribution of

A Z-bar pivoted to the chassis frame and the rear axle prevents road spring wind-up caused by torque reaction, and modifies the rear roll stiffness to produce the desired degree of understeer

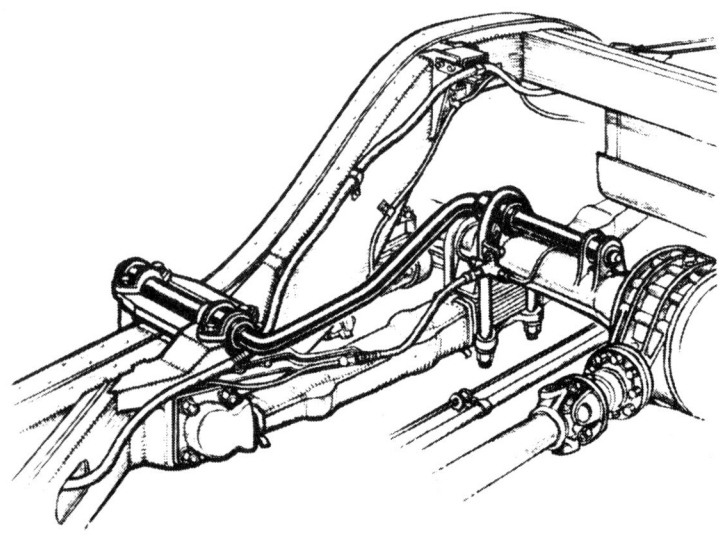

The new S.U. carburettor has auxiliary drillings in conjunction with the needle valve to adjust the slow running, and a diaphragm member which forms the seal for the jet block assembly. A small lever with screw adjustment is used to vary the height of the jet block for carburettor tuning

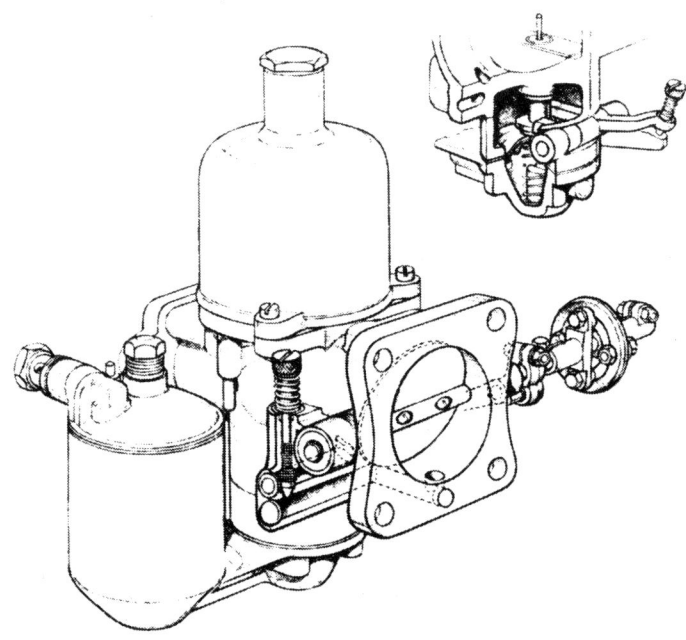

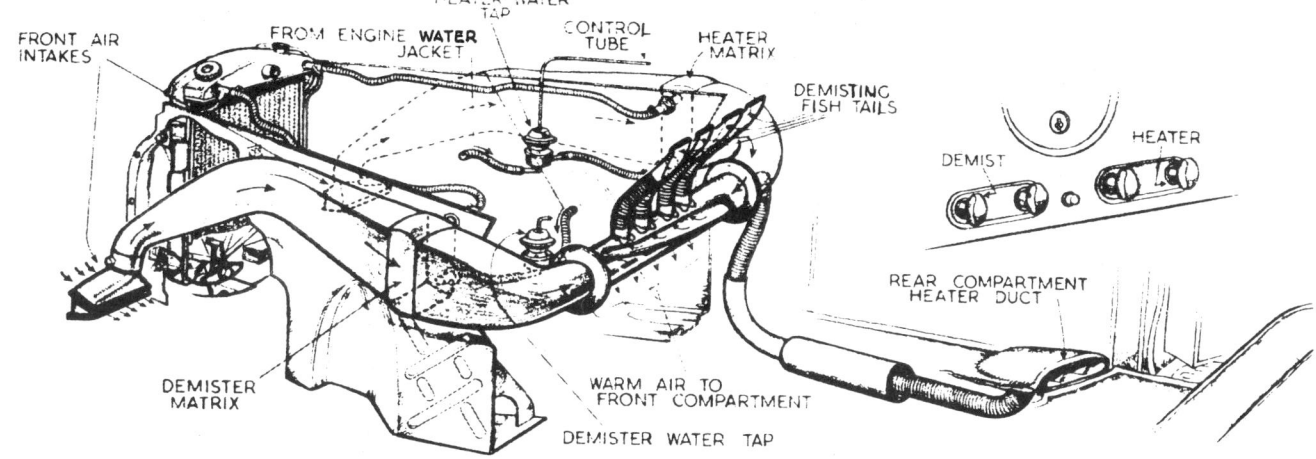

Layout of the heating system. Fans are provided to assist the flow through both heater units, and the speed of these is controlled by multi-position switches

SILVER CLOUD AND SERIES S
. . . . continued

braking between front and rear is 1.23 to 1. Automatic adjustment is provided for the front brakes, and there is a special safety device to prevent the brake shoes from wearing out against the drums and to indicate when relining is necessary. This consists of a high rate spring which, in effect, over-rides the automatic adjustment, with the result that free pedal travel becomes noticeable after a predetermined amount of lining wear has taken place. Manual adjustment is necessary for the rear brakes, and this automatically adjusts the hand brake.

The most noticeable change in the front end is to be observed in the new suspension. A conventional independent arrangement with long and short wishbones and coil springs is now employed. This change has been brought about in order to increase the permissible amount of wheel movement. With the new system 3in of bump and 4in of rebound are provided.

In the new suspension the wishbones are half-trailing, with the inner fulcrum bearings set at an angle of 62½ deg to the longitudinal centre line of the chassis. The fulcrum bearings for the lower wishbones are bolted on to the main front cross member, while those for the upper wishbones are formed by the damper unit. Both upper and lower wishbones are channel section pressings with bolted-on bearing and attachment brackets, and additional bolted-on plates and pressings to form the spring mounting and attachment for the rebound rubber. The abutment for the road spring consists of a welded pressing located below the damper. Although the top end of the road spring is finished

flat, the lower end has a pig tail which fits into the pressing bolted to the bottom of the lower wishbone assembly.

Lubricant is piped to all front suspension pivots with the exception of those provided for the front damper, and screwed bushes are used in all suspension joints. Caster angle adjustment is provided by moving the inner ends of the top wishbones along the squared ends of the damper spindle and re-clamping in the correct position, suitably shaped steel blocks being placed between the channel section wishbone members, the centre flange of which is cut back to provide the necessary flexibility. Bolted-on lugs also provide attachment for the anti-roll bar, which is supported by rubber bushes and runs in front of the suspension unit. To prevent vibration the bar has a centre rubber bush bearing.

Steering and track rods are located behind the front wishbones, and the system consists of a three-piece track rod with two slave levers pivoted to the rear of the front cross member. To ensure that accuracy is maintained, lugs attached to the inner wishbone fulcrums provide the pivot points for the slave levers, thereby ensuring that the correct relative distance between the slave lever pivots and the wishbones is maintained. A lug extending back from the left slave lever is connected to a link pivoted to the forward facing lever on the steering box. The steering box itself is located inside the frame member, and has a forward facing lug on its casing so that the frame

attachment point is in line with the cross link (viewed from above), thereby preventing slight frame deflections from affecting the steering.

Although the rear suspension is conventional with half-elliptic leaf springs and a half-floating rear axle, a number of changes have been made. To simplify the frame and enable straight side members to be used, the springs are now placed closer together so that they are on the inside of the chassis frame. This arrangement also tends to make for greater interior body space as the frame side members run closer to the wheel arches. The new layout also increases the roll understeer characteristics. During the development stages it was found necessary to reduce the stiffness of the rear springs in order to improve the rear seat ride and this in turn reduced the rear roll stiffness, with the result that the car then had rather too much understeer. Further, it was found necessary to reduce spring wind-up brought about by torque reaction.

These two factors could have been controlled by the use of a rear anti-roll bar and torque arms, or some other form of link mechanism. However, it is very difficult to accommodate an anti-roll bar on the rear suspension (unless it is of a peculiar shape) and to provide, as well, clearance to permit rear axle movement. The Rolls-Royce engineers solved the problem by fitting a Z-bar, one end of which is pivoted to the frame, the other end to the top of the right-hand axle

Half of the inlet manifold is formed in the new cylinder head ; the other half is bolted to it.

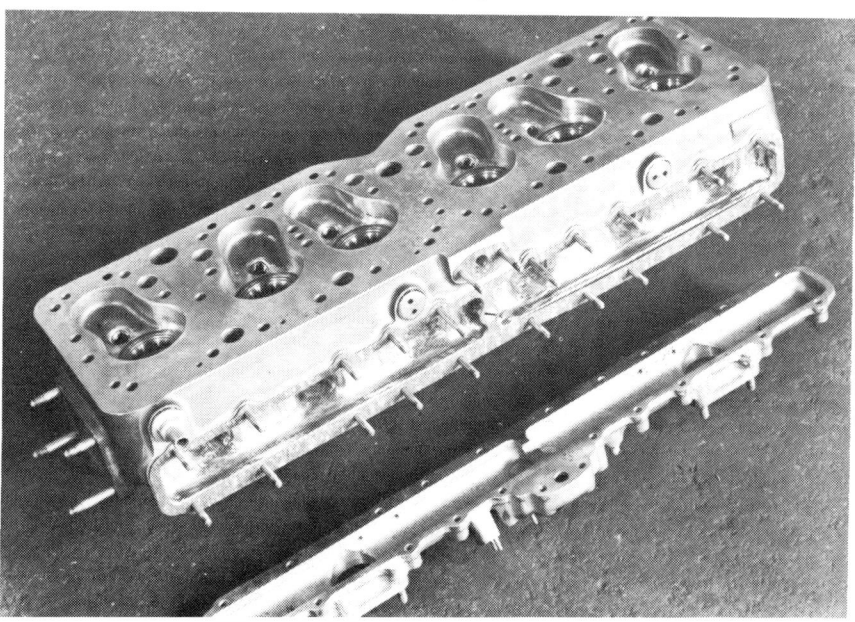

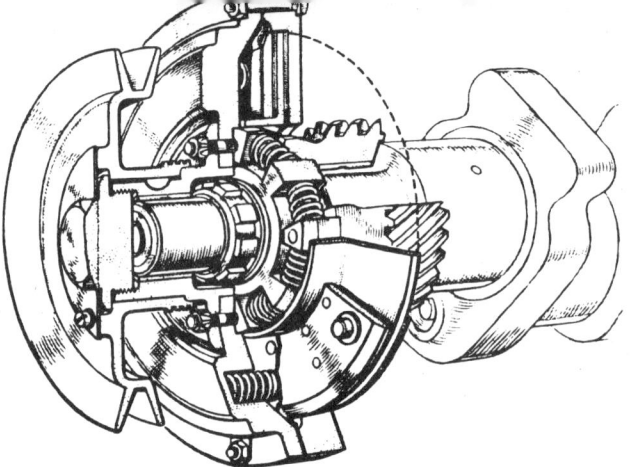

The crankshaft vibration damper and spring drive to the camshaft are located on the front of the crankshaft, and are enclosed by the engine front cover

ing plates spot welded to the upper and lower flange of each section before the main pressings are welded together to form a box. In the centre of the frame there is a deep box section cruciform, drilled to provide the necessary clearance for the propeller-shaft. In addition to the main front cross member, there are two cross members at the rear of the body behind the rear axle centre line.

On a car of this type smoothness and silence are two extremely important requirements. Particular attention has been paid to the body mounts, and these have

SILVER CLOUD AND SERIES S
. . . . continued

casing tube. This bar, in effect, trims the car to provide the correct degree of understeer. The addition of the Z-bar caused a considerable increase in the loading on the front spring eye, located almost directly beneath it, under braking. It was, therefore, necessary to increase the size of the rubber bush, which is now housed in a wrapped and welded spring eye.

The leaf springs are double grooved. To reduce road noise rubber interlining is placed between the top four leaves. The leaves are Parkerized to assist retention of lubricant, and the complete spring is packed with Ragosine 204G lubricant containing 20 per cent molybdenum disulphide. The springs are, of course, enclosed in gaiters which greatly reduce wear by excluding grit.

Improved damping is provided on both front and rear suspensions, giving greater fluid flow, so that the whole of the fluid is circulated as opposed to a small quantity of it continuously. The ride control, which modifies the setting of the rear dampers, has been altered. It is now electrically controlled and alters the "slow leak" on the dampers; operating the switch on the steering column gives instantaneous change, and when in the hard position the damping is twice as

hard as that provided when in the normal position.

Produced in 16-gauge 20-ton steel, the chassis frame is 50 per cent stiffer torsionally between axles than on the previous models. This increase has been brought about without noticeably increasing the weight, the figures for the old and new frame being 286 lb and 300 lb respectively. The side members are of box section, composed of two "top hat" section pressings, with additional stiffen-

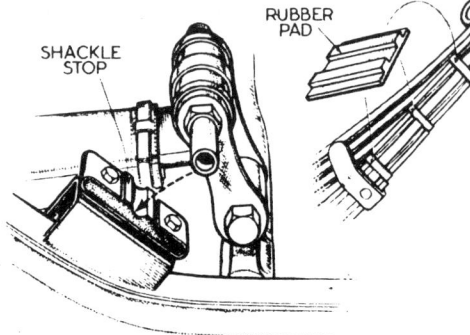

To prevent the rear spring shackle from going "over centre," a shackle stop is built on the top of the frame, and this engages with an extension on the outer end of the shackle bolt

The crankshaft now has integral balance weights. This sub-assembly shows the shaft with a vibration damper and fan pulley at the front, and thin disc fly-wheel and a starter ring at the rear

A forward extension on the steering box brings its frame attachment point close to the ball joint on the steering lever, thereby reducing inaccuracies and vibrations that might occur as a result of frame deflection. Note the pipe around the lower end of the steering box which supplies lubricant to the steering lever joint

been placed at the greatest possible distance from the chassis longitudinal centre line in order to provide the maximum amount of rock control with relatively soft rubbers. Further, it has been found that to reduce noise all body mounts must be equally loaded. To solve this problem the housings for the mountings can be adjusted, and to ensure that all twelve mounts are equally loaded, the body is attached to the front pair of mounts, and air jacks are placed underneath the remainder. The air pressure then applies a uniform loading, and the mountings are then secured. Two additional body mountings are provided on the rear arms of the cruciform to prevent floor vibrations.

In producing the new body the aim has been to provide a car with faster and more modern lines, and also provide extra width in both front and rear compartments. The main body panels are in 20-gauge steel, although 18- and 16-gauge light alloy are used for the doors, luggage locker and bonnet panels. To resist corrosion, zinc-plated steel is used for the sills and bulkhead. To improve visibility and give the car a lighter appearance, thin, polished, stainless frames are used for the top halves of the doors. Like the door

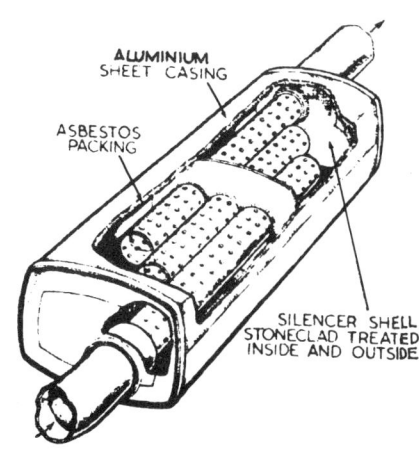

A heritage from the coachbuilder's trade, the razor-edge treatment blends well with the curves and still the "finest car in the world" shuns the flush-sided treatment

The first silencing chamber consists of a stoneclad treated steel box surrounded by asbestos, with an aluminium casing

panels, the fuel tank is also in light alloy, as are the fuel feed pipes.

Both the Rolls-Royce and Bentley now have completely new heating and demisting systems. In effect, there are two complete heat exchanger units, one on each side of the engine compartment. The combined output varies from 8 kw at 30 m.p.h. to 11 kw at 80 m.p.h. Both heating units have forward facing air intakes mounted low on each side of the main engine radiator. These are provided with special intake ducts which, in addition to the forward opening, have a diagonal grille and a rear outlet slot. The purpose of this is to prevent insects and foreign bodies from being drawn up into the main heater matrix. In addition, if the main forward facing grille becomes blocked with snow, the heater will still function because air can then be drawn through the narrow slot at the rear of the duct. The right-hand unit supplies air to the windscreen, the left-hand heater discharges it along the toe-board in the front compartment and via an additional tube into the rear of the body. This enables the temperature at the bottom and top of the car to be varied, and that very desirable combination of warm air at the bottom of the car and cool, fresh air around the driver's face can easily be provided. As on previous models, the electric element rear window demister is still retained.

In keeping with the remainder of the car, much thought and detail development have been given to the design of the seats. Basically the upholstery consists of a spring case with a Dunlopillo overlay, and in place of individual seats there is a single bench in the front. To increase the comfort and prevent the effects of weight on one side of the cushion being transferred to the other side (from driver to passenger, or vice versa), a measure of damping is provided by a vertical diaphragm fitted midway in the cushion. Another instance of detail development work is the use of a flexible panel under the tray behind the rear seats. This re-

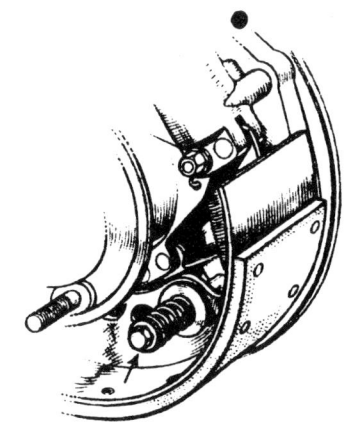

To permit more accurate adjustment a low-rate spring is used for the shakeback stops on the brake shoes

duces boom. The new cars also have greater luggage carrying capacity. No part of the car can be analysed in detail without bringing to light a most interesting development story, and there is little doubt that these fine new cars will carry on the makers' tradition and reputation.

SPECIFICATION

Engine.—6 cyl, 95.25 × 114.3mm, 4,887 c.c. Compression ratio 6.6 to 1. B.h.p.—not quoted. Maximum torque—not quoted Seven-bearing crankshaft. Overhead inlet valves, side exhaust valves operated by single side four-bearing camshaft.

Transmission.—Fluid coupling and four-speed automatic transmission. Overall ratios: top 3.42 to 1; third 4.96 to 1; second 9.0 to 1; first 13.03 to 1. Reverse 14.7 to 1.

Final Drive.—Half-floating rear axle with hypoid gears; ratio 3.42 to 1 (12 to 41). Four-pinion differential.

Suspension.—Front: independent, wishbones and coil springs; anti-roll bar. Rear: half-elliptic leaf springs with Z bar. Rolls-Royce hydraulic dampers. Suspension rate (at the wheel): front, 92.5 lb per in; rear, 127 lb per in. Static deflection: front, 10in; rear, 9in.

Brakes.—Hydraulically operated two trailing shoe, front; hydro-mechanical interlinked leading and trailing, rear. Mechanical servo assisted. Drums: 11¼in dia, 3in wide, front and rear. Total lining area 240 sq in (120 sq in front).

Steering.—Rolls-Royce cam and roller. Ratio (straight ahead) 20.6 to 1. Five turns from lock to lock.

Wheels and Tyres.—8.20-15in tyres on 6L × 15in rims. Five-stud fixing.

Electrical Equipment.—12 volt, 57 ampère-hour battery. Double-dip head lamps. 60-36 watt bulbs.

Fuel System.—18-gallon tank. Oil capacity 16 pints.

Main Dimensions.—Wheelbase 10ft 3in. Track, front 4ft 10in; rear 5ft 0in. Overall length 17ft 8in. Overall width 6ft 2¾in. Overall height 5ft 4¼in. Ground clearance 7in. Frontal area 26.4 sq ft. Turning circle 41ft 8in. Weight (with 5 galls fuel) 4,228 lb. Weight distribution 49.7 per cent front.

Price.—Bentley: Basic £3,295, British purchase tax £1,374 0s 10d, total £4,669 0s 10d. Chassis £2,465. **Rolls-Royce:** Basic £3,385, British purchase tax £1,411 10s 1d. Total £4,796 10s 1d. Chassis £2,555.

Although the bench-type front seat has a one-piece cushion, the squab is divided. Both parts can be adjusted individually for rake, and this adjustment also results in a variation in available leg room

Adjustable body mountings are provided so that all the rubbers can be set to a predetermined load when the body structure is bolted to the chassis

Craftsmanship

A four-door, six-light sports saloon on the Rolls-Royce Silver Cloud chassis. The usual sharp-edged shoulder of the bonnet has now been rounded off

PAR EXCELLENCE

Wooden patterns hang from the rafters, and a full size drawing is examined in the body building shop

EVEN though a beautifully made object, whether it be a work of art or a machine, may be beyond one's financial reach, there is great pleasure to be had from examining it, and even more from watching its creation.

One of the most respected names in coachbuilding is that of Freestone and Webb, who specialize in the manufacture of bodies of the highest quality on Rolls-Royce and Bentley chassis. This firm believes that it may be unique among the few who still practise the art in this country, in offering a body which, *ab initio*, is entirely to a customer's individual requirements. Among the other great coachbuilders the tendency is for a standard range of bodies to be made, choice of colour, upholstery, trim and the like being left to the customer.

As bespoke tailoring costs more than the ready-made garment, so does the individual coachbuilt car body, and only the more discriminating and well-endowed will call at the Willesden works for a fitting. Here, in consultation with the designer, Mr. Hedges, the style will be decided upon

and a pencil sketch made. This is followed by an ink drawing containing the important internal dimensions, which is sent to the customer for approval.

At this stage the design must be passed also by Rolls-Royce, whose reputation would not be enhanced by the fitting to one of their chassis of a freakish or ugly body which might be requested by an eccentric customer. Objection must be a tricky and, one hopes, rare event, for the customer expects to get what he asks for, though his æsthetic taste may not reach the height of his bank balance.

Consider the difficulties which beset the designer of bodies for these large chassis. Admitted that the larger the car is the easier it is to give it graceful, flowing lines. But spaciousness is usually expected, too, with ample seating capacity and luggage accommodation—a nine-seater was under construction at the time of our visit—and this makes it very difficult to avoid a bulky appearance.

It is hard to say whether the body built out over the rear wheels is dictated by the demand for space or merely to

The ash frame takes shape for an outsize nine-seater body. The windscreen pillars and frame have yet to be assembled

Craftsmanship

PAR EXCELLENCE...

conform to the current fashion; probably both are responsible. Nevertheless, such a body is no match for the elegance and litheness achieved in previous years with the separate and distinct treatment of front and rear wings, though these designs are now dated in the public mind.

It is a matter for rejoicing that the classic Rolls-Royce radiator has been retained, albeit farther forward than it used to be. Its uncompromising profile is not easily reconciled with generous body curves, and the knife-edge style is ideally suited to it. On the other hand the Bentley radiator permits greater liberties to be taken, and large radius curves can repeat the theme stated at the beginning.

The next step in the creation of a Freestone and Webb body is the making of a full-size drawing. This will occupy a whole wall of the drawing office and as several views—elevation, plan, front and rear—all appear on the same sheet with all the details of fittings, the layman is at a loss when he attempts to read it.

From this drawing the setting-out department makes the templates which enable the frame members to be formed to the precise shape, but not the exact size required, for some material is left so that the bodybuilders may make an accurate fit with mating members. Lap joints generally are used, although the mortise and tenon is to be seen, for example, where cant rail meets pillar. All joints are screwed and glued and reinforced by steel brackets.

Sufficient metal is used, apart from panelling, for it to be called a composite structure. The floor, rear seat pan, rear wheel arches, boot platform and spare wheel housing are steel pressings purchased from Rolls-Royce and spot-welded together as a unit. On a steel and timber sub-frame the body structure is erected. Centre pillars are either of wood or fabricated T-section steel; more recently, a box section aluminium alloy pillar has been adopted to reduce weight. The windscreen pillars are particularly to be admired for the slenderness which belies their strength. Their construction, and that of the light alloy centre pillars, is shown in accompanying sketches.

Tracings from the main drawings are made to enable the coach fitters to work on the metal parts for the frame and such interior fittings as occasional seat mechanisms and picnic table components. All door window frames are made from brass strip brazed together and, like the massive brass door hinges, they are heavily chromium-plated over deposits of copper and nickel. The joiners also receive tracings for interior woodwork, of which there is always a great deal in this class of body.

Before the last war, panel beating was done entirely from the drawing, but armament work made us all jig-conscious

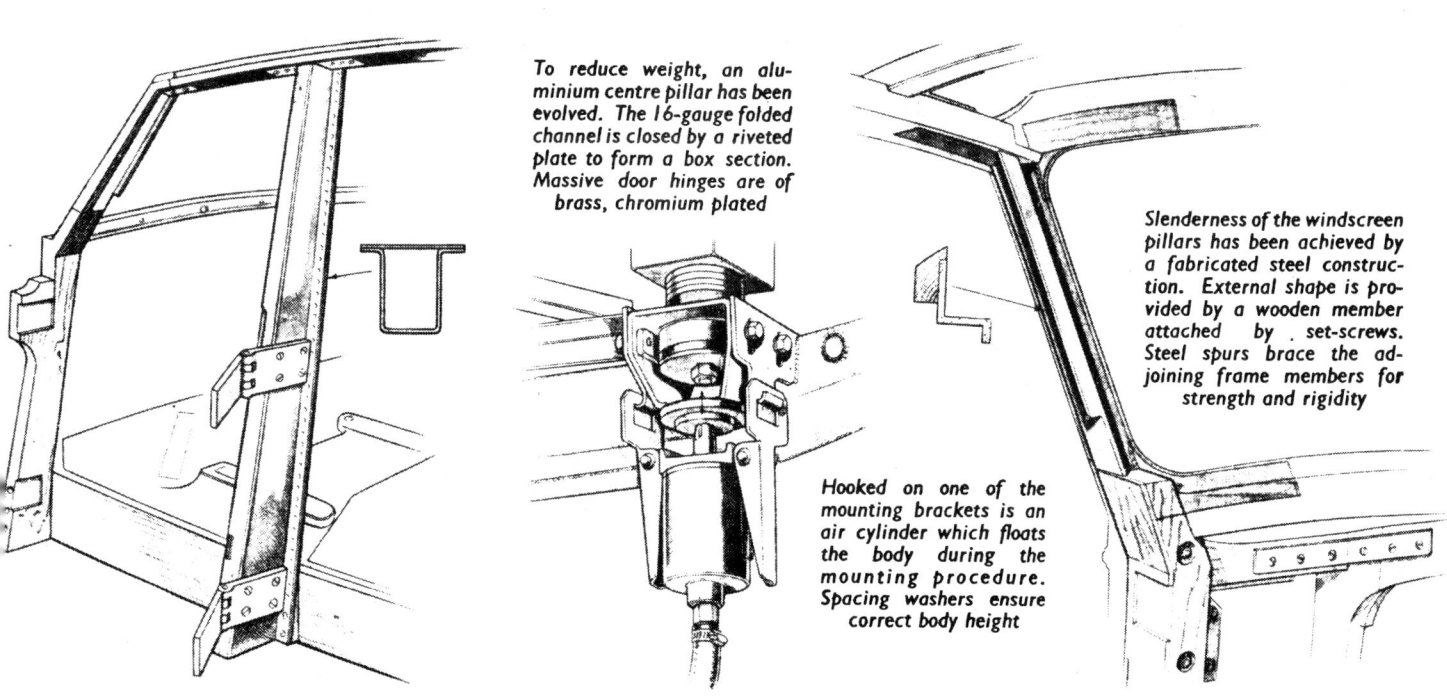

To reduce weight, an aluminium centre pillar has been evolved. The 16-gauge folded channel is closed by a riveted plate to form a box section. Massive door hinges are of brass, chromium plated

Hooked on one of the mounting brackets is an air cylinder which floats the body during the mounting procedure. Spacing washers ensure correct body height

Slenderness of the windscreen pillars has been achieved by a fabricated steel construction. External shape is provided by a wooden member attached by set-screws. Steel spurs brace the adjoining frame members for strength and rigidity and nowadays complex panels, such as front and rear wings, are made on wooden jigs. It matters not that one wing only may be formed on it—the jig must be made. All panels are in half-hard aluminium and are not preformed (excepting the wings) but are beaten and manipulated into shape in position on the frame, and joined by welding with the torch.

The painter has been with the company since 1926, when they were establishing their reputation with the building of fabric-covered Weymann bodies on the 3-litre Bentley chassis. At least twenty coats are applied—primers, fillers, stopper, gun-glaze, undercoat and six coats of cellulose lacquer or more if it is metalescent finish. Application is by spray gun and rubbing down is by hand; polishing follows the road test, which is a story in itself.

All bodies on the Silver Cloud and S-type Bentley chassis are mounted in accordance with a procedure evolved by Rolls-Royce. Ten Silentbloc bushes along the side-members are used and, with the body in position on these, an air cylinder connected to each bracket floats the body at a pressure of 50 lb. sq in. This ensures that the weight is supported uniformly over all mountings before the bolts—in elongated holes—are secured. These, in common with all screwed fastenings on the body, are tightened to a predetermined torque.

The finest materials are used for the upholstery and interior trim, and a wait of up to twelve weeks for delivery of skins of the quality required for seats is not unusual. All interior woodwork, in cellulosed matching veneers, is to the customer's choice.

Timber construction is well suited to this highly specialized type of body, because of the flexibility it affords to meet individual requirements. On the score of weight it shows up less well, and although frames are treated against the diseases to which wood is heir, export to tropical climes would be to tempt providence and termite attack. The proportion of metal used in these bodies has grown, and it seems likely that the traditional ash will yield to light alloys and steels in due course. If it does, one can be sure that the same superlative craftsmanship will prevail.

Here there are two provisos—the continuance of demand and the training of young craftsmen. In these days of credit squeezes and market uncertainty, one can but hope that captains of industry and commerce will continue, by their custom, to support houses such as this.

All members of the thirteen different trades practised at Freestone and Webb are perfectionists who take great pride in their work. Such skill and attitude of mind are rare these days, and Major Williams, the managing director, who was chief tester in the original Bentley company, is concerned at the reluctance of youngsters to persevere with an apprenticeship in bodybuilding. Without them there can be no one to inherit the tradition of Willesden, and there is no method of producing bodies of such quality other than by the wholehearted devotion of craftsmen to their tasks.

DONALD PETERS.

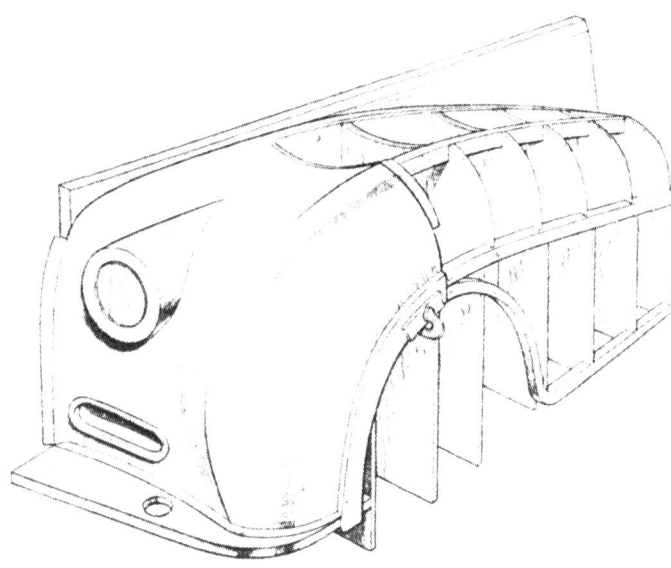

Wooden jigs are used to obtain the intricate shapes of front wing panels

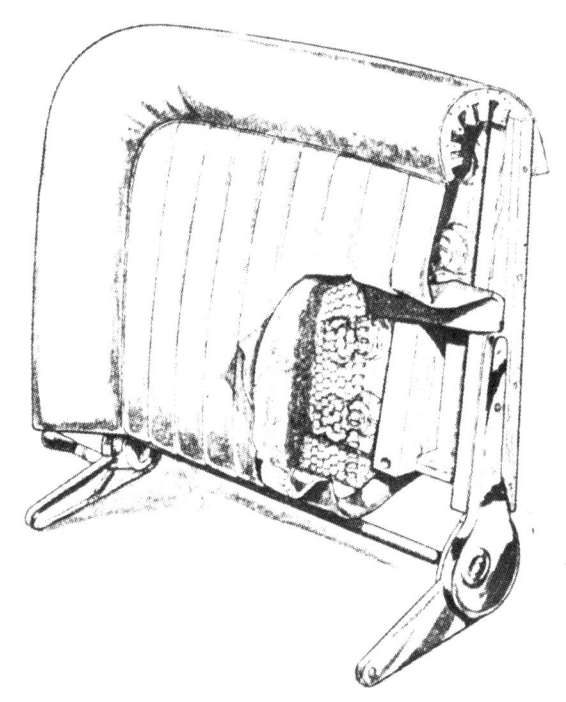

Front seat squabs have spring loaded hinges and a control to adjust angle. Below the cotton wool padded flutes are a horse hair mattress, spring mattress, helical springs and brass webbing. The roll is of foam rubber

West of England cloth is used for the upholstery of this seven-seater limousine on a Rolls-Royce Silver Wraith chassis. Below the quarter light are controls for the radio

Freestone and Webb's 1954 Earls Court Show Silver Wraith limousine

H.J. Mulliner's touring limousine on a 1957 Silver Wraith chassis

H.J. Mulliner and Harold Radford joined forces to produce this Silver Cloud estate car in 1959

There are no external changes on the Rolls-Royce Silver Cloud four-door saloon. Air conditioning and power-assisted steering are available as optional extras in export models

REFINEMENTS

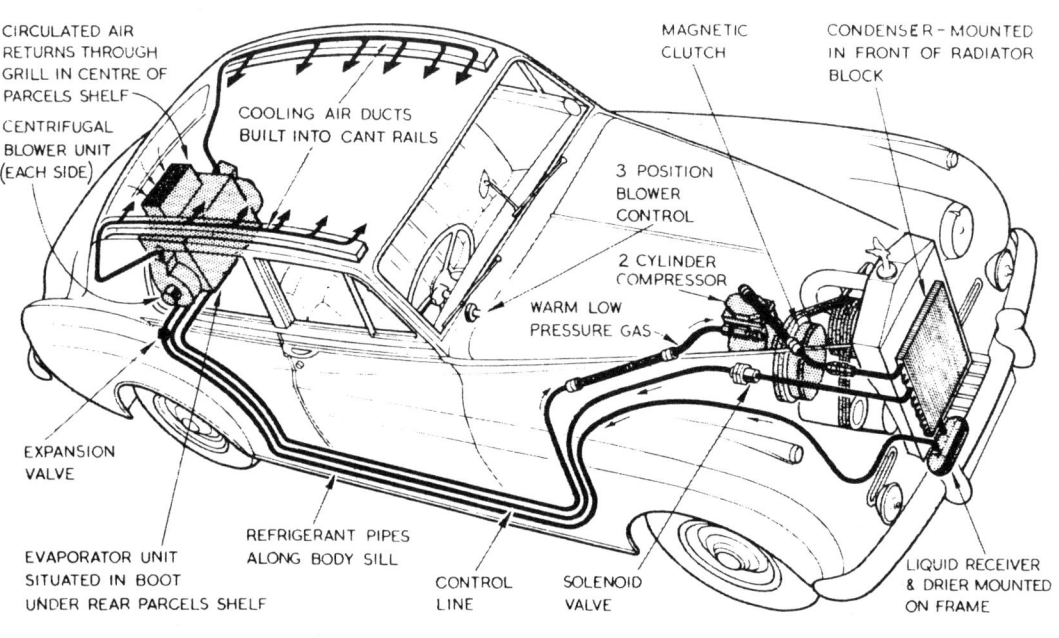

CIRCULATED AIR RETURNS THROUGH GRILL IN CENTRE OF PARCELS SHELF

CENTRIFUGAL BLOWER UNIT (EACH SIDE)

COOLING AIR DUCTS BUILT INTO CANT RAILS

MAGNETIC CLUTCH

CONDENSER - MOUNTED IN FRONT OF RADIATOR BLOCK

3 POSITION BLOWER CONTROL

2 CYLINDER COMPRESSOR

WARM LOW PRESSURE GAS

EXPANSION VALVE

EVAPORATOR UNIT SITUATED IN BOOT UNDER REAR PARCELS SHELF

REFRIGERANT PIPES ALONG BODY SILL

CONTROL LINE

SOLENOID VALVE

LIQUID RECEIVER & DRIER MOUNTED ON FRAME

The cooling air of the conditioning unit is circulated through ducts built into the roof cant rails. Under maximum operating conditions the engine-driven compressor of the refrigeration system requires 5 h.p. to drive it. With the air-conditioning system inoperative, the compressor is disconnected by means of the magnetic clutch

AIR CONDITIONING AND POWER-ASSISTED STEERING FOR EXPORT ROLLS-ROYCE AND BENTLEY : INCREASED POWER FOR CONTINENTAL

WITH a large proportion of the Rolls-Royce and Bentley production sold in overseas markets, most of them crossing the Atlantic, it is not surprising that air conditioning and power assistance for the steering are to be made available. The air conditioning system is available as an optional extra on the Rolls-Royce Silver Cloud and Silver Wraith, and on the S series Bentley. Similarly, power-assisted steering is available as an export optional extra on all these models, but also can be supplied on any Silver Wraith chassis sold in the United Kingdom. The complete refrigeration plant for the air conditioning unit is imported from the U.S.A. On the Bentley Continental, for which increased engine power is now provided, only the power-assisted steering is available as an optional export extra.

The air conditioning or refrigerator unit works on the vapour cycle system, which uses a straightforward series layout of compressor, condenser and evaporator. The gaseous cooling medium (Freon 12) is quite harmless and practically non-toxic, though it requires a few simple precautions to guard against a higher-leak tendency than those of most other refrigerants.

It is not necessary for the refrigeration plant to provide a large drop of air temperature. In countries where the system is needed, the occupants of the car usually dress according to the climate—the ladies wear light filmsy dresses and the men cool linen suits, often without jackets. Investigation has shown that the inside air temperature of a car tends to run about 10 deg F higher than ambient. Thus, if the outside air temperature is between 78 and 82 deg F the comfortable inside temperature is around 68 deg F. The wors conditions are when a car is left standing in the sun with all doors and windows closed. Even under these circumstances, if the engine is running at fast idle, the inside temperature can be reduced to the normal operating range within three minutes with the blower control set in its high position. The air is changed at a rate of 300 cu ft per minute at this setting, which gives a complete change of the inside air every 1½ minutes.

On switching on the refrigeration unit, the engine is automatically set to fast idle, to prevent the engine from stalling, due to the power required to drive the compressor. Maximum refrigeration rate is reached at a road speed of 30 m.p.h.

The cycle of operations in the refrigera-

tion begins with the compressor inlet valve, through which the vapour enters at a relatively low temperature and pressure. On the down-stroke of the compressor piston the automatic suction valve is opened by the pressure differential, and vapour enters the cylinder. On the up-stroke the suction valve closes and the vapour is compressed until it opens the discharge valve, so that the high pressure refrigerant is forced into the condenser. Here the heat of compression and the heat absorbed by the refrigerant in the cooling coil is imparted to the air flowing over the tubes, and the refrigerant liquifies.

The liquid refrigerant next flows into the receiver, which acts as a storage tank and contains a strainer-drier to remove dirt and moisture. Still in a liquid state, the refrigerant enters the expansion valve, the function of which is to meter the flow to the evaporator by throttling it, so that some of the refrigerant flashes into vapour. The remaining liquid is cooled down to saturation temperature at the expansion valve outlet. This valve is also the dividing point between the high and low pressure and temperature sides of the system. No adjustment of the valve is provided, and it will maintain superheat from −30 deg F to +50 deg F.

FROM CREWE

Steering power assistance is obtained by a slight initial axial movement of the worm, which circulates the oil under pressure from the pump to a chassis-mounted actuating cylinder

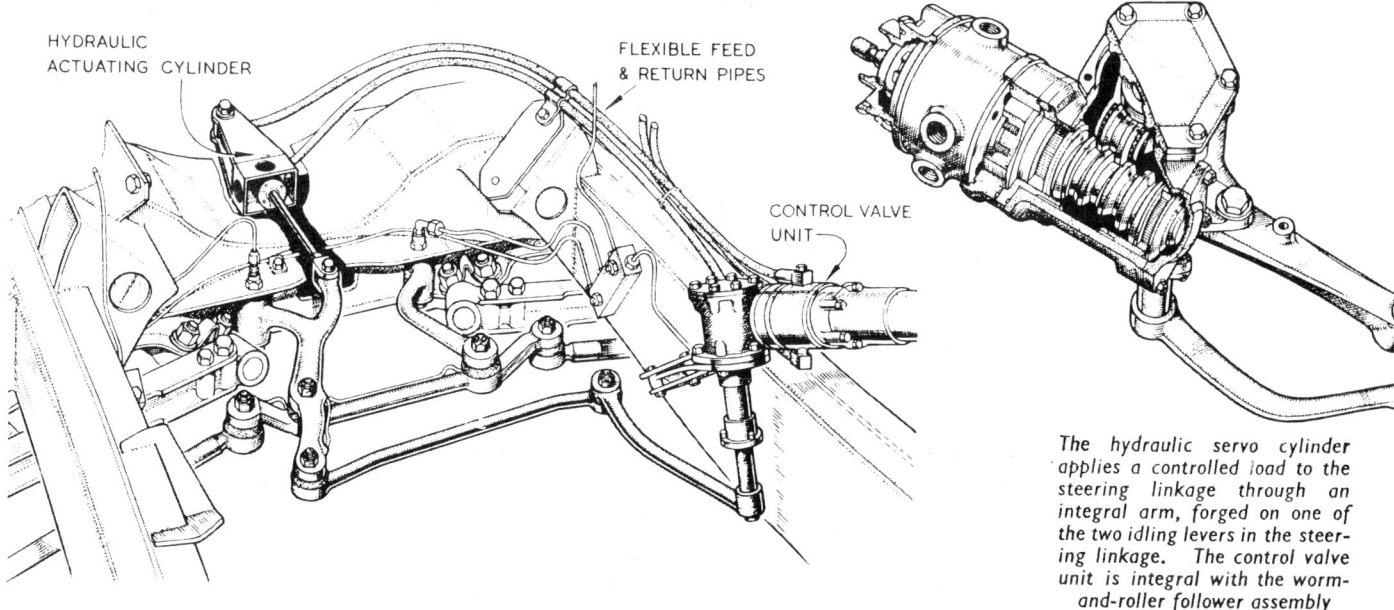

HYDRAULIC ACTUATING CYLINDER

FLEXIBLE FEED & RETURN PIPES

CONTROL VALVE UNIT

The hydraulic servo cylinder applies a controlled load to the steering linkage through an integral arm, forged on one of the two idling levers in the steering linkage. The control valve unit is integral with the worm-and-roller follower assembly

The liquid and vapour next enter the cooling coil of the evaporator unit, where the remaining liquid evaporates, absorbing heat from the air blown through it from the inside of the car. This is the refrigeration stage, in which the air is cooled by the latent heat of vaporization of the refrigerant in the coil. The completely vaporized refrigerant is finally drawn back to the compressor.

Triple wedge-type vee-belts from the crankshaft pulley drive the dynamo and fan pulley on the water pump shaft. The fan pulley has three additional grooves, two for the compressor drive and one for the power steering pump when fitted. A two-cylinder reciprocating type compressor with its own lubrication system is used. The suction and exhaust valves are of reed type, discharging through a common valve plate located between the block and head.

A magnetic clutch is provided in the compressor drive pulley, with a spring-

The two-cylinder compressor of the refrigeration system is belt-driven from the fan pulley. Great attention has been paid to the installation and fittings of the refrigerant pipes to eliminate possible leaks. The hydraulic circuit of the power-assisted steering has its own self-contained oil and filtration system

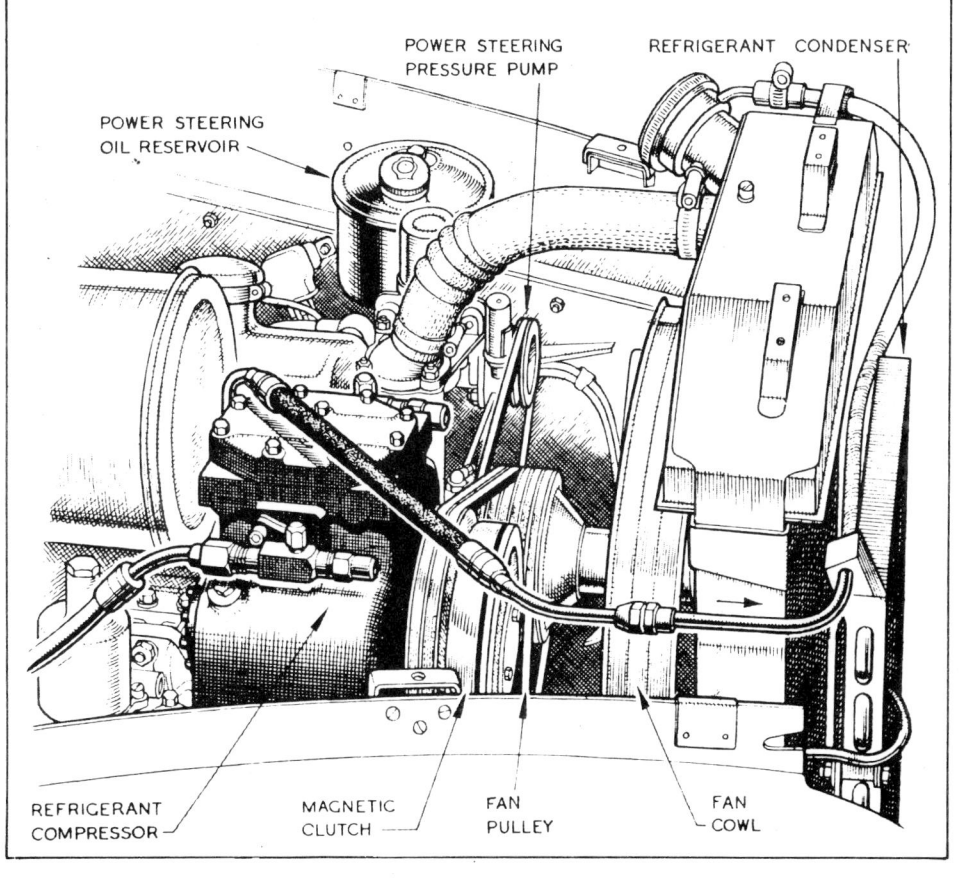

POWER STEERING PRESSURE PUMP

REFRIGERANT CONDENSER

POWER STEERING OIL RESERVOIR

REFRIGERANT COMPRESSOR

MAGNETIC CLUTCH

FAN PULLEY

FAN COWL

Hooper's
Silver Cloud saloon
with division

Refinements from Crewe...

loaded drive plate attached to the compressor crankshaft. When the electromagnetic coil (mounted in the pulley) is not energized, the pulley assembly freewheels on a double roller ball bearing. With the car blower control switched on and the electromagnet simultaneously energized, the drive plate is attracted to the pulley and the compressor brought into action.

The condenser unit, made of finned tubes for rapid heat dissipation, is located in front of the engine radiator block to take maximum advantage of ram effect. For low road speed conditions, the engine fan has been increased in capacity and provided with a cowl. Housed under the parcel shelf in the luggage boot, the evaporator unit contains the twin air blowers and has a substantial filter.

The solenoid valve is fitted in a by-pass line between the pressure side of the compressor and the inlet of the evaporator. It controls the flow of gaseous refrigerant in the by-pass, and mixes it with liquid refrigerant from the expansion valve; the proportion of mixing regulates the degree of cooling imparted to the air in the car. The blower speed and temperature control switch is an integral unit, mounted on the dash; switching on energizes the magnetic clutch and the solenoid valve.

Power-assisted Steering

True hydraulic power assistance, as distinct from power operation, is achieved in the Rolls-Royce designed steering mechanism. It does not become operative until the driver applies one pound of turning effort to the rim of the steering wheel; thereafter equal assistance is provided, i.e., for each pound of driver effort there is one pound of assistance. This ratio obtains until the driver exerts about 8 lb, after which an increased rate of assistance is provided. Under parking conditions with little or no motion of the road wheels, it might be necessary to exert a maximum rim effort of 12 lb which would not tax the frailest of drivers. The important feature of the Rolls-Royce system is that the driver retains a desirable degree of feel, even when motoring on ice or mud.

With power assistance, higher-geared steering is used with a steering box ratio of 18.7 to 1—the unaided manual ratio is 20.6 to 1.

Hydraulic pressure is supplied by a Hoborn-Eaton pump driven by a single wedge belt from the fan pulley, and it has its own built-in filter. There is a separate oil tank for the system, and when the engine is running 1¼ gallons of oil circulate continuously. With no steering wheel movement, this flow is by-passed through the control valve system.

The control valve assembly is mounted in tandem with a Marles hour-glass worm-and-roller follower. When the steering wheel is turned, resistance is met by the worm which is displaced axially (the movement is .008 to .010in), permitting the oil to flow through the distributor to the actuating ram which is mounted on the chassis and connected to one of the centre track rod idling levers. The hydraulic ram is mounted on a single pivot point to accommodate the small arcuate movement of its geometry.

The valves in the control unit are deliberately set to operate at high loads, so that they are not sensitive to any dirt which may escape the pump filters. A piston attached to the worm shaft presses on a valve plate through a series of springs and plungers. These springs control the steering wheel rim load at which assistance becomes operative. Oil pressure on the valve from the piston thrust load tends to centre the valve plate and maintains feel in the steering.

Should the hydraulic assistance system fail, mechanical connection is still retained, with a slight increase in back lash at the steering wheel. This results from the 0.008 to 0.010in axial movement built into the worm to operate the hydraulic control valve. A safety valve in the circuit automatically cuts out the servo should the wheel be turned against a kerb or similar obstacle.

Continental Power

Power output has been increased on the Bentley Continental engine for this year. It is not the policy of Rolls-Royce to publish engine output figures, but the modifications have provided an increase of 13 per cent over previous power. The compression ratio has been increased to 8 to 1 (previously 7.25 to 1) and the inlet valve heads are larger. The twin S.U. diaphragm-type carburettors now have 2in diameter throats, instead of the 1⅜in diameter on the earlier engines.

There are no changes in the Rolls-Royce Silver Cloud this year, but the six-cylinder engine of the Silver Wraith is now equipped with twin S.U. carburettors to improve engine breathing.

The bodies for the Silver Cloud and "S" Series Bentley are assembled at the Crewe factory of the Rolls-Royce Company from individual pressings and sub-assemblies supplied by the Pressed Steel Company of Oxford. In each range, specialist coachwork is available from H. J. Mulliner, Park Ward, James Young, Hooper, and Freestone and Webb.

H. J. Mulliner's fully-coachbuilt drophead coupé Silver Cloud with cloth-lined power-operated hood was shown at the 1956 London Motor Show

Minifon portable wire recorder in the central folding armrest

A handsome and dignified car, the Silver Wraith is large, but the space is all usefully employed and there are no unnecessary bulges or ornamentation

Luxury Limousine

Rear armrests carry, on the offside, the H.M.V. radio controls and, on the nearside, fitted mirrors, notebook, cigarette case, lighter and TV selector switch

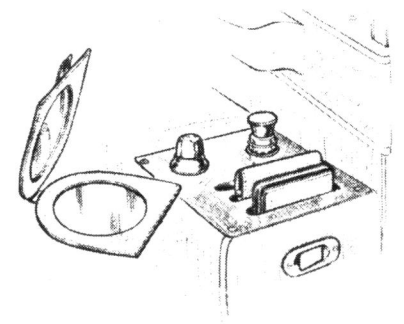

IT is most frustrating to know the answer to a question and not be able to put it into words. That is how I feel when people ask me "What justification can there be for paying £9,000 for a car?" Since, from the point of view of the ordinary man, we are in the financial realms of Eastern potentates, the reply might be that if I had three wives, I would rather buy them one luxurious limousine and three mink coats than three mink coats and a pony and trap.

But this is, in fact, unfair, because at that price the rich foreigner could have the car and buy a mink coat for the Chancellor of the Exchequer, whose share of the £9,000 home sale price is £3,000.

When, infrequently, I ride in one of these vehicles either as the driver or the rear-seat resident, I have no doubt about the difference and the value. It is not just the ride, the comfort and the equipment—it is the way you feel and the up-lift to the morale, enabling you to make bigger, better decisions, ignoring the trivialities and diversionary influences.

On a more serious note, there is no doubt that space, comfort and silence in a Rolls-Royce Wraith limousine are such that a man can usefully apply himself to his work, and if he needs relaxation, he can find that, too. With the aid of a wire recorder or secretary, ordinary office work can continue while mobile, and in privacy.

Turning again to the driver, it should not be thought that a very large car of this kind is difficult to handle. A responsibility, yes, but for sweetness of control and lack of effort few, if any, cars are its equal. Thus the owner and his wife would not hesitate to take the limousine out for a drive, even though it is designed to have a professional at the wheel. The front seats are comfortable and the compartment is well equipped. It has its own radio speaker and volume control and, of course, a share of the heat. The glass partition dividing it from the rear is raised and lowered electrically.

Seat adjustment, which is in the fore-and-aft sense only and inadequate for long arms and legs, is the only cause for criticism. The view through the large screen from the high sitting position is exceptionally good.

Power Steering

The particular car I sampled—a Park Ward Silver Wraith, seven-passenger limousine—carries a good deal of the extra equipment which is offered to special order with the coachwork. In addition, it is provided with Rolls-Royce power-assisted steering and the engine is of the latest mark, similar to the S-series and with twin S.U. carburettors. Automatic transmission with individual gear selection at the driver's discretion is a standard feature and, of course, servo-assisted brakes.

Power steering I consider to be almost essential for manoeuvring large vehicles today. The Wraith weighs 47 cwt, and because of the dimensions, it is on occasions a laborious business to park or turn in drives, mews or city streets. Power assistance, as provided by the Rolls-Royce system, is then most welcome. With power, the steering gear ratio is reduced from 20.6 to 1 to 18.7 to 1, and the steering wheel can be smaller.

Introduced last show time, the design was described and illustrated in *The Autocar* of 5 October 1956. Briefly, it comprises an hydraulic pump, belt-driven from the fan pulleys; a power cylinder which applies a controlled load to the steering linkage; a fluid reservoir with filter element, and, at the base of the steering column, flow control and relief valves with plunger and springs. Detail functioning is shown in the diagram.

It will be seen that the flow of oil to the hydraulic ram is controlled by a spool valve, which is located by reaction plungers. The plungers are exposed to oil pressure on the inside, and are also pressed outwards by primary springs. In circumstances calling for heavy steering loads, oil pressure builds up on the inside of the plungers, and at a predetermined point they collapse secondary springs, which then allow steering assistance up to maximum pressure of the constant output pump without manual load increasing.

From the driver's point of view, the power assistance helps as follows. First, in an Irish sense, it permits him up to 1 lb of manual force on the steering wheel without interfering (before first displacement of spool valve against primary springs). In practice this is sufficient for the tiny, sensitive movements which, together with a floating grip, give accurate and positive control of the car at speed. Sufficient road feel also comes back to the driver's hands, although he cannot receive a pronounced reaction from the wheels.

If the manual force exceeds 1 lb, as it always will when turning or cornering, assistance is applied automatically to the extent of 48 per cent of the load applied on the steering wheel, up to a maximum of 6 lb. Over 6 lb, as in slow-speed manoeuvring and perhaps sharp turns, the hydraulic pressure is allowed to give assistance up to the maximum pressure provided by the pump. (Collapse of secondary springs by plungers.

The pump output is controlled by a flow valve, which passes a steady $1\frac{1}{4}$-$1\frac{1}{2}$ gallons per minute, regardless of pressure. The pressure itself varies between 15 lb sq in at idling speed to 600 lb sq in (on the Silver Cloud and S Bentley the maximum is 500 lb sq in).

A driver knowing nothing of the power-assisted steering would find that if his automatic transmission selector was at neutral, the car stationary and the engine turning fast, he would be able to turn his wheel from lock to lock unexpectedly easily (but it would be better for the tyres if he did not try it).

When manœuvring slowly he (or his wife or chauffeur) would find the big limousine as light to handle as a Morris Minor. He would find steering when driving to be entirely normal to the feel, except that it would be pleasantly light and effortless. And he would fail to find any cause for complaint about undue sensitiveness or over-correction on long, high-speed straights. A very discerning driver at first might experience a little over-anxiety on the part of the steering to round fast bends. The assistance then seems greater than might be expected. This would be more apparent in a Bentley, driven as such a car would be, than in the more stately gait of the Wraith. Lest this point seems to be over-emphasized, I repeat that few would notice the effect at all.

Rolls-Royce power-assisted steering is undoubtedly a desirable fitment, but it is not cheap. The cost is £110, plus £55 purchase tax to home buyers.

Mobile Television

Although the coachwork special equipment on the Wraith was incidental to our assessment on this occasion, I freely confess that to watch television while being driven home was an intriguing experience, although reception was a long way from perfect. The Ekco equipment fitted is, in fact, a mains/portable set, and it is styled in beneath the central cocktail cabinet.

The quality of reception of B.B.C. and I.T.V. television programmes varied according to conditions and distance from the stations, and was better when the car was stationary than when moving. In Central London there was a good deal of interference on the screen, but the picture was quite bright and clear. In outer London and to a range of perhaps 30 miles, the picture generally was good when stationary but frequent "snow-storms" were experienced when driving. Approaching London from the West, no picture could be obtained until we neared Henley, but it then came in rapidly, and at Maidenhead was quite acceptable.

Fine workmanship is seen in the installation of the television and cocktail cabinet in the Park Ward limousine. Two occasional seats fold forwards

Sound reception was good at all times, and V.H.F. radio can also be received.

Perhaps the set's most profitable use at present is for watching one sporting event while attending another. One can also view one end of a racecourse while observing from the other.

No provision is made for darkening the interior of the car, and the bright picture desirable for daylight viewing seems more subject to interference than the duller picture required at night.

If the television set is removed from the car it must receive power from an outside source, but it carries its own telescopic aerial on the back of the case. When installed in the Wraith, it uses an extra long, whip-type aerial which it shares in this case with the H.M.V. radio, a two-way selector switch being provided. The set costs £99 3s 4d (purchase tax to be added, £45 2s 8d), and the cocktail cabinet in unit with it costs £46 10s (plus £11 10s tax). This accounts for the whole double installation, including the interconnected folding doors to the cabinet and its automatic lighting.

Motor show visitors last autumn may have examined the television installation in a Wraith and seen, as well, the Minifon wire recorder installed in the central armrest. This equipment works well, and

can play back through the radio speaker circuit. It costs £96 15s or £109 5s with tax added. The electrically operated glass partition is standard equipment, but powered windows are extra, the four actuators cost £140, and £70 purchase tax.

M. A. S.

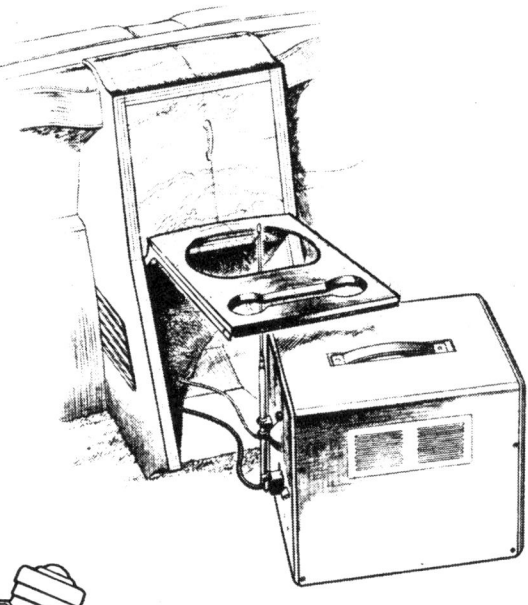

The Ekco television is portable but has no built-in power source. It carries its own telescopic aerial

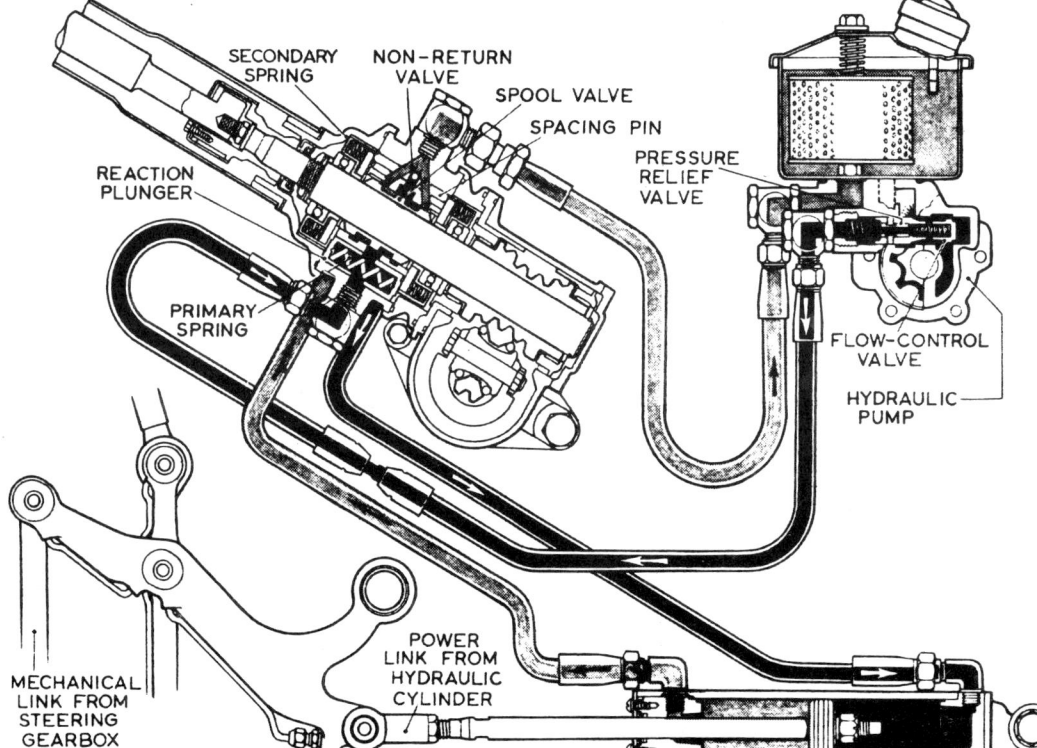

Layout and components of the power-assistance system for Rolls-Royce and Bentley steering. Flow here applies to the case of a light load, right-hand turn. High pressure is indicated by dark fluid lines. Normal manual steering remains in the unlikely event of power failure

SECONDARY SPRING

NON-RETURN VALVE

SPOOL VALVE

SPACING PIN

PRESSURE RELIEF VALVE

REACTION PLUNGER

PRIMARY SPRING

FLOW-CONTROL VALVE

HYDRAULIC PUMP

MECHANICAL LINK FROM STEERING GEARBOX

POWER LINK FROM HYDRAULIC CYLINDER

The lines of the Silver Cloud are well balanced; the bumpers wrap round at the corners. The radio aerial can be lowered from inside. There are sills protected by the doors. These visitors to the Brussels International Exhibition clearly are interested in the car

Autocar ROAD TESTS | 1683

Rolls-Royce Silver Cloud

THIS is the first occasion on which a full road test has been carried out on the latest model of the Silver Cloud, although on 7 October, 1955, we published a test report on the Series S Bentley, which differed from its contemporary Silver Cloud only in frontal appearance. Since the Bentley test neither model has changed markedly, but developments and improvements, of which there are many minor ones, include a higher compression ratio (8.0 instead of 6.6 to 1) and to the actual car now under review is fitted Rolls-Royce power-assisted steering. The differences resulting from the higher power output and assisted steering proved to be considerable. Brake horsepower is not quoted by Rolls-Royce, but the improvement in the already high performance suggests that it has been stepped up appreciably.

Belgium and Holland were used as the testing grounds for high-speed driving, with French roads to recapture appreciation of the model's "grand touring" character. Although sheer speed is not a major consideration in a car of this type, it is no less pleasing to find that the peak is now 106 m.p.h. (101 was the best achieved with the Series S).

Like the other car, the Silver Cloud reached exactly the same maximum in each direction, and its consistency was further confirmed while making the series of each-way runs necessary for the compilation of the performance data as a whole. This consistency is an impressive feature of the car.

In the more important field of acceleration the improvement makes 90 m.p.h. possible from a standing start in 34.1 seconds (39.4 previously) and the standing quarter-mile takes 18.8 instead of 19.7sec. The power continues to be delivered smoothly from the moment of getting away from rest. At traffic speeds of 16 to 20 m.p.h., when automatic high ratio is still retained, there is sometimes a slight engine harshness at pick-up; again at maximum engine speeds in all ratios the presence of the engine can be felt. However, in the wide cruising range it is particularly sweet.

The automatic transmission, standard on these cars, has maxima on the three lower gears of 22, 34 and 63 m.p.h. respectively. No cruising speed can be quoted with any precision, for there is no fuss even at the maximum. Certainly, 90 m.p.h. can be maintained on suitable roads from one tankful to the next—barely 200 miles, allowing a reason-

The back window is sufficiently large to give adequate rearward visibility, while appropriate privacy is achieved in the rear compartment for occasions on which the car is chauffeur-driven

There are separate, central arm-rests on the divided backrests of the front seats, and a small lever is provided for each occupant for adjustment of backrest rake. The folding tables in the rear compartment have ashtrays above them, and the sides of the rear seat sweep round to support occupants' shoulders and then to form armrests. Facing picture: The traditional Rolls-Royce radiator and mascot are continued. Fog lamps play a dual role as winking indicators

able margin. The tank capacity could, with advantage, be increased. On two occasions this speed was maintained almost without pause between Brussels and Ostend, the car's occupants enjoying what must surely be a unique degree of quietness. As long as the windows are shut, conversation may be carried on in drawing-room tones or the radio heard clearly at low volume.

There is a small price to pay for the extra power—the tickover on this car did not have quite the silkiness of old. This subtle change must be related carefully to the car; it amounted to no more than that the driver can detect the engine tick-over by feel rather than sound—with a little less difficulty than before.

The transmission control has five positions and, in concert with throttle pedal kick-down, a variety of techniques may be used for gear selection. At speeds of less than 60 m.p.h. it is possible to change to third by pressing the pedal fully down, or into second if the speed is very low. As the lower ratio then takes up coincident with the application of full engine power, the result is a little abrupt. This changing technique is normally reserved for emergency use.

With the quadrant set at position 4, all changes are automatic, and should a change-down be wanted while top is in engagement then instead of kicking down one may simply move the lever one notch to position 3. The quadrant lever never requires to be used in this way, but it is useful if, say, the driver wants to prepare for quick overtaking; while held up and, therefore, using a light throttle opening, he can make the car change down by moving the lever. With 3 selected the box remains automatic on all gears but now engages third gear at once, as and when the speed falls below 60 m.p.h. Similarly, in position 2, second is held, but this is an emergency position for very steep, long descents.

The other positions on the quadrant, neutral and reverse, are safeguarded by a button on the tip of the lever; the button must be pressed to get out of neutral or into reverse. Another customary safety factor is that the engine cannot be started unless neutral is selected. The particular car tested did have

a tendency to creep sometimes from a standstill with any one of the driving positions selected. There was no difficulty when starting from cold; the automatic choke, interconnected to the throttle, set the engine speed slow enough even first thing in the morning, so that manœuvring out of a garage, for example, presented no problem.

The power-operated steering is a joy; just enough effort is required of the driver for some feel to be retained, but all the work is taken out of parking manœuvres. The wheel gives little kick-back from road surfaces whatever their condition. The difference which the assistance makes to town driving is well worth having, and no snags were encountered to offset the advantages. The steering is more sensitive than previously, and one cannot detect the operation of the servo at any time. In the event of failure of the power mechanism, normal steering remains. Power-assisted steering should not be judged on less than a day's driving. The tyres' increased propensity to squeal probably results from cornering faster, unconsciously, with the aid of the power-steering, and the low pressure recommended for the front tyres further to reduce road-shock transmission to the steering wheel.

With a weight of some two tons, and with the high speed capability, something very special is required in the matter of brakes and suspension if safety is to be achieved. Of Rolls-Royce mechanical servo drum brakes there is little which has not already been said; little which is not known, if only by repute. For a maximum retardation on dry concrete of 94 per cent a pedal pressure of only 80lb is required. This pressure is not much in terms of driver effort, while 94 per cent is the sort of braking power that will fling any oddments on the seats to the floor. More than 60 per cent efficiency—the equivalent of the hardest braking power ever likely to be used in normal driving—requires only 50lb pressure. The newcomer to the model may startle himself by the result of using too high a pressure on the pedal, but it requires no skill, only an hour or two at the controls, to master the art of the soft touch, to enjoy the benefits of smoothly progressive four-square, fade-free stopping power

The instruments, surrounded by polished walnut, are neatly lettered in white on black. Below the radio controls is a pull-out table. The ride control switch is on the steering column. The luggage locker is deceptively long, and the spare wheel has a separate compartment. Illumination is now provided automatically when the lid is open

Silver Cloud . . .

which Rolls-Royce provide in return for so little effort. The hand brake is under the facia, reasonably easy to reach (if not entirely to hand), light, and fully effective in action.

The suspension of the Silver Cloud proved a little softer than that of the Bentley. The comfort of the ride remains of an extremely high standard, for combined with the soft, almost spongy feel experienced at slow and medium speeds is sufficient stability to enable remarkably high averages to be maintained even on winding roads of indifferent quality.

If a corner is taken fast, or in emergency it is necessary to make a quick change in direction at high speed, the initial feeling is that the suspension may prove too soft and imprecise—but this is not, in fact, confirmed by the car's behaviour; it will rise to the sudden difficulty well. There is more roll than was found with the Series S, though its extent is far short of giving any suggestion of wallow. There is a Normal and Hard switch on the steering column which varies the setting of the rear dampers to a slight degree. In practice the difference between the settings is difficult to detect; many owners would prefer a rather harder optional setting for use when driving fast.

The standard Silver Cloud, though without a fixed division, is equally well suited to chauffeur- or owner-driving. Front and rear compartments have similar choice leather upholstery and deep pile carpets; the facia and window surrounds are of superbly matched and polished walnut. The extraordinarily comfortable seats wrap round the shoulders at the rear. At the front there is a single seat with separate backrests, each instantly adjustable for rake. There is a wide central armrest at the rear, while a pair are used at the front so that, if desired, the front passenger can have maximum comfort while the driver enjoys all the elbow room he requires.

The steering column is not adjustable, but is well sited for most drivers—and a little too long for some. Particularly when power assistance is fitted, some drivers might also prefer a smaller wheel. The positioning of the two pedals is comfortable for a driver of any height. To the left of them, in addition to the dip switch, is the miniature pedal for the automatic chassis lubrication. The speedometer can be seen easily through the wheel. It is very nearly accurate, reading at high speed only one per cent slower than the car's true speed. The needle moves smoothly past the clear, white-on-black numerals.

Minor instruments, grouped in a dial on the left, while not quite so easy to read are, at least, comprehensive. The fuel gauge has a warning light which operates when petrol runs low, and a line on it for oil level; when the driver presses a control button the oil level reading is given. (During the test, including all the high-speed Continental motoring, the sump required no topping up.) Other gauges include water temperature, oil pressure, and the ammeter.

There are some differences in the operation of the switches, chiefly for ignition and lights, which have their own central, circular panel. Removal of the key now acts as the master switch; without it even the side lights or radio cannot be put on. However, it is possible to switch on whatever may be required and then remove the key; with the key out, nothing can be turned off. Therefore, in addition to the benefit of a complete master control, no one (including children left in the car) can tamper with settings when the key is removed. The lights include fog lamps with yellow bulbs which also act as powerful winkers, under-bonnet and luggage locker lights and, in addition to the usual interior arrangements, lights for vanity mirrors in the rear corners.

Extra touches of luxury are provided by a pull-out table mounted centrally under the facia (incorporating a wide ashtray) and hinged tables let into the rear of the front seat backrests. All the tables are of polished walnut matching the facia. Visibility is very good for a car of this character. As many of these cars are frequently chauffeur-driven, the privacy afforded the rear passengers seems appropriate. It is not achieved at the cost of any serious blind spots, and the slim windscreen pillars of the curved screen scarcely interrupt forward vision.

The heating and ventilating system fitted as standard operates silently, and is capable of precise adjustment. The rear compartment is now equipped with vents, and the temperature and distribution of air can be adjusted to meet any requirement at the screen, and in the front or rear.

A centrally hinged bonnet enables one side or the other to be opened. The layout beneath is one of the car's most impressive aspects to the enthusiast; not only is the density of components in the large space productive of awe, but the cleanliness gives the air rather of a laboratory than of machinery. One wonders how room was found for the quite

On each side of the rear seat is a vanity mirror with its own light, and with space for storing cosmetics. The engine compartment is well filled and the cleanliness of its contents is unrivalled. Although most owners would be unlikely to attempt servicing, components requiring regular attention remain easy to reach

Rolls-Royce Silver Cloud . . .

massive needs of the steering power assistance—and marvels that units for high-capacity refrigeration equipment can be added here.

The carpeted luggage locker is deceptively large, particularly in fore and aft length. The shape permits ordinary suitcases to be carried, but best advantage of the space would be taken with fitted cases. The spare wheel has its own compartment under the floor, with the jack. It can be reached without disturbing luggage. On the car tested the lock was sometimes difficult to operate.

The Rolls-Royce is a car of tradition, and few of its owners would welcome radical changes or unconventional design features. At a time when, for a number of cumula-

tive reasons, quality of finish and attention to details of trim and fit cannot receive as much attention on production cars as they did in the past, this make continues to attain the highest standards—little short even of the best seen in any of its predecessors.

A difficulty in appraising the Rolls-Royce lies in the exceptionally wide range of attributes which its designers have set out to achieve. Size and weight have not been allowed to reduce cornering safety; high performance is combined with silence. In these and other matters compromises may have been made, but few people once familiar with the car would not agree that the decisions have been taken with wisdom. There is no doubt that the car fully justifies the admiration, even glamour, which attaches to its name throughout the world in countries where cars of quality are understood and appreciated.

ROLLS-ROYCE SILVER CLOUD

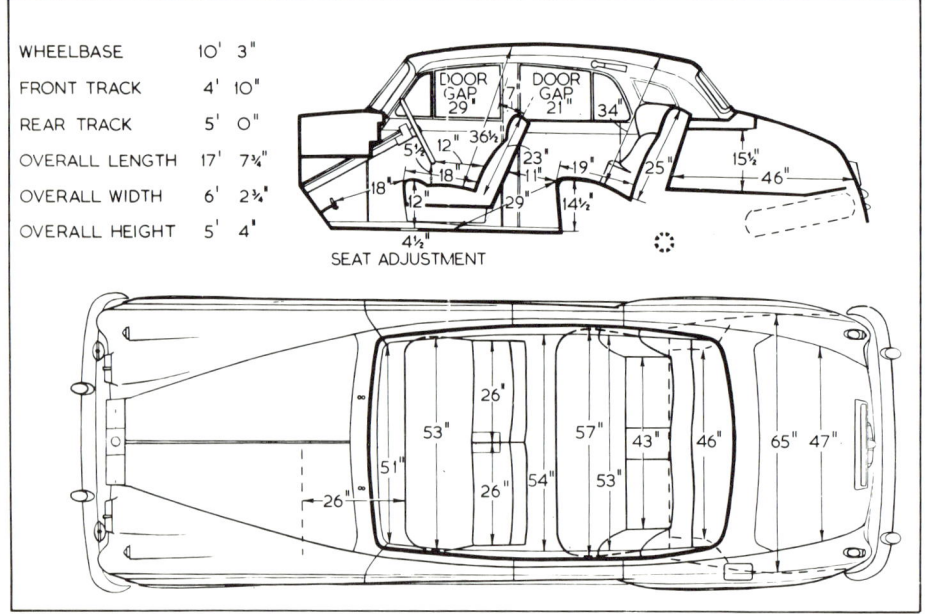

WHEELBASE	10' 3"
FRONT TRACK	4' 10"
REAR TRACK	5' 0"
OVERALL LENGTH	17' 7¾"
OVERALL WIDTH	6' 2¾"
OVERALL HEIGHT	5' 4"

Measurements in these ⅛in to 1ft scale body diagrams are taken with the driving seat in the central position of fore and aft adjustment and with the seat cushions uncompressed

---

DATA

PRICE (basic), with standard saloon body, £3,795.
British purchase tax, £1,898 17s.
Total (in Great Britain), £5,693 17s.
Extras: Power-assisted steering, £110 plus £55 purchase tax. Refrigeration, £385 plus £192 10s purchase tax.

ENGINE: Capacity: 4,887 c.c. (298.2 cu in).
Number of cylinders: 6.
Bore and stroke: 95.2 × 114.3 mm (3.7 × 4.5in).
Valve gear: o.h.v. inlet, s.v. exhaust.
Compression ratio: 8 to 1.
M.P.H. per 1,000 r.p.m. on top gear, 25.

WEIGHT: (with 5 gals. fuel), 37 cwt (4,144lb).
Weight distribution (per cent): F, 52; R, 48.
Laden as tested: 40 cwt (4,480lb).
Lb per c.c. (laden): 0.92.

BRAKES: Type: Rolls-Royce/Girling.
Method of operation: hydro-mechanical, servo assisted.
Drum dimensions: F, 11¼in diameter; 3in wide. R, 11¼in diameter; 3in wide.
Lining area: F, 120 sq in. R, 120 sq in. (120 sq in per ton laden).

TYRES: 8.20—15.00in.
Pressures (lb sq in): F, 19; R, 26 (normal).

TANK CAPACITY: 18 Imperial gallons.
Oil sump, 16 pints.
Cooling system, 28 pints.

TURNING CIRCLE: 41ft 8in (L and R).
Steering wheel turns (lock to lock): 4¼.

DIMENSIONS: Wheelbase: 10ft 3in.
Track: F, 4ft 10in; R, 5ft.
Length (overall): 17ft 7¾in.
Height: 5ft 4in.
Width: 6ft 2¾in.
Ground clearance: 7in.
Frontal area: 26¼ sq ft (approximately).

ELECTRICAL SYSTEM: 12-volt; 57 ampère-hour battery.
Head lights: Double dip; 60-36 watt bulbs.

SUSPENSION: Front, Independent, coil springs and wishbones. Rear, Semi-elliptic. Anti-roll bars front and rear.

PERFORMANCE

ACCELERATION: from constant speeds.
Speed Range, *Gear Ratios and Time in sec.

M.P.H.	3.42 to 1	4.96 to 1	9.00 to 1	13.06 to 1
10—30..	—	—	3.6	—
20—40..	—	5.9	—	—
30—50..	8.9	6.0	—	—
40—60..	9.4	6.7	—	—
50—70..	11.1	—	—	—
60—80..	13.0	—	—	—

*Figures obtained avoiding kicking-down.

From rest through gears to:

M.P.H.			sec.
30		..	4.1
50		..	9.4
60		..	13.0
70		..	18.4
80		..	25.0
90		..	34.1
100		..	50.6

Standing quarter mile, 18.8 sec.

SPEEDS ON GEARS:

Gear			M.P.H. (max.)	K.P.H. (normal and max.)
Top	..	(mean)	106	170.6
		(best)	106	170.6
3rd	..	..	63	101.4
2nd	..	..	34	54.7
1st	..	..	22	35.4

TRACTIVE RESISTANCE: 20 lb per ton at 10 M.P.H.

TRACTIVE EFFORT:

			Pull (lb per ton)	Equivalent Gradient
Top	..	..	245	1 in 9.1
Third	..	..	415	1 in 5.3
Second..		..	540	1 in 3.9

BRAKES (at 30 m.p.h. in neutral):

Efficiency	Pedal Pressure (lb)
23 per cent	25
62 per cent	50
90 per cent	60
94 per cent	80

FUEL CONSUMPTION:
12 m.p.g. overall for 960 miles. (23.5 litres per 100 km).
Approximate normal range 10–15 m.p.g. (28–19 litres per 100 km).
Fuel, Premium grade.

WEATHER: Sunny, no wind.
Air Temperature 56 deg F.
Acceleration figures are the means of several runs in opposite directions.
Tractive effort and resistance obtained by Tapley meter.
Model described in *The Autocar* of 29 April 1955.

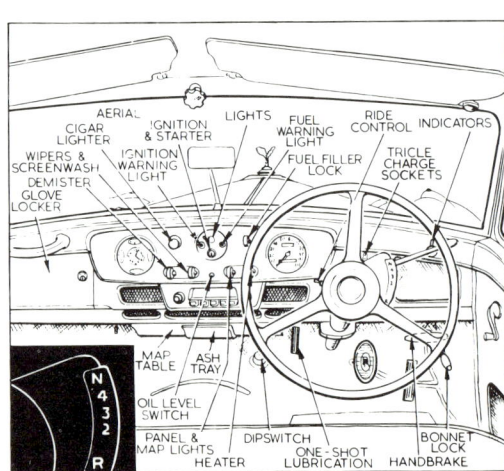

SPEEDOMETER CORRECTION: M.P.H.

Car speedometer:	10	20	30	40	50	60	70	80	90	100
True Speed:	10	21	31	42	52	62	71	81	91	101

Rolls-Royce 6¼-Litre Vee-Eight

Advanced New Design Constructed Mainly of Aluminium

ROLLS-ROYCE achievement in a wide engineering field covering automobiles, aero engines and industrial units was once ascribed, unfairly if facetiously, to the triumph of development over design. But there is a grain of truth in this statement, for this famous company has a proportionately larger development staff than any other British manufacturer. The result of this policy is that continual detail improvements are incorporated, unheralded, and radical design changes are rather infrequent.

Now a completely new vee-8 engine, constructed largely of aluminium, is to replace the present in-line six-cylinder unit in all models. Otherwise the S series Rolls-Royce and Bentley continue unchanged, except for detail improvements, including a new ventilating system, for which a refrigeration unit can be supplied as an optional extra to give full air conditioning.

After being in production for 13 years, the Silver Wraith is replaced by a new Phantom V, powered by the same vee-8 engine as the new S.II series. This Phantom V, with a wheelbase of 12ft and an overall length of 20ft, is the largest Rolls-Royce ever made. As with the Wraith, only bodies built by specialist coachbuilders will be fitted to the chassis. Details of these models and of the air-conditioning system appear later.

When standards of smoothness are as high as Rolls-Royce set—and these are very high indeed—there comes a time when a basic engine, particularly if it is a large-capacity six-cylinder, can be stretched no more. The superseded six-cylinder engine was first introduced with a capacity of 4,256 c.c. and a bore and stroke of 89 × 114mm for the Silver Wraith in 1946. Basic design had begun before 1939, and development work on a limited scale continued through the war years. In 1951 the bore was increased to 92mm (capacity 4,566 c.c.); in 1955 bore became 95.25mm and stroke 114.3mm (capacity 4,887 c.c.).

Throughout its life this engine has used the overhead inlet side exhaust valve arrangement. When first introduced, with a stroke to bore ratio of 1.25 to 1 and a compression ratio of 6.4 to 1, there were advantages in this F head layout. The combustion chamber was compact, and good inlet gas flow could be obtained.

Five years ago it became apparent to the Rolls-Royce engineers that a new power unit was required. If the engine was to have greater capacity, six cylinders in line could not be contemplated, as the resulting unit would be too long, and be ex-tremely difficult to make sufficiently rigid to eliminate vibrations. It was obvious that the vee-8, with its inherent stiffness and short overall length, was best suited to the capacity envisaged. Moreover, if considerable use was made of aluminium, there would be no increase in weight, and no company has greater experience of aluminium in engines than Rolls-Royce.

With the adoption of the new vee-8 engine, a considerable increase in displacement has been made, from 4,887 c.c. to 6,230 c.c. (380 cu in), and it is obvious that the engine is deliberately restricted on the carburettor side, leaving plenty of development in hand when the need arises to increase performance.

Noticeably over-square proportions have been chosen for the new engine, which has a bore of 4.1in (104.14mm) and a stroke of 3.6in (91.44mm)—a stroke to bore ratio of 0.88 to 1. Undoubtedly several considerations influenced this choice. The short stroke enables the overall width of the engine—often a drawback with the 90 deg vee-8 layout—to be kept down. This is assisted further by the use of a relatively short connecting rod—6½in between centres. Thus the centre to stroke ratio is 1.805—quite short even by modern standards—but this is of little consequence, for in vee-8 engines using a 90 deg spacing for the crankpins there are no unbalanced secondary forces to be influenced by angularity of the connecting rod.

The short stroke also permits the use of high revs, and although no figures have been issued for the engine, 5,000 r.p.m. involves a mean piston speed of only 3,000ft per min. Greatest advantage of the proportions is undoubtedly that the comparatively large cylinder bore permits the use of in-line valves, in conjunction with an efficient wedge-shaped combustion chamber for good burning. At the same time, each valve can have an individual port, and be so spaced that ample coolant passages can be provided round each port and the profile of the combustion chamber contained within the cylinder bores.

Layout is very straightforward and simple, obviously with an eye to ease of machining. There is one main casting for the cylinder block and crankcase, identical heads which can be changed from side to side, a two-piece front cover, and —for the first time on a Rolls-Royce engine—a pressed steel sump. Side-by-side connecting rods are used, and thus the two banks of cylinders are offset relative to each other. The right-hand block, designated A (the left-hand being B), is the forward one, and the cylinder offset is 1in. The four cylinders on each bank are equally spaced at a distance of 4.75in.

With a bore of 4.1in, it is obvious that the top lands are comparatively narrow. In fact, the radial thickness and depth of the top flange at the joint face is approximately 0.31in; it stands approximately 0.003in proud of the block joint face, and a corrugated steel gasket is used. There is a correspondingly small seating, on which the liner is pulled down by the cylinder head bolts. It has a radial width of approximately 0.1in, but its crush area, arising from the large cylinder bore, is considerable.

This type of construction is based on wide past Rolls-Royce experience with the Phantom III and aero engines. Many engines use a much wider top flange, but Rolls-Royce hold that this leads to bending of the top face, and hence distortion. The R.-R. theory is that narrow flanges, in conjunction with a thick (approximately 0.93in) top deck around the water jacket bore, give the greatest rigidity.

The three compression rings on the piston are outside the water jacket at the top of the stroke—a feature often criticized by some engineers in the past. Thoughtful analysis shows that at high engine speeds the time when the rings are outside the jacket is infinitesimal and, moreover, the use of an aluminium block with its good thermal conductivity ensures an even temperature over a considerable length around this point. A round rubber ring in the deck at the top, and two square-section rings at the bottom of the liner—all three seated in the cylinder block—seal the coolant.

The vee-8 layout results in a deep, short and rigid crankcase. Babbit-lined shells are used for the camshaft bearings

Combustion chambers are fully machined, and the sparking plug threads cut directly in the aluminium

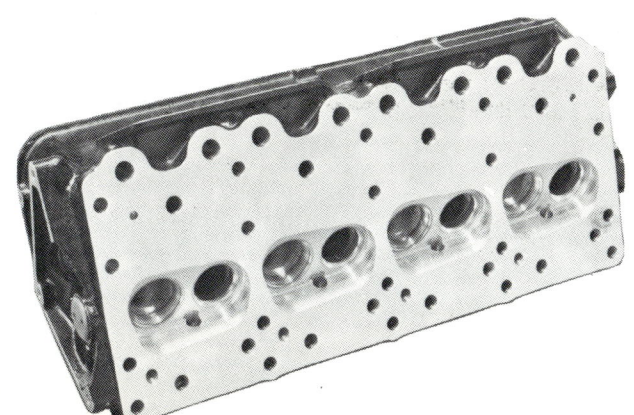

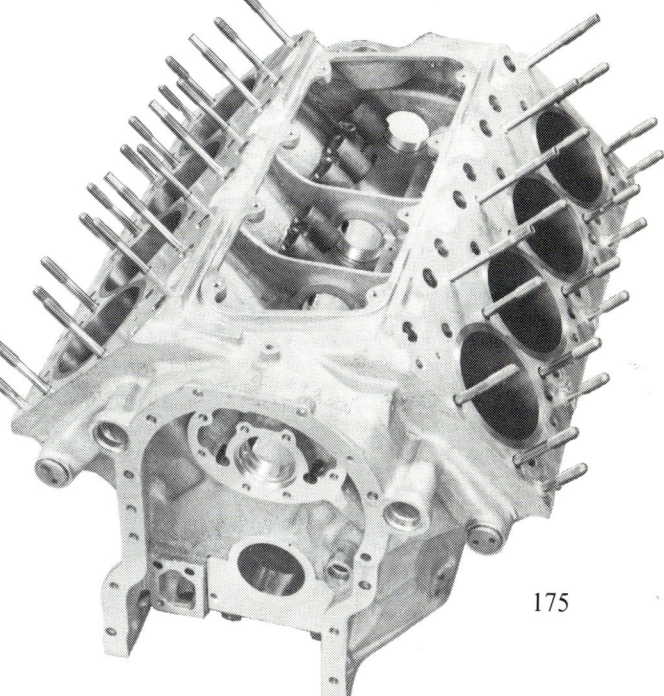

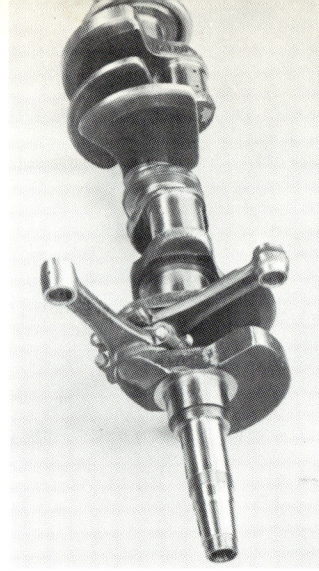

Left: A valve cover removed to show the rocker gear: single valve springs are used. The automatic choke plate in the air trunking is seen in its closed position. Right: The five-bearing, four-throw shaft, showing disposition of balance weights and the front two connecting rods fitted

Rolls-Royce Vee-Eight . . .

The sump joint face is well below the crankshaft centre line, and there are five main bearings, the forged duralumin caps of which fit in deep saddles, each with two $\frac{7}{16}$in dia studs. Copper-lead is used for the big ends and the five main bearings. The diameter of the mains is $2\frac{1}{2}$in, and the front four bearings are all of 1.062in wide; the rear one is 1.44in.

Steel, heat-treated and oil quenched to a 65-ton condition, is used for the crankshaft, which has an orthodox 90 deg crankpin layout—Nos. 1 and 4 throws are diametrically opposed, and the two centre ones are also 180 deg apart, these two being 90 deg out of phase with the two end throws. The only out-of-balance force in the vee-8 engine is a transverse rocking couple, counterbalanced by having a heavier mass of balance weights on the outer throws, which, in this instance, are 1.05in wide. Those on either side of Nos. 2 and 4 mains are 0.65625in wide. There are no balance weights on the centre main, but the webs are again 0.65625in wide.

From each main bearing a diagonal oil hole connects to its adjacent big end—the three intermediate mains feed two big end bearings, and the outer ones one each. In each big end journal there are two cross holes, one for each rod, drilled at right angles and offset 0.4in from the centre line. Each journal is 2.25in diameter and 2in wide, the bearing shells in each rod being 0.81in wide. The connecting rod is an H-section steel forging,

horizontally split, secured by two $\frac{3}{8}$in dia bolts which are a press fit in the rod, to eliminate a stress-raising shoulder and prevent turning during tightening.

Each aluminium slipper-type piston—the skirt is cut away on the non-thrust side, in line with the gudgeon pin—has three 0.078in-wide compression rings (the top one chromium-plated) and a composite oil control ring above the gudgeon pin, which is fully floating, of $\frac{7}{8}$in dia. There is a recess in the piston crown, presumably to provide for future increases in compression ratio as it is filled in.

At the front end of the crankshaft a single helical gear drives the camshaft, which is mounted in four bearings and situated in the tunnel between the two banks of cylinders. The half-speed gear of the camshaft is made from forged aluminium, the material used also on the superseded six-cylinder engine. Rolls-Royce claim that a gear drive can be made quieter than a chain and, moreover, it has a much longer life; aluminium is chosen for the camshaft gear because it keeps down the inertia mass—an aid to quietness. Between the hub and the gear teeth the centre is formed with a series of corrugated flutes for stiffness, and to eliminate the metallic ring often associated with a gear drive.

Forward of the helical gear on the crankshaft is a bronze and steel spiral drive for the oil pump, which is mounted in the front timing chest. Helical displacement gears are used for the pump, which has an integral relief valve with pre-set adjustment; surplus oil is returned to the inlet side of the pump.

From the main gauze pick-up filter a pipe leads to a full flow filter, made by British Filters, at the front of the cylinder block on the left-hand side. From the filter the oil is fed to a cast recess in the camshaft front bearing, then to two drilled galleries running the length of the cylinder block on either side of the camshaft. From these galleries the oil is taken alternately to the back feed grooves of the main bearing housings and to the tappet blocks for supplying the hydraulic tappets, as shown in the cross-section drawing. The cast-iron tappet blocks are in groups of 3, 2, 3 along each bank.

With an all-aluminium engine and its associated problems of high coefficient of expansion, self-adjusting tappets are almost indispensable. They have also incidental advantages in permitting the use of shorter quietening ramps on the cam form, and hence wider effective valve timings and lower accelerations, simplifying the design of the spring. The Rolls-Royce tappet design is based on the American Chrysler, and initial production will come from the U.S.A., but plans have been made for eventual manufacture at Crewe.

Within the main tappet body is a plunger assembly consisting of the plunger, into which is pressed the bottom seating for the push-rod, the valve retainer and its spring, and the non-return valve, which has a near knife-edge seating. Oil is fed from the main gallery through the tappet block to an annular groove and hole in the body, and thence through a radial hole in the inside of the plunger. During the dwell period, when the engine valve is

Left: Layout of the two-tier induction system and its water jacketing. Right: Component parts of two important assemblies. The pad on the connecting rod cap is machined for weight grading

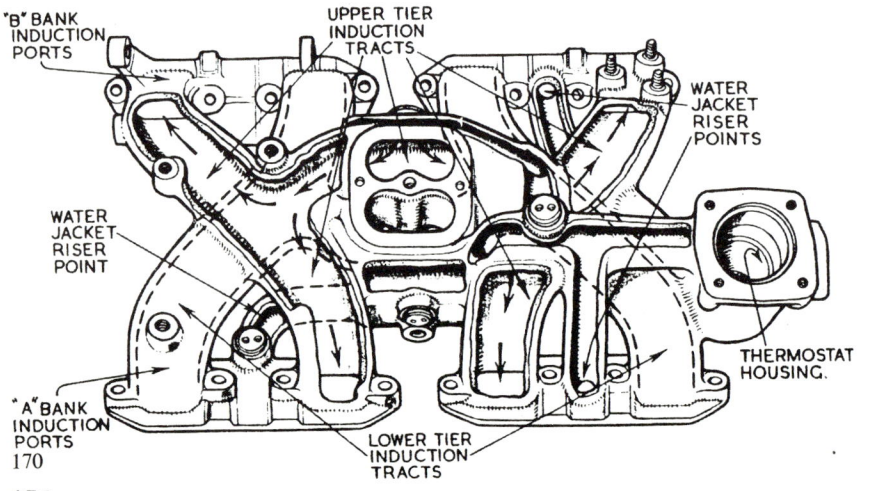
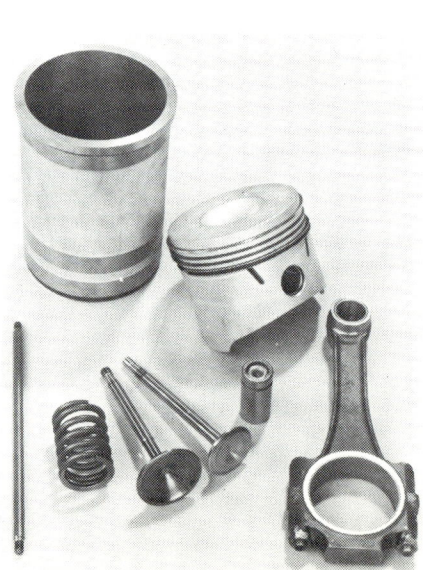

170

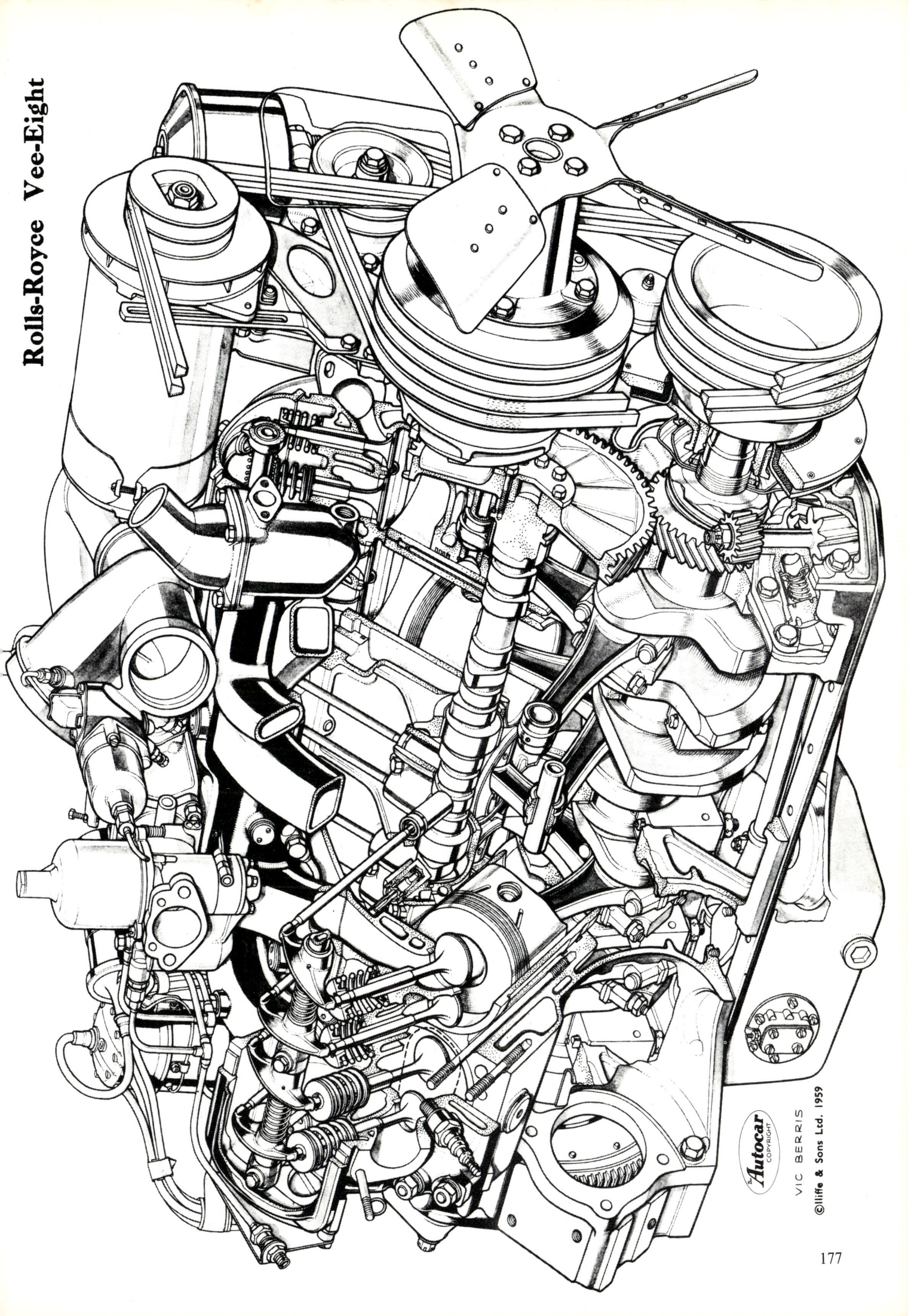

Rolls-Royce Vee-Eight

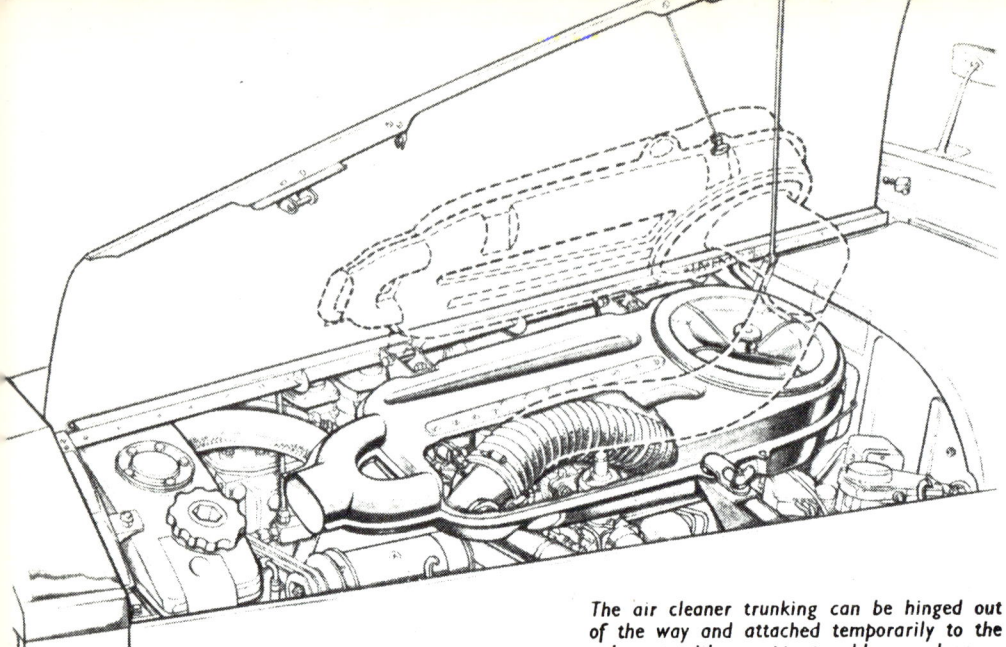

The air cleaner trunking can be hinged out of the way and attached temporarily to the bonnet with a support cable, as shown

Component parts of the hydraulic assembly are manufactured to extremely fine limits. The face which contacts with the cam has a 30in spherical radius to induce rotation

on its seating, the oil can pass through the non-return valve to the lower well in the tappet body. The strut load on the push-rod, which takes up the valve clearance during this period, is determined by the oil leak through the non-return valve; the clearances here are very small, and closely controlled during manufacture. As the cams turn and the engine valves begin to open, the main pressure oil feed is cut off, the non-return valve is pressed on to its seating and the plunger raised on the column of oil trapped below the non-return valve.

It is important that there should be no aeration in the oil if the system is to function satisfactorily. This is achieved by having the oil feed from the two main galleries low in the circuit; air is taken out by means of a continuous controlled leak through the hollow push-rods, which have case-hardened steel ends for the seatings and Bundy tubing for the tubular portion. A separate low-pressure oil system is used for lubricating the rocker shaft.

The cylinder head is an aluminium casting with shrunk-in, cast-iron inserts for the valve seats. The combustion chamber is substantially wedge-shaped, with the in-line valves set at an angle of 28 deg from the vertical centre line. There is a considerable area of squish, most of it directed towards the plug, which is on the outside of the head, biased slightly towards the exhaust valve. The sparking plugs are situated beneath the exhaust manifold, and are not very accessible with the engine installed in the chassis. The inlet ports, of rectangular section at the manifold joint face, are of considerable length. Bronze guides are used for the exhaust valves, which are of KE 965 steel; they are Stellited on the face and stem end, and the head is Brightrayed all over.

Each rocker shaft is supported on **five** separate pedestals, each with a single stud passing through the centre line of the shaft. These studs are an extension of the inner cylinder holding-down studs; there are 20 7/6th-dia studs for each cylinder head. They are made of austenitic steel, and the four main ones round each bore extend well into the crankcase casting.

Firing order is A1, B1, A4, B4, B2, A3, B3, A2—the engine fires down A bank in the sequence 1, 4, 3, 2, and in B bank 1, 4, 2, 3. The induction system, fed through two 1¾in S.U. diaphragm type carburettors, built especially for Rolls-Royce, is arranged to give equal intake impulses. The two carburettors are placed transversely across the engine, and the two separate induction systems (although contained in a common manifold) are arranged in two tiers—looking at the top of the engine the pipes for the right-hand carburettor are above those for the left. From the central gallery for each system, the induction track crosses from the outer cylinder on one bank to the nearest inner one on the other bank, and the same at the other end of the engine, as shown in the diagram.

On the air side of each carburettor, a U-shaped trunking connects to a central elbow which contains an automatic choke for cold starting. This is controlled by a thermostat in one of the exhaust manifolds, and there is a cam and link mechanism from the throttle spindle of the choke valve to the enrichment jet in the diaphragm assembly. Above the engine is a long air intake silencer and cleaner. It is fixed, by wing nut, to the central elbow, with a flexible bellows so that it can be lifted up and hooked to the bonnet lid during adjustments on top of the engine.

A four-groove pulley on the front of the crankshaft drives the accessories through narrow-wedge belts. Two are for the triangulated drive from the crank to the water pump, on the end of which is a five-bladed fan, and the oil pump for the power-assisted steering, which is now standard on all models. The water pump has a two-branch feed to cross galleries near the top joint face of each cylinder bank. These feed into jackets which are connected by cored holes along the block, and thence through three holes on the lower side of each cylinder, so that water at high velocity is directed to the exhaust valve regions.

On the outer side the system is split, with a take-off point between the pairs of inlet ports on each head. It is then routed through the inlet manifold to form a heating jacket for the induction system, and thence to a housing containing the thermostat connected to the inlet side of the pump. All castings containing water jackets are anodized in a partly machined condition to resist corrosion, and cylinder liners are varnished on their outsides for the same purpose.

The two outer belts drive the dynamo, which is mounted on top of the engine, and operates at approximately twice engine speed. A triangulated drive with longer belts is used when the compressor for the refrigeration system is fitted.

Dry weight of engine and gear box is 890 lb—approximately 10 lb less than that of the superseded six-cylinder in the same condition. Thus there has been no penalty in weight for a 27½ per cent increase in capacity; overall length is shorter, but width is increased.

Among many Rolls-Royce traditions is one of never publishing engine powers—when asked they merely say "enough"—but many readers are interested in such matters, and some estimations are not out of place. Based on an examination of inlet valve area and porting efficiency, the old six-cylinder 4.8-litre engine probably developed approximately 182-185 b.h.p. as installed. It would seem that there has not been a great increase in maximum horsepower with the new engine, for although it has a much bigger displacement, the two carburettors are only 1¾in dia, whereas, latterly, on the six-cylinder

SPECIFICATION

ENGINE		Phantom V	Silver Cloud
No. of cylinders	...	8 vee	
Bore and stroke	...	104.4 x 91.44mm (4.1 x 3.6in)	
Displacement	...	6,230 c.c. (380 cu in)	
Valve position	...	O.h.v., hydraulic tappets	
Compression ratio	...	8.0 to 1	
Carburettor	...	2 S.U. diaphragm type, 1.75in dia	
Fuel pump	...	S.U. twin electric, independent pumps	
Tank capacity	...	23 Imp. gals (104.5 litres)	18 Imp. gals (81.82 litres)
Sump capacity	...	12.5 pints (7.1 litres)	
Oil filter	...	Full flow	
Cooling system	...	Centrifugal pump and fan	
Battery	...	12 volt 67 ampere hour	

TRANSMISSION			
Automatic	...	Fluid coupling. Four forward speeds; steering column change lever	
Overall gear ratios:			
Top	...	3.89 (direct)	3.08 (direct)
3rd	...	5.64	4.46
2nd	...	10.23	8.10
1st	...	14.86	11.75
Rev.	...	16.72	13.27
Final drive	...	Hypoid bevel, 3.89 to 1	Hypoid bevel, 3.08 to 1

CHASSIS			
Brakes: front	...	Hydraulic, servo assisted	
rear	...	Hydro-mechanical, servo assisted	
Drum dia, shoe width		11.25 x 3.0in	
Suspension: front	...	Independent, coil springs. Anti-roll torsion bar	
rear	...	Asymmetric, semi-elliptic leaf springs	
Dampers	...	Hydraulic; ride control on rear	
Wheels	...	Bolted on pressed steel with disc	
Tyre size	...	8.90—15in	8.20—15in
Steering	...	Cam and roller, power assisted	
Steering wheel	...	Three-spoke	
Turns, lock to lock	...	4.25	

MANUFACTURER'S DIMENSIONS			
Wheelbase	...	12ft 0in (368cm)	10ft 3in (312cm)
Track: front	...	5ft 0.88in (155cm)	4ft 10in (147cm)
rear	...	5ft 4in (162.5cm)	5ft 0in (152cm)
Overall length	...	19ft 10in (604.5cm)	17ft 7.75in (538cm)
Overall width	...	6ft 7in (200.6cm)	6ft 2.75in (190cm)
Ground clearance	...	7.25in (18.41cm)	7in (17.8cm)
Turning circle	...	48ft 9in (14.86m)	41ft 8in (12.7m)

Rolls-Royce Vee-Eight...

engine they were 2in dia. Irrespective of cylinder displacement there is a limit to the amount of air which the carburettor will pass; it is estimated, therefore, that these control the peak figure on the new engine, which would be around 200 b.h.p.

There is, of course, a considerable increase in torque arising from the larger capacity, improving acceleration and smoothing out gear changes in the automatic transmission, which remains basically unchanged. This greater torque has enabled the final drive to be equipped with higher and strengthened gearing, raising full throttle change points through the gears from 20, 36 and 70 m.p.h. to 23, 40 and 78 m.p.h.

••

WHILE the principal technical interest in the Rolls-Royce programme centres on the new vee-8 engine, described on the preceding pages, numerous modifications have been made to the series S.2 saloons. In addition, the imposing new Phantom V limousine chassis, and the luxury bodywork that various specialist coachbuilders are designing for it, will fill a place in the range of British cars that was formerly the prerogative of the Silver Wraith, production of which has now ceased.

There are many detail changes on the S.2 chassis. The previous pressed steel

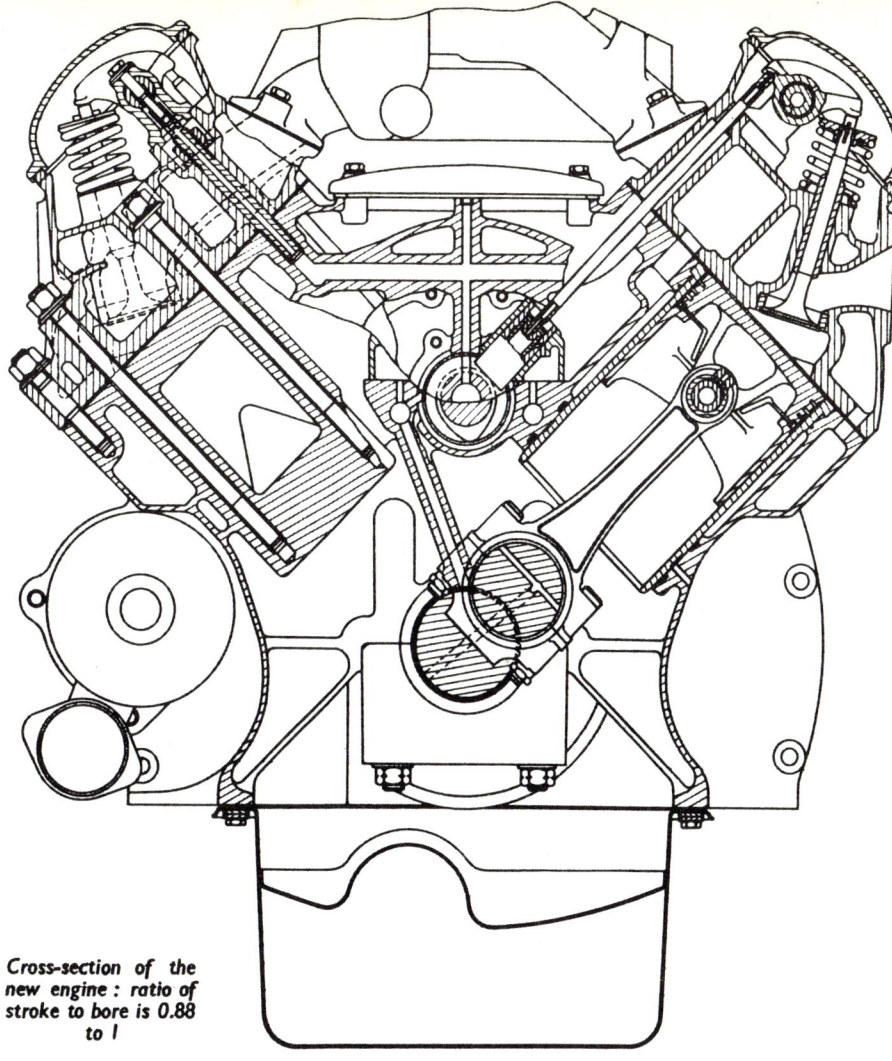

Cross-section of the new engine : ratio of stroke to bore is 0.88 to 1

Largest Rolls-Royce Ever Built

New Phantom V Limousine — Modifications to S.2 saloons

swept-back wishbones for the front suspension are replaced by forgings, and the centralized chassis lubrication system is discarded. Each greasing or oiling point has been provided with a reservoir, so that attention to these is required only at intervals of 10,000 miles or one year, whichever is the shorter.

Extra width of the vee-8 engine has necessitated the cam and roller steering box, with its inbuilt valves for the power assistance system (described in *The Autocar* of 5 October 1956), being moved

rearwards, and from the inside to the outside of the frame. To maintain the column position the box is provided with a pair of spiral input gears. The power valving assembly and its shaft are mounted horizontally and the output spindle, on the lower end of which is the steering arm, vertically. The steering wheel is closer to the facia panel, its diameter is reduced by 1in, and it has a much thinner rim section; improvement in the driving position results.

Basically the braking system, with its

duplicated hydraulic circuit, is unchanged, but there are minor improvements. The mechanical servo, consisting of a clutch driven from the final drive shaft of the gear box, has been speeded up to reduce delay, and the ratio of braking on the front wheels increased from 1.36 to 1 to 1.66 to 1. Rear roll stiffness has been reduced by shortening the arm of the Z-bar at the axle end; this bar also prevents the rear axle from rocking on its springs.

On all models a completely redesigned internal ventilation system in its standard form supplies cool or heated fresh air for the occupants, but the same basic circuit can be equipped with refrigeration units to give full air conditioning, at a relatively moderate extra charge of £275 basic. The new system is described in detail on pages 268-9 of this issue.

There are no changes to the body styling other than the two air intake grilles at the front, which now have black painted mesh instead of the former plating. The offside grille is now the sole air intake, and the horns are placed behind the other grille. The facia layout is revised, an improvement being the provision of a separate clock with external setting and adjustment. Basic prices are increased by approximately 10 per cent, but these now

Engine and transmission ready for installation, in this case a Bentley. This unit is fitted with a refrigerant pump for air conditioning. The Lucas starter is of the pre-engaged solenoid type

179

Exceptionally well balanced proportions make the massive Phantom V limousine a delight to behold. Its luggage compartment is unusually large for this type of car. The interior view (left) emphasizes the spaciousness of the passenger compartment of this Park Ward model

PRICES

ROLLS-ROYCE	U.K. list £	U.K. P.T. £ s. d.	Total £ s. d.
Phantom V chassis	3,130		3,130 0 0
Park Ward limousine	6,285	2,619 17 6	8,904 17 6
Silver Cloud II chassis	2,985		2,985 0 0
l.w.b. chassis	3,045		3,045 0 0
saloon	4,095	1,707 7 6	5,802 7 6
BENTLEY			
S.2 chassis	2,890		2,890 0 0
l.w.b. chassis	2,950		2,950 0 0
saloon	3,995	1,665 14 2	5,660 14 2

include the previously optional extra power steering.

Apart from its obviously greater length, the Phantom V chassis is very similar to that of the S.2 series, power unit and transmission being identical. The front suspension uses many common parts, although the forged, swept-back wishbones are 1in longer. The rear axle is similar externally; it is located on asymmetrical leaf springs, mounted inside the frame members as on the S.2; they are fitted with gaiters, packed with lubricant for life. There is no Z-bar, as in the S.2, for controlling axle movement and providing a degree of roll stiffness, this being achieved by the asymmetrical axle mounting, which also reduces axle hop tendencies.

The brakes, with 11.25in dia drums and 3in wide shoes, are the same size, and are mechanical servo-assisted. They are of the Autostatic Girling design, in which the shoes remain in constant contact with the drum. Front brakes are of two-trailing type, while at the rear they are trailing and leading, with an inter-shoe linkage to convert them into the equivalent of a fixed cam brake for equal lining wear. The mechanical servo operates on the front and rear systems through the master cylinder. In addition to operating the servo, the brake pedal is also connected to the rear brakes through a mechanical linkage, and sup-

plies 30 per cent of the effort needed to apply the rear brakes, the remaining 60 per cent being provided by the servo.

Compared with the more familiar Silver Cloud, the wheelbase of 12ft is 1ft 7in longer, the front track 2.87in wider at 5ft 0.87in, and at the rear, 4in wider at 5ft 4in.

Designed to carry spacious and, therefore, heavy bodywork, the frame is new and obviously very substantial. The deep box section side members are cruciform-braced amidships. These bracings converge into a large diameter tubular section through which the static portion of the two-piece propeller shaft passes, and there is another box section cross-member at its mid point. Power-assisted steering is the same as for the S.2.

Within the Rolls-Royce group itself limousine bodies for the Phantom V will be produced by Park Ward, James Young and H. J. Mulliner, and in all models the makers have produced cars that are mainly designed to be chauffeur driven. They are intended to provide really luxurious transport of the type needed in modern business and political circles for important guests and executives, and Rolls-Royce even hint that the vast space they provide may well attract some private buyers who are tired of the physical contortions necessary when entering or leaving the average modern car.

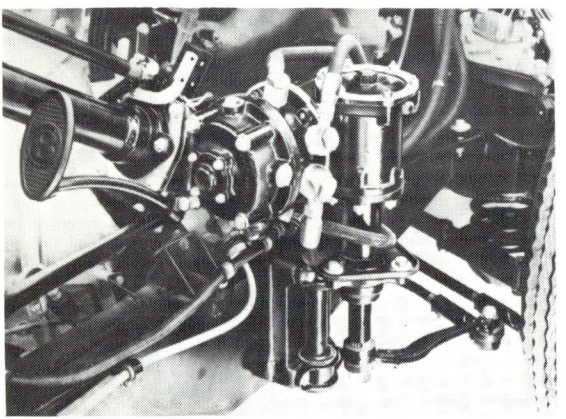

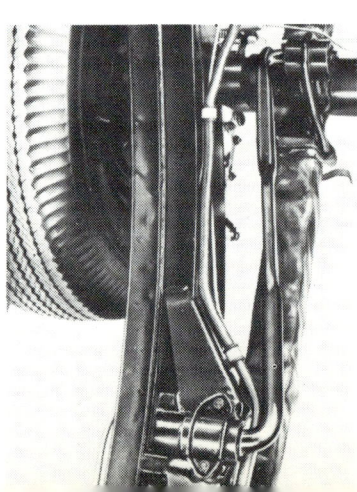

Above left: New mounting position for the steering box which incorporates the valving for power assistance hydraulic circuit. Left: Modified Z-bar, with shorter arm at the axle end, fitted to the right rear spring

Forgings are now used for the front wishbone arms. Visible are the two brake pipes for the duplicated system and the intake for air conditioning

New facia layout for a left-hand drive S.2 model. On the top rail are the two deflector controls for the fresh air system. Beneath the under-panel ashtray is the pull-out drawer deflector fitted to the recirculatory side of the air conditioning circuit

Only outward change from the former series S models is that the Bentley S.2 has black grilles to the inlets flanking the radiator. Formerly these were chromium plated

Typical of these bodies is one built by Park Ward, using some of their techniques described in our issue of Sept. 4. It has a steel framework with aluminium and light alloy panels and components, and is very extensively sound insulated. A boot unusually large for a limousine is provided, yet the overall proportions are extremely well balanced.

The method of construction has kept the weight low in relation to size, and particularly noteworthy are such features as the ease of entry through the very wide doors and the exceptional leg room.

Hinged footrests give alternative positions for use when the rear seat only is occupied or when the occasional seats are in use as well, and in neither case are the rear seat passengers in the least degree cramped for space.

Full adjustment is provided on the driver's seat, and from this position he can also operate all the car's windows when the optionally extra electrical window control mechanism is fitted. The driver has control over the ventilating and heating system, and the full air conditioning apparatus when fitted, while a separate knob on the division panel in the rear compartment allows the occupants to adjust the air circulation to their liking.

Interior fittings available include occasional seats facing inwards and a cocktail cabinet. Upholstery may be in English hide or West of England cloth, and the interior woodwork is veneered with French figured walnut.

Dry weight of the Phantom V chassis, without spare wheel or radiator shell, is 1ton 6cwt 3qtr. The Rolls-Royce Silver Cloud II complete weighs 2ton 1cwt 2qtrs.

Optional refrigeration

Available at extra cost on the Silver Cloud II is the Rolls-Royce underwing refrigeration system which extends the scope of the existing heating and ventilation system. As the drawing shows the system is installed under the righthand front wing and uses two evaporators to cool and dehumidify the air entering the car through either the lower recirculatory system or the upper fresh air system.

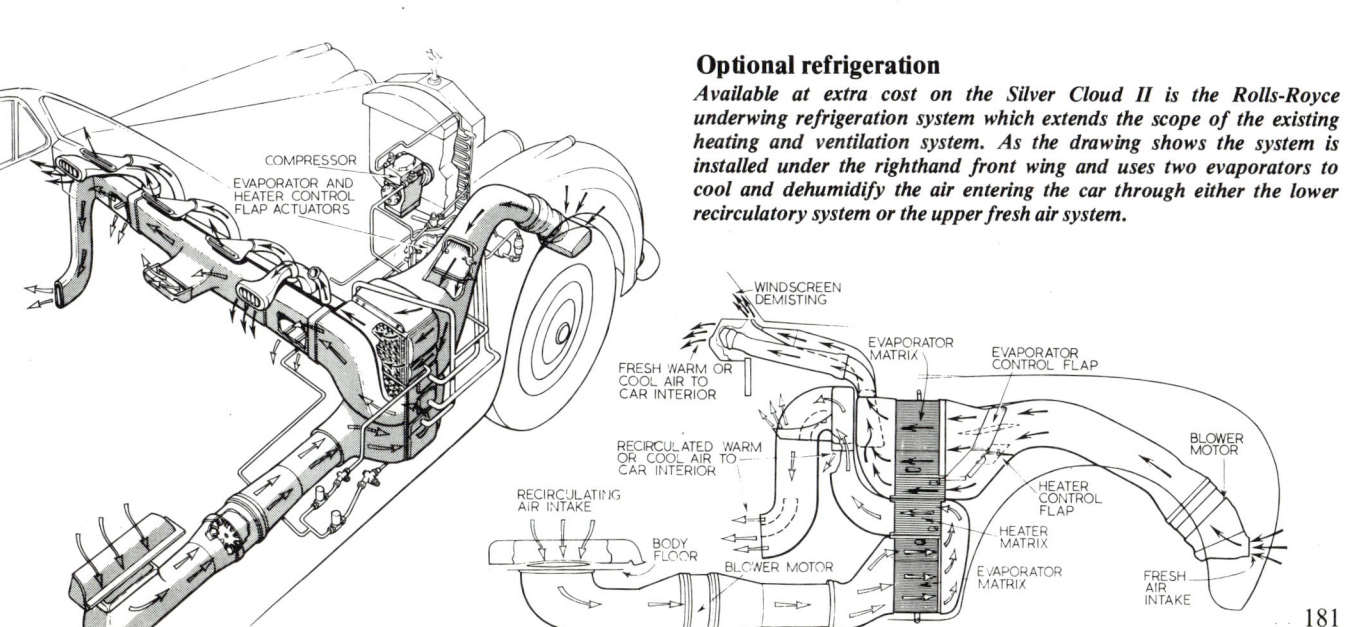

181

Phantom V Rolls-Royce for Her Majesty the Queen

ONE seldom has the privilege of studying at close quarters the great cars in which members of the Royal Family travel, so that it was with considerable interest that we accepted an invitation from Mr. Charles Ward, of Park Ward, Ltd., to inspect the latest addition to the Royal Mews.

It consists basically of a Park Ward 7-passenger limousine body on a standard long-wheelbase Phantom V Rolls-Royce chassis, to which is fitted the new vee-8 engine; in fact, below the waistline, the body panels are entirely standard. Above this point, however, the most obvious change is that the roof-line has been raised by 5in. throughout its length.

The rear part of the roof itself—back, top, and curved quarters—is panelled in one large Perspex moulding, with which considerable trouble has been taken to avoid optical distortion. The remainder of the roof to the rear compartment is of

glass, but at the rounded edges, where this section merges into the vertical body areas above the doors, Perspex is again used.

When the car is not being used for ceremonial occasions, complete privacy can be obtained in the rear compartment. The main, glass roof-light is closed by means of an electrically operated sliding panel; similar, sliding panels are also fitted to the smaller, curved Perspex areas, these being operated by hand. The large Perspex moulding at the rear of the body is obscured by a specially fitted "dome" which, when in position, merges with the rest of the roof. It is made in two parts, of aluminium, and is lined first with a layer of cellular plastic material, then with pale grey West of England cloth to match the upholstery of the rear compartment. This "dome" takes slightly under a minute to fit, and a space of about ⅜in. has been allowed between Perspex and dome, so that it can be put in place when the Perspex is wet.

At one time, while the car was being designed, the possibility of using two layers of Perspex was considered, privacy in the rear compartment being obtained by filling the area between the layers with an opaque fluid.

Throughout the rear compartment, plain and unpleated West of England cloth is used, the floor being carpeted with curly wool-mohair rugs, with underlays of Wilton carpet. Walnut curl veneer, cross-banded with French walnut, is used for the lower half of the central division, and for the door trim panels. The front compartment is upholstered in navy blue West of England cloth.

Separate radios are fitted to the front and rear of the car, a control panel being set out in the rear central armrest; a special speaker for this set is built into

the rear central part of the front seat backrest. When the set in the passenger compartment is switched on, a red light shows on the facia panel—whereupon the chauffeur operates the electrically raised aerial.

Full air-conditioning is provided, enabling the passengers to introduce cooled, heated or fresh air to the rear compartment. Heater elements are located in the forward part of the rear seats, just above the floor, with an air intake between them. Through these, warm air can be introduced into the car by means of a recirculatory system. Refrigerated air is supplied through three small ducts along the window-sills at either side of the rear seats; through these, cool air can be directed at the face or shoulders. Finally, fresh air can be introduced through ducts at either end of the central division, at floor level.

All these air supplies are controlled by means of three knobs set into the central armrest, each knob having three positions —"Off—Half—Full." Also built into the armrest is a small locker, inside the lid of which is a vanity mirror mounted on a ball-joint. The armrest, together with all its in-built controls, can be folded away.

All windows to the rear compartment, together with the glass central division, are electrically raised and lowered by means of controls on the outer armrests. When the rear doors are opened the running boards (normally obscured by the doors) are lit up, also tungsten lighting automatically illuminates the rear compartment; for ceremonial occasions, fluorescent strip lighting also is fitted.

The car is finished in dark maroon below the waistline, and black above. Overall length is 19ft 8¼in., width 6ft 7in., and height (normally laden) 6ft 1in. Tubeless 8.90 by 15 tyres are fitted.

Outwardly the eight-cylinder Rolls-Royce Silver Cloud II is almost indistinguishable from its six-cylinder predecessor; but improvements to the chassis complement increase performance, while heating and ventilation of the interior are much more efficient

EVERY year the Best Car in the World gets a little better; sometimes there are only minor modifications in hidden parts of the chassis to carry it forward, while very occasionally a completely new or redesigned type is introduced. The most recent big advance was the introduction of a 6·23-litre vee-8 engine, which now powers the Rolls-Royce Silver Cloud II and Phantom V chassis, as well as the Bentley S2 and Continental. With single camshaft and pushrods to operate the overhead valves via hydraulic tappets, it replaces a 4·9-litre straight six with overhead inlet and side exhaust valves. At the same time the chassis of the Silver Cloud II, subject of this test, was improved in several respects concerning suspension, braking and steering; passengers are kept comfortable by a much more comprehensive heating and ventilation system.

Since a primary interest of this road test for many people will be the increase in performance of the Silver Cloud II relative to its predecessor, of which a report was published on 16 May 1958, a few comparative figures follow, those of the earlier car being bracketed. The latest car proved very considerably faster, achieving a mean maximum of 113·1 m.p.h. (106); it accelerated from zero to 60 in 11·5sec (13·0), to 80 in 21·1sec (25·0) and to 100 in 38·5sec (50·6). Of even greater significance, perhaps, is the very rapid rate of acceleration from quite high speeds in top; the new Silver Cloud required only 8·5sec to reach 80 from 60 m.p.h., a 65 per cent improvement over its predecessor.

Maxima in the indirect gears of the test car were: 21 m.p.h. in first (22), 50 in second (34) and 70 in third (62). For the car to reach its peak in second the automatic change has to be over-ridden by moving the selector lever to position 2 on its quadrant, 50 m.p.h. being the highest speed recommended by the makers' handbook.

It seems remarkable that this significant step-up in performance has been achieved without materially affecting the car's fuel consumption, for the overall figure, covering a mileage exceeding 1,500, was 11·8 m.p.g., whereas the earlier car had returned 12·0 m.p.g. For a 60-mile country run in which 60-65 m.p.h. was not exceeded, the consumption figure was 17·5 m.p.g., whereas with the 1958 car 15 m.p.g. was not bettered.

Before attempting to start the engine from cold one is instructed by the owner's handbook to depress the accelerator pedal fully and release it "to allow the fast idle cams on the carburettor controls to position themselves in relation to engine temperature and thus set the throttle to the correct opening for starting." Then the ignition key is turned to operate the starter. Mild weather during the test gave no opportunity to try the car's quick-starting ability in extreme conditions. When assessing the behaviour of a vehicle in this class, the standard of judgment is naturally raised to a degree where a shortcoming,

so small that it could be ignored in a lesser car, cannot pass unnoticed. Thus one must report that, even when the engine had reached normal running temperature, its idling was neither completely smooth nor silent. It tended to run rather hot when the car was held up in dense city traffic, and would then occasionally stall.

As soon as the car moved off from rest, the engine smoothed out and thereafter maintained the standard of refinement expected of a Rolls-Royce, right up to maximum speed. Indeed, if one accelerates on part-throttle and drives generally in the manner of an experienced chauffeur, then the passengers may be almost divorced from awareness of the engine propelling them. Hard driving, using full throttle and maximum speeds in the indirects, brings about a little commotion, most of it apparently from the six-bladed cooling fan. No sound-deadening material lines the undersides of the bonnet tops.

Even from outside the car the single exhaust is quiet, so that no sound of it reaches the passengers. The Silver Cloud II is not constrained on long journeys by any particular cruising speed range, since it remains astonishingly effortless even when held almost to its maximum. It will be seen, in the data tables, that it consumes fuel at the rate of 12·3 m.p.g. at a constant 90 m.p.h., whereas the consumption graph climbs rather steeply thereafter. One might therefore regard 90 m.p.h. as a logical cruising speed (where conditions permit), having regard to fuel consumption and tyre wear. With such a performance potential, combined with first-class stability and superb braking, this Rolls-Royce can record very high journey average speeds. Its 18-gallon fuel tank allows little more than three

From this angle the boot looks much smaller than it really is. An inspection lamp is on the left of the spare wheel

hours driving between refills if an average of, say, 60 m.p.h. is being maintained. A green light on the instrument panel warns the driver when three gallons remain in the tank.

It cannot be said that the Rolls-Royce automatic gearbox has kept pace with current developments across the Atlantic. A four-speed epicyclic unit, mated to a fluid flywheel, it is based on the General Motors' Hydramatic transmission. A limitation of its design lies in the spacing between gear ratios, a wide gap between second and third being apparently unavoidable. Nevertheless, all upward changes are acceptably smooth, the more so when the car is accelerated on part-throttle. Yet the makers recommend in their handbook that deliberate downward changes should be made by flicking the selector lever, rather than by using the throttle pedal kick-down; while this advice seems somewhat contrary to the purpose of a fully automatic transmission, it certainly results in smoother operation.

In particular, a kick-down change from third to second (possible only at 21 m.p.h. or below) resulted in a quite violent jerk—sometimes even rear tyre squeal; by use of the selector lever the operation was still none too smooth with the throttle open to any degree. On the overrun, with throttle closed, its operation was much smoother, although by this method there was a three- to four-second delay between disengagement of third and second taking over. With second selected there is no governor to prevent engine over-speeding, whereas from third there is an automatic change to top at a predetermined limit (70 m.p.h. on this particular car), whether the selector is placed at 3 or 4.

A great asset of the Rolls-Royce transmission is the ability to use the gears to assist in braking this heavy car—especially useful when, for instance, crossing the Alps with a full complement. With reverse selected and the ignition switched off, a positive transmission lock holds the car safely on any gradient—an almost essential device on this car, of which the parking brake would not hold it on a 1-in-4 slope when lightly laden. This lock is released when the lever is moved to neutral, before the engine can be started, when it may be necessary to hold the car with the footbrake.

While most other large British cars, as well as quite a few of medium size, have now adopted disc brakes, Rolls-Royce maintain their allegiance to the drum type. Ever since these manufacturers adopted four-wheel brakes in the 'twenties their cars have been renowned for remarkable braking performance, aided by a mechanical friction-type servo driven off the gearbox. This type of servo is still used, although over the years its speed of rotation has been stepped up to increase efficiency and reduce lag.

Rolls-Royce provide unparalleled security from failure by duplicating their hydraulic lines and by including also a mechanical linkage to the rear wheels, so that there are three independent systems. Probably this installation represents a peak in efficiency and smoothness of drum braking never achieved by any other concern, and the effortless way

A silent, high-speed drawing-room for four: beside the front passenger's seat cushion is a trigger for adjusting rake of the backrest. Back-seat passengers have folding picnic tables; their feet could relax better on a sloping floor

in which this heavy car can be brought to rest from high speeds instils great confidence. Only in endurance against fade are they inferior to discs, but their rate of recovery after overheating is rapid. At very low speed, if one application is followed by another in quick succession, the servo may not have time to come to grips again; consequently a much higher pedal pressure is then required.

Power assistance for steering is now standard Rolls-Royce equipment. An hydraulic pump, belt-driven from the crankshaft pulley, feeds an external ram, of which one end is anchored to the chassis, the other to an idler-lever in the steering linkage. It is controlled by valves incorporated in the cam-and-roller steering box. The steering wheel is now an inch smaller in diameter than those of earlier Silver Clouds, and is mounted slightly nearer the facia to improve the driving position.

Anyone taking the wheel of this car without knowing that the steering was assisted would obviously suspect this because of the low effort required, but would sense no loss of feel. Indeed, this is just how powered steering should be, with assistance in constant proportion to normal effort, and with no lag in reaction or tendency to exaggerate the driver's movements. There is no appreciable kick-back through the wheel. Parking the car in a confined space is made easy by a combination of this assistance, a quite compact turning circle and a clear view of the side lamps on each front wing from the driving seat. At full speed on M1 on a still day, the car ran straight as an arrow with

Left: While almost as sumptuous as it looks, the back seat has very small side armrests. In the quarters are recesses containing mirrors and reading lamps; the one seen here also holds a cigarette lighter. The rear panel of each door window is fixed. Right: With power steering standard, the wheel is of quite small diameter; it has a particularly comfortable rim. The T-handle parking brake is apt to catch a knee when pulled out. A group of four switches enables the driver to control all windows—invaluable when travelling alone. Adjustable air vents at each end of the screen rail are new

Rolls-Royce
Silver Cloud II . . .

practically no call for correction; on a less excellent road surface there was more need for concentration, to control an occasional tendency to wander.

A two-way electric switch on the steering column selects Normal or Hard setting of the rear suspension dampers, the latter for high-speed driving or to compensate for a full load of passengers and baggage. This makes an appreciable difference to cornering stability in particular, without stiffening the ride too much. A very high standard of riding comfort is expected and achieved, that on the rear seat being especially relaxed. So efficient is the damping that even a large bump is felt once only, the car thereafter levelling out without any pitch. It is not prone to wallow, despite low-frequency spring rates, and body sway or roll also is strongly resisted.

While certain forms of road irregularity can be felt more than might have been anticipated, no rear axle hop or other behaviour suggestive of excess unsprung masses was experienced. The large-section Dunlop tubeless tyres were quiet-running, except over the coarser type of road dressing which always induces noise, nor was there much squeal from them when sharp corners were taken fast.

A comprehensive array of black-dialled instruments is carried in a central panel, adaptable for right- or left-hand drive. It includes a push-button whereby the fuel gauge can be made to show oil sump level. The speedometer reading became rather optimistic above 70 m.p.h., showing 110 at a true 102 m.p.h. By pushing in the switch for the two-speed wipers, screen-washing jets are fed by an electric pump. Typically, the switch incorporates a temperature control to break the circuit, should the wipers be overloaded.

Concealed from view above the instrument panel is a small green map-reading lamp, but there is no lamp in the glove locker. Two fog lamps are controlled from the main lighting switch, their double filament bulbs also sharing duty as flashing signals; one cannot have head and fog lamps lit simultaneously. On the test car the head lamp beams were inadequate on both main and dipped filaments for fast

driving; this did not appear altogether attributable to faulty adjustment. There is no provision for signal-flashing the head lamps. Potentially useful red tell-tales above the side lamps passed insufficient light to be seen by the driver.

Heating and ventilation are controlled by two switches on the facia, with such a wide choice of combinations of temperature, boost and direction that a full description is impossible here. There are two adjustable fresh air outlets recessed in the wooden capping above the facia, by which front seat occupants may receive a refreshing cool breeze on their faces in warm weather; there is also a separate recirculating intake from the floor of the rear compartment. The only criticism of an otherwise very efficient and versatile system was that, when very little extra warmth was required, the lowest heat setting gave a bit too much. Having this system allows one to travel comfortably with all windows shut, when the car becomes almost uncannily quiet, except for a little wind whistle behind the front screen pillars.

A much appreciated demisting element, almost invisible in the rear window glass, has a switch beside it—that is, remote from the driver. However, as it is wired through the ignition circuit, the obvious routine is to leave it switched on throughout the cold-weather months.

Separate backrests of the bench front seat have a much finer adjustment for rake than is usual, whereby any driver must find a correct and comfortable angle; they are not of the fully reclining type. It almost goes without saying that the seat is extremely comfortably shaped and upholstered, all trim being in top grain hide. In addition to folding armrests in the squabs, there are rests on each front door, adjustable for height. Three can be squeezed abreast on the front seat, when one appreciates how small is the hump in the floor over the transmission.

Electric window lifts (an optional extra) were fitted to the test car; they are so convenient that one very soon becomes reluctant to return to a car without them. Rather surprisingly, a hearty slam was needed to close the doors, even with a window open. Great travelling comfort for two is afforded by the luxurious rear seat, of which the backrests are just high enough to support the head if one slouches sufficiently. Although there is a wide shelf forward of the back window, no map pockets are included in the door trim; the backs of the front seats are occupied by folding picnic tables. An H.M.V. radio is standard in the Rolls-Royce, with a single rectangular speaker beneath the instrument panel. On this car its quality of reproduction was scarcely up to the standard of the rest of the vehicle.

At first sight the luggage compartment may appear less spacious than it is in fact, because it extends far back behind the lid hinges. Main dimensions are over 5ft long, 3ft 10in. wide and up to 15½in. deep. The spare wheel is in a separate compartment beneath, and secured by a typical Rolls-Royce lever and spring pad mechanism. The boot is lit automatically through a mercury switch when the counterbalanced lid is lifted. Rear lamp, stop lamp, brake-light and signal bulbs are reached through hinged access panels.

While few Rolls-Royce owners are likely to do their own maintenance, the schedule suggested in the handbook is not very demanding. Although centralized chassis lubrication is no longer fitted, main greasing points are fed from individual reservoirs which need topping up only at 10,000-

Rolls-Royce Silver Cloud II . . .

mile intervals. These include 10 points on the front suspension, 11 on the steering mechanism. A small set of hand tools, together with spare lamp bulbs and a tyre pressure gauge, are stored in a tray beneath the luggage boot floor. A very efficient hand pump and geared jack are clipped in place beside the spare wheel.

Without purchase tax, the Silver Cloud II costs a little over £4,000. Before the war its mighty forbear, the 7.3-litre vee-12 Phantom III, cost about £2,750 for a typical touring limousine. A two-door Morris Eight was then £128, whereas the basic price of its current equivalent is £416—well over three times as much. These proportionate increases should be borne in mind when assessing the value for money of today's Rolls-Royce cars.

Only by adopting advanced production methods and thereby increasing yearly output can a superlative machine like this be made today at a price its clientele can afford. The Rolls-Royce is one of very few surviving top quality cars; the maintained standard of overall excellence is rewarded by full order books, and a world reputation which has never stood higher.

ROLLS-ROYCE SILVER CLOUD II

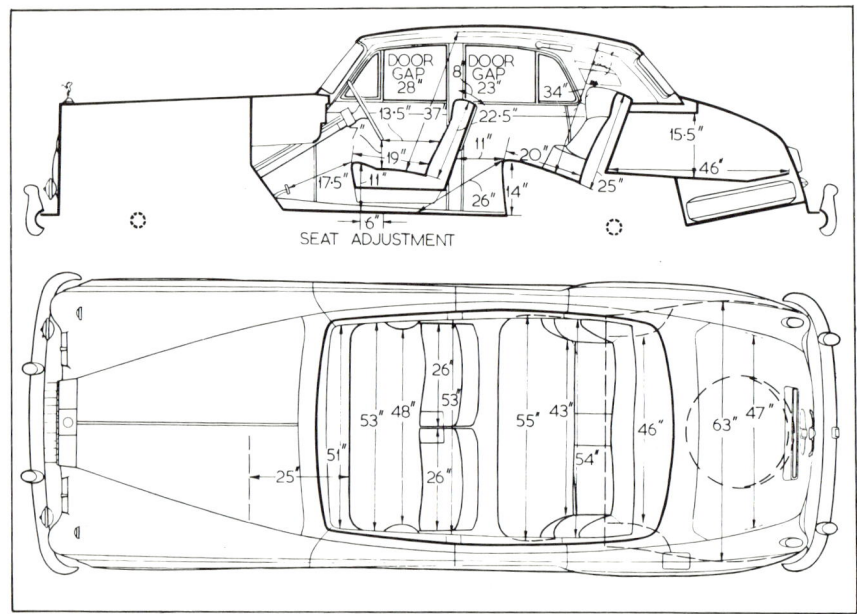

PERFORMANCE

ACCELERATION TIMES (mean):

Speed range, Gear Ratios and Time in Sec.

M.p.h.	3·08 to 1	4·46 to 1	8·10 to 1	11·75 to 1
10—30	..	—	—	3·0	—
20—40	..	—	4·9	3·5	—
30—50	..	7·6	5·1	4·5	—
40—60	..	7·8	5·4	—	—
50—70	..	8·1	6·8	—	—
60—80	..	8·5	—	—	—
70—90	..	11·9	—	—	—
80—100	..	17·4	—	—	—

From rest through gears to:

30 m.p.h.	..	3·8 sec.
40	,,	..	5·9 ,,
50	,,	..	8·3 ,,
60	,,	..	11·5 ,,
70	,,	..	15·5 ,,
80	,,	..	21·1 ,,
90	,,	..	27·4 ,,
100	,,	..	38·5 ,,

Standing quarter mile 18·2 sec.

MAXIMUM SPEEDS ON GEARS:

Gear			M.p.h.	K.p.h.
Top	..	(mean)	113·1	182·1
		(best)	115·0	185·2
3rd	..	..	70	113
2nd	..	..	50	80
1st	..	..	21	34

TRACTIVE EFFORT (by Tapley meter):

		Pull (lb per ton)	Equivalent gradient
Top	..	270	1 in 8·2
Third	..	390	1 in 5·7
Second	..	680	1 in 3·1

BRAKES: (at 30 m.p.h. in neutral):

Pedal load in lb	Retardation	Equiv. stopping distance in ft
25	0·28g	108
50	0·68g	44
75	0·81g	37·5
80	0·87g	34·7

FUEL CONSUMPTION (at steady speeds in top gear):

30 m.p.h.	19·5 m.p.g.
40 ,,	18·4 ,,
50 ,,	17·4 ,,
60 ,,	16·4 ,,
70 ,,	14·9 ,,
80 ,,	13·5 ,,
90 ,,	12·3 ,,
100 ,,	9·5 ,,

Overall fuel consumption for 1,559 miles, 11·8 m.p.g. (23·9 litres per 100 km.).

Approximate normal range 10—17·5 m.p.g. (28·2—16·1 litres per 100 km.).

Fuel: Premium grade.

TEST CONDITIONS: Weather: Dry and sunny, no wind.

Air temperature, 56 deg. F.

Model described in *The Autocar* of 25 September, 1959.

STEERING: Turning circle,

Between kerbs, L, 43ft 4in. R, 42ft 10in.
Between walls, L, 45ft 3in. R, 44ft 9in.
Turns of steering wheel from lock to lock, 4·25.

SPEEDOMETER CORRECTION: M.P.H.

Car speedometer	..	10	20	30	40	50	60	70	80	90	100	110	120
True speed:	..	10	20	30	40	50	59	68	76	84	93	102	112

DATA

PRICE (basic), with standard saloon body £4,095.
British purchase tax, **£1,707 7s 6d.**
Total (in Great Britain), **£5,802 7s 6d.**
Extras: Electric window lifts **£92 1s 8d** (inc. P.T.)
Refrigeration system, £389 11s 8d (inc. P.T.) (H.M.V. radio fitted as standard).

ENGINE: Capacity, 6,230 c.c. (380 cu. in.)
Number of cylinders, 8 in vee.
Bore and stroke, 104·4 × 91·44mm (4·1 × 3·6in.).
Valve gear, o.h.v., self-adjusting tappets.
Compression ratio, 8·0 to 1.
M.p.h. per 1,000 r.p.m. in top gear, 27·8.

WEIGHT: (With 8 gals fuel), 40·4cwt (4,522lb).
Weight distribution (per cent); F, 49·5; R, 50·5.
Laden as tested, 43·4cwt (4,858lb).
Lb per c.c. (laden), 0·78.

BRAKES: Type, Rolls-Royce Girling drum. 2 T.S. front, L and T rear. Method of operation: F, hydraulic; R, hydro-mechanical. Mechanical servo assistance, and duplication of hydraulic system.
Drum dimensions: F and R, 11·25in. dia; 3·0in. wide.
Lining swept area: F, 212 sq. in. R, 212 sq. in. (196 sq. in. per ton laden).

TYRES: 8·20—15in. Dunlop tubeless.
Pressures (p.s.i.): F, 22; R, 27. (All conditions).

TANK CAPACITY: 18 Imperial gallons.
Oil sump, 13 pints.
Cooling system, 21 pints.

DIMENSIONS: Wheelbase, 10ft 3in.
Track: F, 4ft 10·5in.; R, 5ft 0in.
Length (overall), 17ft 7·75in.
Width, 6ft 2·75in.
Height, 5ft 4in.
Ground clearance, 7in.
Frontal area, 26·4 sq. ft. (approximately).

ELECTRICAL SYSTEM: 12-volt; 67 ampère-hour battery.
Head lamps, double dip; 60—36 watt bulbs.

SUSPENSION: Front: Independent, coil springs and wishbones, with anti-roll bar. Rear: Live axle on asymmetric, semi-elliptic leaf springs.

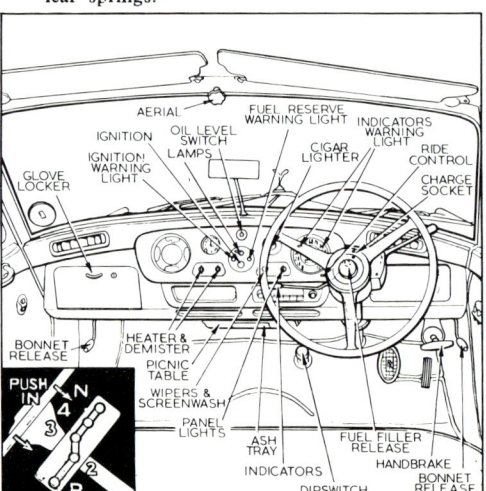

Special coachwork on Silver Cloud II. Above: Harold Radford Countryman conversion. Above right: H. J. Mulliner convertible, modified from standard saloon

Above: Park Ward long wheelbase with division. Below: Special eucalyptus veneers on a James Young long wheelbase saloon

Coachwork on Phantom V

Above: Sweeping and stately lines of James Young's touring limousine. Note particularly the sloping tail made possible by the model's 12ft 1in. wheelbase. Right: Park Ward's 1959 seven passenger limousine. At Earls Court in 1960 James Young showed the first of four sedancas de ville they built (below) and a seven-passenger limousine (below right). Bottom picture: An exclusive design exhibited by Henri Chapron, who built the car, at the 1961 Paris Salon. In fact the car was ordered by Nubar Gulbenkian from Hooper and Co. just before they stopped building bodies and the car was designed by Osmond River of Hoopers. He then supervised the building of his creation by Chapron. Note particularly the distinctive lamp treatment

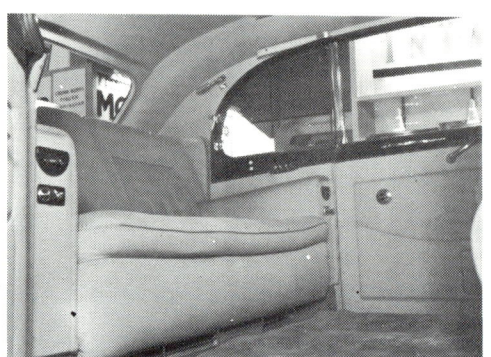

ROLLS-ROYCE SILVER CLOUD III

BENTLEY S3

Crewe-cut, 1963 style: Immediate recognition points for the new Rolls-Royce Silver Cloud III are the paired headlamps, bolder wings with recessed parking-signalling lamps, and more discreet bumper overriders. A second glance reveals that the classic radiator shell has been lowered by about 1½in

MORE POWER, MORE PASSENGER SPACE, BETTER LIGHTING, EASIER STEERING

VERY high grade cars such as the Rolls-Royce and Bentley are made in such relatively small numbers that the fruits of constant research and development can be embodied quickly on the production line. This is a more or less constant process, but modifications of a somewhat basic nature, in particular those which have a sufficiently marked effect on performance or appearance to justify a new series or model designation, are naturally introduced together.

Both the Rolls-Royce Silver Cloud and the S-series Bentley—identical in all except radiator shell and bonnet—advance a major step and are now designated the Silver Cloud III and S3 respectively. In brief, they have more power, an improved lighting system with paired headlamps, reduced steering effort, and increased passenger space in the back.

Firm to their tradition, Rolls-Royce do not reveal power output figures, but claim a seven per cent increase to this unknown quantity for the latest version of their 6,230 c.c. vee-8 engine. This results from a rise in compression ratio, now 9·0 to 1 instead of 8·0 (the lower ratio being optional to suit markets where 100 octane fuels are not available); and from the replacement of 1¾in. S.U. HD6 carburettors

lowered the specific fuel consumption.

To meet the higher power, the chrome molybdenum steel crankshaft is now nitride-hardened, and larger diameter gudgeon pins are fitted. These are now offset in the pistons, the better to withstand the increased thrust and contributing also to quieter running. Crankcase breathing is drawn into the engine intake through sealed ducting, to avoid the possibility of fumes escaping.

Extra power-assistance has been provided for the cam-and-roller steering gear, reducing the maximum load at the wheel rim to 6lb. While this brings about an appreciable saving in effort for normal

by 2in. HD8s. A new vacuum advance-retard mechanism for the ignition distributor, supplementing the centrifugal weights, together with the raised compression, are said by the makers to have

driving, its effect is most marked during low-speed manœuvring and parking. Plenty of "feel" is retained in this system, and the hydraulic power valves remain closed up to ½lb load. There are

Above: This is the Bentley S3, which shares the senior partner's amendments. Driving vision is improved over the steeply sloping bonnet. From the rear only the overriders are new, and the earlier type is retained for export cars. Left: Sealed crankcase breathing into the induction is new, and the ignition distributor now has a supplementary vacuum advance-retard control

189

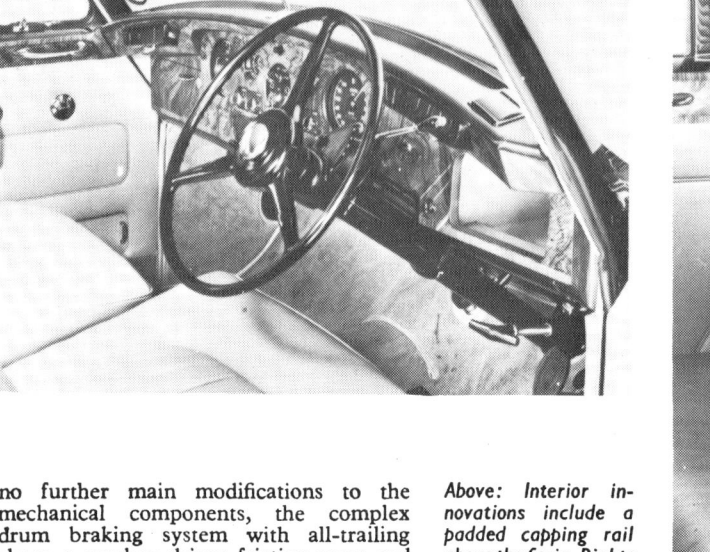

no further main modifications to the mechanical components, the complex drum braking system with all-trailing shoes, a gearbox-driven friction servo and three independent systems being retained.

A four-headlamp system is now standardized, all being Lucas sealed beam units of 5¾in. dia. The inner, long-range lamps each have a single filament, the outer units two filaments—one slightly out of focus to add spread to the main beams, the other for dipped beam. Wattage for the main beams is up from 120 to 150. Parking and direction-signalling lamps are now combined in neat oval units recessed in the wings; the twin fog-lamps are retained. Except for the North American market, smaller and simpler overriders are fitted to the bumpers.

More Seat Room

Inside the cars are important changes in that individual front seats, each with its own centre-folding armrest, have become standard equipment, although the one-piece bench remains optional. In the back two valuable extra inches of legroom have been found, the seat cushion being moved back by that amount. Most of this has resulted from making the backrest more upright—and certainly no less comfortable. Also, the previously rather "aggressive" corner padding has been reduced; this allows greater effective width for seating three abreast, as well as being more comfortable to lean against in any circumstances.

There are five new standard colours—Astral blue, Antelope, Dusk grey, Pine green and Garnet. The four discontinued colours (Velvet green, Midnight blue, Opal and blue-grey) can still be specified, but now are at extra cost. Other listed supplementaries include electric window-lifts, a refrigeration system, tinted glass and fitted suitcases for the boot.

While this completes the particular innovations for the Silver Cloud III and Bentley S3, the later Silver Cloud IIs and S2s had quite a few features which had been progressively incorporated without any fanfares, and which are continued on the new cars. Those which follow are especially noteworthy. The heating and ventilating installation has two ventilating matrices for independent fresh air and recirculating systems, the latter with improved delivery to the middle of the rear floor. A ram position has been added to the fresh air circuit. A headlamp flashing button has been

Above: Interior innovations include a padded capping rail above the facia. Right: Less prominent corner bolsters save space, allowing three abreast in greater comfort. There is extra leg-room, too

incorporated in the direction indicators lever, and there is a tell-tale lamp in circuit with the ignition switch to warn the driver when the handbrake is on.

For the standard Radiomobile receiver (there is a choice between three) a second speaker has been added on the rear parcels shelf, with a balance control for adjusting the front and rear outputs. Footrests are provided for those riding in the back, who also have ashtrays of an improved design. There is a map reading lamp on the facia, the instrument panel lighting is more powerful, the switch for the electrical demisting element in the rear window is on the facia instead of in the back compartment, and the driving mirror is better supported to resist vibration. In the luggage boot there is a detachable metal panel covering the spare wheel, which lies horizontal below the boot floor.

Other Rolls-Royce and Bentley types—the long-wheelbase Silver Cloud III and S3, the huge Phantom V and the S3 Continental—naturally all incorporate the revised engine and other changes. Of the coachbuilt cars in series production,

there is a new two-door sports saloon by Park Ward on the Continental chassis, and the Phantom V seven-passenger limousine (Park Ward and H. J. Mulliner) has a modified rake to the screen as well as a completely redesigned boot.

Price increases have brought the Silver Cloud III and Bentley S3 standard saloons up to £6,277 17s 9d and £6,126 12s 9d respectively, the previous figures being £5,913 10s 3d and £5,769 2s 9d. Current chassis prices for these two cars are £3,135 and £3,035.

During an afternoon spent on the Oulton Park racing circuit in Cheshire, when examples of the latest products were tried in direct comparison with a Rolls-Royce Silver Cloud II, we were able to confirm the gain in performance and to appreciate the sensitive control provided by the unusually light steering. These fine cars have always felt smaller than they look to drive, and the increased close-range field of view over the lowered bonnet adds to this impression. Further remarks concerning the handling of the Silver Cloud III and S3 must await a full Road Test.

Autocar's representatives were given the run of the Oulton Park racing circuit for an afternoon, to sample the increased power and lightweight power-steering of the new cars

Park Ward's 1963 Silver Cloud III two-door saloon used steel and alloy panels

Earls Court 1963 marked the last appearance of a Rolls-Royce chassis, a Silver Cloud III, at a motor show

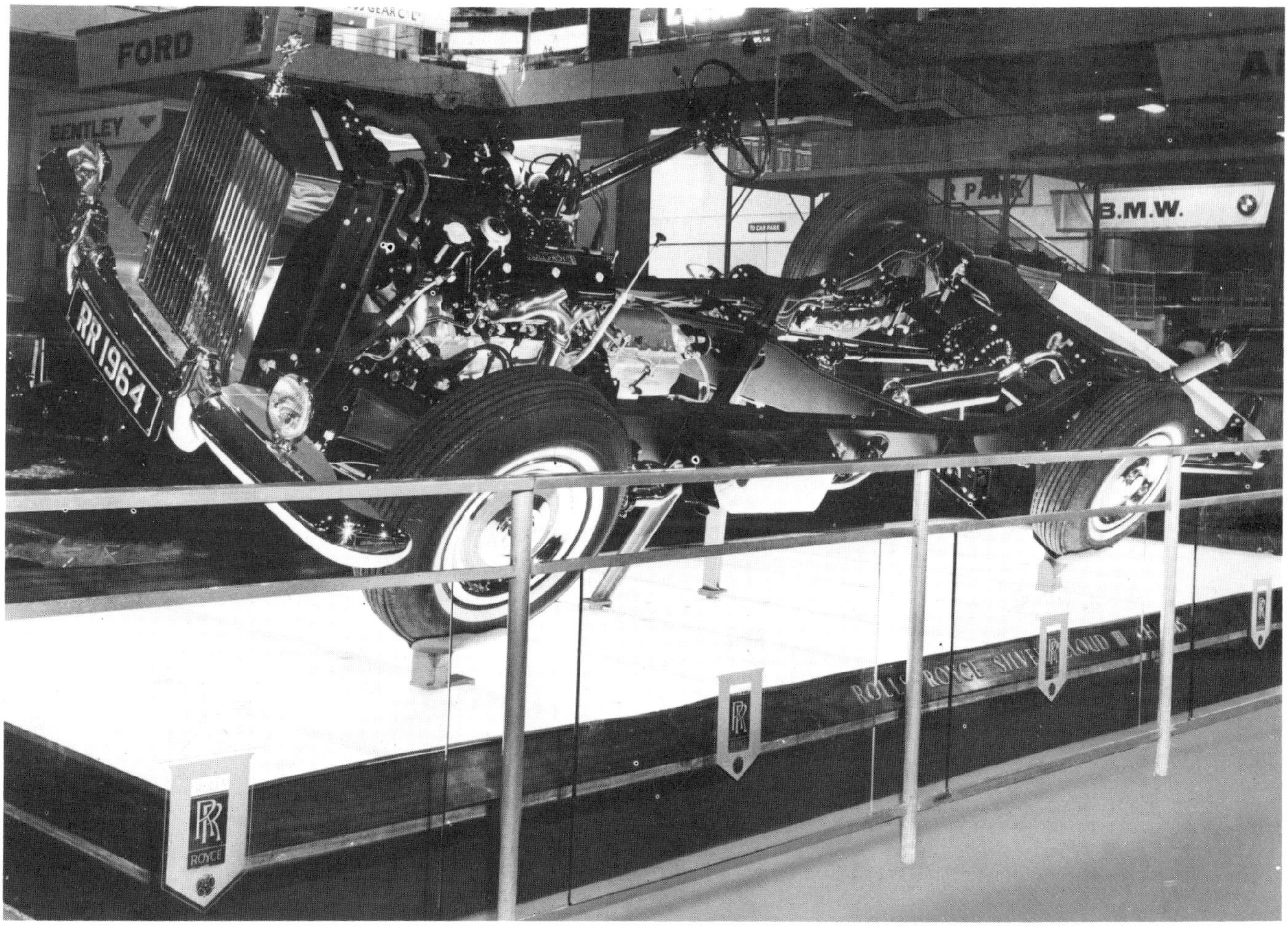

Charles Sykes' Spirit of Ecstasy now cast in nimonic steel

ALL   FOR THE

RONALD BARKER AND GORDON HORNER GO SIGHTSEEING ROUND THE ROLLS-ROYCE AND BENTLEY PLANT AT CREWE

FOR your first visit to Rolls-Royce you brush your best suit specially carefully and think respectful thoughts as you wait in the plain, almost austere entrance hall under that earnest shield bearing the motto: QUIDVIS RECTE FACTUM QUAMVIS HUMILE PRAECLARUM—*Whatever is rightly done, however humble, is noble,* or words to that effect. You are before the high altar of the motoring world, and might reasonably expect a formal reception by suave and rather stuffy executives. And if that's what you *wanted*, you will be very disappointed. There is just no ice to thaw, and within moments you can sense an atmosphere as clear and unaffected as anywhere else.

One of the carefully guarded legacies from Sir Henry Royce (who died almost 30 years ago) is a maxim which remains a cornerstone of the company's engineering philosophy: That the Ship is greater than the Captain. The men are, so to speak, the servants of the product and the personality cult is discouraged; executives'

Automatic — save for anti-sediment stirrer — Paint dish — body receiving first prima

Brush painting the waist line
Jack Hassall
POOL 5

BEST

Engine Balancing: drilling through jig to crank damper

office doors carry simply their names, not ranks or titles in the company. The Car Division's top men are all quite approachable human beings.

These days, with the standard of automobile design and engineering so high even among quantity-produced vehicles, it becomes more and more difficult to maintain a balance on the top perch. Surely the greatest problem at Crewe must be to create and develop new designs and structures to the highest possible standard of excellence, when the development costs can be spread over only about 1,500 cars a year. This explains, for instance, why R.R. chose to develop their automatic transmission from an established American one of proven quality, rather than to start from scratch. It is entirely of R.R. manufacture, even including the nuts and bolts. No one at Crewe, incidentally, is under any illusion that this transmission is completely smooth, but it has the overwhelming asset of transmitting full engine braking on the overrun through any of the four gears. Where a compromise has to be biased towards smoothness or controllability (and thus safety), the latter wins.

This is typical of the sort of thinking one finds at Crewe. They have certain basic precepts which other manufacturers may by-pass to follow a fashion, but not R.R. Cars, they tell you, are built for humans, who have to live in an atmosphere and see out. To this end certain basic engineering dimensions (such as seat to roof measurements) and numbers (such as pedal spring rates) have been fixed from experience over many years and are now recorded in the R.R. archives.

Pedals must move in arcs natural to the movements of the driver's foot, so pendant pedals are out. The benefits of through-the-floor pedals are deemed worth the extra trouble of sealing the slots and protecting the pedal cross-shafts from road throw-up.

They have ready answers to all the usual questions—why not disc brakes, independent rear suspension and so on; but here's one you may not have thought of: Why not left-foot braking? The answer is that you can still do it with the small R.R. pedal if you wish, but it isn't encouraged for the simple reason that during heavy braking with a light pedal load, the left foot may be needed as a prop to support the weight of the driver's body against the car's rapid deceleration. Feel and touch—those are favourite words of the R.R. engineers, for whom ergonomics are more important than aerodynamics. Controls must be correctly placed and function at a reasonable pressure loading, progressively (steering and pedals) and precisely. It is in such details that the pseudo-super-cars are usually shown up by comparison.

Have R.R. an Oscar to help them with their basic seating dimensions? Yes, but just to be different they call him

Charlie, and he "has got our flavour about him." He starts at a quarter-scale and has a movable head acting as a datum point for noise measurement. Can you still hear the clock ticking? Maybe, but the company has spent less money making the clock noisy than on making the car quiet.

If one expects to find a factory as eat-off-the-floor spotless as a power-house—well, this isn't. A great deal of work has been done in it over the years, and one cannot keep everything looking brand new. But it is clean and orderly, and once again the atmosphere is right. One can see that pride in workmanship is not just a superficial *mise en scène* put on for the special benefit of the visitor.

A casual stroll through the mainstream of this factory would not distinguish it greatly from others in the same line of business, but it is in the creeks and bywaters that the special interest lies. We didn't do the grand tour, but snooped about here and there to find detail indications of the R.R. tradition being maintained. It is a factory of contrasts, where modern machine tools and assembly methods have pushed up production way beyond pre-war levels, but where a human is always on hand to inspect, to adjust, to add a little hand-finishing, to check and inspect again.

We started in the woodshop, and if foreman George Williams had had his way, we would have spent the day there. The processes and craftsmanship involved in timber-

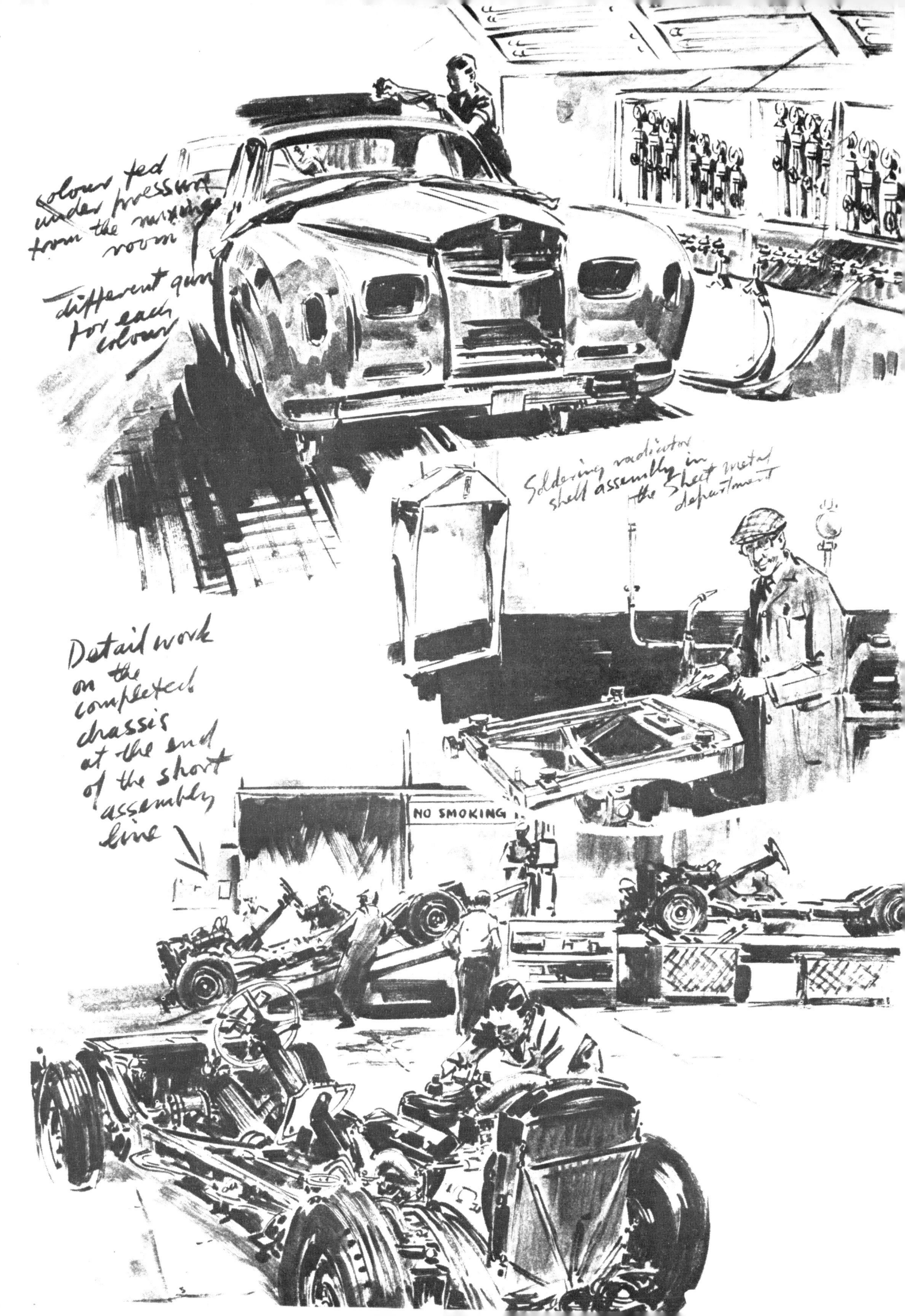

colour fed under pressure from the mixing room

different gun for each colour

Soldering radiator shell assembly in the sheet metal department

Detail work on the completed chassis at the end of the short assembly line

NO SMOKING

ALL FOR THE BEST . . .

ing the standard R.R. and Bentley saloons interiors are almost beyond belief until one has seen them. First we inspected the veneers in their raw state—wafer thin (0·022in.) translucent slices across the grain of Circassian (from the Caucasus mountains) walnut trees.

All veneered panels are jointed down the middle, and the grains are meticulously matched to produce a mirror image "picture" which even on a humble ashtray is symmetrical; and a pair of picnic tables or ashtrays appear virtually identical. On the reverse side of every wooden panel are the part and log numbers: if one picnic table, say, is damaged in a car in the U.S.A. the owner has only to quote these references and a replacement will be prepared with a veneer *from the same log,* since a portion of each is held in storage.

Most veneers are laid over black walnut, mahogany, beech or ash, but the windscreen capping rail and instrument panel are plastic mouldings overlaid with real wood. After a critical check for moisture content, all veneers are glued in place under rubber air-bags in a steam-heated press. There are nearly 700 woodshop jigs. . . . The finished items are stopped up with filling, sprayed with five coats of lacquer with intervening rubbings-down by hand, then finally buffed to a high sheen. Your reporters were so ungracious as to comment that they would prefer to see a semi-matt finish. If not so scratch- and weather-resistant it would look less artificial. In the trim shop we saw Connolly hides being matched for grain and texture—and every car requires six to eight of them, or about 300 sq. ft.

Next visit was to the tappet room, where the vee-8 engine's hydraulic valve lifters are fine ground to very close tolerances. If you must have hush, it's the only way. First the bore is taken to within three ten-thousandths of an inch, then this finished dimension automatically sets an electronic machine that grinds the piston to match—with a running clearance of two tenths (0·0002in.). The parts are then washed by ultra-sonic vibration and assembled submerged in paraffin before undergoing a leak-down test, also in paraffin, under a 50lb weight. Timed over an eighth of an inch

of travel, the piston must not take fewer than 20 nor more than 80sec. Tappets are matched in three groups by timing, 20-40, 30-60 and 60-80sec., then sealed in plastic containers and dispatched to the engine assembly line.

All moving components of the engine are weighed and balanced individually before assembly, and the engine, complete with the fluid coupling torus, is then dynamically balanced to fine limits on an Avery machine. At the front there are jig-bushes through which the operator can drill metal from the edge of the damper flange; at the back, small balance plates are added if necessary to the torus bolts.

On every crankshaft forging is included a small test piece which is detached and checked in the laboratories before the shaft may be machined. One could elaborate on so many details of the engine's bits and pieces, their assembly, inspection, testing and so forth, but perhaps the most significant pointer is that, on average, the daily production is limited to about six.

All engines are motored for three to four hours, and a proportion is bench run for 24 hours under varying loads, then stripped for close inspection before reassembly and more testing—all this apart from the extensive road-testing later.

ENTASIS—that's a word not found in every dictionary, but they know all about it in the radiator assembly shop; not the actual radiator, that is, but the classic R.R. shell. The Shorter Oxford defines it as the "almost imperceptible swelling of the shaft of a column." The same applies to the apparently flat surfaces of the R.R. shell, of which every component has a slight convexity to make it look flat rather than concave from a distance. Originally brass was used, then German silver (nickel, zinc and copper alloy), but for the past 30 years or so stainless steel. The outer surfaces are polished before being united with soft solder, the front plate and its mating components having mitre-milled edges to ensure an invisible joint. It is a fascinating process to watch, and requires the utmost skill from conscientious craftsmen. Finally, the completed assembly is buffed to the customary perfection. Why does a Bentley cost less than an otherwise identical Rolls-Royce? Because the Bentley shell is merely a brass pressing, although definitely of Top Brass, of course.

All bought-out components are checked on special rigs, and nothing is left to chance. This applies even to tiny elec-

ALL FOR THE BEST...

minimum, together with any likelihood of creaks and rattles developing.

When completed, the cars are started for the first time and run on a roller machine for the equivalent of 50 miles. Here everything that can be is checked by a single tester; after adjustment the same tester runs it through the same drill with Mr. Fox, chief tester, and one or two assistants. All oils are changed and the car then takes to the road for its first outing, when the body is also tooth-combed. A wash, further inspection, and off it goes to the finishing shop.

Anyone with any doubts about the firm's confidence in and plans for the future (following some rather bleak statements last year) should take a look at the new paint shop, with the first-in-this country deep-dip for water-soluble primer, for which great things are claimed. Body shells progress on automatic conveyor tracks, and there is capacity for much higher output.

The processes include a seemingly endless succession of degreasing washes in alkali solution, hot and cold rinses, oven bakings, priming and filling, repeat baking, sealing of joints and inspection.

When the body finally leaves to join its chassis, it looks perfect: yet after the final road testing, back goes the complete car to the paint shop again to be completely flatted once more, resprayed and passed through a drying oven. After more polishing, it is closely inspected under bright lights and may even receive a further complete spray and polish. Women now give it a thorough cleaning inside, then the quality engineers take another look. . . . All in all, it will have taken four to six weeks for one of these cars, after leaving the assembly line, to pass through the various finishing stages—including about 150 miles on the road—before being handed over to the sales department. Perhaps, when you arrived at Crewe, you wondered why these cars cost so much. A day's sight-seeing there, and the wonder changes: How *can* they be produced at the price?

trical relays, the carburettors' automatic choke and so on, Generators are tested for noise, starters for load capacity, thermostats for operating temperatures, power steering pumps for quietness and efficiency. The factory makes its own suspension dampers, which are tested on a special rig which "draws a picture" or graph of their behaviour on bump and rebound as well as the differential between hard and soft ride settings. Every rear axle road spring has its actual poundage, free camber, loaded camber and serial number recorded on a plate on its gaiter.

Each car passes along the assembly line with its History Book, bearing the customer's name and special requirements, in which every such detail is noted for a permanent record. Snags and corrections are signed for, and the inspectors' responsibilities remind one of the rigours of an aircraft factory.

One of the showpieces on the assembly line, where the body is united with the chassis, is the "milking machine" which Horner has drawn. It pulls the chassis down on its springs to simulate the laden condition before the ready-painted body is lowered into position, and appropriate spacers are added to ensure equal loadings at each mounting point. In this manner local strains are reduced to the

Silver Ghosts on the Long Walk from Windsor Castle in the 1977 Silver Jubilee Tribute

An £80,000 Black Cherry

We try our most expensive car yet —a 1973 Rolls-Royce Phantom VI Landaulette for sale secondhand at the price quoted above

By Warren Allport

Above left: A car the size of the Phantom really gives H. J. Mulliner Park Ward's craftsmen scope with superb veneers and luxurious red Draylon upholstery. Note the Sony television above the cocktail cabinet and fold-down occasional seats and picnic tables in the division. The rear armrest on the driver's side houses the controls for the heater and refrigeration and the interior lighting. The seat height adjustment buttons are in the front of the seat armrest and the electric intercom is positioned low down. Above: From the front the landaulette looks very like the limousine. Left: From above the huge size of the Phantom, nearly 20ft long, becomes apparent. Below: The author tries the landaulette's rear seat with the hood down

Continued

Phantom VI to an exclusive Lex-Mead specification with sumptuous interior

An £80,000 Black Cherry

(Continued)

MENTION TO the average person that you have been to drive an £80,000 Rolls-Royce and the immediate reaction is one of complete incredulity. How can any car be worth so much money is the response. Yet by Rolls-Royce prices, £80,000 is not even any sort of a record. A sum that by most people's reckoning would buy a good-sized country house comes into perspective when one realises that the owner of such a car probably has a £400,000 house. He, or she, might well compare the cost of such a car with a private helicopter at £90,000-plus and the cost would pale into insignificance alongside much larger sums for a yacht or private jet. A Rolls-Royce Phantom is quite likely to be purchased on impulse without any consideration of the cost, in much the same way as the buyer would a box of special cigars or a bowl of black cherries. For the man who wants the ultimate in Rolls-Royces for use on high days and holidays with a chauffeur at the wheel, then that car has to be a Phantom VI. Cream of the handbuilt Phantoms is the state landaulette, probably 10 times more exclusive than the limousine which is itself a rarity, with only about 20 cars a year now being built.

The landaulette which is the subject of this article features a special specification, developed by Lex Mead of Maidenhead who supplied the car new in September 1973. The lady owner, who already had a Silver Shadow and a Corniche drophead coupé, paid £33,000 for the Phantom and took it to Cannes for the summer season, accompanied by a hired chauffeur. Upon her return, and after covering around 3,000 miles, the car was sold. It seems that she hadn't realised that a Phantom VI is not really an owner-driver car — and she didn't have a chauffeur. The second owner also kept the landaulette for only a few months after which it was exported to Japan. The import duty alone on that transaction is said to have been £40,000. This may account for why the car was virtually unused for two years out there. Upon its return to England in January this year the car was purchased by Lex Mead Maidenhead who recently sold it for £80,000 — so its history has come full circle.

The specification of the "standard" Phantom VI includes all that is best of the coachbuilder's art. But underneath the beaten 16swg aluminium body panels is an all-metal framework of steel and light alloy which long ago replaced the traditional ash frame of the coachbuilt body. The latter is mounted upon a massive cruciform-braced box-section chassis — no monocoque construction here — which carries the running gear. It is in the interior, though, that the

work of the craftsmen of Rolls-Royce Motors' Mulliner Park Ward division is most apparent. A customer buying a Phantom expects, and gets, the finest wood veneers to the door fillets, facia and division, while folding occasional seats enable five passengers to be carried in the *rear* compartment. Deep pile carpets, an electrically-operated division between chauffeur and passengers, electrically-operated door windows, a cocktail cabinet complete with two cut glass decanters and four glasses, and separate refrigeration units for front and rear compartments are all included in the standard limousine specification.

The exclusive state landaulette differs from the limousine in having a power-operated hood which folds back from the division and renders the Phantom an open car as far as the rear passengers are concerned. One of the prime objects of the state landaulette is to ensure that the rear passengers are readily visible on important occasions and it is therefore possible to raise the height of the rear seat by some 3½in. for this purpose. Twin striplights at roof level to the rear of the glass division provide lighting so the occupants can be seen at night, while if the rear passengers wish to stand on ceremonial occasions there is a substantial grab rail above the division.

To this already impressive list of equipment have been added certain items to make up what may be called the Lex Mead Phantom VI specification; we have previously tried a

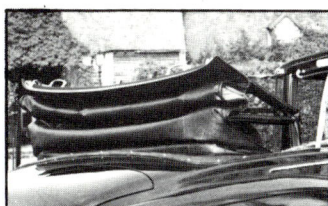

Above: With the hood up the landaulette looks very much like the limousine, though side quarter and rear windows are different

Left: This is as far down as the hood folds without the manual assistance needed to fit the protective cover

limousine with this equipment fitted (see *Autocar* 27 April 1972). Probably the most noticeable difference in a car to the Lex Mead specification is the use of Dralon velvet, in this case a deep red, to the rear compartment. This alone completely transforms the interior compared with the normal West of England cloth. Nylon rugs to the rear compartment, picnic tables folding out from the division, a Radiomobile Stereo 8 tape player and a Sony black and white television above the cocktail cabinet, an electric intercom to maintain the seclusion of the rear compartment while giving the chauffeur instructions, clock and barometer to the rear of the division and a Blaupunkt stereo VHF radio are all added for the convenience of rear passengers. Exterior embellishments include stainless steel trim to wheel arches and sills, badge bar and a vinyl-covered roof to the front; the glass roof panel and flag staffs on the front wings are part of the state landaulette specification. Aids to faster progress include Lucas halogen fog and head lamps and Fiamm Avanti air horns, while in the event of a disaster there is a fire extinguisher clipped to the front of the driving seat!

Specification

Engine: Aluminium alloy with wet liners, V8-cyl. 104.1 x 91.4mm (4.1 x 3.9in.), 6.230 c.c. (380 cu. in.); CR 9.0 to 1; Ohv, hydraulic tappets; 2 SU HD8 carbs, Bhp and torque not quoted. 2 SU electric fuel pumps.

Transmission: Front engine, rear-wheel drive. Rolls-Royce Motors Hydra-matic fluid flywheel automatic. Gearbox ratios 3.82, 2.63, 1.45, 1.00, rev 4.30. Final drive, hypoid 3.89. Top gear mph/1,000 rpm 22.5.

Chassis: Box section with cruciform bracing. Rubber-mounted body with alloy panels on steel and light alloy framework.

Suspension: ifs, double wishbones, coil springs, Rolls-Royce Motors lever dampers, anti-roll bar. Rear: live axle, asymmetric semi-elliptic leaf springs, Rolls-Royce Motors lever damper with normal/hard settings controlled by switch on steering column.

Steering: Cam and roller with variable power assistance. 18.7 to 1 ratio. 4.25 turns lock-to-lock.

Brakes: Rolls-Royce Motors/Girling (mechanical servo); three independent systems (2 hydraulic, 1 mechanical). 11.25in. front and rear drums.

Dimensions: Wheelbase 12ft 1in. (368cm); front track 5ft 0.87in. (155cm); rear track 5ft 4.0in. (162cm). Overall length 19ft 10in. (604cm); width 6ft 7in. (210cm); height 5ft 9in. (175cm). Turning circle 48ft 9in. (14.85m). Unladen weight 6,720lb (3,051kg). Max payload 1,300lb (590kg).

Others: Tyres 8.90-15in. cross ply 6.0in. rims. Battery 12 volt, 68 a/h. CAV 75 amp alternator. Fuel tank 23 gallons (104.6 litres). Engine sump and filter 14.5 pints (8 litres). Gearbox 21 pints (11.9 litres). Cooling system 28.5 pints (16 litres).

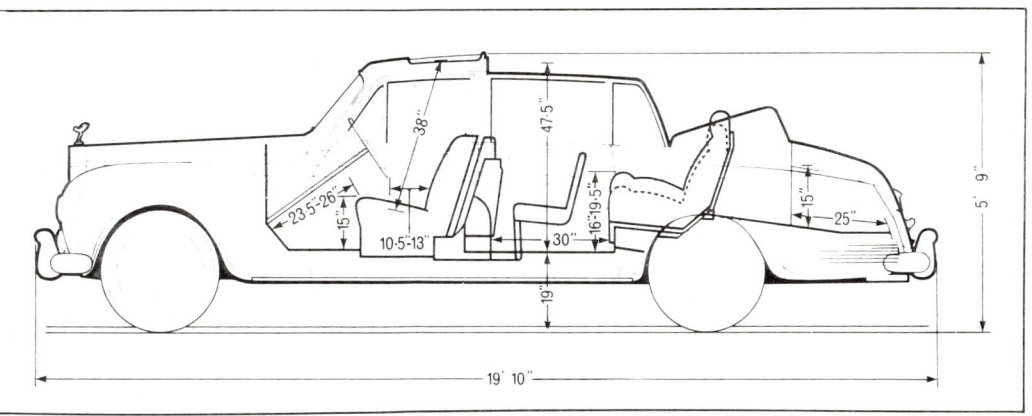

An £80,000 Black Cherry

(Continued)

From the rear seat

This is defeinitely not the sort of car you buy to drive yourself, so it is from the luxury of the rear seat that its performance on the road will be judged by most owners. I elected to be driven a short distance — it was a very cold day — with the hood down first. The actual operation of lowering the hood is not difficult. Two toggle-type catches above the division are first released and then a switch beneath the facia can be operated to activate the electro-hydraulic folding back of the hood. This takes but a few moments, but it then requires some work — and ideally two people — to button on the hood cover.

Once on the move, and with the rear seat in its highest position, it is surprising just how protected one is from wind buffeting. From the neck downwards wind protection is good and one remains surprisingly warm thanks to a good output from the recirculatory heater beneath the rear seat. With the hood down and seat raised you will be easily seen by those outside the car and must expect to attract considerable attention. It must be admitted, though, that the view into the car would be much improved if the rear quarter windows, which are fixed, could be wound down out of the way. It is a pity that the space needed to store the folded hood prevents this. There is also a good view out of the car, both over the chauffeur's head and to the sides and rear. It feels almost like sitting on top of the world looking down at the pedestrians and lesser cars.

With the hood up again I took my place on the back seat once more as the car wound along the A423 towards Henley-on-Thames. So good was the fit of the hood that there was a complete absence of wind noise. As I sat making notes on the car's equipment I could have been in a limousine, so little did the outside world intrude. Only the pvc rear window, which had misted up, gave the game away. A change of road surface and an adverse camber left me in no doubt that I was in a landaulette, for not only could the massive chassis be felt flexing, the doors were seen to move up and down against the body. With a car of this size and weight, this sort of movement is inevitable unless there is a roof structure to provide additional stiffness. The ride itself is good, and shows that a live rear axle and semi-elliptic leaf springs can work well on a big car such as this. I doubt if the use of independent rear suspension would improve the side comfort at low to medium speeds.

With a trained chauffeur at the wheel a rear seat passenger has no sensation of speed and it is impossible to tell how fast the car is going. Only hard driving, when the car rolls

Above: It is almost impossible to tell this is a soft top once the hood is in position. Note Dralon seat upholstery of "mobile office". Below: The rear compartment can seat five

quite appreciably, gives the game away and the rear passengers can literally be flung about if the car is cornered hard.

In the driving seat

I ask the chauffeur to stop and join photographer Peter Cramer in the back of the car. I slide in behind the wheel, at once feeling cramped and wanting to move the driving seat further back. I ask if the seat is right back and am told it is; the division prevents any more rearward movement. I reach behind me and fasten the seat belt which seems strangely out of place amid the walnut and leather. A turn of the ignition key to

the right of the steering wheel and the big 6.2-litre V8 engine comes to life so quietly that I have to rev it to make sure it is running. Left foot on the brake pedal, move the mechanical selector for the automatic transmission into position 4, reach beneath the facia and release the umbrella handbrake. Let the footbrake off, indicate right and accelerate gently out of the lay-by. We're off.

Initial reactions are still of the cramped driving position which leaves the steering wheel in my lap and much nearer than I really like. The cam and roller power assisted steering is very light — almost too light — and lacks feel. I make a lot of minor steering corrections to keep the car running straight. An S-bend approaches and I go in with the power on, winding on lock to counteract the understeer. The roadholding is good and the Phantom shows no sign of sliding on the wet tarmac, though there are loud complaints from Peter Cramer in the back that he is being thrown around. From the driving seat everything feels comfortably under control and the high driving position with a good view of the front wings makes it very easy to place the car on the road.

Another bend approaches and I try the brakes, reassured by their powerful response with plenty of feel. No worries here, even if the all-drum system with gearbox-driven mechanical servo does date back to

Left: The driver, shown operating the wiper switch, sits nearer the facia than it appears in this wide angle picture. Note the large steering wheel. The chauffeur has his own radio

1924. I accelerate gently round the bend giving those in the rear an easier time before putting my right foot hard down on the straight. The acceleration for a big car weighing around three tons is impressive. There is no noise, no fuss, just a surge of power as the V8 gets into its stride, though driven in this way the Hydramatic gearbox upchanges can be felt. I glance at the speedometer and find it showing 85 mph. It feels more like 50. I ease back to 70 mph and make a mental note to check the speedometer as we approach the next bend. It would be all too easy to go in far too fast, so little sensation of speed is there even from behind the wheel.

It starts to rain and I grope for the wiper switch. Sitting so near the facia means I must look down to find the correct switch but eventually with advice from the rear I find the right kidney-shaped knob. I wish the knobs were not all so alike, but then realise that a chauffeur would soon know their positions so perhaps it's not so important after all.

With dusk falling I deem it prudent to switch on the lights and reach for the switch. This time I find it easily, located in its own panel by the ignition key. I am now used to driving the Phantom which seems to have shrunk appreciably. With the division up it seems as though the back of the car finishes there — only a look in the interior mirror confirms that there is indeed a lot of car behind me. Certainly it doesn't feel big and unwieldy from the driving seat despite being almost 20ft long and over 6ft wide. A lay-by looms up through the dusk. I indicate, brake, and pull in to change places with Lex Mead's driver.

From the comfort of the back seat I watch my mobile office head back towards Maidenhead before settling back to complete my notes. I see from my notebook that a new model to this specification delivered now would cost £105,000 — or more likely £125,000 by the time a car ordered was delivered. At £80,000 our Black Cherry seems a bargain and will probably turn out to be a sound investment. I wonder if the Editor will let me add it to my expenses? □

Rolls-Royce Silver Cloud III 6,230 c.c.

AS Gertrude Stein might have said, " A Rolls is a Rolls is a Rolls." To so very many people one Rolls-Royce is little different from another so long as it bears the magic name and, at first glance, the current Silver Cloud III seems to have changed little from its immediate predecessor apart from the paired headlamps. Close observers will note that there are no sidelamps on the more highly domed wing-tops and that the bonnet line falls away a little more to the front. These changes, with others to the mechanical specification, were introduced for the last London Motor Show.

Modifications made at that time also included an increase in power of some seven per cent for the vee-8, 6,230 c.c. engine; extra power assistance for the cam-and-roller steering gear; the fitting as standard of individual front seats; 2in. more legroom for rear-seat passengers; and greater effective width of the rear seat. Each new feature is important in itself, and typifies the care taken by the makers to maintain their claim of producing the Best Car in the World.

It is true to say that the gap between a Rolls-Royce and its competitors, in many respects, is narrower today than it has ever been. This does not imply that Crewe standards are any lower, but is a compliment to the progress other concerns are making. Today there are American vee-8 cast iron engines that are even quieter than the present Rolls-Royce power unit, which is built largely of aluminium, while the latest American automatic transmissions and some suspension systems are in advance of those fitted to the Silver Cloud. It is in sheer all-round quality that Rolls-Royce still preserve their lead over all other makers.

Although Rolls-Royce dispense with any bonnet padding for sound damping, the engine is barely audible inside the car except when stationary and idling. From outside it can

be heard, but most of what noise there is appears to come from the fan. The increased engine power, compared with that of the Silver Cloud II (*Autocar* Road Test, 13 May 1960), comes from a rise in compression ratio from 8·0 to 9·0 to 1 and the use of larger, 2in. S.U. HD8 carburettors. A new vacuum advance-retard mechanism for the distributor is fitted.

By any standards, the performance of this big and heavy car is impressive. A standing start quarter-mile time of 17·7sec is exceptionally good for a large saloon, as is the best top speed of 117 m.p.h. Both these figures improve on those of the previous model, which were 18·2sec and 115·0 m.p.h. respectively. The effect of the extra power in the latest engine shows up most at the higher engine speeds. Although acceleration times for the two cars are very similar up to 80 m.p.h., from that speed to 100 m.p.h. in top gear took 15·0sec for this car compared with 17·2sec for the last.

Quite apart from the results achieved it was the consistent way that the Rolls-Royce performed under the stresses of repeated full-bore runs which aroused admiration. The engine temperature indicator hardly moved, none of the usual "hot smells" was apparent, and after the hardest

PRICES		£	s	d
Standard saloon		4,565	0	0
Purchase Tax		951	12	1
	Total (in G.B.)	5,516	12	1
Extras (including P.T.)				
Seat belts for front seats (pair)		16	6	4
Sundym glass (Supplied as standard on cars fitted with refrigeration, at no extra cost)		15	2	1
Electrically operated windows		84	11	8

Make • ROLLS-ROYCE   Type • Silver Cloud III 6,230 c.c.

Manufacturers : Rolls-Royce Ltd., 14-15 Conduit Street, London, W.1   *Front engine, rear-wheel drive*

Test Conditions

Weather ... Dry and bright, with 8-15 m.p.h. wind
Temperature ... 19 deg. C. (66 deg. F.). Barometer 29·6in. Hg.

Dry concrete and tarmac surfaces

Weight

Kerb weight (with oil, water and half-full fuel tank)
40·9cwt (4,578lb-2,080kg)
Front-rear distribution, per cent F. 50·6; R, 49·4
Laden as tested .... 43·9cwt (4,914lb-2,229kg)

Turning Circles

Between kerbs .... L, 43ft 4in.; R, 41ft 10in.
Between walls ...... L, 45ft 3in.; R, 43ft 10in.
Turns of steering wheel lock to lock .... 4·3

Performance Data

Top gear m.p.h. per 1,000 r.p.m. .... 27·8
Engine revs. at mean max. speed ... 4,160 r.p.m.

FUEL AND OIL CONSUMPTION

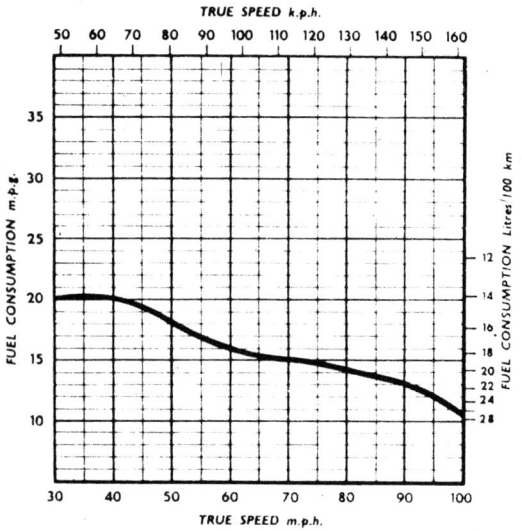

FUEL .... Super premium grade
(100 octane RM)
Test Distance .... 1,377 miles
Overall Consumption .... 12·3 m.p.g.
(23·0 litres/100 km.)
Normal Range .... 11-17 m.p.g.
(25·7-16·6 litres/100 km.)
OIL: SAE 10W/30 ... Consumption negligible

MAXIMUM SPEEDS AND ACCELERATION (mean) TIMES

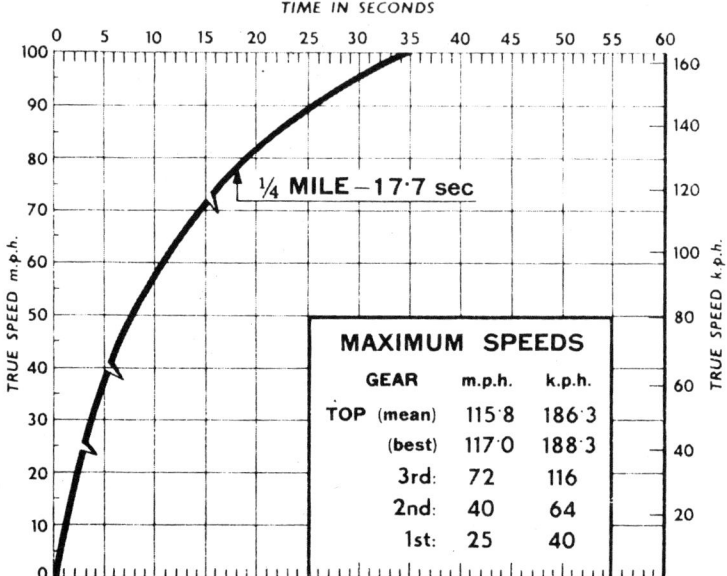

¼ MILE — 17·7 sec

MAXIMUM SPEEDS		
GEAR	m.p.h.	k.p.h.
TOP (mean)	115·8	186·3
(best)	117·0	188·3
3rd:	72	116
2nd:	40	64
1st:	25	40

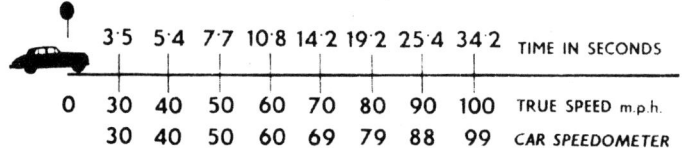

TIME IN SECONDS	3·5	5·4	7·7	10·8	14·2	19·2	25·4	34·2
TRUE SPEED m.p.h.	30	40	50	60	70	80	90	100
CAR SPEEDOMETER	30	40	50	60	69	79	88	99

Speed range, gear ratios and time in seconds

m.p.h.	Top (3·08 to 1)	3rd (4·46 to 1)	2nd (8·10 to 1)
10—30	—	—	2·9
20—40	—	4·9	3·1
30—50	7·9	4·9	3·8
40—60	8·0	5·4	—
50—70	8·5	6·3	—
60—80	9·5	—	—
70—90	11·7	—	—
80—100	15·0	—	—

BRAKES	Pedal Load	Retardation	Equiv. distance
(from 30 m.p.h. in neutral)	25lb	0·28g	107ft
	50lb	0·71g	42ft
	75lb	0·96g	31·3ft
Handbrake		0·14g	213ft

HILL CLIMBING AT STEADY SPEEDS

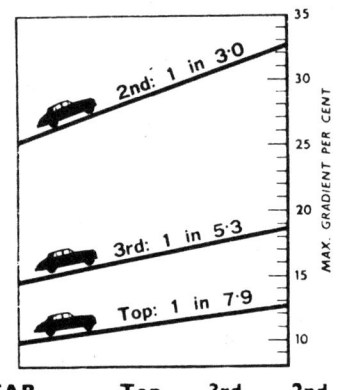

2nd: 1 in 3·0
3rd: 1 in 5·3
Top: 1 in 7·9

GEAR	Top	3rd	2nd
PULL (lb per ton)	280	410	690
Speed range (m.p.h.)	35–55	38–46	28–34

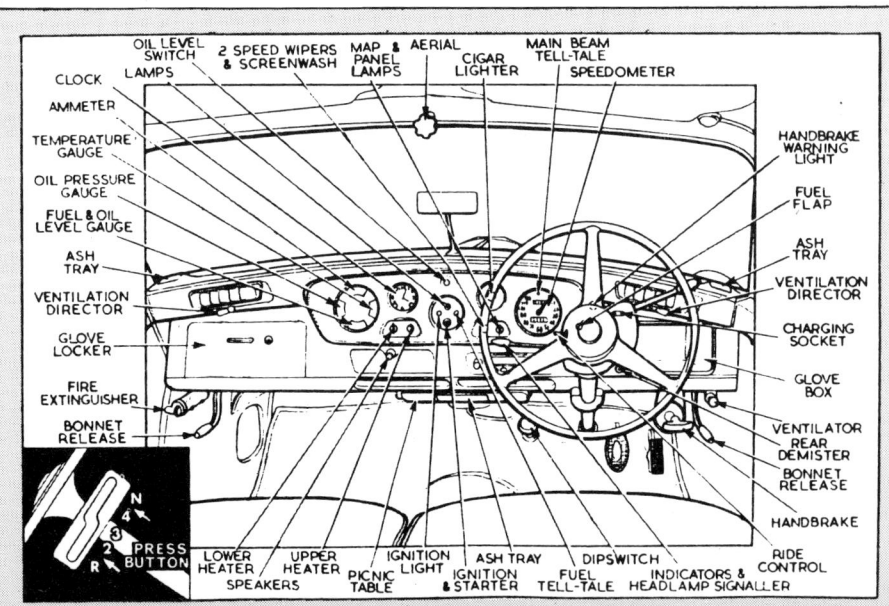

OIL LEVEL SWITCH — CLOCK — AMMETER — TEMPERATURE GAUGE — OIL PRESSURE GAUGE — FUEL & OIL LEVEL GAUGE — ASH TRAY — VENTILATION DIRECTOR — GLOVE LOCKER — FIRE EXTINGUISHER — BONNET RELEASE — 2 SPEED WIPERS & SCREENWASH — PANEL LAMPS — MAP & PANEL LAMPS — AERIAL — CIGAR LIGHTER — MAIN BEAM TELL-TALE — SPEEDOMETER — HANDBRAKE WARNING LIGHT — FUEL FLAP — ASH TRAY — VENTILATION DIRECTOR — CHARGING SOCKET — GLOVE BOX — VENTILATOR REAR DEMISTER — BONNET RELEASE — HANDBRAKE — RIDE CONTROL — INDICATORS & HEADLAMP SIGNALLER — FUEL TELL-TALE — DIPSWITCH — ASH TRAY — IGNITION & STARTER — IGNITION LIGHT — PICNIC TABLE — UPPER HEATER — LOWER HEATER SPEAKERS — PRESS BUTTON

Front-seat backs are adjustable for rake very easily, there are movable armrests on the front doors and even the footrests for rear-seat passengers can be altered for angle

Rolls-Royce Silver Cloud III . . .

acceleration tests and maximum speed runs the power unit went quietly back to its smooth and even light running, ready for the next effort.

Fractional variations in fuel consumption can still be of importance even to Rolls-Royce owners, so it is satisfactory to note that the engine modifications mentioned have also reduced the car's thirst for petrol. The overall figure for 1,377 miles of mainly fast driving was 12·3 m.p.g. of 100 octane grade. The last Silver Cloud did 11·8 m.p.g. on premium petrol, so the better consumption very nearly offsets the extra cost of the grade of fuel now specified.

Starting, in neutral only, is immediate, the N position being reached by pressing in a lock button on the end of the lever. The handbrake should be on, for fast idle for warming up caused the test car to creep when a driving gear was selected. On another car tried, with lower idling speed, there was no creeping.

The lock button also protects reverse from accidental engagement, but movements between positions 2, 3 and 4 can be made without it; there is a step in the gate between 2 and 3. In R, with the car stationary and the engine switched off, a solenoid-operated positive transmission lock comes into operation. This is a necessity rather than a luxury in the III, which, like its immediate predecessor, has a handbrake that will not hold the car on a really steep gradient.

Once used to the automatic transmission, a good driver can so control the throttle that the passengers barely notice the changes. It is a four-speed epicyclic design with a fluid coupling (not a torque converter). For the best performance the makers recommend letting the box make automatic changes throughout on full throttle. On the test car these occurred at 25 m.p.h., 40 m.p.h. and 70-72 m.p.h. One could kick-down to 3rd from top below 66 m.p.h., and from 3rd to the very low 2nd only below 22 m.p.h.

A useful feature of the Rolls-Royce transmission is the ability to hold 2nd and 3rd for sparing the brake linings in hilly country. In 2 the car will start and stay in that gear, unless an extreme gradient forces an automatic change down to 1st, which can only happen at a walking pace, but it is possible to over-rev in this 2nd hold position, and the recommended maximum speed is 50 m.p.h. In 3rd hold there is a governed change-up to top if the road speed rises above about 72 m.p.h. This gear selector position is useful for driving in heavy traffic and avoids the frequent shifts into and out of top at low speeds. To kick down from 3rd to 2nd can produce a hefty transmission "thud" and spin the rear wheels, even on a dry surface; in the wet it is an action to be avoided for obvious reasons.

Ride comfort is superb on good surfaces. It is also very satisfactory on other types, with the reservation that the suspension arrangements and the big tyres do produce a firmness of ride allied to tyre noise which is accentuated by

A centre-hinged bonnet is a rarity today. The "works" are as beautifully finished as the car's exterior

The petrol filler cap on the nearside wing is opened electrically from the driving seat. Wheel trims are now of stainless steel

the overall quietness. This is pretty well damped out before most passengers would be aware of it, but the more sensitive have described it as an impression of the car's having "big feet."

With more power assistance, the steering is now extremely light at any speed. The power mechanism simply augments the driver's own efforts at the slim-rimmed wheel without in any way trying to take command or failing to help at certain points. In spite of the lightness, there are still 4.3 turns of the wheel from lock to lock, a low ratio which is maintained deliberately by the makers for two reasons. One is that, should power assistance fail, the car would remain quite easy to drive. The other concerns what Rolls-Royce lightly term the "sneeze factor"—a margin for slight error by the driver if something disturbs his concentration at high speed, when a twitch at the wheel on "quicker" steering might take the car off its line.

Directionally the Silver Cloud is generally stable, as might be expected, but its undoubtedly large "sail area" does mean that at times it will be forced slightly off course by strong and gusty winds. Poor road surfaces also have their effect, and at over 100 m.p.h. the steering seems to urge the driver to repeated small corrections—which, in fact, are largely unnecessary. Pitching or heeling are negligible, a squeal of protest from a tyre is a rarity, and the rear tyres grip well on wet roads. As usual, there is a two-way switch for giving normal or hard setting of the rear dampers, but one needs to use the hard setting only when the car is carrying a big load. On *pavé* it handles and rides well, and on a "washboard" type of surface settles down to level and almost vibration-free progress at 50 m.p.h. and above.

Renewed experience confirms our previous impression that the Silver Cloud is one of the "smallest" big cars to drive. The fall-away of the bonnet and the visible front

wing tips help in placing it accurately on the road, while the power steering and the surprisingly small turning circle make parking far easier than expected. It is a car that quickly gives the driver confidence—once his apprehension at piloting such a costly mass is allayed—while its precision controls and excellent road behaviour encourage him to handle it as neatly and skilfully as he can. In other words, it is a true driver's car which brings out the very best in him.

While the modern, low-built car may offer advantages by its correspondingly low centre of gravity in respect of suspension, it has lost something that the Rolls-Royce still retains, a commandingly high seating position. Driving the Silver Cloud, one realizes how much better is the all-round vision resulting from the greater height above the road and how much easier—and safer—it is to see over and round obstructions.

Triple-safety Brakes

Rolls-Royce remain faithful to their own excellent type of drum brakes, which maintain the make's reputation for highly efficient stopping power. The hydraulic systems are duplicated and there is also a mechanical linkage to the rear wheels—three operating mechanisms in all to guard against any possible failure. The driver's own efforts at the pedal are assisted as usual by the Rolls-Royce mechanical friction servo, which works efficiently and unobtrusively. It reacts instantly on first application of the brakes, but should the pedal be released quickly and immediately reapplied there is a lag in servo action, particularly noticeable when creeping in traffic or inching one's way into a confined space like a garage.

Apart from this the brakes are splendid, and very quickly recovered from some slight fade which occurred after several applications at high road speeds.

There is nothing ornate about the interior furnishings of the Silver Cloud. Opulent, yes, in the best sense of that term, with everything in extremely good taste. The test car's windows were fitted with glass tinted faintly blue, which is standard for models having fully refrigerated air conditioning and optional on others. Several of us would have preferred clear glass, as the tint does give a slightly darkening effect and distorts natural colours somewhat. An optional extra on the test car that did get universal approval was the electrical operation of all door windows. There is an unobtrusive rocking switch beneath the sill on three doors, while the driver's door has four switches controlling all the windows. One of the operating motors was surprisingly audible, but the others very quiet.

Quality of the hide upholstery, the polished wood trim and the carpeting is beyond reproach, of course, and the front seats give so much fore-and-aft movement that none of the test staff complained of insufficient adjustment.

The rear seat cushion is now 2in. farther back than on the Silver Cloud II, and the corner padding less obtrusive. Complete luxury for two and good comfort for three passengers result. In the right quarter are a reading

The boot is rather shallow, but larger than it appears at first sight. Under the floor are the spare wheel and fitted tools

Rolls-Royce Silver Cloud III . . .

lamp, mirror and a cigar lighter, in the left a lamp and mirror. Above each door is a pull strap and there are ashtrays and picnic tables behind each front seat.

At first sight the facia looks complicated, but all the controls are placed logically and are easy for the driver to reach, even when wearing a safety belt. The instrument dials—some of them rather remote—have clear white markings on black faces and the adjustable night illumination for them is just right. While the speedometer is not directly in front of the driver in the fashionable manner, it is not too far off the forward line of vision; it was exceptionally accurate, even being correct at 110 m.p.h.

Certainly the most effective ventilating and heating arrangements we have yet experienced are those now standard on Rolls-Royce cars. The system is a double one, the "upper" circuit being for fresh air and the "lower" for recirculating air. Either or both can be used for hot or cold air, and there are special vent arrangements to the rear compartment. During the course of the test, when the weather was warm, we also drove a similar car fitted with the optional underwing refrigeration unit. Not only does this provide cooled air but it will remove the moisture.

The refrigerating unit, engaged through a magnetic clutch, works only while the engine is running, and is controlled by extra positions on the normal ventilating system switchgear. The noise of the moving air when the blowers are working at their maximum is rather obtrusive when the car is at rest, but is scarcely heard when on the move at above 30 m.p.h. or so.

With all windows shut, the full refrigeration system will lower the internal temperature some 8 deg. F. in about 5 min, but more important is that a flow of cold air is available almost immediately after switching on. This produces a rapid cooling effect for the occupants, whatever the interior or exterior temperatures. It is fitted as an extra for £332 5s 10d, including tax.

Paired headlamps—the principal distinguishing features of the latest models—provide exceptionally good road illumination, probably helped by the fact that they are mounted higher than on most cars. A flasher switch is operated by pulling up the stalk of the traffic indicator switch.

So many refinements and fittings are found on the Silver Cloud that one cannot note them all within the scope of a Road Test. They include an electrically demisted back window; remote, electrical opening of the petrol filler flap; three ashtrays, a picnic table and a cigar lighter for front seat occupants; and an H.M.V. transistor radio with two speakers and a balancing switch. However, stiff sun visors and vestigial padding across the top rail of the facia make little concession to present-day fashions.

It is a pity that a connoisseur's car like the Rolls-Royce remains far beyond the dreams of the vast majority of the world's motorists, but good to know that cars of this quality can be built still and that there is a healthy market for them. They set a standard that is really appreciated best when one returns to driving lesser cars.

Specification

Scale: 0.3in. to 1ft.
Cushions uncompressed.

ENGINE
Cylinders ... 8 in 90 deg vee
Bore ... 104mm (4.1in.)
Stroke ... 91.5mm (3.6in.)
Displacement ... 6,230 c.c. (380 cu. in.)
Valve gear ... Overhead, pushrods and rockers, self-adjusting hydraulic tappets
Compression ratio 9 to 1 (8.0 to 1 optional)
Carburettors ... Two S.U. HD8
Fuel pumps ... Two S.U. electric
Oil filter ... British Filters, wire mesh replaceable element

TRANSMISSION
Gearbox ... Rolls-Royce four speed automatic
Overall ratios ... Top 3.08, 3rd 4.46, 2nd 8.10, 1st 11.75, reverse 13.25
Final drive ... Hypoid bevel 3.08 to 1

CHASSIS
Construction ... Separate chassis, box section; steel body with aluminium doors, bonnet top and boot lid

WHEELS
Type ... Pressed steel disc, 5 studs, 6in. wide rim
Tyres ... 8.20—15in. Dunlop tubeless

SUSPENSION
Front ... Independent by coil springs, anti-roll bar. Lever arm hydraulic dampers
Rear ... Live axle on half-elliptic leaf springs; hydraulic dampers electrically controlled by two-position switch. Single radius rod
Steering ... Rolls-Royce power-assisted, cam and roller. Wheel dia., 17in.

BRAKES
Type ... Rolls-Royce drum and servo
Dimensions ... F. 11.25in. dia., 3in. wide shoes R. 11.25in. dia., 3in. wide shoes
Swept area ... F. 212 sq. in., R. 212 sq. in. Total: 424 sq. in. (196 sq. in. per ton laden)

EQUIPMENT
Battery ... 12-volt 67-amp. hr.
Headlamps ... Four Lucas sealed beam 37.5-50-watt outer lamps, 37.5-watt inner lamps
Reversing lamp ... One, standard
Electric fuses ... 8
Screen wipers ... Two-speed electric, self-parking
Screen washer ... Standard, electric
Interior heater ... Standard
Safety belts ... Extra
Interior trim ... English hide seats, cloth roof trim
Floor covering ... Wilton deep pile carpet
Starting handle ... No provision
Jack ... Benelift or triple screw
Jacking points ... Two each side
Other bodies ... L. w. b. saloon with division; convertible by H. J. Mulliner, Park Ward Ltd.
Fuel tank ... 18 Imp. gallons (inc. 3 gal reserve)
Cooling system ... 21 pints (including heater)
Engine sump ... 12 pints SAE 10W/30. Change oil every 6,000 miles; change filter element every 6,000 miles
Gearbox ... 20 pints approved automatic transmission fluid. Change oil every 24,000 miles
Final drive ... 1.6 pints SAE 90EP. Change oil every 24,000 miles
Grease ... 21 points every 12,000 miles
Tyre pressures ... 22 F and R, 27 p.s.i. (all conditions)

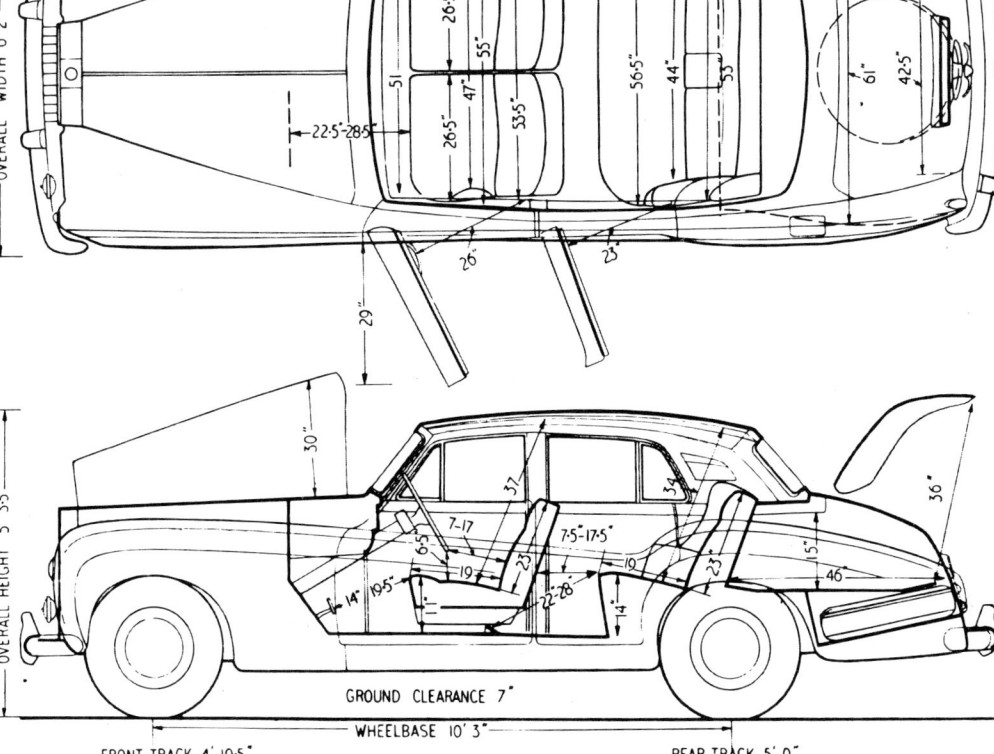

OVERALL LENGTH 17' 6.25"
OVERALL WIDTH 6' 2"
OVERALL HEIGHT 5' 3.5"
GROUND CLEARANCE 7"
WHEELBASE 10' 3"
FRONT TRACK 4' 10.5"
REAR TRACK 5' 0"

Now at last we can see the fruits of their long labours and researches in the Rolls-Royce Silver Shadow—alias Bentley T Series—which conceals beneath an almost austerely orthodox new body a wealth of mechanical innovation. In fact, it possesses more individuality and advanced engineering than this company has ever displayed before in a new model.

It is, for instance, the first Rolls-Royce product to incorporate the following features:

A monocoque steel body shell, with separate front and rear sub-frames for engine and transmission, steering, suspension and wheel assemblies; all-independent suspension with automatic height control; four-wheel disc braking powered by dual high-pressure hydraulic systems; a recirculating ball steering

Frontal aspect of the Series T Bentley, identical to the Silver Cloud except for its radiator and bonnet pressing

present Rolls-Royce and Bentley clientele, the new model is considerably more compact outwardly than its predecessors in every main dimension—$4\frac{1}{4}$ in. lower, $6\frac{3}{4}$ in. shorter, and $3\frac{3}{4}$ in. narrower, yet enveloping increased space for passengers and their baggage. The wheelbase has been reduced by $3\frac{1}{2}$ in. from 10 ft 3 in. to 9 ft $11\frac{1}{2}$ in., and front and rear tracks are now equal at 4 ft $9\frac{1}{2}$ in.—compared with 4 ft $10\frac{1}{2}$ in. front and 5 ft rear for the Cloud.

Several factors have contributed to the increased passenger space within an outwardly less bulky shell. First, dispensing with a separate chassis frame and having a fixed transmission line and final drive unit have allowed the floor and rear seat to be lowered several inches. The luggage boot has also gained from the static final drive assembly, as well as from a more boxy shape and having the spare wheel stowed in a hinged tray beneath it instead of inside. Moving the engine

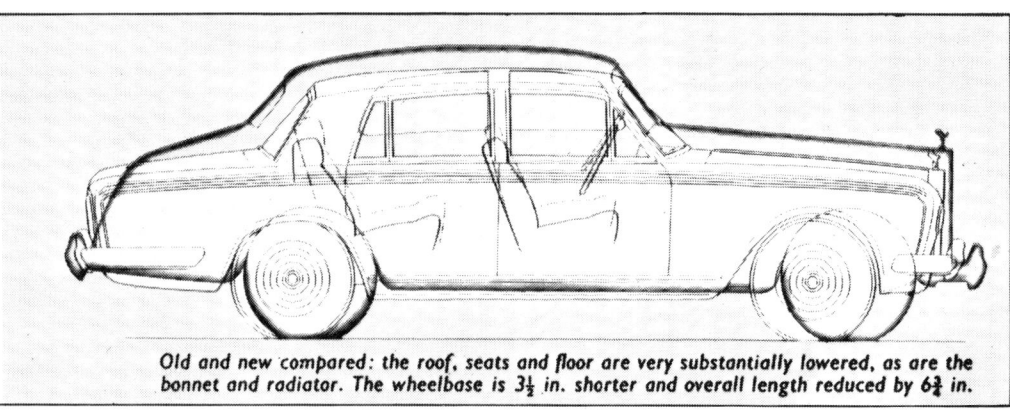

Old and new compared: the roof, seats and floor are very substantially lowered, as are the bonnet and radiator. The wheelbase is $3\frac{1}{2}$ in. shorter and overall length reduced by $6\frac{3}{4}$ in.

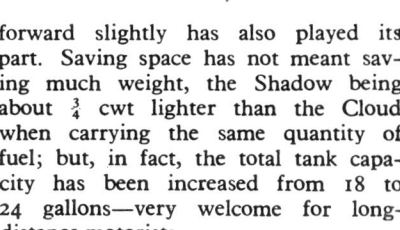

AFTER

ROLLS-ROYCE ADOPT

A decade ago, when the six-cylinder Rolls-Royce Silver Cloud I and Bentley SI were safely hatched after the long incubation period that must lie behind any complex piece of machinery aspiring to near-perfection, the engineers at Crewe were already resetting their sights for the next generation of super cars.

gear with integral power assistance; electric actuation for the gear range selector, as well as for three-way front seat adjustment and window-lifts. In fact, the only direct legacies from the superseded car are its 6.3-litre vee-eight engine and four-speed automatic transmission, both with several interesting innovations.

To conform with current trends and the known preferences of many of the

forward slightly has also played its part. Saving space has not meant saving much weight, the Shadow being about $\frac{3}{4}$ cwt lighter than the Cloud when carrying the same quantity of fuel; but, in fact, the total tank capacity has been increased from 18 to 24 gallons—very welcome for long-distance motorists.

Once again the classic Rolls-Royce radiator shell has been re-proportioned to match the greatly lowered bonnet line, and once again without appearing as a traditionalist anachronism. In fact, it seems to have withstood the transformation perhaps more elegantly than the Bentley shell, which has lost some of its grandeur and distinction. No doubt Rolls-Royce archivists will be quick to remark upon a reversion to the proportions and dimensions of the early Edwardian era.

Still safe on her draughty perch is the Silver Lady mascot, now easy to detach when entering countries where her rigid posture contravenes road safety laws; with the bonnet open one can unscrew her from her pedestal with a special key. Those who live in such

Lighting switches and other minor controls are of traditional design and quality, but the instrument dials (apart from the clock) are now all in front of the driver, and the two-spoke steering-wheel is another innovation. At each side of the centre panel are adjustable outlets for cool air

RR 1966

THE CLOUD-THE SHADOW

MONOCOQUE BODY. ALL INDEPENDENT SELF-LEVELLING SUSPENSION, DISC BRAKES

countries can now specify (at extra cost) a spring-heeled Lady.

Of all the Shadow's mechanical features, the most significant and intriguing is the high-pressure hydraulic system serving the suspension height control and braking system. There are, in fact, two independent circuits. Each is served by an identical single-plunger pump set in the vee between the cylinder banks and actuated through a short pushrod from the camshaft. Mounted low on the left side of the crankcase are two spherical accumulators with butyl separators, inflated with nitrogen to 1,000 p.s.i. The hydraulic pumps pressurize these to 2,500 p.s.i. (maximum), at which point pressure regulating valves (built under licence from Citroën) incorporated in the housing above each accumulator open a by-pass back to the reservoir. Accumulators not only store a reserve supply of fluid under pressure, but also damp down sharp fluctuations in pressure when any service is in demand.

One system—from the forward pump —is responsible only for a 47 per cent share of the total braking which is

divided front and rear in the ratio 31 to 16. The other provides a further 31 per cent (of the total) for the front only, and also feeds the suspension's height control circuits. Each front disc has two independent two-cylinder calipers, and each back one a single, four-cylinder caliper. One pair of cylinders in each rear caliper is served by an ordinary hydraulic system with master

cylinder and no servo assistance. This normally provides the remaining 22 per cent of total braking, but its main purpose—apart from the safety factor of having three distinct circuits—is to give the driver 'feel' through the pedal. In the master cylinder circuit is a 'G conscious' pressure limiting valve of the ball-and-ramp type to reduce the likelihood of rear wheel locking.

→

Left: In the back are picnic tables of a new pattern, with ashtrays beneath. Cigarette lighters are in the door armrests, which also contain red lamps, lit when the doors are open. Slots in the carpet are above safety harness anchorages. Right: Other luxuries in the back include a compartment let into the folding armrest and mirrors in each quarter

ROLLS-ROYCE SILVER SHADOW ...

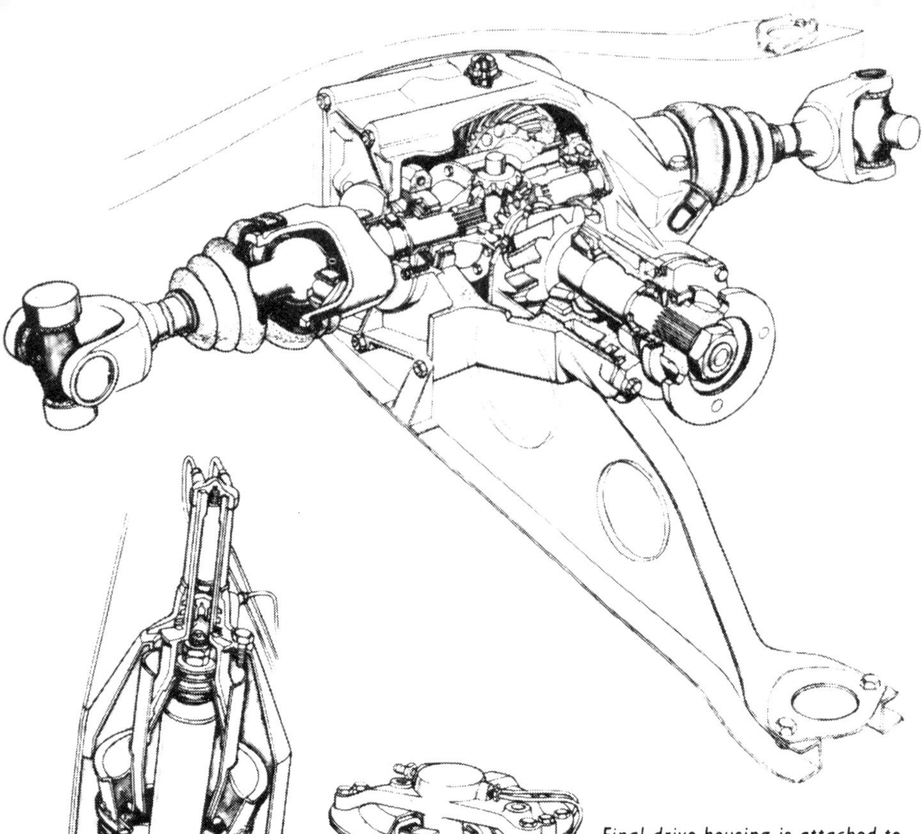

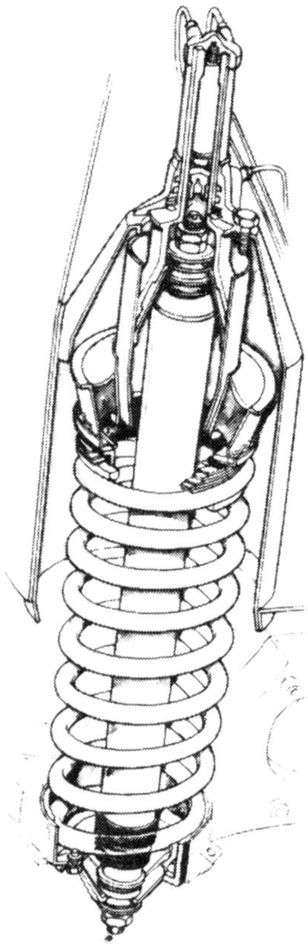

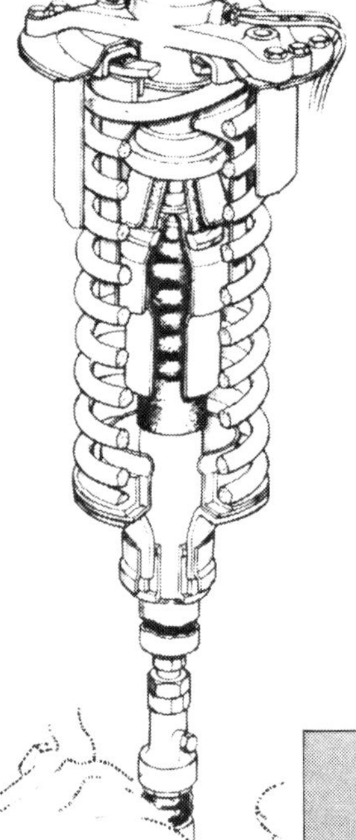

Loss of pressure in either high-pressure circuit is indicated by its own tell-tale lamp, failure of any one of the three foot-brake systems not affecting the others. It will be appreciated from the foregoing remarks that, were two to fail, one would be left with four-wheel braking, or front or rear brakes only depending on which circuit was left in action. The parking brake, of course, provides a fourth system—operating mechanically on the pistons served by the master cylinder. The 11 in. Girling discs are wound around their peripheries with stainless steel wire—not under tension—to absorb high frequency squeal. They are 'tuned' individually, and usually need 30-35 coils which are then trapped by a welded steel band. When the friction pads are worn to the extent that replacements will soon be needed, a warning lamp on the instrument panel is lit.

When considering the Rolls-Royce system of height control it is important to understand right away that this does not directly affect the normal functioning of the car's suspension, and there is no constant fore-and-aft interaction in the manner of the Citroen hydro-pneumatic system or the B.M.C.'s Hydrolastic. In the Rolls-Royce design the levelling action occurs very slowly indeed while the car is moving, about ten times quicker when it is stationary. Thus the normal functioning of the coil springs and Girling telescopic dampers (not adjustable, incidentally) is unaffected; on the move, the height control mechanism has little to do but compensate for the reduction in load over the back wheels as the fuel tank empties.

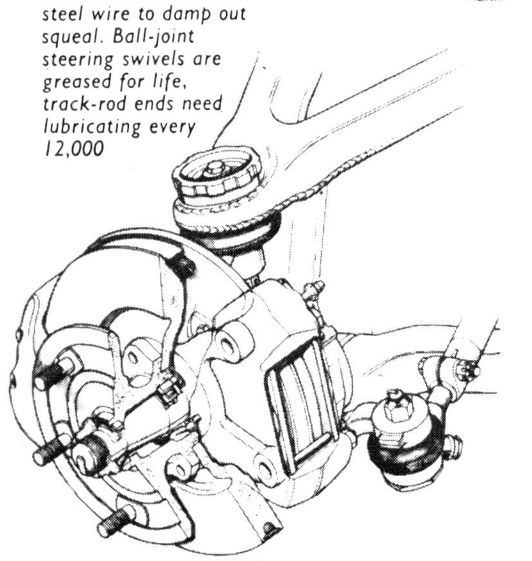

Final drive housing is attached to sub-frame's rear cross-member, a substantial torque arm uniting it with the front one. Inner universal joints are constant velocity ball-and-trunnion type

Far left: Individually matched rate-control shims are inserted between top of rubber-insulated rear spring and its abutment

Left: Front suspension unit, connected to lower wishbone, is more compact than rear one

Below: Layout and functioning of hydraulic services. Broken lines show high-pressure feed from solenoid valve

Each front brake has two twin-cylinder calipers supplied by independent high-pressure systems. Periphery of disc is bound with stainless steel wire to damp out squeal. Ball-joint steering swivels are greased for life, track-rod ends need lubricating every 12,000

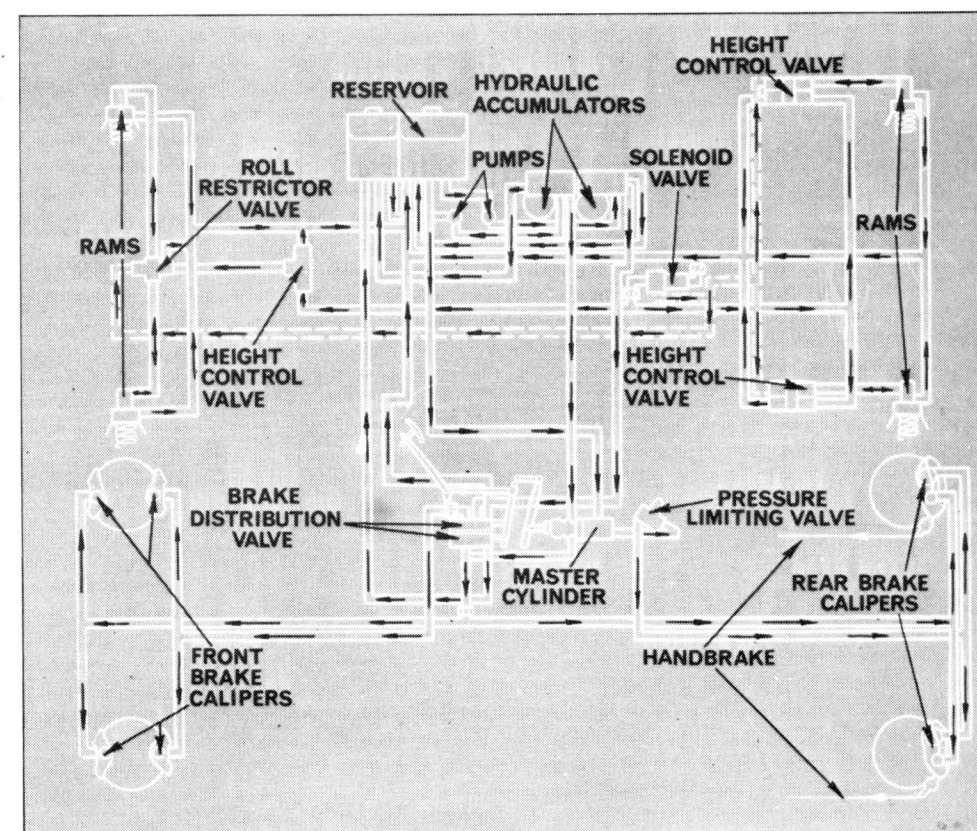

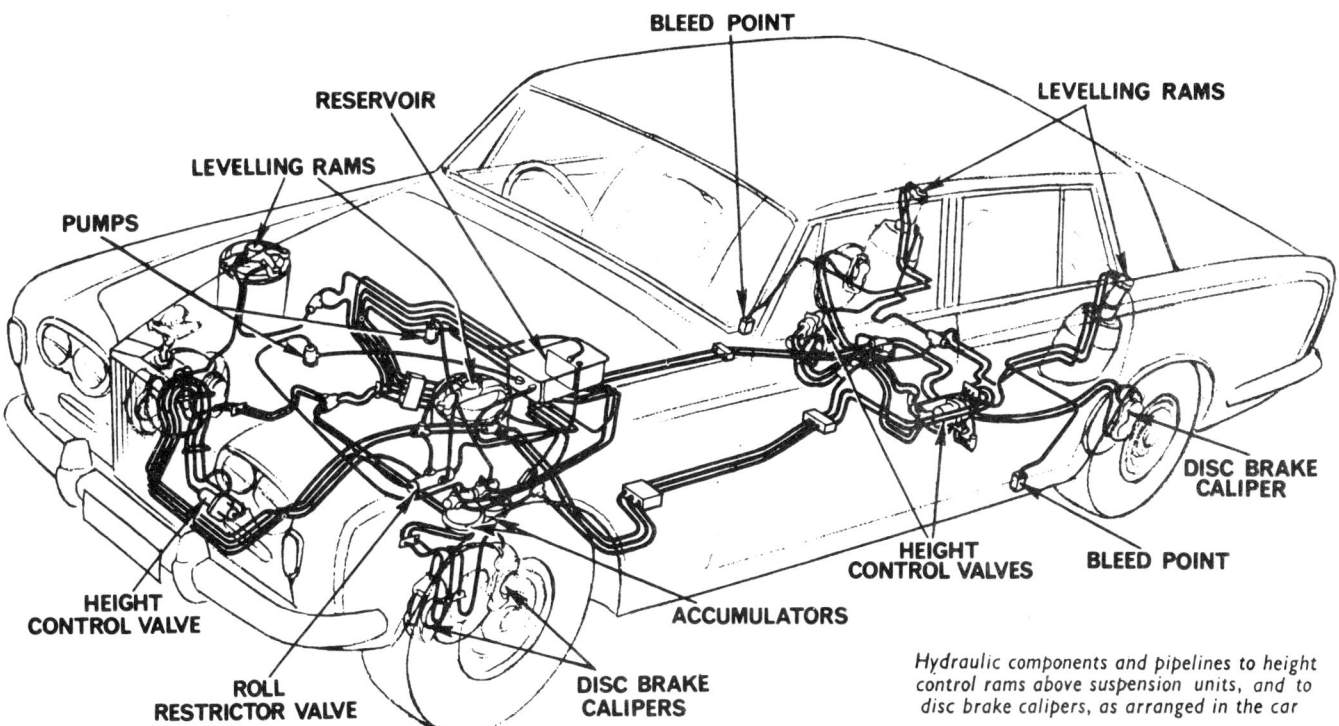

BLEED POINT

RESERVOIR

LEVELLING RAMS

LEVELLING RAMS

PUMPS

DISC BRAKE CALIPER

HEIGHT CONTROL VALVE

HEIGHT CONTROL VALVES

BLEED POINT

ROLL RESTRICTOR VALVE

ACCUMULATORS

DISC BRAKE CALIPERS

Hydraulic components and pipelines to height control rams above suspension units, and to disc brake calipers, as arranged in the car

In simple terms, the object is to keep the basic trim of the car constant regardless of the load carried or variations in weight distribution. The need for rapid levelling occurs only while the car is at rest, when immediate reactions are required to reset the trim as passengers enter or alight, or as the fuel tank is replenished. How this two-speed functioning is achieved will be explained a little later in the text, after considering the fundamental components and action of the system as a whole.

A hydraulic ram with 3 in. stroke is incorporated above each upper spring abutment; any static compression of the spring beyond the prearranged neutral setting for the height control (or levelling) valves causes this ram to extend by the same amount, so that the car, in effect, is then supported on a column of oil. If the car is heavily laden and carrying a boot full of luggage, for instance, then the rear springs will be much more compressed than the front ones, and the rams above them are extended that much further. Since the basic geometrical relationship between the suspension arms and the body structure thus does not vary with the load carried, the bump and rebound stop clearances also remain constant regardless of load, and much greater vertical wheel movements can be provided than with conventional suspensions.

There are three height control valves, one attending to both front rams, one for each at the back; apparently with an individual valve for each corner the system would never reach a state of equilibrium. The valves for the rear suspension are bolted to the sub-assembly's forward cross-member and linked to the trailing arms, whereas the single front one, bolted to that sub-frame, responds to rotary movements of the anti-roll bar. Between this valve and

the levelling rams is a roll restriction valve. As well as dividing the flow between the two rams, it also restricts cross-flow between them, which otherwise would allow one ram to empty into the other and the car to roll.

When any door is opened, or if the gear selector is in neutral, a solenoid valve in circuit with the interior courtesy lamps and the selector is energized. It opens to pass fluid at high pressure to an overriding piston in each rear height control valve and in the front roll restrictor valve. In each of these there is a small, counterbored shuttle which normally provides a very restricted bleed path around it to the ports feeding the levelling rams. The solenoid-controlled piston pushes this

shuttle against a spring loading, to bring a cross-drilling in the shuttle in line with the outlet ports, thereby permitting unrestricted flow—and hence rapid levelling.

With the car at rest and unladen it 'sits on its springs' with the rams unpressurized. The minimum system pressure for their operation is about 1,150 p.s.i. While the accompanying diagram should help to clarify the hydraulic circuits, to describe the precise design and operation of the individual components is beyond the scope of this article. After much experimenting with air springs, incidentally, the Rolls-Royce engineers decided that steel ones set fewer problems, particu-

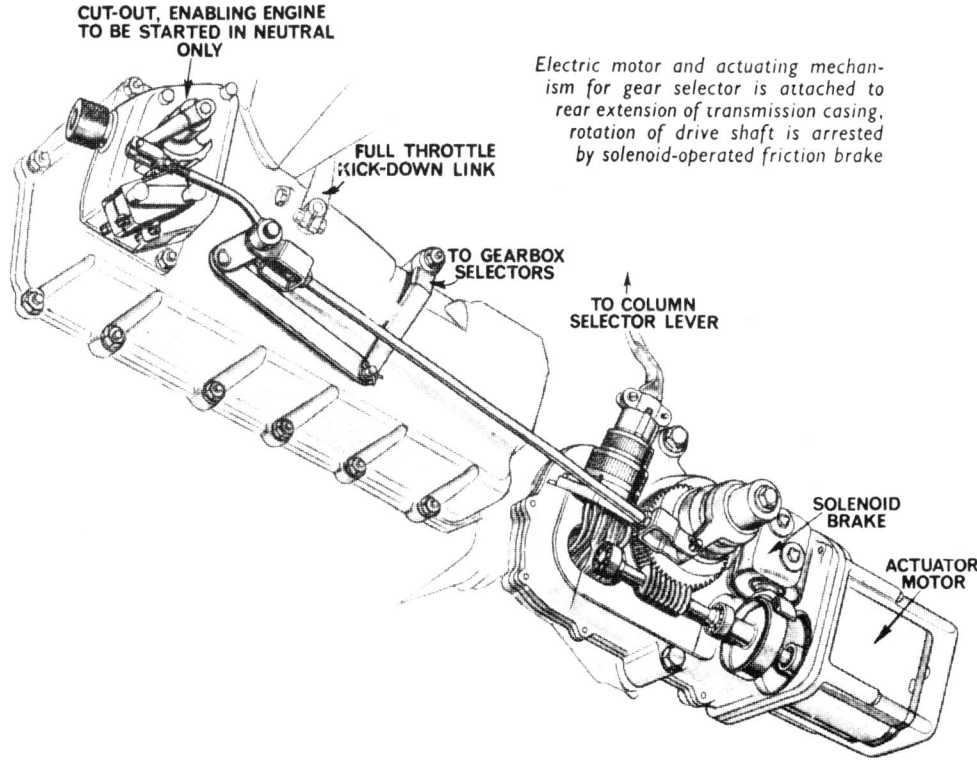

CUT-OUT, ENABLING ENGINE TO BE STARTED IN NEUTRAL ONLY

FULL THROTTLE KICK-DOWN LINK

TO GEARBOX SELECTORS

TO COLUMN SELECTOR LEVER

SOLENOID BRAKE

ACTUATOR MOTOR

Electric motor and actuating mechanism for gear selector is attached to rear extension of transmission casing, rotation of drive shaft is arrested by solenoid-operated friction brake

ROLLS-ROYCE SILVER SHADOW...

Tail end of the new Rolls-Royce shows much larger rear window and squared-up boot

larly in very cold weather—and moreover cannot go flat overnight.

In attaching the front and rear subframes to the main structure, great pains have been taken to evolve mountings flexible enough to suppress road noise without giving the car spongy handling. The rear one is composite. It consists broadly of two vertical cross-members—one carrying the suspension trailing arms, the other the final drive unit, the only direct link between them being a sheet metal torque arm bolted to the right-hand side of the final drive casing. Its front end is attached through a flexible rubber coupling to a pick-up point on the forward cross-member.

A new type of resilient metal mounting is now used to attach these cross-members to the main structure. Developed by Delaney Gallay and called *Vibrashock*, it looks rather like a pan scrubber, embodying a stainless steel mesh claimed to have more closely controllable and constant characteristics than rubber. Supplementing the vertical mounts at each end of the forward cross-member is an arrangement to give it a measure of horizontal compliance—freedom of movement, that is. Below are two long tubular stays linking the cross-member to points well forward on the underside of the main structure, and bolted to the back of it are two upright

forged steel horns of which the tops are sandwiched between two *Vibrashock* mountings. This movement is restricted by a small double-acting hydraulic damper.

Vic Berris's masterly cutaway drawing shows how the pivots of each trailing arm are angled to provide progressive changes in the wheel's attitude as it moves above or below the static mean. When the car is cornered fast, the outer rear wheel assumes a negative camber (that is, leans in at the top) which increases stability and cornering power. The rear-end geometry provides complete freedom from lift when the brakes are applied hard. Roll-centre is about 4 in. above ground level, near the parallel roll axis.

Constant velocity inboard universals on the half-axles are the ball-and-trunnion Detroit type, and the outers normal Hooke-type Hardy-Spicers.

Carrying the entire front assembly—engine, transmission, steering and suspension—is a rigid, box-section subframe welded from sheet steel pressings, with four-point attachment to the car body underframe. The *Vibrashock* mountings in this case are supplemented by heavy coil springs. A short Panhard rod anchored between a point on the front of the sub-frame and the main structure provides positive trans-

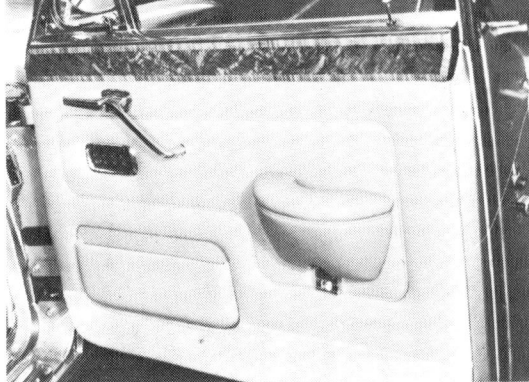

Driver's door has a map pocket, adjustable armrest, switches for all four electric window lifts

verse location. The upper suspension wishbones are one-piece fabrications from sheet steel, whereas the very long two-piece lower links are substantial forgings. Their trunnion axes are tilted to provide about 68 per cent anti-dive under heavy braking. Front wheel range of movement is given as 4 in. on both bump and rebound; at the back it is $3\frac{1}{2}$ in. on bump, $5\frac{1}{2}$ in. on rebound.

An American (Saginaw) recirculating ball steering gear, with constant ratio (19·3 to 1) and a built-in ram for the power assistance, is new to Rolls-Royce. It is fed, as on the Silver Cloud, by a belt-driven Hobourn-Eaton pump and compared with the earlier car the steering load—already light—is reduced still further, as is the turning circle. The column is divided and kinked for safety (and, of course, convenience of installation), having one rubber coupling and one ball-and-trunnion type. A lever-arm hydraulic damper is incorporated in the steering idler. The two-spoke steering-wheel defies tradition for a Rolls-Royce or Bentley; we must try to get used to it. At least it has the same slender rim section and diameter as the old three-spoke article.

Now that Harry Grylls, chief engineer at Crewe, no longer has to explain away drum brakes and a live rear axle, we might ask him: Why not fuel injection for the vee-8 engine? To shift the sparking-plugs

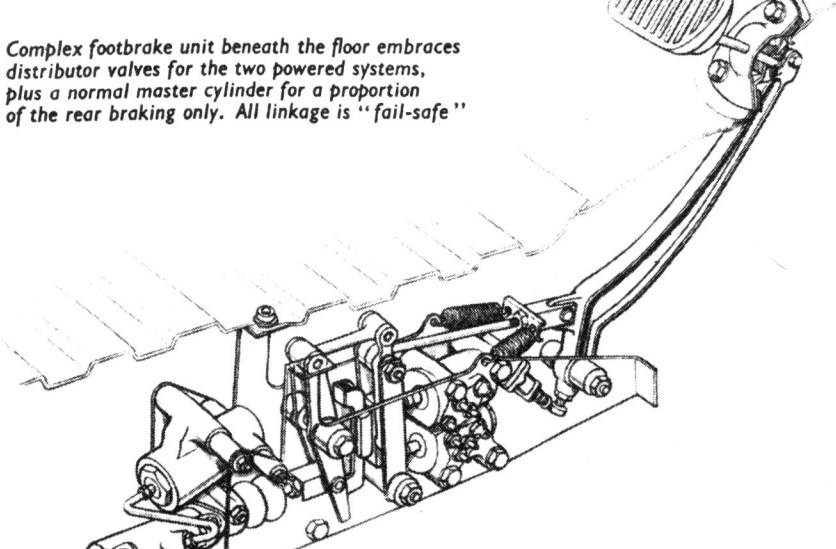

Complex footbrake unit beneath the floor embraces distributor valves for the two powered systems, plus a normal master cylinder for a proportion of the rear braking only. All linkage is "fail-safe"

Specification

ENGINE

Cylinders	8 in 90 deg vee
Cooling system	Water; pump, fan and thermostat
Bore	104·1 mm (4·10 in.)
Stroke	91·4 mm (3·60 in.)
Displacement	6,230 c.c. (380·5 cu. in.)
Valve gear	Overhead in-line, pushrods and rockers, hydraulic tappets
Compression ratio	9·0 to 1; option 8·0
Carburettors	2 diaphragm type S.U. HD8
Fuel pumps	2 S.U. electric
Oil filter	Full-flow, renewable paper element

TRANSMISSION

	Automatic 4-speed with fluid coupling and electric selection
Gear ratios	Top 1·00; Third 1·45; Second 2·63; First 3·82; Reverse 4·30
Final drive	Hypoid bevel, 3·08

CHASSIS AND BODY

Construction	Steel monocoque with separate front and rear sub-frames. Alloy doors, bonnet, boot lid

SUSPENSION

Front	Independent, double wishbone geometry, coil springs, Girling telescopic dampers, automatic hydraulic height control, anti-roll stabilizer
Rear	Independent, single trailing arms, coil springs, Girling telescopic dampers, automatic hydraulic height control

STEERING

Type	Saginaw recirculating ball, integral power assistance
Turns, lock-to-lock	4; steering-wheel dia. 17 in.

BRAKES

Make and type	Rolls-Royce-Girling, front discs each with two single calipers, rear discs each with one dual caliper, power assistance from two engine-driven hydraulic pumps, three independent foot-brake systems
Dimensions	F and R, 11 in. dia.
Swept area	F, 227sq. in.: R, 286sq. in. Total 513sq. in.

WHEELS

Type	Pressed steel disc, five studs, 6in. wide rim

ROLLS-ROYCE SILVER SHADOW...

from their previously inaccessible position beneath the exhaust manifolds, and place them where they can be reached with ease above the manifolds, has meant a considerable redesign of the head. The new combustion chamber shape, shown in cross-section on these pages, allegedly adds about 2 per cent to a maximum output which the manufacturers will never reveal.

The engine is three-point mounted, the single front mounting being on a bridge piece bolted between the steering box on one side and idler arm casting on the other. Rear mountings are on the sub-frame itself. Three silencers are included in the exhaust system, all of them stainless steel, the front one being lagged with asbestos and sheathed in aluminium for heat and sound insulation.

Hydraulic accumulator has butyl diaphragm separator between the nitrogen chamber (below) and oil. Valves above return pump delivery to reservoir when pressure exceeds 2,500 p.s.i.

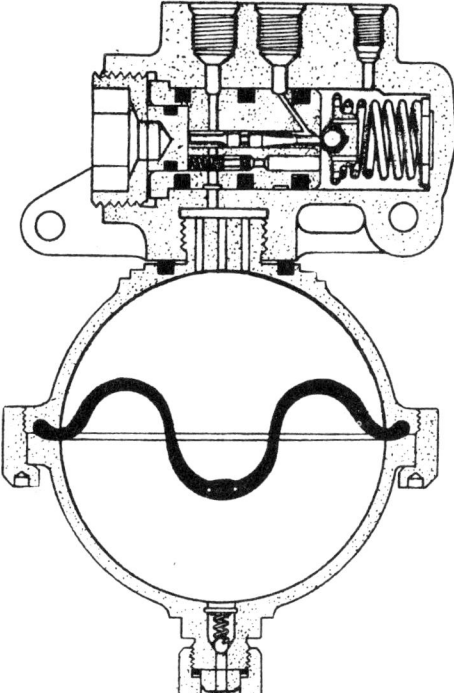

To achieve a low bonnet line the header tank has been divorced from the radiator; there is no overflow catch-tank. For the same reason the air cleaner has been buried down in the forepart of the right-hand wing beside the radiator, and leads to the twin S.U. diaphragm-type carburettors through flexible trunking.

For the first time, also, the bonnet is a one-piece aluminium pressing hinged on counterbalanced links just behind the radiator shell. It is lined with a heavy quilt for sound-deadening —another innovation for Rolls-Royce —and released or pulled shut positively by a substantial lever under the facia.

While retaining their 4-speed automatic transmission with simple fluid coupling, Rolls-Royce have incorporated several significant improvements. The main casing and some of the internal castings are now of aluminium instead of iron, the oil sealing is said to have been improved, and a free-wheel has been added for first and second, particularly to smooth out the big jump down from third to second. But with the second speed hold selected the free-wheel is inoperative and there is full engine braking.

A nice innovation is an electric motor to do the main physical labour of selecting the gears; the driver has a small lever, finger-light to move, which sends its instructions through a five-way switch. The electrical circuits are protected by an overload switch; if this should cut out for any reason, it can be reset by pressing a red button in the fuse box. For emergency get-you-home use there is a tommy bar in the tool-kit; for direct manual changes one inserts this in a hole in the top of the gearbox, after lifting the carpet.

The electric motor is bolted to the back of the aluminium casing containing the actuating mechanism, the whole unit being attached to the rear extension of the transmission casing. There are mechanical links to the selector levers.

Electrical services are supplied by a 12-volt battery with negative earth, charged by a 35-amp dynamo; cars equipped with the optional refrigeration unit have an alternator instead. Considerable use is made of printed circuits, these being employed behind the fuse box, under the seat switches, in the coolant level probe, for the relay box under the bonnet, and for the air-conditioning switches if fitted. Multi-pin sockets are also used where practical. Typical of the Rolls-Royce approach to motoring safety is a system of relays

Engine installation in the Bentley showing the cold-air ducting for the carburettors from a filter housed in the off-side wing. The tops of the suspension units can be seen each side

ROLLS-ROYCE

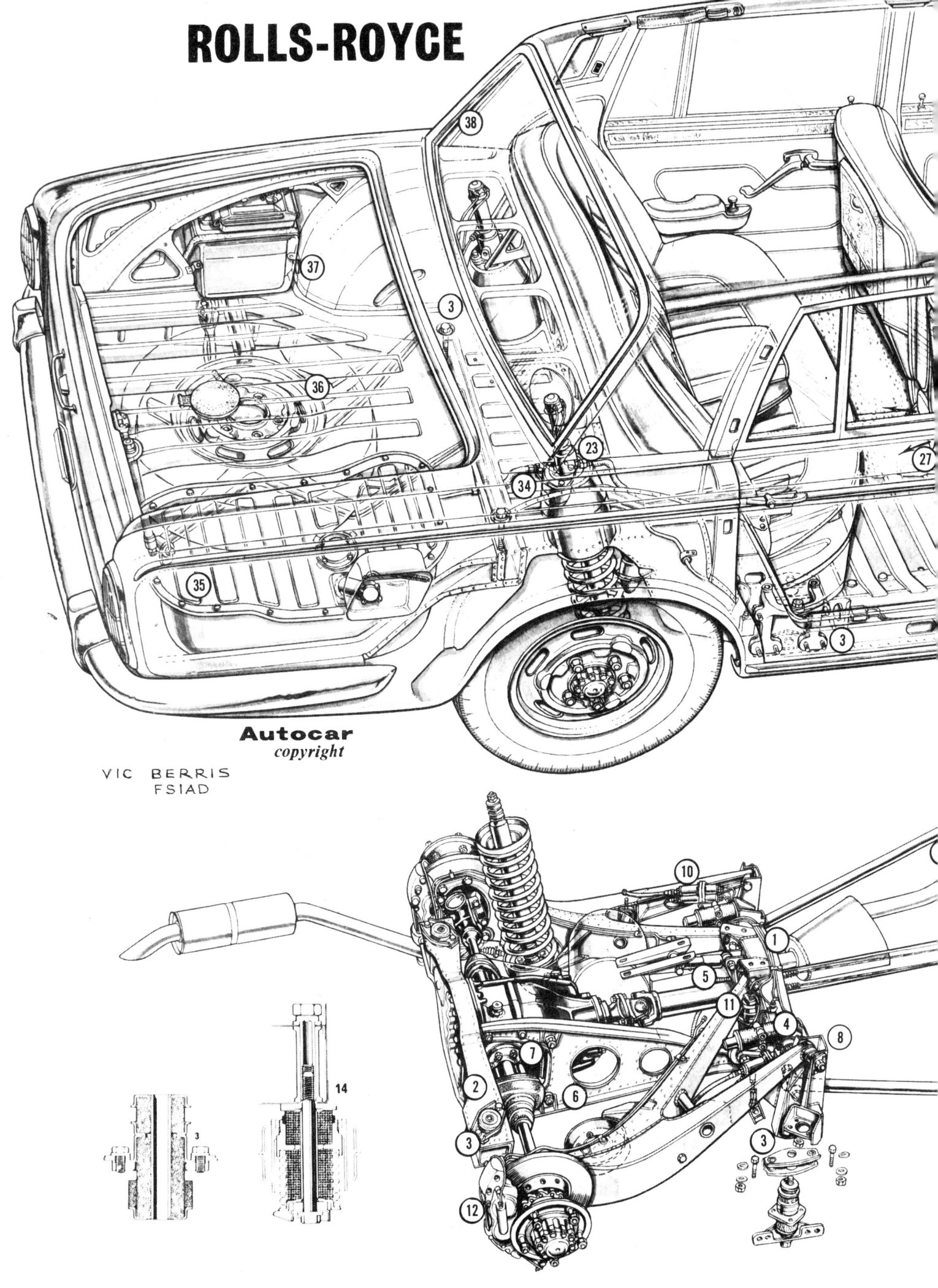

Autocar
copyright

VIC BERRIS
FSIAD

Sub-frame mountings embody new compressible bushes of stainless steel mesh. They provide closely controlled freedom of movement to absorb shock and road noise

SILVER SHADOW

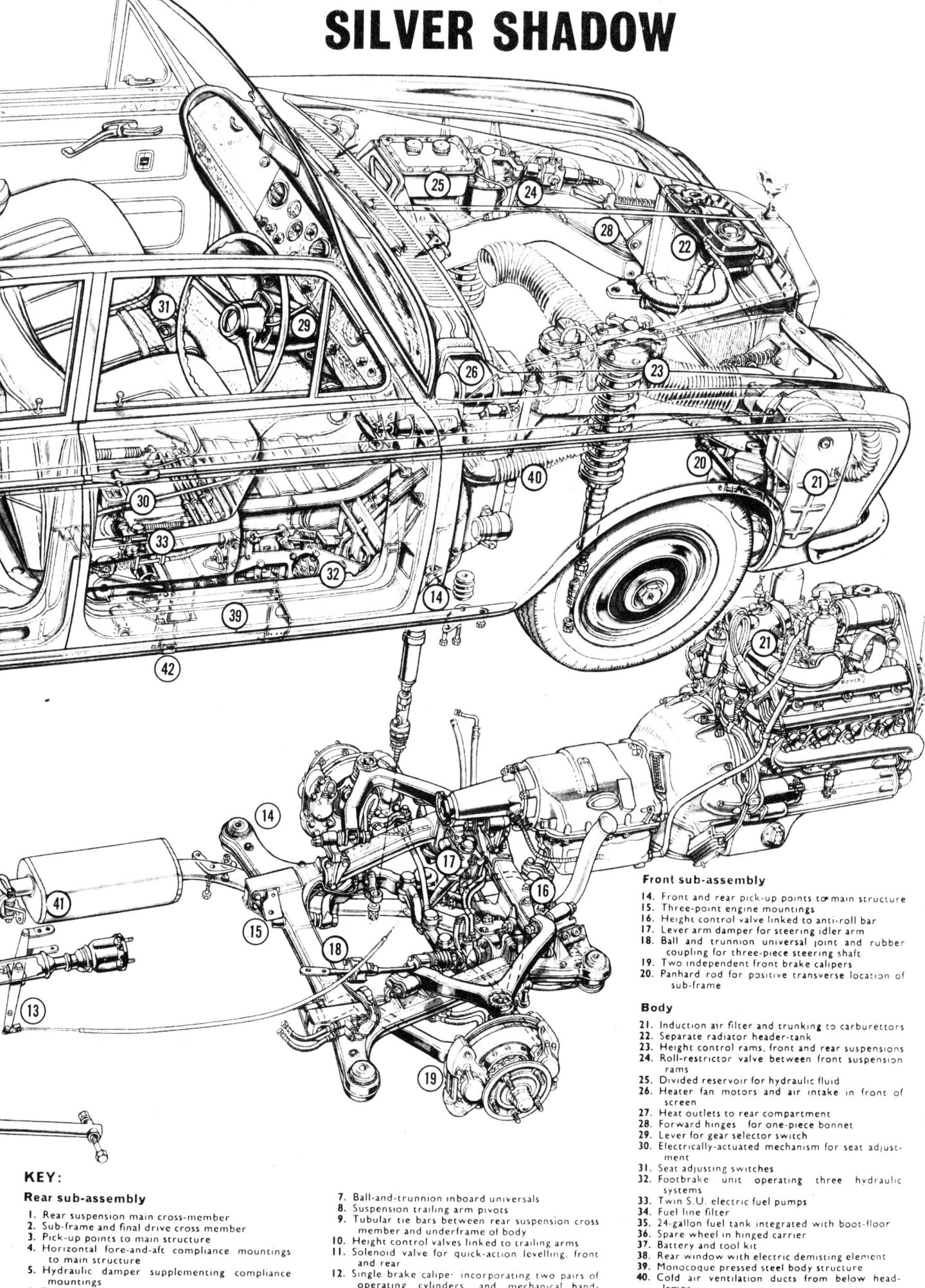

Front sub-assembly

14. Front and rear pick-up points to main structure
15. Three-point engine mountings
16. Height control valve linked to anti-roll bar
17. Lever arm damper for steering idler arm
18. Ball and trunnion universal joint and rubber coupling for three-piece steering shaft
19. Two independent front brake calipers
20. Panhard rod for positive transverse location of sub-frame

Body

21. Induction air filter and trunking to carburettors
22. Separate radiator header-tank
23. Height control rams, front and rear suspensions
24. Roll-restrictor valve between front suspension rams
25. Divided reservoir for hydraulic fluid
26. Heater fan motors and air intake in front of screen
27. Heat outlets to rear compartment
28. Forward hinges for one-piece bonnet
29. Lever for gear selector switch
30. Electrically-actuated mechanism for seat adjustment
31. Seat adjusting switches
32. Footbrake unit operating three hydraulic systems
33. Twin S.U. electric fuel pumps
34. Fuel line filter
35. 24-gallon fuel tank integrated with boot-floor
36. Spare wheel in hinged carrier
37. Battery and tool kit
38. Rear window with electric demisting element
39. Monocoque pressed steel body structure
40. Cold air ventilation ducts from below head-lamps
41. Exhaust system with four stainless steel silencers
42. Central jacking points

KEY:

Rear sub-assembly

1. Rear suspension main cross-member
2. Sub-frame and final drive cross member
3. Pick-up points to main structure
4. Horizontal fore-and-aft compliance mountings to main structure
5. Hydraulic damper supplementing compliance mountings
6. Torque arm bolted to final drive casing, coupled to rear suspension cross member
7. Ball-and-trunnion inboard universals
8. Suspension trailing arm pivots
9. Tubular tie bars between rear suspension cross member and underframe of body
10. Height control valves linked to trailing arms
11. Solenoid valve for quick-action levelling, front and rear
12. Single brake caliper incorporating two pairs of operating cylinders, and mechanical handbrake caliper
13. Mechanical linkage to handbrake caliper

Tyres	8·45-15 in. low profile

EQUIPMENT

Battery	12-volt 64 amp. hr
Generator	Lucas 35-amp
Fuel tank	24 Imp. gallons (109 litres) (warning lamp for 3-gal. reserve)
Cooling system	28 pints (16 litres)
Engine sump	14·5 pints (8 litres)
Gearbox and fluid coupling	24 pints (13·6 litres)
Final drive	4 pints (2·3 litres)

DIMENSIONS (manufacturer's figures)

Wheelbase	9 ft 11·5 in. (304 cm)
Track: front and rear	4 ft 9·5 in. (146 cm)
Overall length	16 ft 11·5 in. (517 cm)
Overall width	5 ft 11 in. (180 cm)
Overall height (unladen)	4 ft 11·75 in. (152 cm)
Ground clearance (laden)	6·5 in. (16·5 cm)
Turning circle	38 ft (11·6 m)
Kerb weight (with half-full fuel tank)	40·6 cwt, 4,546 lb. (2,062 kg)

PERFORMANCE DATA

Top gear m.p.h. per 1,000 r.p.m.	26·2

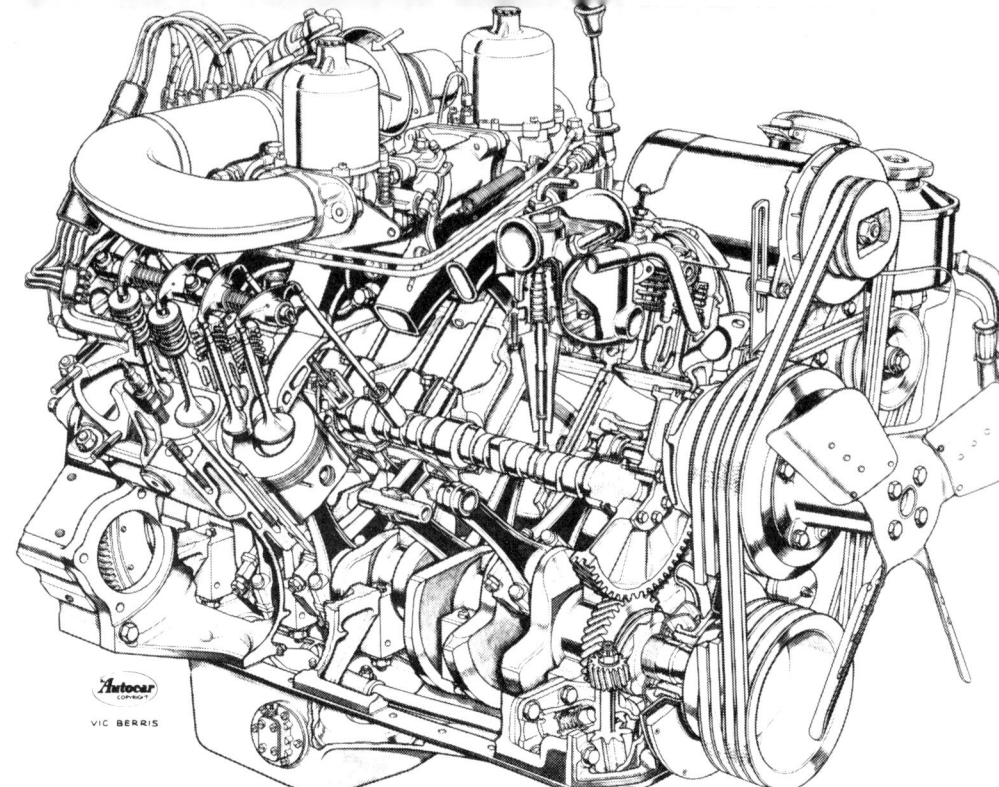

Autocar COPYRIGHT

VIC BERRIS

Revised engine showing new and enlarged porting with sparking-plugs now accessible above exhaust manifold. One of the two camshaft-driven hydraulic plunger pumps can be seen in the drawing above

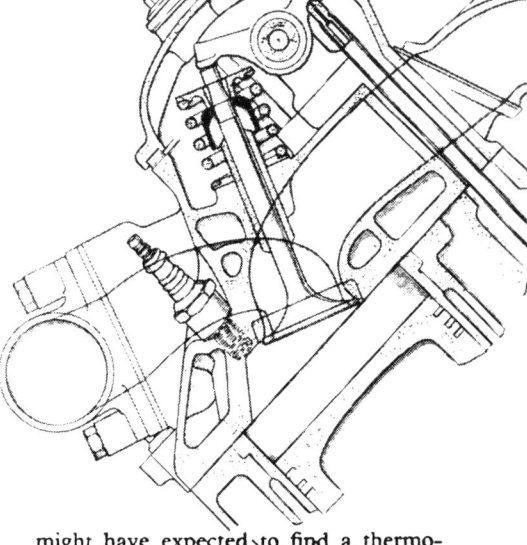

by which, if one filament in either of the outer headlamps fails, the other is lit automatically without delay.

As well as for the window lifts and seat adjustment, electric operation is used to raise and lower the radio aerial, demist the back window by built-in heater wires, and release the fuel filler trap-door. Separate switches on the dash illuminate right or left side and tail lamps for parking, and when these are lit the ignition cannot be switched on. An automatic red warning lamp for following traffic is built into the armrest on each back door.

It must have been a momentous decision to go over to a unitary structure for the chassis frame and body, made easier, of course, by the sad reduction in the number of specialist coachbuilders; and of the survivors, the biggest (H. J. Mulliner and Park Ward) belongs to Rolls-Royce anyhow. Pressed Steel, who have been responsible for the standard steel bodies for Rolls-Royce and Bentley cars for many years past, have been entrusted with the new composite structure. Without the subframes added, it has a torsional stiffness of about 10,000-11,000 lb per degree.

Although the Silver Cloud III and Bentley S3 will remain in production for the time being in standard and long wheelbase forms to carry the specialist bodies, there seems no reason why the Shadow structure should not be adapted for this purpose. Practically all the many Italian special bodies are based on integral structures of some sort.

Inevitably the Shadow will be now somewhat dwarfed beside most of the U.S. extravaganza, but the Rolls-Royce attitude is that, since they obviously cannot make their car in two sizes—one to suit their home customers and another for Americans—the home buyer must have preference. While an extra 2in. of shoulder room and the fact that the back seat is now ahead of the wheel arches have made the Shadow a bit more spacious than the standard Cloud, it is still essentially a four-seater, the cushions being rolled and bolstered to make a third person in the back feel little more welcome than a grub in a lettuce leaf. For four, the seating is, of course, extremely comfortable. There are the usual folding picnic tables behind the front seats, together with ashtrays and lighters, and small vanity mirrors in the quarters between side and rear windows. Footroom is generous, the small transmission tunnel being unobtrusive, and there are loose footrests.

All adjustments of the front seats, except that of varying the included angle between cushion and backrest, are now performed electrically. Back or front of the cushion can be lifted or lowered independently. Two simple switches—one for each seat—govern every movement; they are placed above the transmission tunnel between the front seats.

The Rolls-Royce and Bentley driver will no longer sit head and shoulders above most other motorists, but it is good to find that the Rolls-Royce pedal levers still disappear through the toe board, as distinct from the pendant type. On the restyled instrument panel, still with wood veneer facings, the main dials are now directly in front of the driver instead of grouped in the centre.

There are warning lamps or tell-tales for low level of fuel, handbrake left on (or stop-lamp bulb failure), lack of hydraulic pressure in either system, engine oil pressure, low coolant level and ignition.

Air intake for the standard heating and ventilation system is now just in front of the windscreen, supplemented by two fresh air pick-ups ducted from the front of the car to outlets each side of the scuttle and through the facia. There are independent blowers left and right, and one can divide the flow up and down in the usual way as well as having it delivered at different temperatures. Floor-level outlets are ducted to the rear compartment, but lack the means to close them. One

might have expected to find a thermostatic device in the system to hold any desired temperature more or less constant, and possibly extractor vents to encourage through-flow as this is known to increase heater efficiency considerably. It would be a pity if one needs to open a window to encourage this.

The layout of the refrigeration unit has been completely revised. On the former car the main components were housed in the right-hand front wing valance, but in the latest one space has been found for the evaporator behind the facia, as well as heater matrices which were also previously housed in the wing. As before, the compressor is belt-driven from the crankshaft and the condenser placed just ahead of the radiator.

Prices of these outstanding new models, including purchase tax, are increased by £924 in the case of the Rolls-Royce, £1,003 for the Bentley. The Silver Shadow is listed at £5,425 basic, £6,556 with tax, and the Bentley T-Series costs £5,375 basic, £6,496 with tax. ∎

Rolls-Royce Silver Shadow 6,230 c.c.

AT A GLANCE: An exceptionally comfortable and refined car, with soft springing and high, effortless cruising speed. Powerful and progressive brakes. Steering generally good but slow response when driving fast. Car quiet, tyres often relatively noisy. Lavishly equipped and important services duplicated. Has a finish to be proud of—inside and out.

MANUFACTURER:
Rolls-Royce Ltd., Pyms Lane, Crewe, Cheshire

PRICES:
Basic	£5,425	0s 0d
Purchase Tax	£1,244	19s 0d
Total (in G.B.) ..	£6,669	19s 0d

EXTRAS (inc. P.T.)
Refrigeration system ..	£178	4s 7d
Inertia reel seat belts—front (pair) ..	£19	19s 7d

PERFORMANCE SUMMARY
Mean maximum speed	115 m.p.h.
Standing start ¼-mile.. ..	17·6 sec
0-60 m.p.h.	10·9 sec
30-70 m.p.h. (through gears)	10·9 sec
Fuel consumption ..	13 m.p.g.
Miles per tankful	360

FOR so long accepted as the best car in the world, and probably still so, the Rolls-Royce is inevitably judged by the highest standards. This means that even minor criticism, acceptable in a lesser car, is likely to be regarded as very serious. Today such standards are no longer entirely realistic. The mechanical parts of ordinary inexpensive cars have become so much better; expensive cars can simply add top quality materials, luxurious equipment, a desirable elaboration of services, and a lot of personal and individual attention to details of design and finish. Relatively, but not actually of course, no expense is spared to please the customer; even so there is no reason to expect design miracles of a Rolls-Royce, though every reason to look for top quality in the broadest sense.

This Silver Shadow we have been testing is the latest of its kind, just nicely run in at 4,500 miles. It includes those modifications which are "part of the continuous process of development and improvement which Rolls-Royce carries out" discreetly and usually without mention.

If you look under the bonnet at the extremely full engine compartment, you will detect, from the necessary complication and the quality of detail design and finish around the aluminium vee-8 engine, where a fair proportion of the cost goes. The car was fully described in *Autocar* of 8 October 1965 but such is the extent of the equipment and the elaboration of systems and reserve systems that we have provided a page of refresher notes at the end of this test report.

First and foremost, the Silver Shadow is a superlative journey car for driver as well as for passengers. Those of us who took the car to France and Switzerland, as well as across England, were unanimous in our favourable comments on a complete absence of tiredness or tension at the end of a long day on the roads. The ride is considerably more level and comfortable than in the Silver Cloud this Shadow replaces, and the damping over humps or hollows is very good indeed. Cobbles, including the rough test sections at M.I.R.A., are traversed with the minimum of disturbance to passengers.

Suggestions that this car is less imposing or that you sit too low are no more than first impressions of traditionalists; the same kind of thing was said of previous models when they were new.

Contributing to the relaxed travel are the elaborate air conditioning system, the eight-way power adjusted front seats with additional recline control, the mechanical quietness and the excellent look-out all round. On the negative side is tyre noise, which, according to whether the car is on smooth tarmac or on coarse dressed or ribbed surfaces, varies from quiet to noisy. Passengers sitting back in the rear seats hear more from the tyres than those in front and there is additional rumble when cornering. In contrast, there is very little wind noise so you can talk normally or listen to the radio (balanced front and rear speakers) at 100 m.p.h. This Rolls-Royce is a gentle car by nature, and one wonders if it has not been developed with more than an eye on the American market where straight-line speeds seldom exceed 80 m.p.h., brisk acceleration is essential and a soft ride is demanded.

Our test car had the slightly stiffer home suspension but was still softly sprung by British standards. It became a bit flustered if hurried through a combination of bends. This is because there is quite a lot of initial roll in front as you go into, or alter line through, a bend; and of course a reversal left to right or vice versa doubles the effect. So winding roads are better taken sedately. Even so, when we hurried the car round the test road circuit at M.I.R.A. on both dry and wet occasions, the roll proved to be firmly restrained after the first lean-over, and the adhesion was outstanding. We never made the back wheels slide.

Several people have asked expect-

TEST CONDITIONS
Weather: Cloudy, dry. Wind: 15-20 m.p.h.
Temperature: 18 deg. C. (64 deg. F.)
Barometer: 29·1in. Hg.
Humidity: 46 per cent
Surfaces: Dry concrete and asphalt

WEIGHT
Kerb weight 41·6 cwt (4,660 lb-2,067 kg) (with oil, water and half-full fuel tank)
Distribution, per cent: F, 54·6; R, 45·4
Laden as tested: 45·1 cwt (5,048 lb-2,243kg)

Figures taken at 4,100 miles by our own staff at the Motor Industry Research Association proving ground at Nuneaton.

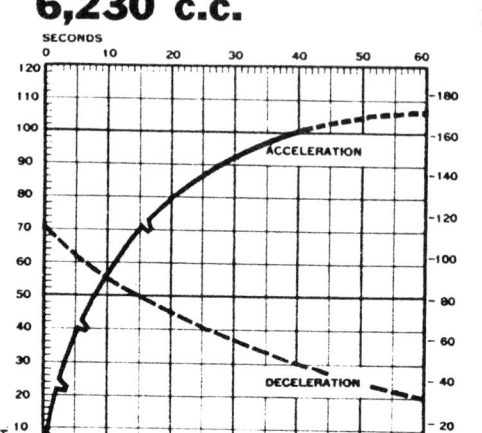

MAXIMUM SPEEDS

Gear	m.p.h.	k.p.h.	r.p.m.
Top (mean)	115	185	4,390
(best)	118	190	4,500
3rd	72	116	4,000*
2nd	43	69	4,350
1st	24	39	3,500*

*Maximum engine speed limited by automatic transmission in these gears

Standing ¼-mile 17·6 sec 76 m.p.h.
Standing Kilometre 33·0 sec 96 m.p.h.

FUEL CONSUMPTION

TIME IN SECONDS	3·4	5·3	7·8	10·9	14·3	19·7	26·9	37·8	
TRUE SPEED M.P.H.	30	40	50	60	70	80	90	100	110
INDICATED SPEED	31	41	52	62	72	82	92	102	112

Mileage recorder 1·2 per cent over-reading.　　　Test distance 2,285 miles.

Speed range, gear ratios and time in seconds

m.p.h.	Top (3·08)	3rd (4·46)	2nd (8·10)	1st (11·75)
10— 30	—	—	2·9	—
20— 40	—	4·8	3·3	—
30— 50	7·2	5·1	—	—
40— 60	7·5	5·7	—	—
50— 70	8·5	6·8	—	—
60— 80	10·5	—	—	—
70— 90	13·1	—	—	—
80—100	15·8	—	—	—

(At constant speeds—m.p.g.)

30 m.p.h.	19·6
40	17·9
50	16·5
60	15·2
70	14·4
80	13·1
90	11·6
100	10·0

Typical m.p.g. Fast Continental touring 11 (25·7 litres/100km)
Typical m.p.g. Gentle touring 15 (18·8 litres/100km)
Calculated (DIN) m.p.g. 13·1 (21·6 litres/100km)
Overall m.p.g. 12·2 (23·2 litres/100km)
Grade of fuel, Premium (96·8-98·8 RM)

OIL CONSUMPTION
Miles per pint (SAE 10W/30) .. 800

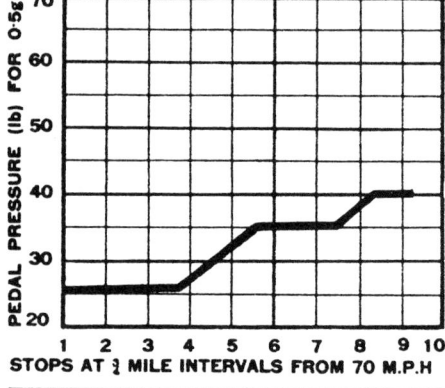

STOPS AT ¼ MILE INTERVALS FROM 70 M.P.H.

BRAKES (from 30 m.p.h. in neutral)

Load	g	Distance
25lb	0·43	70 ft
50 „	0·75	40 „
75 „	0·88	34·2 „
90 „	0·97	31·0 „
Handbrake	0·29	104 „

Max. Gradient 1 in 6

TURNING CIRCLES
Between kerbs, L, 37ft 8in.; R, 39ft 0in.
Between walls L, 40ft 0in.; R, 41ft 2in.
Steering wheel turns, lock to lock, 4·25

HOW THE CAR COMPARES.
MAXIMUM SPEED (mean) M.P.H.

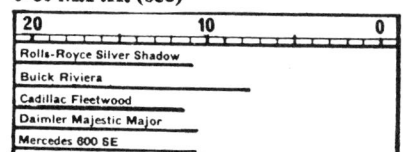

90　100　110　120　130
- Rolls-Royce Silver Shadow
- Buick Riviera
- Cadillac Fleetwood
- Daimler Majestic Major
- Mercedes 600 SE

0–60 M.P.H. (sec)
20　10　0
- Rolls-Royce Silver Shadow
- Buick Riviera
- Cadillac Fleetwood
- Daimler Majestic Major
- Mercedes 600 SE

STANDING START ¼-MILE (sec)
30　20　10
- Rolls-Royce Silver Shadow
- Buick Riviera
- Cadillac Fleetwood
- Daimler Majestic Major
- Mercedes 600 SE

M.P.G. OVERALL
0　10　20
- Rolls-Royce Silver Shadow
- Buick Riviera
- Cadillac Fleetwood
- Daimler Majestic Major
- Mercedes 600 SE

PRICES

Rolls-Royce Silver Shadow	£6,670
Buick Riviera	£4,402
Cadillac Fleetwood	£5,164
Daimler Majestic Major	£2,749
Mercedes 600SE	£8,968

Right: A comfortable, luxuriously fitted rear compartment for two people and with room for three. Note the red warning lamps in the backs of the arm rests. Left: Large, deeply, upholstered seats with eight-way electric adjustment and recline. Workmanship on leather and wood is of high order for a semi-production car

Rolls-Royce . . .

antly "What do you think of the steering?" and we wonder what answers they expected. It is of power-assisted, recirculating-ball type. It is sensitive and lighter than previously and has constant ratio. We think it is good except in one respect, and that is the response around the neutral position. From the straight ahead point the wheel has to be moved up to a sixth of a turn before the nose of the car follows—almost leisurely. The slower you drive the less apparent is this slow response.

One result is that gusty side winds, and uneven cambers such as we met across France, take the car from side to side before the driver can check it. A second result is that corners must be taken early and held firmly or the car will run wide. Third, we did not find it easy to place the car to an inch—to six inches, yes. The more pronounced understeer, disguised in part by the power steering, no doubt arises from the forward position of the engine and the 55 per cent front, 45 per cent rear weight distribution.

In other respects the steering is good and the car's own directional stability is excellent at all speeds, the new independent rear suspension coping admirably on rolling Continental roads. With tyre noise and steering in mind we look forward to trying a Shadow on radial covers one day.

Performance, as we have said earlier, has an American (and now home) market bias towards the 0–70 m.p.h. bracket. The acceleration from a standstill is excellent for this sizeable car. By speeding the engine up in gear and holding momentarily on the foot brake—a reasonable procedure where a maximum getaway is desired—we recorded a best standing quarter-mile time of 17·5sec on more than one occasion. The acceleration continues vigorously to about 75 m.p.h., when the automatic up-change to top occurs (and if set at 3, the

manual hold is also over-ridden). Thereafter it is quite brisk up to 90. Occasionally, in France, when beginning to overtake at about 70 m.p.h., we were "left hanging" with no kick-down and insufficient punch in top (4). Left-hand drive export cars, like one we sampled in Geneva, are better placed, having an American-type three-speed transmission with torque converter, which gives about 85 m.p.h. in middle ratio, so closing the big gap of the Rolls-Royce 4-speed epicyclic box.

The gear lever is light and sweet to use now that an electric selector is incorporated. Changes are very smooth — often undetected — either when selected or automatic. The single exception is the occasional jerk of a double kick-down that can occur, for example, when turning on to, and pulling away up, a steep hill.

Maximum speed these days is little more than a talking point; in favourable conditions owners may get 120 m.p.h. from the Shadow. A representative mean top speed is 115 m.p.h., but more important is the effortless all-day cruising speed of around 100 m.p.h. at which, incidentally, fuel consumption is 10·0 m.p.g. A Conti-

nental journey figure of 13 m.p.g. is normal, or in Britain up to 15 m.p.g. The 24-gallon tank thus gives a range of over 300 miles. The combination of very brisk acceleration and high cruising speeds returned unexpectedly high journey averages even when we were not trying particularly hard. We would plan on an easy 400 miles a day across Europe and expect to have a good lunch and time for a bath before dinner.

Rolls-Royce take tremendous trouble over their brakes and are using discs all round for the first time. They are excellent, with a reassuring bite, light pressure and more than average progression. One of our drivers thought there was a fraction of delay as compared with the early drum and engine-servo system of the Silver Cloud II which we re-tested at the same time (*Autocar*, 2 March)

The best stopping figure of 0·97g was difficult to record consistently, although the figure was always over 0·9g on dry surfaces. The rebound after the initial weight transfer forward would sometimes allow one wheel to lock prematurely. The tyres would also grip much better on some smooth surfaces than others. Con-

A formidable array under the bonnet can be sorted out quickly. Fillers are high and accessible and sparking plugs are now angled up for removal above the manifolds. Design and quality of parts is excellent

A large but unobtrusive tail with wrap-round bumper provides ample luggage space without upsetting the good balance of the car's appearance

sistent wet-road stops of 0·89g were usually good.

In rain we found that the first application of brakes after some miles without use, as on motorways, gave weaker and less even response. This is a well-known characteristic of cold, wet discs and pads. If our test car is representative, Rolls-Royce will have to think again about the hand parking brake. With a man's hard pull it gave a best figure of only 0·29 and barely held the car on a 1-in-6 slope.

With the 4-speed automatic transmission there is no "Park" position for the selector, but if reverse is selected and the engine switched off, a positive parking lock engages. On one occasion the reverse cone stuck in engagement with the selector back in neutral.

Intricate details of the air conditioning system and its controls are described elsewhere. A driver quickly learns to use them, and we do not know of another car which can produce so many different currents or blasts of hot, warm or icy cold outside or recirculated air on request. The numerous flap valves have actuators which buzz when operating "so you know they are working." If we say

that when the next Rolls-Royce is designed we hope it will have just as good and flexible a system but with fewer (and safer) control knobs, we are not being ungrateful for this one, which does its job very well indeed. The engine warm-up to give heating was slow. With the refrigeration system goes tinted glass all round, and there is an efficient electrically heated rear window.

The refrigerator control overrides all the heater controls. The amount of cold air delivered is adjusted with the aid of one main blower motor with four strengths and two adjustable outlets for fresh air. In addition, an air-conditioning flap which looks like a drawer in the middle of the instrument panel, can be opened to allow a very large extra flow into the car.

The eight-way front seats, controlled by a tiny horizontal "joy stick" working in the natural sense, are well shaped and luxuriously padded, with just the right amount of firmness in the cushions. Leather is used generously for seats and trim. Some people thought that the rear seat cushions should be at least an inch longer fore-and-aft; otherwise they, too, are very comfortable. Small,

separate, wedge-shaped footrests are provided. There are folding central armrests front and back, also ashtrays, lighters, the usual two folding tables, mirrors, a reading and a general lamp and a map pocket for each rear passenger.

A four headlamp system is used which, considering the relatively small diameter of the individual lamps, provides an unusually penetrating full beam. The dipped position is well cut off and gives an adequate spread of light. No separate auxiliary lamps are provided.

Among lighting details in the exceptionally complete system may be noted the parking lamp selector switch—left or right. This is in circuit with the starter, which cannot be energised if either parking lamp is on. If the main lighting switch is pulled out, though everything else is locked off, it lights a small lamp above the ignition keyhole.

There are four warning lamps in a group: reds for the two brake accumulators; green to warn that only three gallons of fuel remain; and amber to show both that the handbrake is on or that a stop lamp bulb has failed. To test these warning lamps, switch on the ignition and press the oil level button. In addition to indicating oil level on the petrol gauge, the four warning lamps should all show.

A switch above the rear view mirror is for hazard warning and it has its own tell-tale. This causes all four front and rear signal lamps to flash automatically—as allowed by new safety regulations. Door-open red warning lamps are provided only for the rear doors and they are situated in the backs of the armrests. They are switched on also by the front doors. In a tray under the facia is a businesslike fuse box with all its 20 circuits labelled on a separate pull-out panel.

In the carpeted boot there is an auxiliary or charging socket to save baring the battery terminals behind their covers. Here also is a fitted tool- ▶

A trimmed and carpeted boot of generous capacity. The carefully packed tools are laid out for inspection and the battery uncovered. Just visible behind it is the accessory socket

kit and, in the floor under the carpet, a small cover which lifts to expose the spare wheel valve for checking pressure. Inertia reel harness is provided in front, and all doors have safety locks. It is a pleasure to insert and turn the key and feel the smooth action of the Rolls-Royce Yale locks after the rubbishy stuff on some other cars. Perhaps a master lock for the doors and boot lid will be introduced

one day; we have found it a great convenience on certain other cars in this class.

R-R and Bentley owners of a few years ago asked for a smaller, livelier car but with more room inside; this Shadow is 6·75in. shorter (16ft 11·5in.) and 3·75in. narrower (5ft 11in.), yet it has greater internal and boot space than the Silver Cloud III. It is also 4·5in. lower but it weighs fraction-

ally less. It feels a smaller and more stable car to handle in traffic or on the open road, and you can see out better all round. Having lived with the Rolls-Royce Silver Shadow for several weeks, we have no hesitation in describing it as a worthy successor to the Clouds and Phantoms. Nor have we any doubts that fortunate owners will enjoy tremendous satisfaction and service from their Shadows. ■

SPECIFICATION : ROLLS-ROYCE SILVER SHADOW (FRONT ENGINE, REAR-WHEEL DRIVE)

ENGINE
Cylinders	8, in vee
Cooling system	Water; pump, fan and two 90 deg thermostats
Bore	104mm (4.10in.)
Stroke	91.4mm (3.60in.)
Displacement	6,230 c.c. (380.5 cu. in.)
Valve gear	Overhead; hydraulic tappets, pushrods and rockers
Compression ratio	9.0-to-1
Optional	8.0-to-1
Carburettors	2 SU HD8
Fuel pump	2 SU electric
Oil filter	Full flow, renewable element
Max. power	Not disclosed by manufacturer
Max. torque	Not disclosed by manufacturer

TRANSMISSION
Gearbox	Rolls-Royce automatic epicyclic with fluid flywheel
Gear ratios	Top 1.0; Third 1.45; Second 2.63; First 3.82; Reverse 4.30
Final drive	Hypoid bevel, 3.08-to-1

CHASSIS AND BODY
Construction	Integral, with steel body, aluminium alloy bonnet, boot lid and doors; sub-frames for running gear

SUSPENSION
Front	Independent, coil springs, wishbones, telescopic dampers, anti-roll bar. Automatic hydraulic height control
Rear	Independent, coil springs, single trailing arms, telescopic dampers. Automatic hydraulic height control

STEERING
Type	Recirculating ball, with Saginaw power assistance
Wheel dia.	17in.

BRAKES
Make and type	Rolls-Royce Girling, front discs each with two single piston calipers, rear discs each with one dual piston caliper, three independent foot brake systems
Servo	Power assistance from two engine-driven hydraulic pumps
Dimensions	F, 11.0in. dia. R, 11.0in. dia.
Swept area	F, 227 sq. in. R, 286 sq. in.
Total	513 sq. in. (228 sq. in.) per ton laden

WHEELS
Type	Pressed steel disc, 5-stud fixing 6.0in. wide rim
Tyres: make	Dunlop, Avon or Firestone (Dunlop RS5 on test car)
—type	Low-profile cross-ply tubeless
—size	8.45—15in.

EQUIPMENT
Battery	12-volt 64 amp. hr.
Alternator	Lucas 11AC 45-amp
Headlamps	Lucas four headlamp system 100/37.5 watt
Reversing lamp	Standard
Electric fuses	20
Screen wipers	2-speed self-parking
Screen washer	Standard, Lucas electric
Interior heater	Standard, air-blending
Safety belts	Extra
Interior trim	Selected English hide seats, pvc headlining
Floor covering	Wilton carpet
Starting handle	No provision
Jack	Screw pillar
Jacking points	2, one each side under sills
Windscreen	Laminated
Underbody protection	Bitumastic on all surfaces exposed to road
Other bodies	H. J. Mulliner, Park Ward and James Young 2-door saloons

MAINTENANCE
Fuel tank	24 Imp gallons (107 litres) (low level warning lamp)
Cooling system	28 pints (including heater) (16 litres)
Engine sump	14.5 pints (8 litres) SAE 10W/30. Change oil every 6,000 miles; change filter element every 6,000 miles
Gearbox	24 pints ATF. Change oil every 12,000 miles
Final drive	4.5 pints SAE 90EP. Change oil every 24,000 miles
Grease	6 points every 12,000 miles
Tyre pressures	F, 26; R, 26 p.s.i. (normal driving)

PERFORMANCE DATA
Top gear m.p.h. per 1,000 r.p.m.	26.2
Mean piston speed at mean max speed	2,630 ft per min
B.h.p. per ton laden.	Not disclosed

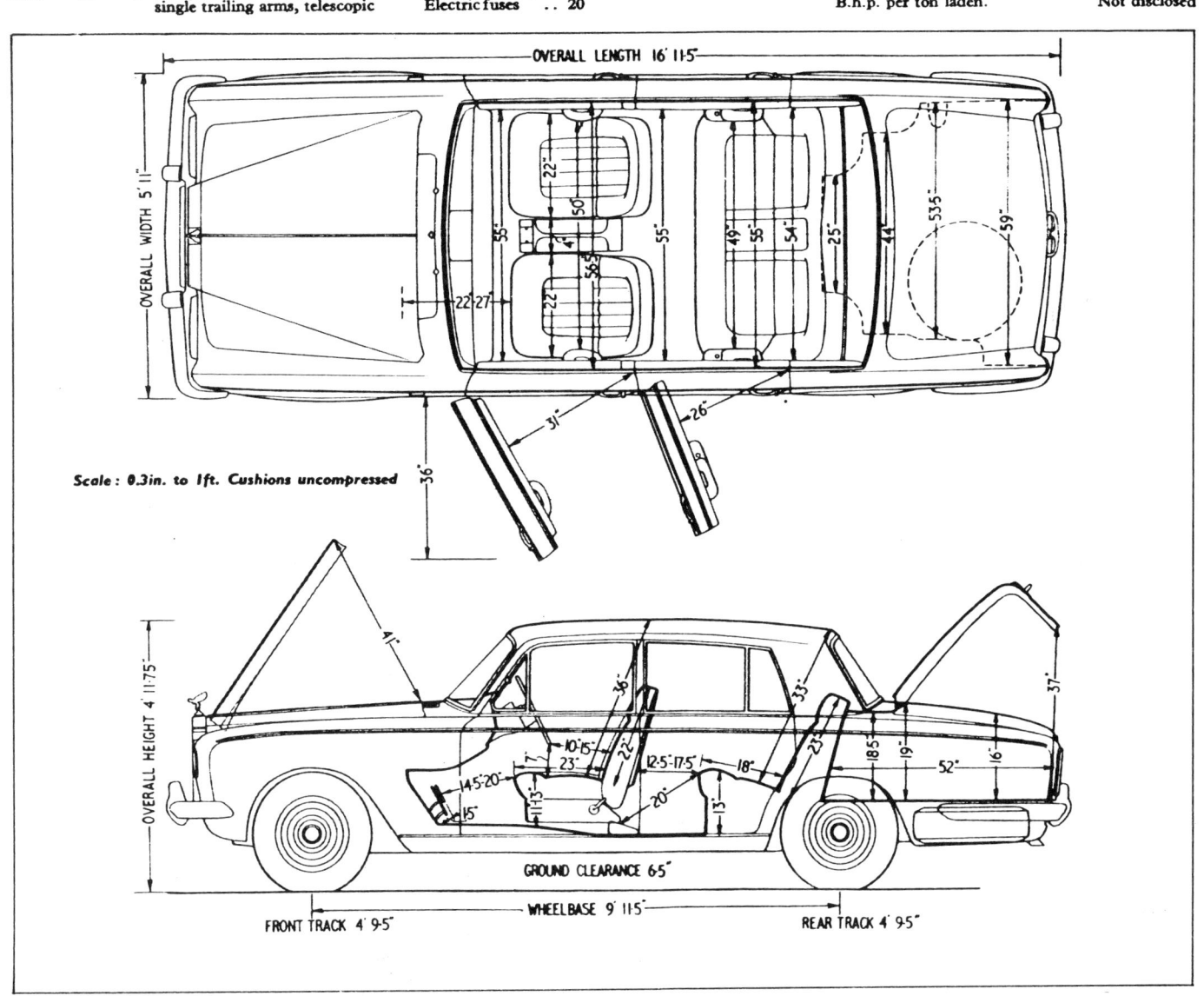

Scale: 0.3in. to 1ft. Cushions uncompressed

OVERALL LENGTH 16' 11·5"
OVERALL WIDTH 5' 11"
OVERALL HEIGHT 4' 11·75"
GROUND CLEARANCE 6·5"
WHEELBASE 9' 11·5"
FRONT TRACK 4' 9·5"
REAR TRACK 4' 9·5"

New Rolls-Royce CORNICHE

By Geoffrey Howard

More power, better interior and revised trim details for two-door H. J. Mulliner, Park Ward models

It was singularly appropriate that just when the overall fortunes of the company had suffered a devastating setback, Rolls-Royce should launch a new car. Of course there had been virtually no warning in the car division that a financial crisis was brewing, and being still a very solvent and profitable offshoot of the main aero-engine division, Rolls-Royce cars had specific instructions from the official receiver to continue as normal.

At first glance the idea of taking a small party of British journalists to the South of France to try the new model seemed totally incongruous with the immediate state of the company. Judged objectively the setting was absolutely right for sampling this new model, which is specifically named after the three roads which link Nice with Monte Carlo at different levels up the hillsides that rise so dramatically from the deep blue of the Mediterranean in this region. And after all, as David Plastow (managing director of the car division) pointed out, the whole operation cost substantially less than half one of the new cars.

Out-of-season Nice is still a busy place and an impending film festival brought many visitors to the town. The sight of no fewer than nine brand new Rolls-Royces lined up in front of the airport created quite a stir. When they moved off in a ragged sort of convoy along the *Promenade des Anglais,* the crowds out walking in the warm winter sunshine stared in wonderment. We felt like the liberation troops entering Paris and the whole scene began for me to take on a dream-like quality that never faded until we splashed down on to the wet tarmac at Gatwick the next day.

Above: Formidable line-up outside Nice airport. On the left is David Plastow, managing director of the car division

Below: The two-door saloon is particularly elegant in this view. Coachwork is by H. J. Mulliner, Park Ward

As well as introducing a new car, Rolls have instigated a new policy whereby the special-bodied models are to be engineering and styling leaders for the standard production cars of the future. The two-door saloon and convertible built by H. J. Mulliner, Park Ward have therefore been made more different from the standard Silver Shadow and will in future be known as the Corniche, in either Rolls or Bentley guise. They have a new, more powerful engine, a revised facia incorporating a rev counter, a wood-rimmed 15in. dia. steering wheel, new wheel trims and a deeper (fore and aft) radiator shell.

The engine is the latest 6,750 c.c. version of the Silver Shadow vee-8 unit with 10 per cent more power and better breathing in the upper rev ranges. Retiming the camshaft, removing the Federal anti-smog equipment, increasing the bore of the exhaust system from 2 to $2\frac{1}{4}$in. and fitting a more efficient air cleaner have all played their part in improving the engine characteristics. Because it does not comply with the US regulations on exhaust emissions this engine cannot be fitted to cars destined for the North America market; they will have the normal 6,750 c.c. Silver Shadow engine.

To improve engine cooling in heavy traffic the drive ratio to the fan has been stepped up, and the new wheel trims allow more air to get to the brakes.

The name Corniche was already registered by Rolls-Royce before the war when it was a prototype Mark V Bentley with a body incorporating some unusual aerodynamic features, built by van Vooren of Paris. It had completed 15,000 miles of endurance testing

8 ☛

New Rolls-Royce CORNICHE...

on the Continent when war broke out and it was blown up by a bomb while waiting to be shipped home on the quayside at Dieppe. *Corniche* itself can be translated as cornice, which in mountaineering terminology means an overhanging outcrop, hence the three coast roads along the Mediterranean cliffs.

By comparison with the last Silver Shadow we tested, which had the original 6,230 c.c. engine, the Corniche is a much more lively car. It really feels now as if the engine is large enough for the huge size and weight of the body, and its step off the mark from rest is now most impressive. At the top end it will run quite easily into the red sector on the rev counter (from 4,500 to 6,000 rpm) even in top gear (4,500 rpm is equivalent to 118 mph). The claim that the car will exceed 120 mph is therefore undoubtedly true, the example I drove reaching this speed on several occasions without any difficulty.

Smooth automatic transmission

Despite the extra torque, gearshifts in the three-speed General Motors automatic transmission are as silky smooth as ever and barely detectable most of the time. When using the selector to get engine braking on a descent it is very easy to stay in intermediate by mistake, so near silent is the engine.

No claims are made for suspension improvements, but there has been a progressive programme of development in this department and the latest car is much better than previous ones. Most of our criticisms of poor directional stability and slow steering response have been answered and the new small wheel helps a lot in giving the driver more feel of what is going on. There is still very strong understeer, largely disguised by the power steering, and excellent straight line running. Rolls now have their tyres made specially by Dunlop, Firestone and Avon, the car I drove being on Firestone F100 radials. There were some out-of-balance tremors at about 100 mph, but much less bump thump than before and no harshness.

One Rolls-Royce passing through the Franco-Italian border at Menton might cause little comment, two in close proximity take longer to clear, and with nine altogether we were in trouble on the Italian side. They were

Below: Rolls-Royce Corniche in convertible form, still a very popular version

Above: Script for the Corniche nameplate is in traditional Rolls style

suspicious of £115,000 of rolling bullion naturally enough and had not Rolls-Royce (France) thought to have a smooth-talking solicitor on hand our driving might have been confined to France alone. As it was we were able to make our way slowly to Genoa and then rush quite a way up the Turin *autostrada* before retracing our steps to Monaco and a night's stop at the Vistaero hotel, appropriately situated on the *Grande Corniche* overlooking the Cap Martin.

The price of the Corniche is about 10 per cent more than that of the previous two-door model, the saloon costing now just over £12,829 as a Rolls-Royce and £12,758 as a Bentley. The convertible is about £600 more. We look forward to carrying out a full test of the Corniche saloon later this year.

The Ultimate in Luxury?

A Unique Rolls-Royce Phantom VI

By Warren Allport and Stuart Bladon
Photography: Ron Easton

SINCE their one-model policy ended with the demise of the Silver Ghost in 1925, Rolls-Royce have offered a large model, capable of carrying the most spacious coachwork of the specialist coachbuilders and bearing the name Phantom. Before the war the smaller 20, 20-25 and 25-30 hp cars were made in comparatively large numbers compared with their larger brothers, the Phantoms. This trend is still continued today with almost 2,500 Silver Shadows a year being built at Crewe while a mere 50 Phantom VI models, one of which is the subject of this article, are produced.

The current Phantom VI has changed little since the introduction in 1959 of the Phantom V, on which it is based. This means, of course, that it belongs far more to the era of the Silver Cloud than to that of the Silver Shadow; for instance the Phantom VI's box-section chassis, all-drum brakes with a gearbox-driven servo, and semi-elliptic leaf spring rear suspension were all Silver Cloud features. This apart, the Phantom VI offers exceptional comfort for the rear seat passengers with all the prestige attached to the largest and most expensive Rolls-Royce limousine. This is a car that commands attention on occasions when even a Silver Shadow might pass unnoticed.

The Phantom VI was designed primarily as a chauffeur-driven car, and its large 145 in. wheelbase allows H. J. Mulliner,

Park Ward Ltd to mount on this chassis a limousine body built to the traditional high standards of the specialist coachbuilder. There is almost no limit to the individual alterations from the basic specification that H. J. Mulliner, Park Ward can make for a customer on a Phantom, but unfortunately very few customers seem to have any idea of the special features that could be provided. With this in mind, Rolls-Royce distributors Lex Mead (Maidenhead) Ltd have ordered for stock —this itself is most unusual as Phantom's are normally built to customer's specific order—a Rolls Royce Phantom VI with a number of modifications which make it unique. The majority of these changes have been made to the interior of the rear compartment, but even from the outside it is at once apparent to the Rolls-Royce connoisseur that this is no ordinary Phantom VI limousine.

Forward hinged doors and modified rear wings

Externally the car is finished in Black over Garnet, instead of the plain black which most customers specify even though the car can be finished in any colour the customer wishes; and on each front wing is a flagstaff mount. Stainless steel trim strips have been added along the sills and round the wheelarches and the chrome waist mouldings have been extended rearwards to meet the roofline. Above the

driving compartment is a glass roof panel with interior curtains that run on a pair of transverse rails. This glass panel makes the driving compartment seem very light and airy with a distinct sense of being in an open car. Further careful study of the exterior will reveal that this is one of the first Phantom VI cars to be fitted with forward-hinged rear doors—a feature now standard on all Phantoms. On this particular car the rear wing line has been modified to give a chopped-off effect and hooded rear lamps —very similar to those used on Bentley Continental S3 models—are incorporated. To afford the owner greater privacy, Purdah glass—which makes it almost impossible to see in while giving only a slightly darkened view of the world outside to the occupants—has been installed in the rear quarters, and the rear door windows have Sundym tinted glass. A badge bar at the front and Lucas quartz iodine headlamps complete the changes to the exterior of the car.

Luxurious interior fittings

Upon opening the massive rear door one enters a world that whispers opulence and luxury. Standard Phantom equipment includes the walnut veneered cocktail cabinet with two cut glass decanters and four glasses and space for two bottles. Even a corkscrew is provided, having its own special place in the cocktail cabinet. Also provided as standard equipment are

the walnut veneered division and garnish rails, the two occasional folding seats, full air conditioning, electrically-operated division and door windows twin interior lamps, cigar lighters in each armrest, heater controls in the right hand armrest, and a radio.

To this already luxurious specification has been added special deep red Draylon velvet upholstery with matching headlining. This gives an immediate impression of luxury and is perhaps the most striking single feature of the car. There are also matching velvet head cushions for the rear seat and velvet curtains to the rear window and quarterlights. Seated on the right side of the rear seat the owner can certainly feel master of the ship. In the armrest are the heater and refrigeration controls and situated just behind these is the electric intercom to the chauffeur so that he can be given instructions without need to lower the division and interrupt the privacy in the rear compartment. At the front of each armrest are ashtrays, and switches for the twin overhead lights and for the electrically operated division.

Mounted in the centre of veneered quarter panels just above the cigar lighters are the two switches for electrical adjustment of the rear seat. This enables the seat, fixed on the usual Phantom, to be moved forwards and at the same time the rake of the backrest is altered from a sitting to a semi reclining position. The seat is a

few inches higher than standard. The movement of the seat can be stopped at any intermediate position if required.

Just ahead of each armrest, in the rear of the door, is the switch for the electrically-operated door window, while in each rear quarter is a swivelling reading lamp with

integral switch. Swivelling eyeball nozzles in the roof on each side and beside the occasional seats provide cool air when the refrigeration system is in operation—a special feature of the Phantom VI is the provision of separate refrigeration units for the front and rear compartments. In the

Specification

FRONT ENGINE
REAR WHEEL DRIVE

ENGINE

Cylinders	8, in 90 deg. vee
Main bearings	5
Cooling system	Water; pump, fan with viscous coupling and thermostat
Bore	104.14 mm (4.1 in.)
Stroke	91.44 mm (3.6 in.)
Displacement	6,230 c.c. (380 cu. in.)
Valve gear	overhead, hydraulic tappets
Compression ratio	9.0-to-1 Min. octane rating: 100
Carburettors	2 SU HD8
Fuel pumps	2 SU electric

TRANSMISSION

Gearbox	Rolls-Royce 4-speed automatic
Gear ratios	Top 3.89
	Third 5.64
	Second 10.23
	First 14.64
	Reverse 16.72

CHASSIS and BODY

Construction	Closed box-section chassis with cruciform centre bracing; aluminium panelled body with steel and light alloy framework

SUSPENSION

Front	Independent; coil springs, wishbones, anti-roll bar hydraulic dampers
Rear	Live axle, asymmetric semi-elliptic leaf springs, adjustable hydraulic dampers

STEERING

Type	Power assisted cam and roller

BRAKES

Make and type	Girling, all drum, dual circuit
Servo—make and type	Rolls-Royce mechanical
Dimensions	F 11.25 in. dia., 3 in. wide shoes
	R 11.25 in. dia., 3 in. wide shoes

DIMENSIONS

Wheelbase	12 ft 1 in. (368 cm)
Track: front	5 ft 0.8 in. (155 cm)
Track: rear	5 ft 4 in. (163 cm)
Overall length	19 ft 10 in. (604 cm)
Overall width	6 ft 7 in. (201 cm)
Overall height (unladen)	5 ft 9 in. (175 cm)
Ground clearance	7.3 in. (18 cm)
Turning circle	48 ft 9 in. (1,485 cm)
Unladen weight (standard car)	5,768 lb (2,619 kg)

The Ultimate in Luxury?

left hand armrest is the switch for the electrically operated radio aerial in the right front wing, while the centre armrest has a front-hinged lid which lifts up to reveal a travelling companion consisting of a leather-covered cigarette case and notebook and two mirrors. Situated ahead of the **rear seat** are the two folding **occasional seats** with the walnut veneered drop-down cocktail cabinet between them.

Tape player, radio and television

Immediately above the cocktail cabinet is installed a Lear Jet stereo tape player and radio and higher still behind two doors which open from the centre outwards, is a small Sony television. This has its own electrically operated aerial in the left front wing; the aerial switch is located inside the cabinet on the left hand side.

We obtained a very good picture when the car was stationary, but there was some slight interference when on the move. However, this was not bad enough to detract from the enjoyment of being able to watch television while on the move—a really fascinating experience. Above the occasional seats are two veneered picnic tables which fold out from the division (with television doors closed). The division

Sony television installed above the cocktail cabinet and Lear Jet radio and stereo tape player

incorporates an ashtray for each occasional-seat occupant. For ease of entry and exit there are leather covered grab handles on the rear door pillars.

The front compartment is primarily the domain of the chauffeur, but even here the velvet headlining is to be found and there is a separate Radiomobile radio for the chauffeur's use. Upholstery of the front compartment is in dark red Connolly hide with carpets to match. Under the chauffeur's command are the usual driving controls—the car has a four-speed Rolls-Royce automatic gearbox which permits manual hold of any of the three higher gears, and variable power assisted steering —as well as a switch for the division, switches for all four windows on the

On the Road

IT seemed wise to let our insurance company know that they would be covering a £17,550 vehicle for the day, and once this had been arranged we were kindly allowed to drive the Phantom VI, this being the first time one of these splendid cars has been entrusted to us. However, we had previously enjoyed a reasonably long spell with the basically similar Phantom V when Mead provided one for a Used Car Test in 1970.

Perhaps the most awesome moment is when one approaches the car preparatory to driving it, when it is advisable to brush away any thoughts of the hours and hours of craftmanship which would have to be summoned up and paid for if one did so much as to biff one of those glistening wings. Once the driving door has been opened, however, and one has placed a foot on the inset running board and climbed up into the driving seat, the whole car begins to seem smaller. The driver looks down on the arched wings with their proud flagstaffs, and even the angular bonnet looks fairly short from the driving seat. A further passing thought is the one which many must have when they travel in a Rolls-Royce—that the occupants of the car certainly get the most inelegant view of that quite beautiful radiator mascot.

The separate starter button has long since been removed, and the key is turned to fire the starter, producing a distant but surprisingly loud clonk and whirr, followed by the smooth purr of the engine. The noise level from the vee-8 engine seems more in the Phantom than in the Silver Shadow, but you still certainly could not call it noisy. Also inferior is the transmission selector, as the lever works through a mechanical linkage instead of the electric selection of the Silver Shadow transmission, and its movement is a little notchy.

Gear changes are smooth enough, although it is only by careful manipulation of the throttle that they can be made imperceptible to passengers. On long gradients one can sense that the engine is beginning to toil slightly, pulling the car up the hill in its fairly high top gear. It requires movement of the selector down to third, to make the transmission change down as there is no part throttle kickdown.

For all its size, the car accelerates really impressively when the power is used to rush swiftly past slower traffic, and one always has the feeling that still more acceleration is in hand, perhaps because of the natural reluctance to use full throttle.

The driver has a commanding view of the road ahead and the car seems much smaller than it really is.

The steering seemed appreciably better, and less prone to wander, on the Phantom VI than it had been on the used Phantom V. In all conditions it takes very little effort, due to the vigorous power assistance, and tends to disguise the considerable understeer on corners. As the car is pulled fairly fast round a tight bend there is quite a lot of sway and tyre scrub, and a strong sensation that there are decided limits beyond which the car would go scrubbing straight on into the undergrowth. After these researches, photographer Ron Easton's voice came through on the intercom from the rear compartment with "Steady on the bends, there, please," and one appreciated something of the surprise the chauffeur must experience each time an intruding mechanical voice breaks into his private world in the front of the car.

He does, however, enjoy the best ride, recalling memories of the old joke about her ladyship in the back acting as a suspension damper to give her chauffeur the best ride. Little of the slight wheel bump and rear-end float over undulations is felt in the driving compartment.

The brakes, with mechanical servo assistance, give very good response, but without the superb smoothness of the later all-disc system used on the smaller cars. There is also still that momentary heart-stopping lack of response for a split second when the car has stopped on a gradient and starts to run back.

One is certainly reminded that motoring has progressed a long way since the Phantom was designed; on the other hand it is remarkable how much pleasure the car gives to the driver, and how delightfully easy it has been made to control such a large vehicle. □

The rear wing line has been altered to accommodate this special rear lamp treatment which is very similar to that used on Bentley Continentals in the 1960s

driver's door, a solenoid-operated fuel filler flap, and special Fiamm Avanti GT Trumpet air horns, operated by a foot-switch.

It goes without saying that one expects the highest standards of finish obtainable on a car such as this and H. J. Mulliner, Park Ward have seen to this in their usual way, even down to the specially dyed rugs to the rear compartment and the matching of the veneers round the car to give a mirror image from one side to the other. After all, this attention to detail accounts for the majority of the £17,550 that this car cost—and that is at a pre-increase (though post-Budget) price. A similar car now would cost around £18,275 or nearly the price of two Silver Shadows. □

Testing a chassis until a component broke, then redesigning the component until when tested again it did not fail formed the basis of the philosophy laid down by Sir Henry Royce. To make such testing practical within a short period of time Rolls-Royce were to be found using a dynamometer, to which cams could be fitted to simulate the pounding of a rough road, as early as 1911 though the scene at Derby depicted here is in the 1930s

Rolls-Royce Corniche

6,750 c.c.

You have to wait a long time for a new Corniche, but the latest models have many improvements and more standard equipment. The quiet, smooth engine, matched to an excellent automatic transmission makes the Corniche faster than the Shadow, with only marginally worse fuel consumption. The ride and handling have been improved, and the road noise levels reduced. It is expensive —but we think the high price is justified.

IN MOST people's eyes the Rolls-Royce Corniche is the absolute ultimate in cars. Not just a Rolls-Royce, it is a coachbuilt two-door coupé commanding a current list price of just over £16,000 and at present in such short supply that delivery is quoted at over three years. At pre-crisis auctions prices of as high as £28,000 have been reached for secondhand examples, although this is a long way from the real market value of around £17,000. Like a piece of select property or a rare antique, a Rolls-Royce is an appreciating investment and as such can be readily justified by company accountants.

When the Corniche was launched three years ago it followed the lines of the previous Shadow-based H. J. Mulliner, Park Ward two-door model, but was given more of a separate identity by using a special engine developing 10 per cent more power. The actual output is still undisclosed, but since the capacity was increased from 6·2 to 6·7 litres in 1970, the claim of "adequate" has been fully justified.

Somehow with a car like a Rolls-Royce, actual performance figures seem beneath its considerable dignity. Since the Corniche is a more sporting version and obviously aimed very much at the owner driver, we feel there is more justification for discussing its speed and acceleration in detail.

Compared with the Silver Shadow we tested in November 1972, the Corniche reached a mean maximum 3 mph higher at exactly 120 mph, with a best one-way run at 122 mph. At this latter speed the rev counter needle was just a whisker below the start of the red sector at 4,700 rpm, which is about as near as practice can get to theory whatever the car. On a slight down grade we had to lift off to prevent over-revving.

From a standing start the Corniche shot away with about a yard of wheelspin to record 0 to 50 mph acceleration time of 6·8sec (0·8sec quicker than that of the Shadow) and a 0 to 60 mph time of only 9·6sec (10·2sec for the Shadow). From rest to 100 mph took exactly 30sec (3·6 sec quicker than with the Shadow), which is no mean achievement for a saloon the size and weight of the Corniche.

Most of these gains have been brought about by improvements in the efficiency of the engine (re-timed camshaft, large-bore exhaust system, revised air cleaner) so fuel consumption suffers very little in consequence despite more eager feet on the pedals. Overall for close to 1,400 miles, which included a trip to northern France for maximum speed measurements and a lot of UK driving before the present fuel-saving campaign, we recorded 11·9 mpg. This is less than a five per cent drop on the 12·4 mpg we obtained with the Shadow in 1972. On a typical run away from London we returned over 13 mpg with ease, but during a spell of thick fog in heavy city traffic the consumption fell to less than 10 mpg, which is about the same as should be expected

A badge reading Corniche identifies the car at the rear, but although following the general lines of the Silver Shadow, the styling is quite distinctive

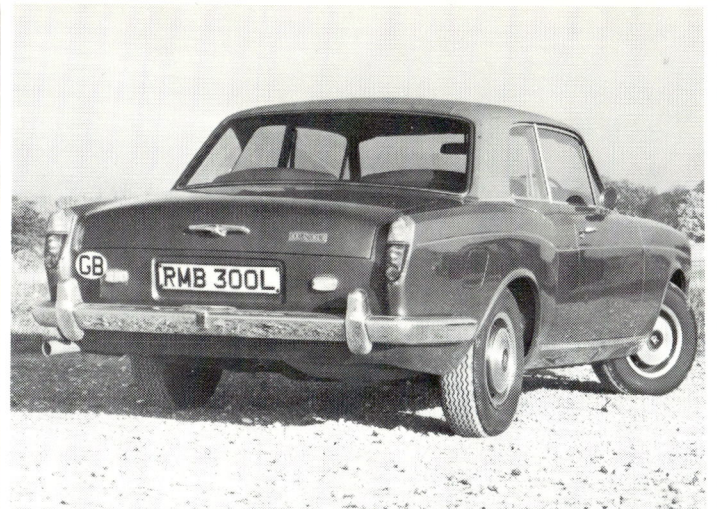

on a fast Continental trip with cruising speeds around 100 mph, speed limits permitting. The tank holds 24 gallons, so the useful range is poor, at just over 200 miles.

The engine starts first turn of the key but engagement is a noisy, out-of-character affair which surprises by-standers and sounds very loud inside a garage. When running, the engine is quiet and completely without temperament, but on the test car the hot idle was rather lumpy. An automatic choke takes care of all temperature variations.

Compared with the last Shadow we drove with the 6·7 litre engine, smoothness and refinement have been improved and there was none of the harshness we complained of in our last test. When the driver of the Corniche opens up to accelerate, there is a detectable and obviously intentional increase in engine noise which amounts to no more than a pleasant and very subdued power hum, like an electric motor speeding up.

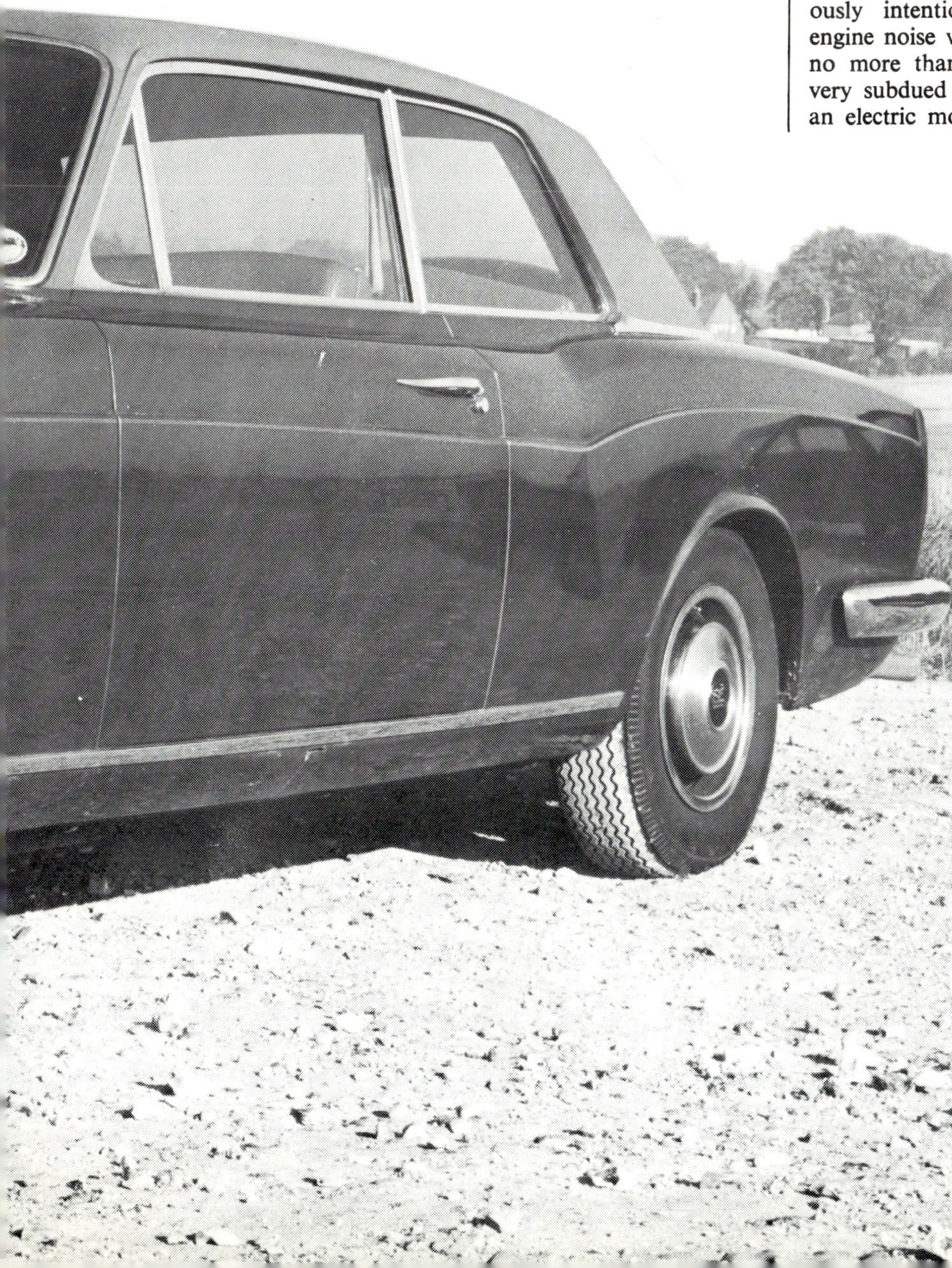

It is louder than on the regular Shadow, but in no way offensive. The rest of the time the near silence of the engine is a continual marvel and its sweetness throughout the range was delightful. These characteristics in a V8, with its secondary balance problems, are a remarkable achievement.

Rolls-Royce engineering policy is to make small but continuous improvements so that no version is immediately out of date but an owner changing his car after, say, three years will notice many worthwhile gains. We were impressed with how much progress has been made recently with the suspension, this nearly new 1974-specification demonstrator incorporating all the latest changes.

In the past we have felt that in the Rolls-Royce book ride took a decisive precedence over handling and we went to great lengths in our 1972 Shadow test to analyse the behaviour over all manner of surfaces and commented in detail on the limitations. In the final score we had to admit to being disappointed overall. The story now has changed considerably and the balance between ride and handling is a much better compromise. Steering response, for a start, is quicker and although understeer is still predominant, with power on the Corniche has much nearer neutral characteristics. In a brutal steering-pad test we got the car drifting sideways with front and rear tyres smoking equally, just to prove the point.

On the road there is still some vagueness in the steering about the straight-ahead position, accentuated to a large extent by the ultra-light servo assistance, but it is much easier than before to position the car accurately on sweeping bends or in narrow lanes. The small, 15in. dia wood-rimmed steering wheel which was fitted to the early Corniches has been replaced by the standard 16in. Shadow plastic wheel, which does not help, yet we soon settled in the big car and had enough confidence to flick it through the twists at remarkably high speeds.

The biggest deterrent to this kind of driving is the body roll which throws occupants across the large slippery seats and tilts the horizon alarmingly. Actual cornering power is good, but for fast driving there are too many attitude changes, both laterally and in the fore and aft direction; although very effective anti-dive is built into the front suspension geometry, rear-end squat under hard acceleration is a real nuisance.

Improvements in ride are just as noticeable, road noise levels being much reduced (although whether this is due to engineering development or more a characteristic of the two-door bodywork, we cannot say for sure). On some coarsely-dressed surfaces, tyre roar begins to intrude, but on the kind of smooth tarmac that covers most main roads one can only marvel at the overall interior quietness. Abroad on French undulations we would have preferred stiffer damping, the rear suspension occasionally contacting the bump stops (despite no back seat passengers) and the general motion being rather like crossing a gentle swell at sea. On level main roads and the *autoroutes* the Corniche stormed along in perfect comfort with superb stability and no detectable wind noise.

For a few years now, Rolls have been using General Motors automatic transmission imported from the USA, the system employing a conventional three-speed epicyclic gearbox with torque convertor. This unit meets the exacting Rolls-Royce standards without modification and it behaved impeccably on the test car. Shift quality was an excellent match for the silky engine, and with sensitive part-throttle downshifts it gives the car a very lively response. At full throttle the gearbox changes up automatically at around 4,000 rpm, which must be close to the peak of the power curve because we could not improve on the acceleration times by holding to higher revs. At 4,000 rpm, maximum speeds are 42 and 73 mph in low and intermediate and the transmission will not kick down above 66 and 29

mph respectively. Low is prevented from engaging above 40 mph, to protect the engine. There is an electric selector on the steering column which is isolated in Park by the ignition switch, thus eliminating the need for a steering lock.

A powerful servo ensures light pedal efforts with the four 11in. disc brakes, which are ventilated at the front, and there was virtually no fade a stabilized temperature. The handbrake is impressively powerful, recording 0.4g on its own from 30 mph and holding the heavy car securely on a 1-in-3 gradient. It is mounted in a slightly awkward position under the right of the facia and needed its full 9in. travel on the test car. Hydraulic circuits are duplicated for the servo system and backed up by a third non-servo installation, so any sort of brake failure is statistically out of the question.

Comfort and Equipment

For £15,000 the buyer has a right to the highest standards of luxury and in most respects he is unlikely to be disappointed with the Corniche. Full air conditioning is standard, best Connolly hide is used for the seats and trim, and wood veneer for the facia and door cappings is accurately matched with spare panels from the same part of the same tree held and indexed at the factory. Being painted and trimmed at the Mulliner, Park Ward factory at Willesden, the Corniche received even more individual treatment than the Shadow, a justification in part for its premium price.

Front seats are large and very sumptuous affairs with folding armrests on the inside edges of the backrests and an adjustable armrest on each door. The inboard armrests quarrel with the seat belt buckles if lowered after fastening and we found it very difficult to get the buckle tongues past the door armrests. Seat belt arrangements are very poor in the Corniche and something the factory should attend to without delay.

Apart from being rather hard and slippery, as is so often the case with leather, the seats are comfortable and reasonably well shaped. You tend to sit on them, rather than in them, but support is quite well arranged. The multi-way joystick power adjustment levers are on the door trims with a much too coarse rake

adjustment at the base of the backrest in line with the hinge. The steering column is fixed and several drivers found it too close to their chests once they had set the seat for comfortable pedal reach.

Getting into the back seat requires a stiff button to be pressed at the top of the backrest, to release it, and the rather heavy assembly to be swung forward. It is then a case of squeezing past the seat belt and exposed inertia reel before settling back in superb luxury and with a surprising amount of legroom. Assistance is needed to get out again as the front door must be opened first and its release is out of the reach of someone in the back. These criticisms aside, the Corniche must surely be the roomiest two-plus-two coupé on the market.

Facia layout is similar to that of the Shadow, except for the addition of a rev counter on the extreme right and a slightly different centre console arrangement. The glass of the rev counter picks up reflections from the side window and is often impossible to read. In a car like this with such an excellent automatic transmission it serves little purpose anyway. At night we found the instrument lighting patchy.

Heating and Air Conditioning

On all Bentley and Rolls-Royce models full air conditioning is standard and once the rather complex controls have been mastered, it works very effectively. Temperature is selected by a progressive rotary knob which is pulled out through four positions to regulate the volume of heated air, a multi-speed booster fan working independently. With practice the system can be set and controlled easily, but we have to question whether something simpler on the lines of that used by Cadillac and now Jaguar would not be more in keeping with this sort of ultimate car. The positions of the various outlets and the balance of flow rates has been well thought out. Far from being something for the occasional heat-wave, the air conditioning was useful on nearly every trip even in winter.

A considerable number of items which normally cost extra are included in the standard price, and the quality has not been skimped to permit this.

There is still a wide choice available to the customer and some of these alternatives were fitted to the test car. One of the most satisfying was a Bosch Frankfurt FM stereo radio instead of the standard pushbutton AM unit, with four speakers. It adds £77.46 to the price. Apart from poor installation of the rear speakers which was not noticed in the front, the quality was most impressive, especially when stereo was being broadcast by the commercial radio stations. In contrast the eight-track Radiomobile cartridge player was disappointing and we would have preferred the alternative Bosch four-track cassette machine which costs £17.87 extra.

Also standard is an automatic cruise control which maintained the speed to within 1 mph of the setting chosen. It is engaged by pressing a button when the required speed is reached, switching it out or touching the brake cancelling this command immediately. It can be overridden in use by depressing the accelerator against extra pressure.

Living with the Corniche

When the total invoice of the car delivered is close to £15,500 and the wait can amount to around four years, one expects a lot from the Corniche. We found the test car stood up to the closest scrutiny of every detail and felt that a buyer would be well pleased with his possession.

After the first 3,000-mile service, the Corniche needs attention every 6,000 miles, when the cost alternates between £40 and £50, assuming a typical labour charge of £3.50 per hour. The warranty period lasts for an impressive three years while replacement of components like brake pads, dampers, starter or alternator is no more expensive than on much cheaper cars. The stainless-steel exhaust system, which should last several years without trouble, is expensive at just under £260, but that is a fair price for long life and quality materials.

Owner checks are made extra simple by the traditional sump level gauge that works through the fuel gauge and in many ways the Rolls can be run without attention, like a washing machine or television. Circuits for the several warning lamps and overheating warning buzzer can be tested by pushing a button on the facia.

Another of the standard luxury items is centralized locking

The Corniche is available only with two-door bodywork – saloon (as tested) or convertible. The huge doors open wide for easy access, and the luxurious thick squabs of the front seats tip forward for entry to the rear compartment, after the chrome button at the top of the backrest has been pressed. The engine compartment is a magnificent, if daunting, sight. Below, the world famous mascot is spring-loaded for pedestrian safety. A further refinement is a drop-down panel beneath the facia carrying the fuses and relays

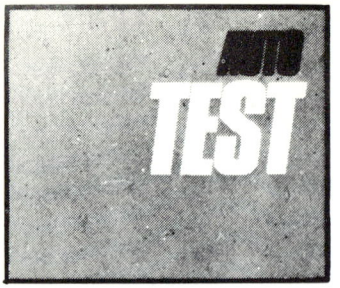

Rolls-Royce Corniche

operated by a two-way button on the trim panel of the two doors. It locks both these and the boot, the latter being released only with the key or by pushing a button inside the glove locker which can itself be locked with the boot lid key. The luggage can thus be left secure while the car is driven by an attendant. After closing both doors the interior lamp stays on with a time switch for about 10sec.

Conclusions

In the light of advances made recently by Mercedes, we would like to see a few more engineering features on this excellent British product. High on our list would be anti-squat suspension to prevent the tail dipping under acceleration, and aero-

Comparisons

MAXIMUM SPEED MPH
Jaguar XJ12C .... (£5,243) 146
Citroen SM .... (£6,369) 139
Mercedes-Benz 450SEL.. (£9,582) 134
Rolls-Royce Corniche (£15,104) 120
Fiat 130 Coupé .... (£5,970) 116

0–60 MPH, SEC
Jaguar XJ12C .... 7·4
Mercedes-Benz 450SEL ..... 9·1
Citroen SM .... 9·3
Rolls-Royce Corniche ..... 9·6
Fiat 130 Coupé .... 10·6

STANDING ¼-MILE, SEC
Jaguar XJ12C .... 15·7
Mercedes-Benz 450SEL ..... 16·7
Rolls-Royce Corniche ..... 17·1
Citroen SM .... 17·1
Fiat 130 Coupé .... 17·7

OVERALL MPG
Fiat 130 Coupé .... 20·6
Citroen SM .... 17·9
Mercedes-Benz 450SEL ..... 14·7
Rolls-Royce Corniche ..... 11·9
Jaguar XJ12C .... 11·4

Performance

ACCELERATION SECONDS

True speed mph	Time in secs	Car speedo mph
30	3·2	30
40	4·9	39
50	6·8	49
60	9·6	58
70	12·7	68
80	16·9	79
90	23·2	92
100	30·0	103
110	—	113

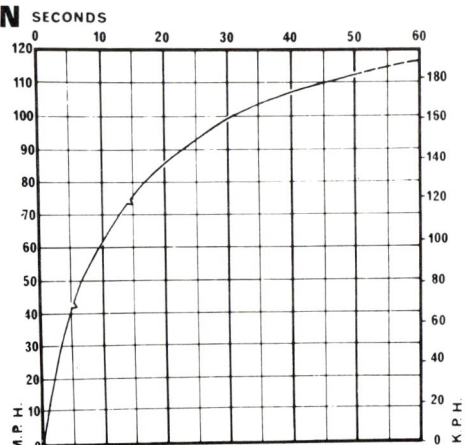

Standing ¼-mile
17·1sec 81 mph

Standing kilometre
31·8sec 101 mph

Mileage recorder: accurate.

GEAR RATIOS AND TIME IN SEC

mph	Top (3·08– 6·28)	Inter (4·56– 9·30)	Low (7·64– 15·59)
10–30	—	—	2·5
20–40	—	3·7	3·0
30–50	—	4·2	3·8
40–60	6·6	5·0	—
50–70	7·6	6·1	—
60–80	9·0	7·8	—
70–90	11·2	—	—
80–100	13·1	—	—

GEARING
(with 205VR–15in. tyres)
Top .... 26·2 mph per 1,000 rpm
Inter .... 17·7 mph per 1,000 rpm
Low .... 10·6 mph per 1,000 rpm

MAXIMUM SPEEDS

Gear	mph	kph	rpm
Top (mean)	120	193	4,600
(best)	122	196	4,660
Inter	83	134	4,700
Low	50	80	4,700

BRAKES
FADE (from 70 mph in neutral)
Pedal load for 0·5g stops in lb

1	20	6	30–40	
2	25	7	30–40	
3	25–30	8	35	
4	28–32	9	35	
5	30–35	10	35	

RESPONSE (from 30 mph in neutral)

Load	g	Distance
20lb	0·45	67ft
40lb	1·00	30·1ft
50lb	1·05	28·7ft
Handbrake	0·40	75ft
Max Gradient	1 in 3	

Consumption

FUEL
(At constant speed—mpg)

30 mph	19·1
40 mph	18·7
50 mph	18·1
60 mph	17·2
70 mph	15·8
80 mph	14·1
90 mph	12·3

Typical mpg .. 12·5 (22·6 litres/100km)
Calculated (DIN) mpg 14·4
(19·6 litres/100km)
Overall mpg .... 11·9 (23·7 litres/100km)
Grade of fuel Super, 5-star (min. 100RM)

OIL
Consumption (SAE20W50)   500mpp

TEST CONDITIONS
Weather: Fine Wind: 0 mph
Temperature: 10 deg C. (50 deg F).
Barometer: 30·1in. hg. Humidity: 93 per cent.
Surface: Dry. concrete and asphalt
Test distance: 1,366 miles.

Figures taken by our own staff at the Motor Industry Research Association proving ground at Nuneaton and on the Continent.

Dimensions

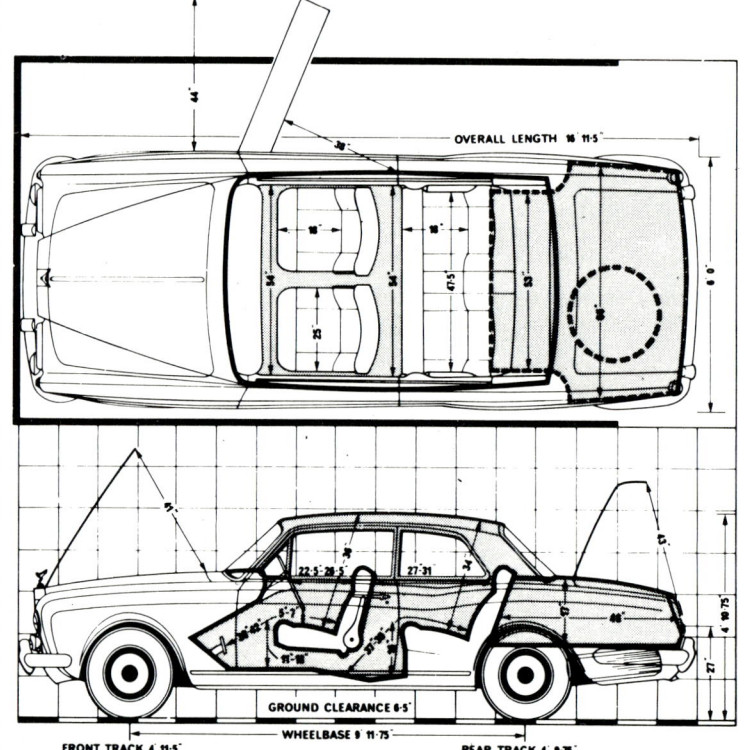

STANDARD GARAGE
16ft × 8ft 6in.

TURNING CIRCLES
Between kerbs
L, 38ft 9in.; R, 38ft 0in.
Between walls
L, 40ft 11in.; R, 40ft 2in.
Steering wheel turns, lock to lock: 3·4.

WEIGHT
Kerb weight 430cwt (4,816lb–2,190kg) (with oil, water and half-full tank).
Distribution, per cent
F, 53·2; R, 46·8.
Laden as tested: 46·0cwt (3,156lb–2,340kg).

dynamic guttering to prevent the side windows from becoming obscured in wet weather. An additional detail would be a push-button trip reset, like that used on various cheap Fords.

These few points apart, we feel the latest Corniche sets very high standards at the top end of the luxury car market and is well deserving of the consider-able esteem in which it is held. Whilst its price is extremely high, it is easy to see where the money has been spent and as a non-depreciative asset it is unique in the modern car field. □

MANUFACTURER:
Rolls-Royce Motors Ltd., Pyms Lane, Crewe, Cheshire.

PRICES		EXTRAS (inc. VAT)	
Basic	£13,390 00	*Everflex roof covering	£184.71
Special Car Tax	£1,115 83	*Bosch Frankfurt AM FM stereo	
VAT	£1,450 58	radio in lieu of standard	£77.46
Total (in GB)	£15,956.41	*Bosch cassette player in lieu	
Seat belts	Standard	of 8-track cartridge unit	£17 87
Licence	£25 00	*Fire extinguisher	£11.81
Delivery charge (London)	Varies	*Fitted to test car	
Number plates	£5.65		
Total on the Road (exc. insurance)	£15,987.06	TOTAL AS TESTED ON	
Insurance	Group 7	THE ROAD	£16,278.91

Specification

Rolls-Royce Corniche

FRONT ENGINE
REAR WHEEL DRIVE

ENGINE
Cylinders	8, in 90-deg. vee
Main bearings	5
Cooling system	Water; pump, thermostat and viscous-coupled fan
Bore	104·1mm (4·1in.)
Stroke	99·1mm (3·9in.)
Displacement	6,750 c.c. (412 cu. in.)
Valve gear	Centre camshaft, hydraulic tappets
Compression ratio	9·0-to-1. Min. octane rating: 100RM
Carburettors	2 × SU HD8
Fuel pump	2 × SU electric
Oil filter	Purolater full-flow, renewable element
Max. power	Not disclosed
Max. torque	Not disclosed

TRANSMISSION
Gearbox	GM automatic, 3-speed with torque converter
Gear ratios	Top (auto) 1·0–2·1
	Inter 1·50–3·15
	Low 2·50–5·25
	Reverse 2·00–4·20
Final drive	
Mph at 1,000 rpm in top gear	

CHASSIS AND BODY
Construction	Integral steel body and chassis, aluminium alloy doors, boot lid and bonnet

SUSPENSION
Front	Independent; coil springs, double wishbones, anti-roll bar, telescopic dampers
Rear	Independent; coil springs, semi trailing arms, anti-roll bar, telescopic dampers, automatic ride height control

STEERING
Type	Power-assisted recirculating ball
Wheel dia.	16·0in.

BRAKES
Make and type	Rolls-Royce/Girling ventilated disc front, plain disc rear. Three independent hydraulic circuits, operating twin front calipers and dual-piston rear.
Servo	Two independent engine-driven pumps
Dimensions	F 11·0in. dia.
	R 11·0in. dia
Swept area	F 227 sq. in., R 286 sq. in. Total 513 sq. in. (223 sq. in./ton laden)

WHEELS
Type	Pressed steel disc, 5-stud fixing 6·0in. wide rim.
Tyres—make	Avon, Dunlop or Firestone
—type	Radial ply tubeless
—size	205-15in.

EQUIPMENT
Battery	12 volt 71 Ah
Alternator	CAV 55 amp
Headlamps	Lucas 200/75 watt (total)
Reversing lamp	Standard
Electric fuses	20, plus thermal cutouts for head-lamps, gear selector and door locks.
Screen wipers	2-speed, plus intermittent delay
Screen washer	Standard electric
Interior heater	Standard, with air-conditioning
Heated backlight	Standard
Safety belts	Standard, inertia reel
Interior trim	Connolly hide seats, cloth headlining
Floor covering	Wilton carpet, with nylon rugs
Jack	Screw pillar
Jacking points	1 each side, under sills
Windscreen	Laminated
Underbody protection	Zinc-coated steel, phosphate dip primer, bitumastic compound.

MAINTENANCE
Fuel tank	23·5 Imp. gallons (107 litres)
Cooling system	28·5 pints inc. (heater)
Engine sump	14·5 pints (8 litres) SAE 20W50. Change oil every 6,000 miles. Change filter every 6,000 miles.
Gearbox	18·6 pints. SAE ATF. Change every 12,000 miles.
Final drive	4·5 pints. SAE 90EP. Change every 24,000 miles.
Grease	6 points every 12,000 miles.
Valve clearance	Self adjusting
Contact breaker	0·014in.—0·016in. gap; 26–28 deg. dwell.
Ignition timing	5 deg. BTDC (stroboscopic at 800 rpm)
Spark plug	Type: Champion N14Y. Gap 0·023–0·028in.
Compression pressure	N.A.
Tyre pressures	F 28; R 28 psi (normal driving) F 28; R 32 psi (full load).
Max. payload	1,000lb (454kg)

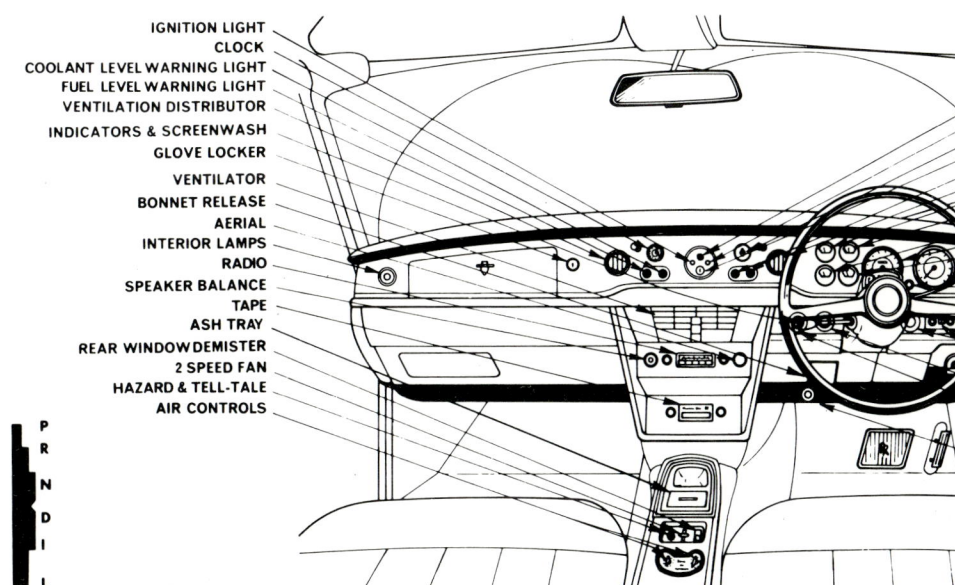

Labels (left): IGNITION LIGHT, CLOCK, COOLANT LEVEL WARNING LIGHT, FUEL LEVEL WARNING LIGHT, VENTILATION DISTRIBUTOR, INDICATORS & SCREENWASH, GLOVE LOCKER, VENTILATOR, BONNET RELEASE, AERIAL, INTERIOR LAMPS, RADIO, SPEAKER BALANCE, TAPE, ASH TRAY, REAR WINDOW DEMISTER, 2 SPEED FAN, HAZARD & TELL-TALE, AIR CONTROLS

P R N D I L

Labels (right): LAMPS, OIL PRESSURE WARNING LIGHT, WIPERS 2 SPEED & INTERMITTENT, IGNITION & STARTER, BRAKE WARNING LIGHTS, VENTILATION DISTRIBUTOR, FUEL GAUGE, AMMETER, COOLANT TEMPERATURE GAUGE, SPEEDOMETER, OIL PRESSURE GAUGE, REV COUNTER, SELECTOR, TRIP RESET, PANEL LAMPS RHEOSTAT, INTERIOR LAMPS, AUTOMATIC SPEED CONTROLS, PARKING LAMPS, HANDBRAKE, FUEL FLAP CONTROL, FUEL OIL LEVEL INDICATOR & WARNING LIGHT TEST SWITCH, HEADLAMP DIPSWITCH

Servicing

	3,000 miles	6,000 miles	12,000 miles	Routine Replacements:	Time hours	Labour	Spares	TOTAL
Time Allowed (hours)	2·75	9·00	9·50	Brake Pads – Front (set)	1·00	£3.50	£20.19	£23.69
Cost at £3.50 per hour	£9.62	£31.50	£33.25	Brake Pads – Rear (set)	0·60	£2.10	£10.09	£12.19
Oil Change	£2.84	£3.25	£9.06	Exhaust System	6·25	£21.88	£258.50	£280.38
Oil Filter	—	£3.30	£3.30	Dampers – Front (pair)	5·00	£17.50	£24.64	£42.14
Breather Filter	—	—	—	Dampers – Rear (pair)	7·75	£27.13	£24.64	£51.77
Air Filter	—	—	—	Replace Half Shaft (exchange)	1·00	£3.50	£41.80	£45.30
Contact Breaker Points	—	£1.57	£1.57	Replace Generator (exchange)	0·80	£2.80	£25.41	£28.21
Sparking Plugs	—	—	£2.94	Replace Starter (exchange)	2·00	£7.00	£29.70	£36.70
Total Cost:	**£12.46**	**£39.62**	**£50.12**					

THE DELTA BECOMES CAMARGUE

New two-door model, styled by Pininfarina, is the most expensive Rolls-Royce saloon yet.
Few mechanical changes, but very advanced automatic air-conditioning system.

By J. R. Daniels, B.Sc. Photographs Ron Easton

THERE IS one very nice thing about being Rolls-Royce (or Mercedes or, presumably, Cadillac): one is not confined to a market sector like everyone else. If in doubt, one can always move up. For the prestigous few, the sky is the limit. With this in mind, Rolls-Royce approached Pininfarina in 1969 with a commission for a new car to form the top end of the Rolls-Royce range. At that time—in the days of the old company, one notes, before the debacle of 1971 —there was already a project, well on the way to fruition, for a replacement two-door Silver Shadow, which was ultimately launched as the Corniche. The Pininfarina car was to be superior to the Corniche in several well-defined ways, but most of all in terms of accommodation.

The brief given to Pininfarina was a strict one. The car had to be based on the existing Silver Shadow platform and running gear. The styling had to be dateless and dignified—as befitted the top of the range and one of the most expensive cars in the world. The resulting design will not please everyone—no design ever does; but Rolls-Royce are happy with the way Sergio Pininfarina has met the specification, and the company have high praise for him as an engineer as well as a stylist.

The engineering aspect was important, because the new car had naturally to meet all present and foreseen safety requirements. This aim in particular has been handsomely achieved, to the extent that all the main safety tests—even the barrier test—were carried out on one body which, as it were, had the dents knocked out of it after each·one before proceeding to the next.

The body is entirely conventional in construction. The Silver Shadow platform is modified (as it is for the Corniche) to accept the bigger, two-door body, and the structure is built up from steel pressings. The only aluminium panels are the doors, boot lid and bonnet. All this work is carried out at the London works of Mulliner Park Ward, after which the shells are sent to Crewe for priming and painting, and mechanical assembly, before being returned to London for interior trimming and finishing.

Based as it is on the normal Shadow platform with its 120 in. wheelbase, the Camargue is not substantially bigger than the other cars in the range, but it *is* bigger and heavier. Compared with the Corniche saloon it is 3.5 in. wider and just ¾ in. lower; the length remains the same, except for American-market cars which will have the bumpers mounted on extensions, adding a further 3 in. to the overall length and bringing it to rather more than 17 feet. Kerb weight is quoted at 5,175 lb, almost 200 lb more than the Corniche, slightly more even than the Corniche convertible.

For this increase in size and weight, one gains a good deal of interior space so that the Camargue is a full—indeed, relaxed— four/five seater. Rolls-Royce say the back seat is no less than 8.5 in. wider than the one in the Corniche, while there is 3 cubic feet more luggage space. Fuel tank capacity is only slightly reduced, at 23½ instead of 24 gallons. Access to the back seat is made as easy as possible by having extremely wide doors, the armrests extending all the way to the trailing edge and incorporating separate door handles for the back seat passengers.

Why is such a massive car built in two-door form? According to David Plastow, Rolls-Royce Managing Director, that is what the market wants. The Camargue is intended as the ultimate personal car, very much for the owner-driver. It will spend much of its time with one or two occupants. Besides, the choice of two rather than four doors makes possible a more attractive styling treatment. There is certainly no prospect of a four-door version.

Engineering changes

Ever since the formation of Rolls-Royce Motors from the 1971 ashes, it has been policy to introduce technical advances on the small-volume, coachbuilt models. This is not a case of asking the customer to act as a guinea-pig: Rolls-Royce could hardly afford to take that attitude. But innovations in the Corniche and the Camargue can be built almost as hand-crafted prototypes, while at the same time production and service staff have a chance to get used to the changes without having to cope with them on every car. When capacity and experience have reached a sufficient level, the changes can be added to the rest of the range. The process can be seen at work in, for instance, the ventilated front disc brakes which were used first on the Corniche but are now standard on the Silver Shadow also.

The major innovation in the Camargue is a fully-automatic air-conditioning system painstakingly developed over the past eight years and claimed by Rolls-Royce to be superior to anything else in the field. Apart from this, a modicum of extra power has been sought (to compensate for the extra weight) by adding a more efficient twin-pipe exhaust system.

From the driver's point of view, the air-conditioning system is childishly simple. There are three controls, two of them temperature selectors for face and foot level respectively, the third a mode switch which allows him to leave the system to its own devices, or to override it in extreme situations or more likely, out of personal whim —since the system can cope with most situations without trouble. Beneath the facia and under the bonnet, the air of simplicity evaporates, although even here the basic principles are clear enough.

The system is a closed loop, constantly measuring temperature inside and outside the car, comparing it with the demands set up on the temperature selectors, and automatically adjusting the valves and fans accordingly. A great deal of work went into the positioning and calibration of the temperature sensors, and the only obvious one is mounted above the door header rail on the passenger side. Others are set into the padding above the facia (where it is affected by and can compensate for the radiant heat effect of direct sunlight) and beneath the facia to measure foot-level temperature. The external sensors are situated inside the rear bumper. Two more behind the radiator shell serve an external air temperature gauge and an ice warning.

The system uses solid-state electronic control, the main control module having 28 transistors mounted on circuit cards for ease of checking and replacement. The output from the computing circuits controls two sets of relays, one for selecting higher temperatures and the other for lower ones; the air-blending valves themselves are moved by mechanical linkages from two servomotors with calibrated cam drives. At the same time, the speed of the two booster fans is controlled by the output from a separate module. This output is "chopped" (switched on and off very rapidly) to vary the amount of current reaching the fan motors. This is a more efficient way of controlling their speed than to feed the current through a varying resistance, which wastes a good deal of electricity in the form of unwanted heat.

The workings of the air conditioning system are further complicated by a number of override devices. One of these prevents the system from operating when the engine is cold, for instance, and other undesirable combinations of valve position and fan speed (some of them discovered during development testing) are inhibited by position- or temperature-sensing switches. One point made very strongly by the Rolls-Royce engineers is that the system will

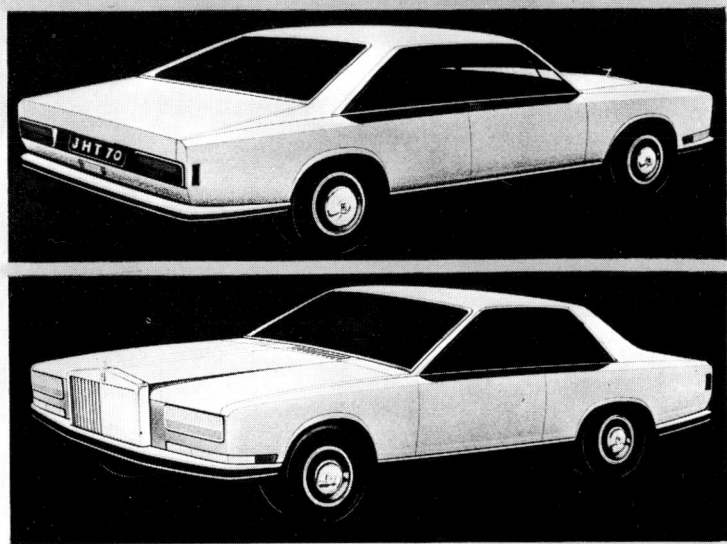

From some angles, Farina's styling is reminiscent of the Fiat 130 Coupé, arguably his most attractive recent design. But the front of the car is dominated by the very large Rolls-Royce grille, which is in fact rather larger than the stylist wanted it. The styling sketches (left) show how little the design was otherwise changed from the initial concept. One alteration concerned the black panel beneath the window sill line, which Pininfarina intended to be a contrasting colour

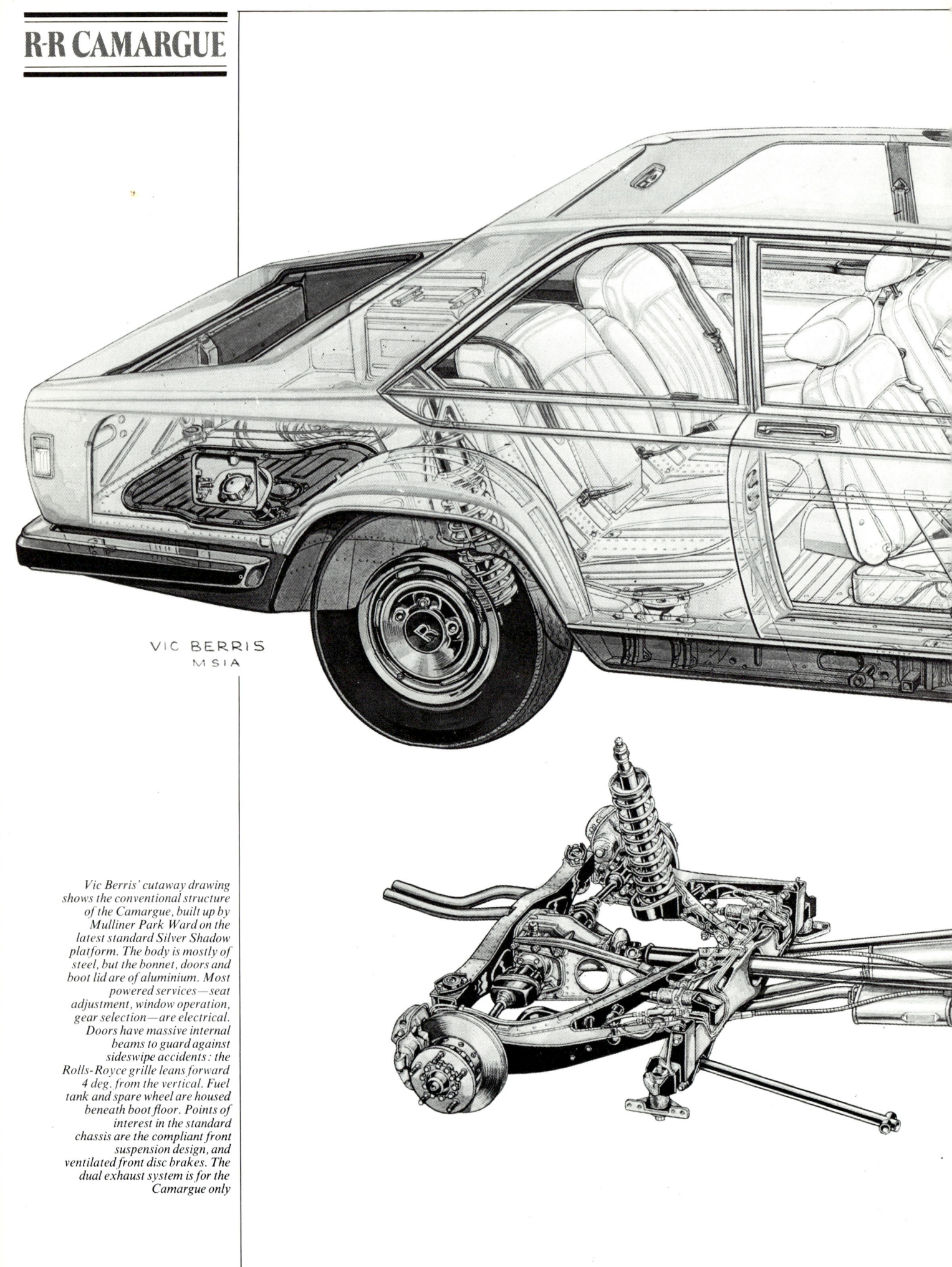

VIC BERRIS
M SIA

Vic Berris' cutaway drawing shows the conventional structure of the Camargue, built up by Mulliner Park Ward on the latest standard Silver Shadow platform. The body is mostly of steel, but the bonnet, doors and boot lid are of aluminium. Most powered services—seat adjustment, window operation, gear selection—are electrical. Doors have massive internal beams to guard against sideswipe accidents: the Rolls-Royce grille leans forward 4 deg. from the vertical. Fuel tank and spare wheel are housed beneath boot floor. Points of interest in the standard chassis are the compliant front suspension design, and ventilated front disc brakes. The dual exhaust system is for the Camargue only

AUTO
CAR
COPYRIGHT

R-R CAMARGUE

attain the selected temperature as quickly as it can; there is nothing to be gained by overriding it.

On the air side of the system, *all* incoming air is cooled and dehumidified in the refrigeration system before passing to the heating and air-blending unit. Air is fed into the cabin at the base of the screen, via two face-level "eyeball" inlets, a slatted vent in the centre of the lower facia, and into the front footwells. Air extraction is via slots in the rear parcels shelf. The heated rear window, interestingly, has no control of its own, but works automatically in conjunction with the rest of the air-conditioning system.

compression ratio of 7.3:1, enabling them to run on lead-free fuel), but in other areas the intention is to replace the SUs with a four-choke downdraught Solex carburettor. When this is done, compression ratio will be reduced to 8:1 without any loss of power, while the conventional ignition system will be supplanted by the transistorised Lucas Opus unit.

The three-speed General Motors transmission continues in use, its ratios unchanged, and a final drive of 3.08:1 in conjunction with HR70-15 tyres gives overall gearing of 26.2mph per 1,000 rpm. The tyres, made to Rolls-Royce specification, are supplied by Avon, Dunlop or Firestone; fabric-breaker construction is used at the moment but steel-belted tyres are being investigated. Steer-

safer. Apart from the veneer backing, the instruments have something of an aircraft look to them, each in its separate case, all the dials round and clearly marked. The minor controls, styled by Pininfarina, are to the same format.

The selector for the automatic transmission (an electric switch rather than a mechanical lever, as in all Rolls-Royce cars) is mounted to the right of the steering column and has the speed-control selector incorporated in its handle, a welcome and logical move. The speed control, capable of holding any speed up to the limit of full throttle, is standard on the Camargue. The other column-mounted control is on the left: the usual indicator/dip/flash control.

The speedometer is very large, but there is no rev counter, nor

Driving the Camargue

Rolls-Royce chose to launch the Camargue in Sicily—a well-judged move, giving sufficient warmth to test the air-conditioning system, combined with some shocking roads which included one pass which took the route above the snowline in the northern mountains.

One's first impression of the car is that it is big: very big. It feels every inch of its 75-inch width to begin with, and although the feeling wears off to some extent one can never fling it into gaps with abandon, certainly not in the narrow main streets of the upland Sicilian villages. There is still a question mark over the steering, at least for the enthusiast: it is extremely light and to my mind still almost devoid of feel, and there is a suggestion of vagueness

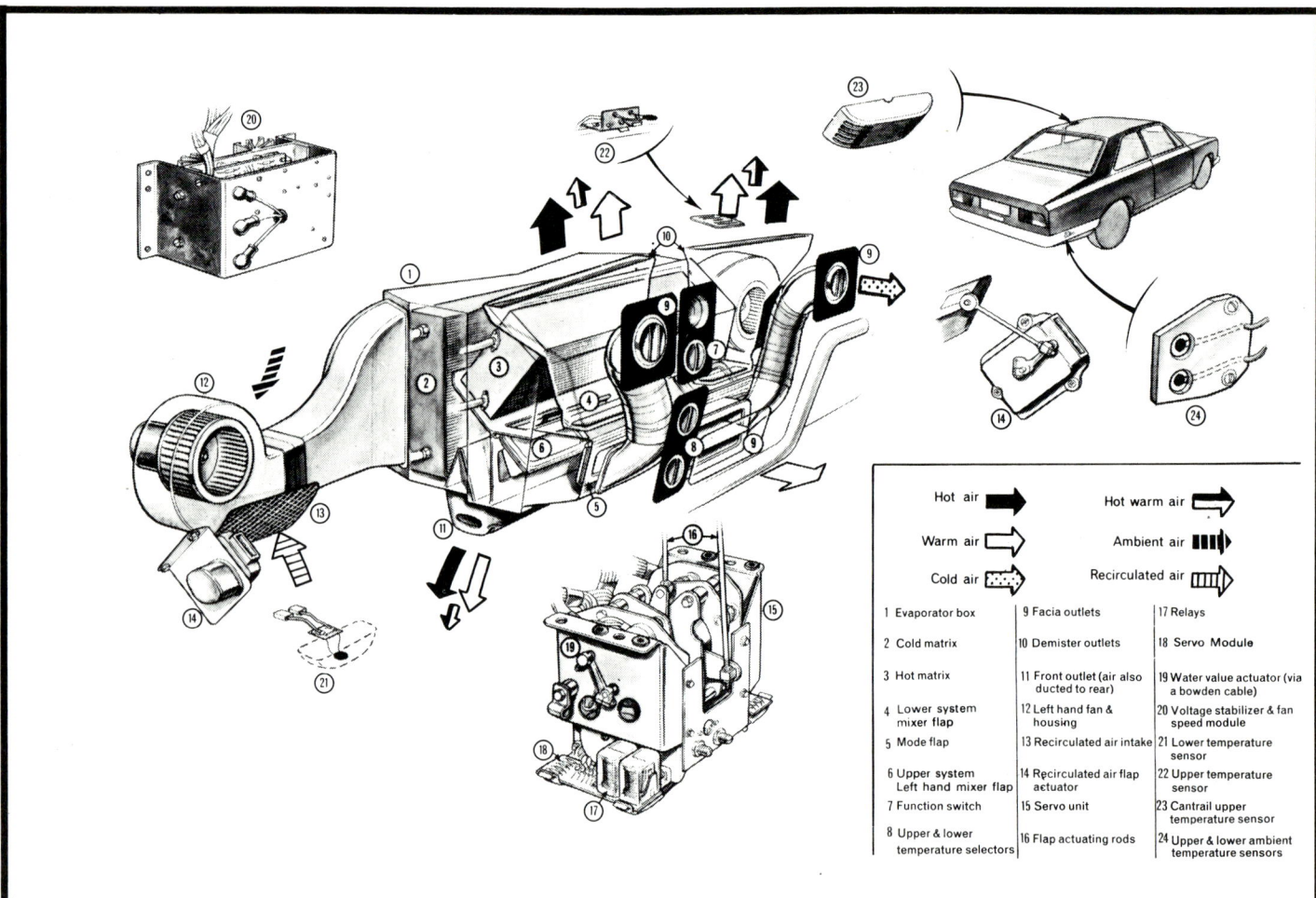

Hot air ➡		Hot warm air ⇨
Warm air ⇨		Ambient air ❙❙❙❙▸
Cold air ⬜⬜▸		Recirculated air ⬜⬜▸

1 Evaporator box	9 Facia outlets	17 Relays
2 Cold matrix	10 Demister outlets	18 Servo Module
3 Hot matrix	11 Front outlet (air also ducted to rear)	19 Water value actuator (via a bowden cable)
4 Lower system mixer flap	12 Left hand fan & housing	20 Voltage stabilizer & fan speed module
5 Mode flap	13 Recirculated air intake	21 Lower temperature sensor
6 Upper system Left hand mixer flap	14 Recirculated air flap actuator	22 Upper temperature sensor
7 Function switch	15 Servo unit	23 Cantrail upper temperature sensor
8 Upper & lower temperature selectors	16 Flap actuating rods	24 Upper & lower ambient temperature sensors

Few mechanical changes

Under the bonnet, the Camargue has a familiar look, since all its main mechanical units are carried across more or less directly from the Silver Shadow. This applies not only to the engine, but to the GM automatic transmission and the final drive.

The first few Camargues, intended mainly for the British market where they can be "kept an eye on" will have what is virtually the standard Corniche engine with two SU carburettors and a compression ratio of 9:1. These will be retained for all American and Japanese-market cars (but with the much lower

ing, as in other cars in the range, is by power-assisted recirculating-ball gearing. The steering column is collapsible and the wheel, of 15½ in. diameter, is dished.

In terms of equipment, the Camargue is lavish without being in any way gimmicky. The air conditioning system is of course the biggest single "extra", although it is built-in. A Bosch Frankfurt AM/FM radio, and a Pioneer quadraphonic cartridge player, are also part of the standard package. The instrument panel, while looking traditionally wooden, actually consists of high-quality veneer applied directly to an alloy base—lighter and much

any oil-pressure or water temperature gauges—the Camargue is not intended as a super-sports car. Apart from the speedometer, in fact, the four smaller dials are an ammeter, fuel gauge, clock, and external air temperature gauge. An impressive battery of warning lights in the centre of the facia light up (for checking) whenever the engine is started. These lights include warnings for failure of a headlamp main beam, a stop lamp or a direction indicator, as well as guarding against the several non-crucial failures possible in the triplicated braking system, which might otherwise go unnoticed until a second failure.

John Hostler's detail drawing shows the fully-automatic air-conditioning system, in many ways the most interesting feature of the new car. Five sensors generate demands which operate the many valves as well as regulating the speed of the two fans

about the straight-ahead position. On the other hand one must accept this is what the former Cadillac owner probably wants—certainly what he has been used to; one wonders how much Rolls-Royce dare try to educate their customers to higher standards.

The Camargue is one of those cars where one must be careful to

*Right: The Camargue facia appears to be traditional wood, but is actually thin veneer over an alloy base, for safety and lightness. There is no rev counter, oil pressure or water temperature gauge
Below: Centre console contains radio and stereo unit, central warning lamp panel and air-conditioning controls*

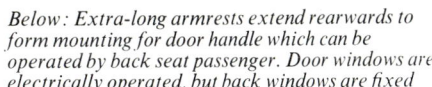

Below: Extra-long armrests extend rearwards to form mounting for door handle which can be operated by back seat passenger. Door windows are electrically operated, but back windows are fixed

Left: Despite two-door design, Camargue back seat is spacious indeed, and very comfortable. Two lights (one spot, one flood) are set in each rear quarter panel. Below: Back seat passengers are provided with their own inertia-reel three-point safety belts

distinguish between steering and handling. If one can come to terms with the steering, helped by the design of the wheel with a rim much thicker than that in the Shadow, the handling is a definite advance on anything Rolls-Royce have offered in recent years. It proved no real effort to keep up with a competently-driven (by the local police) Alfetta which set us an enthusiastic pace. There was very little roll, and the tail could be persuaded to run slightly wide on the tighter corners, then pinned down with a burst of power at the exit. In the limit, one sensed a tendency towards scrubbing understeer, but it was never a problem even down a long and twisting descent.

The ride was well up to the standard set by previous models and does not seem to have suffered in any way from the increased roll stiffness. It was possible to cover extremely bad, broken surfaces in comfort, with no sign of distress from the car except over single very bad bumps, when there was sometimes a loud crash from the suspension—but still very little felt inside the car.

The transmission was totally beyond reproach: in the normal way, changes of ratio simply cannot be felt. The downshift points are well judged, and almost the whole drive (except for the long descent to the north coast, some 3,000 feet in five miles of hairpin bends) was run with the selector at "D". In the same way, the brakes are worthy of very high praise. There was a suggestion of increased effort towards the end of the descent, but that was all: and this with four up and some luggage aboard, giving a running weight little, if any, short of three tons.

Seat comfort is good, though the tallest driver in the party was short of the last inch of rearward movement, while the air-conditioning system lived up to every claim made for it. The one point worth mentioning is that the Rolls-Royce selected datum for head-level temperature seems too high (the foot-level one is just right) and by common consent the upper selector was turned well into the blue-for-cool sector. The temperature limits of the selectors are 63 deg F at the cool end and 91 deg F at the other extremity; if the selectors are linear, our head temperature could not have been set at more than 70 deg. Again, however, one must appreciate the different tastes of (say) the American and Saudi-Arabian markets.

No attempt was made to measure the performance—that must await a full *Autocar* Road Test—but an indicated 122 mph was sustained for several minutes on the Palermo-Messina *autostrada*. This agrees well with the claim of just under 120 mph maximum, and it would seem the Camargue should return much the same figures as the Corniche.

If it is possible to niggle at one

R-R CAMARGUE

The Rolls-Royce Personal Car

aspect of the Camargue, it is in the area known in the industry as "NVH"—noise, vibration and harshness. This is not to say the Camargue is noisy in absolute terms: at 70 mph it is virtually noiseless. But in terms of its own class there is a disappointing build-up of noise from that point on, both road rumble and a measure of wind noise, and at 110 mph voices must be raised slightly to converse. On our car—which, it must be remembered, was a pre-production specimen and perhaps not entirely typical especially where wind noise was concerned —there was also a vibration period, felt more in the back than the front, with a peak at 105 mph. With the near-universal spread of speed limits, however, this is something of an academic point.

Designed to succeed

The post-1971 team at Crewe, ably led by David Plastow, have shown plenty of awareness of the way their product must be developed. All the current cars are much more roadworthy, in the fullest sense of the term, than was (say) the original Shadow. They handle better, they have better brakes, and the road noise problem of the first cars is at least half conquered. The revised, compliant front suspension, the ventilated front disc brakes, the low-profile radial-ply tyres have all been thrown into the battle, and all have played their part. Now we have the Camargue which is much more of an improvement in several directions than it might seem on paper. This is not just a prettier, two-door Shadow, but a distinct advance, not least in the splendid air-conditioning system which entirely justifies the time and money spent on it. The Camargue is additional to the existing Silver Shadow and Corniche models.

The Camargue is now in production at the rate of one a week (each car takes nearly six months to go through the whole production process) and it is hoped to step up that rate to two a week by the end of 1975. Even at that, the order book is full for at least a year to come, many orders having been placed during the last few months on a whatever-it-looks-like, whatever-it-costs basis. It is intended purely as a Rolls-Royce model, though to quote David Plastow, "If anyone asked us for a Bentley, we would certainly quote him a price". At the time of writing, a price was not being quoted at all.

Happy with the excellence of their 1974 figures, and in particular their export record, Rolls-Royce are looking to the Camargue to increase their turnover in export and overall terms. On the face of it, it cannot fail to do so.

THERE HAVE always been Rolls-Royce owners who preferred to drive themselves and who often had the designs of their Rolls-Royce bodies, as carried out by the various coachbuilders, adapted to their needs—C. S. Rolls' own 1908 40/50 h.p. ballooning car is but one example —but through the years until now there has always been a big formal car as the top model of the Rolls-Royce range. As far back as the 1930s a move was made towards an owner-driver situation with the introduction by a number of coachbuilders of what were termed close-coupled saloons. In those days, of course, Rolls-Royce supplied only chassis, though there was a range of suggested coachwork styles, and to some extent the newly acquired Bentley name —the first Rolls-Royce designed Bentley appeared in 1933—also catered for the owner-driver. The majority of Rolls-Royces, however, continued to be chauffeur driven.

After World War II, the introduction of the smaller Bentley Mk VI, to be followed soon afterwards by the large formal Rolls-Royce Silver Wraith, again catered for the owner driver, especially in the form of the coachbuilt Bentley Continental which had a two-door body. From this point onwards there is a definite evolution of the personally owned and driven Rolls-Royce. Yet though the Silver Dawn and Cloud went a considerable way towards being owner-driver cars —as a great many of them were used—they were, dare I say it, the basic models of the range, with coachbuilt Silver Wraiths and Phantoms as the most expensive Rolls-Royces.

During the 1950s and early 1960s the coachbuilt Bentley Continental models had built up a following of owner-drivers and the introduction in 1963 of the Park Ward-designed Bentley Continental two-door saloon body on a Rolls-Royce Silver Cloud III chassis resulted in what may be termed the first standard design for a Rolls-Royce personal car. There were, of course, many two-door Rolls-Royces prior to this, but these were individual coach-built cars, as opposed to coachbuilt to a standardized design. The success of this formula resulted in the Silver Shadow two-door and Corniche coachbuilt models which followed, leading up to the Camargue which represents the ultimate development of the personalized owner-driver Rolls-Royce so far.

Where the Camargue differs from all the previous owner-driver Rolls-Royces is in the shift of emphasis from the formal chauffeur-driven car as the flagship of the Rolls-Royce fleet to this impressive and luxurious two-door saloon. No longer does the millionaire who wants the most expensive Rolls-Royce have to forego the pleasure of driving.

Asked if he saw the Camargue as a successor to the Bentley Continental, David Plastow was quick to point out that the Continental was really a different sort of car and had been designed as a lightweight with a higher maximum speed than the standard saloon of the day. The Camargue, of course, does not pretend to be lightweight nor does it claim extra performance but by the time the S3 Bentley Continentals were being produced in the 1960s demand by owners for thicker seats, radios, electrically operated windows, refrigeration and a host of other weight-adding items to personalize their Continentals had nullified the painstaking efforts of H. J. Mulliner body designers in paring down the weight.

This was certainly the situation by the time the H. J. Mulliner, Park Ward Rolls-Royce Silver Cloud III (pictured above), using the Park Ward designed Bentley Continental body, came on the scene in 1963. The sales brochure for that model described it as being "for the owner who requires a car of particular distinction" which is precisely where the new Camargue comes in, providing a very exclusive top of the range personal car for the man who wants—and is willing to pay for—something appreciably different from the factory-built Silver Shadow or coachbuilt Corniche.

If you think that the Camargue, as the most expensive Rolls-Royce production model, means that the company's cars have been getting relatively more expensive over the years then you may be surprised to learn that in fact this is not so. A 1923 40/50 h.p. "Silver Ghost" limousine cost £2,800— a vast sum in those days—while just prior to World War II the big and complicated V12 Phantom III Sedanca cost £2,870. In relation to these prices the post-war cars have been getting ever cheaper while at the same time becoming more complicated—witness the current Silver Shadow. Looked at in those terms the price of the Camargue puts it back on the price scale of the exclusive Rolls-Royces of years ago, while providing a degree of refinement that would have gratified Sir Henry Royce. **Warren Allport**

Rolls-Royce Corniche (ghosted) and Camargue 2-door saloons compared

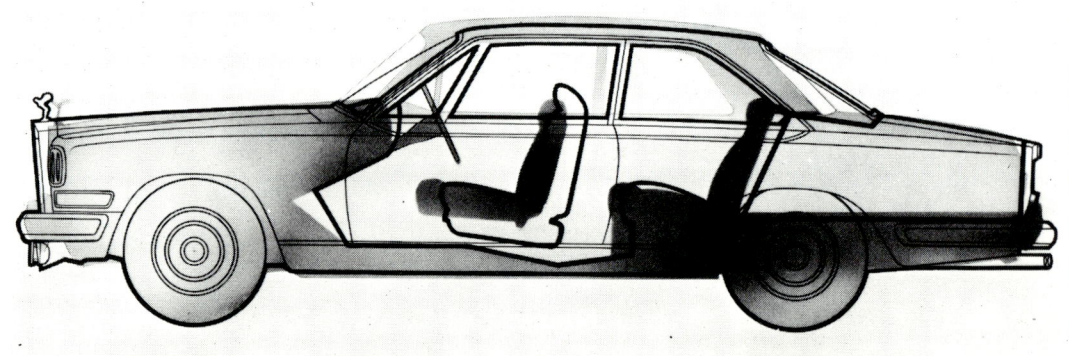

Rolls-Royce Silver Shadow

Cheapest Rolls-Royce offering refinement and finish equalled by few manufacturers.
Quiet V8 engine giving improved economy with adequate performance.
Smooth automatic transmission and good brakes.
Much improved steering response and roadholding but softer ride.

As dignified as the House of Commons, the latest Silver Shadow has changed little outwardly though there have been a number of specification changes under the bonnet

IT IS NOW just over 10 years since Rolls-Royce launched the Silver Shadow, a departure from tradition in so many ways. Now, for some people, the Shadow and its relatives the Corniche and Camargue (which share the same floorpan) *are* the tradition. Part of that tradition is the Rolls-Royce policy of continuous development, so that the Silver Shadow of today is a very different animal from the earliest cars. *Autocar* last published a Silver Shadow test in November 1972, by which time the engine had already grown from 6,230 to 6,750 c.c., and the three-speed General Motors transmission had become standard. Since then the engine has been changed again, not in size but in compression ratio which has come down from 9-to-1 to 8-to-1, permitting the use of four-star petrol with a lower lead content. Lucas Opus electronic ignition is now used and helps to maintain a consistently low level of exhaust emissions, helped also by the thermostatically-controlled air intake. Carburation is still by two SU instruments, with the fuel pumped by twin SU electric pumps.

On the chassis side, several changes have been made to the suspension to obtain better compliance (for lower road noise) without compromising geometry and therefore handling. At the same time the tyres have become lower and wider, the 205-15 covers of the 1972 car being replaced by 235/70-15 size. The former triple braking system has been replaced by a simpler — still fully-duplicated — double system.

Rolls-Royce are no more insulated from the effects of inflation than anyone else, and it is sad to note that the price of a Silver Shadow has risen from the £10,550 of our 1972 test car, to £17,813 today. This does, however, underline what many owners have found, that a Silver Shadow can turn out to be an investment.

Performance and economy

As always, Rolls-Royce quote no power or torque output for the V8 engine. By comparing the performance with that of other cars, however, one can make an intelligent guess. The peak power must be a good deal less than the 225 bhp of the much quicker Mercedes 450SEL, for instance, and indeed it is doubtful if the Rolls-Royce engine produces an honest 200 bhp (DIN). What is more difficult to determine is the engine speed at peak power, and hence the intelligence of the overall gearing.

Such a low power output from an engine of this size, corresponding to less than 30 bhp per litre, argues that the designers have sought other qualities than sheer performance, in particular quietness and reliability. Rolls-Royce have always termed their power output "sufficient" and one can hardly argue with a maximum speed of 116 mph and a 0-60 mph time of 10.6sec. A higher maximum speed would be increasingly useless, and greater acceleration is difficult to use without disturbing passengers.

What seems certain is that little power has been lost with the lowering of the compression ratio. Compared with the 1972 test, the present car is just 1 mph slower at its maximum and has lost only 0.3sec in the standing start acceleration to 60 mph, despite being 80 lb heavier at the kerb and being tested in worse conditions. It all but held its own in acceleration right through to 100 mph, but the 110 mph figure was well down, indicating that some of the top-end eagerness has been lost.

The overall gearing gives a relatively modest 25.8 mph per 1,000 rpm, so that the 116 mph mean maximum is reached at 4,500 rpm which must be fairly close to the power peak. Certainly that peak, when reached, is followed by a rapid strangling of the engine. It is worth noting that while the Intermediate ratio will run to 94 mph, the 70-90 mph time is slower in Intermediate than in top. When running the standing-start accelerations, we found that any attempt to hold the transmission beyond the natural full-throttle change-up points (44 and 74 mph) resulted in a slower time, so there is absolutely nothing to be gained by fiddling with the transmission selector. In the wet conditions of the test, it proved possible to spin the wheels briefly when leaving the line, if the torque converter was brought up to the stall point against the brakes.

Rolls-Royce claim the engine changes have made the Silver Shadow appreciably more economical, and this was borne out by almost all our figures, whether at steady speeds or in normal driving. The steady-speed figures show the "hole" at 30 mph typical of almost all today's emission-controlled cars, so that it is actually more economical to cruise at a steady 40 mph (which is the only speed at which the big car bettered 20 mpg). After that there is a steady decline

all the way to 11 mpg at a steady 100 mph. The only speed at which the latest car proved marginally inferior to the 1972 model was at 80 mph (14.7 against 15 mpg).

In overall terms, the latest car achieved 13.6 mpg against the 12.4 mpg of the previous test. This may not sound much, and it certainly doesn't lift the Shadow much higher in the economy league table, but it *is* a 10 per cent improvement and as such, well worth having.

Above: The latest engine has an 8.0 to 1 compression ratio and Lucas Opus electronic ignition. The underbonnet area looks less accessible than most routine items are. The refrigeration compressor is mounted on top of the engine at front

Naturally, it is a figure that reflects our usual harder than average driving, and a more usual result would be about 15 mpg which incidentally coincides with the predicted DIN touring consumption. Given gentle driving, up to 18 mpg should be possible but clearly, nobody is ever going to see the right side of 20 mpg except in freak circumstances.

Handling and brakes

The first thing that must be said under this heading is that Rolls-Royce know their market. It is a market that does not demand Ferrari-style handling and steering, and it doesn't get it. One is actually driven to question the fairness of one's own criticisms, since the *Autocar* test staff are — perhaps regrettably from their point of view — a long way from being typical Silver Shadow owners. Even so, there are some points where the car might be improved even in the most general view.

The steering is reasonably geared with 3.6 turns of the wheel between extremes of a lock which, for this size of car, is by no means bad: well under 40ft. On the other hand the steering is still extremely light, the assistance very powerful, and it takes a gentle hand at the wheel to detect even a suggestion of feel. It might be argued that this would be a good thing for a chauffeur, driven back to relying on the same senses as those of his passengers. At the

same time, one wonders if it is really a good thing to be so divorced from any idea of what the front wheels are trying to do, and how close to the limit of adhesion they may be. If it is permitted to take the Shadow's two obvious competitors as yardsticks, the steering is much more Cadillac than Mercedes — not surprisingly perhaps, since the steering gear like the transmission comes straight from General Motors.

If the lack of feel does not matter as much as it once did, that is because the latest Shadow is massively stable. We commented in 1972 that the car was much improved in stability compared with the earliest examples (which were decidedly deficent in this respect, at least by today's standards). The further changes to the suspension, and the adoption of low-profile tyres, have made things better still so that the Silver Shadow of today sits on the motorway, running arrow-straight with no need for the driver to correct its course more than occasionally. Even strong, blustering sidewinds do little to push the car off line, and this is all to the good.

Cornering behaviour depends very much on the driver's approach. If the Shadow is driven smoothly, as we trust all chauffeurs will, there is a steady build-up

Above: The wide low profile 235/70HR-15 radials are the only outward change on the latest car

of understeer, smooth and predictable but quite quick, scrubbing off speed unless a lot more power is applied. Rougher driving — which requires some confidence, given the inertia involved — can result in the tail swinging mildly out of line, in which case speed is scrubbed off even more quickly. Increasing the tyre pressures by 6psi all round, to those recommended for driving at over 110 mph, has little effect on the stability but improves the cornering behaviour quite noticeably. At high speed, however, a slight tendency to oversteer can then be detected (and became moderately disturbing when the car was entering the steep MIRA banking at 120 mph). The roadholding is good at all times, and excellent in the wet, thanks to the Avon tyres fitted to the test car.

Rolls-Royce Silver Shadow

Above: A 120 in wheelbase makes for a roomy passenger compartment. The side marker lamps are illuminated with the sidelamps. Right: Hefty overriders and a substantial bumper protect the bodywork from minor scrapes. The rear fog warning lamps are standard

GB 100 LG

The brakes are rather lighter than before, and those familiar with older Shadows may notice the lower brake pedal — now nicely levelled with the accelerator — and reduced pedal travel. Given the lower effort, it would have been easy to over-servo the brakes, but this has not happened. Instead the action is so beautifully progressive that the car is one of the easiest to stop smoothly with no suggestion of a final jerk — doubtless something that was accorded high priority during development. We were expecting a disappointing ultimate performance on the wet track but the wide Avons hung on superbly to record 0.96g before all four wheels slid with considerable reluctance. Stability and control under heavy braking are far better than average.

Our brake fade test showed no problem whatever. To begin with the brakes proved a little speed-sensitive, but once they were fully warmed their performance was absolutely consistent with no increase whatever in pedal travel or effort. Clearly the four big discs are well up to their exacting task of stopping well over two tons of car. The handbrake also did well, recording 0.3g when used alone before locking the back wheels on the wet surface; it held securely on the 1-in-3 MIRA test hill, on which the Silver Shadow restarted — as one would expect — with contemptuous ease.

Comfort and convenience

This is the area in which the Silver Shadow might be expected to excel, and generally it does so, though it is not without its weaker points. The ride is helped by the self-levelling arrangement which ensures that the rear springs are always working around their mid-point whatever the load condition.

The self-levelling can sometimes be felt working when the car has been brought to a quick halt, but most of the time it goes quietly about its task and some owners might never be aware of its existence.

In other ways, the suspension is fairly conventional with a front linkage arrangement which corresponds to double wishbone geometry, and semi-trailing arms at the rear. Suspension travel is long and the springing correspondingly soft; the damper settings are also on the soft side, though not so much as to induce the upsetting vertical heave so often encountered in the full-sized American car. Instead the softness is felt more when the car reaches the bottom of a ramp, or when it traverses a single hump, when it lifts or dives more than one might expect. On rough surfaces the damping works well, while the big wheels stand the car in good stead. Roll angles are not high, but are probably more than many designers would think desirable today. It should not be inferred from this that the Silver Shadow's ride is poor in any way; it is

extremely good, though biased towards those who prefer soft rather than sporting feel. If it no longer seems exceptional, that is because so many manufacturers have managed to improve the ride of their cars in the past few years.

The front seats are power-adjusted by miniature "joysticks" in the centre console, and their range of adjustment is sufficient to cater for a very wide range of drivers. Although the steering column is not adjustable, most drivers seem able to arrive at a comfortable and efficient sitting position, though really short people may have more trouble. The seats themselves are less satisfactory. Both cushion and squab are very thick slabs of beautifully leather-upholstered springing. They lack sufficient shaping to give proper sideways support — even our heaviest driver found he didn't sink very far into them — and several testers thought the squab was badly shaped to support the small of the back. It helps that one can adjust the tilt of the seat, but even so there is a tendency on long trips to slide

Specification

ENGINE

	Front; Rear drive
Cylinders	8, in 90 deg vee
Main bearings	5
Cooling	Water
Fan	Viscous
Bore, mm (in.)	104.1 (4.10)
Stroke, mm (in.)	99.0 (3.90)
Capacity, cc (in.)	6,750 (411.9)
Valve gear	ohv
Camshaft drive	Chain
Compression ratio	8.0-to-1
Octane rating	97RM
Carburettor	2 SU HD8

TRANSMISSION

Type	General Motors three-speed automatic with torque converter

Gear	Ratio	mph/1000rpm
Top	1.0	25.80
Inter	1.48	17.43
Low	2.48	10.40
Final drive gear		Hypoid bevel
Ratio		3.08-to-1

SUSPENSION

Front—location	Double wishbones
springs	Coil
dampers	Telescopic
anti-roll bar	Yes
Rear—location	Semi-trailing arms
springs	Coil
dampers	Telescopic
anti-roll bar	No

STEERING

Type	Recirculating-ball
Power assistance	Yes
Wheel diameter	15.7 in.

BRAKES

Front	11.0 in. dia. disc
Rear	11.0 in. dia. disc
Servo	Hydraulic, engine-driven

WHEELS

Type	Pressed steel disc, 5-stud fixing
Rim width	6.0 in.
Tyres—make	Avon (on test car)
—type	Radial-ply tubed
—size	235/70-15in.

EQUIPMENT

Battery	12 volt 71 Ah
Alternator	55 amp
Headlamps	Four-lamp system, 270/75 watt (total)
Reversing lamp	Standard
Hazard warning	Standard
Electric fuses	21
Screen wipers	2-speed plus intermittent
Screen washer	Electric
Interior heater	Air blending
Interior trim	Leather seats, Ambla headlining
Floor covering	Carpet
Jack	Screw pillar type
Jacking points	1 each side under sill
Windscreen	Laminated
Underbody protection	Zinc plating plus bitumastic overall

MAINTENANCE

Fuel tank	23.5 Imp galls (107 litres)
Cooling system	28.5 pints (inc. heater)
Engine sump	14.75 pints SAE 20W/50
Gearbox	5 pints Dexron
Final drive	4.5 pints SAE 90 EP
Grease	6 points
Contact breaker	Lucas Opus ignition
Ignition timing	15 deg BTDC (stroboscopic at 1,200 rpm)
Spark plug—type	Champion N14Y
—gap	0.030 in.
Tyre pressures	F24; R28 psi (normal driving)
Max payload	1,000 lb (454 kg)

Maximum Speeds

Gear	mph	kph	rpm
Top (mean)	116	187	4,500
(best)	120	193	4,650
Inter	94	151	5,400
Low	56	90	5,400

Acceleration

True mph	Time secs	Speedo mph
30	3.8	30
40	5.6	40
50	7.6	50
60	10.6	60
70	14.1	70
80	19.0	80
90	25.8	91
100	36.5	103
110	60.7	115

Standing ¼-mile:
18.1 sec, 78 mph
kilometre:
33.3 sec, 97 mph

mph	Top	Inter	Low
10-30	—	—	2.3
20-40	—	—	3.4
30-50	—	4.9	4.2
40-60	—	5.6	—
50-70	—	6.7	—
60-80	10.0	8.8	—
70-90	12.5	14.9	—
80-100	21.1	—	—
90-110	32.8	—	—

Consumption

Fuel
Overall mpg: **13.6**
(20.8 litres/100km)
Calculated (DIN) mpg: 15.0
(18.8 litres/100km)

Constant speed:

mph	mpg
30	19.3
40	20.1
50	19.6
60	18.3
70	16.5
80	14.7
90	12.8
100	11.0

Autocar formula
Hard driving, difficult conditions
  12.2 mpg
Average driving, average conditions
  15.0 mpg
Gentle driving, easy conditions
  17.7 mpg
Grade of fuel: Premium, 4-star
(97RM)
Mileage recorder: 0.8 per cent
  over reading

Oil
Consumption (SAE 20W/50)
  2,000 miles/pint

Brakes

Fade (from 70 mph in neutral)
Pedal load for 0.5g stops in lb

	start/end		start/end
1	27/24	6	30/30
2	29/27	7	30/30
3	30/30	8	30/30
4	30/30	9	30/30
5	30/30	10	30/30

Response (from 30 mph in neutral)

Load	g	Distance
20lb	0.45	67ft
30lb	0.60	50ft
40lb	0.75	40ft
50lb	0.90	33ft
60lb	0.96	31ft
Handbrake	0.30	100ft

Max. gradient 1 in 3

Test Conditions

Wind: 10-17 mph
Temperature: 8 deg C (46 deg F)
Barometer: 29.5 in Hg
Humidity: 80 per cent
Surface: wet asphalt and concrete
Test distance 2,120 miles

Figures taken at 17,000 miles by our own staff at the Motor Industry Research Association proving ground at Nuneaton.

All Autocar test results are subject to world copyright and may not be reproduced in whole or part without the Editor's written permission

Regular Service

Interval	3,000	6,000	12,000
Engine oil	Yes	Yes	Yes
Oil filter	No	Yes	Yes
Gearbox oil	No	No	Yes
Spark plugs	No	No	Yes
Air-cleaner	No	No	Yes
C/breaker	No	No	Yes

Total cost £15.48 £42.37 £74.69
(Assuming labour at £4.30/hour)

Parts Cost

(including VAT)

Brake pads (2 wheels)—front	£19.63
Brake pads (2 wheels)—rear	£17.92
Silencers (stainless)	£331.35
Tyre—each (typical advertised)	£38.15
Windscreen	£60.35
Headlamp unit	£3.37
Front wing	£83.24
Rear bumper	£86.40

Warranty Period
36 months/50,000 miles
  (mechanical)
12 months (bodywork)

Weight

Kerb, 42.4 cwt/4,752 lb/2,156 kg
(Distribution F/R, 53.9/46.1)
As tested, 45.7 cwt/5,117 lb/
2,332 kg

Boot capacity: 22.5 cu. ft.

Turning circles:
Between kerbs L, 39ft 8in; R, 39ft 2in
Between walls L, 41ft 3in; R, 40ft 9in
Turns, lock to lock 3.6

Test Scorecard

(Average of scoring by *Autocar* Road Test team)

Ratings: 6 *Excellent*
5 *Good*
4 *Better than average*
3 *Worse than average*
2 *Poor*
1 *Bad*

PERFORMANCE	5.00
STEERING AND HANDLING	4.67
BRAKES	4.60
COMFORT IN FRONT	4.58
COMFORT IN BACK	5.14
DRIVER AIDS	4.25
(instruments, lights, wipers, visibility etc)	
CONTROLS	4.00
NOISE	5.17
STOWAGE	5.67
ROUTINE SERVICE	3.10
(under bonnet access: dipstick etc.)	
EASE OF DRIVING	5.00

OVERALL RATING **4.49**

OVERALL LENGTH 16' 11.5"
OVERALL WIDTH 5'11"
OVERALL HEIGHT 4' 11.75"
GROUND CLEARANCE 6"
WHEELBASE 10' 0"
FRONT TRACK 4' 9.5"
REAR TRACK 4' 9.5"

Comparisons

	Price £	max mph	0-60 sec	overall mpg	capacity c.c.	power bhp	wheelbase in.	length in.	width in.	weight lb	fuel gall	tyre size
Rolls-Royce Silver Shadow	**17,813**	**116**	**10.6**	**13.6**	**6,750**	**—**	**120**	**203½**	**71**	**4,752**	**23.5**	**235/70-15**
Fiat 130	5,721	113	11.4	15.7	3,235	165	107	187	71	3,560	17.5	205-14
Jaguar XJ12	7,496	146	7.4	11.4	5,343	285	113	195	70	4,152	20	205/70-15
Mercedes 450SEL	11,312	136	9.0	14.1	4,520	160	105	181½	68	2,690	15.2	195-14
Opel Commodore GS/E	5,068	115	10.7	18.1	2,784	225	116½	199	73½	3,870	21	205/70-14
Volvo 264	5,896	104	12.7	18.6	2,664	140	104	193	67	3,195	13.2	185/70-14

forward into a slouched position which eventually gives backache. In fact, while the seats look tremendously impressive, they are far from being the best seats available from an ergonomic point of view. The leather upholstery is standard, but Rolls-Royce will of course supply almost any alternative (at a price).

By contrast with the front seats, the back seat is a model of good shaping and comfort. There is plenty of head and knee room for very large passengers, as indeed there should be with a 120in. wheelbase. Entry and exit are easy and if anything, the ride feels better than it does in the front. One is forced to the overall conclusion that it is nicer to ride in the back of the car than in the front: a relic of a former order of priorities?

The major controls are an odd mixture of good and bad. Many people may be surprised to find that the standard steering wheel is a thin-rimmed plastic affair, which seems small in relation with the bulk of the car. The two pedals are well offset to the right, leaving plenty of space to rest the left foot (which has the responsibility of operating the dipswitch). The transmission selector is mounted on the right of the steering column and is very easy to operate, the only danger for a newcomer being a tendency to confuse it with the indicator stalk mounted opposite. At least one staff member frightened himself by selecting neutral when intending to signal a left turn. The transmission itself is almost, but not totally, unobtrusive. We noticed an occasional slight thump when engaging Drive at rest, and the kick-down from Intermediate to Low can certainly be felt. For the rest, it is possible to

Above: Instrumentation appears more comprehensive than it actually is, though there are numerous warning lamps. Push-pull knobs control the central fresh air outlets. Surrounding the clock are (l to r): Panel light switch, radio balance control, electric aerial switch, wiper switch. The main lighting switch and the ignition/starter switch are to the right of the steering column. Right: A Pioneer quadrophonic cartridge player (top) and a Bosch Frankfurt AM/FM stereo radio are both standard. Ahead of the ashtray are the electric seat adjustment "joysticks." Controls for the upper and lower heating systems and refrigeration are central on the console. Below: The boot release switch is positioned in the glove locker so that this can be locked leaving luggage in the boot safe when the car has to be handed to others for parking at hotels

detect ratio changes if one is concentrating and listening for them; but passengers with their minds on higher things will inevitably be unaware of the transmission. If the driver hangs on to Low for an unreasonable time, a safety change up takes place at 56 mph, which corresponds to 5,400 rpm. The handbrake, while effective, is poorly placed, tucked away under the facia on the right. We noticed this especially when having to lean right forward to reach it when restarting on the 1-in-3 hill.

The minor controls are "traditional" and poor by modern standards. The lights switch on the right is a rotary knob selecting side, head and fog lamps in turn. It is matched by a smaller switch on the left which selects the three wiper speeds (two steady, one intermittent). The wiper switch especially calls for the driver to lean well forward to reach it. Screen washing is controlled by a much handier switch on the end of the indicator stalk, which also brings in the wipers for several strokes.

The heater controls, mounted in the centre console, are by contrast easy to reach and operate. The system is not of course a simple heater, but also offers a recirculating circuit with refrigeration (as distinct from the complete fresh-air conditioning system seen on the Camargue, and now also the Corniche). The heater controls select

upper and lower temperature indepently, flow being controlled by pushing the knobs in (less flow) or pulling them out. Both hot and cold air are available in copious quantity, and the separation of upper and lower flows makes it easy to control distribution. Fan speed is separately controlled. The only possible criticism here is that the coarsely-spaced detents of the temperature selectors can make it tricky to achieve exactly the right degree of warmth.

For the driver, one pleasant and mildly surprising aspect of the Silver Shadow is the excellent visibility. The front corners of the car can be clearly seen, and the tail is visible for reversing without any undue craning of the neck. A weaker spot is the wipers, which clear small arcs and on the test car

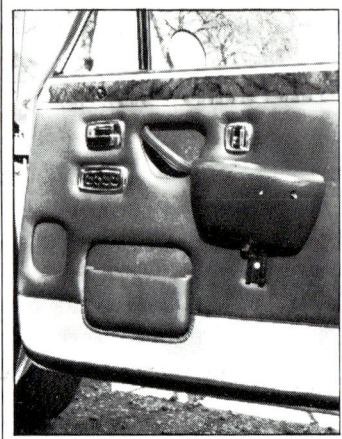

Above: Four switches on the driver's door control the electrically-operated windows and there is remote adjustment of the door mirror. Above the adjustable armrest is the switch for the central locking system

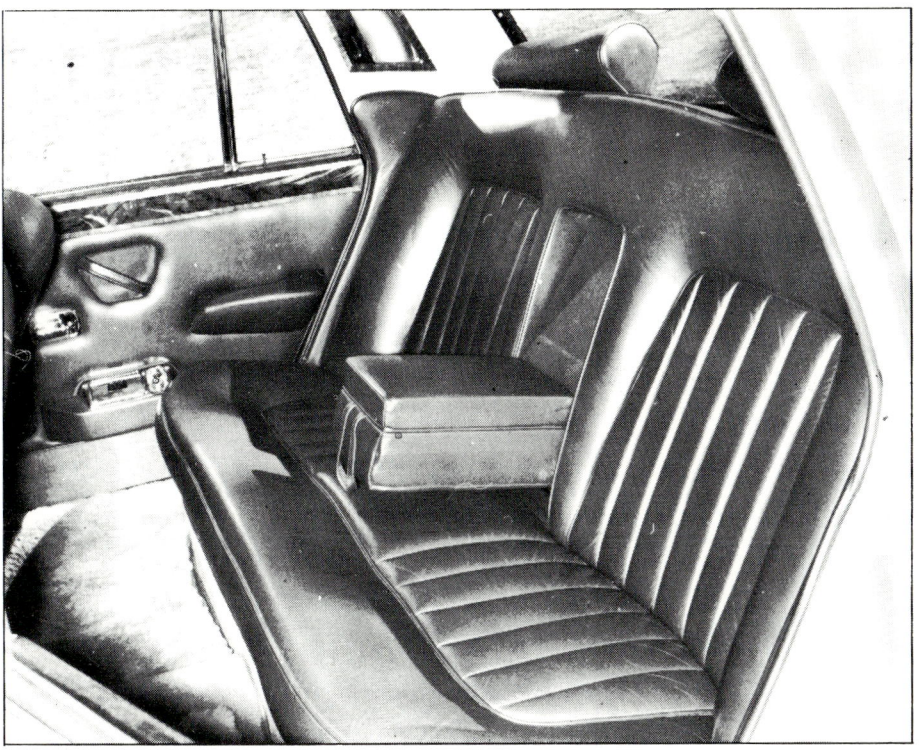

Back seat legroom is generous and there are moveable footrests. Headrests, a reading lamp and mirror in each rear quarter, and an ashtray and cigar lighter in each rear door are provided

at least, did not adhere all that well to the screen at high speed. The headlamps are extremely good on main beam, and well-controlled on dip, though owners may specify halogen headlamps if they need even more light.

Where silence is concerned, the Silver Shadow remains mildly disappointing. Rolls-Royce are not alone in discovering that very wide radial-ply tyres create and transmit a lot of road noise, not only through the suspension mountings but also by air-transmission to the wheel arch interiors. In its latest form the Shadow is certainly better than it was but it is still far from silent. It is quiet enough to fool many passengers they are riding in silence until they notice a change in "background quality" when the car crosses from one surface to another. On smooth asphalt, the Shadow is indeed *very* quiet; on ribbed concrete, it is noticeably less so. This is all a matter of degree, but thrown into more prominence by the Shadow's excellence in other respects. The engine *can* be made to emit a characteristic V8 throb when accelerating flat-out at low speed, but for the most part one is not aware of it. The transmission is quiet at all times. At high speeds in the test car there was a whisper of wind noise, untypical in our experience, from the top of the driver's door — a less than perfect seal, perhaps. In these circumstances it is inevitable that the road rumble will be noticed, and there is certainly quite enough of it to drown the ticking of a clock. There is also, on these latest tyres, an element of bump-thump over transverse road joints, while a large pothole or raised drain cover may give rise to a single loud crash as the car passes across.

Living with the Silver Shadow

One does not, of course, "live with" the Silver Shadow as one might with a lesser car. Few owners will be concerned with washing it — though except for its sheer size, the job is easy — or with doing their own servicing (which is assuredly much more tricky). When it *has* to be lived with, as on a long Continental journey, it has all the equipment needed to ease the strain of life. The long list of standard equipment includes a Bosch Frankfurt AM/FM radio and electrically-retractable aerial, and a Pioneer quadrophonic cartridge player (the much more sensible cassette system may be specified at a small extra cost). Other, lesser items such as the heated rear window and the fog lights one takes for granted.

There is unlikely to be any problem with stowing luggage. The boot is very large, and loading is helped by a feature missing in so many cheaper cars – the absence of a sill over which cases must be humped. Interior stowage for odds and ends is also much better than average, a greatly-appreciated point. The fuel tank, with its remotely-operated filler cover, holds 23½ gallons. This is sufficient for a range of well over 300 miles, though it is disconcerting to discover that the fuel gauge calibration is far from linear, and that the needle wavers when the car is driven on twisting roads.

Speaking of the fuel gauge highlights one odd point of the Silver Shadow: its lack of instruments. It could be argued that this is no bad thing, but there must be keen owners who long for more information than is provided by a speedometer, ammeter, fuel contents gauge and clock. Under the bonnet, things are not as bad as they might at first appear. No big V8 engine is the easiest unit to maintain, but the Rolls-Royce unit is not as bad as it looks. Many of the apparent complications are due to items not immediately associated with the operation of the car, such as the refrigeration compressor. Others, like the Lucas Opus distributor, are mounted high and clear of encumbrances. In other words, although the initial picture is daunting, the Silver Shadow by no means conspires to defeat the keen owner-driver.

In conclusion

It is not easy to sum up the Silver Shadow. A hard-bitten road tester may assess it in terms of performance or ride or handling; but how is he to take into account the feeling which overcomes him when he steps into the back of the car, in full public view, after it has called for him in the morning? Of such feelings are reputations made. In cold-blooded terms, one is entitled to ask if any car is worth nearly £20,000. Included in our comparison tables are three cars costing less than a third as much, though with comparable performance and in each case, at least something of their own sophisticated aura. Yet the Silver Shadow sells. It not only sells, it maintains its value in a unique way. Personal feelings apart – and there are many whose personal feelings will transcend what *Autocar* has baldly to say about specific output or handling or road noise or minor control layout – we should all be grateful that one manufacturer continues to work to a different, and higher, set of standards. And we British should be grateful above all that that manufacturer continues to be one of our most successful exporters. Is it wrong that such a car, so well developed and carefully assembled, should continue in the face of all economic adversity to be a symbol of success in Britain too? ☐

The boot is large and luggage loading is helped by the lack of a sill. Small tools and spare bulbs are housed in a fitted tray on top of the battery. The spare wheel winds down from under the boot floor

MANUFACTURER:	
Rolls-Royce Motors Ltd.,	
Pyms Lane,	
Crewe, Cheshire	

PRICES	
Basic	£15,225.00
Special Car Tax	£1,268.75
VAT	£1,319.50
Total (in GB)	**£17,813.25**
Seat Belts	Standard
Licence	£40.00
Delivery charge (London)	£38.60
Number plates	£6.48
Total on the Road	
(exc. insurance)	**£17,898.33**
Insurance	Group 7
EXTRAS (inc. VAT)	
Halogen headlamps	£22.81
Cassette player	£29.83
Non-standard carpet	£22.81
Non-standard paint	£119.92
Everflex roof covering	£310.05
Woolcloth upholstery	£64.93
TOTAL AS TESTED	
ON THE ROAD	**£17,898.33**

Improved Rolls-Royce saloon with rack and pinion steering, revised front suspension and fully-automatic air conditioning

SILVER SHADOW II

Above: Recognition points on the Series II cars are the black polyurethane-faced bumpers, the front air dam and the chromium plated twin exhaust tailpipe

BY ANY NORMAL standard, the Rolls-Royce Silver Shadow is now an elderly design. It was, after all, first seen in 1965. But normal standards do not apply to the Shadow. For one thing, the usual laws of the market-place seem not to apply to the most expensive cars. You have only to look at the eternally strong demand for the Shadow, and its buoyant second-hand value, to see that. Then again, the Shadow of today is very different from its counterpart of 10 years ago. It takes an expert eye to sort them out, but under the skin the changes — which we recall on page 44 of this issue — have been extensive and all to the good. Last but not least, it is a long and expensive business to develop a new model, the more so if it has to meet the elevated standards of Rolls-Royce. Eventually no doubt there will be a new Silver Shadow (or Silver Something); according to some rumour-mongers, it was imminent. But with the advent of the Silver Shadow II (alias Bentley T2), the prospect of an all-new car has receded by at least three years.

Even though the Shadow II is not a new car, it answers a lot of the criticisms thrown at Rolls over the years, especially by enthusiastic owner-drivers. The general European — perhaps even American — view was that the handling had been improved by various changes to the front suspension and by the adoption of wider and better tyres; but that the steering remained woolly, vague and devoid of feel. This is answered by one of the major changes on the Shadow II, the adoption of rack and pinion steering in place of the recirculating-ball system. Another major change is the incorporation of the fully-automatic air-conditioning system first seen on the Camargue and later adopted for the Corniche. There have been several alterations to the engine specification in the interests of lower exhaust emissions and noise levels. A completely new instrument panel includes several new instruments in a much neater layout, while externally the new version may be identified by a chin-type spoiler under the front bumper, and by the bumpers themselves which are now of the American pattern.

Steering and suspension

The new rack and pinion steering has been developed by Burman, and there are many points of similarity with the Rover 3500 system. There was little difficulty substituting the rack for the previous cross-member running beneath the engine, but it had to be modified to accept an offtake from the centre of the rack, rather than from one end, since Rolls-Royce favour steering links of equal length. The gearing is not as high as in the Rover, but is still "quick" for so large a car, at 3.5 turns from lock to lock.

Together with the rack and pinion steering, the geometry of the front suspension has been altered to improve response by keeping the wheel more upright during cornering. This is achieved by raising the mounting point of the upper "wishbone" (which comprises a transverse link and a compliant link). Tyre life is improved and understeer substantially reduced — indeed, too much for the liking of Rolls-Royce, who have reduced the diameter of the rear anti-roll bar to partially offset the effect.

Two advantages of the new steering system which must, to an extent, have been unlooked-for are the lower weight, and the damping effect within the rack which does away with the need for a separate damper as fitted with the previous system. All told, the rack and pinion arrangement is 27lb lighter than its recirculating-ball predecessor — not much in a car of the Shadow's weight, but well worth having. The tyres remain unchanged on the Shadow II: Rolls are still looking at steel-braced tyres, but are not yet ready to make the change.

Engine changes

The self-cancelling effect of the suspension changes is mirrored in the revised engine, in which a slight power loss on the inlet side is balanced by a gain from the adoption of the Corniche-type twin exhaust system with its lower back-pressure. The main difference on the inlet side is the use of twin SU HIF7 carburettors in place of the old HD8s; the new units have a smaller choke and therefore tend to sacrifice power at the top end, though they gain in mid-range torque. As always, Rolls are not prepared to discuss actual power outputs but the loss in power is at least regained by the dual exhaust system, while there is also some benefit in fuel consumption. The advantages of the new SU HIF carburettors are mainly those of cleaner exhaust emissions. The units are tamper-proof, and have temperature compensation for fuel density which leads to lower

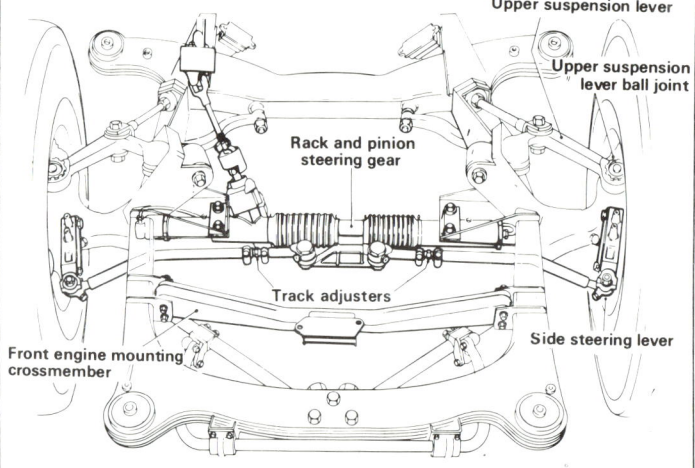

Changes to the front suspension geometry keep the wheels more upright when cornering and reduce body roll thereby taking some load off the tyres. The Burman rack and pinion steering is power assisted

Upper suspension lever

Upper suspension lever ball joint

Rack and pinion steering gear

Track adjusters

Side steering lever

Front engine mounting crossmember

carbon monoxide emissions at idle, and to easier cold starting. An incidental advantage is that the latest carburettors are not "handed," but may be used on either bank of cylinders.

A second change concerns the cooling system, in which the single viscous-coupled fan has been replaced by a larger seven-bladed unit, in tandem with an electric fan mounted ahead of the radiator. The main object is to reduce noise, since the slower, 1,700 rpm maximum of the viscous-coupled fan will clearly be better in this respect. The electric fan is set to operate at a coolant temperature of about 105degC, which means it should only operate at high ambient temperatures.

A final engine change which may — indeed, should — go unnoticed by the owner is the discarding of the traditional felt-element oil filter in favour of the throw-away canister which is now almost universal. Rolls say that they were contemplating this change in any case, but that access problems associated with the rack and pinion steering made it a necessity.

New facia

The first impetus for a change in facia design came from the need to accommodate the new control layout for the automatic air-condi-

Below: Extensively revised facia. The electronic speedometer reads up to 999,999 and the steering wheel incorporates a squashable section between the wheel boss and column to ensure that in an accident the weight of an unbelted driver is taken by the whole wheel rim. To the left of the steering column are the two rotary controls for the air conditioning temperature selection. A new panel contains warning lights for brake circuit pressure (2), parking brake, low brake fluid, low coolant, overheating, low washer fluid, stop lamp failure, icy conditions and low fuel

Above: Under the bonnet there have been a number of changes. Tamper-proof SU HIF7 carburettors are now fitted to give easier emission control and a cartridge-type oil filter replaces the felt-element type. The windscreen washer reservoir has been moved to an under-wing location and is of a massive 8.5 pints capacity. A new 20 in. viscous-coupled cooling fan is supplemented by an electrically driven fan ahead of the radiator

tioning. This system now becomes a universal fitting in Rolls-Royce cars (except for the Phantom VI). It functions exactly as described in detail in our original Camargue description, though the dial controls of the more expensive car have given way to thumbwheel selectors for upper and lower temperature. These work on the same principle, but save space on the facia. As before, Rolls recommend that once an owner has set the controls to his own liking, he should leave them alone; there is nothing to be gained in speed of warm-up, for instance, by over-riding the controls. The system is designed to achieve the desired operating condition as quickly as possible.

The adoption of the system means a considerable expansion in production for the various electronic and electro-mechanical units. When first introduced, in the Camargue, it could be built on a hand-made, "bread-board" basis but in the succeeding period things have become much better organized. Thanks to careful development, the electronics were right from the start, but assembly and test methods have been improved to cope with the far greater production flow. Apart from the different control arrangement, owners will notice that the familiar centre console housing the heater has been deleted and the controls moved to the facia to the left of the steering wheel.

Instead of the old instrument arrangement which to some eyes looked both sparse and ugly, with a single large dial for the speedometer set somewhat off-centre and small accompanying dials for the minor instruments, the new facia has two large, matched, symmetrically-spaced dials. One is the speedometer, a new electronic instrument of great accuracy and improved reliability; the use of an electric rather than a mechanical connection has cut down noise, and there is now a press-to-reset trip mileage recorder.

The second of the two large dials is a four-in-one instrument containing fuel, water temperature, oil pressure gauges and ammeter. In a sense this is a return to Vintage standards but the result is tidy and impressive. Less readily appreciated is the new placing of the electrical systems panel — the fuses, relays and junction boxes — which is now fitted in the knee trim padding below the glovebox on the passenger's side. Apart from making the panel more accessible, the new arrangement also leaves room for an airbag, should it ever be required (not that Rolls confess themselves in favour of the idea).

The final introduction to the facia is another new instrument, potentially very useful. This is an ambient air temperature indicator, which will serve not only to remind occupants how hot or cold it really is outside, but also should give warning of slippery conditions if the temperature falls towards freezing point.

Complementing these changes are others of a more cosmetic nature. The steering wheel is now leather-covered and is of smaller (15¼in.) diameter; a new ashtray is provided by the driver's right hand; and a revised-shape exterior mirror with internal adjustment.

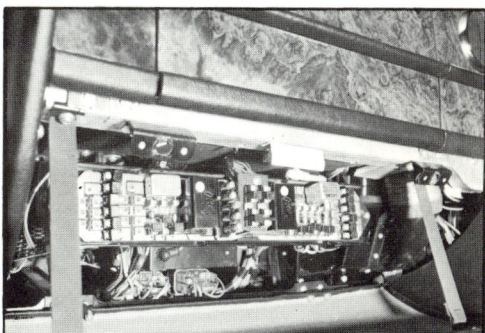

Left: The redesigned external mirror is remotely controlled from inside the car and complies with recent EEC legislation. Below: All the fuses are now located behind a drop-down cover in the lower facia on the passenger side

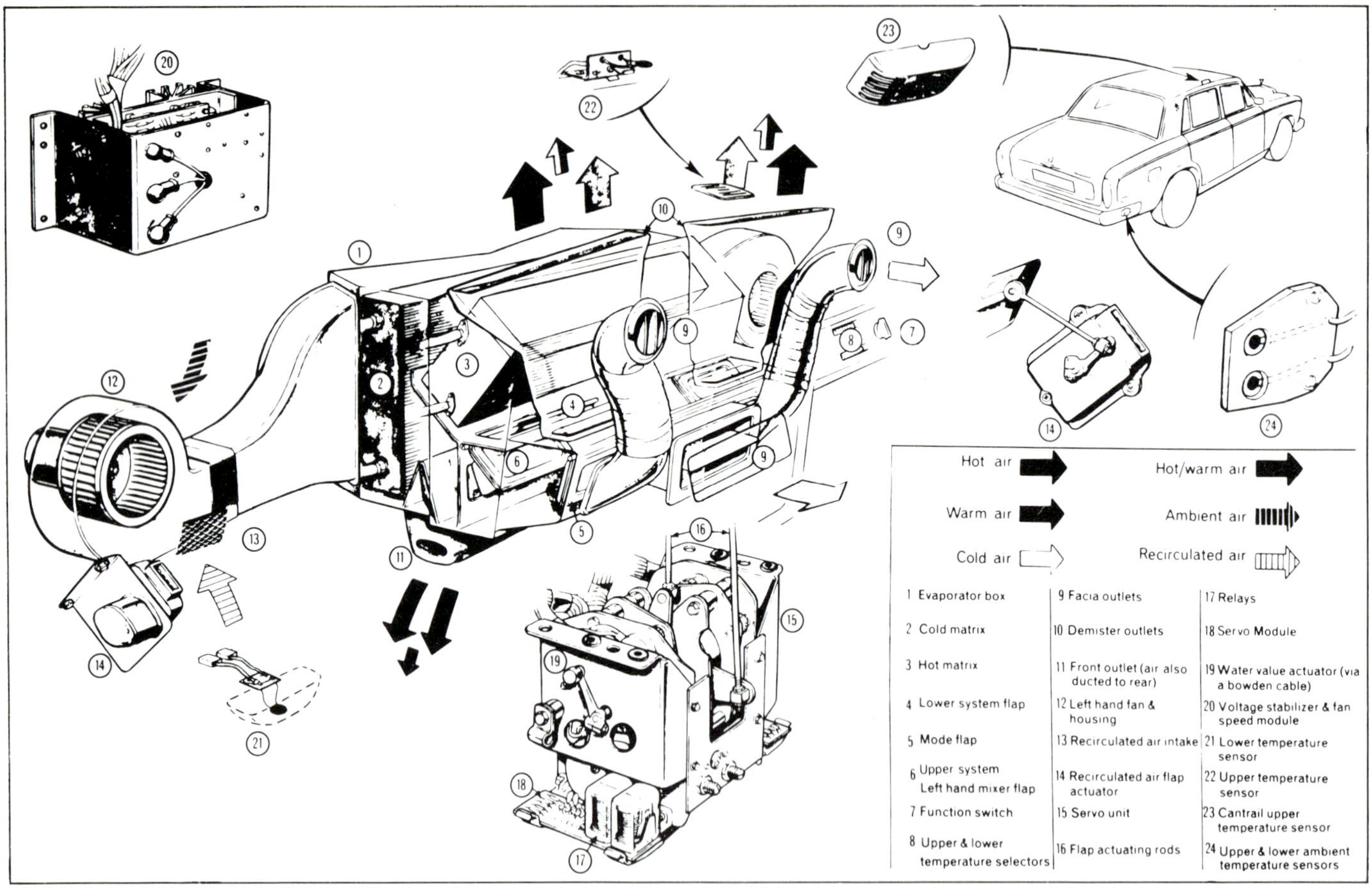

Hot air ▶	Hot/warm air ▶
Warm air ▶	Ambient air ‖‖‖◀
Cold air ▷	Recirculated air ‖‖‖▽

1 Evaporator box	9 Facia outlets	17 Relays
2 Cold matrix	10 Demister outlets	18 Servo Module
3 Hot matrix	11 Front outlet (air also ducted to rear)	19 Water value actuator (via a bowden cable)
4 Lower system flap	12 Left hand fan & housing	20 Voltage stabilizer & fan speed module
5 Mode flap	13 Recirculated air intake	21 Lower temperature sensor
6 Upper system Left hand mixer flap	14 Recirculated air flap actuator	22 Upper temperature sensor
7 Function switch	15 Servo unit	23 Cantrail upper temperature sensor
8 Upper & lower temperature selectors	16 Flap actuating rods	24 Upper & lower ambient temperature sensors

Above: An important part of the revised specification is the automatic air conditioning system as already fitted to the Corniche and Camargue. There is completely independent temperature control of upper and lower systems and all air passes through the refrigeration unit for dehumidification. A 13-second delay is applied to the fan motors to freeze air already in the ducts and prevent windscreen misting. When heat is required from a cold start the fans do not work until coolant temperature reaches 44deg C unless defrost is selected. Operation of the electrically-heated rear window is automatic
Below: The Series II version is the first to carry the Silver Shadow name actually on the car

Body changes

The most immediately obvious external change is the adoption of American-style bumpers. This is not quite as bad as it sounds, because they are mounted in the "retracted" position, thanks to the elimination of the shock-absorbing struts required on the far side of the Atlantic. The hard polyurethane inserts of the bumpers mean there is no need for overriders. Overall length is an inch greater than for the previous model, though still three inches less than that of the American-market cars.

Less obvious, but important at higher speeds, is the air dam or spoiler (Rolls prefer to call it an anti-lift panel) under the nose. It is made of plastic, and is detachable; its size is a compromise between aerodynamic effect and ground clearance — the development team admit to having brought a prototype back from rough country more than somewhat tatty. While some manufacturers claim a drag reduction from the use of an air dam, Rolls merely say that straight-line stability is improved, especially in a gusting sidewind.

Otherwise, externally, the radia-

tor shell is now half an inch thicker than before, there is a Silver Shadow II (or Bentley T2) badge on the boot lid and chromed twin tailpipes. Considering all the changes it is an achievement to have held the weight increase down to 80lb, for a kerb weight of 4,930lb. American specification cars weigh all but 5,000lb and, incidentally, are not fitted with the air dam as the effect of this is not reckoned to be significant at their 55 mph limit.

The changes apply across the Shadow / Corniche / Camargue range, though the latter two do not have the Mark II designation.

Above: From the side only the bumpers and twin exhaust tail pipes distinguish this as the Series II version
Right: The first of the new Bentley T2 Series cars to be built. Mechanically the Bentley is identical to the Rolls-Royce Silver Shadow, only the radiator, bonnet and badging are different

Specification

Engine: V8 cyl. 104 1 x 99 1 mm (4.1 x 3 9 in). 6,750 c.c. (412 cu. in). CR 8 0 to 1. OHV. 2 SU HIF7 carbs. — bhp at — rpm. max torque — lb. ft at — rpm.

Transmission: Front engine, rear-wheel drive. Automatic gearbox. ratios 1.00. 1.50. 2.50, rev 2.00. Top gear mph/1,000 rpm 26.3. Final drive ratio 3.08.

Suspension: ifs. coil springs. wishbones. telescopic dampers. anti-roll bar. Rear. independent. coil springs. wishbones. telescopic dampers. anti-roll bar. automatic ride height control. Steering. Burman rack and pinion (power assisted).

Brakes: RR/Girling (power hydraulics). 11.0 in. front discs. 11.0 in. rear discs.

Dimensions: Wheelbase. 10 ft 0.06 in. (305 cm). front track 5 ft. 0 in. (152 cm). rear track 4 ft. 11.6 in. (151 cm). Overall length. 17 ft. 0.5 in. (519 cm). width 5 ft 11.3 in. (181 cm). height 4 ft. 11.75 in. (152 cm). Turning circle. 39 ft. 0 in. (11.9 m). Unladen weight. 4,930 lb. (2,237 kg). max. payload. 1,000 lb. (455 kg).

Others: Tyres 235/70 HR-15 in. 6 in. rims. fuel 23.5 galls (107 litres). alternator 75 amps

SILVER SHADOW II

Driving impressions

Early in January, we were able to spend some happy hours driving the Silver Shadow II round a partly snowbound circuit from the Crewe factory. It was cold enough, and road conditions bad enough, for us to appreciate some of the virtues of insulation offered by the car. It is not just insulation from the cold that counts, but from the road surface and even, seemingly, from some of the cares of workaday driving.

To begin with, the air-conditioning system does its job just as well as in the Camargue. Some people look on air conditioning purely in its refrigerating sense, and see no point in it if the ambient temperature is less than 80degF; yet a good system ensures comfort at all times, and the Rolls-Royce system is one of the best. In the Shadow, the controls are not as impressive to look at as those in the Camargue, and may not perhaps give the same feeling of precision. But that is a personal view, and in fact they work in exactly the same way. The most important thing for the driver is that they are "set and forget" controls, ensuring the same atmosphere inside the car whether it is freezing or boiling outside. The system also takes care of switching the heated rear window without the driver having to worry about it. Incidentally, a larger (75amp) 12-pole alternator is now fitted to cope with extra electrical loads.

It takes only a few hundred yards to discover that the rack and pinion steering has made a tremendous difference to the Silver Shadow. The steering is no longer quite as light as it was — it now needs a firm push with one finger instead of being to all intents and purposes weightless. There are two great gains, in feel and precision. While in the previous model it was not always easy to tell when the front wheels were close to their limit, the Shadow II gets the message back to its driver sufficiently well to permit rapid progress over packed snow and rutted ice. Now there is a certain "bite" when the front

wheels are hanging on well, and a suggestion of vagueness (not unlike the permanent impression of its predecessor) when they are being asked to do too much.

The precision of the steering is also a major gain. Gone is the feeling that the car is waiting for a split second to give its driver a chance to change his mind. The response to any steering wheel movement is immediate and crisp. It is not overdone; as we have already said, the gearing is modest and there is no danger from that mythical American beast, the "sneeze factor". Seasoned Rolls-Royce drivers may find it mildly startling for a few minutes, but it is difficult to believe that anyone will end up claiming he preferred it the old way. The strain of always allowing for its delayed-action response has gone.

There is no doubt also that cornering behaviour, and handling limits, have been improved. The engineers at Crewe seem inclined to dismiss the revised front suspension geometry as a minor change, but that belies its effect. With the previous model in mind, we took some time to work our way up to the limits of the new one. The lack of front-end-roll when cornering is most noticeable, and at times it is almost as though the front wheels are determined to drag the car in the direction in which they are pointing. Since, as we have said, the driver can now always be sure which way they *are* pointing, the

effect is greatly reassuring. When the car is cornered extremely hard, especially if the entry to the corner is abrupt rather than smooth, it is now the back end which feels as though it may flick outwards, or at least that it is being dragged along willy-nilly; whereas previously one always felt the limit would be set by the front wheels sliding straight ahead.

For the rest, we felt the car to be better in several respects, even though in some cases no engineering changes were claimed. For instance, the ride in the test car felt pleasantly firmer. It was just as good as before at soaking up poor surfaces, yet it seemed not to suffer from the upsetting "floating" feeling of previous Shadows. Rolls-Royce say that the spring and damper rates remain unchanged, but it is possible that the suspension changes have also had a second-order effect on the ride. As for performance, we were unable to take figures but felt there was a touch more liveliness about the car, most of all in the important range from 30 to 70 mph. At the higher speed one could begin to feel the effect of the chin spoiler, steadying the car nicely and endowing it with better natural stability than before, even in the evil, snow-laden sidewind.

Noise levels remain low, but we were unable to detect any real improvement due to the new fan layout. As with all large, massively-tyred cars, road noise is the major problem area, the more so on

the kind of surface on which we were travelling.

For many owners, however, the most successful and obvious feature of the new car will be its much improved instrument and minor control layout. The electronic speedometer is admirably accurate and steady, and as a kind of party trick also reads accurately when the car is reversing. The whole facia looks much more pleasant, with none of the sparse lop-sidedness of its forebear, and the new four-in-one instrument is cleverly laid out so that everything is fine as long as the two side needles are horizontal, and the upper one vertical (the fuel gauge needle is the lower one). The driver may therefore quickly check without having to sort out which gauge is which. There is, of course, also a comprehensive set of warning lights. The minor controls, mostly grouped by the driver's right hand, have been given different-shaped knobs to help identify them without looking. Another improved feature is the cruise control system, which is now electronic instead of relying on a mechanical speed sensor. This has permitted the addition of an "inching" facility for small speed changes without disengaging the system. The "resume speed" facility is retained.

As is to be expected these changes have added to the price of the Silver Shadow II or Bentley T2 which now cost a total of £22,809.15 — an increase of £3,147 of which the automatic air conditioning alone must account for a considerable part. The important thing, however, is that a great many worthwhile improvements have been made, not only in the area of comfort but also in re-establishing the Shadow as a capable and worthy road car, an area in which it had been somewhat left behind. No doubt it will continue to sell well, as it deserves to. It has been in full production at Crewe since before the turn of the year, and the change-over of models should not interrupt the smooth and increasing flow of cars from the factory. **JRD**

Production changes

THE ORIGINAL Silver Shadow, announced in October 1965, was the most complex Rolls-Royce model to go into production. For Rolls-Royce Ltd it broke new ground in several new areas — their first monocoque, all-independent self levelling suspension and disc brakes both using high pressure hydraulics. Under the bonnet was an improved version of the 6,230 c.c. V8 engine, which had powered the Silver Cloud III, coupled to a four-speed, R-R Hydra-matic gearbox. First cars were not delivered to customers until 1966, since when the model has gone from strength to strength and has included some 2,000 modifications to Series I cars.

First significant changes were in 1968 when a rear anti-roll bar was added and the front bar enlarged (July) and the cooling fan became viscous coupled (September). November saw the fitting of the GM 400 three-speed, automatic

transmission which had been standard on export lhd cars from the start. Further important changes followed in May 1969 with a revised interior to meet American Federal Safety Standards. Substantial padding was added around the facia, instruments and controls were repositioned and the heater controls brought together in a central console. Interior door handles were recessed and exterior side-marker lamps added. In the autumn swing-needle SU carburettors were fitted and the front height control deleted. November 1969 saw the standardization of air conditioning, an alternator and a stainless steel exhaust system. A smaller 16in. steering wheel was fitted in February 1970 followed by the 6,750 c.c. engine in July. Centralized door locking and four radio speakers took effect that September. In March 1971 ventilated wheel discs and windscreen wash/wipe became standard and in August the steering ratio was increased.

Changes for 1972 included compliant

front suspension and radial-ply tyres (August) and electrical additions (September) with delay switch for interior lights, eight warning lamps, intermittent wipe and centralized boot locking. Through-flow ventilation was fitted from November.

The summer of 1973 saw the fitting of ventilated front disc brakes (June) and quartz halogen fog lamps (July). Standard equipment from December 1973 were internally-adjustable door mirror, eight-track stereo cartridge player, headrests to rear seats and an automatic speed control. In April 1974 low profile radial-ply tyres were fitted with consequent changes to the suspension, an increase in wheelbase from 119.7in. to 120.062in. and "eye-brows" for the wheelarches. An improved in-car-entertainment specification in October 1974 included a Pioneer QP-444ER quadrophonic tape player with four 5 watt channels plus a Bosch Frankfurt AM/FM stereo radio, both as standard. Mechanical changes aimed at

greater efficiency were the hallmark of 1975 with a number of improvements taking effect from August. Better fuel consumption resulted from a reduction of the compression ratio to 8.0 to 1, a distributor with vacuum advance control, a thermostatically-controlled carburettor air intake and the Lucas Opus electronic ignition system. Changes to the braking resulted in a new duplicated system without a conventional master cylinder. Rear fog warning lamps were also added.

Final changes to the Series I cars came in 1976 when grooveless front main bearing shells, giving a greater bearing area, were fitted to the engine (March), and air-cored gauges giving a damped reading were substituted in August.

These improvements are, of course, carried through to the new Series II cars which have a number of other important changes already described in the previous pages. **WA**

Royal Phantom

A special body for the Queen's new Rolls-Royce

By Warren Allport

Above: With the hardtop in place for less formal use there is only a very small rear window. The boot line is special as are the reversing lamp cluster and boot handle. Rear quarter windows can have screens fitted for extra privacy. Right: The Perspex dome provides the visibility of an open car with the advantage of weather protection. Below right: The hardtop folded and stowed. The chauffeur's luggage is affixed by the two straps

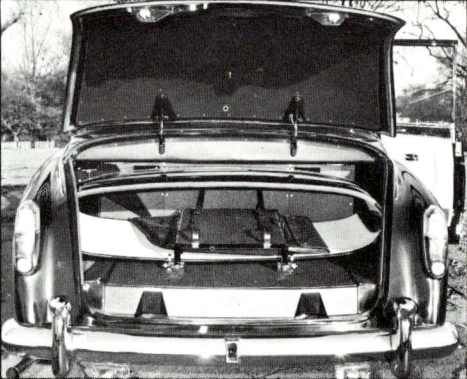

TODAY, 29 March, Her Majesty the Queen will be presented with the Rolls-Royce Phantom VI special limousine commissioned by the Society of Motor Manufacturers and Traders as a Silver Jubilee gift from the British Motor Industry. Unfortunately an industrial dispute at the Mulliner Park Ward division of Rolls-Royce Motors prolonged the 12 months build time of a car such as this by several further months and so prevented the car being delivered during 1977 as had been planned when the project was started early in 1976. A further delay was unavoidable when Rolls-Royce Motors decided to incorporate in this Phantom a number of mechanical changes that may be introduced on production Phantoms later. When one realises that the newest Rolls-Royce in HM The Queen's stable up to now is the Phantom V delivered in 1961, and that an almost identical Phantom V delivered in 1960 and a pair of straight-eight Phantom IVs delivered in 1950 and 1955 make up the remainder of the quartet of official cars, the reasons for wanting to provide the very latest specifications for a car that is likely to be in use for 20 years or so are obvious.

To deal with the mechanical changes first, the modifications can be briefly summed up by saying that the royal car now has the 6.7-litre engine and three-speed GM 400 Turbo Hydra-matic torque convertor transmission to the same specification as fitted to Silver Shadow II models, plus the Silver Shadow-type high pressure dual circuit hydraulic braking system applied to the drum brakes. Other Phantoms at present still have the 6,230 c.c. engine as fitted to Silver Shadow I in 1966 plus the four-speed Rolls-Royce Motors Hydra-matic transmission with take

off for the mechanical friction disc brake servo which dates back to 1924. It sounds simple to say that the bigger engine and new gearbox have been fitted, but of course with Rolls-Royce Motors' typical thoroughness a number of changes to the chassis have been undertaken as well. The single front engine mounting is now smaller and the rear mountings, one on each side of the transmission bell housing, have been moved 2in. further aft in the chassis. The propeller shaft, which is made up of two sections, has been redesigned with three constant velocity joints and a splined fitting resulting in an increase in diameter from 2.25in. to 2.75in. Some four per cent more power is delivered by the 6,750 c.c. engine.

A very noticeable difference between the production Phantom VI and the royal car's chassis is the plumbing for the high pressure servo braking system with the twin master cylinders for the two separate circuits now filling what was a space beside the chassis cross-bracing aft of the gearbox. The mechanical rear brake actuation, working off the handbrake linkage but activated by the brake pedal, has been retained as a long stop in the unlikely event of failure of both hydraulic systems. Under the bonnet the positioning of the large rectangular brake fluid reservoir on the nearside is an immediate recognition point for the latest braking system.

Going almost unnoticed among the braking changes are the thicker ribbing on the brake drums themselves, while inside a new lining material is used. One of the biggest benefits of the new system is the lack of a time-lag while the servo winds up at slow speeds and when manoeuvring. The pedal also has a harder feel and there is less pedal free travel, plus a reduction in pedal pressures. Rolls-Royce Motors figures for a 0.5g stop with the car fully laden show a reduction in pedal pressure from 63 to 48lb, and for a 0.8g stop from 96 to 68lb.

Other changes in the Phantom body area that may be applicable to production cars later include the provision of centralized door and boot locking (but not boot locking on the royal car), and a revised facia panel. Incorporated in the latter to the right of the speedometer is a Silver Shadow II-type panel containing warning lamps for loss of pressure in No 1 or 2 brake circuit (two separate lamps), low brake fluid, parking brake on, low coolant level, fuel level 3 gallons or below, rear fog lamps and their switch. On the steering column gear selector positions 1-4 have now been replaced by the more familiar PRNDIL and on the road with the selector in D Rolls-Royce Motors say that full-throttle upward changes take place at 35 and 52 mph, while using kick-down results in upward changes at 38 and 66 mph. In the low and intermediate positions there is no safety upchange, so the driver must not exceed 38 and 66 mph respectively. Official Government fuel consumption figures for the new specification Phantom VI are 9.9 mpg for the ECE 15 driving cycle simulating typical town driving, 15.0 mpg at a constant 56 mph and 12.4 mpg at a constant 75mph.

From the first moment one sees the new royal Phantom it is reconizable as HM The Queen's car because of the deep windscreen which has resulted from raising the whole roof structure by 4in. to give increased headroom and the fitting of a moulded Perspex roof section over the rear compartment. The styling itself thus closely follows that of Canberra, the first royal Phantom V. The success of this design for state use can be appreciated when it is stated that after 18 years of experience with Canberra this Perspex roofed design was considered preferable to a landaulette. After all the special limousine has all the advantages of enabling the occupants to be clearly seen thanks to the large glass area and Perspex roof which render the interior light and airy, without the disadvantages of getting wet if it rains or being buffeted by the wind. For a car which is very much a working vehicle and will be used in all weathers, besides covering a considerable mileage in a year, these are important considerations.

For use on less formal occasions, or when greater privacy is required such as when travelling at night, the moulded Perspex roof section can be covered with a detachable black hardtop with a tiny rear window. The hardtop itself it made of aluminium to which is bonded a soundproofing layer before the cloth headlining is fitted. When not required this hardtop can be removed by undoing four budget locks with a special key and is then folded in half before being stowed in the boot. A ¼in. gap between Perspex dome and hardtop allows the latter to be fitted when wet. In addition to the Perspex dome over the rear seats there is a glass roof panel. This can be obscured by an

Left: Special fittings hand made in brass under the eagle eye of Roy Aldridge, superintendent of the Mulliner Park Ward experimental and special bodies department where the royal car was built

electrically-operated sliding cover, while manually operated sliding covers obscure the side roof panels. With the hardtop on and the sliding roof covers closed the car is fairly private, but even greater seclusion can be obtained by fitting the screens to the rear quarter windows. These screens, normally carried in the boot, clip inside the rear quarter windows, presenting a black side to the outside world and a cloth trimmed inside to the rear compartment occupants.

The external paintwork of the car is in the royal colours of Black over Royal Claret (a deep red) and the royal coat of arms are emblazoned on both rear doors. As presented by the SMMT the Phantom VI is equipped with a kneeling version of the famous Spirit of Ecstasy mascot. This is uni-

que to the Queen's car, not having been used on other post-war Phantoms though a similar mascot was used on Silver Wraith and Silver Dawn models. It is expected that the Queen's personal mascot of St George slaying the dragon will replace the kneeling lady on ceremonial occasions. Other special exterior features are the special boot lid — higher than normal to allow the hardtop to be stowed — with a completely different boot handle and lock made possible because the car does not carry number plates. At the front a skirt panel has been fitted to conceal the power steering mechanism. A pair of quartz halogen foglamps are fitted at the front and red foglamps at the rear. Mounted in the centre of the roof above the

windscreen is the circular blue police identification lamp, with the fittings for a shield with coat of arms and flagstaff immediately behind it. The shield can be illuminated at night, all the necessary electrical connections being built into the roof socket. A special clamp fitting for the bumpers enables them to be removed by undoing two bolts on each, thus reducing the length by 9 in. to fit in the garage on the Royal Yacht *Britannia.*

The rear compartment

It is the little detailed items of equipment fitted to the interior of HM The Queen's car that make it really special and set it apart from other Phantoms. For the first time on a royal Phantom the colour for the West of England cloth upholstery has been changed from the usual grey to a very pale blue called Baroda Blue. The same colour cloth is used for the headlining and there are matching Wilton carpets and lambswool rugs. It may come as a surprise to some to discover that there is no television or even a cocktail cabinet in the rear compartment. Instead there is a veneered storage unit, for four cassettes, replacing the cocktail cabinet with an Asprey winding clock above it. Twin folding occasional seats are fitted and fold away into the division but the usual footrests for the rear seat passengers are omitted. For such a big car the rear seat is not as wide as one might imagine and would be a squeeze for three adults. This is not important however as it usually carries only two members of the royal family, so the fold down armrest has been made extra wide to accommodate a Radiomobile cassette player and AM push-button radio plus the control buttons for the heating/air conditioning in a sloping console at the front. The buttons have been coloured red and green — for port and starboard respectively as Prince Philip is a naval man — and allow the heating and air conditioning controls (duplicated in the outer fixed armrests) on the side of the car on which the button is depressed to control the rear compartment temperature. Obviously with two sets of temperature controls only one set can be worked at once, which is what the central changeover switch regulates. Also to be found in the central armrest under the hinged lid are an adjustable mirror and a Philips model 185 portable dictating machine complete with two tiny spare tapes and two spare Mallory Duracell batteries. As well as the heater controls each fixed side armrest also incorporates switches for the four interior roof lights — they stay on for seven seconds after the door is closed but can be overridden by the driver — and the four fluorescent strip lights. Fitted in the rear quarter just above the armrests are switches for the electrically-operated division glass, door windows and roof blind.

Like all Phantoms the royal car has a comprehensive heating and air conditioning system, but modifications unique to this car are a fresh air intake, mounted on the boot saddle just below the rear window, for the refrigeration system and the fitting of a second water tap in the heater matrix. These modifications boost the

Above: Changes from the normal facia include a warning lamp panel to the right of the speedometer, a modified gear selector quadrant and a special switch panel for the police lamp and shield illumination. Below: The new and longer GM gearbox and the power braking system installed in the chassis

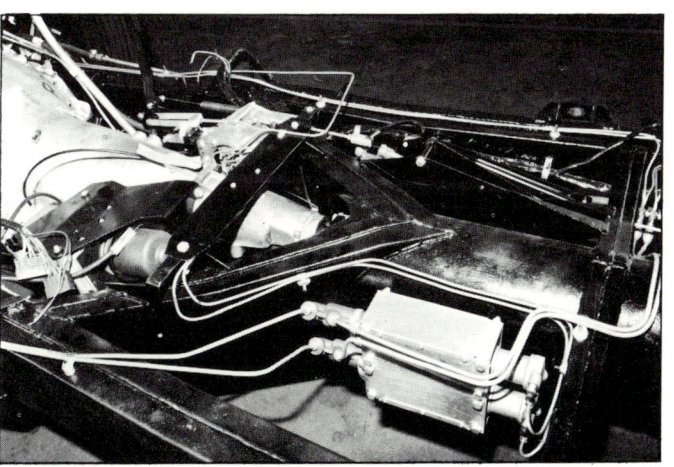

Royal Phantom

normal heating and refrigeration to the rear compartment, and even permit heating and refrigeration to be operated simultaneously. The rear heating system is the normal recirculatory one with ducts beneath the front of the rear seat. Refrigerated cool air is expelled into the rear compartment through vents in the front of each side armrest and there are also three adjustable vents in each rear quarter, just level with the side window, to give additional face-level cooling. These six vents were hand made in brass, including the control flaps, and are unique to the Queen's car. In hot weather the Perspex dome can render the rear like a hothouse — hence this extra cooling provision.

Two small items in the rear of the car typify the attention to detail of the Mulliner Park Ward craftsmen under the supervision of engineering manager Ted Holland. The rear seat cushion behind the driver, where the Queen sits, is softer than that on the other side because Her Majesty is lighter than Prince Phillip. The running boards too are non-standard, having a smooth instead of ribbed rubber finish to avoid the Queen catching her heel when alighting from the car.

Chauffeur and detective

The front compartment is the domain of the royal chauffeur and detective but it, too, has its special equipment. In the roof is housed the electric motor for the roof blind, with a flap immediately ahead of this concealing the fittings for the Royal Standard and coat of arms. Mounted on the top facia roll are twin mirrors, while in the space normally occupied by a centre armrest is to be found the telephone handset for the two-way radio. Whatever comes over the radio is also broadcast through a speaker in the front passenger door, and the coiled lead to the handset is long enough for it to be used by the rear compartment occupants.

Below: Retractable sun vizors and the shield mounting in the front roof. Access for the Royal Standard is through the roof flap. Bottom: The special chauffeur's step

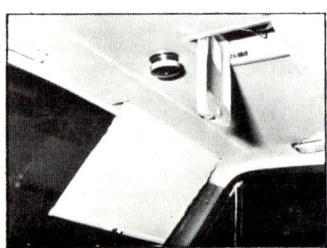

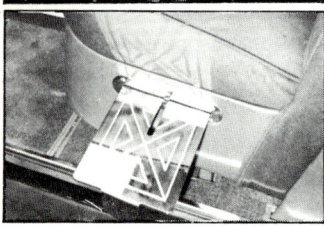

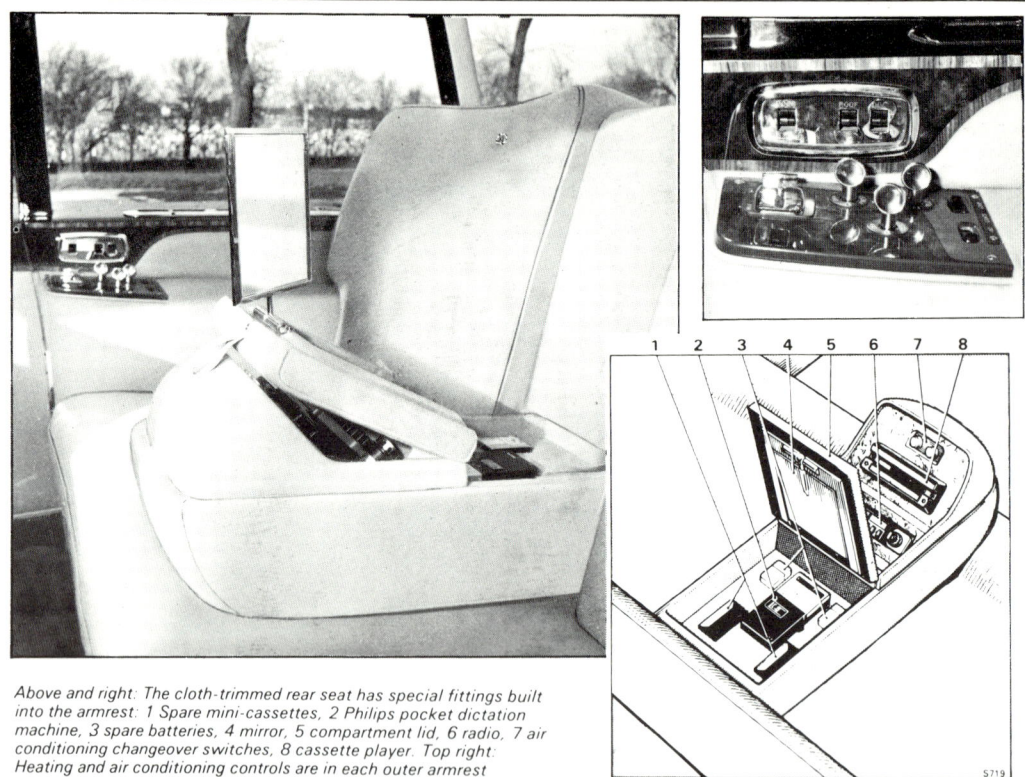

Above and right: The cloth-trimmed rear seat has special fittings built into the armrest: 1 Spare mini-cassettes, 2 Philips pocket dictation machine, 3 spare batteries, 4 mirror, 5 compartment lid, 6 radio, 7 air conditioning changeover switches, 8 cassette player. Top right: Heating and air conditioning controls are in each outer armrest

Left: There are two occasional seats and no rear footrests. Above: Normal cocktail cabinet is replaced by cassette storage (all four cassettes are of Guards bands) and clock which swivels for winding

Illumination of the police lamp and coat of arms is controlled from a switch panel just to the left of the steering wheel. Two final special features are a tool tray beneath the front seat and a pull-out step at the side of the front passenger seat to enable the chauffeur to climb up to affix or dismount the Royal Standard and coat of arms.

Thus not only does the Queen's new Rolls-Royce have the most advanced specification of any Phantom VI yet built, it also has a distinctive custom-built body with a host of very special equipment. The only thing that is not special about the car is the standard of workmanship, for Rolls-Royce Motors and their Mulliner Park Ward coachbuilding division's craftsmen work to only one standard — the best. □

Specification

(Chassis PGH 101)

Engine: Aluminium alloy with wet liners. V8-cyl. 104.1 × 99.1mm (4.1 × 3.9 in.). 6.750 c.c. (412 cu. in.). CR 8.0 to 1. ohv hydraulic tappets. 2 SU HIF 7 carbs. Bhp and torque not quoted. 2 SU electric fuel pumps. Lucas Opus Mk II electronic ignition.
Transmission: Front engine, rear-wheel drive. GM 400 Turbo Hydra-matic torque convertor automatic. Gearbox ratios 2.50. 1.50. 1.00. rev 2.00. Final drive hypoid 3.89. Top gear mph/1,000 rpm 22.5.
Chassis: Hermetically sealed box section with cruciform bracing. Rubber mounted body with alloy panels on steel and light alloy framework. galvanized steel floor and sills. Centralized door locking.
Suspension: ifs. double wishbones. coil springs. Rolls-Royce Motors lever dampers. anti-roll bar. Rear. live axle. assymmetric semi-elliptic leaf springs. Rolls-Royce Motors lever damper with normal/hard settings controlled by switch on steering column.
Steering: Cam and roller with variable power assistance. 18.7 to 1 ratio. 4.25 turns lock to lock.
Brakes: Rolls-Royce Motors/Girling with high pressure hydraulic power assistance. Dual hydraulic circuits. plus mechanical linkage to rear wheels. 11.25 in. front and rear ribbed brake drums. 3in. wide shoes.
Dimensions: Wheelbase 12ft 1 in. (368 cm). front track 5 ft 0.87 in. (155 cm). rear track 5 ft 4.0 in. (162 cm). Overall length (with bumpers) 19 ft 10 in. (604.5 cm). (without bumpers) 19 ft 1 in. (581.6 cm). width 6 ft 7 in. (201 cm). height 6 ft 1 in. (185.4 cm). Ground clearance 7.25 in. (18.4 cm). Turning circle 52 ft 0 in. (15.85 m). Unladen weight 6,790 lb (3,080 kg). Max payload 1,300 lb (590 kg).
Others: Tyres 8.90-15 in. cross ply. 6.0 in. rims. Battery 12 volt 95 a/h. CAV 90 amp alternator. Fuel tank 23 gallons (104.6 litres). Engine sump and filter 14.5 pints (8 litres). Gearbox/torque convertor (dry) 18.6 pints (10.6 litres). fluid change and renewal of intake strainer 8 pints (4.5 litres). Cooling system 35 pints (20 litres).

Index

Alpine Eagle, 40/50 hp	42, 77
Alpine, Trial of	40
Automobile Division, Research	137, 140
Barker, Cabriolet	44
Phantom III	115
Phantom III Limousine	110
40/50 hp	84
40/50 hp Tourer, 1919	46
40/50 hp Tourer, 1925	68
Bentley S3	189
Series S	156
S-Type, refinements, 1956	166
T2	250
Camargue	234
Chapron, Phantom V	188
Cockshoot 40/50 hp Limousine	46
Cooke Street workshops	19
Corniche	222
Road Test	228
Crewe factory, tour of	192
Derby Works, 1930's	227
Engine, 6¼-litre, V-eight	175
Freestone & Webb, Silver Cloud	162
Sports Saloon	130
Silver Wraith	130, 165
Gurney and Nutting, New Phantom Weymann saloon	82
Silver Wraith	134
Hamshaw, Alpine Eagle	42
Hives, Lord	6
Hooper, Silver Cloud Saloon	168
Silver Wraith	134, 135
20/25 hp	80
40/50 Limousine	56
India, R-R cars for	44
Johnson, Claude	6
Laundaulet, 8-cylinder	27, 29
Mulliner, Park Ward, Corniche	222
Mulliner, Phantom II	129
Phantom IV	148
Mulliner & Radford, Silver Cloud Estate	165
Mulliner, Silver Cloud coupé	168
Silver Wraith	145, 165
'New Phantom'	72
Paris Salon, 1904, R-R cars at	8
Park Ward, New Phantom coupé-de-ville	83
Phantom III Pullman	110

Phantom V	182, 188
Silver Cloud III	191
20/25 hp	105
40/50 1921 Saloon	51
Phantom I, replica body	80
New	81
II	96, 98, 129
II Continental, Road Test	101
III	106, 112, 115
III, Road Test	109
IV	132
IV, for Princess Elizabeth	148
V	182, 188
V Black Cherry	198
V, Limousine	179
V, Park Ward	180
VI	224
VI, Royal	252
Pininfarina, Camargue	234
Plastow, David	6
R.A.C. Tourist Trophy 1905	20
1906	30
1906, experiences	31
Regent Carriage Co. 40/50 hp coupé	44
40/50 hp saloon	44
Research–Automobile Division	137, 140
Rolls: The Hon. C. S.	6
Rolls: C.S. & Co., advertisement	9
Rolls-Royce automobiles 1905	10
1910 refinements to	38
Royce: Sir Henry	6
Servo Brakes, Road Test	65
Silver Cloud	156, 162, 168
Estate	165
Refinements 1956	166
Road Test	171
II, Harold Radford Countryman	187
II, Mulliner, convertible	187
II, Park Ward	187
II, Road Test	183
III	189, 191
III, Road Test	203
Silver Dawn	131, 144
Saloon, Road Test	152
Silver Ghost	60, 79

cutaway	58
at Windsor	197
the story of	34
Silver Shadow	209, 242
Road Test	217
II	248
Silver Wraith	125, 130, 165, 196
Limousine	169
Sedanca de Ville, Road Test	145
Specifications: basic table	7
Sportsman's Coupé, advance of	87
Two-seater, 1921	50
Waring Brothers, 40/50 hp saloon	68
Weyman, New Phantom	81
Windovers Ltd, New Phantom	71
Wraith	116
details on the	119
road test	122
Young, James, Phantom V	188
10 hp, 1905, 2 cyl.	14, 57, 78
20 hp 4-cyl. 1905	78
20 hp Tourist-Trophy car 1905	23
20 hp Six cylinder 1922	61
20 hp, six cylinder 1926 Road Test	75
20 hp Saloon, 1929 Road Test	85
25 hp, 1931, Road Test	97
20/25 hp 1933	80
Modification	94, 99
Sports Saloon	130
1935, of Sax Rohmer	105
Touring Saloon Road Test	103
40/50 hp 1906	32
1919	46
armoured car	45
Carbiolet 1921	54
Cabriolet 1922	56
gas driven	45
Limousine	45
Limousine 1922	56
London–Edinburgh Trial	39
1920 model, on the road	47
1921, Road impressions	52
1922, road test	55
OHV, 1925	69
6¼-litre, V-eight engine	175